Y0-ABF-162

THE PAPERS OF

THOMAS JEFFERSON

BARBARA B. OBERG
GENERAL EDITOR

THE PAPERS OF
Thomas Jefferson

Volume 39
13 November 1802 to 3 March 1803

BARBARA B. OBERG, EDITOR

JAMES P. MCCLURE AND ELAINE WEBER PASCU,
SENIOR ASSOCIATE EDITORS

TOM DOWNEY AND MARTHA J. KING,
ASSOCIATE EDITORS

W. BLAND WHITLEY, ASSISTANT EDITOR

LINDA MONACO, EDITORIAL ASSISTANT

JOHN E. LITTLE, RESEARCH ASSOCIATE

PRINCETON AND OXFORD
PRINCETON UNIVERSITY PRESS
2012

Published by Princeton University Press, 41 William Street,
Princeton, New Jersey 08540
In The United Kingdom:
Princeton University Press, 6 Oxford Street,
Woodstock, Oxfordshire OX20 1TW

ISBN 978-0-691-15671-2

Library of Congress Number: 50-7486

This book has been composed in Monticello

Princeton University Press books are printed on
acid-free paper and meet the guidelines for permanence
and durability of the Committee on Production
Guidelines for Book Longevity of the
Council on Library Resources

Printed in the United States of America

DEDICATED TO THE MEMORY OF

ADOLPH S. OCHS

PUBLISHER OF THE NEW YORK TIMES

1896-1935

WHO BY THE EXAMPLE OF A RESPONSIBLE

PRESS ENLARGED AND FORTIFIED

THE JEFFERSONIAN CONCEPT

OF A FREE PRESS

ADVISORY COMMITTEE

CONSULTANTS

SUPPORTERS

THIS EDITION was made possible by an initial grant of $200,000 from The New York Times Company to Princeton University. Contributions from many foundations and individuals have sustained the endeavor since then. Among these are the Ford Foundation, the Lyn and Norman Lear Foundation, the Lucius N. Littauer Foundation, the Charlotte Palmer Phillips Foundation, the L. J. Skaggs and Mary C. Skaggs Foundation, the John Ben Snow Memorial Trust, Time, Inc., Robert C. Baron, B. Batmanghelidj, David K. E. Bruce, and James Russell Wiggins. In recent years generous ongoing support has come from The New York Times Company Foundation, the Dyson Foundation, the Barkley Fund (through the National Trust for the Humanities), the Florence Gould Foundation, the "Cinco Hermanos Fund," the Andrew W. Mellon Foundation, the Pew Charitable Trusts, and the Packard Humanities Institute (through Founding Fathers Papers, Inc.). Benefactions from a greatly expanded roster of dedicated individuals have underwritten this volume and those still to come: Sara and James Adler, Helen and Peter Bing, Diane and John Cooke, Judy and Carl Ferenbach III, Mary-Love and William Harman, Frederick P. and Mary Buford Hitz, Governor Thomas H. Kean, Ruth and Sidney Lapidus, Lisa and Willem Mesdag, Tim and Lisa Robertson, Ann and Andrew C. Rose, Sara Lee and Axel Schupf, the Sulzberger family through the Hillandale Foundation, Richard W. Thaler, Tad and Sue Thompson, The Wendt Family Charitable Foundation, and Susan and John O. Wynne. For their vision and extraordinary efforts to provide for the future of this edition, we owe special thanks to John S. Dyson, Governor Kean, H. L. Lenfest and the Lenfest Foundation, Rebecca Rimel and the Pew Charitable Trusts, and Jack Rosenthal. In partnership with these individuals and foundations, the National Historical Publications and Records Commission and the National Endowment for the Humanities have been crucial to the editing and publication of *The Papers of Thomas Jefferson*. For their unprecedented generous support we are also indebted to the Princeton History Department and Christopher L. Eisgruber, provost of the university.

FOREWORD

DURING THE period covered by this volume, 13 November 1802 through 3 March 1803, Thomas Jefferson never left the nation's capital, forgoing even one of the brief visits to Monticello that he treasured. At the start, he was busy preparing his annual message to Congress, referring it to members of his cabinet and taking their suggestions under consideration. By mid-November, he had a draft ready for the scheduled opening of the session on 6 December, but members of Congress trickled in. While the House of Representatives had a quorum by the 7th, on the 10th Jefferson reported that there was still "no senate, nor any prospect of one for several days." Only 12 senators had arrived. Finally, on 15 December, Meriwether Lewis delivered copies of the message to the House and Senate. Jefferson's words were resoundingly optimistic as he observed that the nation enjoyed prosperity and economy at home and was "still blessed with peace and friendship abroad." He briefly noted the achievements of the previous year and described the challenges that remained. Among these were calculating the impact of the restoration of peace on American trade with Europe; preparing for a change in foreign relations if the cession of Louisiana to France took place; keeping watch on the harbor of Tripoli to determine whether reinforcements were needed; "marking the boundaries" with Indian nations; and weighing the construction of a dry dock in Washington to preserve navy vessels when not at sea.

Jefferson's message avoided the issue that loomed largest, at least for the western states: the October order by the acting Spanish intendant of Louisiana, in apparent violation of the Treaty of 1795, withdrawing the right of Americans to store goods awaiting export at New Orleans. Jefferson received the news not long before the opening of Congress. Westerners demanded a vigorous response against this threat to their economic well-being, grimly predicting, as Governor James Garrard of Kentucky wrote, that Spain's action would "at one blow cut up the present and future prospects of their best interests by the roots." The clamor from the west was echoed by Jefferson's political opponents in the east. Some, such as Senator James Ross of Pennsylvania, pressed for acquiring New Orleans by force if necessary. Federalists called for the president to permit open debate in Congress and to make public all papers and correspondence related to the potential consequences of the retrocession of New Orleans and the Louisiana territory to France. Jefferson, however, preferred a more confidential, behind-the-scenes approach to the whole issue, one that would rely on diplomacy rather than confrontation.

On the final day of 1802, Jefferson received Pierre Samuel Du Pont's letter of 4 October recommending various steps that might lead to a mutually acceptable accord between France and the United States. Jefferson was happy to rely on his "private friendship" with Du Pont to persuade him to use his good offices with the French government to keep the two nations at peace. Jefferson also took the adroit step of naming James Monroe as special envoy to proceed immediately to Europe. There he would join Robert R. Livingston in negotiating a resolution of the problem. Monroe received letters of credence for both France and Spain, and he was to go to Paris first, then, depending upon what he learned there, to Madrid if necessary. Because he owned land in the west and was reputed to be a strong advocate of free navigation of the Mississippi, Monroe's participation would help to deflect "all further inflammatory proceedings meditated by the Federalists." He was also popular in France, where he would be called upon to handle not just the right of deposit but the more complex and far-reaching consequences of the retrocession.

Jefferson was also convinced that the future course of the country depended upon the transfer of large sections of land owned by Native American nations to the United States. The prospect of French troops arriving in the Louisiana Territory and supporting Indian refusals to part with their soil persuaded the president that he must move expeditiously to carry out his plans for confirming the boundaries and, eventually, for assuming ownership of Indian property. With the Indians, Jefferson's language was gracious, respectful, and conciliatory. He assured delegations led by Seneca leaders Handsome Lake, Cornplanter, and Farmer's Brother that he would "watch over" their interests and renew the "chain of friendship." The president cajoled, explained, and offered incentives and an accommodation of their wishes, but he was also firm. He insisted to Owl and other members of the Miamis and Delawares who had traveled to the capital to meet him that the government desired to live "in peace and friendship" with them, and had even gone so far as to give up territory that their ancestors had ceded and therefore by "right" belonged to the United States. Jefferson concluded by declining their offer to deduct the travel expenses from the next year's annuity. He assured the delegation that the government would absorb those costs "with satisfaction."

When the president wrote privately to Secretary of War Henry Dearborn or William Henry Harrison, governor of the Indiana Territory, however, his words were candid and his directions emphatic: persuade Indian nations to live within greatly reduced borders, adopt an agricultural economy, and relinquish all claims to terrain east of the Mississippi. What the Indians considered to be their territory must ultimately belong to the United States. To Jefferson, the bargain seemed reasonable: the Indians had an abundance of land, which the United States needed, and in exchange the United States could supply them with "necessaries, with which we abound." Above all, the nation must secure its boundary on the Mississippi and the federal government had "paramount sovereignty" over the western territories.

In contemplating the west, and especially its commercial possibilities for the United States, Jefferson sought to find a route to the Pacific Ocean and raised the possibility of sending a party to search for it. He suggested the idea in the draft of the annual message that he sent to his cabinet for review, but on the advice of Secretary of the Treasury Albert Gallatin he held the matter for a separate, confidential communication. This message, read in the House on 18 January, discussed the continuation of the Act for Establishing Trading Houses with Indian tribes and its effect on commerce. Jefferson encouraged Congress to look at commercial possibilities to the west and proposed that "an intelligent officer with ten or twelve chosen men" explore the Missouri River and the country beyond. The endeavor would be useful to the country in many ways. It would promote commerce, provide valuable intelligence on Indian tribes, and advance "the geographical knowledge of our own continent." He requested and received an appropriation of $2,500, then wrote to his friends and fellow members of the American Philosophical Society, Benjamin Smith Barton, Robert Patterson, Benjamin Rush, and Caspar Wistar, informing them of the expedition and asking their help in preparing Meriwether Lewis, its appointed leader. Lewis, while "brave, prudent, habituated to the woods, & familiar with Indian manners & Character," was lacking in knowledge of botany, natural history, mineralogy, and astronomy.

Although critical matters of state confronted him, Jefferson's daily life in the President's House was brightened for six weeks in the late fall and early winter by the visit of Martha Jefferson Randolph and two of her children—Thomas Jefferson, age ten, and Ellen, age six—and Martha's younger sister, Mary Jefferson Eppes. Jefferson had long urged his family to come to Washington, and although he left few details of their sojourn, the reports of others indicate that they were well received. While in residence the young women attended their father's dinner gatherings, accompanied him to religious services in the hall of the House of Representatives, and participated in some of the social life of the capital. They attended the president's levee on New Year's Day, along with the members of the cabinet, foreign diplomats, Federalist and Republican members of Congress, and some "strangers." Manasseh Cutler, a Federalist congressman from Massachusetts, found Martha and Mary to be "well-accomplished women—very delicate and tolerably handsome." Margaret Bayard Smith observed that Mary was "beautiful, simplicity and timidity personified." Her older sister was "rather homely," with a "delicate" resemblance to her father, and had a "countenance beaming with intelligence, benevolence and sensibility." Delighting in the company of the two young women, whom she visited at the President's House and received in her own home several times, Smith also lavished praise on granddaughter Ellen, who was fond of poetry and "without exception one of the finest and most intelligent children" she had ever met. Thomas Jefferson Randolph years later recalled making a trip with the coachman, unbeknownst to his mother and grandfather, to the navy yard, where he was received with salutes. After the pleasures of these six weeks, the family's departure for home a few days after New Year's was painful. Mary wrote of the sorrow of seeing her father "turn back alone" as she and her sister rode off anguished at the thought of the "unsafe & solitary manner" in which he slept upstairs. They wished he were at home, with them (William Parker Cutler and Julia Perkins Cutler, *Life, Journals, and Correspondence of Rev. Manasseh Cutler, LL.D.*, 2 vols. [Cincinnati, 1888; repr. Athens, Ohio, 1987], 2:113-16; Margaret Bayard Smith, *The First Forty Years of Washington Society*, ed. Gaillard Hunt [New York, 1906], 34-5; Malone, *Jefferson*, 4:171-4).

Monticello continued to require Jefferson's attention and funds. He alerted Craven Peyton that he would have to postpone and reduce the payments on what he owed for the Henderson lands. The nailery had "long been a dead expense instead of a profit," and he intended to put it under new direction. The low pitch of a section of the roof allowed water to seep in under the shingles, and he sketched out a plan to lay sheet iron over the roof in a system of gutters and ridges to remedy the problem.

His expenses for entertaining, both personal and official, mounted. A hamper containing 50 bottles of champagne was opened on 7 December and finished on 19 December; 125 gentlemen had dined during that period and this, Jefferson calculated, resulted in "2. bottles to 5. persons." About three weeks later, he paid Carlos Martínez de

Irujo for another 200 bottles of champagne. Jefferson subscribed to the Georgetown balls and attended the annual horse races at the track just west of the President's House. He paid for his subscription for two prints of Niagara Falls. He made two anonymous contributions to the sufferers from a fire in Portsmouth, New Hampshire, supported the rebuilding of Dickinson College, donated to the Jefferson Monticello Academy in South Carolina, subscribed to the construction of a market in the capital, and noted several smaller sums given "in charity" (MB, 2:1086-93).

As he had often done before, Jefferson expressed his longing to retire from public life. Madame de Corny, one of his circle of friends from his years in France, agreed. She had seen his second annual message and worried that Louisiana was giving him trouble. She urged him to "hasten the end of his presidency." To Madame de Tessé, also in Paris, for whom Jefferson was gathering a selection of seeds to plant in her gardens, he claimed that he would return to Monticello, possibly in 1805 but by 1809 "at the latest." There he would turn to gardening and, in order to reap the rewards of his labor within a year, he would plant not trees, which were a lengthy undertaking, but flowers.

ACKNOWLEDGMENTS

MANY individuals have given the Editors the benefit of their aid in the preparation of this volume, and we offer them our thanks. Those who helped us use manuscript collections, answered research queries, assisted with translations, or advised in other ways are William C. Jordan, Princeton University; Neil Ann Stuckey Levine for German translations; in the libraries at Princeton, Karin A. Trainer, University Librarian, and Elizabeth Z. Bennett, Colleen M. Burlingham, Stephen Ferguson, Daniel J. Linke, Deborah T. Paparone, AnnaLee Pauls, Ben Primer, and Don C. Skemer; Timothy Connelly of the NHPRC; James H. Hutson, Barbara Bair, Julie Miller, and the staff at the Manuscript Division of the Library of Congress, especially Frederick J. Augustyn, Jennifer Brathovde, Jeffrey Flannery, Joseph Jackson, Lia Kerwin, Patrick Kerwin, Bruce Kirby, and Lewis Wyman; Peter Drummey and the library staff of the Massachusetts Historical Society, especially Nancy Heywood for providing digital scans; Susan Halpert, Houghton Library, Harvard University; Robert C. Ritchie, Sara N. Ash Georgi, Juan Gomez, and Olga Tsapina at the Huntington Library; James W. Campbell of the New Haven Museum and Historical Society; Anna Berkes, William L. Beiswanger, and Lucia C. Stanton of the Thomas Jefferson Foundation at Monticello; Nicole Bouché, Regina Rush, and the staff of Special Collections at the University of Virginia Library; Beatriz Hardy and Susan A. Riggs, Swem Library, the College of William and Mary; Sara Bearss and Brent Tarter, Library of Virginia; Dennis Northcott and the staff of the Missouri Historical Society; Martin Levitt, Roy Goodman, Charles B. Greifenstein, and Earl E. Spamer of the American Philosophical Society; Patrick Spero, formerly of the APS and now at Williams College; James N. Green of the Library Company of Philadelphia; the staff of the New York Public Library; the Gilder Lehrman Institute of American History and Jean W. Ashton and Edward O'Reilly of the New-York Historical Society; Charles M. Harris of the Papers of William Thornton, and our fellow editors at the Thomas Jefferson Retirement Series at Monticello, the Adams Papers at the Massachusetts Historical Society, the Papers of George Washington and the Papers of James Madison at the University of Virginia, the James Monroe Papers at the University of Mary Washington, and the Papers of Benjamin Franklin at Yale University. For assistance with illustrations we are indebted to Alfred L. Bush of Princeton and Bonnie Coles of the Library of Congress. Stephen

Perkins and Jason Bush of dataformat.com provided essential technical support for us with the XML preparation of these volumes. We thank Alice Calaprice for careful reading and Jan Lilly for her unparalleled mastery of what a Jefferson volume must be. We appreciate especially the support and leadership of Peter J. Dougherty, Director of Princeton University Press. Others at the Press who never fail to give these volumes the benefit of their expertise are Adam Fortgang, Dimitri Karetnikov, Neil Litt, Elizabeth Litz, Clara Platter, Linny Schenck, and Brigitta van Rheinberg.

For many volumes of *The Papers of Thomas Jefferson*, Robert W. Hartle skillfully and patiently assisted us with transcriptions and translations of French documents. We extend our deepest gratitude for his knowledge and dedication.

EDITORIAL METHOD AND APPARATUS

1. RENDERING THE TEXT

Julian P. Boyd eloquently set forth a comprehensive editorial policy in Volume 1 of *The Papers of Thomas Jefferson*. Adopting what he described as a "middle course" for rendering eighteenth-century handwritten materials into print, Boyd set the standards for modern historical editing. His successors, Charles T. Cullen and John Catanzariti, reaffirmed Boyd's high standards. At the same time, they made changes in textual policy and editorial apparatus as they deemed appropriate. For Boyd's policy and subsequent modifications to it, readers are encouraged to consult Vol. 1: xxix-xxxviii; Vol. 22: vii-xi; and Vol. 24: vii-viii.

The revised, more literal textual method, which appeared for the first time in Volume 30, adheres to the following guidelines: Abbreviations will be retained as written. Where the meaning is sufficiently unclear to require editorial intervention, the expansion will be given in the explanatory annotation. Capitalization will follow the usage of the writer. Because the line between uppercase and lowercase letters can be a very fine and fluctuating one, when it is impossible to make an absolute determination of the author's intention, we will adopt modern usage. Jefferson rarely began his sentences with an uppercase letter, and we conform to his usage. Punctuation will be retained as written and double marks of punctuation, such as a period followed by a dash, will be allowed to stand. Misspellings or so-called slips of the pen will be allowed to stand or will be recorded in a subjoined textual note.

English translations or translation summaries will be supplied for foreign-language documents. In some instances, when documents are lengthy and not especially pertinent to Jefferson's concerns or if our edition's typography cannot adequately represent the script of a language, we will provide only a summary in English. In most cases we will print in full the text in its original language and also provide a full English translation. If a contemporary translation that Jefferson made or would have used is extant, we may print it in lieu of a modern translation. Our own translations are designed to provide a basic readable English text for the modern user rather than to preserve all aspects of the original diction and language.

2. *TEXTUAL DEVICES*

The following devices are employed throughout the work to clarify the presentation of the text.

[. . .]	Text missing and not conjecturable.
[ ]	Number or part of a number missing or illegible.
[roman]	Conjectural reading for missing or illegible matter. A question mark follows when the reading is doubtful.
[*italic*]	Editorial comment inserted in the text.
<*italic*>	Matter deleted in the MS but restored in our text.

3. *DESCRIPTIVE SYMBOLS*

The following symbols are employed throughout the work to describe the various kinds of manuscript originals. When a series of versions is recorded, the first to be recorded is the version used for the printed text.

Dft	draft (usually a composition or rough draft; later drafts, when identifiable as such, are designated "2d Dft," &c.)
Dupl	duplicate
MS	manuscript (arbitrarily applied to most documents other than letters)
N	note, notes (memoranda, fragments, &c.)
PoC	polygraph copy
PrC	press copy
RC	recipient's copy
SC	stylograph copy
Tripl	triplicate

All manuscripts of the above types are assumed to be in the hand of the author of the document to which the descriptive symbol pertains. If not, that *fact is stated*. On the other hand, the following types of manuscripts are assumed *not* to be in the hand of the author, and exceptions will be noted:

FC	file copy (applied to all contemporary copies retained by the author or his agents)
Lb	letterbook (ordinarily used with FC and Tr to denote texts copied into bound volumes)

Tr transcript (applied to all contemporary and later copies except file copies; period of transcription, unless clear by implication, will be given when known)

4. LOCATION SYMBOLS

The locations of documents printed in this edition from originals in private hands and from printed sources are recorded in self-explanatory form in the descriptive note following each document. The locations of documents printed from originals held by public and private institutions in the United States are recorded by means of the symbols used in the National Union Catalog in the Library of Congress; an explanation of how these symbols are formed is given in Vol. 1:xl. The symbols DLC and MHi by themselves stand for the collections of Jefferson Papers proper in these repositories; when texts are drawn from other collections held by these two institutions, the names of those collections will be added. Location symbols for documents held by institutions outside the United States are given in a subjoined list.

CSmH	The Huntington Library, San Marino, California
CU-BANC	University of California, Berkeley, Bancroft Library
CtHi	Connecticut Historical Society, Hartford
CtY	Yale University, New Haven, Connecticut
CtY-Br	Yale University, Beinecke Rare Book & Manuscript Library, New Haven, Connecticut
DLC	Library of Congress
De-Ar	Delaware Department of State, Division of Historical and Cultural Affairs, Hall of Records, Dover
DeHi	Delaware Historical Society, Wilmington
FMU	University of Miami, Coral Gables, Florida
G-Ar	Georgia State Department of Archives and History, Atlanta
ICHi	Chicago Historical Society
KyU	University of Kentucky, Lexington
MB	Boston Public Library
MHi	Massachusetts Historical Society, Boston
MWA	American Antiquarian Society, Worcester, Massachusetts
MdHi	Maryland Historical Society, Baltimore
MoSHi	Missouri History Museum, St. Louis

NBLiHi	Long Island Historical Society, Brooklyn
NBuHi	Buffalo & Erie County Historical Society, Buffalo, New York
NHi	New-York Historical Society, New York City
NN	New York Public Library
NNC	Columbia University, New York City
NNFoM	Forbes Magazine, New York City
NNMus	Museum of the City of New York
NNPM	Pierpont Morgan Library, New York City
NPV	Vassar College, Poughkeepsie, New York
Nc-Ar	North Carolina Office of Archives & History, Raleigh
NcD	Duke University, Durham, North Carolina
NhPoS	Strawbery Banke, Portsmouth, New Hampshire
NjHi	New Jersey Historical Society, Newark
PHC	Haverford College, Pennsylvania
PHi	Historical Society of Pennsylvania, Philadelphia
PPAmP	American Philosophical Society, Philadelphia
PPCP	College of Physicians, Philadelphia
T	Tennessee State Library and Archives, Nashville
Vi	Library of Virginia, Richmond
ViC-M	The Thomas Jefferson Foundation, Monticello
ViU	University of Virginia, Charlottesville
ViW	College of William and Mary, Williamsburg, Virginia
VtMS	Office of the Secretary of State, State Papers Division, Montpelier, Vermont

5. *NATIONAL ARCHIVES DESIGNATIONS*

The National Archives, recognized by the location symbol DNA, with identifications of series (preceded by record group number) as follows:

RG 42	Records of the Office of Public Buildings and Public Parks of the National Capital	
	LRDLS	Letters Received and Drafts of Letters Sent
RG 45	Naval Records Collection of the Office of Naval Records and Library	
	LSO	Letters Sent to Officers
	LSP	Letters Sent to the President
	MLS	Misc. Letters Sent

RG 46 Records of the United States Senate
- EPEN Executive Proceedings, Executive Nominations
- EPFR Executive Proceedings, Foreign Relations
- EPIR Executive Proceedings, Indian Relations
- LP Legislative Proceedings
- LPPM Legislative Proceedings, President's Messages
- LPPMRSL Legislative Proceedings, Petitions, Memorials, Resolutions of State Legislatures
- LPRC Legislative Proceedings, Records Collection

RG 56 General Records of the Department of the Treasury
- CL Circular Letters
- MLS Misc. Letters Sent

RG 59 General Records of the Department of State
- CD Consular Dispatches
- DD Diplomatic Dispatches
- DL Domestic Letters
- GPR General Pardon Records
- LAR Letters of Application and Recommendation
- LOAG Letters from and Opinions of Attorneys General
- MCL Misc. Commissions and Lists
- MLR Misc. Letters Received
- MPTPC Misc. Permanent and Temporary Presidential Commissions
- NL Notes from Legations
- PTCC Permanent and Temporary Consular Commissions
- RD Resignations and Declinations

RG 75 Records of the Bureau of Indian Affairs
- LSIA Letters Sent by the Secretary of War Relating to Indian Affairs

RG 76 Records of Boundary and Claims Commissions and Arbitrations

RG 104 Records of the Mint
- DL Domestic Letters

RG 107 Records of the Office of the Secretary of War
- LSMA Letters Sent by the Secretary of War Relating to Military Affairs
- LSP Letters Sent to the President
- MLS Misc. Letters Sent
- RLRMS Register of Letters Received, Main Series

RG 217 Records of the Accounting Officers of the Department of the Treasury
- MTA Misc. Treasury Accounts

RG 233 Records of the United States House of Representatives
- PMRSL Petitions, Memorials, Resolutions of State Legislatures
- PM President's Messages
- RCSH Reports and Commissions Submitted to the House

RG 360 Records of the Continental Congress
- PCC Papers of the Continental Congress

6. *OTHER SYMBOLS AND ABBREVIATIONS*

The following symbols and abbreviations are commonly employed in the annotation throughout the work.

Second Series The topical series to be published as part of this edition, comprising those materials which are best suited to a topical rather than a chronological arrangement (see Vol. 1: xv-xvi)

TJ Thomas Jefferson

TJ Editorial Files Photoduplicates and other editorial materials in the office of The Papers of Thomas Jefferson, Princeton University Library

TJ Papers Jefferson Papers (applied to a collection of manuscripts when the precise location of an undated, misdated, or otherwise problematic document must be furnished, and always preceded by the symbol for the institutional repository; thus "DLC: TJ Papers, 4:628-9" represents a document in the Library of Congress, Jefferson Papers, volume 4, pages 628 and 629. Citations to volumes and folio numbers of the Jefferson Papers at the Library of Congress refer to the collection as it was arranged at the time the first microfilm edition was made in 1944-45. Access to the microfilm edition of the collection as it was rearranged under the Library's Presidential Papers Program is provided by the Index to the Thomas Jefferson Papers [Washington, D.C., 1976])

RG Record Group (used in designating the location of documents in the National Archives)

SJL Jefferson's "Summary Journal of Letters" written and received for the period 11 Nov. 1783 to 25 June 1826 (in DLC: TJ Papers). This register, kept in Jefferson's hand, has been checked against the TJ Editorial Files. It is to be assumed that all outgoing letters are recorded in SJL unless there is a note to the contrary. When the date of receipt of an incoming letter is recorded in SJL, it is incorporated in the notes. Information and discrepancies revealed in SJL but not found in the letter itself are also noted. Missing letters recorded in SJL are, where possible, accounted for in the notes to documents mentioning them or in related documents. A more detailed discussion of this register and its use in this edition appears in Vol. 6: vii-x

SJPL "Summary Journal of Public Letters," an incomplete list of letters and documents written by TJ from 16 Apr. 1784 to 31 Dec. 1793, with brief summaries, in an amanuensis's hand. This is supplemented by six pages in TJ's hand, compiled at a later date, listing private and confidential memorandums and notes as well as official reports and communications by and to him as Secretary of State, 11 Oct. 1789 to 31 Dec. 1793 (in DLC: TJ Papers, Epistolary Record, 514-59 and 209-11, respectively; see Vol. 22: ix-x). Since nearly all documents in the amanuensis's list are registered in SJL, while few in TJ's list are so recorded, it is to be assumed that all references to SJPL are to the list in TJ's hand unless there is a statement to the contrary

V Ecu

f Florin

£ Pound sterling or livre, depending upon context (in doubtful cases, a clarifying note will be given)

s Shilling or sou (also expressed as /)

d Penny or denier

₶ Livre Tournois

℘ Per (occasionally used for pro, pre)

7. *SHORT TITLES*

The following list includes short titles of works cited frequently in this edition. Since it is impossible to anticipate all the works to be cited in abbreviated form, the list is revised from volume to volume.

ANB John A. Garraty and Mark C. Carnes, eds., *American National Biography*, New York and Oxford, 1999, 24 vols.

Annals *Annals of the Congress of the United States: The Debates and Proceedings in the Congress of the United States . . . Compiled from Authentic Materials*, Washington, D.C., Gales & Seaton, 1834-56, 42 vols. All editions are undependable and pagination varies from one printing to another. The first two volumes of the set cited here have "Compiled . . . by Joseph Gales, Senior" on the title page and bear the caption "Gales & Seatons History" on verso and "of Debates in Congress" on recto pages. The remaining volumes bear the caption "History of Congress" on both recto and verso pages. Those using the first two volumes with the latter caption will need to employ the date of the debate or the indexes of debates and speakers.

APS American Philosophical Society

ASP *American State Papers: Documents, Legislative and Executive, of the Congress of the United States*, Washington, D.C., 1832-61, 38 vols.

Bear, *Family Letters* Edwin M. Betts and James A. Bear, Jr., eds., *Family Letters of Thomas Jefferson*, Columbia, Mo., 1966

Bedini, *Statesman of Science* Silvio A. Bedini, *Thomas Jefferson: Statesman of Science*, New York, 1990

Betts, *Farm Book* Edwin M. Betts, ed., *Thomas Jefferson's Farm Book*, Princeton, 1953

Betts, *Garden Book* Edwin M. Betts, ed., *Thomas Jefferson's Garden Book, 1766-1824*, Philadelphia, 1944

Biog. Dir. Cong. *Biographical Directory of the United States Congress, 1774-1989*, Washington, D.C., 1989

Biographie universelle *Biographie universelle, ancienne et moderne*, new ed., Paris, 1843-65, 45 vols.

Brigham, *American Newspapers* Clarence S. Brigham, *History and Bibliography of American Newspapers, 1690-1820*, Worcester, Mass., 1947, 2 vols.

Bryan, *National Capital* Wilhelmus B. Bryan, *A History of the National Capital from Its Foundation through the Period of the Adoption of the Organic Act*, New York, 1914-16, 2 vols.

Bush, *Life Portraits* Alfred L. Bush, *The Life Portraits of Thomas Jefferson*, rev. ed., Charlottesville, 1987

CVSP William P. Palmer and others, eds., *Calendar of Virginia State Papers . . . Preserved in the Capitol at Richmond*, Richmond, 1875-93, 11 vols.

DAB Allen Johnson and Dumas Malone, eds., *Dictionary of American Biography*, New York, 1928-36, 20 vols.

DHSC Maeva Marcus and others, eds., *The Documentary History of the Supreme Court of the United States, 1789-1800*, New York, 1985-2007, 8 vols.

Dictionnaire *Dictionnaire de biographie française*, Paris, 1933- , 19 vols.

DNB H. C. G. Matthew and Brian Harrison, eds., *Oxford Dictionary of National Biography, In Association with The British Academy, From the Earliest Times to the Year 2000,* Oxford, 2004, 60 vols.

DSB Charles C. Gillispie, ed., *Dictionary of Scientific Biography*, New York, 1970-80, 16 vols.

Durey, *Callender* Michael Durey, *"With the Hammer of Truth": James Thomson Callender and America's Early National Heroes*, Charlottesville, 1990

DVB John T. Kneebone and others, eds., *Dictionary of Virginia Biography*, Richmond, 1998- , 3 vols.

EG Dickinson W. Adams and Ruth W. Lester, eds., *Jefferson's Extracts from the Gospels*, Princeton, 1983, *The Papers of Thomas Jefferson*, Second Series

Esarey, *William Henry Harrison* Logan Esarey, ed., *Messages and Letters of William Henry Harrison*, Indianapolis, 1922; repr., New York, 1975, 2 vols.

Evans Charles Evans, Clifford K. Shipton, and Roger P. Bristol, comps., *American Bibliography: A Chronological Dictionary of All Books, Pamphlets and Periodical Publications Printed in the United States of America from . . . 1639 . . . to . . . 1820*, Chicago and Worcester, Mass., 1903-59, 14 vols.

Foner, *Thomas Paine* Philip S. Foner, ed., *The Complete Writings of Thomas Paine*, New York, 1945, 2 vols.

Ford Paul Leicester Ford, ed., *The Writings of Thomas Jefferson*, Letterpress Edition, New York, 1892-99, 10 vols.

Gallatin, *Papers* Carl E. Prince and Helene E. Fineman, eds., *The Papers of Albert Gallatin*, microfilm edition in 46 reels, Philadelphia, 1969, and Supplement, Barbara B. Oberg, ed., reels 47-51, Wilmington, Del., 1985

Grainger, *Amiens Truce* John D. Grainger, *The Amiens Truce: Britain and Bonaparte, 1801-1803*, Rochester, N.Y., 2004

HAW Henry A. Washington, ed., *The Writings of Thomas Jefferson*, New York, 1853-54, 9 vols.

Heitman, *Dictionary* Francis B. Heitman, comp., *Historical Register and Dictionary of the United States Army*, Washington, D.C., 1903, 2 vols.

Heitman, *Register* Francis B. Heitman, *Historical Register of Officers of the Continental Army during the War of the Revolution, April, 1775, to December, 1793*, new ed., Washington, D.C., 1914

Higginbotham, *Pennsylvania Politics* Sanford W. Higginbotham, *The Keystone in the Democratic Arch: Pennsylvania Politics 1800-1816*, Harrisburg, 1952

Jackson, *Lewis and Clark* Donald Jackson, ed., *The Letters of the Lewis and Clark Expedition, with Related Documents, 1783-1854*, 2d ed., Urbana, Ill., 1978

JCC Worthington Ford and others, eds., *Journals of the Continental Congress, 1774-1789*, Washington, D.C., 1904-37, 34 vols.

JEP *Journal of the Executive Proceedings of the Senate of the United States . . . to the Termination of the Nineteenth Congress*, Washington, D.C., 1828, 3 vols.

JHR *Journal of the House of Representatives of the United States*, Washington, D.C., 1826, 9 vols.

JS *Journal of the Senate of the United States*, Washington, D.C., 1820-21, 5 vols.

King, *Life* Charles R. King, ed., *The Life and Correspondence of Rufus King: Comprising His Letters, Private and Official, His Public Documents and His Speeches*, New York, 1894-1900, 6 vols.

Kline, *Burr* Mary-Jo Kline, ed., *Political Correspondence and Public Papers of Aaron Burr*, Princeton, 1983, 2 vols.

L & B Andrew A. Lipscomb and Albert E. Bergh, eds., *The Writings of Thomas Jefferson*, Washington, D.C., 1903-04, 20 vols.

LCB Douglas L. Wilson, ed., *Jefferson's Literary Commonplace Book*, Princeton, 1989, *The Papers of Thomas Jefferson*, Second Series

Latrobe, *Correspondence* John C. Van Horne and Lee W. Formwalt, eds., *The Correspondence and Miscellaneous Papers of Benjamin Henry Latrobe*, New Haven, 1984-88, 3 vols.

Leonard, *General Assembly* Cynthia Miller Leonard, comp., *The General Assembly of Virginia, July 30, 1619-January 11, 1978: A Bicentennial Register of Members*, Richmond, 1978

List of Patents *A List of Patents granted by the United States from April 10, 1790, to December 31, 1836*, Washington, D.C., 1872

McLaughlin, *Jefferson and Monticello* Jack McLaughlin, *Jefferson and Monticello: The Biography of a Builder*, New York, 1988

Madison, *Papers* William T. Hutchinson, Robert A. Rutland, J. C. A. Stagg, and others, eds., *The Papers of James Madison*, Chicago and Charlottesville, 1962- , 33 vols.
Sec. of State Ser., 1986- , 9 vols.
Pres. Ser., 1984- , 6 vols.
Ret. Ser., 2009- , 1 vol.

Malone, *Jefferson* Dumas Malone, *Jefferson and His Time*, Boston, 1948-81, 6 vols.

Marshall, *Papers* Herbert A. Johnson, Charles T. Cullen, Charles F. Hobson, and others, eds., *The Papers of John Marshall*, Chapel Hill, 1974-2006, 12 vols.

Mattern and Shulman, *Dolley Madison* David B. Mattern and Holly C. Shulman, eds., *The Selected Letters of Dolley Payne Madison*, Charlottesville, 2003

MB James A. Bear, Jr., and Lucia C. Stanton, eds., *Jefferson's Memorandum Books: Accounts, with Legal Records and Miscellany, 1767-1826*, Princeton, 1997, *The Papers of Thomas Jefferson*, Second Series

Miller, *Treaties* Hunter Miller, ed., *Treaties and Other International Acts of the United States of America*, Washington, D.C., 1931-48, 8 vols.

NDBW Dudley W. Knox, ed., *Naval Documents Related to the United States Wars with the Barbary Powers*, Washington, D.C., 1939-44, 6 vols., and *Register of Officer Personnel and Ships' Data, 1801-1807*, Washington, D.C., 1945

NDQW Dudley W. Knox, ed., *Naval Documents Related to the Quasi-War between the United States and France, Naval Operations*, Washington, D.C., 1935-38, 7 vols. (cited by years)

Nichols, *Architectural Drawings* Frederick Doveton Nichols, *Thomas Jefferson's Architectural Drawings, Compiled and with Commentary and a Check List*, Charlottesville, 1978

Notes, ed. Peden *Thomas Jefferson, Notes on the State of Virginia*, ed. William Peden, Chapel Hill, 1955

OED J. A. Simpson and E. S. C. Weiner, eds., *The Oxford English Dictionary*, Oxford, 1989, 20 vols.

Papenfuse, *Maryland Legislature* Edward C. Papenfuse, Alan F. Day, David W. Jordan, and Gregory A. Stiverson, eds., *A Biographical Dictionary of the Maryland Legislature, 1635-1789*, Baltimore, 1979-85, 2 vols.

Parry, *Consolidated Treaty Series* Clive Parry, ed., *The Consolidated Treaty Series*, Dobbs Ferry, N.Y., 1969-81, 231 vols.

Pasley, *Tyranny of Printers* Jeffrey L. Pasley, *"The Tyranny of Printers": Newspaper Politics in the Early American Republic*, Charlottesville, 2001

Peale, *Papers* Lillian B. Miller and others, eds., *The Selected Papers of Charles Willson Peale and His Family*, New Haven, 1983-2000, 5 vols. in 6

PMHB *Pennsylvania Magazine of History and Biography*, 1877-

Preston, *Catalogue* Daniel Preston, *A Comprehensive Catalogue of the Correspondence and Papers of James Monroe*, Westport, Conn., 2001, 2 vols.

Prince, *Federalists* Carl E. Prince, *The Federalists and the Origins of the U.S. Civil Service*, New York, 1977

PW Wilbur S. Howell, ed., *Jefferson's Parliamentary Writings*, Princeton, 1988, *The Papers of Thomas Jefferson*, Second Series

RCHS *Records of the Columbia Historical Society*, 1895-1989

Rowe, *McKean* G. S. Rowe, *Thomas McKean, The Shaping of an American Republicanism*, Boulder, Colo., 1978

RS J. Jefferson Looney and others, eds., *The Papers of Thomas Jefferson: Retirement Series*, Princeton, 2004- , 8 vols.

S.C. Biographical Directory, House of Representatives J. S. R. Faunt, Walter B. Edgar, N. Louise Bailey, and others, eds., *Biographical Directory of the South Carolina House of Representatives*, Columbia, S.C., 1974-92, 5 vols.

Seale, *The President's House* William Seale, *The President's House*, Washington, D.C., 1986, 2 vols.

Shaw-Shoemaker Ralph R. Shaw and Richard H. Shoemaker, comps., *American Bibliography: A Preliminary Checklist for 1801-1819*, New York, 1958-63, 22 vols.

Shepherd, *Statutes* Samuel Shepherd, ed., *The Statutes at Large of Virginia, from October Session 1792, to December Session 1806 . . .*, Richmond, 1835-36, 3 vols.

Smith, *St. Clair Papers* William Henry Smith, ed., *The St. Clair Papers, The Life and Public Services of Arthur St. Clair*, Cincinnati, 1882, 2 vols.

Sowerby E. Millicent Sowerby, comp., *Catalogue of the Library of Thomas Jefferson*, Washington, D.C., 1952-59, 5 vols.

Stanton, *Free Some Day* Lucia Stanton, *Free Some Day: The African-American Families of Monticello*, Charlottesville, 2000

Stets, *Postmasters* Robert J. Stets, *Postmasters & Postoffices of the United States 1782-1811*, Lake Oswego, Ore., 1994

Sturtevant, *Handbook* William C. Sturtevant, gen. ed., *Handbook of North American Indians*, Washington, D.C., 1978- , 14 vols.

Syrett, *Hamilton* Harold C. Syrett and others, eds., *The Papers of Alexander Hamilton*, New York, 1961-87, 27 vols.

Terr. Papers Clarence E. Carter and John Porter Bloom, eds., *The Territorial Papers of the United States*, Washington, D.C., 1934-75, 28 vols.

TJR Thomas Jefferson Randolph, ed., *Memoir, Correspondence, and Miscellanies, from the Papers of Thomas Jefferson*, Charlottesville, 1829, 4 vols.

Tulard, *Dictionnaire Napoléon* Jean Tulard, *Dictionnaire Napoléon*, Paris, 1987

U.S. Statutes at Large Richard Peters, ed., *The Public Statutes at Large of the United States . . . 1789 to March 3, 1845*, Boston, 1855-56, 8 vols.

VMHB *Virginia Magazine of History and Biography*, 1893-

Washington, *Papers* W. W. Abbot, Dorothy Twohig, Philander D. Chase, Theodore J. Crackel, Edward C. Lengel, and others, eds., *The Papers of George Washington*, Charlottesville, 1983- , 56 vols.

Confed. Ser., 1992-97, 6 vols.

Pres. Ser., 1987- , 16 vols.

Ret. Ser., 1998-99, 4 vols.

Rev. War Ser., 1985- , 20 vols.

WMQ *William and Mary Quarterly*, 1892-

Woods, *Albemarle* Edgar Woods, *Albemarle County in Virginia*, Charlottesville, 1901

CONTENTS

CONTENTS

1803

CONTENTS

APPENDICES

ILLUSTRATIONS

Following page 322

BROADSIDE FROM THE MISSISSIPPI HERALD

Americans who relied on the Mississippi River and its tributaries to ship the produce of their farms to market received terrible news in the fall of 1802. Juan Ventura Morales, the Spanish official at New Orleans known as the intendant, revoked the policy that allowed U.S. citizens to deposit their goods at the port without paying customs duties while awaiting transshipment (see John Brown to TJ, 26 Nov.). The handbill illustrated here, which was printed in Natchez on the evening of 28 Oct. 1802, captures the urgency of the information. Beneath its dramatic headline, the sheet announces: "By an Express arrived this evening from New-Orleans, we have received the following important intelligence, which we hasten to give to our readers." There follows an extract of a letter written 19 Oct. by a "gentleman in New-Orleans" to an unidentified friend in Natchez. Officials had already prohibited the unloading of flour from two boats that had come down the Mississippi and cargoes of cotton and other goods from Natchez were sure to meet the same fate. This measure, the letter writer reported, "must produce infinite embarrassment, as well as much loss to many of the citizens of the United States." Following the extract of the letter is an English translation of Morales's proclamation, signed by the intendant on 16 Oct. and countersigned by Peter Pedesclaux, the Spanish government's clerk and notary in Louisiana. Jefferson probably never saw this handbill, but the agitation spawned by Morales's decree played a role in the decision to send James Monroe to Paris to parley for New Orleans.

The *Mississippi Herald*, a Natchez newspaper established by Andrew Marschalk only a few months earlier, produced the broadside. The handwritten note visible at the top of the sheet directed this copy of the handbill to "Capt. Joseph Vedal"—meaning José Vidal, the commander of a Spanish outpost and settlement located across the Mississippi River from Natchez (Brigham, *American Newspapers*, 1:426; José Montero de Pedro, *The Spanish in New Orleans and Louisiana*, trans. Richard E. Chandler [Gretna, La., 2000], 121-4; Madison, *Papers*, *Sec. of State Ser.*, 5:387).

Marschalk printed the announcement on a sheet about 7 inches by 11 inches in size. The image illustrated here was created from a photostat at the Library of Congress of an original in the Papeles de Cuba of the Archivo General de Indias in Sevilla, Spain (Douglas C. McMurtrie, *A Bibliography of Mississippi Imprints, 1798-1830* [Beauvoir Community, Miss., 1945], 38, fig. 20; Shaw-Shoemaker, No. 2914).

Courtesy of the Library of Congress.

DRY DOCK

The Peace Establishment Act, approved just before Jefferson took office in March 1801, reduced the size of the United States Navy to 13 frigates. The statute called for six of the frigates to remain in service, with the others to be "laid up in convenient ports." In 1802, Jefferson developed a different plan for storing warships in one place for efficiency and economy. In November he asked Benjamin Henry Latrobe to design a great dry dock at Washington. A rectangular reservoir 175 feet wide and 800 feet long, Jefferson informed Latrobe, could accommodate 12 frigates. If the facility could be built near the navy yard on the Eastern Branch (the Anacostia River), no pumps would be needed to fill the huge basin, for a canal could bring water from the Potomac by natural flow (U.S. Statutes at Large, 2:110-11; Vol. 33:250n; Vol. 37:682-3; Vol. 38:90-1, 542-3, 619-21).

Illustrated here are Latrobe's diagrams for "the principal Dry Dock or Naval Arsenal," giving graphic form to the president's specifications. The architect and engineer prepared these drawings by early December, in pencil, ink, and watercolor on a sheet approximately 20 inches by 33 inches in size. Along the middle of the paper is a top-down plan of the dry dock, in the dimensions asked for by the president. Below that is an elevation drawing of one of the long sides of the structure, which would be open to the air along the sides. Latrobe also made elevation drawings of the ends of the building, seen here at either end of the plan view. His finely detailed illustrations showed how a dozen 44-gun frigates would fit into the basin, three abreast by four deep, their masts and rigging removed and the hulls propped up to hold the ships upright after the water was drained away. At the top of the sheet are two cross sections. Latrobe also drew plans, not shown here, for the feeder canal from the Potomac and for a lock system to raise the ships 24 feet from the level of the Eastern Branch to the dry dock above. Latrobe signed the corner of the sheet: "B. Henry Latrobe Engineer Decr. 4th. 1802." Latrobe's reports and beautifully rendered designs confirmed the president's suppositions about the project. Jefferson included a proposal for the dry dock in his annual message to Congress in mid-December, but Congress did not make an appropriation and the facility was never constructed (Darwin H. Stapleton, ed., *The Engineering Drawings of Benjamin Henry Latrobe* [New Haven, 1980], 116-24; Vol. 38:619-21; Robert Smith to TJ, 8 Dec.; Annual Message to Congress, 15 Dec.).

Courtesy of the Library of Congress.

CROSS SECTION OF DRY DOCK

Seen here is one of the two cross-section views from Latrobe's sheet of diagrams of the dry dock. Jefferson saw the facility's immense tank, which would be made of stone, as similar to a canal lock in its construction. It must be covered, however, to protect the ships from the elements, particularly the harsh rays of the sun. He knew that the dimensions he gave Latrobe would allow for a roof: "over a bason," he wrote, "not wider than 175. feet, a roof can be thrown, in the manner of that of the Halle au blé at Paris." Jefferson first saw the large domed roof of the Halle aux Bleds, the grain market in Paris, in 1786. He studied the design, an elegant system of arched ribs, and adapted it for the dome on his house at Monticello. To cover the long, rectangular ship basin, the roof would need to be a section of a cylinder rather than a dome, but the concept of using curved laminated ribs would be the same. With "no underworks to support it," Jefferson wrote, such a roof would not interfere with the movement of ships in and out of the dry dock.

Where the spaces between the ribs in the dome of the Halle aux Bleds were filled with windows to admit light, in Latrobe's design the dry dock would have been roofed in sheet metal (Stapleton, *Engineering Drawings*, 116-17; McLaughlin, *Jefferson and Monticello*, 213, 219; Vol. 38:90, 619-20; Annual Message to Congress, 15 Dec.).

This cross section also shows the gates that were to connect the dry dock to the lock system. Above the gates Latrobe painted the masts of ships in the distance, as they might appear if the vessels were anchored on the Eastern Branch, 24 feet lower than the water level of the dry dock when its reservoir was filled. Raised runners, labeled 1, 2, and 3, are visible at the bottom of this cross section. They were to support the keels of three rows of ships. Latrobe labeled this diagram "Fig V. Section of the Arsenal, looking to the Harbor."

Courtesy of the Library of Congress.

VIEW OF WASHINGTON

In this scene, the two buildings in the far background are the President's House (left) and the Treasury Building (right). The view is toward the northwest. The large brick building at the right edge of the picture is Blodget's Hotel, designed by James Hoban on a commission from Samuel Blodget, Jr., who intended the building to be the prize of a lottery. That venture failed, and in 1800 the structure became the home of Washington's first theater. The federal government purchased the building in 1810 to house the Post Office and Patent Office, and Congress met there after British troops damaged the Capitol in 1814.

This view in watercolors, 9 inches high and about 13½ inches wide, is by Nicholas King, who became surveyor of the city in 1803. He probably painted the scene in the period 1799 to 1801. King advertised two engravings for sale by subscription in 1801, one of the President's House and executive office buildings, the other depicting the Capitol (Margaret Burri, "A New View of Blodget's Hotel," *Washington History*, 2 [1990], 103-6; Ralph E. Ehrenberg, "Nicholas King: First Surveyor of the City of Washington, 1803-1812," RCHS, 69-70 [1971], 34, 54-5; Bryan, *National Capital*, 528, 631n; Vol. 35:657; Vol. 38:234; Samuel Hanson to TJ, 11 Feb. 1803).

Courtesy of the Huntington Library, San Marino, California (HM 52665).

LETTER FROM THOMAS JEFFERSON RANDOLPH

Thomas Jefferson Randolph wrote this letter to his grandfather in February 1803, when he was ten years old. The undated document is printed in this volume at 24 Feb., the day Jefferson received it (see also a letter from the president to the boy—calling him "my dear Jefferson"—at 21 Feb.). Master Randolph had recently visited his "Grand Papa" in Washington with his mother, younger sister, and aunt. They arrived on 21 Nov. and stayed for several weeks in the President's House. During that visit, he later recalled, the youngster made an impromptu visit to the navy yard accompanied only by coachman Joseph Dougherty. The escapade drew a reprimand from the boy's mother but amused his grandfather. Years later, Thomas Jefferson Randolph published the first edition of his grandfather's papers (Malone, *Jefferson*, 4:172; Vol. 36:657n; Statement of Account with Meriwether

Lewis, 21 Nov.; TJ to John Wayles Eppes, 22 Nov.). This document is in the Randolph Family Papers (1783-1909, n.d., accession no. 6225).

Courtesy of Special Collections, University of Virginia Library, Charlottesville.

SENECA MOTHER AND CHILD

Several leaders of the Seneca Indians communicated to Jefferson in the winter of 1803. Farmer's Brother, an ally of Red Jacket, led a delegation to meet with the president, and Cornplanter and Handsome Lake sent letters. Divided over the course to be followed in response to the transformations they and other Native Americans were facing, the Senecas spoke to Jefferson in multiple voices. He, however, had formed a unified policy toward all Indians, to hem them in "systematically" while encouraging and requiring them to become yeoman farmers (see the memorandum for Henry Dearborn at 29 Dec., the letters to Cornplanter and others on 11 Feb. and to Handsome Lake on 12 Feb., and the address to Farmer's Brother and others at 14 Feb.; for divisions among the Senecas see also Vol. 38:273, 274-5n, 342-4, 628-31).

The unidentified Seneca woman captured in this 1808 portrait illustrates that transitional period in which she lived. Her skirt may have been made of blue muslin cloth that was included in her tribe's annuity from the United States government. The textiles of her robe, which has a ruffled edge and a blue stripe, were very likely also of manufactured origin, but she uses it in a traditional fashion, as a garment and to help her carry her child. She wears leggings, one of which is visible at her ankle, and no shoes. She is on a chair, but appears to perch on it rather than sitting comfortably (William N. Fenton, "The Hyde de Neuville Portraits of New York Savages in 1807-1808," *New-York Historical Society Quarterly*, 38 [1954], 133, 136; William C. Sturtevant, "Patagonian Giants and Baroness Hyde de Neuville's Iroquois Drawings," *Ethnohistory*, 27 [1980], 341).

An amateur artist, Henriette Hyde de Neuville, made the portrait in pencil and watercolor in New York State in 1808. She and her husband, Jean Guillaume Hyde de Neuville, a royalist exile from France, first came to the United States in 1807, bearing a letter of introduction to Jefferson from Madame d'Houdetot. They traveled through western New York that year and returned to spend a few summers in the small town of Angelica, where several prominent French émigré families had houses. The town (named for Jefferson's friend Angelica Schuyler Church) was on the Genessee River, on land formerly possessed by the Senecas and not far from their reservations in the western end of New York. The Hydes lived in America until 1814, and again from 1816 to 1822, when Jean Guillaume, then a baron, was the French minister to the United States. Henriette Hyde's drawings and watercolors provide a visual record of people, towns, and scenes neglected by professional portraitists and landscape painters. Reflecting her inexperience with the English language when she made this portrait of woman and child, she titled it "Squah of Seneca tribe with his papou." She dated the picture August 1808. The work (New-York Historical Society accession number 1953.209) is $7\frac{1}{4}$ inches high and $5\frac{7}{8}$ inches wide (Jadviga M. da Costa Nunes and Ferris Olin, *Baroness Hyde de Neuville: Sketches of America, 1807-1822* [New Brunswick, N.J., 1984], 1-10, 35; *Dictionnaire*, 18:117-19; Jacques

Faugeras, *Hide de Neuville: Irréductible adversaire de Napoléon Bonaparte* [Paris, 2003], 108-130; Sturtevant, *Handbook*, 15:512; RS, 4:374n; Madame d'Houdetot to TJ, 16 Aug. 1806, and Jean Guillaume Hyde de Neuville to TJ, 22 Dec. 1807, both in DLC).

Collection of the New-York Historical Society.

"SAUVAGE DE BALSTON SPRING"

Soon after they arrived in the United States, the Hydes set out for Niagara Falls and stopped over at Ballston Spa, about 30 miles north of Albany. Known for its mineral waters, Ballston Spa offered visitors hotels and bathhouses and was a vacation spot for members of the social elite of New York City. It was there that Henriette and Jean Guillaume Hyde de Neuville first encountered Native Americans. The Indians at Ballston struck Monsieur Hyde as "à peu près civilisés," somewhat more civilized, than the people he later saw on reservations in New York State. We do not know how many Native Americans he saw in the resort town, but they were not as barbaric as he had expected them to be: apart from the tone of their skin, he decided, there was little to identify them as native people. He recorded that his wife drew one of them, a girl of large stature. The sketch illustrated here, labeled as a picture of a "Sauvage de Balston Spring" made in July 1807, is likely one of the portraits Henriette Hyde made of that young woman. Neither of the Hydes made note of her tribe. Jean Guillaume noted only that she was of the "country" (*patrie*) of Atala. That comment merely identified her as an American Indian, for the title character of François René de Chateaubriand's novel *Atala*, first published in 1801, was a fictional woman of the Natchez Indians living in the lower Mississippi Valley in the late 17th or early 18th century. The Hydes met Chateaubriand at Cadiz just before they embarked for the United States, and Jean Guillaume Hyde and the author began a lasting friendship. On Hyde's arrival in the New World, Atala represented his and many Europeans' idealized American *sauvage*. As Hyde had to acknowledge, even on his visits to reservations he never encountered the exotic "sauvages belliqueux" who roamed an idyllic state of nature in Chateaubriand's romance. Atala's hold on Hyde was powerful, though, and he faulted the young woman who sat for her portrait at Ballston Spa for lacking the fictional heroine's charm and grace. Henriette Hyde de Neuville, too, was influenced by romanticized depictions of New World natives, for a watercolor she made of "an indian and his Squah" was a copy of a published depiction of Patagonians. Nevertheless, her portraits of the Indians who posed for her in New York State appear to be accurate representations of her subjects (Jean Guillaume Hyde de Neuville, *Mémoires et souvenirs du Baron Hyde de Neuville*, 3 vols. [Paris, 1888-92], 1:451-9; François René de Chateaubriand, *Atala and René*, trans. Rayner Heppenstall, introduction by Robert Baldick [London, 1963], vi-xv, 6, 10; *Dictionnaire*, 18:117-18; Sturtevant, "Patagonian Giants," 331-48; da Costa Nunes and Olin, *Baroness Hyde de Neuville*, 7-9; Nancy Goyne Evans, "The Sans Souci, a Fashionable Resort Hotel in Ballston Spa," *Winterthur Portfolio*, 6 [1970], 111-14; Richard H. Gassan, *The Birth of American Tourism: New York, the Hudson Valley, and American Culture, 1790-1830* [Amherst, Mass., 2008], 9-28, 107-8).

The individual portrayed here was perhaps a Mohawk, for that nation once occupied the region to the west of Ballston and Mohawks knew the springs there long before the place became a resort. Most of them left the area by the end of the Revolutionary War, however. She may have been one of the Stockbridge Mohicans, the remainder of a group that earlier had lived in the upper Hudson Valley and western Massachusetts. The American Revolution had displaced them, too, and in the early 19th century they lived near the Oneidas in central New York. There is a good chance that whatever her tribal affiliation may have been, the young woman in the picture was, like the imagined Atala, a Christian. Whatever her identity, in the span of her parents' lifetime and her own, Indians in that region went through great changes in where and how they lived. In this portrait she wears moccasins, leggings, ear loops, and, like the Seneca mother in the facing illustration, a blanket wrap or robe. Those articles may have adhered to traditional designs, but her pretty hat, a manufactured article, did not (Fenton, "Hyde de Neuville Portraits," 126-7; Sturtevant, "Patagonian Giants," 340; Sturtevant, *Handbook*, 15:198, 209, 475-8; TJ to Farmer's Brother and Others, 14 Feb., and to Dearborn, 15 Feb., in this volume). This drawing in pencil (New-York Historical Society accession number 1953.216) is $8\frac{1}{8}$ by $6\frac{3}{8}$ inches in size. Henriette Hyde de Neuville made another picture of this young woman at Ballston, a head-and-shoulders portrait without her robe and hat, in watercolor, pencil, charcoal, gouache, and ink (N-YHS accession 1953.217).

Collection of the New-York Historical Society.

"MAD TOM IN A RAGE"

According to a widely circulated account, Thomas Paine's first act after setting foot on the wharf in Baltimore on a late-October day in 1802 was to find a tavern, quaff some brandy, and credit Thomas Jefferson for making possible his return to the United States after an absence of 15 years. Paine's opponents despised him as an apostate: if he was in a state of grace when he wrote *Common Sense*—which he penned as "a hireling," they decided—he damned himself by affronting Christianity in *The Age of Reason* and attacking the first president in the confrontational *Letter to George Washington.* Federalist newspapers labeled him an "infidel" and compared him to Benedict Arnold. His heresy, involving both religion and politics, was complete. Not only did he show no sign of remorse, he now trumpeted his cordial relationship with the equally heretical Jefferson. Their enemies condemned them, each as the particular friend of the other: Paine was "*Mr. Jefferson's affectionate friend*" and Jefferson was "the friend of the author of the '*Age of Reason.*'" The duo's "united exertions" could "*destroy the reputation of Washington and with it the administration of our government*," Federalists proclaimed (*Philadelphia Gazette*, 2 Nov.; *Alexandria Advertiser*, 10 Nov.; *New-York Herald*, 13 Nov.; Georgetown *Olio*, 18 Nov.; *Washington Federalist*, 26 Nov.; Boston *Mercury and New-England Palladium*, 30 Nov.; John Keane, *Tom Paine: A Political Life* [London, 1995], 455-63; ANB).

That union of president and polemicist, bonded together for allegedly nefarious purpose, is the subject of the cartoon illustrated here. Although this copy is untitled, at least one extant issue of the print has a caption, "Mad Tom in a Rage." The print is undated and the artist and printer have not been identified, yet the image contains language and visual symbols associated with Paine's return to the United States. He is shown to be in league with the Devil—who is Thomas Jefferson. Together they tug at a strong pillar that represents the United States government and bears the names of Washington and Adams. Paine, a brandy bottle at his feet, strains at the rope and says of his task, "Oh! I fear it is stronger rooted than I expected but with the assistance of my Old Friend & a little more Brandy I will bring it down." Jefferson-as-Lucifer, embracing Paine from behind to help him pull, declares: "Pull away Pull away my Son dont fear I'll give you all my assistance." Some of the papers sticking out of Paine's pocket are untitled, labeled only with the word "Manuscript," but the anonymous artist took care to identify two of the sheets. One has the partial title "Letters to the Citizens of," signifying the essays that Paine began to publish, soon after his arrival, as *Letters to the Citizens of the United States*. Their contents were so inflammatory that even William Duane, a political ally of Paine and no stranger to polemics, wished that Paine would exercise some restraint (see Duane's letter to Jefferson at 26 Nov.). The other partial title is "3d Part of," a reference to a rumored third installment of *The Age of Reason*, which, Federalists warned each other in November 1802, Paine was readying for publication under Jefferson's patronage (*New-York Gazette and General Advertiser*, 13 Nov.; *Salem Gazette*, 16 Nov.; Hudson, N.Y., *Balance, and Columbian Repository*, 16 Nov.; Providence, R.I., *United States Chronicle*, 18 Nov.; New York *Commercial Advertiser*, 22 Nov.; John Rhodehamel, *The Great Experiment: George Washington and the American Republic* [New Haven, 1998], 140).

An eagle defending the pillar of government from Paine echoes a motif from an earlier anti-Jefferson cartoon, "The Providential Detection," in which the American eagle fends off Jefferson to protect the Constitution and the independence of the United States. In that caricature, Jefferson was not Satan but certainly an acolyte of the Prince of Darkness, who lurks to one side (Vol. 29:xxxvii, 318 [illus.]). Not surprisingly, Paine frequently found himself linked to demons or the Devil by cartoonists and satirists. Nor was this the first representation of Paine as "Mad Tom"; caricaturists called him that as early as 1791. The nickname was not coined for him, but was rather a well-worn trope. Sometimes in the form "Tom of Bedlam," it stretched back at least as far as Shakespeare's *King Lear*. A 17th-century song, still sometimes heard in American music halls during Jefferson's presidency, kept the figurative image alive. In 1806, during a bitter political war between Duane and Thomas McKean, Duane's *Aurora* called the Pennsylvania governor "*old mad Tom*." The newspaper also schooled its readers on the longevity of the song, which contained the line, "I am old *mad Tom*, behold me" (Jack Fruchtman, Jr., *Thomas Paine: Apostle of Freedom* [New York, 1994], 274 [illus.]; Keane, *Paine*, 202 [illus.]; Stanley Wells, "Tom O'Bedlam's Song and King Lear," *Shakespeare Quarterly*, 12 [1961], 311-15; John P. Cutts, "Jacobean Masque and Stage Music," *Music and Letters*, 35 [1954], 199; Niels Herold, "On Teaching the Madness of *King Lear*," *Journal of Narrative Technique*, 27 [1997], 253, 257-9; New York *Chronicle Express*, 30 May 1803; Newburyport, Mass., *Merrimack Magazine and Ladies' Literary Cabinet*, 3 May 1806; Baltimore *American*, 19 Nov. 1806; *Philadelphia Aurora*, 26 Dec. 1806; Rowe, *McKean*, 360-76).

"Mad Tom in a Rage," like "The Providential Detection," was published as an individual print—political cartoons did not yet appear on the editorial pages of newspapers. As was the case with all engravings of the era, cartoons were expensive to produce (some were colored by hand). They did not circulate in large numbers, which limited their influence. This vivid depiction of Paine as "Mad Tom" aided by the demon Jefferson must have been seen primarily by people who were already committed to the political opinions it expressed. The image is approximately 10½ inches in height and 7¾ inches in width (Noble E. Cunningham, Jr., *The Image of Thomas Jefferson in the Public Eye: Portraits for the People, 1800-1809* [Charlottesville, 1981], 111-13; James C. Kelly and B. S. Lovell, "Thomas Jefferson: His Friends and Foes," VMHB, 101 [1993], 134-6).

Courtesy of the Houghton Library, Harvard University, American Prints No. 200.

Volume 39

13 November 1802 to 3 March 1803

JEFFERSON CHRONOLOGY

1743 • 1826

1743	Born at Shadwell, 13 Apr. (New Style).
1760	Entered the College of William and Mary.
1762	"quitted college."
1762-1767	Self-education and preparation for law.
1769-1774	Albemarle delegate to House of Burgesses.
1772	Married Martha Wayles Skelton, 1 Jan.
1775-1776	In Continental Congress.
1776	Drafted Declaration of Independence.
1776-1779	In Virginia House of Delegates.
1779	Submitted Bill for Establishing Religious Freedom.
1779-1781	Governor of Virginia.
1782	His wife died, 6 Sep.
1783-1784	In Continental Congress.
1784-1789	In France as Minister Plenipotentiary to negotiate commercial treaties and as Minister Plenipotentiary resident at Versailles.
1790-1793	Secretary of State of the United States.
1797-1801	Vice President of the United States.
1801-1809	President of the United States.
1814-1826	Established the University of Virginia.
1826	Died at Monticello, 4 July.

VOLUME 39

13 November 1802 to 3 March 1803

21 Nov.	His daughters and two of his grandchildren arrive in Washington, remaining until 5 Jan.
22 Nov.	Removes Arthur St. Clair as governor of the Northwest Territory.
15 Dec.	Sends second annual message to Congress.
17 Dec.	House of Representatives requests information regarding the closure of the port of deposit at New Orleans.
23 Dec.	John Wayles Eppes reports on confrontation between James Thomson Callender and George Hay.
27 Dec.	Sends plans for dry dock at Washington to Congress.
28 Dec.	Indiana memorial calls for suspension or repeal of the ban on slavery in the Northwest Ordinance.
29 Dec.	Sends memorandum on Indian policy to Henry Dearborn.
1 Jan.	Cabinet meets to discuss New Orleans and the Floridas.
11 Jan.	Nominates James Monroe to be minister extraordinary and plenipotentiary to France and Spain.
18 Jan.	Makes confidential request to Congress for appropriation of $2,500 for an expedition up the Missouri River.
16 Feb.	Senator James Ross introduces resolutions authorizing the seizure of a place of deposit on the Mississippi River.
19 Feb.	Endorses "a few prosecutions" against Federalist newspaper editors in Pennsylvania.
25 Feb.	Sends circular letter to governors on the importance of the militia system to national defense.
28 Feb.	Offers Lewis Harvie position as private secretary in place of Meriwether Lewis.
3 Mch.	Second session of the Seventh Congress ends.

THE PAPERS OF
THOMAS JEFFERSON

Receipt from Vincent Ducomb

MRS DALLAS philadelphia Novbre 13th 1802

Bougt of Vincent DuComb

2 Dressed wigs $19— $38—

Recd the above in full

VINCENT DUCOMB

MS (DLC); in an unidentified hand, receipted and signed by Ducomb; endorsed by TJ: "Ducomb."

MRS DALLAS: Arabella Maria Smith Dallas, the wife of prominent Philadelphia lawyer Alexander James Dallas and a close friend of the Gallatins and Madisons, was known for her lavish entertaining (Raymond Walters, Jr., *Alexander James Dallas, Lawyer, Politician, Financier, 1759-1817* [Philadelphia, 1943], 111-13; James Robinson, *The Philadelphia Directory, City and County Register, for 1803* [Philadelphia, 1802], 66; Mattern and Shulman, *Dolley Madison*, 398).

VINCENT DUCOMB, a Philadelphia perfumer residing at 58 Walnut Street, was treasurer of the Mutual Assistance Society of Hair Dressers and Surgeon Barbers. In addition to Paris perfumes, he sold hair powder, braids, curls and ringlets, shoe polish, and cigars (Robinson, *Philadelphia Directory for 1803*, 76; Philadelphia *General Advertiser*, 18 Oct. 1791; *Claypoole's American Daily Advertiser*, 27 Sep. 1799; *Philadelphia Gazette*, 18 June 1801, 2 Feb. 1802; MB, 2:1145).

For the WIGS TJ ordered for his daughters' visit to Washington, see Martha Jefferson Randolph to TJ, 29 Oct.

From Gibson & Jefferson

DEAR SIR Richmond 13th. Novr. 1802

Your favor of the 9th. inclosing 150$ in bank notes is received. We are Very respectfully Yr. Mt. Obt. servts.

GIBSON & JEFFERSON

RC (MHi); in George Jefferson's hand and signed by him; at foot of text: "Thos. Jefferson esqr."; endorsed by TJ as received from George Jefferson on 18 Nov. and so recorded in SJL.

To Benjamin H. Latrobe

DEAR SIR Washington Nov. 13. 1802.

Your favor of the 9th. is recieved as that of the 8th. had been the day before. on recieving that of the 8th. I was immediately sensible I had omitted in mine to say any thing on the subject of a just compensation for the preliminary business of a survey, estimate &c. I therefore referred your letter to the Secretary of the Navy (who was now returned, having been absent at the date of my letter) and he yesterday wrote to you to assure you of a proper compensation, and at the same time to mr George Harrison to make you an advance of[1] (I believe) one hundred dollars. the work I propose is to contain the vessels we now possess, but that finished, and answering, as cannot be doubted, another will be proposed for building vessels under, and laying them up as built. so that the two will take some time for construction. the first however we should push as much as possible, to get our present vessels put out of the way of decay. I shall hope to see you here as soon as possible, because our estimate must be ready before the meeting of Congress. Accept assurances of my esteem & respect. TH: JEFFERSON

PrC (DLC); at foot of text: "B. H. Latrobe esq."

See Latrobe's letter of 9 Nov. for THAT OF THE 8TH, which has not been found.

On 12 Nov., the SECRETARY OF THE NAVY wrote to Latrobe "that we shall not fail to provide an adequate compensation for the Services you may render." On the same day, Smith asked GEORGE HARRISON, the navy agent at Philadelphia, to call on Latrobe, find out if he needed any funds before he left for Washington, and offer him $100 as an advance (DNA: RG 45, MLS; NDQW, Dec. 1800-Dec. 1801, 374).

[1] TJ here canceled "what should be necessary."

From Craven Peyton

DEAR SIR Stumpisland 13th. Nov. 1802

In Answar to yours of 2d inst. I am happy to inform you the payments named is quite sufficient. in consequence of the friendly aid of my Attorney M. Stewart of Richmd. I have reciavd. sufficient time to enable me to make payment without makeing a sacrafice, which woud. of been more pleasing than for you, to of been put to Any inconvenience, although farthar time was what I had no conception of at the time I write you last. shoud. you wish me to engage some person for the next year to Occupy the House & cultivate the feald you will please Inclose the widows conveyance with James' Obligation, which will be my authority to Act. John has no idea of the sale & will make use of every shift rathar then part with the proparty. I think the buiseness had bettar be still done in my Own name Untill the purchase can be made of Kee. As there is no person Undar the sun Acquainted with the sale to you there is no probability of Kee raising in price untill the purchase can be made which I am in hopes will be shortly. howevar Any commands shall be surely[1] attended to.

With Real Respt. Yr. Mst Obt C PEYTON

RC (ViU); endorsed by TJ as received 19 Nov. and so recorded in SJL.

THE TIME I WRITE YOU LAST: Peyton to TJ, 27 Oct. 1802.

PURCHASE CAN BE MADE OF KEE: probably Joshua Key, one of the twelve children of Martin and Ann Key of Albemarle County. TJ's financial memoranda for 18 Mch. 1803 regarding future land payments due indicated the possibility that Joshua Key's land might be purchased (Woods, *Albemarle*, 245; MB, 2:1094).

STILL DONE IN MY OWN NAME: for TJ's earlier understanding with Peyton on the covert nature of the Henderson land transactions, see Vol. 33:18 and Vol. 35:343n.

[1] MS: "shully."

From Nicolas Gouin Dufief

[before 14 Nov. 1802]

Mr. Dufief a l'honneur d'observer à Monsieur Jefferson, qu'il n'epargnera ni soins, ni travail pour faire disparaître les Gallicismes & autres fautes qui se trouvent dans son Ouvrage. Il consultera à ce sujet, des personnes qui ont la reputation d'être versées dans la connaissance de la Langue Anglaise—

Il a toujours présent a l'esprit cette Maxime Judicieuse de Boileau—

Sans la Langue en un mot, L'auteur le plus divin,
est toujours, quoi qu'il fasse, un méchant écrivain—

Il se propose aussi de faire quelques legers changemens dans la distribution de chaque Vocabulaire, afin que l'ordre des matieres, peigne autant qu'il est possible les progrès de l'esprit humain & du Langage—

Son Vocabulaire des noms d'objets physiques, sera rangé suivant l'ordre des Besoins de l'homme en Societé—

Il est Son très respectueux Serviteur

EDITORS' TRANSLATION

[before 14 Nov. 1802]

Mr. Dufief has the honor of informing Mr. Jefferson that he will spare no care or work to remove the gallicisms and other errors from his work. To this end, he will consult those who are known to be knowledgeable in the English language.

He is always conscious of Boileau's judicious maxim:

Without language, in a word, the most divine author
Is always a bad writer, no matter what he does.

He also proposes to make some minor changes in the distribution of each glossary, so that the order of contents will represent, as closely as possible, the progress of the human mind and of language.

His list of the nouns for physical objects will be arranged to match the order of human needs in society.

He is his most respectful servant.

RC (DLC); undated. Recorded in SJL as received 14 Nov.

OUVRAGE: see Dufief to TJ, 9 Nov.

MAXIME JUDICIEUSE DE BOILEAU: Dufief quoted two lines from *L'Art poétique* by Nicolas Boileau, a work first published in 1674 (Jean-Pierre Collinet, ed., *Nicolas Boileau: Satires, Épîtres, Art poétique* [Paris, 1985], 25, 231).

From J. P. P. Derieux

MONSIEUR Richmond ce 14. Nov. 1802.

J'ai reçu par Mr. G. Jefferson la lettre que vous m'avés fait L'honneur de m'ecrire Le 28. oct. et jose prendre la liberté de vous supplier de voulloir bien agreer mes plus sinceres remerciments du certifficat que vous avés eu la bonté dy joindre.

J'ai eu le bonheur il y a quelques jours de me procurer une si bonne recommandation auprés du Capitaine du navire le Triton destiné pour le Hâvre, a present en chargement a City-pointe, qu'il m'a promis de me donner gratuitement mon passage, a condition seulement que je fournirois mes provisions pendant la Traversée; et je suis depuis a essayer de m'employer dans quelqu'office a Richmond pour tacher de gagner le peu qu'il m'en couteroit pour les acheter, et faire mon voyage du Hâvre a Paris. Mais ici les places pour ecrire sont si longtemps sollicitées avant même qu'elles soient vacquantes, que je crains beaucoup de perdre L'occasion si favorable de ce navire qui doit partir du 23. au 25. de ce mois.

J'ai L'honneur d'etre dans les Sentiments du plus profond respect Monsieur Votre très humble et très obeisst Serviteur

P. DERIEUX

EDITORS' TRANSLATION

DEAR SIR, Richmond 14 Nov. 1802

I received from Mr. G. Jefferson the letter that you did me the honor of writing on October 28. I am taking the liberty of asking you to accept my sincere thanks for the certificate that you were kind enough to enclose.

A few days ago, I had the good fortune of obtaining such a good recommendation to the captain of the *Triton*, a ship bound for Le Havre and currently being loaded at City Point, that he promised me free passage in return for furnishing my own provisions during the crossing. Since then, I have been seeking work in some office in Richmond to try to earn the modest amount needed to buy provisions and pay for the trip from Le Havre to Paris. But here, with positions for clerks sought out before they are even vacant, I greatly fear losing the very favorable opportunity of taking this ship, which must leave between the 23d and 25th of this month.

I have the honor, Sir, of being your most respectful, humble and obedient servant.

P. DERIEUX

RC (DLC); endorsed by TJ as received 19 Nov. and so recorded in SJL.

To the National Institute of France

CITIZENS PRESIDENT
AND SECRETARIES Washington Nov. 14. 1802.

I have recieved the letter wherein you have been pleased to announce to me that the National institute of sciences and arts[1] had elected me a foreign associate for the class of moral and political sciences: and I recieve it with that sensibility which such an expression of respect from a body of the first order of science, is calculated to inspire. Without pretensions to those qualifications which might do justice to the appointment, I accept it as an evidence of the brotherly spirit of Science, which unites into one family all it's votaries of whatever grade, and however widely dispersed through the different quarters of the globe.

Accept, Citizens President and Secretaries, for yourselves and your associates, the assurance of my high consideration and respect.

TH: JEFFERSON

RC (Max Thorek, Chicago, 1946). PrC (DLC). Recorded in SJL as to the National Institute with notation "President & Secretaries." PrC (same); dated 3 Nov.; salutation: "Mr. President," and so worded in final paragraph; with one other variation noted below. Recorded in SJL as to the National Institute with notation "Vincent Presidt of."

TJ had received four signed copies of the LETTER of 26 Dec. 1801 in which François André Vincent, the president of the organization, and two of its secretaries, Noël Gabriel Luc de Villar and François Jean Gabriel de La Porte du Theil, informed him of his election to the National Institute (Vol. 36:208-9).

EXPRESSION OF RESPECT: in March 1803, a text of TJ's letter began to appear in American newspapers. Labeled "From a Paris Paper of February 1," the published version was dated "March 14, 1802." The text read: "I have received a letter, in which you have the goodness to announce to me, that the National Institute of the Arts and Sciences have elected me a foreign associate for the class of moral and political sciences. I receive this favor with a degree of sensibility equal to the respect which a body of *savans* of the highest character naturally inspires. Without pretending to any claim to the title of one of their colleagues, I accept it as a proof of the spirit of fraternity, which unites in one family all who cultivate science and letters, whatever part of the world they inhabit. Accept for yourselves, citizens president and secretaries, and for your colleagues, the assurance of my high consideration and respect" (New York *Morning Chronicle*, 28 Mch. 1803). Over the next several weeks, a number of newspapers throughout the country reprinted the text. Many editors published it without comment, but some Federalists used the occasion to mock TJ. The *New-York Herald* of 2 Apr., for example, called attention to the terms "savans" and "spirit of fraternity." On 8 Apr., Samuel Harrison Smith's *National Intelligencer* responded to the criticism of the letter "said to have been written by the President." Suggesting that the false wording was the result of the translation of the original letter into French, then back into English, and declaring that it was now possible "to give a correct copy of the original," the *Intelligencer* published the letter in the form in which TJ had written it. Other newspapers then began to reprint the corrected wording. Some Republican editors chided their counterparts at "distinguished federal prints" who had tried to turn a few expressions in a faulty text into a political issue. A comment in the New York *American Citizen* of 13 Apr. and in other papers noted that the authentic letter "contains not one of the phrases carped at." On 18 Apr., the editors of the *Gazette of the United States* printed the corrected version but wondered why the president "would be at the pains of furnishing an authenticated copy of this letter," since on other occasions he had refused to confirm or refute letters attributed to his pen (Baltimore *Federal Gazette*, 1 Apr.; Harrisburg, Pa., *Oracle of Dauphin*, 4 Apr.; *Albany Centinel*, 5 Apr.; Worcester, Mass., *National Aegis*, 6 Apr.; *Washington Federalist*, 6 Apr.; New Bedford *Columbian Courier*, 8 Apr.; Elizabethtown *Maryland Herald*, 13 Apr.; Richmond *Virginia Argus*, 13 Apr.; *Providence Gazette*, 16 Apr.; Charleston *City Gazette*, 16 Apr.; New York *Republican Watch-Tower*, 16 Apr.; Hudson, N.Y., *Bee*, 19 Apr.; Amherst, N.H., *Farmer's Cabinet*, 21 Apr.; Portsmouth *New Hampshire Gazette*, 3 May 1803).

[1] Preceding four words lacking in 3 Nov. version.

To Connecticut Republicans

SIR Washington Nov. 15. 1802.

Expressions of confidence from the respectable description of my fellow citizens, in whose name you have been pleased to address me, are recieved with that cordial satisfaction which kindred principles and sentiments naturally inspire.

The proceedings which they approve were sincerely intended for the general good: and if, as we hope, they should in event produce it, they will be indebted for it to the wisdom of our legislative councils, and of those distinguished fellow labourers whom the laws have permitted me to associate in the general administration.

Exercising that discretion which the constitution has confided to me in the choice of public agents, I have been sensible, on the one hand, of the justice due to those who have been systematically excluded from the service of their country, and attentive, on the other, to restore justice in such a way as might least affect the sympathies and the tranquility of the public mind. deaths, resignations, delinquencies, malignant & active opposition to the order of things established by the will of the nation, will, it is believed, within a moderate space of time, make room for a just participation in the management of the public affairs; and that being once effected, future changes at the helm will be viewed with tranquility by those in subordinate stations.

Every wish of my heart will be compleatly gratified when that portion of my fellow citizens which has been misled as to the character of our measures and principles, shall, by their salutary effects, be corrected in their opinions, and joining with good will the great mass of their fellow citizens, consolidate an union which cannot be too much cherished.

I pray you, Sir, to accept for yourself, and for the general meeting of the Republicans of the state of Connecticut at New Haven whose sentiments you have been so good as to convey to me, assurances of my high consideration and respect. TH: JEFFERSON

PrC (DLC); at foot of text: "William Judd esquire, Chairman." Tr (NcD: Ephraim Kirby Papers); in Judd's hand. Recorded in SJL "Connecticut Republicans. Judd Wm."

YOU HAVE BEEN PLEASED TO ADDRESS ME: see Connecticut Republicans to TJ, 27 Oct. 1802.

To Nicolas Gouin Dufief

SIR Washington Nov. 15. 1802.

I have duly recieved two rolls of the work on language you propose to publish, and it is with regret, but with truth, I am obliged to assure you that so unremitting are the duties of my office, the things which I am bound to do, that I scarcely ever can command one moment to read any thing but official papers. piles of these are always lying till I can read and dispatch them. not therefore to retard your publication, which you expressed a desire to commence, I was about returning the rolls unread with my apology, when last night I accidentally got an half hour which I could dispose of. I gave a cursory perusal to your preliminary discourse, and run over some of the phrases, yet not so as to be able to form a judgment of the merit of the work. the proposition to teach a language by phrases is new *as a method*; altho', besides infants learning their native tongue, we have seen persons learn a foreign language in that way: and I have observed they are less apt to run into barbarisms, as Je suis froid, for I am cold, &c. than those who learn single words, & put them together of themselves. I have observed that to understand modern latin, you must understand the native language of the writer, & to find the meaning of a phrase must retranslate it into his language. that the genders in French must be learnt by memory I am convinced, since there are few rules where the exceptions are not as numerous as the words it embraces. the position of the adjective before or after the substantive, when to use the active & when the reflective verb, which of the auxiliaries etre, & avoir, is proper to each verb, are difficulties which your method may conquer: I am sure the common one has not done it. your pupils will doubtless understand their subject the better for learning also the common principles of grammar. for the higher, they must ascend into the highest regions of metaphysics. I can see by what you have done that your work will be eminently useful, and ask permission to subscribe for half a dozen copies for the different members of my family. Accept my salutations & best wishes.

TH: JEFFERSON

PrC (DLC); at foot of text: "Mr. Dufief."

PRELIMINARY DISCOURSE: the introduction to Dufief's *Nature Displayed* (see Dufief to TJ, 9 Nov.).

I CAN SEE BY WHAT YOU HAVE DONE: Dufief quoted this sentence from TJ's letter in advertisements for subscriptions to his book. When the book appeared in 1804, TJ's name topped the list of subscribers (*Gazette of the United States*, 21 Dec. 1803; Nicolas Gouin Dufief, *Nature Displayed, in her Mode of Teaching Language to Man*, 2 vols. [Philadelphia, 1804], 2:[435]).

From Benjamin H. Latrobe

DEAR SIR

Philadelphia, Novr. 16th. 1802.

The Post came in so late to-day, that I cannot prepare to leave Philadelphia in compliance with your favor of the 13th. before Thursday morning (the day after tomorrow). I shall then come on by the Mail, and by using my utmost exertion to accomplish the object, in which you have pleased to engage me, prove how gratefully sensible I am of the honor you have done me by your confidence.

I am with true respect Yr. faithful hble Servt

B HENRY LATROBE

RC (DLC); at foot of text: "The President of the U.S."; endorsed by TJ as received 19 Nov. and so recorded in SJL.

To Samuel Harrison Smith

Nov. 16. 1802.

Th: Jefferson returns his thanks to mr Smith for the volume sent him. he incloses the account of a lifeboat which he thinks may be interesting to the seaports of the US. should mr Smith think proper to publish it at any time, and should he believe it would attract more attention to publish the first paragraph of the letter from mr Tatham to Th:J. (which alone relates to the subject) he is free to do it.

RC (DLC: J. Henley Smith Papers); address torn; addressed: "Mr Sam[uel] [...]." Enclosure not found, but see below.

Smith published an abridged ACCOUNT OF A LIFEBOAT invented by Henry Greathead as well as the FIRST PARAGRAPH OF THE LETTER from William Tatham to TJ, 1 July 1802, as the lead story of the *National Intelligencer*, 26 and 29 Nov. 1802.

To Dabney Carr

DEAR SIR Washington Nov. 17. 1802.

I inclose you a letter from Colo. Newton of Norfolk. will you be so good the first time you pass Monticello to call there, look for the act which he desires, and get it copied by some of the young men in Charlottesville for which trouble I will have paiment made the Copyer, and then inclose the copy to me and I will inclose it to[1] Colo. Newton. your friends here are all well, tho Sam and his wife have both had very severe bilious attacks, from which they are just recovered. my love to my sister and respects to mrs Carr. affectionate salutations to yourself.

TH: JEFFERSON

PrC (MHi); at foot of text: "Mr. Dabney Carr"; endorsed by TJ in ink on verso. Enclosure: Thomas Newton to TJ, 6 Oct.

A letter of 30 Nov. from Carr, recorded in SJL as received 7 Dec., has not been found. On 1 Jan. 1803, TJ recorded paying Carr $1 for a COPY of the "act concerning Norfolk" (MB, 2:1089).

[1] Preceding seven words interlined.

To Nicolas Gouin Dufief

SIR Washington Nov. 17. 1802.

There has been a book written lately by DuMousnier in answer to Barruel, and to the diatribes of the Anti-philosophers, which from my knolege of the man I am sure must be good. should a copy of it come to your hands I shall be happy to obtain it. in the original, I mean, for it has been translated into English, but I never read translations. Accept my salutations & best wishes. TH: JEFFERSON

PrC (DLC); at foot of text: "M. Dufief"; endorsed by TJ in ink on verso.

The BOOK that TJ sought was Jean Joseph Mounier's *De l'influence attribuée aux philosophes aux franc-maçons et aux illuminés sur la révolution de France*, published at Tübingen and in other cities in 1801. The work was a refutation of the *Mémoires pour servir à l'histoire du jacobinisme* of Augustin BARRUEL, who blamed the French Revolution on a conspiracy of freemasons and Illuminati against religion and monarchy. TJ in January 1800, writing to Bishop James Madison, deemed Barruel's argument "the ravings of a Bedlamite" (Vol. 31:349-52).

MY KNOLEGE OF THE MAN: in August 1789, Mounier was one of eight French political leaders who attended a dinner at TJ's residence in Paris organized by the Marquis de Lafayette to negotiate a compromise on critical constitutional issues and avert, in Lafayette's words, "a civil war" (Vol. 15:354-5, 390-1, 548, 551n; Vol. 25:58).

The Scottish Episcopal bishop James Walker TRANSLATED Mounier's book into English as *On the Influence Attributed to Philosophers, Free-Masons, and to the Illuminati, on the Revolution of France* (London, 1801).

From Robert Hewes

SR Boston Novmr. 17th. 1802

I make free to do myself the Honour to present your Exelency by the hand of my Frind Doctr. Eustis one of my Books of the Horse Sabre Exercise—made by the French and Austrians—which is a Compleat defence for man and horse—if you Should see fitt in a General order to make it the Exercise of our Cavalry—I have a Large Number of the Books on hand and will allso Teach one man of Each Company if they Apply to me—at present—our Cavalry are truely Millitary Monsters haveing no Sistem of Exercise. I have allso sent one Book to the war Office to General Dearborn—who you will please to Converse with upon the Subject. as to Myself—my Frind Doctr. Eustis has known me from a Child and will Give you all the Nesesary Information. Sir, Being Like Other Citisens, one of the Great Majority of the Nation, who are frinds to the present

Administration I take the Liberty to Subscribe myself your Frind and humb. Serv. ROBT. HEWES

RC (DLC); endorsed by TJ as received 8 Jan. 1803 and so recorded in SJL. Enclosure: *Rules and Regulations for the Sword Exercise of the Cavalry*, revised and corrected by Robert Hewes (Boston, 1802; Shaw-Shoemaker, No. 3028).

The son of a prosperous Boston tallow chandler, Robert Hewes (ca. 1751-1830) established a variety of business enterprises during his life, including a glue factory, a soapworks, and one of the pioneering glass manufacturing establishments in the United States. He was also well known as a fencing instructor, especially in the use of the cavalry sword. Besides his edition of *Rules and Regulations*, Hewes also published a revised and corrected edition of *An Elucidation of Regulations for the Formations and Movements of Cavalry* in 1804 (DAB; Boston *Columbian Centinel*, 27 Oct. 1798, 16 Mch. 1803; Boston *Constitutional Telegraphe*, 23 Dec. 1801; Shaw-Shoemaker, No. 6240).

From Peter S. Marks

SIR Sweet Springs 17th November 1802

Seventeen months since I recievd a letter from your secretary covering the proceedings of the Court Martial by which I was Tried, in which letter your sentiments respecting the Trial was Contained. Mr. Lewis says that you directed him to inform me that you thought my Case a hard one, but that no remedy Could be applied in a millitary point of View but when ever an opportunity offered Suted to my wishes I should be thought of. I have waited patiently during the above mentioned time, have never thought otherways but that you would think of me when an opportunity should offer—you declared to Mr. Lewis that you did not think that I had forfeited the Confidence of the executive. if I have not I cant help thinking but I ought to calculate on your doeing me the justice that Could not formerly be obtained. I hope sir you will not think me impertinent when I ask what I have to depend on, it is time for me to get into some way of obtaining a subsistance, at present I have none. If you should think it improper for me to hold an appointment under the General Goverment, I must in Justice to my self publish the whole of the proceedings of the Court, together with the opinions of a number of Gentlemen on that Subject which I have in writeing.

I am Sir with Respect PETER MARKS

RC (DNA: RG 59, LAR); endorsed by TJ as received 26 Nov. and "employment" and so recorded in SJL.

For the LETTER from Meriwether Lewis and the PROCEEDINGS OF THE COURT MARTIAL, see Marks to TJ, 20 May 1801.

To Thomas Newton

Dear Sir Washington Nov. 17. 1802.

Your favor of the 6th. is recieved. I have no doubt the act you desire is in my printed collection. I have written to mr Dabney Carr my nephew, & an attorney, to desire he will, in passing Monticello, call there, find the act, and have it copied & forwarded to me, and I shall on reciept of it send it on to you. I am happy in this & every other occasion of being useful to you, and of rendering some reciprocity for the many commissions I trouble you with. Accept my friendly salutations and great respect. Th: Jefferson

PrC (MHi); at foot of text: "Colo. Thomas Newton"; endorsed by TJ in ink on verso.

Because he did not receive Newton's favor of 6 Oct. until 10 Nov., TJ assumed that Newton had misdated it. have written: TJ to Dabney Carr, 17 Nov.

Drafting the Annual Message to Congress

I. REFERRAL OF THE DRAFT TO JAMES MADISON, 18 NOV. 1802

II. REFERRAL OF THE DRAFT TO ALBERT GALLATIN, 19 NOV. 1802

III. GALLATIN'S REMARKS ON THE DRAFT, [19-21 NOV. 1802]

IV. STATEMENT OF RECEIPTS AND EXPENDITURES, [ON OR BEFORE 21 NOV. 1802]

V. REFERRAL OF THE DRAFT TO HENRY DEARBORN, 22 NOV. 1802

VI. DEARBORN'S REMARKS ON THE DRAFT, [23 NOV. 1802]

VII. ROBERT SMITH'S REMARKS ON THE DRAFT, [ON OR BEFORE 25 NOV. 1802]

VIII. REFERRAL OF THE DRAFT TO LEVI LINCOLN, [25 NOV. 1802]

IX. LINCOLN'S REMARKS ON THE DRAFT, 25 NOV. 1802

EDITORIAL NOTE

At the close of the first session of the Seventh Congress in May 1802, the House of Representatives and the Senate adjourned to the first Monday in December, which would fall on the 6th (*Annals*, 11:306, 1296). Jefferson had a partial draft of his annual message ready by 18 Nov., the day on which he asked James Madison to look it over (see Document I). The drafts of the second annual message have not been found, however. The earliest version that survives is a final version in Jefferson's hand, printed in this volume at 15 Dec.

No written comments by Madison about the draft message are extant (nor are there any for the first annual message; see Vol. 35:614). The draft that Jefferson asked Madison to review was incomplete—lacking, Jefferson noted, a conclusion and the parts "respecting the treasury department." Jefferson must have completed the sections pertaining to the Treasury while Madison looked over the rest of the document, for Albert Gallatin received the draft on the 19th, and, as his remarks on the text make clear, by that time it included the paragraphs on finances (Documents I-III below). After Gallatin saw the draft, the president sent it to Henry Dearborn, then to Robert Smith, and finally to Levi Lincoln. They perhaps all reviewed the same copy: Lincoln, for one, certainly saw pages that someone else had scrutinized before him, for he mentioned a spot "already marked" with a question (Document IX). Jefferson had used a similar process in drafting his first annual message in 1801, sending it to his advisers in succession. His plan in November 1802, as he stated at the outset, was to let the members of the cabinet see the draft individually, then meet with them as a group (Vol. 35:611-52; Documents I-II, V, and VIII). There is no record of that meeting.

In preparing his first annual message, Jefferson gave each section a heading in the margin. Those section titles were in place through the drafting process, then Jefferson had Meriwether Lewis omit them from the final version received by Congress (Vol. 36:53). The headings served a purpose as he constructed the annual message, but he did not consider them part of the finished state of the document. He employed a similar process in November 1802. The final copy in his hand contains marginal headings, which did not appear in the versions seen by the House and Senate (see 15 Dec.). And, as he had done with the 1801 message, he assigned the section headings in the early stages of drafting. When Gallatin reviewed the text on 21 Nov., he called some portions of it by the titles they had in Jefferson's later fair copy, such as "Naval estimates" and "Dry dock" (see Document III below and the message at 15 Dec.).

Gallatin's comments, read in conjunction with Jefferson's fair copy, reveal something of the contents of the early stage of the document. Jefferson put marks in the margin of Gallatin's suggestions according to the action he took on each item: "qu" for topics to be queried; "+" for suggestions he accepted, and "–" for one rejected suggestion (Gallatin's request that he eliminate or scale back the proposal for a dry dock at the Washington navy yard). Sections seen by Gallatin that remained in the finished version include the introduction and the paragraphs on countervailing duties, naval estimates, the dry dock, American seamen discharged in foreign ports, Mississippi Territory and the agreement with the Choctaws, the militia, Louisiana, Native Americans in the northwestern territories, finance, and estimates. Topics that Jefferson modified according to Gallatin's suggestions (and perhaps those of other advisers) included the addition of a separate paragraph on the Georgia boundaries; shrinking the part on naval estimates, language about the authority to act; modification of the discussion of the dry dock, including the excision of the phrase "singular advantage" mentioned by Gallatin; and the addition of language Gallatin suggested regarding Louisiana (Document III).

In his comments on the portion of the message relating to finances, Gallatin underlined a passage at the beginning of each of the items he numbered

1 and 4-8. Those underlined phrases were quotations from Jefferson's draft. An examination of the finished message indicates that the president eliminated, modified, or augmented his language in those passages in accordance with Gallatin's comments. Jefferson did not take up Gallatin's suggestions of adding something to the message about the admission of Ohio as a new state and omitting the Wabash salt spring. Nor did he mention the expiration of the law regarding trading houses as Gallatin suggested. He followed the Treasury secretary's advice to remove a section on "Missouri"—which introduced the idea of "an expedition out of our own territory" in Gallatin's words (Document III)—and put that topic in a message to Congress on 18 Jan. in which he also brought up the trading houses. Whereas Jefferson and Gallatin exchanged several communications about finances during the drafting phase of the first annual message in 1801 (see Vol. 35:624-30, 632, 636-8), in November 1802 there was only one document of that sort from Gallatin, an accounting of receipts and expenditures for the 12 months that ended 30 Sep. 1802 (Document IV below).

A section relating to extradition of foreign seamen who deserted from their ships in the United States was in the draft when Gallatin saw it and as late as Smith's review a few days after that (Documents III and VII). All we know about that passage is what can be inferred from the two advisers' comments about it. Both questioned its appropriateness for the message, and it was gone by the time Jefferson made his clean copy of the final state of the manuscript.

Dearborn received the draft from the president on 22 Nov. and replied the following day (Documents V and VI). He made only two comments. Jefferson was apparently following Dearborn's advice when he stated, in the final message, that success with the dry dock at Washington could lead to the construction of similar facilities elsewhere. Jefferson did not incorporate Dearborn's other suggestion, about a magazine and armory in South Carolina.

No note from Jefferson asking Smith to read the draft has survived, but the secretary of the navy probably received the pages about 24 Nov. Jefferson received Smith's remarks, which like Dearborn's were brief, on the 25th (Document VII). On that day also, Jefferson asked Lincoln to give the message "scrupulous" but prompt attention (Document VIII).

Lincoln's response (Document IX) was more extensive than Dearborn's or Smith's. Jefferson marked Lincoln's comments as he had Gallatin's, using "+" or "–" in the margin to signify acceptance or rejection of a suggestion. The text of the finished message shows that Jefferson did not incorporate Lincoln's advice about the introductory section. Jefferson did alter the end of the second paragraph of the message (on discriminating duties) to follow the attorney general's phrasing. The final wording of the message implies that Jefferson did use phrasing from Lincoln's third paragraph (for the section on discriminating duties) and perhaps from Lincoln's third paragraph, about the Mississippi Territory. (In the latter case, it is difficult to know if Lincoln was providing new wording, which Jefferson then followed with some modification, or if Lincoln was urging a modification of existing language that Jefferson chose to leave unaltered.) Lincoln advised changing "a measure of urgency" to "a desirable measure" in the section on the Mississippi Territory, but Jefferson ultimately used neither phrase in his final version.

Gallatin and Smith both acknowledged the significance of the paragraph on the Louisiana cession to diplomatic relations, and they used almost the same expression to characterize its importance. According to Gallatin, that passage was "the most delicate part" of the address, and Smith praised Jefferson's skillful handling of "the delicacy of the Case" (Documents III and VII). In terms of domestic politics, Gallatin argued that "political enemies," as well as opponents of Washington as the capital city, would attack the plan for the dry dock. But only Lincoln directly addressed the broader political context in which Jefferson's communication to Congress would be received. Several times in his remarks, the attorney general speculated about how "the opposition" or "the minority" would react to portions of the message (Document IX).

The serial examinations of the draft message by the advisers took one week, from Jefferson's referral of the document to Madison on 18 Nov. to his receipt of Lincoln's comments on the 25th. That was less than half the time the same process had taken in November 1801. Gallatin's comment to Jefferson in Document III that the "things you want to be done" in the 1802 message "are very few" acknowledged that this communication to Congress was less complex than the one of the previous year. Jefferson and his cabinet had also worked out a procedure in 1801 that made for an efficient vetting of the draft of the second annual message.

Although Gallatin, in his remarks on the draft, referred to the message as "the speech," there is no evidence that Jefferson considered breaking the precedent he had established in 1801 and delivering the message as an oration rather than a written communication. Probably well before the anticipated convening of Congress, he made his fair copy, revised it with a few changes, and had Lewis write out the copies for the houses of Congress. After Lewis had done so, Jefferson made a late addition to the end of the paragraph on the dry dock, which he inserted in the margin of his retained copy and Lewis squeezed in as an interlineation on the versions for the House and Senate (see note 12 to the message at 15 Dec.). Jefferson reviewed Lewis's work and signed the three documents—his own copy and the two he would send to Congress. His final act in the composition of the message was to write the date of its submission, 15 Dec., on each of those manuscripts.

I. Referral of the Draft to James Madison

Nov. 18. 1802.

Will you give the inclosed a serious perusal, and make such corrections, in matter & manner as it needs, & that without reserve, & with as little delay as possible, as I mean to submit it in like manner to the other gentlemen, singly first, & then together. the part respecting the treasury department is not yet prepared. a concluding paragraph is also to be added, when we see if any other matter is to be inserted.

RC (DLC: Madison Papers, Rives Collection); addressed: "The Secretary of State"; endorsed by Madison with notation "enclosing draft Message to Congress." Not recorded in SJL. Enclosure not found.

II. Referral of the Draft to Albert Gallatin

Nov. 19. 1802.

Th:J. sends to mr Gallatin the draught of his message to Congress which he prays him to revise both as to substance & form, and to favor him with his amendments or strictures freely adhibited,[1] & with as little delay as he can, because it is proposed to be submitted to each gentleman singly in the first instance, and then to a meeting, which will involve time.

RC (NHi: Gallatin Papers); addressed: "The Secretary of the Treasury"; endorsed. Not recorded in SJL. Enclosure not found.

[1] Preceding two words interlined.

III. Gallatin's Remarks on the Draft

Dear Sir [19-21 Nov. 1802]

I hope that your administration will afford but few materials to historians; and we have already a favorable symptom in the difficulty under which we are to collect materials for a message. The things you want to be done are very few & seem confined to the following points—

1st. *Countervailing duties if necessary.* To this there can be no objection; but might not the advantage resulting from a mutual abolition of duties between Great Britain & America, be placed on more positive ground than the shape in which it stands &a. "Whether this would produce a due equality is a subject &a." and does not the conduct of Great Britain on that occasion deserve a *freer* style of approbation?

qu.

2d. *Foreign seamen deserting.* I had rather omit this altogether. It does not seem of sufficient importance: the authority though derived from the general commercial power vested in Congress may be considered as rather constructive than positive: its exercise will be unpopular as was that given to the French by the treaty, & which was accordingly defeated,

qu.

whenever practicable, by placing the most rigid litteral construction on the article of the treaty. See case of Capn. Barré of the "Perdrix"—Dallas's rep.

3d. *Naval estimates* under which head three objects seem to be recommended

1st. a conditional authority in the Executive to increase the force
2d. purchase or building smaller vessels
} both of which are unexceptionable

qu. 3d. authority for our vessels to act offensively in case of war declared or waged by other Barbary powers—

I do not & never did believe that it was necessary to obtain a legislative sanction in the last case: whenever war does exist, whether by the declaration of the United States, or by the declaration or act of a foreign nation, I think that the executive has a right, & is in duty bound, to apply the public force which he may have the means legally to employ, in the most effective manner to annoy the enemy. If the instructions given in May or June 1801 by the Navy department to the commander of the mediterranean squadron shall be examined, it will be found that they were drawn in conformity to that doctrine; and that was the result of a long cabinet discussion on that very ground. It is true that the message of last year adopted a different construction of the constitution; but how that took place I do not recollect. The instructions given to the commanders to release the crews of captured vessels were merely because we did not know what to do with them; & there was some hesitation whether the instructions should not be to give them up to the Neapolitans. What have been the instructions given in relation to Morocco, in case war had been found to exist?

– 4th. *Dry dock.* I am *in toto* against the recommendation—1st. because so long as the Mediterranean war lasts, we will not have any money to spare for the navy—and 2d. because if dry docks are necessary, so long as we have six navy yards, it seems to me that a general recommendation would be sufficient, leaving the legislature free either to designate the place or to trust the Executive with the selection. It is highly probable that Congress will adopt the last mode if the recommendation is general, and that they will designate another place if this shall be specially recommended. At all events I would strike out the word "singular" preceding "advantage," and modify the expressions of the whole paragraph so as to prevent any possible attack on the ground of partiality to the city. The moment the Potowmack is mentioned, political enemies, & the enemies of this place will unite in representing the plan of a dry dock as proposed for the purpose of obtaining a navigable canal from that river to the Eastern branch. Quere, by the bye, whether the charter of the Potomack company would permit taking water above the little falls?

\+ 5th. *Seamen discharged abroad* Should not the recommendation to legislate be more strongly expressed? and the fact of the expence having been partly defrayed from the contingent fund simply stated? omitting the words "thought to come &a" which seem to imply doubt—

\+ 6th. *Settlement of the Mississipi territory*, instead of being connected only with the Choctaw boundary, depends almost entirely on the Georgia cession & legislative ratification, which, being now binding on Congress, positively enjoins the opening of a land office, for the purpose of raising the money due to Georgia: this, perhaps, will preclude the idea of a settlement condition; but after having read over the Articles of agreement with that State, the President will probably be induced to new model that part of the message. Some notice may be taken of the provision contemplated for satisfying former claims, also for quieting settlers under Spanish titles posterior to the treaty of 1795. We expect on that subject communications from Gov. Claiborne to whom the Commissrs. have written officially.

7th. *Militia law* seems almost a matter of course. What are the defects of the present system? & could any specific improvement be recommended? I think that the important point is to provide that the middle & southern States militia should have arms as well as the eastern. Shall it be done by the public purchasing the arms & selling them, or by rendering it penal, as well to attend without arms, as not to attend on review days?

\+ 8th. *Missouri* seems, as it contemplates an expedition out of our own territory, to be a proper object for a confidential message. I feel warmly interested in this plan, & will suggest the propriety that Gen. Dearborn should write immediately to procure "Vancouver's survey" one copy of which, the only one I believe in America, is advertised by F. Nichols No. 70 Chesnut St. Philada. *Price* with all the charts 55 dollars.

\+ The other parts of the message are only statements of facts, on which, (except in relation to finances) only two parts have struck me—1st *Louisiana*, which might perhaps be reserved for the confidential message; but if left in this, I had rather place the taking possession by the French on hypothetical ground, saying, after the word "war" will, if it shall be carried into effect, make a change &a.; but this being the most delicate part of the speech, will, I presume, be the subject of a cabinet consultation.—2d. *Indians* who, it seems to
\+ me, occupy too much space in the message in proportion to the importance of the subject—The Wabash salt spring might be omitted; it is a topic which awakens the objections to the salt tax. On the other hand it might be well, once more to remind Congress that the trading houses law will expire on the 4th of March.

Is not the admission of the new State in the Union a subject of sufficient importance to be inserted in the message?[1]

Finances

\+ 1. *ratio of increase greater than any former year.* Probable but not certain.

\+ 2. only $4\frac{1}{2}$ millions dollars in treasury on 30th Septer. 1802

\+ 3. *to pay from the treasury*—say within one year—or perhaps add those words after the words "5 millions of principal"

\+ 4. *Expences contemplated in treasury statement* &a. The expences there contemplated were those then authorized by law, before the reduction of establishments & before the repeal of the internal duties—It should be "contemplated last year by Congress"

qu? 5. *reduce offices &a.* I doubt the propriety of repeating this year this admonition—Mint Comrs. of loans—& marines are the only possible objects—Other to as great an amount will probably soon take place.

\+ 6. "*I have already discontinued*" &a. Whenever the collection was closed the offices have ceased by law, without any act of the President. It would be better to speak in general terms—saying that some of the officers &a. have already been discontinued, in others they will &a. but in a few &a.

\+ 7. *We have had no occasion* &a. I had rather say "It has not yet been thought necessary" &a.

\+ 8. *shall be faithfully applied*—I would like the introduction of the words "in conformity to the provision of the law of last session"—or any other allusion to that law showing in a striking point of view the federal misrepresentation of that law.

\+ 9. The Statement to be made by the Comer. of the sinking fund is directed to be made annually *by law*: two of that board, the Vice Prt. & Chief justice are officers independent of the Presidt.; perhaps the Presidt. should not say that such statement will be laid before Congress.

\+ 10. *Estimates*. The War estimate spoken of in another part of the message makes part of the general estimates for the year and they are always sent all together—civil, foreign interc. military, naval, & miscellaneous. The other part of the message says that the *military* estimate is *now* laid before Congress; which is not correct.

Note. Under that head "War estimate" one item has been introduced which requires a specific authority vizt. 20,000 dollars for holding treaties.

I enclose a rough sketch of the expences & receipts for the year ending 30th Sept. 1802. It is not yet correct for want of some accounts which will be obtained within 2 or 10 days; but it is sufficiently so for any general conclusions.

The President's directions to make free remarks have been very freely followed. As to style I am a bad judge; but I do not like, in the first paragraph, the idea of limiting the
\+ quantum of thankfulness due to the supreme being; and
\+ there is also, it seems, too much said of the Indians in the enumeration of our blessings in the next sentence.

With sincere respect & attachment Your obedt. Servt.

Albert Gallatin

RC (DLC); undated; "qu," "+," and "–" notations by TJ in margin; for emendation by TJ in pencil, see note 1 below; endorsed by TJ as received from the Treasury Department on 21 Nov. and "Message" and so recorded in SJL. Enclosure: Document IV.

WHETHER THIS WOULD PRODUCE A DUE EQUALITY: see, at 15 Dec., the third paragraph of the text of the annual message.

The section on FOREIGN SEAMEN DESERTING did not appear in the finished message. In the draft version, TJ may have suggested a need for legislation concerning the extradition of deserters from foreign warships. This was a politically volatile matter, for some deserted seamen, wanted by the British government for capital offenses, claimed to be American citizens and victims of impressment by the Royal Navy. In the much-publicized cases of Jonathan Robbins at Charleston and Hugh Jones at Norfolk, mariners accused of mutiny were extradited from the United States and taken to Jamaica for execution. In early 1801, a Virginia law passed in response to Jones's extradition made it a felony to deliver up "to be transported beyond sea," or elsewhere outside the United States, anyone entitled to the protection of the state's laws. The penalty upon conviction would be imprisonment for a term of one to ten years. The act went on to declare that if the person who was transported outside the United States should be "tried and condemned by any court, either civil or military, for any criminal offence pretended to have been committed by such person at any place whatsoever," and was then "actually executed under the authority of the court passing sentence upon him," then whoever had turned that person over to foreign authorities could be "adjudged a felon, and suffer death in like manner as aiders, abettors and counsellors of murder in the first degree" under the state's penal laws. British chargé d'affaires Edward Thornton declared that the law violated the Jay Treaty, which required the extradition of people accused of murder or forgery. Thornton filed a protest in mid-October 1802, only a few weeks before TJ began to draft the annual message, after William Davies, the collector of customs at Norfolk, cited the Virginia statute as the reason why he could not turn over a deserter from a British ship who had joined the crew of a U.S. revenue cutter. Madison sent a circular to U.S. district attorneys on 19 Oct., asking on the president's behalf if laws in their states made any provision for the return of deserted seamen to the countries that claimed them. Writing to Thornton on 9 Nov., Madison stated that the law of nations did not require the delivering up of deserted sailors from ships of war and that the United States and Great Britain had not in the Jay Treaty extended the right of extradition to such cases. "It follows that the effect of applications in such cases must depend on the local laws existing on each side," Madison wrote, and he suggested that in Britain the law would "immediately interpose its defence against a compulsive recovery of deserters." In some American states the law was "probably similar" to that of Britain, and in other states "it is understood that the recovery of seamen deserting from foreign vessels can be effected by legal process." In conclusion, Madison wrote, "the President cannot interpose the orders which are wished; however sensible he may be of the beneficial influence which friendly and reciprocal restorations of seamen could not fail to have on the commerce and confidence which he wishes to see cherished between the two nations" (Madison, *Papers*, *Sec. of State Ser.*, 4:27-8, 32-3, 104-5; *Acts Passed at a General Assembly of the Commonwealth of Virginia. Begun and Held at the Capitol, in the City of Richmond, on Monday the First Day of December One Thousand Eight Hundred* [Richmond, 1801], 39; Vol. 31:180, 181-2n; Vol. 34:163-4, 206).

CASE OF CAPN. BARRÉ: under Article 9 of the 1788 consular convention between the United States and France and a 1792 act to implement it, a consul or vice consul could obtain the arrest of deserters from his country's ships, and federal courts were to give "all aid and assistance" necessary. In 1794, Jean Baptiste Henri Barré, the captain of the French corvette *La Perdrix*, deserted his ship in an American port, and a French vice consul asked John Laurance, who was then the U.S. district judge for New York, to issue a warrant for his arrest. The judge, declaring that the language of the convention required French officials to produce the original ship's roll as proof that Barré was a deserter, refused to give the warrant. Edmund Randolph, the secretary of state, asked Attorney General William Bradford to seek a writ of mandamus in the Supreme Court to overturn Laurance's decision. When the case was argued in the February 1795 term, the Supreme Court ruled that it did not have authority to issue a writ of mandamus, and Laurance's ruling was left to stand. In 1800, in debates in the House of Representatives following the Robbins episode, Gallatin cited Barré's case as an instance in which the executive branch left questions about the extradition of deserters to the courts (Parry, *Consolidated Treaty Series*, 50:398-9; DHSC, 6:522-6; Alexander J. Dallas, *Reports of Cases Ruled and Adjudged in the Several Courts of the United States, and of Pennsylvania, Held at the Seat of the Federal Government*, 3 vols. [Philadelphia, 1799], 3:42-54; U.S. Statutes at Large, 1:254-7).

Orders from Samuel Smith as acting secretary of the navy to Captain Richard Dale on 20 May 1801 were what Gallatin recalled as INSTRUCTIONS GIVEN IN MAY OR JUNE 1801. The orders, which were the result of a cabinet meeting of 15 May, empowered Dale to respond aggressively should he find that any of the Barbary Coast states were engaged in war against the United States (Vol. 34:114-15). DIFFERENT CONSTRUCTION: with reference to the engagement between the *Enterprize* and a Tripolitan ship, TJ in his December 1801 annual message said that the navy was "unauthorised by the constitution, without the sanction of Congress, to go beyond the line of defence." In February 1802, Robert Smith instructed the Mediterranean squadron to deposit the CREWS of captured Tripolitan ships "on the Barbary shore, or at any other convenient place, so as not to subject the U.S. to the expence of maintaining them" (NDBW, 2:56; Vol. 36:59). For instructions to the navy IN RELATION TO MOROCCO, see Robert Smith to TJ, 16, 27 Aug. (first letter), 1 Sep.

STRIKE OUT THE WORD "SINGULAR": the passage that Gallatin sought to modify in the section on the dry dock does not appear in the final version of the message.

OMITTING THE WORDS "THOUGHT TO COME &A.": the phrase does not appear in the finished message.

For the ARTICLES OF AGREEMENT between the United States and the state of Georgia concerning western lands, see Vol. 37:300-1, 343-5.

TJ took out the section on MISSOURI and the proposed EXPEDITION.

The Philadelphia publisher and bookseller Francis Nichols offered for sale George VANCOUVER'S *A Voyage of Discovery to the North Pacific Ocean, and Round the World; in Which the Coast of North-West America Has Been Carefully Examined and Accurately Surveyed*, 6 vols. (London, 1801), the published record of the British naval expedition commanded by Vancouver from 1790 to 1795 (*Philadelphia Gazette*, 19 Nov.; H. Glenn Brown and Maude O. Brown, *A Directory of the Book-Arts and Book Trade in Philadelphia to 1820: Including Painters and Engravers* [New York, 1950], 89; DNB).

SAYING, AFTER THE WORD "WAR": see the section on Louisiana in the message at 15 Dec. for TJ's incorporation of Gallatin's suggestion.

TJ did not excise the reference to the WABASH SALT SPRING and did not, in the final state of the message, mention the law pertaining to TRADING HOUSES or the admission of Ohio as a NEW STATE. Regarding the approaching expiration of the law on trading houses, see TJ to the Senate and the House of Representatives, 18 Jan. (first message).

EXPENCES CONTEMPLATED: see the section on finances in the message for TJ's incorporation of Gallatin's suggested wording.

PROPRIETY OF REPEATING THIS YEAR THIS ADMONITION: in his first annual message in 1801, TJ noted that "the great mass of public offices" could only be reduced through legislation (Vol. 36:60-1).

In the finished message, TJ omitted the subject of DISCONTINUED offices.

In the section on internal taxes, TJ evidently removed the clause "We have had no occasion" and substituted Gallatin's phrasing, "IT HAS NOT YET BEEN THOUGHT NECESSARY."

LAW OF LAST SESSION: the "Act making provision for the redemption of the whole of the Public Debt of the United States," passed 29 Apr. (U.S. Statutes at Large, 2:167-70; Vol. 37:158-9n). What Gallatin characterized as MISREPRESENTATION of the statute by Federalists focused on three of its provisions: one that allowed borrowing to cover payments due in Holland from 1803 to 1806, at five percent annual interest and five percent in charges, in which case a sum equal to what was deferred on the European debt would be applied to "the present debt of the United States"; a provision that authorized the use of the Bank of the United States, or another institution or an individual, as agent for the payment of the overseas debt, for a commission of one fourth of one percent, which critics said would amount to $5,000 per year; and authorization for the employment of an agent in Europe, with compensation of up to $3,000 per annum (*New-York Evening Post*, 6 May; *Boston Gazette*, 27 May). In a paragraph published on 11 Oct. under the title "Genevan Financiering," the editors of the *Trenton Federalist* commented: "Thus it appears that our present rulers, so far from relieving us from debt, mean only to *change* our *creditors*, by providing that Government might at a great expense '*Borrow from Peter to pay Paul.*'" For TJ's handling of this issue in the finished message, see, in the text at 15 Dec., the section on internal taxes and reloans.

TJ removed all reference to a statement to come from the commissioners of the SINKING FUND.

SPECIFIC AUTHORITY: the act for military appropriations for 1803, approved 3 Mch., allocated up to $20,000 for defraying expenses of treaties with Indians. The sum would include "any unexpended balance of former appropriations for the same object" (U.S. Statutes at Large, 2:227-8).

It is not known if TJ made any alteration to the FIRST PARAGRAPH of the message in accordance with Gallatin's suggestions.

[1] TJ here wrote in the margin "if official information be recd."

IV. Statement of Receipts and Expenditures

[on or before 21 Nov. 1802]

A Sketch of the Receipts and Expenditures of the United States for the year ending 30th Septer. 1802

Expenditures

	Civil department Dollars	592,975. 3	
	Miscellaneous domestic expences	305,642.36	
	Intercourse with foreign nations	321,654.97	
	French convention	226,502.89	
	War & Indian departments	1,474,449.14	
	Naval establishment	1,035,355.—	
	Public debt	8,310,753.17	
(a)	Do. do. due to Bank & discharged from the proceeds of Bank shares sold	1,287,600.—	
	As yet unascertained principally for light houses & expences of coasts	32,302.16	
	Total expenditures		13,586,934.72
	Balance in Treasury 30th Septer. 1802		4,541,470.58
			18,128,405.30

Receipts

Revenue vizt		
Impost & tonnage	12,298,937.56	
Public lands	179,575.52	
Postage	50,500.—	
Fines, Patents, old debts	5,095.75	
		12,534,108.83
Arrears of *former* revenue		
internal duties	813,798.08	
direct tax	226,804.19	
Bank dividends	39,960.—	
		1,080,562.27
Incidental		
Public vessels & property sold	245,472.25	
Prize money	31,943.22	
(a) Sale of Bank shares	1,287,600.—	
		1,565,015.47
Total receipts		15,179,686.57
Balance in Treasury on 1st Octer. 1801		2,948,718.73
		18,128,405.30

Payments of public debt pr. above		8,310,753.17
Of which was due for interest vizt.		
on domestic debt & loans	3,611,848.74	
on foreign debt	462,731.—	
	4,074,579.74	
loss on exchange estd.	55,000.—	4,185,579.74
bills protested not yet repd.	56,000	
Principal Paid from the Treasury		4,125,173.43
Do. do. from sales of Bank shares		1,287,600.—
Total principal paid		5,412,773.43

Comparative view on gain during the year.

Balance in Treasury 30th Sept. 1802	4,541,470.58
Do— do—1st Octer. 1801	2,948,718.73
Difference gained	1,592,751.85
Principal public debt paid from the Treasury	4,125,173.43
Total gained during the year Drs.	5,717,925.28

MS (DLC: TJ Papers, 126:21781); undated; entirely in Gallatin's hand; endorsed by TJ. Enclosed in the previous document.

For the sale of 2,220 SHARES of the Bank of the United States to obtain guilders for payment of the Dutch debt, see TJ to Gallatin, 7 Oct.

TOTAL EXPENDITURES: the sum of the line items as Gallatin listed them is $13,587,234.72. The figure of $13,586,934.72 is presumably correct, however, because changing it would put expenditures and receipts out of balance. It seems most likely that Gallatin made a transcription error when he copied one of the amounts for expenditures.

PRIZE MONEY: during the undeclared war with France, if a U.S. Navy ship captured a vessel "of equal or superior force," the prize was "the sole property of the captors," but if the prize was of "inferior force," the United States got half the proceeds (NDQW, Dec. 1800-Dec. 1801, 312-13, 471).

For an example of PROTESTED bills of exchange on Amsterdam in significant amounts, see Vol. 37:198.

COMPARATIVE VIEW ON GAIN: although the figures vary slightly, Gallatin based his report to Congress on the state of the Treasury on conclusions drawn here. After reviewing receipts and expenditures for the year and estimating costs for 1803, Gallatin stated that the balance of specie in the Treasury had increased from $2,948,718.73 on 1 Oct. 1801 to $4,539,675.57 on 1 Oct. 1802, a difference of $1,590,675.84 in favor of the Treasury. When the payment of $4,152,869.66 on the principal of the public debt was added to that amount, the actual difference in favor of the United States was more than $5,740,000. If expenditures were kept within limits, Gallatin concluded, no new source of public revenues would be required in 1803. Gallatin attached to the report a statement on revenues from duties on imports for the last two years, a statement on the sale of public lands during the preceding year, signed by Joseph Nourse and dated 6 Dec. 1802, and proceedings of the 7 June 1802 meeting of the sinking fund commissioners, respecting the sale of Bank of the United States shares and payment of the Dutch debt. Gallatin completed the report and dated and signed transmittal letters to the speaker of the House and the president of the Senate on 16 Dec. (MS in DNA: RG 233, RCSH, 7th Cong., 2d sess., in a clerk's hand, with report signed and dated by Gallatin; MS in DNA: RG 46, LPRC, 7th Cong., 2d sess., in a clerk's hand, with report signed and dated by Gallatin; printed in ASP, *Finance*, 2:5-9). Both the House and the Senate received the Treasury Department report on Monday, 20 Dec. The Senate ordered it printed and the House referred it to the Committee of Ways and Means (JS, 3:247; JHR, 4:254). William Duane printed the documents for the House committee as a *Letter from the Secretary of the Treasury, Accompanying His Report, Prepared in Obedience to the Directions of the Act, Supplementary to the Act Intituled "An Act to Establish the Treasury Department"* (Washington, D.C., 1802; Shaw-Shoemaker, No. 3323).

V. Referral of the Draft to Henry Dearborn

Nov. 22. 1802.

Will Genl. Dearborne be pleased to examine the inclosed with rigour & suggest any alterations he would think for the better. if he can return it tomorrow it will be desireable, because when individually examined by all the gentlemen, I propose to submit it to them collectively. TH:J.

RC (DLC); addressed: "The Secretary at War"; with Dearborn's reply at foot (see the next document). Not recorded in SJL. Enclosure not found.

VI. Dearborn's Remarks on the Draft

[23 Nov. 1802]

May it not be expedient to intimate that if a dry dock at this place should succeed, that others at more Northern ports may be likewise proper for such Ships as may be hereafter built.

---

will it not be proper to make some mention of the measures taken for commencing the establishment of a Magazine & Armoury in S. Carolina.—

RC (DLC); in Dearborn's hand, written at foot of the preceding document; undated; endorsed by TJ as a letter from the War Department of 23 Nov. received on that day and "Message" and so recorded in SJL.

In the section of the annual message relating to the proposed DRY DOCK, TJ incorporated Dearborn's suggestion about holding open the possibility of building such facilities in other ports.

MAGAZINE & ARMOURY: see Dearborn to TJ, 31 July. TJ did not mention that subject in the annual message.

VII. Robert Smith's Remarks on the Draft

[on or before 25 Nov. 1802]

If a more summary process be wanted to enforce a specific performance of the Contract of foreign Seamen, ought it not to be a subject of diplomatic adjustment?

The Cession of Louisiana is expressed with an accurate attention to the delicacy of the Case. But ought it not to be a separate Confidential Communication? Will it not otherwise produce in France great sensibility and in G. Brittain too high an expectation?

RC (DLC); undated, entirely in Smith's hand; endorsed by TJ as received from the Navy Department on 25 Nov. 1802 and "Message" and so recorded in SJL.

VIII. Referral of the Draft to Levi Lincoln

TH:J. TO MR LINCOLN. [25 Nov. 1802]

Will you be so good as to give the inclosed a scrupulous examination, and suggest any alterations for the better, and without any reserve. the sooner you return it the better, as, when it has been separately examined and amended by the gentlemen, I mean to ask their joint attendance to consider it finally.

RC (MHi: Levi Lincoln Papers); undated or date clipped; endorsed by Lincoln as 25 Nov. 1802; with unrelated notations by Lincoln on verso. Not recorded in SJL. Enclosure not found.

IX. Lincoln's Remarks on the Draft

SIR— Novr 25—1802

considering the great captiousness of the opposition, I respectfully, suggest for consideration whether the following alteration, would be of any advantage viz—after the word, *Yet*, in the ninth
+ line of the first paragraph, to insert, *our revenues are.*

– Instead of the word *fiscal*, in the last line of the same paragraph, to use the word, *needless*, or *unnecessary*, to guard against a construction, that may infer the idea of oppression merely from the term *fiscal*—

In the close of the 2d. Paragraph, Instead of saying it rests with the legislature to meet &c. pointing out one particular measure to be pursued; would it not put it more out of the power, of party captiousness which might consider it as incroaching, to say it *rests with the legislature to decide whether they will meet inequalities abroad by countervailing inequalities at home, or adopt any other measures to remove the evil*—

I likewise have my doubts on the last paragraph. On the 2d page which has been already marked with a quere—

In the close of the 2d Paragraph of the last page of the first sheet. would it be as well to bring the object wished for into the view of the legislature in a manner less pointing to a particular measure to be adopted—and instead of saying *in this case* &c—to say, *in*
+ *such a case, a monopoly which prevents population, would be injurious, and actual habitation being made a condition of acquiring*[1] *a complete title, very beneficial*—

My doubts are, as it now stands, 1st. whether the opposition would not say it looked like directing the legislature. 2dly. If the condition of settling ought to refer to any titles already existing, if any there are now without it.

This difficulty particularly applies also to the last line in the same paragraph—If there is any weight in it, would it not be
+ best, to say, instead of, "*becomes a measure of urgency as well as justice*"—*becomes a desirable measure*

I have Sir perused the message with great attention & equal pleasure, it is a most valuable collection of facts & sentiments, & must make a very useful impression. In obedience, to directions I have stated without reserve the doubts which occurred to me—am sensible of the impropriety of expressing positively ideas, as substitutes for the ones objected to—the design was only the more fully to explain my difficulties—I can see no fair objections that the opposition can make to any part of the message, and no possible ones but those which I have mentioned—perhaps the – word "*false*" in the first Paragraph of the last page but two, may be exchanged for one more palatable to the minority.

I am Sir with the highest esteem most respectfully yours

LEVI LINCOLN

RC (DLC); addressed: "The President of the United States"; "+" and "–" notations by TJ in margin; endorsed by TJ as received 25 Nov. and "Message" and so recorded in SJL.

Lincoln's remarks on the FIRST PARAGRAPH relate to the phrases that read, in the finished message at 15 Dec., "yet our income sufficient for the public wants" and "unoppressed by fiscal exactions."

RESTS WITH THE LEGISLATURE: see the section on discriminating duties in the annual message.

MONOPOLY WHICH PREVENTS POPULATION: for TJ's apparent incorporation, with alterations, of this suggestion from Lincoln, see the section of the message relating to Mississippi Territory. In that section also, TJ removed the reference to a MEASURE OF URGENCY, but did not substitute the term "desirable measure."

The word "FALSE" appears in the section of the annual message on internal taxes, in the phrase "false objects of expence."

[1] Lincoln underlined this word with two strokes.

From Nicolas Gouin Dufief

MONSIEUR, 18. de Novembre. 1802

J'ai été infiniment touché de votre lettre obligeante en me renvoyant mes papiers. Le vif désir de savoir votre opinion de mon travail, m'a empêché de considérer que le Philosophe de *Monticello* était changé en homme d'etat à Washington, & que les soins importans dont vous êtes chargé, pouvaient enlever tous vos momens

Recevez donc mes excuses pour vous avoir importuné. Vos observations judicieuses au sujet du langage, prouvent combien cette matiere abstraite vous est familière, & les remarques que vous faites sur quelquesunes des difficultés les plus délicates de la langue Française, font voir aussi que vous avez honoré cette langue d'une attention profonde.

Je vais passer l'hiver entier à m'efforcer de rendre tout mon ouvrage digne de l'approbation que vous avez accordée à la partie qui vous en a été soumise.

J'ai l'honneur d'être, Monsieur, avec cette foule de Sentimens que vous inspirez à ceux qui ont l'avantage de vous connaître Votre très dévoué Serviteur. N. G. DUFIEF

EDITORS' TRANSLATION

SIR, 18 Nov. 1802

I was infinitely touched by your kind letter accompanying the return of my papers. My keen desire to know your opinion of my work prevented me from considering that the philosopher of Monticello had been transformed into a Washington statesman and that the important tasks entrusted to you could absorb all your time.

Please accept my apologies for having disturbed you. Your judicious observations on the subject of language prove your familiarity with this abstract matter. Your remarks about some of the most subtle difficulties of the French language illustrate, further, that you have honored this language with a profound attention.

I shall spend the entire winter trying to make my work worthy of the approval you have given to the part you have seen.

With the myriad of sentiments that you inspire in those who have the good fortune to know you, I have the honor of being your most devoted servant.

N. G. DUFIEF

RC (DLC); at foot of text: "Thomas Jefferson, President des Etats-Unis"; endorsed by TJ as received 22 Nov. and so recorded in SJL.

VOTRE LETTRE: TJ to Dufief, 15 Nov.

OBSERVATIONS JUDICIEUSES: in promoting subscriptions to his forthcoming book, Dufief characterized TJ's letter of the 15th as "replete with ingenious and truly philosophical ideas on language, with some useful hints for the improvement of this work, that bespeak a profound knowledge of the genius of the French language" (*Gazette of the United States*, 21 Dec. 1803).

From Albert Gallatin

DEAR SIR 18th Nover. 1802

I enclose the letter which had been intended for Mr Short. The bill purchased for that object amounts to *2439 Guilders current money of Holland* (not *banco*), and will be sent to Messrs. "Wilhem & Jan Willink and N. & J. & R. Van Staphorst" our bankers at Amsterdam. Those gentlemen will be instructed to inform Mr Livingston our minister at Paris of the acceptance of the bill, and to hold the proceeds at his disposition. It will be necessary that, in writing to Mr Livingston, you should inform him accordingly.

Respectfully your obedt. Servt. ALBERT GALLATIN

RC (DLC); at foot of text: "The President"; endorsed by TJ as received from the Treasury Department on 18 Nov. and "letter to W. Short for books" and so recorded in SJL. Enclosure: TJ to William Short, 16 July.

The BILL of exchange, for the equivalent of $1,000, was for the purchase of books for the congressional library (TJ to Short, 16 July).

WRITING TO MR LIVINGSTON: see TJ to Robert R. Livingston, 20 Nov.

From George Helmbold

HONORED SIR, Philadelphia, Novr 18. 1802

I hope you will not deem me impertinent for addressing myself to you without your having any previous knowledge of me.

I am the same person that published a full length portrait of you. By printing a german paper in this city for near three years, and by the vile conduct of an agent I sent to Virginia, North Carolina &c. to sell prints for me I am reduced to the disagreeable necessity of asking a loan of *one hundred and fifty dollars* of you, which I pledge my sacred honor to repay in three months from the time I receive it.

I am about erecting a printing office in Lancaster, with an expectation of obtaining a part of the public work the profits of which will enable me to discharge my obligation to you.—

I have tried several honorable expedients to obtain so much money, but, although I have at least three times as much due me for prints, in different places in the U.S. I cannot raise it, unless your known liberality will induce you to assist me.

I remain, With great respect, Your humble Servant,

GEO: HELMBOLD, JUN.

RC (MHi); at foot of text: "His Excellency Thos. Jefferson"; endorsed by TJ as received 21 Nov. and so recorded in SJL.

For Helmbold's FULL LENGTH PORTRAIT of TJ, see Vol. 33:529-30, Vol. 34:xlii.

GERMAN PAPER: *Neue Philadelphische Correspondenz* (Vol. 33:529n).

From William S. Jacobs

SIR Philadelphia Novr. 18th 1802.

I take the liberty of sending you my Inaugural Dissertation, With a Copy of "the Students Chemical Pocket Companion." In doing this, I am directed More by a desire of evincing to you, the grateful sensations created by a recollection of the politeness you shew me, When I had the honor of living With Doctor Wistar, than a desire of praise, if there should be any real merit in the performance—

I am With Much esteem W. S. JACOBS

RC (DLC); endorsed by TJ as received 24 Nov. and so recorded in SJL with notation "with 2. books." Enclosures: (1) Jacobs, *Experiments and Observations on Urinary and Intestinal Calculi* with dedication to Caspar Wistar, adjunct professor of anatomy, surgery, and midwifery at the University of Pennsylvania, "as a mark of respect and gratitude, for numerous favours conferred upon his obliged friend" (Philadelphia, 1801; Sowerby, No. 850). (2) Jacobs, *The Student's Chemical Pocket Companion* (Philadelphia, 1802; Sowerby, No. 849).

William Stephen Jacobs (1772-1843), a native of Brabant, Belgium, studied medicine in Austria, was drafted into the French army, and served in European military hospitals before sailing to America in 1794. He became a dissector at the medical school of the University of Pennsylvania, where he took his degree in 1801. His chalk drawings of the claws of the megalonyx became engravings for TJ's paper on the subject published by the American Philosophical Society. In addition to election to the APS in 1802, Jacobs was a member and librarian of the Chemical Society of Philadelphia and an honorary member of the Philadelphia Medical Society. In 1803, he moved to St. Croix where he remained until his death (Wyndham Miles, "William Stephen Jacobs," *Journal of Chemical Education*, 24 [1947], 249-50; Vol. 29:xxxix, 300n).

To Edward Preble

Th: Jefferson asks the favor of Capt Preble to take a family dinner with him tomorrow at half after three

Thursday Nov. 18. 1802

Tr (TJ Editorial Files); 1961 typescript of RC in possession of Dundas Preble Tucker, La Jolla, California; addressed: "Capt Preble."

Edward PREBLE, a moderate Federalist from Maine who had served with a Massachusetts sloop during the American Revolution, received an officer's commission in the United States Navy in April 1798 during the Quasi-War with France. The following year he was promoted to captain and took command of the frigate *Essex*. Plagued by ulcers and digestive disorders throughout his life, he offered his resignation from the navy in April 1802 but was instead granted indefinite furlough. He had been in Washington only a few days when he received this invitation. He also met with Madison and Robert Smith, who considered him for future naval assignments upon the restoration of his health. In 1803, he took command of the third U.S. squadron to be sent to the Mediterranean and distinguished himself during the war against the Barbary pirates (ANB; Christopher McKee, *Edward Preble: A Naval Biography, 1761-1807* [Annapolis, Md., 1972], 88, 99-100, 105-6; Vol. 35:489n).

From John Dawson

Dear Sir, Fredericksburg Nov. 19. 1802

Will you permit me to present to your acquaintance and civilities Mr. Carter, who proposes to visit Washington, and whose worth will obtain an excuse for the freedom which I now take.

Accept an assurance of the highest esteem J Dawson

RC (MHi); endorsed by TJ as received 21 Nov. and so recorded in SJL with notation "by mr Carter." Enclosed in Landon Carter to TJ, 21 Nov. 1802.

From James Jackson

Sir, Savannah, Novr 19h, 1802.

I have to acknowledge the receipt of your two several favors, since my leaving Congress, the first in May last reached me whilst it was dubious whether I should live or die—a state in which I remained for upwards of ten weeks, a most violent fever succeeded that illness and prevented that answer your high rank & my estimation of your Personal and publick Character immediately demanded—I am happy to find that Mr. Mitchels conduct was placed in that point of view as to give you satisfaction—he is among the foremost of our Republicans and receives the abuse of Federal partizans on that account—One of the supposed Authors of the Story about him and one of the most inveterate enemies of your administration, has since fallen by his hand—Thomas Gibbons whose Character you need not be told has also since I saw you been publickly horsewhipped in the streets of Savanna by Captain Putnam for the attack on him. The Republicans hold their own even at the expence of a little blood in this State & I have no doubt will continue to do so

In compliance with your favor of the 18h Ultimo, I take the liberty to recommend William Bellinger Bulloch and Joseph Welscher Lawyers and Edward Stebbins and John Postel Williamson Merchants as proper persons for Commissioners of bankruptcy for the district of Savannah, all of those Gentlemen are steady Republicans and Men of talents—Another set will be necessary for Augusta, but as I have not been able to compleat a list I must leave the subject until I have the honor to wait on you at Washington, for which place I shall sail via New York on Sunday next

I am Sir with the highest esteem and respect. Jas Jackson

RC (DNA: RG 59, LAR); at foot of text: "Thos Jefferson President U States"; endorsed by TJ as received 7 Dec. and so recorded in SJL.

YOUR TWO SEVERAL FAVORS: see TJ to Jackson, 4 May; TJ's letter to Jackson, recorded in SJL at 18 Oct., has not been found.

FALLEN BY HIS HAND: David Brydie Mitchell killed William Hunter in a duel on 19 Aug. (Norwich *Connecticut Centinel*, 14 Sep.; Vol. 37:393n). Federalist Thomas Gibbons, mayor of Savannah during the 1790s, and Jackson were longstanding political adversaries who fought at least one duel, where neither was injured (ANB; George R. Lamplugh, *Politics on the Periphery: Factions and Parties in Georgia, 1783-1806* [Newark, Del., 1986], 81-6, 171-2). For the accusations against Henry Putnam published in the *Washington Federalist*, see TJ to Abraham Baldwin, 1 May 1802.

After receiving a 10 Dec. letter from Abraham Baldwin acquiescing to Jackson's choices for COMMISSIONERS OF BANKRUPTCY, TJ sent an undated memorandum to Madison listing the four nominees exactly as given by Jackson and noting at a brace, "all of Savanna, to be Commissioners of bankruptcy for Georgia" (MS in ViU; in TJ's hand; with check marks in left margin by each name, perhaps by TJ; addressed: "The Secretary of State"). On 13 Dec., the State Department issued commissions to the four Georgians, and TJ added their names to his ongoing list of appointments (list of commissions in Lb in DNA: RG 59, MPTPC; Appendix I).

WAIT ON YOU AT WASHINGTON: Jackson took his seat in the Senate on 20 Dec., two weeks after Congress convened (JS, 3:241, 247).

From Archibald McCall

SIR Tappa. 19th. Novemr. 1802

Wishing to avoid giving you unnecessary trouble, I have this long waited for answers to many letters I addressed to Messrs. Skipwith & Epps, to know if they would come into the terms you proposed, to pay their proportions with you, of the Loss my Daughter sustained by your sending Willm. Peachey Admr. of Nichs. Flood, Six hundred Pounds—paper Money late in the war, towards part discharge of Mr. Wayles Bond for Specie lent him; And haveing contrary to my expectation received no answer from them, or either of them; I am again compelled Sir, to apply to you, to know if you will agree, & pay her loss, at a day to suit your convenience, & take in the Bond which is in her possession, & settle with them their proportions: and your Act of Justice will undoubtedly induce them, to follow your Example—I shall hope for an answer, and have the Honour to be

Sir Your most Obedt. Servant ARCH'D MCCALL

RC (MHi); endorsed by TJ as received 26 Nov. and so recorded in SJL.

Son of a prominent Glaswegian merchant, Archibald McCall (1734-1814) immigrated to Essex County, Virginia, in the 1750s, established himself as a successful merchant, and married Katherine Flood, daughter of Nicholas Flood, a wealthy doctor and planter. His wife died in 1767, leaving him with two daughters, whom he sent to Great Britain for an education. Of divided loyalties during the Revolutionary period, McCall ran afoul of Westmoreland and Essex County patriots during the Stamp Act crisis but in 1770 added his signature to a non-importation decree. In 1775, the Essex Committee of

Safety exonerated McCall and a business partner of charges that they were supplying Lord Dunmore, Virginia's royal governor, although evidence suggests that McCall had indeed provided foodstuffs to Dunmore's troops before departing for Great Britain. Apparently intending a short visit to his daughters, one of whom soon died in London, McCall ended up remaining in Britain for the duration of the conflict, unable to gain satisfactory permission for his return to Virginia. The layover risked not only his Essex business interests but also the inheritance due his daughter, Catherine Flood McCall, upon the death of her maternal grandfather. McCall returned to Virginia with his daughter when peace was restored, and although eventually he ceded most of his own property to heirs of a business partner in London, his daughter secured her inheritance of two plantations (Hardy Bertram McCall, *Memoirs of My Ancestors. A Collection of Genealogical Memoranda Respecting Several Old Scottish Families* [Birmingham, Eng., 1884], 83; Joseph S. Ewing, ed., "The Correspondence of Archibald McCall and George McCall, 1777-1783," VMHB, 73 [1965], 312-53; James B. Slaughter, *Settlers, Southerners, Americans: The History of Essex County, Virginia, 1608-1984* [Tappahannock, Va., 1985], 53, 58-60, 66; William J. Van Schreeven and others, eds., *Revolutionary Virginia: The Road to Independence*, 7 vols. [Charlottesville, 1973-83], 4:374, 378n; Vol. 1:46).

TERMS YOU PROPOSED: on 14 Feb. 1796, TJ responded to a letter from McCall of 8 Dec. 1795, recorded in SJL as received 16 Dec. Neither letter has been found.

McCall and his daughter had sued William PEACHEY for mismanaging the administration of her grandfather's estate, which was creditor to scores of Virginia individuals and estates, including that of Reuben Skelton, the administrator of which had been John WAYLES. Upon Wayles's death, Skelton's estate became a part of TJ's obligations. In May 1778, TJ recorded making a payment of £130 to Peachey, which he later identified as interest, and on 22 Dec. 1779, a payment of £600, which Peachey entered into Flood's estate account as "By Cash of Governor Jefferson." The McCalls' suit hinged on Peachey's acceptance of Virginia-issued paper money and continental loan office certificates, which they estimated had cost the estate over £14,000 Virginia currency. Never finding relief in the Virginia courts, the McCalls eventually applied for an award from the British commission in charge of assessing the claims of American loyalists (PRO: T 79/4, claim of Catherine Flood McCall; MB, 1:464, 490; Vol. 15:659; Vol. 19:246).

From John Thomson Mason, with Jefferson's Order

SIR George Town 19th Nov. 1802

Inclosed I return to you the transcript of the record of conviction in the case of the United States v Samuel Fumfrey alias Pumphry

Upon the trial the evidence was so strong and so respectable as to exclude all possibility of doubt as to his guilt. From the articles enumerated in the Indictment you will discover it was a little felony. The circumstances were these, the criminal, a free black man, was in the habit of cleaning the boots and shoes of William Duane and his assistant and of performing other little menial services about the store.

This enabled him to observe the situation of the store and the habits of its keeper, they afforded him as he supposed an opportunity of pilfering without danger of detection, he made the attempt, but as the result showed upon false calculations, for hc was detected in the fact.

The Court adjudged him to receive corporal punishment and to pay a fine of one dollar, the former part of the Judgment he has satisfied, for the latter together with the costs of the prosecution he was committed to Jail. His having remained there so long proves his inability to pay them. To remit the fine without also remitting the costs (which I presume have been already paid by the United States) would be to leave him where he is.

I have the honor to be Sir with great respect Your Obedt Servt

J. T. Mason

[*Order by TJ:*]

the fine and costs to be remitted

Th: Jefferson
Nov. 20. 1802.

RC (DNA: RG 59, GPR). Enclosure: proceedings of the U.S. Circuit Court for the District of Columbia, Washington, 22 Mch. 1802, in the trial against Samuel Fumfrey, alias Samuel Pumphry, a free black laborer, indicted for stealing money, books, clothing, and sundry personal articles worth an estimated $14.01 from William Duane and William Kean on or about 1 Mch. 1802; Fumfrey is found guilty and ordered to receive 39 stripes on the back and to pay a fine of $1 and court costs totaling $18.50 and 327$\frac{1}{3}$ pounds of tobacco (Tr in same; attested by Uriah Forrest, clerk of court, 11 Nov. 1802).

TJ issued a pardon for SAMUEL FUMFREY on 23 Nov. 1802, remitting the payment of Fumfrey's fine and court costs (FC in Lb in DNA: RG 59, GPR).

From Joseph H. Nicholson

Sir [Nov.] 19. 1802

I have lately seen it announced in the public Prints that a Convention has been entered into by Spain and the United States for the purpose of settling existing diferences relative to certain commercial Spoliations; and that Commissioners are to be appointed to carry this Object into Effect.

The Place of Commissioner under this Convention will be an important, and I presume, in some Degree, a lucrative one. The United States, no Doubt, will furnish a number of able men well qualified to fill it, and you will of course be under no dificulty in selecting a proper Character for the appointment. It is therefore with very great Difidence, that I beg Permission to draw your atention to Col.

Thomas Rodney, the Father of my early and valued Friend Cæsar A. Rodney of Delaware. I believe you are not personally acquainted with him, but I am sure if you were, you would hold him in high Estimation, as well for the qualities of his Heart, as for the Excellence of his Understanding and the Soundness of his Principles. He is at present in Obscurity, but is an old, and I believe is universally admitted to have been a faithful servant of the Public. From 1776 to 1787 he was constantly either in the field or the Cabinet. He was a member of the State convention of Delaware in 1776, in the Council of Safety likewise, and bore his Part in many of our warmest Engagements. He served as a Volunteer in the gloomy Month of December 1776, and for his Gallantry and good Conduct at the Battle of Princeton, had a Major's Command conferr'd on him. For several Years he was a Member of the old Congress, & considerable Time Judge of the Admiralty Court [...] the State Legislature till the Tories [gained?] [...]. Since that Period he has suffered much, and has experienced the most severe Persecutions. But Persecution has not broken his spirits, nor has Misfortune impaired the Vigor of his Mind. The Temperance and Regularity of his Life secure him an uncommon Stock of good Health, and constant and laborious Research give full Employment to his mental Faculties. But he is poor—is entirely dependent on his Son; and that Son I know to be dependent on his professional Pursuits, the Emoluments of which must hereafter necessarily be diminished. If under these Circumstances and upon farther Enquiry, you should think him worthy of the Place of Commissioner under the Spanish Convention (and his Experience in Admiralty Cases, would, perhaps, peculiarly fit him for it) you would render an essential Service to a most deserving man by conferring it upon him, and I am persuaded would highly gratify some of the best Whigs in Delaware.

I have too little Confidence in my own Judgment to vinture the Recommendation of a character to fill so important an Appointment upon bare Opinions of my own, but ever since I have thought that a Value would be set on Revolutionary Services by the Federal Executive, I have been anxious that this venerable Man should be provided for, and have taken some Pains to make the necessary Enquiries about him—The Information I have uniformly received has corroborated my own Opinion both as to his Character and Talents—

Permit me to offer you my Congratulations on the recent Triumphs of Republican Principles, and to add that

I am, Sir, with the highest Respect & Consideration yr. Ob. Servt.

Joseph H. Nicholson

RC (DNA: RG 59, LAR); torn; endorsed by TJ as received 25 Nov. and so recorded in SJL with notation "Thos. Rodney Commr. Spain" and received from "Centreville."

ANNOUNCED IN THE PUBLIC PRINTS: on 18 Oct. the Baltimore *Federal Gazette* and two days later the *National Intelligencer* carried a letter from Madrid, which noted that on 11 Aug. the plenipotentiaries from the U.S. and Spain had signed a convention calling for the appointment of commissioners from each country to form a board at Madrid to settle spoliation claims (for the convention, see TJ to the Senate, 11 Jan. 1803, fourth letter).

Caesar A. Rodney's income from his law practice would NECESSARILY BE DIMINISHED when he took his seat in Congress (Vol. 37:331n, 386-7).

On this date, Nicholson also recommended Thomas Rodney to the secretary of state (Madison, *Papers, Sec. of State Ser.*, 4:127).

From Robert Smith

Nav Dep
19 Nov 1802

SIR!

I have the Navy Estimates for the ensuing year, prepared in detail, but can not state the aggregate, until it shall be determined how many vessels are to be kept in actual service—on this point therefore I beg leave to request instructions from you.

With the highest respect & esteem I have the Honor to be Sir, your mo ob St.

RT SMITH

RC (DLC); in a clerk's hand, signed by Smith; at foot of text: "President of the United States"; endorsed by TJ as received from the Navy Department on 19 Nov. and "force in Mediterranean. estimate" and so recorded in SJL. FC (Lb in DNA: RG 45, LSP).

From Arsenne Thiébaut de Berneaud

Rome, le 19. Novembre an 1802.
(29. Brumaire an XI. Répain.)

AMI DES HOMMES,

La bonté de votre coeur généreux n'est pas seulement connue des respectables Virginiens et des peuples heureux de l'Amérique Septentrionale, elle a traversé le liquide élément et est venue imprimer votre nom chéri dans toutes les ames sensibles. Depuis la lecture de votre touchant Voyage dans la Virginie, vous vivez tout entier dans mon sein et votre nom ami, depuis cette époque, vient sans cesse agréablement caresser ma sensibilité. Permettez qu'aujourd'hui je vous donne la preuve la plus palpable de mon attachement pour vous, en vous découvrant le motif d'une bonne action.

Vous savez qu'en 1795. les Etats-unis d'Amérique conçurent

l'heureuse idée d'ériger un monument durable pour perpétuer la mémoire de l'immortelle révolution Américaine, et qu'en conséquence l'exécution en fut confiée aux talens connus de *Joseph Ceracchi*, célebre sculpteur de Rome. J'en ai vu la description dans une lettre imprimée, écrite par les Membres du Gouvernement, en Date du 14. fevrier de ladite année, et où j'appris également qu'aussitôt *Ceracchi*, pour répondre à la confiance de la République, préparer son travail, exprimer sa pensée toute entiere en modèles de terre cuite.

Des Circonstances, que vous connaissez mieux que moi, retardèrent la mise en œuvre de ce monument. Je ne vous les déduirai point, leur souvenir rappelle une époque trop facheuse.

De toutes les conditions faites entre les Représentans des Etats et l'Artiste, la récompense de *Ceracchi* fut la promesse solennelle que lui firent plusieurs membres du Gouvernement et plus particulièrement le bon *Washington* et vous, généreux ami, de le considérer, son travail achevé, comme Citoyen des Etats et, à l'instar des Athéniens qui en agirent de même envers le savant *Epiméride*, lui donner les propriétés qui devaient l'attacher au Sol de l'Amérique et lui assurer la jouissance de tous les droits et prérogatives attachés au tître de Citoyen.

Cependant *Ceracchi*, de retour à Rome, attendant toujours l'ordre d'exécuter en marbre son ouvrage, devint suspect au Gouvernement des pretres. Amant-né de l'indépendance, il avait affermi son goût et ses opinions républicaines par le spectacle consolateur de tout un peuple libre. Ses manières franches le firent exiler. Bientôt Rome, sembla renaître à son antique splendeur à la voix de ces mêmes Gaulois qui jadis furent vaincus au pied du Capitole. *Ceracchi* reparut alors à Rome, mais, comme une météore, la liberté ne brilla qu'un moment dans cette cité fameuse. *Ceracchi* fuit la terre maudite, traverse la France et vient à Paris: c'est là que je l'ai connu, c'est là que cet artiste termina sa Carrière.

Depuis mon séjour à Rome, je connais sa veuve et je suis à même de juger de sa situation et des besoins de ses six enfans. Mon cher Mr. *Jefferson*, ce serait une bien douce consolation pour un jeune homme sensible d'ajouter aux jouissances qui résultent d'un voyage dans cette Italie, si pleine de grands souvenirs, le plaisir d'être utile à une famille infortunée. Oh! si mes moyens me permettaient de lui assurer une existence honnête, je ne laisserais pas à d'autres le pouvoir d'usurper sur moi le bonheur de la délivrer de l'horrible situation, dans laquelle elle se trouve plongée, et de l'arracher d'un pays injuste, incapable de sensibilité, de compassion, où elle est exposée au mépris et aux injures des Ministres d'une religion intolérante. Pour satisfaire mon inclination et réparer en quelque sorte, à mes yeux, l'impossibilité réelle dans laquelle je me trouve d'obliger cette pauvre famille, je me suis promis d'améliorer son sort, de lui faire rendre justice, d'appeller sur elle la générosité des ames sensibles, et c'est pour remplir une partie de mon engagement tacite que je vous écris la présente.

Pour vous intéresser en sa faveur, je ne déroulerai point devant vous l'effrayant tableau de la misère: je ne vous montrerai pas la Veuve la plus intéressante, en proie aux larmes amères de la douleur, rongée par un désespoir concentré, manquant de tout, des objets même de la plus urgente nécessité: je ne vous montrerai point six enfans qui demandent sans cesse du pain, des vêtemens et de l'éducation: je ne vous montrerai point une famille entierre éplorée, sans parens, sans amis, sans ressource, enveloppée par l'indigence la plus profonde et qui nuit et jour dévorée de besoins... Non, un tel spectacle épouvanterait votre belle ame et vous déchirerait les entrailles. Il vous suffit de savoir que la famille *Ceracchi* est en proye à toutes les tourmentes de la faim et de la misère, pour vous porter à adopter la proposition que je vais vous faire.

Le travail de *Ceracchi* n'a point été payé. Ne pourriez-vous pas, généreux ami, sous ce prétexte, décider le Gouvernement bienfaisant des Etats Unis à venir au secours de sa veuve et de ses enfans. Il me semble qu'une occasion de faire le bien ne peut être plus heureuse. Voyez à cela, consultez votre bon coeur et laissez vous aller à tout ce qu'il vous dictera. Je suis persuadé qui si vous voulez vous intéresser au sort de la famille *Ceracchi*, vous contribuerez pour beaucoup, sinon à tarir la source profonde de ses maux, du moins à corriger l'âcreté de ses longues infortunes présentes et passées.

Parmi les ouvrages de *Ceracchi* qui sont restés à sa Veuve, il existe un très beau buste Colossal du Général *Georges Washington.* C'est le même qui fut modelé sous les yeux du grand homme à Philadelphie. Il est très ressemblant. Les Etats Unis ne possèdent aucun ouvrage durable qui puisse transmettre à la postérité les traits de ce Héros, dont le nom sera longtems précieux dans les Annales de l'Humanité, en ce qu'il rappellera toujours une foule de belles actions, unies à toutes les vertus publiques et privées. Je n'ignore pas, il est vrai, que le Premier Président des Etats-Unis vit dans tous les cœurs Américains; que le génie de Clio, la divine institutrice des Siècles, redira ses victoires, la bonté de son administration, la sagesse et le Zèle qu'il développa dans la rédaction des lois d'un peuple nouveau-né pour la Liberté; que Boston, Hessians, Trenton, Princeton, Monmouth et Yorck attesteront à jamais son courage et la prudence de ses armes, mais, vertueux *Jefferson*, vous le savez aussi: la reconnaissance et l'admiration demandent à caresser l'œil en même tems qu'elles embrassent, qu'elles occupent, qu'elles enchaînent le Cœur. Le souvenir de *Marc-Aurele* est imprimé sur tous les monumens qui m'environnent, *Jules Capitolin*, *Dion Cassins* et autres auteurs me font connaître toutes les particularités de sa vie qui ne fut un tissu que de bontés et de vertus, cependant si mes yeux ne s'étaient point arrêtés attendris sur cette belle statue équestre qui couronne le sommet du Capitole, il me manquerait tout, je ne serais point satisfait de ma visite à l'ancienne capitale du monde. Il en sera de même pour tout Voyageur qui verra Philadelphie, s'il n'y trouve pas le buste de *Washington*. En s'en retournant, il éprouvera le regret pénible de n'avoir pu imprimer dans sa mémoire les traits du grand homme.

D'après ces motifs que votre goût pour les arts, que votre patriotisme et votre sensibilité développeront mieux que je ne pourrais le faire, j'ose croire que vous prendrez toutes les mesures nécessaires pour déterminer le Gouvernement des Etats Unis, ou quelque Société patriotique à faire l'acquisition de ce buste. Il peut être expédié sans aucune crainte, quoiqu'il soit en terre cuite. Le prix ne se monte qu'à[1]

J'aime à me persuader que ma lettre ne restera point sans réponse, et que vous daignerez prêter tout l'intéret possible aux motifs qui m'ont déterminés à vous l'écrire.

Adieu, mon cher Mr. *Jefferson*, croyez à toute la sincérité de l'amitié que je vous ai vouée et si vous me trouvez digne ou capable de vous être utile, soit en france, soit en Italie, ordonnez, je saisirai toujours avec empressement l'occasion qui se présentera de vous assurer de ma tendre estime et de ma profonde admiration.

J'ai l'honneur de vous saluer. ARSENNE THIÉBAUT

La présente vous parviendra par le moyen du Consul Américain à Livourne, vous aurez sans doute précédement reçu celle que je vous écrivis sur le même objet le 18. Septembre dernier: un Bâtiment parti de Brest a du vous la porter les derniers jours dudit mois.

EDITORS' TRANSLATION

Rome, 19 Nov. 1802

DEAR FRIEND OF MANKIND, (29 Brumaire Year 11 of the Republic)

The goodness of your generous heart is known not only to the honorable Virginians and fortunate people of North America; it has crossed the seas and come to imprint your beloved name on all compassionate souls. Ever since I read about your affecting journey in Virginia, you have been fully alive in my breast. Since that time, your sympathetic name has constantly and pleasantly touched my soul. Allow me today to offer you the most tangible proof of my esteem by sharing the justification for a good deed.

You know that in 1795 the United States of America conceived the excellent idea of building a lasting monument to perpetuate the memory of the immortal American Revolution. Its execution was entrusted to the well-known talents of Giuseppe Ceracchi, the eminent Roman sculptor. I saw the description in a printed letter, written by the members of the government, dated February 14 of that year, where I also learned that Ceracchi, in response to the confidence of the Republic, immediately accomplished his work, fully expressing his idea in terra-cotta models.

Circumstances that you know better than I delayed the implementation of this monument. I will not enumerate them for you, since their memory evokes too unhappy a period.

Among the conditions for compensating Ceracchi, agreed upon between the representatives of the states and the artist, was the solemn promise made by several members of the government and, especially, the estimable Washington and you, generous friend, that when the work was finished, he would be considered a citizen of the States and, following the example of the Athenians toward the wise Epimenides, he would receive land that would attach him to the American soil and ensure him all the rights and prerogatives of a citizen.

When Ceracchi returned to Rome, however, still awaiting the order to execute his work in marble, he became suspect to the government of priests. As a born lover of independence, he had reaffirmed this love and his republican opinions through the inspiring spectacle of an entire free nation. His frank manners resulted in exile. Soon thereafter, Rome seemed to be reborn to her ancient splendor thanks to these same Gauls who were once vanquished at the foot of the Capitol. Ceracchi returned to Rome, but liberty, like a meteor, shone for only a moment above this famous city. He fled the ill-fated land, crossed France, and arrived in Paris. That is where I knew him and where the artist ended his career.

Since coming to Rome, I have met his widow and am in a position to assess her situation and the needs of her six children. Dear Mr. Jefferson, it would be a very great consolation for a sensitive young man to augment the enjoyment of traveling in Italy, rich in historic echoes, with the pleasure of being useful to an unfortunate family. Oh, if I had the means to ensure them an honest existence, I would not allow others to steal the happiness I would feel in saving them from the horrible situation in which they are plunged. I would wrest them from an unjust country, incapable of feeling and compassion, where they are exposed to the disdain and insults of the ministers of an intolerant religion. To satisfy my desire and somehow remediate my absolute impossibility to help this poor family, I have vowed to improve their lives, obtain justice for them, and call upon the generosity of sensitive souls. To fulfill part of my tacit commitment, I am writing you this letter.

To gain your favor on their behalf, I will not unfold the terrifying picture of their poverty. I will not show you the most worthy widow, overcome by bitter tears of sorrow, consumed by intense despair, lacking everything, even the basic necessities. I will not show you the six children, begging constantly for bread, clothing, and education. I will not show you a grieving family, with no relatives, friends or resources, shrouded in the most profound indigence, devoured by need, day and night… No, such a spectacle would terrify your noble soul and tear your entrails. Knowing that the Ceracchi family is assailed by all the torments of hunger and misery is enough to inspire you to accept the plan I am about to propose.

Ceracchi's work was not compensated. Could you not, therefore, generous friend, convince the beneficent government of the United States to come to the aid of his wife and children? I can think of no more appropriate occasion to do good. Consider it. Consult your generous heart and follow your instincts. I am convinced that if you take an interest in the fate of the Ceracchi family, you will contribute enormously, if not to end the profound source of their misfortunes, at least to correct the bitterness of these prolonged misfortunes, past and present.

Among Ceracchi's works, now in his widow's possession, is a very beautiful colossal bust of General George Washington, sculpted in Philadelphia under the eyes of the great man. The likeness is excellent. The United States does not possess any lasting work capable of transmitting to posterity the traits of this hero whose name will long be treasured in the annals of humanity as a reminder of innumerable great actions joined with every civic and personal virtue. I am aware, of course, that the first president of the United States lives in the hearts of all Americans; that the genius of Clio, the divine teacher of the centuries, will repeat his victories, the goodness of his administration, the wisdom and zeal he demonstrated in drafting laws for a people newborn to liberty; that Boston, Hessians, Trenton, Princeton, Monmouth, and Yorktown will forever testify to his courage and his military prudence. But, virtuous Jefferson, you also know this: gratitude and admiration must speak to the eye even as they embrace, fill, and capture the heart. The memory of Marcus Aurelius is imprinted on all the monuments around me. Julius Capitolinus, Cassius Dio, and other authors acquaint me with the details of his life, entirely woven of goodness and virtue. But if my eyes had not paused, in emotion, before this beautiful equestrian statue crowning the summit of the Capitol, nothing else would matter; my visit to the ancient capital of the world would be unsatisfactory. The same is true for travelers who visit Philadelphia without finding a bust of Washington. They will leave with painful regrets at not having been able to imprint the traits of the great man in their minds.

Given all these factors, which your understanding of the arts, your patriotism and compassion will elaborate better than I can, I dare hope you will undertake all the actions necessary to convince the United States government, or some patriotic organization, to acquire this bust. It can be shipped without any risk, even though it is in terra-cotta. The price is only [*blank*].

I would like to believe that my letter will not be unanswered and that you will deign to give all possible consideration to the motives that impel me to write you about this matter.

Farewell, my dear Mr. Jefferson. Accept my sincere friendship. If you find me worthy or capable of being useful, either in France or Italy, give me an order. I shall hasten to seize any occasion to assure you of my warm esteem and profound admiration.

I have the honor of greeting you. ARSENNE THIÉBAUT

This letter will come to you from the American consul in Leghorn. You will undoubtedly already have received the one I wrote on the 18th of last September about the same subject. A ship departing from Brest should have brought it to you at the end of that month.

RC (MoSHi: Jefferson Papers); at head of text: "à M. Jefferson, Président des Etats Unis D'Amérique"; below signature: "poste restante à Rome" (general delivery, Rome); ellipses in original; endorsed by TJ as received 20 Feb. 1803 and so recorded in SJL. Enclosed in Therese Ceracchi to TJ, 3 Dec.

Arsenne Thiébaut de Berneaud (1777-1850) became an author at a young age, having already published, by the time he wrote the letter printed above, *Voyage à l'île de peupliers*, a reflection on his pilgrimage to the original site of Rousseau's tomb, and *Exposition du tableau philosophique des connaissances humaines*, a schema for organizing human knowledge based on Diderot's and Roger Bacon's systems. Thiébaut had left France for Italy because of his republican political sentiments and with a hope, ultimately unsuccessful, of making a journey around the entire Mediterranean basin. After he returned to France in 1808, he wrote on agronomy, natural history, and other subjects, served as secretary of the Linnean Society of Paris, worked in a library, and authored the principal biography of Palisot de Beauvois (Arsenne Thiébaut, *Voyage a l'isle des peupliers: Réimpression en fac-similé de l'édition de 1799*, ed. Tanguy L'Aminot [Reims, 1986], i-vii; J. C. F. Hoefer, *Nouvelle biographie générale depuis les temps les plus reculés jusqu'a nos jours*, 46 vols. [Paris, 1855-66], 45:159-61; Charles C. Gillispie, "Palisot de Beauvois on the Americans," APS, *Proceedings*, 136 [1992], 35; Gérard G. Aymonin, " 'Adansonia,' fêtes champêtres et linnéens français," *Taxon*, 23 [1974], 157, 158).

In 1792, Congress declined to commission Giuseppe Ceracchi's design for a grand MONUMENT to American liberty that the sculptor hoped would answer a 1783 resolution of Congress calling for a statue of George Washington. As Ceracchi promoted his design, he created busts of numerous Americans, including Washington and TJ, who wrote letters of introduction for him. In 1795, a campaign to raise funds by subscription for a modified version of Ceracchi's monument issued a printed circular (the LETTRE IMPRIMÉE mentioned by Thiébaut), but that effort failed. Washington declined when the artist tried to sell him the large bust Ceracchi had made of him. TJ also refused at first when Ceracchi tried to make him pay for his bust, which TJ had understood was a gift, but he relented and paid the sculptor a reduced price (Ulysse Desportes, "Giuseppe Ceracchi in America and his Busts of George Washington," *Art Quarterly*, 26 [1963], 141-79; Vol. 23:229-30, 252, 337, 385-6; Vol. 28:302-4, 347-9; Vol. 29:119-21; Vol. 32:61-2).

The Athenians offered Epimenides of Crete—LE SAVANT EPIMÉRIDE—honors and riches for purifying their religious practices and preparing the way for political reformation, although the only reward he accepted was a branch of the city's sacred olive tree (Bernadotte Perrin, trans., *Plutarch's Lives*, 11 vols. [Cambridge, Mass., 1914; repr. London, 1928], 1:433, 435; Aristotle, *Constitution of Athens and Related Texts*, trans. Kurt von Fritz and Ernst Kapp [New York, 1950], 69, 150).

SA VEUVE: Therese Ceracchi was the sculptor's widow (see 3 Dec.).

JULES CAPITOLIN: the *Historia Augusta*, a compilation of biographies that form a history of Rome in the 2d and 3d centuries, purported to be the work of six authors. One of them, called Julius Capitolinus, received credit for the section that included the biography of Marcus Aurelius. Scholars since the late 19th century have surmised that the *Historia* was probably written by one unidentified individual (T. D. Barnes, *The Sources of the* Historia Augusta [Brussels, 1978], 13-17; Ian Marriott, "The Authorship of the *Historia Augusta*: Two Computer Studies," *Journal of Roman Studies*, 69 [1969], 65-77).

DION CASSINS: in the third century, Cassius Dio wrote a comprehensive history of Rome (T. D. Barnes, "The Composition of Cassius Dio's 'Roman History,'" *Phoenix*, 38 [1984], 240-55).

Thomas Appleton was the U.S. CONSUL at Leghorn (Vol. 37:253).

18. SEPTEMBRE: Thiébaut's earlier letter has not been found and is not recorded in SJL.

[1] Thus in MS; Thiébaut did not complete the sentence.

From John Avery

SIR— Boston Novemr 20th 1802

Agreeable to the direction of the Legislature I have the honor to transmit your Excellency one set of the Maps of the Commonwealth of Massachusetts, for your own use. I have delivered them to the care of the honorable Mr Varnum.—

I have the honor to be Your Excellency's most obedient & very humble Servant JOHN AVERY Secy:

RC (DLC); at foot of text: "His Excellency Thomas Jefferson Esqr Presidt of the United States"; endorsed by TJ as received 8 Jan. 1803 and so recorded in SJL.

John Avery (1739-1806) of Boston was a Harvard graduate and active patriot during the American Revolution. In 1780, he was elected the first secretary of the Commonwealth of Massachusetts, a position he held until his death (John L. Sibley and Clifford K. Shipton, *Sibley's Harvard Graduates: Biographical Sketches of Those Who Attended Harvard College*, 18 vols. [Cambridge, Mass., 1873-], 14:384-9).

An 8 Mch. 1802 resolution by the Massachusetts LEGISLATURE directed the secretary of the commonwealth to send one set of state MAPS to the president of the United States. Sets were also to be presented to each house of Congress and to the Library of Congress (*Resolves, &c. of the General Court of Massachusetts. Passed at the Session Begun and Held at Boston, on Thursday, the Fourteenth Day of January, Anno Domini 1802* [Boston, 1802], 68).

From John Carr

DEAR SIR Charlottesville Nov. 20h. 1802

I have ventured to enclose to you the Character of a young man who has served me faithfully for some considerable time. You will see from the enclosed in what degree of Estemation he stands with a respectable part of the citizens of Albemarle. many, very many more who know his worth would have subscribed their names to the enclosed if they had been requested, but I considered the number who have annexed their names as sufficient to place him in such a point of view any where, as to cause him to be well received; It was not designed when obtained, for the purpose it is now enclosed to you, The young man intended to travel to the North western teritory, but engagments he has since made has put it out of his power to make the intended tour; It is his wish now to be engaged in some active employment; and if any office under the general government could be obtaind it would be greatly prefered by him; his merits entitle him to promotion, his industry may be equaled it cannot be surpassed, his integrity is equal to any mans; indeed I consider him a young man of such worth, that it is a pity he should remain in obscurity he is poor but from his known and maked attention to and ability to perform any Business he has heretofore been engaged in, he could obtain any security that might be requird for the faithful performance of any office he might be appointed to fill. If Sir, any employment can be obtained for him, a letter to me in Charlottesville will be recd., with thankfulness, and afford the highest satisfaction, that it has been in my power to with the aid of others to, promote a deserving and meretorious young man.

I am Dear Sir with the highest statements of respect and esteem Your Obt Sert JOHN CARR

RC (DNA: RG 59, LAR); at head of text: "Mr. Jefferson"; endorsed by TJ as received 14 Dec. and "John Johnson for some office or clerkship" and so recorded in SJL. Enclosure: testimonial as to the qualifications of John Johnson, an assistant to John Carr, deputy clerk of the Albemarle County Court and the district court at Charlottesville, 5 Aug. 1802, praising Johnson's "moral Character" as "unblemished" and characterizing him as a "young man of sound Judgment, extraordinary quickness of parts, great steadiness, indefatigable industry, and unwearied attention to business"; that during his tenure of two or three years, his "exemplary" performance has given "perfect satisfaction" to all who have conducted business in the Albemarle courts (MS in same; in John Carr's hand, signed by 31 individuals, mostly attorneys or justices of the peace, including Dabney Carr, Thomas Mann Randolph, William W. Hening, John Walker, and George Divers).

From Albert Gallatin

DEAR SIR Saturday [20 Nov. 1802]

The enclosed communication of Gov. St. Clair to the convention is so indecent, & outrageous that it must be doubtful whether, notwithstanding his approaching political death, it is not incumbent on the Executive to notice it. He calls the Act of Congress a nullity—He misrepresents all its parts, as you will perceive by a recurrence to the Act—He advises them to make a constitution for the *whole* territory in defiance of the law—He asserts that they are entitled to more than one representative, and for that purpose misquotes the case of Tenessee who, (though by the census, under which they were admitted, they were entitled to two members,) obtained only one on the ground of the census of 1790 by which the other States were then represented; and by the census of 1800 by which all the States are now represented *Ohio State* is entitled to only one—&a. &a.

Your's with sincere respect ALBERT GALLATIN

May I keep your message till to morrow? A. G.

RC (DLC); endorsed by TJ as a letter of 20 Nov. 1802 received from the Treasury Department on 20 Nov. and "St. Clair" and so recorded in SJL. Enclosure: see below.

For the 3 Nov. COMMUNICATION by Arthur ST. CLAIR to the Ohio constitutional convention, see Thomas Worthington to TJ, 8 Nov. 1802.

YOUR MESSAGE: see Documents II and III in Drafting the Annual Message to Congress at 17 Nov.

Statement of Account with Edward Gantt

The President in Acct. with Edwd. Gantt for medical Services rendered to the following Persons

		Dr		
1802				
March 22.	To Ursula		15	
	To her Child from April 2nd. to May 13th	1	12	6
	To Betsy Severman, Attendance & Medicine from June 2nd. to 20th.	7	15	
	To Door Keeper		7	6
	To Coachman's Child		7	6
	To Lithe		2	6
	To Mr. le Mar Attendance twice a Day with Medicine Septr. 15 to 28	8	19	4
	To yourself	1	15	9
	To J Dougherty Attendance & Medicine from Octr. 12 to Novr. 20th	2	16	3
	To Betsy Severman Attendance & Medicine from Octr 20 to Nov 2	5	15	
	To Joseph Dougherty from Novr. 4th. to 5th	1	1	3
	To Abraham		2	6
	To Captn Lewis	1	2	6
		£ 32	15	7

MS (DLC); in Gantt's hand; endorsed by TJ: "Gantt Dr."

For TJ's slave URSULA Hughes and HER CHILD, see TJ to Martha Jefferson Randolph, 18 June 1802. They had returned to Monticello in July 1802 (Vol. 38: Appendix IV).

Betsy Süverman (SEVERMAN) and her husband, footman John Christoph Süverman, had left TJ's service on 4 June 1802 (Vol. 34:489n; Vol. 37:536).

DOOR KEEPER: probably William Fitzjames (Lucia Stanton, "'A Well-Ordered Household': Domestic Servants in Jefferson's White House," *White House History*, 17 [Winter 2006], 13; Vol. 37:492n).

COACHMAN'S CHILD: probably a child of TJ's coachman Joseph Dougherty and his wife Mary, who also worked at the President's House (Vol. 34:566n). The child has not been identified by the Editors, but might be the one mentioned in Étienne Lemaire's letter to TJ of 17 Aug. 1802, who died on 14 Aug.

LITHE: possibly Alethia (Lethe) Browning Tanner, an enslaved woman who operated a produce stand near the President's House, which TJ patronized. She reputedly worked for a time at the President's House during TJ's administration. Tanner purchased her freedom in 1810 with the assistance of Joseph Dougherty. She later freed several members of her family and became a leading member of antebellum Washington's free black community (Constance McLaughlin Green, *The Secret City: A History of Race Relations in the Nation's Capital* [Princeton, 1967], 16; Letitia Woods Brown, *Free Negroes in the District of Columbia, 1790-1846* [New York, 1972], 100, 117, 207n; *Special Report of the Commissioner of Education on the Condition and Improvement of Public Schools in the District of Columbia* [Washington, D.C., 1871], 196-7).

ABRAHAM: Abraham Golden, personal servant to Meriwether Lewis (Vol. 37:442n).

From Richard Humpton

SIR Philadelphia 20th. Novr 1802

The bearer of this is Mr. Robert Martin a friend of mine who served as an Officer in the American Revolution in a Regiment that I had the honor to Command in the Pennsylvania Line to the conclusion of the Peace with Great Britain—

Some time after the Peace his family connections required his presence in Europe and when in Paris did himself the honor to wait upon you—also was the bearer of some despatches (from You) to Mr John Adams then Ambassador at the Court of London—

Mr. Robt. Martin has resided since that time several years in the West Indies but from the present dangerous situation there has return'd to America with a view of remaining—

Any thing Sir that you can serve an old Soldier and I can say a good Officer will confer an Obligation upon your

most Obedt. &c. &c. &c. RICHD HUMPTON

RC (DLC); at foot of text: "Thomas Jefferson President of the United States *America*"; endorsed by TJ as received from Richard Hampton on 23 Nov. and so recorded in SJL; also endorsed by TJ: "by mr Martin."

Richard Humpton (1733-1804) was

born in Yorkshire, England. He served as a captain in the British army during the Seven Years' War, after which he settled in Chester County, Pennsylvania. Siding with the Americans during the Revolution, he became colonel of the 11th Pennsylvania regiment of the Continental Army. He subsequently commanded the 10th and 6th Pennsylvania regiments and in 1781 was named superintendent of recruiting for the state's militias. After the war he remained active in military affairs, becoming major general of the third division of the Pennsylvania militia and in 1800 adjutant general for the state (*Aurora*, 22 Dec. 1804; W. A. Newman Dorland, "The Second Troop Philadelphia City Cavalry," PMHB, 49 [1925], 93n; Gregory Fremont-Barnes and Richard Alan Ryerson, eds., *The Encyclopedia of the American Revolutionary War: A Political, Social, and Military History*, 5 vols. [Santa Barbara, Calif., 2006], 2:625-6).

ROBERT MARTIN served under Humpton as an ensign in the 10th Pennsylvania and mustered out of the Continental Army as a lieutenant in 1783. He may have been the same individual who solicited an office from George Washington at the beginning of Washington's presidency (Heitman, *Register*, 382; Washington, *Papers*, *Pres. Ser.*, 2:127).

From Carlos Martínez de Irujo

Capitol Hill Saturday 20th of Novr. 1802

Le Chevalier d'Irujo presents his comps. to Mr. Jefferson & according to his promise, he takes the liberty to sent to him with this two hampers of Champaing which he wishes may prove as good as in reputation—

RC (MoSHi: Jefferson Papers); endorsed by TJ as received 20 Nov. and so recorded in SJL.

To Robert R. Livingston

DEAR SIR Washington Nov. 20. 1802.

Having recieved from mr Short and others a very strong recommendation of M. Pougens a bookseller in Paris, and being desired to direct the procuring thence some books for the use of Congress, I thought to spare your time which is engaged on higher objects, & therefore desired mr Short by the inclosed letter to superintend the purchase, the details of which were to be executed by mr Duane and Pougens. after furnishing mr Duane with his instructions, but before the departure of the letter to mr Short, he arrived in this country; so that Duane's orders are gone but no bill from us to pay for the books. I am obliged therefore now to trouble you with the subject. if the books are come away, they will be to be paid for of course. if not yet packed up, then I will pray you to undertake the office of superintending the purchase committed in the within letter to mr Short. if the books are not sent off before you recieve this, they had better be detained till April, as they suffer more than any thing else by a winter passage. the Secretary of the Treasury will inclose with this letter a bill of exchange, beyond the amount of which I pray you not go, all expences included. Accept assurances of my high esteem & respect.

TH: JEFFERSON

RC (PHC); addressed: "Robert R. Livingston esquire Min. Plenipo. of the US. at Paris"; endorsed by Livingston. PrC (DLC). Enclosure: TJ to William Short, 16 July.

William SHORT had recommended Charles POUGENS to TJ in 1797, and Tadeusz Kosciuszko had commended the bookseller to TJ more recently (Vol. 29:333; Kosciuszko to TJ, [28 July 1802 or after]).

For William Duane's INSTRUCTIONS, see TJ to Duane, 16 July, and for the BILL OF EXCHANGE, see Gallatin to TJ, 18 Nov.

To Thomas Newton

DEAR SIR Washington Nov. 20. 1802.

Your favor of Oct. 25. did not get to my hands till the 17th. instant after I had delivered mine of that day to the post office. in that you will have been informed of the steps I had taken to procure you a copy of the act of assembly you had desired. your kind offer respecting the procuring cyder for me is accepted with thankfulness. if there were people at Norfolk who follow the business of bottling as in most of the large cities, I am persuaded it would be better done there than here. my people (who are foreigners) know nothing of it, nor is there any body in this place who does. hence a great inequality in the bottles, from some being better or worse corked, and an inequality in the casks from their not understanding the true state of the liquor for bottling. if there be persons in Norfolk who follow this & are skilful, I should prefer it's being done there, & forwarded after it is done. if not, I shall still be glad to recieve it in cask and do it ourselves. 6. casks sent on to this place, and three to Gibson & Jefferson in Richmond to be forwarded to Monticello, will be sufficient. the main article is to have it of superior quality. but for this I rely with satisfaction on your friendship. Accept my apologies for this trouble and my assurances of constant esteem and respect. TH: JEFFERSON

PrC (MHi); at foot of text: "Colo. Thomas Newton"; endorsed by TJ in ink on verso.

To Craven Peyton

Dear Sir Washington Nov. 20. 1802.

Your favor of the 13th. came to hand last night: and I am happy that the postponements of paiment will be not inconvenient: and the more so as the dates I proposed were suggested by so strong a desire to fix them as early as possible, that tho' I still trust I can comply with them, yet unforeseen emergencies might throw them forward a month. I now inclose you the deeds, bonds and reciepts respecting mrs Henderson's part & those of the children included in this last purchase; and I think with you that every thing had better still appear under your name, and shall be glad if you will lease for me as you would do for yourself. I should be glad that Key's part should be got, but on a credit till Autumn or for a twelvemonth. Accept my best wishes and friendly esteem. Th: Jefferson

PrC (ViU); at foot of text: "Mr. Craven Peyton"; endorsed by TJ in ink on verso. Enclosures: see enclosures at Peyton to TJ, 27 Oct. 1802.

Statement on Loan Certificates for William Short

Having been the attorney in fact for William Short esquire from my return to America in 1790. to his in 1802. I had occasion to have a correspondence & many conversations with messrs. Pickering & Wolcott the Secretaries of State & the Treasury on the subject of a sum of 9000. Dollars due from the public to mr Short on his mission to Spain. after thoroughly examining into the case, and mr Randolph's suggestions that himself & not the public was the debtor, they acknowleged to me explicitly that the public was responsible to mr Short. mr Pickering so stated it in writing, and an equal inference may be drawn from mr Wolcott's letters; tho' not as strongly expressed as he did to me in conversation. they constantly desired that the money might not be demanded until the trial of the suit against Randolph which was expected to take place constantly at the next court ensuing every conversation. at length when the last 8. per cent loan was to be opened I applied pressingly, that the money should be paid that it might be invested in that stock, and I presented them a short statement of the demand & interest, shewing a balance then due of nearly 8000. D. they observed that the treasury having always money to pay it's debts, never paid interest. I replied that as they had constantly refused to pay a debt which the gentlemen themselves acknoleged they owed, that interest was justly due, & the more so as they would recover it from Randolph. they acquiesced in the justice, and said that being still unwilling to pay till the decision of the suit, they would have 8000 D. subscribed in the name of some one belonging to the Secretary of state's office, to the 8. p. cent loan, which should be in trust for mr Short and should be delivered to him with it's accruing interest when the affair with him should be finally paid. I took for granted this was done, and that that sum was invested in stock for mr Short, till on some enquiry of mr Wagner,[1] he informed me the subscriptions had overflowed so much, that only a sum of between two & three thousand dollars resulted on the subscription for mr Short but that that sum was held for him. I did not enquire in whose name it was subscribed: but such a sum is certainly held in trust by the Secretary of state's office for mr Short. if there be no other stock in this situation but what is stated in the within account in the name of mr Pickering, I should think the conclusion unavoidable that this is the identical stock. Certified this 20th. of November 1802.

TH: JEFFERSON

MS (DNA: RG 59, MLR); entirely in TJ's hand, written on verso of a statement of account in a clerk's hand showing a credit of $2,800 on the books of the Treasury for Timothy Pickering as secretary of state "for the use of the United States," 5 Mch. 1800, consisting of two $1,000 certificates and two $400 certificates of the funded eight percent stock. Not recorded in SJL.

MR PICKERING SO STATED: see Vol. 30:299n. For Oliver WOLCOTT'S LETTERS to TJ in May and December 1800 on the subject of William Short's claim, see Vol. 31:574 and Vol. 32:373-4.

8. P. CENT LOAN: after the eight percent United States loan opened in 1799, Pickering and Wolcott agreed to purchase shares in the name of a government clerk to cover Short's claim. As late as January 1802, TJ thought that the amount invested in the certificates was $8,000 (Vol. 31:504; Vol. 36:456). BETWEEN TWO & THREE THOUSAND DOLLARS: for the subscription in the amount of $2,800, see also TJ to Short, 18 Oct. 1802. On 22 Nov., David Rawn, as acting comptroller, at Gallatin's request certified to Madison that the 28 shares of eight percent stock credited to Timothy Pickering on the Treasury's books constituted the subscription in Short's behalf (Madison, *Papers*, *Sec. of State Ser.*, 4:133).

[1] TJ here interlined and canceled "in 180."

From Landon Carter

Rhodes Tavern
Sunday morning [21 Nov. 1802]

SIR

I take the Liberty to inclose to you a Letter from Mr. Dawson. I beg leave to account for the step by assigning a motive.

My business to the City is an exhibition of a piece of invention for the purpose of procuring a Pattent; and considering it to be a curious piece of mechanism I flattered myself with an expectation you would honor it with your judgement if I had an oppty to bring forward a request—I wish it scanned by the Philosophic Eye which in an enquiry after the principles can be abstracted from the deformities in the Execution—That was the sole effort of an ignorant Clapboard Carpenter as they are vulgarly distinguished in the state I live in

I have the honor to be with perfect respect Sir Your very obt

LANDON CARTER

RC (DLC); partially dated; endorsed by TJ as a letter of 21 Nov. received from Washington the same day and so recorded in SJL. Enclosure: John Dawson to TJ, 19 Nov. 1802.

Landon Carter (1751-1811) of Cleve, a significant landowner and the grandson of Robert "King" Carter, represented King George County in the Virginia House of Delegates in 1780-81. He corresponded with George Washington from 1796 to 1799 on scientific interests including agricultural matters and health remedies. In 1810, he described his invention of a lock and key to Madison, who discouraged his hopes of obtaining patent rights (Madison, *Papers*, *Pres. Ser.*, 2:239n, 254-5; same, *Sec. of State Ser.*, 4:121-2; Washington, *Papers, Ret. Ser.*, 1:32n, 3:60-63).

From Samuel Hanson

DEAR SIR, Washington, Novr 21st. 1802

After a conflict with myself, of more than a week's continuance, I have come to the determination of addressing you on the subject of my deplorable situation. I know that my invaluable friend, Overton Carr, has often applied to you in my behalf; but, as, among his other virtues, may be reckoned an unaffected modesty, he may not have delineated the extent of my distress. He may not have represented to you that, for many weeks, I have been, in a manner, exiled from my family—that my children are billetted about the country upon the benevolence of my friends; two of them being, at this moment, in Maryland, two in Virginia, and two, with their afflicted mother, in New Jersey.

I mentioned to you, Sir, a few days ago, my application for the place of Secretary to the Senate. But, should there be a new appointment, which is doubtful, I have a poor prospect of success, without your advocation. Genl. S. T. Mason promised that he would attend early, with a view to promote my success. But, it is probable that the efforts of my Enemies, i.e. the Bank-Directors, and their Votaries, will be employed against me. These men could not have persecuted me with more rigour had my crime against them been the publication of a *calumny*, instead of the *truth*!

I should have supposed that, on account of my sufferings, their resentment would have been satisfied before this time. As I hope for mercy, Sir, in the World of Spirits—that mercy which is denied me here—I have never heard that my enemies have impeached my integrity! My whole offence against the Directors, was, as I understood, (for they would never, though called on, declare it to me) *contumacy*; a charge which they meant to designate by my impatience of their official obliquities. Now, if this be the amount of my crime, I would ask if my sufferings have not been already sufficient to expiate it? If I am doomed to suffer still more, nothing remains for my persecutors but to sacrifice my children before my eyes.

Sir, be not displeased at the remarks of a Man rendered almost desperate by the keenness of his distress. Nothing is farther from my intention than to say any thing that might be incompatible with the respect that I feel both for your official and private character. With this precaution, permit me to remark that there is something in my fate more analogous to the chimerical incidents of a dream, than to the substantial reality of actual life.

That a Man of unimpeached, and, I am bold to say, *unimpeachable*, character, who counts among his friends some of the worthiest men in the United States, some of whom have been his friends for 30 years—a man who had the good-fortune to conciliate the esteem of the present Chief-Magistrate, and to obtain from him repeated assurances of a competent provision, not only on the score of his good character, and his necessities, but also of his having suffered by a flagrant act of persecution—that such a Man, now considerably descended into the vale of years, and possessed of a large family, should, after renewed assurances of the President's patronage, given for more than 18 months, be compelled, at length, to dismiss his family, for want of the means of subsisting them—is a real fact, that can scarcely be exceeded by any of the fictitious occurrences of a Romance! I might have said that the political creed of this man, "the last, though, perhaps, the least", of his merits, is precisely that of the present administration.

What is the inference, Sir, from this statement? That there is, and has been, an influence operating on the mind of the President, or on his Cabinet, adverse to my interest. With respect to that Cabinet, I have taken no pains, directly or indirectly, to win them to my side. This has been owing, not to want of respect for them, but to respect for myself; a Sentiment that makes it extremely irksome to a Man, unhacknied, as I am, in the ways of solicitation, to perform the part of a courtier. This violence upon my feelings, however, should, for the benefit of my family, have been committed, had I deemed it necessary: But, having, as I hoped, gained the *head* of the Cabinet; and the other members being well acquainted with my pretensions; I considered any other Steps as not only painful, but superfluous.

I confess, Sir, that I do not know what is the precise object of this letter. It is certainly addressed to the *friend of the writer*, rather than to the Chief-Magistrate of the United States. It appears important that you should know my real situation. If you can, with propriety, recommend me as the Successor of Mr. Otis, in case of his removal, I have no doubt of my success. Without your interposition, I have no hopes. There will be the Weight of Bank-Obloquy in one scale, without a preponderating Counter-poise in the other.

To close this doleful subject; permit me to add that my hopes of terrestrial happiness are not sanguine nor extravagant. I discard all prospect of wealth, splendor or distinction. My only prayer to you, Sir, is to employ your influence in enabling an *honest*, yet persecuted, man to be re-united to his family, and to pass, in an unambitious poverty, the remnant of his days in their society; a Society that, though he possessed the wealth of the Indies, would, of all others, be to him the most delightful.

With great respect, I am, Dear Sir, Your most obedt. Servt.

S HANSON of Saml

RC (DLC); endorsed by TJ as received 22 Nov. and so recorded in SJL.

Samuel A. Otis of Massachusetts served as SECRETARY TO THE SENATE from 1789 until his death in 1814. Hanson continued to seek a more lucrative NEW APPOINTMENT even though TJ had nominated him as a bankruptcy commissioner for Georgetown on 8 June 1802 and he had received a clerkship in the State Department in October (*Biog. Dir. Cong.*; Vol. 37:408-9n, 705, 709; Vol. 38:28-9).

From Joseph Marie Lequinio de Kerblay

SIR Newport 21 novembre 1802

Please you permitt one of the truer your governement's mildness and wisdom admirers remember himself respectfully to your Excellency, by the way of our respectable and amiable Senator Mr. Ellery now going away for the Congress? i am not ignorant of your time's high price, and pretend not to Spend it, in vain, with a long and unuseful epistle; but being intitled to your Bounties by your Bounty itself, and by the most graceful persuasion issued from your letters, i Can't neglect, nor refuse myself such a good opportunity of presenting you my humble duties by hand, at least, Since i may not present them now in person. be so good, Sir, i pray, as to accept of them with your usual goodness, and do remain Convinced of my Sincere wishing to possess a little Share in your esteem and of my fond endeavouring to get it.

i am, Sir, of your Excellency, the most respectful, and the most obedient Servant LEQUINIO KERBLAY

RC (MoSHi: Jefferson Papers); at head of text: "to his Excellency Master jefferson president of the united States"; endorsed by TJ as received 10 Dec. and so recorded in SJL.

Statement of Account with Meriwether Lewis

Dr. Thos. Jefferson in Act. with M. Lewis 6th.

1802.		£	s	d	1802		£.	s	d.
Nov. 17th.	To ferriage at Georgetown		6		Nov.	By Cash of			
					16th.	Mr. Barnes	12	0	0
	To Bill at Fairfax C.H.		10	6					
18th.	do. do. at Brown's	1	7						
	do. do. at Elk-run Cch.		10	6					
19th.	do. do at Herring's including Mr. Eppes's bill	2	15	6					
	do. do. at Elk-run Cch.		7	6					
20th.	do. do. at Browns	2	11	3					
	do. do. at Fairfax C.H.		6						
21st.	do. do. at Colo. Ren's	2	13	9					
	do. ferriage at Georgetown		7	6					
	do. ferryman at do.		1	6					
	To. Cash herewith returned		3						
	£	12	0	0		£	12	0	0
	or Dollars	40				or Dollars.	40	0	0

E.E. M. LEWIS

MS (DLC: TJ Papers, 111:19135); in Meriwether Lewis's hand; endorsed by TJ: "Lewis Meriwether. travellg. exp. Nov. 1802."

Meriwether LEWIS, outfitted with fresh horses and a carriage, met TJ's daughters and two of his grandchildren, ten-year-old Thomas Jefferson Randolph and his six-year-old sister Ellen, at the home of John Strode, which was next to Herrin's Tavern (HERRING'S), at the end of the second day of their journey. He accompanied them the 62 miles TJ estimated from there to the Georgetown ferry and into Washington (see Vol. 37:534-5; Martha Jefferson Randolph to TJ, 9 Nov.). On 16 Nov., TJ wrote an order on John Barnes "to furnish Capt. Lewis with 40. Dollars on acct. of Th:J. for the expences of the journey he is to take for his family" (MS in ViU: Mary Kirk Moyer deposit; in TJ's hand; addressed: "Mr. Barnes"; endorsed by Barnes as paid on 16 Nov.; endorsed by TJ). TJ entered the 16 Nov. payment to Lewis in his financial records. On 21 Nov., TJ recorded that he "Recd. back from Capt. Lewis .50 of the money ante Nov. 16" (MB, 2:1086). Stage line operator John H. Barney also submitted an invoice dated 21 Nov. for $50 for Lewis's "use of my Carriage & 4 Horses & Driver 5 Days" (MS in ICHi; in Barney's hand; with order by TJ at foot of text: "Mr. Barnes will be pleased to pay this Th: Jefferson Nov. 22. 1802"; signed by Barney acknowledging payment; endorsed by Barnes as paid in full on 22 Nov.). TJ recorded the order to pay Barney for "carriage & horses to Strode's" in his accounts at 22 Nov. (MB, 2:1086).

E.E.: that is, errors excepted.

To Francis Mitchell

SIR Washington Nov. 21. 1802.

It is but lately that the return of the Secretary of the Navy has enabled me to answer your application for the place of Midshipman. he has examined and finds there is not a single vacancy at present: but they happen pretty frequently, and your name & that of another are set down for the two first vacancies, of which, when they happen you shall be apprised. Accept my salutations and best wishes.

TH: JEFFERSON

PrC (DLC); at foot of text: "Mr. Francis Mitchell"; endorsed by TJ in ink on verso. Recorded in SJL at 20 Nov.

Francis Mitchell received a warrant as a midshipman in March 1803 and served in the Mediterranean in 1804 and 1805. Commissioned a lieutenant in 1809, he saw action commanding a sloop in the naval flotilla at Delaware Bay during the War of 1812, drawing praise as a "gallant officer." He later served less successfully at the Battle of Lake Champlain, where his commanding officer deprecated his bravery and characterized him as "the most profane man in the service." After the war Mitchell took furlough duty but remained on naval registers into the 1820s (NDBW, *Register*, 37; William S. Dudley and Michael J. Crawford, eds., *The Naval War of 1812: A Documentary History*, 3 vols. [Washington, D.C., 1985-2002], 2:182, 200; Christopher McKee, *A Gentlemanly and Honorable Profession: The Creation of the U.S. Naval Officer Corps, 1794-1815* [Annapolis, Md., 1991], 291; *Register of the Commission and Warrant Officers of the Navy of the United States* [Washington, D.C., 1820], 7).

To William Bache

Dear Sir Washington Nov. 22. 1802.

Yours of the 16th was recieved yesterday, and communicated to mr Gallatin. his answer is 'if Doctr Bache will supply me with a list of medicines wanted, in conformity to my former request, I will have the purchase made, and the chest transmittted to his direction at New Orleans. our appropriation is so small that every necessary must be provided with the most rigorous economy.'

On the 1st. inst. I[1] desired mr Jefferson to pay you 143.33 D of which 33.33 D was for Polly Carr, and wrote to you at the same time. but whether I sent the letter to you direct or under cover to mr Jefferson, I do not recollect. I hope you have recieved it. Accept for yourself and mrs Bache my best wishes for a more agreeable journey & voyage than I am afraid you will have, & assurances of my friendly attachment. Th: Jefferson

RC (Christie's, New York City, 5 Dec. 1997 sale, item 62); at foot of text: "Doctr. Wm. Bache."

yours of the 16th: according to SJL, a letter that Bache wrote at Edgehill on 16 Nov. reached TJ on the 21st. The communication has not been found.

Gallatin's answer is not recorded in SJL and has not been found.

[1] TJ here canceled "inclosed to."

From Henry Dearborn

War Department
22d. November 1802

The Secretary of War has the honor of proposing to the President of the United States, that Joseph Morgan, be appointed Superintendant of the Armoury at Springfield in the State of Massachusetts.

FC (Lb in DNA: RG 107, LSP); in a clerk's hand.

After a brief term as master armorer at the Springfield Armory, joseph morgan was appointed superintendent of the facility on 23 Nov. 1802 and served until 1805 (Mason A. Green, *Springfield, 1636-1886, History of Town and City* [Springfield, Mass., 1888], 356; Dearborn to Morgan, 20 Feb. 1802, in DNA: RG 107, LSMA; Dearborn to Morgan, 23 Nov. 1802, in DNA: RG 107, MLS).

From Henry Dearborn, with Jefferson's Note

SIR [22 Nov. 1802]

Will you be so obliging as to inform me whether the Journals and other papers relating to the several Indian Treaties, should accompany the respective Treaties when presented to you.

with respectfull concideration I am Sir Your Huml. Servt

H. DEARBORN

[*Note by TJ*:]

The Senate always expect a communication of all papers throwing light on the treaty, and have called for them when withheld.

RC (DLC); undated; at foot of text: "The President of the United States"; endorsed by TJ as a letter of 22 Nov. received from the War Department on that day and "Communicns to Senate" and so recorded in SJL.

From Nicolas Gouin Dufief

MONSIEUR, Le 22 de Novembre. 1802

Je suis bien fâché de n'avoir point parmi mes livres celui dans lequel, Dumourier, donne si militairement sur les Oreilles, au Calottin Barruel, de tous les Aboyeurs contre les philosophes morts ou vivans, les plus sot & le plus fanatique—Je vais faire une recherche active pour vous le procurer en *Français* & J'espére réussir, s'il est en Philadelphie—

Je deteste comme vous les traductions des bons ouvrages, que l'on peut lire dans la langue Originale—Les pensées des Ecrivains de Génie, ne sont pas ordinairement faciles à traduire; pour les bien rendre, il faudrait avoir un génie presque égal à celui qui les a conçues, & une conformité de goût qui se rencontre rarement, le domaine des Sciences étant si immense—

Une autre circonstance restreindra toujours à un petit nombre les excellens originaux bien traduits; c'est que les hommes les plus capables de réussir dans une entreprise aussi difficile ont communément une grande répugnance à le faire; continuellement occupés de leurs propres idées, ils ne sont gueres bons à suivre lentement & peniblement celles des autres, pour les exprimer avec la fidélité scrupuleuse qu'on exige dans un Traducteur—

Les ennemis le plus violens de Dumourier, ne sauraient lui refuser beaucoup de Génie—Sa maniére Brusque & vive d'arriver a une conclusion, à un résultat quelquefois inattendu, & ses vues politiques souvent profondes doivent rendre ses ouvrages infiniment interessans à ceux qui savent les apprécier—

Recevez de Nouveau mes remercimens pour votre lettre du 15. de ce mois, & agreez l'assurance de ma respectueuse Estime

N. G. DUFIEF

EDITORS' TRANSLATION

SIR, 22 Nov. 1802

I am dismayed not to have among my books the one in which Dumouriez so violently attacks the popish Barruel, the stupidest and most fanatic bad-mouther of the philosophes. I shall undertake a search to procure it for you in French, hoping to succeed if it is available in Philadelphia.

Like you, I detest translations of good works that one can read in the original. The thoughts of writers of genius are not usually easy to translate. To convey them, one must have a genius almost equal to the one who conceived them and have a similar taste. This is very rare, for the realm of knowledge is immense.

Another circumstance will always limit the number of excellent originals that are well translated: those most capable of succeeding in such a difficult endeavor are usually reluctant to undertake it. Perpetually occupied by their own ideas, they are scarcely good at following, slowly and painfully, the ideas of others, in order to express them with the scrupulous fidelity required in a translator.

Dumouriez's most violent enemies would not deny his great genius. His brusque and rapid manner of arriving at conclusions, at sometimes unexpected results, and his often profound political views must make his works infinitely interesting to those who know how to appreciate them.

Receive, once again, my thanks for your letter of the 15th of this month, and accept the assurance of my respectful esteem. N. G. DUFIEF

RC (DLC); at foot of text: "Thomas Jefferson, Président des Etats-Unis"; endorsed by TJ as received from Philadelphia on 26 Nov. and so recorded in SJL.

When TJ wrote "DuMousnier" in his letter of 17 Nov., he meant Jean Joseph Mounier, but Dufief thought he meant the French army officer, government minister, and author Charles François Du Périer Dumouriez, whose name was sometimes spelled DUMOURIER. TJ had asked Dufief to obtain books by Dumouriez in the past (Sowerby, Nos. 233, 3895; Vol. 31:87, 88n; Vol. 32:345n, 415).

To John Wayles Eppes

DEAR SIR Washington Nov. 22. 1802.

The family arrived here yesterday morning, without accident. mr Lilly's order for £40. his wages & £20. for Austin is good. I have lately remitted to John Perry the whole balance due him to the completion of the South East offices; and our bargain is, whenever a compleat job is done & settled it is to be paid for. he says the shop is done, and that it will amount to £60 although he always overcharges & is to be docked down to our agreement. yet I presume I may assume the paiment of his order for £60. and the more readily as you say it will suit you to recieve the whole £120. in March. for in truth I have for four months to come such heavy paiments to make for corn, negro hire, land &c with heavy current expences during a session of Congress, that I shall weather the winter with difficulty with respect to the land including the spring at Pantops. when I come home in March I will lay it off and make a deed adding it to Pantops without any retribution. Accept my affectionate and constant attachment

TH: JEFFERSON

PrC (MHi); at foot of text: "J. W. Eppes."

FAMILY ARRIVED HERE YESTERDAY MORNING: see Statement of Account with Meriwether Lewis, 21 Nov.

LATELY REMITTED: for these transactions totaling £120, or $400, see TJ's financial memoranda recorded at 22 Nov. At 9 Nov., TJ noted that a payment of $108.87 to Gabriel Lilly was for John Perry (MB, 2:1085, 1086). A letter from Perry to TJ of 17 Nov., recorded in SJL as received from Shadwell on 21 Nov., has not been found.

From David Gelston

SIR, New York Novr. 22d. 1802.

Your letter of the 12th instant with its enclosure I have had the honor to receive.

Many of the circumstances related in the anonymous communication are within my knowlege—the Gentleman therein mentioned I am acquainted with, and tho' I feel disposed to render him all the assistance in my power, I do not think it would be prudent in me to appoint him to a more important office.—

I am, Sir, very respectfully, your most obedient Servt.

DAVID GELSTON

RC (MHi); at foot of text: "Thomas Jefferson Esquire"; endorsed by TJ as received 25 Nov. and so recorded in SJL.

GENTLEMAN THEREIN MENTIONED: Walter Bicker, a weigher in the surveyor's office at the New York custom house (TJ to Gelston, 12 Nov.).

Memorandum from Benjamin H. Latrobe

Mr. Latrobe presents his respectful Compliments to the President of the U. States:

In preparing for his survey of the line of Potowmac Canal, Mr L. has obtained access to the records of the Commissioners, which happen to be perfect as to the levels of the Streets N. West of the Presidents house, & South of the large Street K and also as to those of some streets about the Capitol. The page marked by this letter (32) exhibits the level above high water of that part of the Pennsylvania Avenue which is immediately in front of the six buildings. It appears that the level on the highest point marked * is 76 feet $10.^{i}$ $9.^{10}$ above high water. Should the Canal be carried along this line there will of course be a difference between the level of the street & of the Water of 44 feet (the fall at the locks being only $32.^{f}$ 6^{i} or thereabouts.) This difference will Mr. L. fears, be fatal to the idea of carrying the Canal along the line of the Pennsylvania Avenue,—for a navigable tunnel from Rock Creek to the descent of the hill East of the President's house would be cheaper than such an open Canal.

As there is lower Ground both to the right & left of the Pennsylvania Avenue Mr L. examined the book as to a variety of Streets running across or along the lowest situations, & finds that there is not any track between the Pennsylvania Avenue & the high Ground intended for the University, which is lower than from 50 to 54 feet above high Water,—giving a difference between the level of the Streets & of the Water in the Canal of at least 20 feet.—From the bank of the Rocky Creek, North of the Pensylvanian Avenue towards the Tiber, *the hollow*, (which appears to run along the Wide street marked K, & then to follow the Massachusets Avenue to the Tiber) does not seem lower for a very considerable part of its extent than that between the Pennsylvania Avenue and the University hill, so that no advantage would be gained by leading the Canal into that "*uninteresting*" part of the City, as the natural level of the Ground must be about 50 feet above high Water. Of the levels of the streets in this direction Mr L could not find any record in the office of the City surveyor.

It appears[1] from these facts that if the Canal be made not very different in its level from that of the street, the streets near the river must be resorted to. The line indeed of the Cut will be circuitous, & the Ground often disadvantageous,—but the thing is practicable;—

and its execution might perhaps be attended with the advantage of unloading the Country produce near to the Stores from which it must be exported, & which will naturally arrange themselves near the Potawmac.—As the weather forbids operations in the open Air, Mr Latrobe will employ himself in making the drawings of the dock & Locks, untill he receives further instructions from the President, upon whom he will wait at the first convenient moment.—

Washington
Secretary's office P.U.S
Monday morning [22 Nov. 1802]

Mr. N. King is in possession of an accurate detailed plan, & sections of Georgetown, from Fayette street to Rocky Green, which will render Mr Ls. operation through that City unnecessary.—Indeed there does not appear to be more than one weeks surveying necessary to obtain all the requisite data for a very detailed estimate.—

MS (DLC); entirely in Latrobe's hand; partially dated; endorsed by TJ as a document of 22 Nov.

For the residences at Pennsylvania Avenue and 22d Street known as the SIX BUILDINGS, see Vol. 33:595n.

The DETAILED PLAN of Georgetown, from surveys by Nicholas King in 1800, included street gradations and other details (Latrobe, *Correspondence*, 1:231-2n).

[1] MS: "It is appears."

To John Mason

Nov. 22. 1802.

Th: Jefferson asks Genl. Mason's acceptance of three Paccan trees. the bearer brings two; the 3d. will be sent.

RC (CtHi); addressed: "Genl. John Mason." Not recorded in SJL.

To Thomas Mann Randolph

DEAR SIR — Washington Nov. 22. 1802.

The family arrived here yesterday morning without any accident, as Martha will probably inform you by her own letter. I inclose you a letter from Genl. Sumpter, lately recieved. I do not think the aspect flattering from his statement, altho' he supposes no difficulty in an application to the legislature. but we know that applications to legislatures for special dispensations from law are difficult & disagreeable. Dr. Tucker expects daily to recieve an answer from the Govr. of S.

Carolina on the same subject, which shall be communicated to you. I think the principal hope is that the question being stirred, the legislature may soon after their meeting be induced to pass a general law with just qualifications of their former one; and that this may be passed before your people get on. I think it probable the Govr. & Genl. Sumpter will both endeavor to get this done by their friends in the legislature.—the event of the elections of this autumn has shewn a very universal growth of republicanism. Accept assurances of my affectionate attachment. TH: JEFFERSON

RC (DLC); at foot of text: "T M Randolph." PrC (MHi); endorsed by TJ in ink on verso. Enclosure: Thomas Sumter, Sr., to TJ, 31 Oct.

To the Senate and the House of Representatives

GENTLEMEN OF THE SENATE &
H. OF REPRESENTATIVES [on or after 22 Nov. 1802]

I communicate for information a copy of[1] the speech of Arthur St. Clair, governor of the territory N.W. of the Ohio, delivered to the Convention assembled under the act of Congress for enabling that territory to form a constitution & for it's admission into the union, which copy[2] has been transmitted to me through authentic channels. This outrage on the justice and wisdom of the National legislature, as well as on the respect due to it from every citizen, exhibited by an Executive officer at the head of an important member of the union, called for exemplary notice. it was due to these considerations, and equally so to the maintenance of harmony and good understanding between coordinate branches of the government to give prompt and decisive evidence that the Executive countenances none of it's officers in acts or principles of insubordination to the legislative authority. he was immediately removed from office.

Whether the seditious and disorganising suggestions of the speech furnish fit matter of cognisance to[3] the Constitutional tribunals, is for them to consider.

Dft (DLC: TJ Papers, 127:22014); undated; entirely in TJ's hand.

SPEECH OF ARTHUR ST. CLAIR: see Thomas Worthington to TJ, 8 Nov. 1802 and Albert Gallatin to TJ, 20 Nov. 1802.

HE WAS IMMEDIATELY REMOVED: on 22 Nov., James Madison wrote St. Clair and informed him: "The President observing in an address lately delivered by you to the convention held at Chilicothe, an intemperance and indecorum of language towards the Legislature of the United States, and a disorganizing spirit and tendency of very evil example, and grossly violating the rules of conduct enjoined by your public station, determines that your commission of Governor of the North Western Territory shall cease on the receipt of this notification." Madison enclosed St. Clair's dismissal in a letter to Charles Willing Byrd, the secretary of the territory, informing him that no successor had been appointed and that Byrd should assume the functions of the governor's office (Madison, *Papers, Sec. of State Ser.*, 4:131-2).

No evidence has been found to indicate that TJ ever sent this message to the Senate or the House of Representatives.

[1] Preceding three words interlined.

[2] Word interlined in place of "speech."

[3] TJ first wrote "fit matter for the cognisance of" before altering the text to read as above.

To George III, King of Great Britain

GREAT AND GOOD FRIEND,

Rufus King, who for several years has resided with you as the Minister Plenipotentiary of the United States, having desired to return to America, we have yielded to his request. He will accordingly take his leave of you; embracing that occasion to assure you of our friendship and sincere desire to preserve and strengthen the harmony and good understanding so happily subsisting between the two Nations, and which will be further manifested by his Successor. We are persuaded, that he will do this in the manner most expressive of these sentiments, and of the respect and sincerity with which they are offered.

We pray God to keep you, Great and Good Friend under his holy protection.

Written at the City of Washington the Twenty Third day of November, in the year of our Lord one thousand Eight hundred and two.

TH: JEFFERSON

FC (Lb in DNA: RG 59, Credences); in a clerk's hand; below signature: "By the President" and "James Madison Secretary of State." Enclosed in Madison to King, 16 Dec. 1802 (see below). Not recorded in SJL.

In a letter to Madison dated 5 Aug., RUFUS KING requested leave to resign as minister plenipotentiary to Great Britain and return to the United States in April. Madison acknowleged King's request in a private letter of 9 Oct. and sent King his official recall in December along with a copy of TJ's annual message (Madison, *Papers, Sec. of State Ser.*, 3:457; 4:5-6, 192-3, 232).

TAKE HIS LEAVE OF YOU: King gave George III his letter of recall, and had his final audience with the monarch, on 4 May 1803 (same, 5:2-3; King, *Life*, 4:248-50).

To Samuel Hanson

DEAR SIR Washington Nov. 23. 1802.

I recieved last night your favor of the day before. be assured that there is no sort of influence operating on me in what respects yourself; and that your situation & the means of relieving you from it has never been out of my mind. but we have, as you know, put down a great portion of the offices under the US. of those which remain, such as are in this district have been of too little value to be accepted by you; and those of the general government exerciseable here are under the double necessity of requiring talents & qualifications in that particular line which the office calls for,[1] and that these be sought among the different states & distributed with equal hand. in the particular object expressed in your letter, I have already spoken with some of my friends, and will certainly omit no opportunity of doing so with urgency. Accept assurances of my sincere esteem & attachment TH: JEFFERSON

PrC (DLC); at foot of text: "Mr. Samuel Hanson"; endorsed by TJ in ink on verso.

YOUR FAVOR OF THE DAY BEFORE: Hanson to TJ, 21 Nov.

[1] Preceding two words interlined in place of "requires."

To James Monroe

DEAR SIR Washington Nov. 24. 1802.

On reciept of your letter of June 11. in answer to mine of June 3. I wrote to mr King our minister at the court of London, a letter, the copy of which I now inclose you. I trusted we had then time enough to have recieved an answer before the ensuing meeting of the legislature of Virginia. but he probably left England on a visit to the continent a little before the reciept of that letter. as his absence however was not to be long, I am not entirely without hope of an answer before the rising of the legislature which may give us an idea of the probable result. it shall be communicated to you as soon as recieved.

The convulsions prevailing in the French West India islands place in a state of alarm all the nations having possessions in their neighborhood into which Blacks have been admitted. under these circumstances, the dangers which might result to them from any innovation, from any change of position, are opposed to propositions which at other times would be admissible. the similar apprehensions we have experienced ourselves will suggest the difficulties which this branch of our proposition may meet with for a time. but no favorable occasion of attempting it shall be lost. I pray you to accept assurances of my affectionate esteem and high consideration.

TH: JEFFERSON

RC (Vi); at foot of text: "Govr. Monroe"; endorsed by clerks. PrC (DLC). Enclosure: Tr, not found, of TJ to Rufus King, 13 July.

From J. P. P. Derieux

MONSIEUR Petersburg ce 25. Nov. 1802.

N'ayant pu me procurer aucune occupation a Richd. je suis venu a Petersburg, ou il paroit que mon succés ne sera pas meilleur. Le vaisseau sur lequel j'ai l'offre d'un passage Gratis, à eté rétardé dans son chargement, et ne partira d'ici que le second jour du mois prochain.

Je n'espere pas, Monsieur, que telle que soit la distresse de ma presente situation, je puisse d'aucune maniere etre excusable a vos yeux, de solliciter encore vos bontés pour m'y secourir, mais le plus malheureux se livre souvent a L'esperance, plutot qu'au désespoir, et c'est a L'appui de ce sentiment, que je prends La liberté de Supplier vos bontés et votre indulgence. une somme de 5. Doll. me mettroit a même d'acheter des provisions suffisantes pour la Traversée, et je crois qu'autant au plus me conduiroit du Hâvre a Paris; Si vous voulliés bien m'en faire L'avance, je vous prie, Monsieur d'etre persuadé que le premier argent que je recevrai dans la Succession de Mad., Bellanger, sera Certainement employé à vous faire cette remise, ainsi que celles dont vous avés bien voulu m'honorer auparavant.

Si vous voullés bien me faire L'honneur d'une reponse vous m'obligerés, Monsieur de voulloir bien me l'adresser sous le Couvert de Mr Rd. Rambaut Mercht a Petersburg.

J'ai L'honneur d'etre dans les sentiments du plus profond respect et de la plus grande reconnaissance Monsieur

Votre trés humble et trés Obeissant serviteur

PETER DERIEUX

EDITORS' TRANSLATION

SIR Petersburg, 25 Nov. 1802

Unable to find employment in Richmond, I came to Petersburg, where it appears that my success will not be any greater. The ship on which I have been offered free passage has been delayed in its loading and will not leave here until the second of next month.

Whatever the distress of my present situation, I have no hope that you might find it excusable to call upon your goodness once again to help me, but in dire straits, one often turns to hope rather than despair. With this sentiment I take the liberty of begging for your kindness and indulgence. The sum of five dollars would allow me to buy the necessary provisions for the crossing, and I think another equal amount would take me from Le Havre to Paris. If you are willing to advance the funds, I promise, Sir, that the first money I receive from the inheritance of Madame Bellanger will serve to reimburse these and the previous advances with which you have honored me.

If you do me the honor of a response, I would be obliged if you could send it care of Mr. Richard Rambaut, merchant in Petersburg.

I have the honor of being with the most profound respect and the deepest gratitude, Sir,

Your most humble and obedient servant. PETER DERIEUX

RC (DLC); endorsed by TJ as received 30 Nov. and so recorded in SJL.

SOLLICITER ENCORE VOS BONTÉS: TJ gave Derieux $25 "in charity" (MB, 2:1087; see also TJ to George Jefferson, 1 Dec.). Richard RAMBAUT was an émigré from Saint-Domingue (Suzanne Lebsock, *The Free Women of Petersburg: Status and Culture in a Southern Town, 1784-1860* [New York, 1984], 65).

From George Helmbold

HONORED SIR, Philadelphia, Novr 25 1802

You will confer a favor on me by giving me an answer to my request of Thursday last. I hope you will comply with it, as it will enable me to recover that station, in point of property, I once held. I enclose a note, by way of memorandum.

I remain, With respect, Your humble Sevt.

GEO: HELMBOLD, JUN.

RC (MHi); with note by TJ adjacent to closing: "I returned the note to him without answer. TH:J."; at foot of text: "His Excellency Thos. Jefferson"; endorsed by TJ as received 29 Nov. and so recorded in SJL. Enclosure not found.

REQUEST OF THURSDAY LAST: Helmbold to TJ, 18 Nov. 1802.

From John Milledge

SIR Louisville 25th November 1802.

The news papers having announced, that Mr. King has resigned his appointment as minister for the united States, at the court of London—I take the liberty to bring to your view my particular friend—

Elijah Clarke esqr. who you are personally acquainted with, as Secretary to the Legation that succeeds Mr. King—If correct morals, soundness in the Principles of the administration and a Classical education, are good grounds for recommendation, they are all to be found in Mr. Clarke.—

I am with sentiments of high respect, Your Mo Obt. Sevt.

JNO MILLEDGE

RC (DNA: RG 59, LAR); endorsed by TJ as received 10 Dec. and "Clarke Elijah to be Secy. of legn. London" and so recorded in SJL.

By early October 1802, newspapers announced Rufus King's resignation (New York *American Citizen*, 6 Oct. 1802).

Recommended to TJ by Josiah Tattnall, Jr., in a letter of 25 Aug. 1801, ELIJAH CLARKE traveled with Milledge to Monticello and Edgehill in April 1802 (Vol. 35:144; Vol. 37:329-30).

To Thomas Mann Randolph

DEAR SIR Washington Nov. 25. 1802.

I now inclose you Govr. Drayton's answer to Doctr. Tucker by which you will percieve that there is no prospect of getting your negroes through the state of S.C. in the present state of their laws; and as to alterations to be made in these, they are too precarious to affect your plans in the least. you will have to go therefore either through Tennissee or by water. it is said that the former route, besides being scarcely passable for a horse, exposes the people to temptations from the inhabitants which are very dangerous. what would their passage from Richmd. to Savanna by water cost? I know the passage of a gentleman, fed & lodged as such, from Philadelphia to Richmond was but 8. dollars. in this way you could carry little & big, men & women at once, & they would probably be taken in the lump, counting only the grown persons. Mrs. Trist told me there were some wild cherry stocks at Birdwood which would now not be wanting for the family; as I understand you have the direction of their affairs, I shall be glad to take them at their value. mr Dinsmore on your giving him permission, will engage sawyers to cut them up, or perhaps it would be better for mr Lilly to cut and bring the stocks home. Patsy thinks her cough better since the journey. to me it appears very bad. when the carriage comes for them, a spare cloak or two should come as far as mr Strode's. they will have mine to that place. I happened to send them by the stage, and without them they would have suffered, as they moved early, and the mornings were cold. Accept assurances of my affectionate attachment and respect. TH: JEFFERSON

P.S. on searching for Govr. Drayton's letter, it is mislaid, but shall follow as soon as found. you have the result of it.

RC (DLC); at foot of text: "T M Randolph." PrC (CSmH); lacks postscript; endorsed by TJ in ink on verso.

John DRAYTON'S ANSWER of 9 Nov. to Thomas Tudor Tucker warned that "no person has attempted, to carry negroes through this State, without great trouble, risque, & expence." Drayton added that in supporting the law, he had "consistently refused, giving passports for carrying them through this State, or allowing any security to be given, respecting the passing of slaves through this State." He advised that Randolph await an upcoming legislative effort to allow slave importation, and if that should fail, "he may then act in such manner as he shall think most to his advantage & safety" (RC in DLC; endorsed by TJ).

From John Brown

DEAR SIR Frankfort 26th. Novr. 1802

The inclosed Letter reached my Hand this Morning. I hasten to forward it to you by this Days Mail, that you may have the earliest possible information of the Measure to which it relates. There is probably very little produce of the Western Country now at New Orleans, or on its way to that Market, but very large quantities are in readiness for exportation at the first rise of our Rivers, & great loss, & inconvenience may be experienced should the extraordinary Decree said to have been issued by the Intendant be continued in force. A Gentleman lately from that Country informs, that Colo. Fulton in French Uniform, & some other French Officers had arrived at New Orleans, & were engaged in making arrangements for a Body of French Troops daily expected to occupy that important Post.

I had the honor to receive your favor covering a Letter of thanks from the Philosophical Society. Presuming the Letter was intended for a Gentn. of my name who took charge of the Bones referred to, I forwarded it to him by a safe Opportunity, & doubt not but he has reced. it.

The indisposition of Mrs. Brown, & some others of my Family renders it probable that I shall not be able to set out for the Seat of Government before the 5th. Decr. but fully expect to reach it by the 20th. or 25 at farthest.

I have the honor to be with the highest respect & esteem Sir Your most obt. Sert. J. BROWN

RC (DLC); at foot of text: "Thomas Jefferson Esqr."; endorsed by TJ as received 9 Dec. and so recorded in SJL. Enclosure: Meeker, Williamson & Patton to John Brown, 18 Oct., New Orleans, informing him that the intendant has ended the right of deposit at New Orleans without naming a substitute location; this act, "so Unexpected and so extraordinary," has caused the "Utmost Confusion" among those involved in the U.S. trade; it was thought at first that the governor would oppose the decree, but it now appears that he will not do so (RC in same).

EARLIEST POSSIBLE INFORMATION: news of what had transpired at New Orleans had already reached Washington. On 25 Nov., Madison wrote an official communication asking the Spanish minister, Carlos Martínez de Irujo, for an explanation (Madison, *Papers, Sec. of State Ser.*, 4:139-40).

Under Article 22 of the 1795 treaty between Spain and the United States, Americans shipping goods down the Mississippi River were allowed to store items at New Orleans without paying customs duties. After three years, the Spanish could terminate this right of deposit at New Orleans and pick another place on the river to serve the purpose. By a proclamation dated 16 Oct. 1802, Juan Ventura Morales, the acting INTENDANT of Louisiana and West Florida, put an immediate end to the deposit. Morales justified the timing of the decision by explaining that the continuation of the privilege at New Orleans beyond the initial three-year period had been a concession to the United States as a neutral nation while Spain and Britain were at war—a condition that ended with the Amiens peace. According to Article 22, if New Orleans ceased to be the place of deposit, responsibility for designating a new site belonged to the Spanish crown, and Morales, declaring that he had no orders on that matter, did not name a new location. The intendant's decree took Manuel de Salcedo, the governor of Louisiana, as much by surprise as it did American merchants and shippers. Intendants, however, had jurisdiction over commercial affairs and were not subordinate to governors. Salcedo objected to Morales's edict, but could not countermand it. Morales did not reveal to the governor that he was following confidential instructions from the royal government (same, xxv-xxvi; broadside, "Port of New-Orleans SHUT" [Natchez, 28 Oct. 1802; Shaw-Shoemaker, No. 2914, illustrated in this volume]; *Documentos relativos a la independencia de Norteamérica existentes en archivos españoles*, 11 vols. [Madrid, 1976-1985], 1:696-7; Miller, *Treaties*, 2:337; Alexander DeConde, *This Affair of Louisiana* [New York, 1976], 119-20; José Montero de Pedro, *The Spanish in New Orleans and Louisiana*, trans. Richard E. Chandler [Gretna, La., 2000], 113; Duvon Clough Corbitt, "The Administrative System in the Floridas, 1781-1821," in Gilbert C. Din, ed., *The Spanish Presence in Louisiana, 1763-1803*, vol. 2 of *The Louisiana Purchase Bicentennial Series in Louisiana History* [Lafayette, La., 1996], 119).

Newspaper reports noted the presence of Samuel FULTON, who had served as a commissioned officer in the French army and, in the 1790s, was involved in intrigues to reestablish French control of the Mississippi Valley. Fulton had written to TJ from Paris in the spring of 1801 seeking an appointment (Baltimore *Federal Gazette*, 10 Dec.; Nancy Son Carstens, "George Rogers Clark and the French Conspiracy, 1793-1801," in Kenneth C. Carstens and Nancy Son Carstens, eds., *The Life of George Rogers Clark, 1752-1818: Triumphs and Tragedies* [Westport, Conn., 2004], 239-45; Junius P. Rodriguez, ed., *The Louisiana Purchase: A Historical and Geographical Encyclopedia* [Santa Barbara, Calif., 2002], 4-5; Vol. 33:653-4).

YOUR FAVOR: TJ to Brown, 14 Aug. Regarding the LETTER OF THANKS misdirected to Brown, see Vol. 37:351-2 and John Vaughan to TJ, 21 July.

MRS. BROWN: Margaretta Mason Brown. She and Brown had married in 1799. At the Conrad and McMunn boardinghouse in Washington in the winter of 1800-1801, Margaretta Brown attempted, without success, to break custom and obtain a better seat at the dining table for TJ (ANB; Margaret Bayard Smith, *The First Forty Years of Washington Society*, ed. Gaillard Hunt [New York, 1906], 12).

From William Duane

Pennsylvania Avenue
Friday Evening [26 Nov. 1802]

SIR,

My absence from home until this moment prevented my sending an answer to your note before.

Young Coopers name is Thomas Cooper,—he appears to be about 22 years old.

Lacretelle's book I have not here but have written for it by Mail to Philadelphia, and requested it to be sent by some private hand.

Paine's third letter gives me considerable uneasiness, he has in fact commenced the subject of the Age of Reason in it—I have Used every effort of which I am capable to persuade him against it—but nothing will operate on him—I have fairly told him that he will be deserted by the only party that respects or does not hate him—that all his political writings will be rendered useless—and even his fame destroyed—but he silenced me at once by telling me that Dr Rush at the period when he commenced Common Sence told him that there were two words which he should avoid by every means as necessary to his own safety and that of the public—*Independence* and *Republicanism*.

With respect Yours faithfully WM DUANE

RC (DLC); partially dated; addressed: "The President"; endorsed by TJ as a letter of 27 Nov. received 28 Nov. and recorded in SJL as a letter of the 27th received on that day.

FRIDAY EVENING: 26 Nov. was a Friday.

The NOTE to Duane has not been found and is not recorded in SJL.

Thomas COOPER sought an appointment for his son, Thomas Cooper, Jr., as a midshipman in the navy; see TJ to Thomas Cooper, 29 Nov., and Cooper to TJ, 21 Mch. 1803.

LACRETELLE'S BOOK: French politician Pierre Louis de Lacretelle made his name as a writer with his *Discours sur le préjugé des peines infamantes* (Paris, 1784; Sowerby, No. 2362). He was the author of several works, including *Sur le dix-huit brumaire* (Paris, 1800) and *De la convocation de la prochaine tenue des États Généraux en France* (Paris, 1788; Sowerby, No. 2509).

PAINE'S THIRD LETTER: "After an absence of almost fifteen years, I am again returned to the Country in whose dangers I bore my share, and to whose greatness I contributed my part"—so Thomas Paine, writing in Washington, opened a series of letters "to the citizens of the United States." The essays appeared serially in the *National Intelligencer* beginning on 15 Nov. In the third one, dated 26 Nov. and published on the 29th, Paine stated that he had become so notorious among Federalists, "they cannot eat or drink without me. I serve them as a standing dish, and they cannot make up a bill of fare if I am not in it." He characterized the latter part of George Washington's presidency and the entirety of John Adams's administration as a "reign of terror" built on falsehood and lies. Its leaders "were in character the same sort of men" as Robespierre and the leaders of the French Terror. The creators of the American reign of terror, Paine declared, "who were waiting in the devotion of their hearts for the joyful news of my destruction, are the same banditti who are now bellowing, in all the hackneyed language of hackneyed hypocrisy, about humanity, and piety, and often about something they call infidelity, and they finish with the chorus of *crucify him, crucify him*." Paine recounted how he had been slated for execution several times in France, only to be spared from the guillotine each time by circumstance. According to the "outrageous piety" of his enemies in America, he taunted, Providence "must be as bad as Thomas Paine; she has protected him in all his dangers, patronized him in all his undertakings, encouraged him in all his ways, and rewarded him at last by bringing him in safety and in health to the promised land." Paine asserted that during the American Revolution he had supported Washington after "a series of blunders" by the general "nearly ruined the country" and a political faction—including Adams—sought to remove Washington from command of the American armies. Yet later, when Paine faced destruction in France, Washington "left me to perish." Washington, Paine wrote, "accepted as a present (though he was already rich) a hundred thousand acres of land in America, and left me to occupy six foot of earth in France." The first president, Paine explained, "was of such an icy and death-like constitution, that he neither loved his friends, nor hated his enemies." Following the appearance of another essay in December, Duane and other printers compiled the four letters as a pamphlet (Shaw-Shoemaker, Nos. 2837, 2840, 2889). Paine, however, was not finished: he resumed the series in February 1803, writing three more letters that year and adding a final essay in June 1805. Beginning with the sixth installment in March 1803, he wrote in Bordentown, New Jersey, sending most of the last essays in the series to the *Aurora* for publication (*National Intelligencer*, 15, 29 Nov.; Foner, *Thomas Paine*, 2:908-57).

From Robert R. Livingston

SIR Paris 26 November 1802

Not knowing whether an agricultural Society is still in existence in Pennsylvania, I have chosen to adress this to you to whose Institution no useful discovery is foreign—

I had heard here that the ashes of Pyrites were used as a manure, but I could meet with no satisfactory information on the subject till in a little excursion that I made lately into Flanders I was enabled to see the process & to procure the Samples I enclose.

I observed two persons at some distance from the road employed stiring a heap of earth which emitted smoke but no flame visible at that distance—Leaving my post-chaise & going to them I found that the earth they were burning was a Pyrites Sample No. 1 this was laid upon an earthen floor, in the open air in a bed of about thirty feet long & ten wide and about a foot thick it was reduced into small particles like what I enclose, & when dry contained sufficient Sulphur to burn without any addition.—when the fire was checked in time it formed the red ashes No. 2 which was more valuable than the black No. 3—these other were sifted in a fine sive when they were carried many miles on the backs of asses & used as a manure particularly on grass lands in the proportion of about six bushels to the acre—the corn was also dried in it afore it had been steeped before Sowing & very considerable effect was found from this process. You will observe in this a striking resemblance to the effects of Gypsum & indeed it almost demonstrates that Gypsum derives its fertilizing quality from the Sulphuric acid—this is probably disengaged by slow combustion & retained by the earth either in a combined or uncombined State as the earth may or may not be calcarious or as it may or may not contain vegetable matter reducible to ashes with which it would unite—In writing to the agricultural Society of New-york upon this subject I have suggested to them the Idea of trying diluted Sulphuric & other acids as manures the effect of which would be more instantaneous probably than any combination of them with earth—perhaps too this fertilising quality may not be confined to the mineral acids, if not I have proposed to them a trial of the pyroligneous acid which may by easy process be obtained cheaper than any other.

But the samples enclosed may enable the members of Society to find the earth, which I have reason to think by no means uncommon in the United States—I also send small samples of the Clay used in the fabric of china at Seves to aid the recherches of such of their members, as may wish to make it an object of enquiry—

I have the honor to be, Sir with the highest respect Your most Obt hume Servt

Robt R Livingston

RC (PPAmP); in a clerk's hand, signed by Livingston; at foot of text: "Thomas Jefferson Presidt of the United States & of the philosophical society"; endorsed for the American Philosophical Society.

At a meeting of 18 Mch. 1803, the APS received Livingston's letter and the accompanying SAMPLES (APS, *Proceedings*, 22, pt. 3 [1884], 335).

TO THE AGRICULTURAL SOCIETY OF NEW-YORK: Livingston corresponded with Benjamin DeWitt and Samuel L. Mitchill to keep the New York Society for the Promotion of Agriculture, Arts, and Manufactures informed of his observations on agriculture, livestock, domestic architecture, farm technology, and other subjects during his stay in Europe. He discussed the use of burned pyrites as a fertilizer in Flanders in a letter to DeWitt of 10 Oct. 1802 (*Transactions of the Society for the Promotion of Useful Arts, in the State of New-York* [Albany, 1807], 5-22, 69-73).

From Matthew Lyon

Sir Frankfort 26 Novr 1802

A Circumstance has just come to my knowledge which reminds me of my annual tribute of a letter to the President, It is the Death of Judge Clark of the Indiana Territory—Perhaps you may recolect the third person I recomended as Marshal of the District of Vermont in April 1801, his name is James Witherill he is now of the Legislative Council of Vermont and one of the Judges of the County Court or Common pleas of Rutland County, one of the largest & most respectable Counties in that State where it is not uncommon to have 1000 Actions on the doquet, he has been a justice 10 years or upward & has distinguished himself by his upright decissions & his legal knowledge and would have been on the bench long before had not Anti republican prejudices prevailed against him, he is a man of first rate abilities has an excellent english education and extensive information, he is a Politician of a Conciliating disposition & a firm republican he sustains the most irreproachable private charracter. Law has been his favorite Study.

This man I have reason to think from former intimations would gladly accept the office made vacant by the death of Judge Clark—he is an active, Industrious, personable man near forty with a considerable family, he has long wished to come[1] to this country, but the sacrifice he must make in his property which (altho middleing for that country) is not large has hitherto prevented him—I have lately been a tour into the Western part of that Country & liveing near the southerly part of it and where there is a great intercourse with that I have an opportunity to learn what is doing & saying there. The present Governor who was a Violent advocate for the fallen administration now tells the people he has nothing to do with Politics, while his best friends & supporters are exclaiming against the present administration, & in the most nonsensical manner condemning the salutary measures of the last session of Congress. the Secretary & Attorney for the US are the most petulant anti republicans, with one only of the Judges am I acquainted he wishes to be considerd & perhaps really is a republican & a friend to the present Administration, his influence can not be great while the officers of the governors appointment and the most of the people are gennerally afraid to express a sentiment when at home which can in any wise seem to contrast the opinion of the Governor.

The people there ardently wish for the second grade of government they express it by their Conversation when in our Country but they have been checked by him & at home they dare say but little about it.

I cannot but think that Witherills independance & his conciliatory manner would be of great service to that country beside which the Vermonters who have stoped comeing to my neighbourhood for want of sufficient opening would have ample room there & doubtless many would follow him a large number of familes passed by from Vermont last spring & went up Missisipi some are in the Spanish Teritory others in the Indiana.

I presume Mr Isreal Smith will coroborate the Carracter I give of Judge Witherill Mr Bradley who is not so well acquainted with him can have no objection to him, it may be recolected that Vermont is behind most of the States in receiveing Appointments which are not confined to the State, Mr Eaton was not a Vermonter nor of a Vermont family he was from Massachusetts when he got his appointment in the Army. altho resideing at the time as a Studient at Law in Vermont he had renderd Mr Bradley an eminent service & it was supposed for that he got the appointment—

I am Sorry to find my suspicions that Mr Burr wished & maneuverd for the Presidency were but too well founded. he has no partizans in this State, I fear he will have too many amoung the milk & water republicans beyond the Delaware.

Callanders defection might have been expected, the only cause of wonder is that the Tories are not ashamed of him we always were—

The people here are almost universally pleased with the present administration however strange it may seem those in the opposite politics seem not to be feard nor gaurded against, they are plausible & insinuateing, two of that Charracter will probably be candidates for next congress in the lower half of the State one may be chosen if so he will not dare to leave a republican majority, it is however wrong to trust them, Governor McKean has demonstrated that he knew best how to deal with the Anti Republicans—

The Legislature here are occupied with a bill for divideing the State into destricts for the choice of Members of Congress, they have once decided they would have but two destricts three members in each the lower house has since voted they would have six, there seems to be partiality & design in laying out the six, & it is thought that it will go back to two again, this is thought will favor the Candidates in the center of the State—

It would give me great pleasure Sir to see my much valued friend

Witherill name in the list of new Appointments, should it prove otherwise I must conclude it is for the best when it is done by him who holds the most exalted place in the Esteem & Affection of

M LYON

RC (DNA: RG 59, LAR); addressed: "The President of the US"; endorsed by TJ as received 9 Dec. and so recorded in SJL; also endorsed by TJ: "Witherill James. to be Judge Indiana. v. Clarke."

ANNUAL TRIBUTE: Lyon last wrote TJ on 12 Aug. 1801.

William Clarke, former U.S. attorney for Kentucky, took the oath of office as chief justice of INDIANA TERRITORY on 10 Jan. 1801. He died suddenly at Vincennes on 11 Nov. 1802, having presided at a session of the General Court that day (Clarence E. Carter, "William Clarke, First Chief Justice of Indiana Territory," *Indiana Magazine of History*, 34 [1938], 1-2, 5-6, 13; Vol. 32:563n). On 15 Nov., Judge Henry Vander Burgh informed Madison of the death of the chief justice "of a Pleurisy." He noted that the services of the territorial judges were "highly necessary" as the business of the court had greatly increased. Not only did they hold court at the seat of government twice a year, but they also attended sessions as members of the legislature and held circuit courts in the distant counties (RC in DNA: RG 59, LAR, 2:0264-5, endorsed by TJ: "Vanderburg Henry to mr Madison Wm. Clarke, chief justice of Indiana dead"; Madison, *Papers, Sec. of State Ser.*, 4:122). John Griffin, son of Cyrus Griffin, was the third territorial judge. TJ transferred him to the Michigan Territory in 1806 (JEP, 2:11, 30; Cyrus Griffin to James Madison, 3 Oct. 1805, in DNA: RG 59, LAR).

For Lyon's previous recommendation of JAMES Witherell (WITHERILL), see Vol. 33:113, 666. TJ appointed Witherell a judge in the Michigan Territory in 1808 (JEP, 2:81).

President Adams appointed John Gibson, SECRETARY of the Indiana Territory, in May 1800. ATTORNEY FOR THE US: Lyon is probably referring to John Rice Jones, appointed attorney general for the territory by Governor William Henry Harrison (Donald F. Carmony, "Indiana Territorial Expenditures, 1800-1816," *Indiana Magazine of History*, 39 [1943], 241-2; JEP, 1:355; *Terr. Papers*, 7:34; Vol. 36:521n).

SECOND GRADE OF GOVERNMENT: see Thomas T. Davis to TJ, 16 Dec. 1802.

William Eaton was identified as being from Vermont when he received his APPOINTMENT IN THE ARMY as a captain in March 1792. He was born in Woodstock, Connecticut. After graduating from Dartmouth in 1790, he became clerk of the Vermont Assembly (JEP, 1:114-16; ANB).

DIVIDEING THE STATE INTO DESTRICTS: by the act of 13 Dec. 1802, the Kentucky General Assembly divided the state into six congressional districts. Six Republican representatives, including Lyon, were elected to the Eighth Congress (*Acts Passed at the First Session of the Eleventh General Assembly for the Commonwealth of Kentucky* [Frankfort, Ky., 1803], 83-6; *Biog. Dir. Cong.*).

[1] MS: "to come to come."

From John Smith

SIR Chillicothe Nov 26th 1802

The day after to morrow I expect we shall sign the Constitution of this new State; a Copy of which, accompanying an adress will be sent you from our body.

The propositions of the law of Congress I presume will not be accepted without some modification, for which purpose we in all likelihood will send Col. Worthington with instructions to negociate with the National Legislature & adjourn to a day subsequent to his return. The operation of the terms proposed by Congress, would in the opinion of many be partial & excite much discontent in our new State, which would be unfortunate at the moment of our entering into a State Government—This Sir, is the important crisis, to settle the political habits & sentiments of the people in our Country And much depends on the conduct of the general government toward us in the above affair. We are chiefly Republican in theory & I hope Sir that we shall now reduce it to a uniform practice.

I beg that you will excuse the liberty I take in stating to you the little progress we are making in the affairs of our government—And also to recommend to your consideration Charles W Byrd Esqre (who stands high in the esteem of our Republican Friends) to the office of Federal Judge in our State—He has been educated to the law, He would I am confident fill that office with honour as he does that of Secretary. The Republicans would be greatly pleased with him in that situation. They hear Mr McMillen (whom they most cordially despise) is a Candidate—It would be very disagreable to them, from various considerations to hear of his appointment.

The 2d. Tuesday in Jany. next we elect our Governor & Representatives. The first session of the state Legislature is to meet at this place on the first monday in march. I think there is good reason to suppose that they will choose for us two Republican Senators & in consequence we will elect a Representative for Congress of the same politics. Be pleased to accept the assurances of the high consideration & respect with which I am

Sir your most obedient Servant JOHN SMITH

RC (DLC); at foot of text: "Thos Jefferson Esqr. President of the U States"; endorsed by TJ. Recorded in SJL as received 9 Dec.

The Enabling Act of 1802 contained three PROPOSITIONS for the consideration of the Ohio constitutional convention. The first called for setting aside one section in every township for the use of schools. The second would grant several salt springs to the state, provided that the legislature would not lease the same for periods longer than ten years. The final provision would apply five percent of public land sale proceeds toward the construction of federal roads through the state. All three provisions, however, were made on the condition that Ohio would exempt all federal lands sold after 30 June 1802 from state and local taxes for a term of five years after the day of sale. The convention agreed to the propositions on 29 Nov., provided that the land for schools include portions of the U.S. and Virginia military districts, the Connecticut Reserve, and any future Indian land cessions, and that said school lands would be vested in the state legislature. The convention also requested that three percent of the net proceeds from federal land sales be granted to the legislature for road construction. The convention appointed Thomas Worthington to carry the propositions to Washington, who presented them to Congress on 23 Dec. Congress agreed to the modified provisions on 3 Mch. 1803 (Thomas Worthington, *Letter from Thomas Worthington, Inclosing an Ordinance Passed by the Convention of the State of Ohio, Together with the Constitution, Formed and Agreed to by the Convention for the Said State, and Sundry Propositions Submitted to the Congress of the United States. 23 December, 1802* [Washington, 1802; Shaw-Shoemaker, No. 3331], 33-4; U.S. Statutes at Large, 2:175, 225-7).

TJ saw several other letters from Ohio Republicans recommending Charles W. BYRD as FEDERAL JUDGE. On 17 Nov., Thomas Worthington sent separate letters to Gallatin and William B. Giles advocating Byrd's appointment. He wrote Gallatin that Byrd discharged his duties as secretary and governor "with much satisfaction" and deservedly had "the Confidence of the republicans." To Giles, he wrote, "Mr Byrd I am well satisfied will be acceptable to the people here and will discharge the duties of the office with fidelity." On 4 Dec., Edward Tiffin wrote Madison from Chillicothe at the request of several other residents who wanted the president to be informed of their support for Byrd as district judge. Tiffin observed that Byrd stood "high in the estimation of the people—and is a regular Law Character, equal to any which can be selected in the State" (RCs in DNA: RG 59, LAR; both endorsed by TJ as Byrd "to be judge of Ohio").

Prominent Cincinnati attorney and jurist William McMillan (MCMILLEN) served briefly as the delegate for the Northwest Territory in Congress and received an appointment as U.S. attorney for the territory in June 1801. Although previously a Republican, McMillan earned the enmity of the party when he allied with Arthur St. Clair in his effort to redivide the territory along the Scioto River, which, McMillan believed, would have enhanced Cincinnati's future prospects. In his letter to William B. Giles of 17 Nov., Worthington declared that "the president could not appoint a man More Obnoxious to the republicans" than McMillan. On the same date, Joseph Darlinton warned Albert Gallatin from Chillicothe that McMillan's appointment would "prejudice the minds of many against the President" (DNA: RG 59, LAR; endorsed by TJ: "McMillan not to be judge"). He did not receive the federal judgeship for Ohio and in 1803 was an unsuccessful candidate for the state's representative to Congress (Jeffrey P. Brown, "William McMillan and the Conservative Cincinnati Jeffersonians," *The Old Northwest*, 12 [Summer 1986], 117-35; Vol. 33:676; Vol. 36:300-1; Worthington to TJ, 10 July 1803).

From St. George Tucker

Williamsburg Nover. 26. 1802.

St. Geo. Tucker with very respectful Compliments to Mr. Jefferson takes the earliest Opportunity since his return home to forward the history of Connecticut, according to the promise he made at Monticello. He takes the Liberty of referring Mr. Jefferson particularly to the Appendix, which contains some curious particulars.

RC (MHi); endorsed by TJ as received 2 Dec. and so recorded in SJL.

The HISTORY OF CONNECTICUT that Tucker forwarded has not been identified but may have been the first volume of *A Complete History of Connecticut, Civil and Ecclesiastical, from the Emigration of Its First Planters from England, in MDCXXX, to MDCCXIII*, written by Yale graduate and pastor of the church at North Haven, Benjamin Trumbull, and published in Hartford in 1797. Its appendix of "Original papers illustrating the preceding History," contained 26 documents, including old patents for Connecticut, fundamental articles of the colony's original constitution, and the Great Patent of New-England of 3 Nov. 1620. Trumbull's lengthy list of subscribers to the history included many Connecticut citizens and legislators and 10 United States senators, among whom was Tucker's fellow Virginian, Henry Tazewell. Another history that may have been sent to TJ was published in London in 1781 and attributed to Samuel A. Peters writing as "A Gentleman of the Province." His *General History of Connecticut, From Its First Settlement under George Fenwick, Esq. to Its Latest Period of Amity with Great Britain; Including a Description of the Country, and Many Curious and Interesting Anecdotes*, included an "Appendix, wherein new and true Sources of the present Rebellion in America are pointed out; together with the particular Part taken by the People of Connecticut in its Promotion."

From Benjamin H. Latrobe

6 buildings, Washington

Dear Sir, Sunday morning. [28 Nov. 1802]

An unfortunate scratch across the end of my Nose which I received among the briars in the Neighborhood of the Navy Yard, has given me so disgraceful an appearance for the last four days, that I have confined my Labors to the Survey of the Canal, & to my Chamber. I have now nearly finished the Ground work of my Estimate & have every reason to believe, that the Canal from the Locks to the Navy Yard,—perforating bothe the Capitol hill, & that extending from Rocky Creek to Eastward of the Presidents house, cannot be executed for a less Sum than 250.000 Dollars,—of which the perforations will consume 116.320 or thereabout (if the plan of the City be at all correct). If the hill be followed it is possible that 50.000 Dollars of the whole expence may be saved—In two or three days (about Wednesday) I will exhibit to you a compleat Section of the Canal, & the Plans of the Docks & locks, all which are in a greater or less degree of forwardness already. I am with the truest respect

Your faithful hble Servt B Henry Latrobe.

RC (DLC); partially dated; endorsed by TJ as a letter of 28 Nov. received on that day and so recorded in SJL.

To Caesar A. Rodney

DEAR SIR Washington Nov. 28. 1802.

I am indebted to you for several letters giving me pleasing information from time to time of the progress of your election & of it's final result. I have avoided answering because of the use which the disaffected made of our correspondence, by lying imputations on it's object. that I, as well as every other honest man should rejoice at your substitution for that of your predecessor, was right: and altho' he is likely to obtain a more durable birth, it is one where calumnies can do little harm.—the happy effects of our fiscal operations, which already shew themselves beyond all expectation, will forever fix the fate of the fallen party. the prospect which presents itself is really consolatory, and will shew to our constituents that the resources reserved are so abundant if directed with economy, that nothing but war, or federalism getting hold of them, can prevent the extinguishment of the debt within the period contemplated.—on the reciept of your last letter, I enquired after the one you supposed to have been recieved. it was not recieved till a day or two after. altho' not expressed in very positive terms, it was accepted as such, and will some time hence go into effect. but who is to be the successor? this is always the most difficult part of the subject, from which I hope you will relieve us by proper recommendations of the person whose principles & qualifications will be most out of the reach of objection. I cannot omit to congratulate you on the general progress of republicanism evinced by the late elections. the approaching session of Congress will not fail to give a new spur to that progress. Accept assurances of my affectionate esteem and high respect. TH: JEFFERSON

RC (De-Ar); addressed: "Caesar A. Rodney Wilmington"; postmarked 29 Nov.; endorsed by Rodney: "Authorising me to appoint a successor to Al MClane." PrC (DLC).

SEVERAL LETTERS: see Rodney to TJ, 25 Aug., 6 and 15 Oct. YOUR PREDECESSOR: James A. Bayard.

TJ received Rodney's LAST LETTER, undated, on 4 Nov. Rodney referred to a letter that Allen McLane had written to the Treasury secretary, requesting that he be allowed to retain the collectorship at Wilmington, Delaware, at least until the close of the first quarter of 1803. TJ read and endorsed that letter on 3 Nov. (see note at Rodney's letter to TJ, [before 4 Nov.]). TJ had also come into possession of a letter written by McLane to his friend John Steele on 25 Oct. Not realizing that the comptroller was in North Carolina and had resigned, McLane addressed the private letter to Steele in Washington; it was retained in the president's papers. The Wilmington collector noted that he was "much exercised" since the Delaware elections, having heard people declare that his days were numbered. McLane went on to say that his enemies would give the president no rest "till he removes me." Under these circumstances, he was pleading to be left in office only until the next spring. Through great exertions,

McLane asserted, he had "secured dues to the United States to greater amount than ever was secured in any former year, with the least expences to the United States." He contended: "should my enemies be able to prevail on the President to remove me before I reap the fruits of a service rendered at the risk of my life, the greatest injury will be done me, and I shall have cause to complain." He requested that Steele sound out the president on the subject through Gallatin or Madison (RC in DLC; torn at seal; addressed: "John Steele Esquire" and "*private*"; endorsed by TJ: "Mc.lane to mr <*Gallatin*> Steele [. . .]").

To Thomas Cooper

DEAR SIR Washington Nov. 29. 1802.

Your favor of Oct. 25. was recieved in due time, and I thank you for the long extract you took the trouble of making from mr Stone's letter. certainly the information it communicates as to Alexander kindles a great deal of interest in his existence, and strong spasms of the heart in his favor. tho his means of doing good are great, yet the materials on which he is to work are refractory. whether he engages in private correspondencies abroad, as the king of Prussia did much, & his grandmother sometimes, I know not: but certainly such a correspondence would be very interesting to those who are sincerely anxious to see mankind raised from their present abject condition. it delights me to find that there are persons who still think that all is not lost in France: that their retrogradation from a limited to an unlimited despotism, is but to give themselves a new impulse. but I see not how or when. the press, the only tocsin of a nation, is compleatly silenced there, and all means of a general effort taken away. however I am willing to hope as long as any body will hope with me: and I am entirely persuaded that the agitations of the public mind advance it's powers, and that at every vibration between the points of liberty and despotism something will be gained for the former. as men become better informed, their rulers must respect them the more.—I think you will be sensible that our citizens are fast returning from the panic into which they were artfully thrown, to the dictates of their own reason: and I believe the delusions they have seen themselves hurried into, will be useful as a lesson under similar attempts on them in future. the good effects of our late fiscal arrangements will certainly tend to unite them in opinion, and in a confidence as to the views of their public functionaries legislative & executive. the path we have to pursue is so quiet, that we have nothing scarcely to propose to our legislature. a noiseless course, [not] medling with the affairs of others, unattractive of notice, is a mark that a society is going on in happiness. if we can but prevent the government from wasting the labours of the people, under the pretence of taking care of them, they must become happy. their finances are now under such a course of application as nothing could derange but war or federalism. the gripe of the latter has shewn itself as deadly as the jaws of the former. our adversaries say we are indebted to their providence for the means of paying the public debt. we never charged them with the want of foresight in providing money; but with the misapplication of it after they had levied it. we say they raised not only enough, but too much: and that after giving back the surplus we do more with a part than they did with the whole.

Your letter of Nov. 18. is also recieved. the places of midshipmen are so much sought that (being limited) there is never a vacancy. your son shall be set down for the 2d. which shall happen; the 1st. being anticipated. we are not long generally without vacancies happening. as soon as he can be appointed you shall know it. I pray you to accept assurances of my great attachment and respect.

TH: JEFFERSON

PrC (DLC); faint; at foot of first page: "Thomas Cooper esq."

KING OF PRUSSIA: Frederick the Great. Emperor Alexander's GRANDMOTHER was Empress Catherine of Russia (see Cooper to TJ, 25 Oct.).

YOUR LETTER OF NOV. 18: Cooper's letter, dated 18 Nov. at Wilkes-Barre, Pennsylvania, and recorded in SJL as received on the 25th, has not been found.

From Blair McClenachan

SIR, Philadelphia, Novr. 29. 1802.

I must again entreat you, to have the goodness to pardon me for again, troubling you: Nothing less than the pressure of Severe circumstances, could have extorted from me the former application. These circumstances have not Since improved.

The enclosed paper, which my fellow citizens have executed, not only without my Solicitation, but without my privity or knowledge, Shews the place they Still honor me with in their regard, and at the Same time Solicits for me, an office the duties of which, I trust I Should not be incompetent to discharge.

Please, Sir, to accept the acknowledgments, of my gratitude, for the blessings conferred on this happy country, by your administration, and of my most profound personal respect.

BLAIR MCLENACHAN

RC (DNA: RG 59, LAR); endorsed by TJ as received 3 Dec. and "for office" and so recorded in SJL. Enclosure: Recommendation, dated 20 Nov. 1802, signed by Joseph Scott, Mathew Carey, and 59 other members of the general ward committees of Philadelphia elected to form the Democratic Republican ticket for the previous election; they note the "patriotic and disinterested services" of Blair McClenachan during the Revolutionary War and his uniform adherence to those principles of government "recognized in the declaration of Independence" and endorse him "as a citizen worthy, from his long experience in commercial affairs, of filling the office of Purveyor of Public Supplies, now in the possession of one of our most active Political enemies" (MS in same; probably in Joseph Scott's hand, signed by all).

FORMER APPLICATION: see McClenachan to TJ, 6 Jan. 1802.

On 27 Nov., McClenachan informed Gallatin of his application to the president. He noted that the Treasury secretary's Republican friends in Philadelphia would be highly gratified if he used his influence to have him appointed the next purveyor of public supplies. He requested that Gallatin keep him informed of his prospects for that or any other office (RC in DNA: RG 59, LAR; endorsed by TJ: "Mc.lanachan Blair to mr Gallatin"). For Israel Whelen's plans to vacate the purveyor's office in 1803, see Gallatin to TJ, 24 July 1802.

From John Morton

SIR N. York Nov. 29. 1802.

The Editors of the Medical Repository having requested of me a Summary Account of the City of Havana, I beg permission to request your acceptance of a Copy of that Article from their last number.

You will perceive, Sir, that, as there stated, it is *but* a summary: but as I intend collecting all my Notes into one view (those which you did me the honor formerly to peruse being much enlarged & corrected) I shall, at a future day, also request your acceptance of that collection; as a small mark of that sincere respect with which I continue

to remain, Sir, Your ob. Serv JNO. MORTON.

RC (DLC); at head of text: "private"; at foot of text: "Tho. Jefferson Esqr."; endorsed by TJ as received 3 Dec. and so recorded in SJL. Enclosure: John Morton, "Notices Respecting the City of Havanna" (*Medical Repository*, 6 [1803], 228-34).

YOU DID ME THE HONOR FORMERLY TO PERUSE: see Morton to TJ, 3 Feb. 1801.

To Joseph Priestley

DEAR SIR Washington Nov. 29. 1802.

Your favor of Oct. 29. was recieved in due time, and I am very thankful for the extract of mr Stone's letter on the subject of Alexander. the apparition of such a man on a throne is one of the phaenomena which will distinguish the present epoch so remarkeable in the history of man. but he must have an Herculean task to devise and establish the means of securing freedom & happiness to those who are not capable of taking care of themselves. some preparation seems necessary to qualify the body of a nation for self-government. who could have thought the French nation incapable of it? Alexander will doubtless begin at the right end, by taking means for diffusing instruction & a sense of their natural rights through the mass of his people, and for relieving them in the mean time from actual oppression. I should be puzzled to find a person capable of preparing for him the short analytical view of our constitution which you propose. it would be a short work, but a difficult one. mr Coopers Propositions respecting the foundation of civil government; your own piece on the First principles of government; Chipman's Sketches on the principles of government, and the Federalist would furnish the principles of our constitution and their practical developement in the several parts of that instrument. I question whether such a work can be so well executed for his purpose by any other, as by a Russian, presenting exactly that view of it which that people would sieze with advantage. it would be easy to name some persons who could give a perfect abstract view, adapted to an English or American mind: but they would find it difficult perhaps to disengage themselves sufficiently from other pursuits. however if we keep it in view, we may perhaps get it done. your letter to mr Stone shall be taken care of.

Our busy scene is now approaching. the quiet tract into which we are endeavoring to get, neither meddling with the affairs of other nations, nor with those of our fellow citizens, but letting them go on in their own way, will shew itself in the statement of our affairs to Congress. we have almost nothing to propose to them but 'to let things alone.' the effects of the fiscal arrangements of the last session will shew themselves very satisfactorily. the only speck in our horizon which can threaten any thing, is the cession of Louisiana to France. tho' probable, it is not yet entirely certain how far it will be carried into effect.—I am sorry you cannot be absent this winter from the cold of the position in which you are. I have a great opinion of the favorable influence of genial climates in winter, & especially on old persons. altho' Washington does not offer the best, yet it is probably much milder than that in which you are. otherwise it could offer little but the affectionate reception you should have experienced. the notice of me which you are so good as to prefix to your book, cannot but be consolatory, inasmuch as it testifies what one great and good man thinks of me. but in truth I have no pretensions but to have wished the good of mankind with very moderate talents for carrying it into effect. my chief object is to let the good sense of the nation have fair play, believing it will best take care of itself. praying for you many days of life & health, & of leisure still to inform the understandings of man, I tender you assurances of my sincere esteem & attachment & high respect. TH: JEFFERSON

PrC (DLC); at foot of first page: "Dr. Priestley."

LETTER TO MR STONE: a letter, not found, that Priestley had asked TJ to forward to John Hurford Stone; see the first enclosure listed at Priestley to TJ, 29 Oct. See that letter also for the NOTICE of TJ in the dedication to Priestley's *General History of the Christian Church*.

From Stephen Sayre

SIR. Philaa. 29th novr 1802

You may imagine I feel inexpressibly hurt, under your administration, that there are many men kept in office, & others appointed, who have no comparative claims upon your patronage. At last, I am made to understand the cause; for I must not suppose you could, so long neglect a faithful servant, suffering as I have done, thro' a long life, without some very imperious reasons.

I leave it to your own feelings to imagine, what mine are, when supposed, by yourself, or some of your Ministers a criminal in private life. Some of my friends have hinted, that unfavorable impressions might exist respecting Baron de Poelnitz & his Lady. and when I come to reflect upon some paragraphs in the papers, while I was in England, & that you may have read & given credit to those vile & false accusations—also; that the Baron might, after his return to New York, have done much to confirm the Idea I am not so much astonished, as I have been, that I should be the last man, who might hope for your favors.

It is some consolation to me, that you had, by prejudice, cause for that apathy, under which I have so long suffer'd—but I feel still more, that it is in my power to remove it.

I have acted with uncommon circumspection, in every thing which regarded both the Baron & his wife. I foresaw the consequences, which might naturally result, from becoming her Agent, in the absence of her husband, & declined the commission for a long time—I requested her to employ Mr Hamilton—she did so—*but he gave her some offence*. Before I consented to act, I persuaded her to dispose of every thing that she meant to part with, at Vendue, before her departure—she did so, except two negro Servants & her carriage—this appears, in an account now in my possession, signed An: Blecher—made in her name, & dated while she was in New York—and I have now before me, her order to sell those negroes & carriage—I have also receipts for the payment of all her debts, and for money advanced her—for you must be informed, that her income was attached in the city of London, at the time, which had compeled the Baron to go there. I had nothing to do with her affairs, afterwards

It was my misfortune, while in England, to have two suits in chancery agt. the very attorney which the Baron had employd—he had committed a forgery—I endeavour'd to hang him—my papers on the table prove the fact—he of course did all in his power to injure me, by paragraphs & malignant lies.

He represented Lady Ann as living in the Kings Bench while I was there—she never was in that prison—she went over to France as soon as she had made a settlement with the Baron, or soon after, as I beleive.

I have a demand, to this day, against the Baron for above £60. new york cury, cash advanced for his children by my nephew who wrote me that he got no answer from him but abuse. I saw him both in France & England—he never express'd the least dissatisfaction as to my conduct—if he ever held a different Language he has acted very unfairly—

If Sir, these conjectures are well founded—pray—do me the justice to give opportunity of vindicating myself. Name any person of worth, to read & examine my papers—my innocence will be clearly & instantly manifest—every dark & malicious insinuation, as to this, & every other transaction from my infancy to this hour, is as false as those publish'd, by your enemies, to injure your name & character—it fortunately happens—I can prove a negative as to the above charges—and I defy all my enemies to substantiate a single action, either in public, or private life, which can degrade me in the opinion of a candid man. Mr Duane is now at Washington—you know his integrity—will you Sir, condescend to make him the judge in this, or any other matter which may have had an influence on your good opinion

I am most respectfully yours &c &c Stephen Sayre

RC (DNA: RG 59, LAR); at foot of text: "President of United States"; endorsed by TJ as received 2 Dec. and so recorded in SJL.

BARON: Friedrich Karl Hans Bruno von Poellnitz was the former chamberlain at the court of Frederick II of Prussia. His third wife, the LADY Anne Stuart, was the eldest daughter of the third earl of Bute and the divorced spouse of Hugh Percy. The baron and his wife came to the United States in 1782 and settled in New York in 1784. Poellnitz, whom John Adams first brought to TJ's attention in Sep. 1785, conveyed letters on TJ's behalf later that year when he returned to London to attend to his wife's outstanding debt. Lady Anne remained behind to settle their American estate and engaged Sayre as her business agent. The two returned to England amidst rumors that he was also her paramour. She was reputed to have joined Sayre in his quarters at the King's Bench prison, where he was held for his debts (London *Morning Chronicle and London Advertiser,* 14 July 1786; John R. Alden, *Stephen Sayre: American Revolutionary Adventurer* [Baton Rouge, La., 1983], 137-58; Charles Starne Belsterling, "Baron Poellnitz of New York City and South Carolina," *New York Genealogical and Biographical Record*, 80 [1949], 130-41; Vol. 8:525; Vol. 9:89, 91, 93, 95).

AFTER HIS RETURN TO NEW YORK: when the Baron returned to Manhattan by 1788, he became an advocate of experimental farming. In 1790, Poellnitz wrote several essays on the abolition of slavery for the *Gazette of the United States*. After selling his New York property, he moved to Ragtown, South Carolina, where he purchased almost 3,000 acres. His marriage to Lady Anne ended in divorce because of desertion and he married for a fourth time before his death in 1801 (Belsterling, "Baron Poellnitz," 136-9).

From Hippolyte Ferdinand de Widranges

À Lignÿ Près Bar-sur-Oznain, Departement de la Meuse, ce 29 Novembre 1802.

MONSIEUR,

J'ai l'honneur de m'adresser à Vous pour Vous prier de Vouloir bien me donner quelques renseignemens concernant une Nommée Sophie de Bréard, Née française et établie chez les Bostoniens déjà depuis bien des années. Elle doit résider à Philadelphie ou aux environs. Ne connaissant personne dans ce pays, Je prends la liberté de m'adresser à Vous pour savoir par Votre moyen si cette demoiselle De Breard Vit encore et quel est le lieu de sa résidance. Ayant l'avantage d'être son neveu par mon mariage avec Melle de Bréard-d'Attignéville Sa niéce, Je serais fort aise de Pouvoir connaître la seule Tante qui reste à ma femme du côté de son père.

J'ai d'ailleurs des nouvelles importantes à lui communiquer concernant toute Sa famille dont elle Sera Sans doute bien aise d'être instruite. J'attends Votre réponse, Monsieur, pour terminer des affaires de famille, Je Vous aurai mille obligations de ne la differer que le moins possible.

J'ai l'honneur d'être avec la plus parfaite considération, Monsieur, Votre très-humble et très obeissant Serviteur

DE WIDRANGES-BRÉARD

EDITORS' TRANSLATION

Sir,

Ligny near Bar-sur-Oznain, Department of Meuse, 29 Nov. 1802

I have the honor of writing to request information concerning a certain Sophie de Bréard who was born French and settled many years ago among the Bostonians. She is probably living in or near Philadelphia. Not knowing anyone in this country, I take the liberty of approaching you to find out if Mademoiselle de Bréard is still alive and where she lives. I have the good fortune to be her nephew through marriage to her niece, Mademoiselle de Bréard-d'Attigneville, and I would be grateful to know my wife's only remaining aunt on her father's side.

In addition, I have important news to communicate to her about her entire family, which she will undoubtedly be happy to learn. I await your reply, Sir, to conclude family business and would be a thousand times indebted if you could defer as little as possible.

I have the honor of being, with the sincerest regards, Sir, your very humble and very obedient servant.

De Widranges-Bréard

RC (DLC); addressed: "A Monsieur" and "Monsieur Le Président des états-unis d'Amérique"; postmarked Ligny, France; postmarked New York, 30 Aug. [1803]; franked; endorsed by TJ as received 5 Sep. 1803 and so recorded in SJL.

Hippolyte Ferdinand de Widranges (1773-1826), member of an old family of chevaliers of Lorraine, joined the army of royalist exiles in 1791 but returned to France and avoided condemnation as an émigré. In 1798, he married Nicole Marie Joséphine de Bréard. By collateral descent through an uncle, she inherited the titles of comtesse of Cousances and baroness at large of the Holy Roman Empire, and through his marriage to her, Widranges assumed comparable titles. In 1821, Louis XVIII made Widranges a chevalier of the Legion of Honor. Beginning in 1814, Widranges was mayor of Ligny (*Annuaire de la noblesse de France et des maisons souveraines de l'Europe* [Paris, 1859], 212, 216).

From Timothy Bloodworth

Sir

Wilmington N.C. Novr. 30th 1802.

Permit me to express the gratefull sence of my obligation for the favor you have bestow'd, in the appointment of Collector for the Port of Wilmington. Please to accept my sincere acknowledgment, for this evidence of your indulgence. and rest assured, that I shall endeavor by my conduct, to merit your confidence.

When I came into Office, I found it in a deranged Situation, the Deputy Collector, and Naval Officer, holding their Offices in their own Chambers, a considerable distance a part. time, and expence, became necessary to reduce the Office to proper order. Some time elapsed, before I received the Books, and papers, of my predecessor. and at present Some of them Still remain in the hands of their Agent, who has not fully compleated the returns for the last year, and one quarter of the present.

At the request of Mr. Macon, I am enduced to mention to the President, four Gentlemen of reputable characters, to fill the station of commissioners of Bankrupcy. Viz: Joshua Potts, Christopher Dudley, and Caleb D. Howard, Merchants in this Town, and Mr. James Walker, Attorney at Law. Should they meet the approbation of the President, I presume they would perform the duties of the station with fidellity. I beg leave to mention the death of Doctor Peters, surgeons Mate at Fort Johnston, which makes a Vacancy in that office. to Supply that deficiency, I am requested to mention to the President, A Mr. John Griffin, who has heretofore fill'd that office, this Gentleman is a native of Virginia, and nephew to Judge Griffin of Virginia, and also Sam Griffin former Member congress. my short acquaintance with him, prevents me from mentioning his professional abilities, but I am inform'd, he has practised with Success for eighteen months past, and has acquired a knowledge of the disorders incident to the climate.

With every expression of Esteem, and respect, I have the honor to be, Sir. Your Most Obedient, Most Obliged, and very humble Servant.

TIMOTHY BLOODWORTH

RC (DNA: RG 59, LAR); endorsed by TJ as received 19 Dec. and so recorded in SJL with notation "Commrs. bkrptcy."

TJ had appointed Timothy Bloodworth COLLECTOR FOR THE PORT OF WILMINGTON, North Carolina, in February. Thomas Robeson, DEPUTY COLLECTOR, served under the two previous collectors. Carleton Walker assumed the position of NAVAL OFFICER in December 1800 (Vol. 34:484n; Vol. 35:467-9).

REQUEST OF MR. MACON: see TJ to Nathaniel Macon, 18 Oct. 1802. All four of Bloodworth's nominees for commissioners of bankruptcy received appointments with commissions dated 20 Dec. (list of commissions in Lb in DNA: RG 59, MPTPC; Vol. 37:702, 710).

Both Alexander A. PETERS and John GRIFFIN were listed as "Additional" surgeon's mates with the Fourth Regiment of Infantry in the roll of officers published in 1802. On 31 Mch. 1802, Peters was nominated as surgeon's mate at Fort Johnston. Griffin received a commission as a surgeon's mate in the army in 1803. He was identified as a North Carolinian (ASP, *Miscellaneous*, 1:312; JEP, 1:458-9; Vol. 37:144, 155-6).

From James Garrard

SIR, State of Kentucky, Frankfort Novr. 30 1802

Two days ago I received the inclosed letters from Doctr James Speed, and Meeker & Co. from New Orleans; together with a copy of a proclamation issued by Juan Ventura Morales Intendant of the

Spanish Government of Louisiana; and which I do myself the honor to inclose, for your information. The Citizens of this State are very much alarmed and agitated; as this measure of the Spanish government will (if not altered) at one blow cut up the present and future prospects of their best interests by the roots. To you Sir, they naturally turn their eyes, and on your attention to this important subject, their best hopes are fixed. Permit me to request, you will give me information on this business, as soon as you can say with certainty what we may rely on, and let my solicitude on this occasion, be my apoligy for this request.

With sentiments of respect &c signed JAMES GARRARD

Tr (DNA: RG 233, PM, 7th Cong., 2d sess.); in a clerk's hand; at head of text: "The Governor of Kentucky to the President of the U States (Copy)." Enclosures: (1) James Speed to Garrard, 18 Oct., New Orleans, sending a copy of Juan Ventura Morales's proclamation, "which did not issue till this evening"; asserting that if the decree "does not amount to a declaration of war, with the worst consequences to individuals, none of us here understand it. The people of the Mississippi territory will immediately feel its effects, and when to their indignation is joined that of our countrymen in the spring, God knows how it may be possible to prevent hostilities"; with a postscript of 19 Oct. stating that an application to land American property has been denied, and that according to rumor, a second decree will be issued to prohibit U.S. citizens from residing at New Orleans longer than 40 days and to bar American vessels (printed in New York *American Citizen*, 22 Dec., with incorrect date of 13 Oct.). (2) Meeker, Williamson & Patton to Garrard, 18 Oct., New Orleans, informing him of the intendant's decree (printed in same). (3) Proclamation by Morales, 16 Oct. (see John Brown to TJ, 26 Nov.). Enclosed in TJ to the House of Representatives, 22 Dec.

James Garrard (1749-1822), a native of Stafford County, Virginia, was a militia officer, landowner, distiller, salt manufacturer, and Baptist minister before becoming governor of Kentucky in a controversial election in 1796. He won a second term in 1800. As a member of the Virginia House of Delegates in 1786, he supported TJ's bill for religious freedom. Garrard was also an advocate of gradual abolition (ANB).

From Ephraim Kirby

SIR, Litchfield Novemr 30th. 1802

Several of my respectable fellow citizens, understanding there is still a vacancy in the Commission of Bankruptcy in this State, have solicited me to address you on this subject, and to name Majr. William Judd, as a candidate for the appointment.

Majr. Judd's location is convenient and accomodating to the public service. He resides in Farmington, which is much the largest commercial town, (not on navigable waters) in Connecticut. It is situated partly between Hartford and New Haven, about ten miles from the first, and about thirty from the last mentioned place. The intercourse of business between Farmington and Hartford is such, that communications may be made from one to the other almost every hour in the day through out the year. In addition to the conveyance by mail, the communication with New Haven is also easy and frequent.

Major Judd was liberally educated at Yale College, and has since made the law his professional business. He was an active and respectable military officer during the revolutionary war with Great Britain, and has never abandoned the principles for which he then contended. During a long period of federal persecution & oppression in this State, he continued a firm defender of the constitutional principles of our general government. The people of Farmington have often elected him their representative in the Legislature, and he is now a magistrate in the county of Hartford.

Believeing the duty of designating the various official appointments throughout a government as extensive as the United States, where, from remoteness of situation, information respecting candidates, must often be derived from others, to be attended with many difficulties and embarrassments, I have troubled you with a minute detail of circumstances.—There is nothing material within my knowledge, which I have not mentioned.

From a long acquaintance with Major Judd, I believe his talents well adapted to the office of Commissioner of Bankruptcy, and that he will discharge the duties with a fidelity and ability, honorable to himself and satisfactory to the public.

I am Sir most respectfully Your Obedt. Servt EPHM KIRBY

RC (DLC); at foot of text: "The President of the United States"; endorsed by TJ as received 6 Dec. and "Wm. Judd to be Comr. bkrptcy" and so recorded in SJL.

TJ immediately appointed WILLIAM JUDD commissioner of bankruptcy in the place of Jonathan Bull, who had declined the appointment. The State Department issued Judd's commission on 7 Dec. (list of commissions in Lb in DNA: RG 59, MPTPC; Vol. 36:108-9; Vol. 37:708; Gideon Granger to TJ, 8 Aug.).

From Philippe Reibelt

MONSIEUR LE PRÉSIDENT! Norfolk ce 30 Novembre 1802.

Je suis chargé de la part de Madame Felix et de Mr. le Général Kosciusko de remettre à Votre Excellence le Douple de l'acte de Cession faite a cette dame par le Général de sa Terre sur le Scioto, et de recevoir de vos mains non seulement les Titres originaires du

Général et autres Papiers y relatifs en Original, mais aussi les Ordres, et Instructions pour la prise de Possession au Nom de cette dame.

C'est en Consequence de ces Commissions amicales, et dans la Probabilité que Vous n'ayez point avec Vous les dits Titres qui d'ailleurs me peuvent être adressés dans la suite, je dois prier Votre Excellence d'ordonner en attendant l'Expedition des Pieces necessaires à la Prise de Possession.

J'ose joindre la Lettre par laquelle Mr. le Général à bien voulú solliciter pour moi, et mes Compagnons de Voyage votre Protection particuliere, et Vous prie de vouloir bien faire expedier en même Tems une Recommendation pour Mde. Felix, pour moi, et les Autres à Mr. le Gouverneur du Territoire de l'Ouest.

Je parts d'ici Lundi prochain pour Alexandrie. Je serai Probablement dans sept à huit jours à Federal City, Aussitot que j'y serai arrivé, je demanderai de Votre Excellence la Permission de Vous presenter mes Respects personels. Ce n'est que ce devoir qui m'engage à préférer cette Route à celle plus direct pour l'Ohio ou mes Affaires m'appellent incessament.

En attendant je prie Votre Excellence de vouloir bien Agreer les Assurances par Ecrit du Respect le plus Sincere et profond dont un Homme puisse être penetré pour votre Caractére privé, et public, et dont je le suis Constamment depuis que l'on connoit votre Nom en Europe. J'ai l'honneur d'etre Votre Excellence Très obeïssant Serviteur

Philippe Reibelt
Natif Allemand du Palatinat
sur la rive gauche du Rhin
nouveau francais par la
reunion de ce paÿs a la France

EDITORS' TRANSLATION

Mister President! Norfolk, 30 Nov. 1802

Madame Felix and General Kosciuszko have asked me to give Your Excellency the duplicate of the transfer deed from the general for his land on the Scioto River, and to receive from you the general's original titles and related documents, as well as orders and instructions so Madame Felix can take possession of the land.

Fulfilling this friendly mission, and assuming that you do not have the land titles with you (they can be sent at a later time), I beg Your Excellency to provide in the meantime the other documents necessary for Madame Felix to take possession.

I take the liberty of enclosing a letter from the general requesting your special protection for my travel companions and myself. When you send the other documents, could you please include a recommendation to the governor of the Western Territory for Madame Felix, the others, and myself?

I shall leave here next Monday for Alexandria and shall probably be in the Federal City in seven or eight days. As soon as I arrive, I shall request permission from Your Excellency to present my regards in person. This is the sole commitment that prompts me to travel by this route rather than the more direct one to Ohio, where urgent business calls me.

Until then, I beg Your Excellency to accept in writing this assurance of the deepest, most sincere respect a man can feel for your public and personal character, which I have felt since your name has become known in Europe. I have the honor of being your very obedient servant.

PHILIPPE REIBELT
German native of the Palatine lands
on the left bank of the Rhine,
now French because of
the reunion of this region with France

RC (MHi); endorsed by TJ as received 14 Dec. and so recorded in SJL. Enclosures not found.

Philippe Reibelt (d. 1809), educated in German universities, spoke German and French and also knew Latin and Greek. He had served under various European governments, holding such positions as director of archives of the Helvetic Republic, political officer attached to a French army, and the Directory's agent overseeing a Rhineland principality. He was acquainted with Frédéric César de La Harpe, who like Reibelt had ties to revolutionary Switzerland (see Thomas Cooper to TJ, 25 Oct. 1802). TJ described Reibelt as "a strong republican in principle" and "a man of excellent understanding and extensive science" (to W. C. C. Claiborne, 27 Apr. 1806, 3 Feb. 1807). In Baltimore from 1803 to 1806, Reibelt marketed books as the agent of a Parisian firm. He sold volumes to TJ and to the State Department. He also sought to obtain seeds of hard-to-find grain crops and garden plants for TJ. As early as the autumn of 1803, Reibelt hoped to obtain some public office or private position that would allow him to relocate to New Orleans. After a visit to Monticello in September 1805, he expected to buy a farm in Albemarle or Augusta County, but before he could carry out that plan he asked for an appointment as an Indian agent. TJ and Henry Dearborn made him the factor of the government trading house at Natchitoches, but Reibelt put off going there and asked TJ for some other appointment in the western territories. Early in 1807, Dearborn and TJ retracted the appointment. W. C. C. Claiborne, then the governor of Orleans Territory, appointed Reibelt judge of Avoyelles Parish, where he had bought a farm. Reibelt, however, had assisted James Wilkinson in collecting intelligence about Aaron Burr's associates and activities. When, in 1808, a resolution of the territorial legislature forced Claiborne to remove Reibelt from the judgeship for misuse of authority, Reibelt saw the legislature's action as retribution against him by cronies of Wilkinson's political enemy, Daniel Clark. Nevertheless, TJ refused to consider Reibelt for another appointment. He took his family to Havana, where he died a few months after their arrival in 1809 (Reibelt to TJ, 18 Dec. 1802, 30 Sep., 31 Oct. 1803, 12, 18, 31 May, 1 Oct., 16, 19 Dec. 1805, 2, 13 Jan., 3 Feb., 8, 15, 29 May, 5, 26 June, 24 Aug. 1806, 16 Jan., 28 Mch. 1807, 25 Feb., 10 May, 12 Dec. 1808, 15 Feb. 1809; TJ to Reibelt, 7 Mch., 21 June 1805, 10 Jan. 1806, 3 Feb. 1807, 25 Feb., 28 Oct. 1808; TJ to John Barnes, 19 Sep. 1805; Claiborne to TJ, 4 June, 12 Nov. 1806, 3 May 1807, 5 Mch., 16 Apr. 1808; TJ to Claiborne, 3 May 1807; Wilkinson to TJ, 16 July 1808; Madison, *Papers*, *Sec. of State Ser.*, 8:421n; *Terr. Papers*, 9:749;

Betts, *Garden Book*, 305, 356, 367; MB, 2:1138, 1143, 1147, 1171; RS, 1:504-5; 2:394).

SUR LE SCIOTO: in 1800, TJ arranged for the surveying and patenting of 500 acres of military bounty land for Tadeusz Kosciuszko. At that time, Kosciuszko expected to rent out the property, but in July 1802, he sold it in Paris to Louise Françoise Felix, with Robert R. Livingston witnessing the transaction (Miecislaus Haiman, *Kosciuszko: Leader and Exile* [New York, 1977], 129-30; Vol. 31:560, 561n; Vol. 32:101).

RECOMMENDATION POUR MDE. FELIX: when TJ received a letter from Reibelt's wife in 1805, he recorded her name as L. F. F. Reibelt, which suggests that Reibelt married Louise Françoise Felix. The letter, recorded in SJL as written on 2 Oct. 1805 and received the next day, has not been found. Little is known about Reibelt's wife; when she wrote to TJ following her husband's death, she used only her last name (RS, 2:394-5).

From Samuel Elliot

New salem, (County of Hampshire)
RESPECTED SIR. Novr. 1802.

When I address you as the *President* of a great and independent Republic, I am impressed with diffidence & awe; but when I recognize you, as the mild and philanthropic *Jefferson*—when I behold you as the author of several valuable literary productions, and the uniform admirer and friend of Science, and all useful & entertaining lucubrations, my Diffidence, in some measure vanishes, and, clothed with manly confidence, I address you, with the freedom and familiarity of a *fellow citizen* & *friend*.

While surly base, unprincipled wretches as Callender and other impudent declaimers and writers, are poisoning the public Sentiment, and liberally sowing the seeds of dissatisfaction, it may be matter of Joy with you, to find others, who are grateful enough to acknowledge your services & worth, and just enough to render that respect & obedience to you & your administration, which they so justly merit.

Permit me, Sir, to rank among the undeviating supporters of the republican Cause, my respected brother, James Elliot of Brattleboro', Vermont; present Post-Master, and Clerk of the Genl. Assembly of that State. He, with several other genuine disciples of rational Liberty, have boldly & invariably stood forth, the avowed advocates of the (lately proscribed) republican Cause.

During his attendance on the last and very recent Session of the Legislature of that State, he received a Commission from the President, appointing him *Commissioner of Bancruptcy for the District of*

Vermont.—I rejoiced, and my brother felt grateful for this public and presidential notice. The office, in Vermont, cannot be very lucrative, but may be agreable and attended with very little expence. In that State, Republicanism has, decidedly the ascendency, but not in Massachusetts.—The friends to order, headed by such great & virtuous Characters as Gerry, Lincoln, Dearborn, Eustis, Varnum, Geo. Blake, Bacon, Crowningshield, Skinner, with others too numerous to mention, will soon effect a Change, already begun, auspicious to Republicanism

In this part of the State, the federalists must awhile prevail—We are very deficient in republican Characters of any celebrity—The offices have been hitherto engrossed by the river demagogues, generally revolutionary adherents to our enemies, or violent, overbearing federalists.

I have just published a little work which accompanies this Letter; and wishing to present you with one of the pamphlets, have been induced to forward both the letter & the Book.—

Respect for the unfortunate Fayette, and Gratitude for his services, during our struggle for Liberty, when you, with other American worthies, were no less active & useful in the Councils of our Country, induced me to the prosecution of the work.—Altho' it is trifling, being nothing more than an incorrect & incomplete *Tragedy*, yet I hope it may be entertaining to *some*, & disagreable to *none*.

With high respect I am yours Obediently &c. SAML. ELLIOT

P.S. I have procured 600 subscribers for the Work, & shall probably be able to purchase me a little law Library from the profits, against my admission to the bar, next May.

RC (DLC); partially dated; addressed: "Thomas Jefferson Esq. *President of the United States* Washington"; endorsed by TJ as received 19 Dec. and so recorded in SJL. Enclosure: *Fayette in Prison: or Misfortunes of the Great. A Modern Tragedy. By a Gentleman of Massachusetts*, a play, in five acts, on Lafayette's confinement by the Austrians at Olmütz (Worcester, Mass., 1802; Shaw-Shoemaker, No. 2215).

Samuel Elliot (1777-1845) was two years younger than his brother James Elliot, who served as a Republican congressman from Vermont from 1803 to 1809. The family moved from Gloucester to New Salem, Massachusetts, in 1780, after the death of their father, to be raised by their mother Martha Day Elliot, a seamstress. Samuel followed his brother to Guilford, near Brattleboro, in southern Vermont, where they established a law practice in 1803. Samuel served as postmaster at Brattleboro from 1803, when he succeeded his brother, until 1811, when he was replaced. He served several terms as the representative from Brattleboro in the Vermont House and held other local offices, including justice of the peace, register of probate, and Windham County state's attorney. In the 1790s, the Elliot brothers and John H. Palmer wrote newspaper essays, entitled "The Rural

Moralist." In 1803 and 1804, Samuel Elliot delivered the Fourth of July orations at West Springfield, Massachusetts, in praise of the new Republican administration. By 1812, however, in an address before the local Washington Benevolent Society, he denounced the abuses of both parties and wished to harmonize the factions around the "first good old" policies of the Washington administration. In 1844, as a member of the Brattleboro Clay Club, he was elected a delegate to the Whig state convention. Working with representatives from Massachusetts and New Hampshire, he advocated measures for the improvement of navigation on the Connecticut River (ANB, s.v. "Elliot, James"; Stets, *Postmasters*, 243; Samuel Elliot, *Oration Pronounced at West-Springfield, (Mass.) July Fourth, Eighteen Hundred and Three* [Bennington, 1803]; Elliot, *An Address. To the Members of the Washington Benevolent Society, and the Public* [Brattleboro, 1812], 8-15; Brattleboro *Reporter*, 2 May 1803; 6 Feb., 23 Sep. 1809; 11, 18 Mch. 1811; 13 June 1812; 20 Nov. 1813; 4 Nov. 1814; 11 Jan. 1815; 28 Oct. 1817; 1 Sep. 1819; 11 Nov. 1822; Northampton, Mass., *Republican Spy*, 3 July 1804; Worcester *National Aegis*, 10 May 1826; Brattleboro *Vermont Phoenix*, 28 June 1844).

COMMISSION FROM THE PRESIDENT: see Memorandum to James Madison, printed at 18 Oct. 1802.

TJ responded to Elliot on 20 Dec.: "Th: Jefferson presents his compliments to mr Elliot, and his thanks for the poetical production inclosed to him and recieved the last night. he is sensible also to the sentiments of respect and confidence expressed in mr Elliot's letter, and having in view no earthly object but the good of his fellow citizens, he deems their approbation the highest reward they can bestow on him" (RC in Raab Collection, Ardmore, Pennsylvania, 2007; PrC in DLC, at foot of text: "Mr. Samuel Elliot," endorsed by TJ in ink on verso).

To James Dinsmore

DEAR SIR Washington Dec. 1. 1802.

Your's of Nov. 25 is recieved and I have ordered the patera wanting for the tea-room. with respect to the joists for the N. West wing of offices, I leave it to yourself to decide; only let there be no danger of failure for want of due strength. I am quite at a loss about the nail-boys remaining with mr Stewart. they have long been a dead expense instead of a profit to me. in truth they require a rigour of discipline to make them do reasonable work, to which he cannot bring himself. on the whole I think it will be best for them also to be removed to mr Lilly's. in that case it will be necessary for mr Lilly to have a stock of brads of every size for the buildings always in readiness and before hand, as at that distance it will not do to furnish them from hand to mouth. I will write to him on this subject that he may prepare for recieving them. it will be at any rate a nuisance removed from the house. when will you be ready for the Corinthian modillions and eggs & anchors? you must leave the moulding square which is to recieve the latter, because they will be made to fill up the quarter circle thus I am very much disposed to cover the terras at once with tin. I find that it may be done of the thickest tin for 18. Dollars a square; and it will be proof against fire. I presume mr Oldham has hardly made any progress in preparing to plank it, for want of plank. it may therefore lie for consideration. how does mr Fitch get on with the ballusters? does mr Perry keep him supplied with locust stocks for them?—if by the removal of the nailboys to mr Lilly's you should cease to recieve money enough for your current purposes, let me know and I will give you a standing order on mr Higginbotham for supplies of cash as you may want them. Accept my best wishes. TH: JEFFERSON

RC (ViU); at foot of text: "Mr: Dinsmore."

YOURS OF NOV. 25: recorded in SJL as received 30 Nov., but not found. The PATERA was likely one of the circular rosettes applied to the areas between the triglyphs of the frieze in Monticello's tea room. Pateras of the same design but of smaller size also were featured in the tea room's cornice. TJ modeled the design after an illustration of the doric order found in the 1766 edition of *Parallèle de l'architecture antique avec la moderne*, by Roland Fréart de Chambray and Charles Errard (Sowerby, No. 4216; Vol. 37:114-15n). The image was from a building in Albano Laziale, near Rome, probably the church of Santa Maria della Stella, and TJ referred to the example several times in his notes and sketches on the north bow, his architectural term for the tea room ("Monticello: Notebook for Remodelling, [1794-1797]," "Monticello: Remodelling Notes, [begun 1796]," and "Monticello: Architectural Detail (North Bow), ca. 1805," all in MHi; Nichols, *Architectural Drawings*, Nos. 143, 147b, and 176; Roland Fréart de Chambray, *Parallèle de l'architecture antique avec la moderne suivi de Idée de la perfection de la peinture*, eds., Frédérique Lemerle-Pauwels and Milovan Stanic [Paris, 2005], 72-3).

A letter of 1 Dec. from TJ to Gabriel LILLY, recorded in SJL, has not been found.

For the entablature of Monticello's parlor, TJ commissioned Washington artisan George Andrews to make composition ornaments, including MODILLIONS for the cornice, and egg and anchor ovolos. In his financial memoranda the president recorded payments to Andrews on 13 July 1802 and 21 Feb. 1803 (McLaughlin, *Jefferson and Monticello*, 290; MB, 2:1077, 1092).

BALLUSTERS: the balusters may have been intended for any of a few different projects, the balustrade for the hall gallery, banisters for the staircases, or the balustrade for the roof (McLaughlin, *Jefferson and Monticello*, 265-6; Notes on Work to be Done by James Dinsmore, 24 Sep. 1804).

From Alexander Fowler

Fowlers Glenn, near Pittsburgh,
1st, December 1802.

SIR,

I am sorry that Electioneering tactics should have been the means of bringing my name and Character before your Excellency in so deformed a point of veiw; for I find I have not only been represented to the President of the United States, as having relinquished my political principles, but of having become a debaucher and *a sot.*—I feel for the wretched depravity of such men, and lament the dangerous consequences of such wicked traffick. But I can turn the slander, and were I as Independent as I have been, I should have let the slander pass, and not have troubled your Excellency with a single syllable on the subject.—However, as the object of the calumny, was to injure me in the opinion of your Excellency, and administration, it becomes my duty to endeavour to remove the opprobrium.

On the eve of the Election, in October 1801, when a number of the Citizens, unsollicited by me, thought proper to introduce my name to the people of this district, for Congress, the Editor of the *Tree*, a paper established by the Republicans, in which we all bore a share in proportion to our abilities, contrived to open the sluices of destruction against me in various directions, and I was in a twinkling to become as *black* as I had been *fair*. The most unfounded slander is wickedly and artfully propagated against me; and to crown the shamefull business, this Republican press—Shame on such Republicanism!—was shut against me, so that the slander might not only have time to take root, but blossom, and shed its banefull influence; and I was cruelly compelled to fly to the Pittsburgh Gazette a fedral Press, to endeavour to do myself justice; which not passing through the same Channell, my weak attempt proved fruitless and abortive. How disgusting and disgracefull! The palladium of our Liberties; the freedom of the press; the pride of Republicans; and the main-stay, or sheet amber of all that is precious and dear to *Freemen*, is wrested from us by designing ambitious men to suit Electioneering purposes; and I am Sir, as an *old Whig*, (whose sufferings have been manifold and whose reputation for firmness and integrity, I had long vainly conceived was placed above the reach of Slander) by the *hocus pocus* tricks of political Juglers, to be treacherously denounced to your Excellency, and administration, as *a Turn-coat, and a Tory*, Shame, shame, where is thy blush? Conscience where is thy sting?— Alass! Alass! I cannot help feeling on such occassions with heart-felt indignation, and I cannot collect patience to detail such shamefull and nefarious transactions.—I am branded by a Tory paper in philadelphia, *The Gazette of the United States* as "*a renegade English Jacobin*," and by the Editor of the Tree, a Republican paper, "as *a Tory and a turn-coat*," as both appellations springs from the same polluted source, I deem them equally horrible; for it is but too evident, that America, at this moment, is convulsed with *party rage*, and that the vain, and the venal, are struggling in various shapes, and by various means, to bestride our common Country.

With respect to my living Sir, I have ever been accustomed to live sociably with my friends and neighbours, unfortunate as I have been, and humble as I now live, hospitallity still finds a temperary residence under the roof of my humble Cottage; but no Man on earth more abhors the character of *a Sot*, or is less entitled to the detested appellation. With a circumscribed fortune Sir, it required the united efforts of prudence and oeconomey to live *Eighteen years* in the British Kings Service, in the character that I did; and since I became an American Citizen, from a variety of strokes of adverse fortune, I have been compelled to adopt a kind of frugallity, almost bordering on parsimony. I live, may it please your Excellency, on a small Farm, which I cultivate by persevering industry, by which means I have, thank God, learned *to live on little*; and I endeavour, by all the honest means in my power, *to make that little suffice.*

My amiable friend Mrs. E: Trist, knows well, not only my mode of living, but my principles and disposition. I live in 1782, as I did in 1774, and 1775, when that Lady first knew me.—My intimacy with Mr. Trist, her ill treated husband, whose principles were congenial with my own, gave Mrs. Trist an opportunity of knowing my character more particularly than any other person whatever. It was a period that put Men to tryal and *sifted* the Grain from the chaff. I live may it please your Excellency, *now*, as I did *then.* I hold the same principles *now*, that I *then* did; and to keep possession of those principles, and the small share of virtue by which they were acquired, I must continue to pursue my *old tract*, by persevering steadily in every thing I know to be right, with a total disregard of all that can insue from it. By this line of conduct Sir, I have ever been governed, and from it I shall never depart.

But Sir, it is surely the heaviest of all human burthens, for an honest man, who has steered the course that I have done, through a long life, marked with a variety of vicissitudes and misfortunes, to be loaded now in the evening of his life with such unprovoked and unmerited reproach. Newspaper slander may be repelled; but concealed calumny—the secret stab of a lurking assassin, cannot. The slanderer lies secure, for the slander is placed, not only out of the reach of resentment, but of Justice. I am knocked down Sir, and trampled upon by a Ruffian in the dark; and what shall restrain the assassins stab, the brutal intemperance of factious demagogues, or the malignant artifice of slanderers? In my youth I should have answered, *a Bastinade*; but now age and experience tells me, *Government.* I am therefore compelled Sir, by the loud calls of honour, and injustice to a reputation hitherto unsullied, to apply on this occassion to the President of the United States, to whom the slander was communicated, for this Brilliant Epistle, or a Copy thereof; an Epistle "*replete with slander and scurrillity*," and which delineates my character in such false, horrid, and injurious Colours.—Long retired as I have been, from the ways of intriguing, ambitious men, I have still Sir, in my retirement, a longing after *a good name*;—nay, it is the "*immediate jewel of my soul*," and as an injured man, a traduced Whig, and a Gentleman, I hope your Excellency will deliver up to Justice, and to shame, the *branders* of my reputation, the *filchers* of my good name, so that I may strike at the root of the slander, and thereby be enabled to do myself Justice, by removing the opprobrium, and convincing your Excellency and the world, of my innocense, and the purity of my principles, and the baseness and depravity of those of my enemies. The views of such men will then be unfolded, and characters will be seen in their native colours; when, notwithstanding all the transcendent cunning, and low treachery of those *Reputation Butchers*, mouthed, as well as your Excellency, must be convinced, that there is not only, "*something rotten in Denmark*," but that there are more *Callenders* in Denmark than *one*, and more *Vice Presidents*, than *Aaron Burr*. I have the honor to be, with due consideration, and perfect respect,

Sir, Your most obedient humble Servant A: Fowler

RC (DLC); at foot of text: "His Excellency Thomas Jefferson Esquire, President of the United States, &c. &c. &c. Washington City"; endorsed by TJ as received 5 Jan. 1803 and so recorded in SJL.

Alexander Fowler was a lieutenant in the British army in the Eighteenth Royal Irish Regiment of Foot. He served in the Seven Years' War and resigned his commission before acquiring a small farm in western Pennsylvania. A brigadier general in the Allegheny County militia, he became deputy quartermaster at Fort Pitt and, in 1779, auditor of accounts for the Western Department. In the 1790s, Fowler and his son-in-law Andrew Richardson became affiliated with the Republican faction in Pittsburgh known as the Clapboard Junto. At the beginning of TJ's presidency, Fowler expressed his desire for appointment to the local quartermaster or supervisor positions (Leland D. Baldwin, *Pittsburgh: The Story of a City* [Pittsburgh, 1937], 175; Madison, *Papers*, 16:426-8, 17:469-71; Vol. 34:490n).

MY NAME AND CHARACTER: Meriwether Lewis communicated to TJ a report from Pittsburgh that Fowler had Federalist support and was intemperate, insolvent, and politically divisive (Vol. 35:183-4).

A bitter schism within the ranks of the Republican party occurred in Pittsburgh during the ELECTION of 1801. The Clapboard Junto, introducing a district delegate process, nominated William Hoge as Gallatin's replacement in Congress and Thomas Morton to the state senate. At a caucus meeting on 19 Aug. 1801, a faction of other Republicans countered with a ticket that included Fowler for Congress and Richardson for state senator. John Israel, EDITOR of the *Tree of Liberty*, suggested that the Federalists, who did not offer their own candidates in the election, had instigated the Republican schism with the hope of benefiting in the next gubernatorial election (Higginbotham, *Pennsylvania Politics*, 37-8; Russell J. Ferguson, *Early Western Pennsylvania Politics* [Pittsburgh, 1938], 164-5, 173-4; Alston G. Field, "The Press in Western Pennsylvania to 1812," *Western Pennsyl-*

vania Historical Magazine, 20 [1937], 232-4; Gallatin, *Papers*, 5:795-6; Madison, *Papers, Sec. of State Ser.*, 2:133-6; Pittsburgh *Tree of Liberty*, 12 Sep. 1801; Vol. 32:486).

AS BLACK AS I HAD BEEN FAIR: possibly an allusion to Othello, who was "far more fair than black" (Shakespeare, *Othello*, 1.3).

A TURN-COAT, AND A TORY: a member of the Federal Republican committee suggested to John Scull, the editor of the *Pittsburgh Gazette*, that the Clapboard Junto had defamed members of the committee in the *Tree of Liberty* by stigmatizing them as Tories and "*turn coats of faction*" (Brigham, *American Newspapers*, 2:965; *Pittsburgh Gazette*, 24 Sep. 1802).

SHAME, WHERE IS THY BLUSH: Shakespeare, *Hamlet*, 3.4.

MY AMIABLE FRIEND: Elizabeth Trist, who had previously defended Fowler to TJ (Vol. 35:499-500).

SIFTED THE GRAIN FROM THE CHAFF: an allusion to Matthew 3:12.

IMMEDIATE JEWEL OF MY SOUL: a good name in a man and a woman "is the immediate jewel of their souls" (Shakespeare, *Othello*, 3.3).

SOMETHING ROTTEN IN DENMARK: "something is rotten in the state of Denmark" (Shakespeare, *Hamlet*, 1.4).

To George Jefferson

DEAR SIR — Washington Dec. 1. 1802

Mr. Derieux has for years past urged such perpetual demands on me for charity, that I have long since gone beyond the proportion[1] which he had a right to expect of what I can give in charity, and consequently has been[2] infringing on what other objects had a better right to. I have therefore for some time rejected his applications. he makes one now however under circumstances to which I cannot be entirely deaf. I will therefore ask the favor of you to send to him in Petersburg to the care of mr Richard Rambaut mercht of that place twenty five dollars, barely mentioning it to be at my desire, for I cannot write to him myself.

I presume mr Brown did not call for the 285.83 D placed with you for him; because after I sent him the order on you he wrote me to desire I would send the money to Albemarle which I immediately did. Accept assurances of my affectionate attachment

TH: JEFFERSON

PrC (MHi); at foot of text: "Mr. George Jefferson"; endorsed by TJ in ink on verso.

For previous communications related to TJ's purchase of land from Benjamin BROWN, see Promissory Note to Thomas Wells, Jr., 6 Sep.; TJ to George Jefferson, 1 Nov.

[1] Preceding two words interlined.

[2] Preceding two words interlined.

From George Jefferson

DEAR SIR Richmond 1st. Decr. 1802

Your favor of the 22d. ultimo inclosing a letter for Doctor Bache was received here the 25th., but it so happened that it was filed away without my seeing it, and it was not until this morning a few moments before the closing of the Charlottesville mail, that I observed it. Having the day before yesterday received a letter from Dr. B. in which he informed me he had declined going by Norfolk as he intended, and had concluded to go by Philada., I put your letter to him into the post office, and requested that the post master at Charlottesville would forward it, should he have set off before its arrival. I suppose however that it will arrive in time, and conclude likewise it will not be material if it does not; as you will of course see him on his way through Washington.

I am Dear Sir Yr. Very humble servt. GEO. JEFFERSON

RC (MHi); at foot of text: "Thomas Jefferson esqr."; endorsed by TJ as received 5 Dec. and so recorded in SJL.

TJ did not record sending a FAVOR of 22 Nov. to George Jefferson, and none has been found, but see his letter of that day to William BACHE.

Memorial of the Kentucky Legislature

[1 Dec. 1802]

The Memorial

Of the Senate and House of Representatives of the Commonwealth of Kentucky.

Having on a former occasion, when we represented the obstructions to the Navigation of the river Mississippi, experienced the attention and justice of the General Government, in providing by a treaty with the court of Spain, not only for the free navigation of that river, but for what, in our remote situation from the ocean was absolutely necessary to the enjoyment of it, a place of deposit for our produce.—We deem it necessary barely to state to you, that by an infraction of that treaty, we are deprived of these advantages, in violation of the treaty between the United States and the King of Spain, concluded at San Lorenzo el Real, in October 1795. The Intendant of the Port of New-Orleans has by a proclamation of the 18th of October last, forbidden American Citizens to deposit their merchandizes and effects in the said Port, without having assigned to the United States an equivalent establishment on another part of the banks of the Mississippi.

We rely with confidence on your wisdom and justice, and pledge ourselves to support, at the expense of our lives and fortunes, such measures as the honor, and interest of the United States may require.

Printed copy (DNA: RG 46, LPPMRSL, 7th Cong., 2d sess.); date supplied (see below); at head of text: "To the President of the United States, and the Senate and House of Representatives of Congress"; endorsed by a clerk. Printed copy; by Duane and Son by order of the Senate, 28 Dec.; Shaw-Shoemaker, No. 3293.

RELY WITH CONFIDENCE: a pair of resolutions unanimously adopted by the Kentucky House of Representatives on 1 Dec. accompanied the memorial. The first resolution declared that the barring of U.S. citizens from the right of deposit at New Orleans without naming another site was "a direct infraction of the treaty of friendship limits and navigation, concluded in October 1795, between the United States and the king of Spain." The second resolve asked the governor to forward the memorial to the Kentucky senators and representatives in Congress, "to be by them presented to the President of the United States; the Senate and House of Representatives of Congress" (Tr in DNA: RG 46, LPPMRSL; printed copies in same and Shaw-Shoemaker, No. 3293). John Breckinridge presented the resolutions and memorial to the Senate on 24 Dec., and Thomas T. Davis presented the materials to the House of Representatives on 28 Jan. 1803 (JS, 3:248; JHR, 4:312). TJ probably saw the memorial by 17 Dec. On that day Samuel Harrison Smith published the resolutions and the memorial in the *National Intelligencer*, and Madison enclosed them in a letter to Robert R. Livingston. The secretary of state also mentioned the memorial in a dispatch to Rufus King on 23 Dec. John Graham of the American legation in Madrid saw the "very solemn address from the Legislature of Kentucky" in newspapers by 8 Feb. (Madison, *Papers*, *Sec. of State Ser.*, 4:198, 216, 311; TJ to James Garrard, 18 Jan.).

To John Bartram, Jr.

SIR Washington Dec. 2. 1802.

I recieved last night your favor of the 26th. Nov. informing me that the seeds and plants are made up for which I had written to you some time ago. Mr. William Short sets out from this place tomorrow for Philadelphia, and will call on you, recieve and pay you for them. to him therefore be so good as to deliver them, and to accept assurances of my esteem & best wishes. TH: JEFFERSON

PrC (DLC); at foot of text: "Mr. John Bartram"; endorsed by TJ in ink on verso.

Bartram's FAVOR of 26 Nov., received from Kingsessing, Pennsylvania, on 1 Dec., is recorded in SJL but has not been found. TJ had sent Bartram the order for SEEDS AND PLANTS in April, with the expectation that the items might be ready late in the year (Vol. 37:179, 290). See also TJ to Short, 2 Dec.

From Daniel Carroll

Thursday Decr. 2d. 1802

Mr. Danl. Carroll presents his respects to the President, he cannot have the pleasure to dine with him on sunday next, agreable to invitation

RC (MHi); addressed: "The President"; endorsed by TJ.

SUNDAY NEXT: 5 Dec.

To James Madison

TH:J. TO MR MADISON Dec. 2. 1802.

Mr. Nimmo the Commr. of bkrptcy appointed for Norfolk whose Christian name was left blank, is named 'James.'

RC (DNA: RG 59, MLR); addressed: "The Secretary of State."

According to State Department records and TJ's list of appointments, the commission for James NIMMO was dated 24 Nov. Madison sent the document to James Monroe on 29 Nov. with the request that he insert the CHRISTIAN NAME, send it to him, "and inform me of the name you shall insert" (Madison, *Papers, Sec. of State Ser.*, 4:159; list of commissions in Lb in DNA: RG 59, MPTPC; Appendix I).

To William Short

TH: JEFFERSON TO MR SHORT. Dec. 2. 1802.

I recieved last night the inclosed letter, which tho' not signed I know to be from John Bartram. you will percieve by it that he has prepared the plants seeds &c which I ordered for M. de Liancourt at your request. I write to Bartram to day to deliver them to you and that you will pay him for them. while in Philadelphia you will readily get a hack to carry you to his gardens, about a mile on this side of Gray's gardens & 4 miles from the city. they are well worth seeing, and he is the only correspondent who can compleatly answer the wishes & orders of an European botanist. while at Monticello you shewed me a list from Madame de Tessé a part of which I could execute by sending the articles in quantity, but the season was then too early. can you leave me a copy of it, and I will select such articles as I can execute. I shall be happy in every opportunity of serving Madame de Tessé which my occupations will permit. Accept assurances of my affectionate esteem & wishes for a pleasant journey.

RC (DLC: Short Papers); partially addressed "William," remainder of address not found. Enclosure: John Bartram, Jr., to TJ, 26 Nov., not found (see TJ to Bartram, 2 Dec.).

The horticultural items that TJ ordered from John BARTRAM, Jr., at Short's request were for a French agricultural society, probably the Société d'Agriculture du Departement de la Siene (Tulard, *Dictionnaire Napoléon*, 49; Vol. 36:423; Vol. 37:179, 290).

GRAY'S GARDENS: a public pleasure garden or "Vauxhall" on the English model, located on the Schuylkill River at the Lower Ferry. Visitors could stroll through landscaped grounds and enjoy refreshments. The spot was along the route of travelers arriving in Philadelphia from the south or departing in that direction. The gardens were also the site of Independence Day celebrations (Harold Donaldson Eberlein and Cortlandt Van Dyke Hubbard, "The American 'Vauxhall' of the Federal Era," PMHB, 68 [1944], 162-5; MB, 1:765; 2:826, 874).

As she mentioned in a letter to TJ in May, MADAME DE TESSÉ had asked Short to obtain some plants for her garden (Vol. 37:480-1).

From Therese Ceracchi

Rome, ce 3. Décembre 1802.

La tendre amitié que vous avez daigné témoigner à mon époux, pendant son séjour à Philadelphie me fait esperer, généreux Jefferson, que vous aurez la complaisance de lire la lettre cijointe. Elle vous fera connaitre au vrai toute l'horreur de ma situation présente et les besoins urgens de ma nombreuse famille. Les moyens que mon ami ose vous proposer sont faciles, il ne dépendra que de vous d'en voir l'exécution. Un seul mot de vous peut tout. Veuillez le prononcer et la veuve de l'infortuné Ceracchi sortira de l'abyme affreux dans lequel elle est perdue.

Comme mon ami se prépare à un voyage, je vous prierai de vouloir bien nous faire parvenir votre réponse par la voie du Consul Américain à Livourne, sous le couvert de M. Chiassi, Negociant, Place d'Espagne. Cette complaisance de votre part me sera très sensible.

J'ai l'honneur de vous assurer de mes profonds respects et de ma haute Considération. THÉRÈSE CERACCHI

EDITORS' TRANSLATION

Rome, 3 Dec. 1802

The warm friendship you kindly showed my husband during his stay in Philadelphia prompts me to hope, generous Mr. Jefferson, that you will be good enough to read the enclosed letter. It reveals all the horror of my current situation and the urgent needs of my large family. The plan my friend dares propose is simple; its execution rests entirely in your hands. One word from you can make everything happen. If you say that word, the widow of the unfortunate Ceracchi will emerge from the awful abyss in which she is lost.

Since my friend is about to depart, I ask you to respond through the American consul in Leghorn, care of Mr. Chiassi, merchant, Place d'Espagne. I would be very grateful for this kind gesture on your part.

I am honored to assure you of my deep respect and highest regards.

THÉRÈSE CERACCHI

RC (DLC); endorsed by TJ as received 20 Feb. 1803 and so recorded in SJL. Enclosure: Arsenne Thiébaut de Berneaud to TJ, 19 Nov.

Therese Schliesshan Ceracchi met Giuseppe Ceracchi in Vienna, where the artist worked during the early 1780s. They married in 1785. She remained in Europe during her husband's first trip to the United States in the early 1790s, but accompanied him, with their children, on his second trip in 1794. During that stay they lived in Philadelphia and dined on one occasion with President Washington and his family. After her husband's death in 1801, Therese succeeded in selling some of his works (*Giuseppe Ceracchi: Scultore Giacobino, 1751-1801* [Rome, 1989], 45; Ulysse Desportes, "Giuseppe Ceracchi in America and His Busts of George Washington," *Art Quarterly*, 26 [1963], 146, 152, 160, 164, 169).

CONSUL AMÉRICAIN À LIVOURNE: Thomas Appleton was the U.S. consul at Leghorn (Vol. 37:253). The business of Gaetano CHIASSI, a cloth merchant, was a meeting place for political activists during the Roman Republic formed in 1798 (Fabio Tarzia, *Libri e rivoluzioni: Figure e mentalità nella Roma di fine* ancien régime *[1770-1800]* [Milano, 2000], 229; Vol. 30:68n).

From Nicolas Gouin Dufief

MONSIEUR, 4 de decembre 1802

J'ai lu avec mon attention ordinaire votre lettre du 17 Novembre, lorsque je la reçus; ainsi je puis vous rendre compte des idées qu'elle a fait naître, et de l'origine de ma méprise.

Vous me demandiez, il est très vrai, l'ouvrage de *Dumousnier* & non pas celui de Dumourier. Cependant, ce qui m'a porté à croire que vous désiriez le livre du Général, au lieu de celui du Législateur, c'est que le nom du premier est écrit par quelques personnes Dumou*s*rier, probablement à cause de la Voyelle *u* qui est un peu longue. On pouvait aisement en faire *Dumounier* en écrivant tant soit peu vite: cela ne vous est pas arrivé, Monsieur, car vous portez la précision partout.

Je ne connaissais d'ailleurs le celèbre membre de l'assemblée Nationale, que sous le nom de Mounier; ce qui a pu encore achever de me confirmer dans ma bévüe, c'est l'idée qui me faisait regarder Dumourier, que je n'estime que sous quelques rapports, comme très propre à ridiculiser le porte-soutanne Barruel, qui ne mérite gueres d'être refuté sérieusement, comme l'a peut être fait, Mr. Dumousnier, s'il m'est permis, toutefois, de hazarder une opinion sur le genre de son talent, d'après le peu que je connais de cet auteur.

Excusez ma précipitation à Juger dans cette occasion, en faveur des sentimens d'estime et même d'admiration (car Je suis un peu Bolingbrokien) que vous m'avez inspirés.

Votre trés dévoué Serviteur N. G. DUFIEF

P.S. J'ai dans ma bibliothèque particuliere, *La Guerre des Dieux* par Parny: ouvrage qui a eu un succès prodigieux en France. Il est ecrit un peu dans le genre de la *Pucelle*, & est rempli de gaïté, philosophique, aux depens de la Superstition ancienne & moderne. J'ai pensé que si la lecture de ce petit in 18°, était de votre goût, il pourrait servir à vous amuser, et par conséquent à vous délasser dans un de ces momens que vous consacrez à un repos nécessaire. Donnez-moi vos ordres à ce sujet & il vous sera adressé sur le champ. Le croiriez-vous L'Auteur a encouru, par cette charmante production la disgrace du parti Regnant, qui l'a accusé ouvertement d'*Immoralité*, & en conséquence l'a fait exclure de l'Institut National!!

EDITORS' TRANSLATION

SIR, 4 Dec. 1802

When I received your letter of November 17, I read it with my usual attentiveness. I can thus explain the reasoning it evoked and the source of my misunderstanding.

It is true that you requested the book by Dumousnier, not Dumouriez. But what led me to believe that you wanted the general's book rather than the legislator's is that the name of the former is sometimes spelled Dumousrier, probably because of the vowel "u" which is rather long. In haste, one might easily write Dumounier. You did not, Sir, since you are precise in all things. I knew the eminent member of the National Assembly only under the name of Mounier. What finally confirmed me in my mistake was the idea that Dumouriez, for whom I have limited respect, was capable of ridiculing the cassock-wearing Barruel, who scarcely warrants being seriously refuted, as Mr. Dumousnier may have done, if I may venture an opinion about his talent based on the little I know about him.

Forgive my hasty judgment on this occasion, knowing the esteem and even admiration you have inspired in me (for I am a little Bolingbrokian).

I am your most devoted servant. N. G. DUFIEF

P.S. In my private library I have *La Guerre des dieux* by Parny, a work that has had a prodigious success in France. It is written in a style similar to *La Pucelle*, and is full of philosophical gaiety at the expense of ancient and modern superstition. If this little book is to your liking, it might amuse and relax you in one of those moments you devote to necessary rest. Let me know and

I will send it immediately. Believe it or not, this charming work earned its author the disgrace of the reigning party, which openly accused him of *immorality* and then excluded him from the National Institute!

RC (DLC); at foot of first page: "Le President des Etats-Unis"; also at foot of first page: "Tournez la page s.v.p.," with postscript on verso; endorsed by TJ as received 8 Dec. and so recorded in SJL.

DUMOUSNIER: Jean Joseph Mounier (see Dufief to TJ, 22 Nov.).

QUE JE N'ESTIME: for TJ's own negative assessments of Charles François Du Périer Dumouriez, see Vol. 26:389; Vol. 27:62-3.

JE SUIS UN PEU BOLINGBROKIEN: headstrong decisions undermined the political career of the English politician and author Henry St. John, known as Viscount Bolingbroke (DNB).

Évariste PARNY wrote *La Guerre des dieux* ("war of the gods"), a controversial satire in verse published in 1799. The National Institute elected Parny to membership in April 1803 (*Biographie universelle*, 32:167-8; Raphaël Barquissau, *Les Poètes créoles du XVIIIe siècle [Parny, Bertin, Léonard]* [Paris, 1949], 77-91; Amable Charles, Comte de Franqueville, *Le premier siècle de l'Institut de France, 25 Octobre 1795-25 Octobre 1895*, 2 vols. [Paris, 1895-96], 1:148-9).

The full title of Voltaire's LA PUCELLE—*La Pucelle d'Orléans*, or "the Maid of Orléans"—referred to Joan of Arc. The mocking poem generated scandal well before Voltaire published the authorized edition in 1762 (Jennifer Tsien, *Voltaire and the Temple of Bad Taste: A Study of La Pucelle d'Orléans*, published with Gwenaëlle Boucher, *La Poésie philosophique de Voltaire* [Oxford, 2003], 291-311).

From Benjamin H. Latrobe

DEAR SIR, Saturday morning Decr. 4h. 1802

I should be happy to wait upon you with the result of my calculations at 2 o'clock, if you could then make it convenient to devote half an hour to me. I propose that hour because it is the very earliest that I can mention,—and I believe you to be desirous of obtaining the information which I can give as soon as possible; but a later hour will be equally convenient to me.—I am anxious that you should believe that if during my residence here I have been wanting in the respect of personal attendance upon you,—it has been, because my whole time has been engrossed by unremitted attention to the subject you have committed to me;—and that if I could use expressions to which no meaning of adulation could be possibly attached I should not be at loss,—as I am,—to express to you my sense of your personal kindness to me,—and to tell you how much my attachment to your public character, which my parents instilled into me before I saw you, & which has never varied, has spread itself over *that*, which belongs to you as an individual.—I hope you will pardon this involuntary effusion of my feelings,—they are sincere & disinterested,—and I should have much less sensibility than I do, & much less gratitude than I ought to, possess, were I to feel otherwise. I have perhaps taken an improper opportunity to express them,—but my tongue cannot to do,—but my conduct may.—

I am with great truth Your faithfull hble Servt.

B Henry Latrobe

RC (DLC); endorsed by TJ as received 4 Dec. and so recorded in SJL.

For Latrobe's CALCULATIONS and estimates for the proposed dry dock at Washington, see Robert Smith to TJ, 8 Dec. 1802.

From Affinity Megeath

Honord Sir
President of the United States

City Washington
December 4th 1802

may my intretis prevail on your goodness to condesend to notis this scrall. I beg your honor wold please to pardon me, and let the cause that urges me to the ardent task apolligise for the liberty I take my lack of education and want of abilitys, renders me uncapable of placing words with that sence and stile proper to address so greate and worthy a Presedent, from the public charractor your honor barse of humanity and benevolant disposition assurse me to rely on your honours goodness and charity for my conduct I take the liberty with a humble fealing to relait my cirucmstanc. I am a stranger a widow upwards of sixty years of age, my family consists of three daughters the yongest foreteen I traviled with them from Redstone old fort to this place with views to perfect them in branches of neadle work mantumaking and other branches that might assist them to suport in some genteale line of business. I am hapy to mention as a truth that my daughters with honesty at hart do what they can to assist me in compassing these advantages, but my low surcumstances and the little oppertunity this place affords me to git a living that it is with difficulty that I make out from day to day, I am greivd to know that near too years has relapst Since I came to this place and my Dear Childern unperfected in any point of view, all our exertions go to pay house rent and fire wood I occupy a Small building the rent is eighty dollars a yere. I feer from thes circomstances I Shall be obligd to devide the family, it will reach the Childerns feelings very much and a grate trial to me if I could know my Self independant of rent it would be a hapy release, if your honour[1] will pleas to contribit to they relief of a widow and orphins under these distressing circumstances, I shall be under grate obligations and thankfulness at harte and ever feal grateful for the hapy change, one more earnest wish I beg to be indulged with pleas to cause a line to be wrote desiding this matter to me and I will attend the post office to meet with it.

Thes with Sumision to your Superiority

AFFINITY MEGEATH

NB I resid near the war office

RC (DLC); endorsed by TJ as received 6 Dec. and so recorded in SJL.

[1] MS: "homour."

From John Brown

SIR

Frankfort 5th. Decr. 1802

Thinking it probable that the vacancy occasioned by the death of Mr Clark late first Judge for the Indiana Territory has not yet been filled, I take the liberty hereby to recommend to your Notice, William Garrard Esqr. of this State, as well quallified for that Office. Mr Garrard is son of Colo Garrard our present Governor, & now about thirty two years of age. He completed his Education at Carlisle College, & having read Law with attention under the direction of Colo. Geo. Nicholas has been, for eight or ten years past a practitioner at the Bar. He is a Gentn. of sound, independent mind, temperate, of conciliatory manners, & unsullied reputation. Indeed I know of no one among my acquaintances to whom the appointment would be an object, who in my opinion would fill it with greater ability & integrity than Mr Garrard

I have the Honor to be with profound respect Sir Your most obedient[1] & very Hbe Sevt.

J: BROWN

RC (DNA: RG 59, LAR); at foot of text: "Thomas Jefferson Esqr. President of the U. States"; endorsed by TJ as received 24 Dec. and "Garrard Wm. Kentucky. to be judge of Indiana" and so recorded in SJL.

WILLIAM GARRARD was not nominated for the Indiana judgeship, but in March 1808 TJ appointed him a commissioner for settling land claims in the Opelousas District of the Orleans Territory (*Terr. Papers*, 9:778).

CARLISLE COLLEGE: that is, Dickinson College in Carlisle, Pennsylvania.

Virginia native George NICHOLAS, a brother of Wilson Cary Nicholas and Kentucky's first attorney general, had declined appointments as U.S. attorney for Kentucky in 1789 and 1793. He died in Lexington in 1799 (ANB; Mary K. Bonsteel Tachau, *Federal Courts in the Early Republic: Kentucky, 1789-1816* [Princeton, 1978], 68-9; Vol. 24:707n; Vol. 26:507-8; Vol. 31:172n).

On 8 Dec., Brown paid $2.50 to William Hunter for TJ's subscription to the Frankfort, Kentucky, *Palladium*, for the year ending 1 Aug. 1802. Brown had also paid TJ's subscription in 1800 and 1801 (receipt in MHi, dated 8 Dec. 1802, in Hunter's hand and signed by him, endorsed by John Barnes; MB, 2:1018, 1035; Vol. 37:312).

[1] MS: "obedidient."

To John Redman Coxe

SIR Washington Dec. 6. 1802.

The vaccine virus being at present lost in this part of the country, Dr. Gant has sollicited me to endeavor to recover it for him & his brethren of the profession here. the difficulty of keeping up a constant succession of inoculated subjects, and the uncertainty of success from matter which is not fresh, will probably expose every part of the US. to the accident of losing the matter, and render it a thing of common interest to all the Medical gentlemen, while they possess it, to distribute it far & near, in order to multiply their own chances of recovering it whenever the accident of loss[1] may happen to themselves. presuming you retain the matter at Philadelphia, I have to ask the favor of you, on behalf of the faculty here, to send some by post under cover to me, which shall be immediately given to Doctr. Gant. Accept assurances of my esteem & respect. TH: JEFFERSON

RC (PPCP); addressed: "Dr. John Redman Coxe Philadephia"; franked and postmarked; endorsed by Coxe: "recd. 9th. Ansd. 10. {Hansel. 92 9th day Novr. 16th.}." PrC (DLC).

[1] Preceding two words interlined.

From Albert Gallatin

DEAR SIR Monday morning Decer. 6th 1802

The Collectors continue to apply for sea-letters: we have none to send them. Is it intended to discontinue them altogether? If so, what is the proper answer to give to the collectors?

Respectfully your's ALBERT GALLATIN

RC (DLC); endorsed by TJ as received from the Treasury Department on 6 Dec. and "Sea letters" and so recorded in SJL.

In 1793, customs COLLECTORS began to distribute sea letters or passports; see Vol. 34:381n.

From George Jefferson

Dear Sir Richmond 6th. Decr. 1802

I have duly received your favor of the 1st., and have in compliance with your direction forwarded Mr. Derieux $:25.

The draught you mention in favor of Brown was some time since presented by Mr. J. Nicholas, but as you had previously informed us that you had concluded to forward the amount to Albemarle in bank notes, and as the draught was not endorsed so as to give N. a legal right to demand payment, we declined taking it up, and informed him we expected the money was remitted to Mr. B. as you had proposed.

I am Dear Sir Yr. Very humble servt. Geo. Jefferson

RC (MHi); at foot of text: "Thos. Jefferson esqr."; endorsed by TJ as received 10 Dec. and so recorded in SJL.

To Benjamin Jones

Sir Washington Dec. 6. 1802

Your favor of Nov. 15. came to hand in due time, but it has not been till lately I could find time to look through our past account. it was thoroughly impressed on my mind that I had never failed to order paiment for every supply of iron at the term of three months a little more or less. but I find in effect that the two small articles of Sep. 12. sash weights & Oct. 28. bar iron to Stewart, had been forgotten, which added to the last article furnished makes up the balance stated in your account. I accordingly now inclose you a draught on the bank of the US for 186. D 22 c and I state below the supplies & paiments as they appear on my books. I am sincerely sorry for the death of your partner: but not doubting equal fidelity in the executing my commission, I shall continue to send them to you. my nailery has done little lately. it is now under a new direction and will occasion a greater demand for rods & hoop. Accept my best wishes & respects.

Th: Jefferson

		Th: Jefferson in acct. with Roberts & Jones	D[r].
1800.	July 17.	To supply of rods & hoops.	406.62
	Oct. 12	Stoves	73.
1801.	May 22.	Rods	268.12
	June 24	Rods & hoops	218.82

	Sep. 12.	Sash weights 52.[97]		
	Oct. 28.	Stewart Bar iron	[80.22]	133.19
1802.	Apr. 6	Rods & hoops		327.20
	June 22.	Bar iron & steel		52.73
				Cr.
1800.	Oct. 8.	By remittance by Barnes		406.32
1801.	Jan. 7.	do.		73
	Sep. 16	do.		[268.12]
	Nov. 9.	do.		218.82
1802	July 18.	do.		327.20
	Dec. 7	now inclosed		186.22

PrC (MHi); faint; at foot of text, in ink: "Mr. Benjamin Jones"; endorsed by TJ in ink on verso. Recorded in SJL with notation "186.22."

Benjamin Jones (1767-1849), a Philadelphia ironmonger and investor, pursued several business partnerships in the 1790s before going into business with Joseph Roberts, TJ's regular iron merchant, in 1800. After the death of Roberts in 1802, Jones retained TJ's business with his new firm Jones & Howell. TJ continued to purchase iron and lead from Jones until at least 1815. In additon to his merchandising, Jones held an interest in iron furnaces in New Jersey, speculated in land, served as a director of the Delaware Insurance Company of Philadelphia, and was a member of the central committee of the Pennsylvania Society for the Promotion of Manufactures and the Mechanic Arts (Philadelphia *Gazette and Universal Daily Advertiser*, 17 Mch. 1795, 6 Feb. 1797, 13 Jan. 1800; Philadelphia *Inquirer*, 16 Dec. 1829; Philadelphia *North American*, 16 May 1849; "Meeting of the Pennsylvania Society for the Promotion of Manufactures and the Mechanic Arts, held in Philadelphia, on 14th May, 1827" [Philadelphia, 1827], 12; biographical information in PHi: Jones and Taylor Family Papers; RS, 4:634n; Vol. 37:598n).

Jones's FAVOR was recorded in SJL as received from Jones & Howell "for Roberts & Jones" on 19 Nov. but has not been found.

TJ had placed the enslaved workers at his NAILERY under the discipline of Gabriel Lilly, instead of William Stewart (TJ to James Dinsmore, 1 Dec.).

From Levi Lincoln

SIR Washington Decr. 6th. 1802

By the last mail I recd. letters from two very respectable Gent. in the county of Essex, to whom I had written, respecting the political Conduct of Mr Whettimore the Surveyor of Gloucester. As I assured them no use should be made of their names, they are not mentioned. From one of these letters the following is an extract—"I have made particular enquiries respecting Mr Whittemores political conduct, and find it has been (prior to the appoinment of Mr. Gibbaut) uniformly that of a high federalist, using his time and abilities in rendering the present administration unpopular—But since the dismission of Mr Tuck, he has conducted with more caution." The other letter is much more particular, lengthy full & decided—I have no doubt of the statements being correct, and that it would be useful proper, & popular to remove him—

A Mr. Fosdick of Portland has been represented also as a very bitter and open mouthed collector.

I differ very much from many of my friends with respect to the utility of Mr Paine's writings It is to be regreted that he cannot be induced to be silent on the character of General Washington and the christian religion—But republicans I think can better manage, than quarrel with, his treatment of these subjects.

His political writings will certainly be very useful in the eastern States. The violent federalist can say nor do any thing more, than they have said & done—They consider Paine's writings as irresistable in their affects on the public mind, and dread them, as they would a scourge of scorpions. There are no terms to be made with them. The inclosed, which you will be pleased to throw your eye on, at a moment of leisure, exhibits I presume, the republican feeling in reference to Paine & his writings in Massachusetts, They distinguish between his politicks & his religion, & apologise for his attack on Genl Washington on the score of personal sufferings, or neglect—Federalists here already anticipated & exhausted themselves & their invectives on these topicks. Republicans have been defending him, and would now be extremely mortified, to have their friends join with the federalist, in denouncing him—

The P.S to the inclosed, furnishes a specimen of clerical insolence & impudence, in the face of a parish composed of a majority of republicans—

with affectionate esteem I am Sir most respectfully yours

Levi Lincoln

RC (DLC); at head of text: "President of the U. States"; endorsed by TJ as received 6 Dec. and so recorded in SJL. Enclosure not identified.

TJ sought Lincoln's opinion on whether Samuel Whittemore, SURVEYOR OF GLOUCESTER, should be replaced, after Jacob Crowninshield and John Gibaut, the successor to William Tuck as collector at the port, recommended his removal (Gallatin to TJ, 16 Oct.; TJ to Lincoln, 25 Oct. 1802).

Nathaniel F. FOSDICK, Harvard graduate and active Federalist leader at Portland, was appointed collector of customs in 1789 (Washington, *Papers*, *Pres. Ser.*, 2:329n; Prince, *Federalists*, 39-40).

From the Navy Department

[on or before 6 Dec. 1802]

Cost of the Constellation $314–212=15–

The Constellation cost more than any other vessel in the service.

RC (DLC); undated; in an unidentified hand; addressed: "The President of the United States"; endorsed by TJ as received from the Navy Department on 6 Dec. and "Constellation" and so recorded in SJL.

From "A True Republican"

Anne Arundel County Maryland
[ca. 6 Dec. 1802]

My Dear Sir

Take the advice of a true Republican and have nothing to do with Pain for if you keep him with you any longer you will surely Loose your next Election you had better turn him away and give him no more feasts. But I think that you may never stand for president again for Adams will be the next president but god forbid it. Tom Pain that scandilous rascal for you a true Republican to encourage that villain Therefore take my advice and have nothing more to do with him

I am your most Ob Servant A True Republican

RC (DLC); undated; at foot of text: "Mr. Thos. Jefferson President"; endorsed by TJ as received from "Anonymous" on 6 Dec. and "Paine" and so recorded in SJL.

no more feasts: see Paine to TJ, 12 Jan. 1803.

From Francis Deakins

Sir Geo. Town Decr. 7th. 1802

Permit me to inform you we have not been Able to obtain Subscription for the Allegany Turnpike road Agreeable to the Acts of the Legislatures of Virginia & Maryland from Potomack to the Western Navigation, which I had the Honor to lay before you last Winter

There is no monied Capital on the Potomack nor in the Country immediately Interested in this Road, hence Subscriptions of Shares payable in money Cannot be got—but we have good grounds to believe Enough are Willing to become Adventurers Payable in lands at A fair Price. & there Are in New England Companies formed for making turnpike roads whereever there is a demand for their Services—

who would According to the Opinion of Wellinformed men of that Country, Come on & undertake this road on condition of receiving $\frac{3}{4}$ or $\frac{4}{5}$th their pay in lands, they must have Some money to precure provisions Utensils &c. &c.

In New England through Countries quite as Mountanious as that between the Eastern & Western Waters turnpike roads are made for 700 to 1000 Dolls. ₩. Mile—The Country through which this road must pass is but thinly Settled—repairs will be difficult it ought to be So constructed as to require none for a length of time—& it may Cost about 50000 Dolls.

There will be A Subscription immediately in land to the amount of 40000 Dolls.—and with the land if 10000 or 12000 Dolls. in Cash Could be Subscribed—no doubt the road can be made, Perhaps finished in all next year.

I have taken the Liberty of troubling you with this in hope that it may be thought advisable that Congress should give a power some where to undertaking like this—If the Public could take shares to the Amount of 10000 or 12000 Dolls. on the same terms that Individuals would Subscribe—in money, & like them to receive a portion of the toles, they might not Loose even in A pecuniary View—but without a Consideration of this kind. no road can be made in the U. States So important to the union of the Eastern & Western States as this—no where can So Small Sum of Public money be laid out to so much Public Advantage

I have the Honor to be with great respect Sir yr. Most Obedt Servt.

Francis Deakins

RC (MHi); at foot of text: "Thos. Jefferson Esqr. President of the U. States"; endorsed by TJ as received 9 Dec. and so recorded in SJL.

Francis Deakins (1739-1804) was a land surveyor and speculator with extensive interests in western Maryland. Prominent in Georgetown business circles, he served as a director for the Bank of Columbia and of the Maryland Mutual Insurance Company. He ran successfully as a presidential elector in 1796 and 1800, both times supporting John Adams (Fredericktown *Maryland Chronicle, or Universal Advertiser*, 15 Aug. 1787; Hagerstown *Washington Spy*, 23 Nov. 1796; Georgetown *Centinel of Liberty*, 2 Apr. 1799; *Washington Federalist*, 4 Dec. 1800; New York *Commercial Advertiser*, 26 Mch. 1802; Washington, *Papers*, *Pres. Ser.*, 6:647).

For TJ's interest in the TURNPIKE, see Vol. 36:417. In February 1803, the House of Representatives declined a "prayer of the shareholders" of the turnpike company (*Washington Federalist*, 11 Mch. 1803).

From Elizabeth Ford

Honour'd Sir Stafford Cty. Decr. 7th 1802

In Addressing a Gentleman of your Rank and character and to whom I have not the honor of being acquainted I may appear presumtuous; but I Flatter myself that, that goodness of heart for which you are so emminently Distinguished will easily form an Apology for my Singularity. Being Greatly straitened for cash since the Death of my husband looking over his papers finds a sum of the old kind of money which Greatly releav'd my distress'd mind untill I tender'd it as payment and to my Great mortification was told that it was not good by some of the collectors of this County that with the sum of 1518 Dollars it will not benefit me 300 which is a sum I now stand in need of to save me from being Distressd—My Humble petition is that your Honor would use some influence towards the releif of your Distress'd petitioner and Family by receiving of the inclos'd six Bills of a Virginia currency which has been sent to Richmond once by the advice of one of our attorneys but having no friend to act for me these was retur'd not chang'd. your petitioner prays for your benevolent assistance or Pardon the Interruption she may give to your other more Important Business

I have the Honor to be Sir Yr Very Hble Servt.

Elizabeth Ford

NB If your Honor should think proper to consider me Direct to the postmaster in Dumfries if not she prays for to bury it all in oblivion.[1] EF

RC (DLC); at foot of text: "To the President of the United States whom God preserve"; addressed in unidentified hand: "The Right Honbl Thomas Jefferson City of Washington"; franked; postmarked Dumfries, Virginia, 8 Dec.; endorsed by TJ as received 10 Dec. and so recorded in SJL.

postmaster in dumfries: Timothy Brundidge (Stets, *Postmasters*, 256).

[1] MS: "olivion."

To Albert Gallatin

Th:J. to mr Gallatin Dec. 7. 1802.

The short answer to the Collectors is that Sea letters are never given out but in time of war. then they are given in consequence of the stipulations in treaties to ascertain our flag to the other party when belligerent. no Sea letter was ever issued by this government till the commencement of the war between France & Great Britain.—I should except from these observations the case of vessels going on voiages beyond the Cape of good hope; all nations furnish such with sealetters and so did we from the beginning of this government.

I inclose you other papers from Majr. Jackson. I know not why they are sent to me, unless to give him an opportunity of assuring me that I have a very good opinion of him: an assurance which needs some modification. his evidence is a little commonplace compliment in an answer to a letter in which he laid himself out for it. health & friendly salutations.

RC (NHi: Gallatin Papers); endorsed. PrC (DLC). Recorded in SJL as a letter to the Treasury Department of 6 Dec. with notation "Sea letters. Jackson." Enclosures: see below.

ANSWER TO THE COLLECTORS: on 9 Dec., the Treasury secretary issued a circular letter, stating: "It having never been the usage of this government to grant Sea-Letters but in time of war, and then only in consequence of the stipulations in treaties to ascertain our flag to the belligerent parties; the President of the United States is of opinion that the issuing of Sea-Letters is no longer necessary, except in cases where vessels are bound on voyages beyond the Cape of Good Hope." The collectors were to communicate the executive decision to those who applied for sea letters and submit requests to the Treasury Department only for vessels making long voyages. When Philadelphia merchants wanted more information, Gallatin responded to Peter Muhlenberg on 27 Dec., "that the granting of Sea-Letters is not only very troublesome but wholly destitute of utility as well as contrary to usage." Gallatin continued: "It is understood that the English government give no Sea-Letters now that they, like us, are at peace with all the world; and there is no reason for departing from universal practice." The same day, Gallatin applied to the State Department for a supply of sea letters for those vessels sailing beyond the Cape of Good Hope, and on 10 Jan. 1803, he sent ten of them to the Philadelphia collector (Gallatin, *Papers*, 7:796, 854-5, 914).

INCLOSE YOU OTHER PAPERS: according to SJL, TJ had recently received two letters from William Jackson, the Federalist customs surveyor and inspector at Philadelphia. The first was recorded in SJL as a letter of 24 Nov., received from Philadelphia on the 27th, with the notation "T."; the second was of 3 Dec., received by TJ on the 6th. Neither letter has been found. Jackson had previously corresponded with TJ in early 1801 (Vol. 32:541-4; Vol. 33:58-9; Vol. 35:100, 102n, 118n). For TJ's COMMONPLACE COMPLIMENT of 18 Feb. 1801, in response to Jackson's letter of 3 Feb., see Vol. 33:14.

To George Jefferson

DEAR SIR — Washington Dec. 7. 1802

I inclose you three hundred & fifty dollars to cover two drafts I make on you in favr. of Saml. & S. Myers for 150. D. & of Moran for 200. D. which be pleased to honour when presented. affectionate attachment & salutations. TH: JEFFERSON

P.S. Take the reciept, if you please, as paid for S. Dyer.

PrC (MHi); at foot of text: "Mr. George Jefferson"; endorsed by TJ in ink on verso. Recorded in SJL with the notation "350."

For the payment to Joseph MORAN, see TJ to Gibson & Jefferson, 9 Nov.

To S. & S. Myers

Washington Dec. 7. 1802

By desire of mr Samuel Dyer of Albemarle I inclose you an order on Messrs. Gibson & Jefferson for one hundred & fifty dollars for the credit of mr Dyer with you. Accept my respects and good wishes.

TH: JEFFERSON

RC (DeHi); addressed: "Messrs. Samuel & S. Myers Richmond"; franked and postmarked; endorsed as received 10 Dec. and answered on the 11th. Recorded in SJL with the notation "150."

S. & S. Myers was the partnership headed by Samuel Myers (1755-1836), a half-brother and former business partner of Moses Myers of Norfolk. Samuel Myers transferred a successful mercantile business from Petersburg to Richmond during the 1790s and emerged as a leading member of the city's small but potent Jewish community. By November 1800, his business advertised under the name S. & S. Myers, but three years later it was advertising solely under his name (Richmond *Virginia Argus*, 4 Nov. 1800, 1 Dec. 1802, 5 Oct. 1803; Myron Berman, *Richmond's Jewry, 1769-1976: Shabbat in Shockoe* [Charlottesville, 1979], 64-70).

TJ was likely reimbursing SAMUEL DYER on behalf of his carpenter John Perry (MB, 2:1088). A letter of 7 Oct. from Dyer to TJ, recorded in SJL as received 13 Oct., has not been found. TJ's response of 15 Oct. has also not been found.

From Carlos Martínez de Irujo

Wenesday morn—[8 Dec. 1802]

Le Chevalier d'Irujo has the honor to present his complimt. to Mr. Jefferson, & in answer to his polite & friendly notte of yesterday concerning the amount of the champaing, to assure him, that his approbation of it will be for him the highest prize he can expect in this bargain—Le chevalier returns his sincere thanks to Mr. Jefferson for his generous offer of the Madeyra, & he will make use of it if he has occasion for—

RC (MoSHi: Jefferson Papers); partially dated (see TJ to Irujo, 9 Dec.); endorsed by TJ.

NOTTE OF YESTERDAY: the communication from TJ has not been found, and he did not record it in SJL.

CHAMPAING: in his list of wine used during his presidency, TJ noted the receipt of 100 bottles of champagne from Irujo on 1 Dec. (MB, 2:1115).

From Richard W. Meade

SIR Phila., December 8th. 1802.

Having been informed the Commissioners are about to be appointed on the part of the US. to meet those of Spain for the settlement of Certain claims of the American Citizens, I Have taken the liberty of addressing you on the Subject, with a tender of my services.—

I Have not thought it necessary to accompany this Letter with any Recommendations. I flatter myself however that on investigation my character will not meet your disaprobation. My Being a Native as well as my father Mr. George Meade of this City & of Respectable Connections will I am induced to hope, add a little weight to the application.

The Secretary of State was addressed some time since by the Merchants of this place in my behalf for an Agency to prosecute their Claims. I then considered myself as a Plaintiff Since when some fortunate circumstances have occurr'd with respect to my [c]laim which induce me to Consider myself so no longer—If I should be thought capable & worthy of the appointment & [it] should be deemed necessary to procure any Recommendations, I doubt not being able to procure satisfactory ones—

With due Respect & Consideration I remain Sir Your most obt. hum Sevt. R. W. MEADE

RC (DNA: RG 59, LAR); torn; at head of text: "Thomas Jefferson Esqr. President of the U.S."; endorsed by TJ as received 11 Dec. and "to be Commr. to Spain" and so recorded in SJL.

Richard Worsam Meade (1778-1828) was the son of Henrietta Worsam and George Meade, a land speculator and Irish-Catholic merchant in Philadelphia. Richard established a successful mercantile business in Saint-Domingue in the late 1790s. He returned to Philadelphia and in 1801 married Margaret Coates Butler, daughter of a prominent shipowner in Perth Amboy, New Jersey. Meade, as the assignee in bankruptcy proceedings in 1802, oversaw the dissolution of his father's holdings, including tracts of land in Pennsylvania, Virginia, Georgia, and South Carolina. In 1803, Philadelphia merchants sent the younger Meade as their agent to Spain to seek redress for the seizure and confiscation of their vessels in Buenos Aires. He established himself as a merchant, banker, and shipowner at Cadiz and in 1804 began seeking the consulship there in place of Joseph Yznardi, Sr. Meade served as U.S. naval agent at the port from 1806 to 1816. He also collected art and took an interest in the exportation of merino sheep to the United States. His family returned to Philadelphia in 1817, but Meade was detained and confined at Cadiz by the Spanish government until April 1818, when the U.S., to gain his release, threatened reprisals against Spanish commerce. Meade spent the next decade attempting to recover debts owed him by Spain. In 1820, a Spanish tribunal awarded him a certificate of debt for the sum of $491,153.62, but under the 1819 Treaty of Florida, the United States assumed responsibility for the claims of American citizens against Spain. Meade moved back to Philadelphia and then to Washington to settle his account, but he never received reimbursement (DAB; R. W. Meade, "George Meade, A Patriot of the Revolutionary Era," *Records of the American Catholic Historical Society of Philadelphia*, 3 [1888-91], 194, 218-19; *Poulson's American Daily Advertiser*, 8 Mch., 9, 28 Apr. 1802, 19 June 1818; Montrose, Penn., *Susquehannah Centinel*, 16 Aug. 1817; Philadelphia *National Gazette and Literary Register*, 12 Jan. 1826, 18 Dec. 1827; *Alexandria Gazette*, 10 Jan. 1828; NDBW, 6:455-6; Madison, *Papers, Sec. of State Ser.*, 3:548-9; 6:62-3; 8:81-2; Pierce Butler to TJ, 3 Oct. 1804).

SECRETARY OF STATE WAS ADDRESSED: perhaps a letter from Thomas FitzSimons, president of the Philadelphia Chamber of Commerce, to Madison, 18 Sep., which has not been found. In it FitzSimons noted that Philadelphia merchants were sending an agent to Spain to prosecute American claims. Meade, also a member of the Chamber of Commerce, was FitzSimons's nephew (Madison, *Papers, Sec. of State Ser.*, 3:590; Meade, "George Meade," 194, 199; *Philadelphia Gazette*, 2 Nov. 1802; see also Madison to TJ, 14 Aug. 1802). MY CLAIM: Meade later noted that he had lost a large sum of money through Spanish detentions at Buenos Aires. Merchants entrusted him with claims worth almost $1,000,000 when he left for Spain (Richard W. Meade, *The Case of Richard W. Meade, Esq. A Citizen of Pennsylvania, U.S.A. Seized and Imprisoned, 2d of May, 1816, by the Government of Spain, and Still Detained. Cadiz, November 27th, 1817* [Washington, D.C., n.d.], 4-5).

On 9 Dec., James Barbour of Barboursville, Virginia, wrote Madison also offering his services as commissioner under the Convention of 1802 with Spain (RC in DNA: RG 59, LAR, endorsed by TJ: "Barber James to Mr. Madison to be Commr. in Spain"; Madison, *Papers, Sec. of State Ser.*, 4:183-4).

To Thomas Newton

DEAR SIR Washington Dec. 8. 1802.

I have the pleasure now to inclose you a copy of the act of assembly which you desired. it could not be authenticated in any way: but I send you mr Carr's letter, which assures me that it is an accurate copy. Accept assurances of my esteem & great respect.

TH: JEFFERSON

PrC (DLC); at foot of text: "Colo Thomas Newton"; endorsed by TJ in ink on verso. Enclosures: (1) Dabney Carr to TJ, 30 Nov., recorded in SJL as received 7 Dec. but not found. (2) A copy of a 1764 colonial Virginia law pertaining to the Anglican parish in Norfolk (see Vol. 38:454-5).

From Robert Smith

Nav Dep
8 Decr 1802

SIR!

I have the honor to enclose two copies of a report made to me by B. H. Latrobe Esq on the subject of a Dry Dock, at this place, of a size sufficient to contain Twelve frigates of 44 guns—in which report he mentions the site that would, in his opinion, be the best—the works necessary to be erected, accompanied by Drawings—the means of supplying the Dock with Water—& the probable period it would take to complete the works—to which he has subjoined the necessary Estimates, exhibiting the probable cost.

I also enclose two Copies of a Report made to me by Capt Tingey, in pursuance of instructions to examine the streams of water in the neighbourhood.

I have the honor to be with the greatest respect & esteem, Sir, your mo ob Sv

RT SMITH

RC (DNA: RG 233, PM, 7th Cong., 2d sess.); in a clerk's hand, signed by Smith; addressed: "President of the United States"; endorsed by a House clerk. RC (DNA: RG 46, LPPM, 7th Cong., 2d sess.); in a clerk's hand, signed by Smith; endorsed by a Senate clerk. FC (Lb in DNA: RG 45, LSP). Enclosures: (1) Benjamin Henry Latrobe to Robert Smith, Washington, 4 Dec. 1802, presenting plans and estimates for the proposed "dry dock or naval arsenal" at Washington in which 12 frigates of 44 guns could be laid up; since the plan had already been "so far matured by the President of the United States," Latrobe suggests where the works can "most advantageously be erected, & designs and estimates of the works which are necessary to carry it into effect"; since the Eastern Branch of the Potomac contains a bottom mostly of mud, Latrobe strongly recommends locating the locks for entering the dry dock at the end of 9th Street east of the Capitol and bounding the navy yard, where a "Spit of hard gravel" running into the channel will furnish a solid foundation; a valley running up the direction of the street will also save more than half the digging necessary for the works; Latrobe suggests purchasing the lots between 9th and 10th Streets south of the intersection of Virginia and Georgia Avenues, but if such extensive purchases prove impracticable, Latrobe suggests vacating the streets only as far as the navy yard and running the arsenal east to west at right angles with the locks; the latter plan, however, would necessitate the construction of a "turning Dock," the expense of which might offset any savings on land purchases and also render the location and erection of storehouses inconvenient; regarding the necessary works, Latrobe first mentions two locks, each of 12 feet lift, to raise vessels from the Eastern Branch into the dry dock, which would contain 23 feet of water; once the water is drained from the dry dock, vessels would settle on blocks prepared in the slips and thereby, in the words of the president, "be perfectly drained and rendered as safe against decay as the internal timbers of a house"; in the dry dock, vessels may be built or repaired at leisure, and single vessels may be docked for repair between the dry dock and locks without the necessity of filling the dry dock; regarding the naval arsenal, Latrobe emphasizes that it will admit the free passage of air and be built of "solid masonry" to protect it from fire; Latrobe agrees that the president's suggestion to model the arsenal roof after the Halle aux Bleds in Paris "is certainly the cheapest and I think the best," but Latrobe does not include estimates for ornamentation since they are not "within the compass of the arts in America at present"; Latrobe prefers using the Potomac River to supply the dry dock by means of a canal from the locks at the Little Falls canal through Georgetown to Rock Creek, thence through the city to the navy yard; such a canal would fill the works within 12 hours and also convey timber, stores, and provisions to the navy yard from western Virginia, Maryland, and Pennsylvania; at the request of the president, Latrobe has also considered Tiber Creek as a water source, but finds it inadequate; using the water measurements calculated by Thomas Tingey and Nicholas King, Latrobe calculates that it would take 29 days to fill the dry dock using water taken directly from Tiber Creek and Stoddert's Spring, which would be reduced to three days by increasing the dimensions of the canal and constructing a reservoir on Piney Branch; Latrobe estimates that if workmen can be procured immediately from Philadelphia and Washington, the locks can be completed by the end of 1803 and the naval arsenal by the end of 1804; a canal from the Tiber could be completed in 1803, but if not, then the locks only could be filled by means of pumps in three days; a Potomac canal could not be completed before the end of 1805; Latrobe urges workmen to be engaged before the first of March, by which time most have already planned their employment for the season; Latrobe is confident in his estimates for labor and materials, but cautions that there could be significant variation in those for land purchases and because of the uncertain foundation below the bed of the Eastern Branch harbor (Tr in DNA: RG 233, PM, endorsed by a House clerk; Tr in DNA: RG 46, LPPM, endorsed by a Senate clerk). (2) Latrobe, estimate of the cost of constructing the locks, naval arsenal, and canal, Washington, 4 Dec. 1802, calculating $167,968 for excavating, walling, iron work, and pumping for the locks; $222,013 for constructing the walls and roof of the naval arsenal; and $27,295 for masonry, excavating, and land purchases for a canal from Tiber Creek and Stoddert's Spring to the navy yard and a reservoir on Piney Branch, making an aggregate cost of $417,276 (Tr in DLC, in Meriwether Lewis's hand, including recapitulation of aggregate cost at foot of text, endorsed by TJ: "Dry dock at Washington Latrobe's estimate. 1802"; Tr in DNA: RG 233, PM, with recapitulation of aggregate cost at foot of text in TJ's hand; Tr in DNA: RG 46, LPPM, with recapitulation of aggregate cost in TJ's hand at foot of text, endorsed by a Senate clerk). (3) Latrobe, drawings, 4 Dec. 1802, including "Section of Locks" and "Plan of Locks necessary to elevate the Ships into the Arsenal" and a "Plan of the Principal Dry Dock or Naval Arsenal, to contain Frigates in three tier of four ships each," with north, south, and side elevations and sections looking to and from the Eastern Branch (DLC: Prints and Photographs Division; reproduced in Darwin H. Stapleton, ed., *The Engineering Drawings of Benjamin Henry Latrobe* [New Haven, 1980], 119-20). (4) Thomas Tingey to Robert Smith, 22 Oct. 1802 (see Smith to TJ, 23 Oct. 1802). Enclosed in TJ to the Senate and the House of Representatives, 27 Dec. 1802.

To Robert Bailey

SIR Washington Dec. 9. 1802.

A friend of mine in France has asked of me to procure the seeds and plants below mentioned. as this may not be out of your line, and the plants abound in this neighborhood, I will ask the favor of you to make the collection, and pack them well and properly for the sea, labelling each article so substantially as not to be erased. the sooner they are ready the better. should you not have the convenience of having the boxes made, and will send me a note of the sizes, they shall be made here. Accept my best wishes for yourself & family

TH: JEFFERSON

black walnuts. half a bushel
seeds of the Poplar (Liriodendron) half a bushel.
Cedar berries 1. ℔
acorns of every kind. half a bushel to be packed in dry bran.
Sassafras seed. 1. ℔
Swamp laurel. 1. ℔.
Dogwood ½ ℔
white ash seed ½ ℔[1]
Catalpa seed ½ ℔
wild roses of every kind. ½ bushel of seed.

---

12 plants of sassafras.
12. do. of swamp laurel } to be packed in moss, in a box
12 do. of Dogwood

PrC (MoSHi: Jefferson Papers); at foot of text: "Mr. Bailey"; endorsed by TJ in ink on verso.

Madame de Tessé was the FRIEND in France; see TJ to William Short, 2 Dec.; TJ to Madame de Tessé, 30 Jan. 1803; TJ to Bailey, 10, 19 Oct. 1803. For Bailey, who had a nursery in Washington and was formerly a gardener at Monticello, see Vol. 28:256-7 and Vol. 37:100.

[1] Alongside this entry TJ wrote in ink "not here."

From Laurence A. Dorsey

Wilmington N.C.
9th. Decr. 1802.

The Petition of Laurence A. Dorsey a natural born Citizen of America.

Respectully Sheweth

That Your Petitioner for many years past has acted as Deputy of the Cape Fear District to John S. West Esquire Marshal of North Carolina: That he is informed that Mr. West will be out of Office, or that his term of appointment will expire on the tenth instant.

Your Petitioner therefore, being (he flatters himself) fully adequate to the duties of Marshal of North Carolina, solicits that in case the said Mr. West should not be re-appointed, that he Your Petitioner from being long conversant in the duties of the Office, and he hopes also from the Character he has long borne of integrity and industry, that you will appoint him to the Office.

and Your Petitioner shall ever pray &c.

RC (DNA: RG 59, LAR); at head of text: "To the President of the United States of America"; at head of list, on a separate sheet, in the same hand: "We the Subscribers Do respectfully recommend the prayer of the within Petition to the attention of the President," signed by Timothy Bloodworth, William Giles, and 27 others; endorsed by TJ as received 24 Dec. and "to be Marshal N. C. v. West" and so recorded in SJL.

Laurence A. Dorsey served as one of the port inspectors and measurers at the Wilmington, North Carolina, custom house in 1800. Although not a graduate, he was a founding member of the Philanthropic Society established at the University of North Carolina in 1795 for the improvement of its members in English composition, the science and art of debating, and a "knowledge of parliamentary rules and modes of conducting public business." The society also promoted the cultivation of moral and social virtues and lasting friendships (ASP, *Miscellaneous*, 1:276; Stephen B. Weeks, ed., *Register of Members of the Philanthropic Society, Instituted in the University of North Carolina, August 1st, 1795*, 4th ed. [Raleigh, N.C., 1887], 3-5; Kemp P. Battle, *History of the University of North Carolina*, 2 vols. [Raleigh, N.C., 1907-12], 1:76, 85).

JOHN S. WEST had let it be known that because of ill health he probably would not seek another term as marshal of North Carolina. On 10 Oct., however, West wrote the secretary of state that he still had fees to collect and important business to complete. Unless another had been nominated, he requested that Madison "make known to the President my willingness to accept a reappointment" (RC in DNA: RG 59, LAR; endorsed by TJ: "West John S. to mr Madison. to be reappointed Marshal of N.C.").

For a previous recommendation for the North Carolina marshalcy, see note to David Stone to TJ, 3 Nov. 1802.

The imminent expiration of West's commission probably prompted TJ to inquire at the State Department about all commissions for marshals. In an undated memorandum "For the President," the State Department sent "A List of the Marshals of the United States with the dates of their Commissions, terminating four years from thence respectively." West's name heads the list of 19 marshals, with his designation in the North Carolina district in one column and the date of his commission, 14 July 1798, in the second. Only West's entry has an emendation, in an unidentified hand, noting that his commission "was limited to take effect on the 10th Decr. 1798 & expires 10 Decr. 1802" (MS in DNA: RG 59, MCL, in a clerk's hand).

To Carlos Martínez de Irujo

TH: JEFFERSON TO
THE CHEVALR. YRUJO Dec. 9. 1802.

I recieved, my dear Sir, your note of yesterday, and am sensible of the friendly spirit which dictated it. but you must pardon me for repeating my request to inform me of the price of the wine. this is such a transaction of meum & tuum as must follow the same rules between us as between others. it is sufficient obligation to me to spare me so excellent a supply, and if not done on the usual & equal terms would forbid my availing myself of a similar accomodation in future, which in consequence of the superabundance you had mentioned I had contemplated doing. I pray you therefore to fill up the measure of the favor by the information requested, which is indispensable. friendly salutations & respect.

PrC (DLC).

MEUM & TUUM: what is mine and what is yours (OED).

From James Mease, with Jefferson's Note

109 Spruce In Philadelphia [9 Dec. 1802]

with Dr Mease's respectful Compliments.

[*Note by TJ*:]

Dec. 24. 1802.—subscribed to the work, to wit Domestic Encyclopedia 5. vols@ 2.50 D pr. volume.

RC (DLC); undated; addressed: "The President of the uStates"; franked; postmarked 9 Dec.; endorsed by TJ. Enclosure not found, but see below.

DOMESTIC ENCYCLOPEDIA: James Mease, a newly elected member of the American Philosophical Society, proposed an octavo edition in five volumes of Anthony F. M. Willich's compendium, *Domestic Encyclopædia; or, A Dictionary of Facts, and Useful Knowledge*. Mease may have enclosed a proposal for the first volume of his American edition, which was scheduled for publication on 1 Apr. 1802, with additional volumes to appear every three months thereafter. Unlike Willich's London edition, published in 1802, Mease's Philadelphia edition was published by William Y. Birch and Abraham Small in 1803-4, "with additions, applicable to the present situation of the United States" such as TJ's invention of the moldboard plow (Baltimore *Republican*, 28 July 1802; New York *American Citizen*, 11 Jan. 1803; Mease, *Domestic Encyclopædia*, 4:288-92; Mease to TJ, 9 Aug., 5 Dec. 1803, 28 Mch. 1804; Vol. 30:207n).

From Abraham Baldwin

Decr 10th 1802

Abr Baldwin presents his respects to the President of the United States. I have consulted Genl. Merriwether on the subject of your note of yesterday: the persons recommended by Genl Jackson to be commissioners of Bankruptcy for Savannah are not particularly known to us: Mr Bullock has been Attorney General of the State, and Mr Williamson has been member of the General Assembly, we know of no objection to their being appointed

RC (DNA: RG 59, LAR); addresssed: "Thomas Jefferson President of the United States."

Newly elected congressman David Meriwether (MERRIWETHER) had taken his seat in the House of Representatives on 6 Dec. (*Biog. Dir. Cong.*).

NOTE OF YESTERDAY: a letter from TJ to Baldwin of 9 Dec. has not been found, nor is one recorded in SJL.

PERSONS RECOMMENDED: see James Jackson to TJ, 19 Nov. 1802.

From John Redman Coxe

SIR/ Philada. Decr. 10th. 1802

It is with great pleasure I transmit to Dr. Gantt, through you, a portion of Vaccine Infection: It is from a very perfect pock of the 9th day, but is not however quite so recent as I could wish, being nearly three weeks old.—I have been disappointed, in several late instances, of obtaining matter, from the inattention of Parents allowing the Pock to be rubbed off at the period I had anticipated obtaining a copious supply.—Having given away all the freshest Infection I had, I am under the necessity of forwarding this, which I hope will take effect; I shall nevertheless in a few days take the liberty to forward some, more recent, lest this should fail.—

I wish your observation relative to the necessity of distributing the infection was more attended to.—Each days experience proves its propriety;—especially as people are not yet satisfied of the propriety of vaccinating *at all* seasons of the Year.—

With great respect & esteem—I am Sir, Yr. much obliged humble servt. JOHN REDMAN COXE

RC (DLC); at foot of text: "His Excy. Ths. Jefferson"; endorsed by TJ as received 13 Dec. and so recorded in SJL.

To James Dinsmore

DEAR SIR Washington Dec. 10. 1802.

I some days ago wrote directions to mr Lilly for filling the Icehouse: but I forgot one previous requisite, which I must get you to have done. make a long square tube, open at both ends, 6. I. square within, & reaching from the bottom of the well of the icehouse up through the flat roof. the bottom of the tube to be notched thus  to let water run into it at bottom. then make a square bucket about 12. I. high, a little smaller than the internal square of the tube,

so as to run easily up & down inside of that. in the bottom of it make a hole, and nail a bit of stiff leather as a valve, so that when it goes down it may fill with water, & bring it up. put a handle to it like that of a bucket, but fixed, and to this handle tie a rope, by which it is to be worked, whenever it is found that there is water in the well.—I have said that the tube & bucket should be square. yet if they are easily made round, I imagine they may be made tighter, & to work better. in this do as you think best. it had better be fixed immediately and put in, before a season happens for getting ice, as it can not be put in afterwards. accept my best wishes. TH: JEFFERSON

RC (NBLiHi); at foot of text: "Mr. James Dinsmore."

This was the first winter in which TJ had the use of Monticello's ICEHOUSE, which had been built during the preceding spring. By contriving the TUBE to drain meltwater from the icehouse, TJ also helped alleviate the chronic shortage of water on the mountaintop (McLaughlin, *Jefferson and Monticello*, 296, 301-2; Vol. 37:86-7).

From Albert Gallatin

DEAR SIR Dec. 10th 1802

I enclose all the notes & corrections I can make on the appointment list. The office of the Secy. of State can always give more precise description of the offices—

Respectfully your obed. Servt. ALBERT GALLATIN

RC (DLC); addressed: "The President of the United States"; endorsed by TJ as letter of "11" Dec. from the Treasury Department and "Nominations" and so recorded in SJL at 11 Dec. Enclosures: TJ's appointment list has not been found; other enclosures printed below.

ENCLOSURES

I

List of Appointments, with Notes by Gallatin and Jefferson

August
2 Commissions 25— George Wentworth Surveyor for the District of Portsmouth and Inspector of the Revenue for the same.
do. Joseph Farley—Collector for the District of Waldoborough and Inspector of the Revenue for the same.
do. Joseph Wilson, Collector for the District of Marblehead and Inspector of the Revenue for the same—

28th. Abraham Bloodgood, Surveyor for the Port of Albany & Inspector
do. of the Revenue for the same—

S. *do.* Silas Crane, Collector for the District of Little Egg Harbour and Inspector of the Revenue for the same. *his commission as inspector dated 7th July*

S. *do.* John Heard, Collector for the District of Perth Amboy ☞ —The Commissn. for Inspector never issued.[1]

do. Alexander Scott, Collector for the District of Nanjemoy & Inspector of the Revenue for the same.

William White, Surveyor for the Port of East-River and Inspector of the Revenue for the same.

Thomas Archer, Collector of York Town and Inspector of the Revenue for the same.

John Easson, Surveyor of Smithfield and Inspector of the Revenue for the same—

S Benjamin Cheney, Surveyor of the Port of Beaufort ☞ The Commission for Inspector never issued—[but it was approved by Senate]

S James L. Shannonhouse, Surveyor of Newbiggen Creek—☞ The Commission for Inspector never issued. [approved by Senate]

John Rowan, Surveyor of Windsor & Inspector of the Revenue for the same—

Jehu Nichols, Surveyor of Tombstone and Inspector of the Revenue for the same.

Henry Tooley, Surveyor of Slades Creek & Inspector of the Revenue for the same—

Robert Anderson New, Collector of Louisville & Inspector of the Revenue for the same.

Griffin Greene, Collector for the District of Marietta & Inspector of the Revenue for the same.

Daniel Bissell, Collector for Massac & Inspector of the Revenue for the same.

S. The Commission of Silas Crane as collector, & those of John Heard, Benjamin Cheney & James L. Shannonhouse are entered as of 3d of May, and confirmed by the Senate

MS (DLC: TJ Papers, 128:22050); undated; in a clerk's hand; with emendations by Gallatin supplied in italics and two notes by TJ supplied in square brackets.

All of the Treasury Department appointments listed above required two COMMISSIONS, one as collector or surveyor of a port, the other as inspector of the revenue. The Senate had confirmed the nominations of CRANE and HEARD, as collectors only, and CHENEY and SHANNONHOUSE as both surveyors and inspectors during the final days of the last session of Congress. All four had received commissions as surveyor or collector, but, as Gallatin notes above, only Crane had received a commission as inspector and that was a temporary one (see Enclosure No. 2). In his personal, ongoing list of appointments, TJ had entered these four appointees at 14 May 1802, after Congress had adjourned. This perhaps explains why they are included above with recent interim nominations. On his personal list, TJ noted the appointment of Cheney and Shannonhouse as surveyors only, not inspectors (Vol. 33:679; Vol. 37:348-9, 406).

TJ submitted Crane's nomination as inspector of the revenue, along with the other interim appointments, to the Senate on 11 Jan., but he did not submit Heard's nomination as inspector until 2 Feb. (TJ to the Senate, 11 Jan. and 2 Feb. 1803).

[1] At this entry in the margin, Gallatin wrote and canceled "but only one issued."

II

Gallatin's Notes on Appointments, with Jefferson's Orders

The enclosed list contains all the alterations which seem necessary in the President's list, so far as relates to this department.

The errors in that list were

1st. That in every case where an officer is at once, either collector & surveyor of a port, and inspector of the revenue for the same port; he receives two distinct commissions, one as collector or surveyor, as the case may be, and the other as inspector—

2d. Silas Crane is inspector as well as collector of Little Egg harbour. *he was not nominated as such to the Senate, & therefore is now to be nominated.*
Alexr. Scott is collector as well as inspector for Nanjemoy
John Rowan is surveyor as well as inspector for Windsor
All three have received both commissions; only one was inserted in each case in the President's list

3d. John Heard collector Perth Amboy
Benjamin Cheney surveyor Beaufort. *he was approved by Senate as Surveyor & Inspector therefore the latter commn can issue.*
James L. Shannonhouse surveyor Newbiggen Creek. *approved by Senate as Surveyor & Inspector, therefore the commission may issue.*
ought each to have received a commission of inspector of the revenue for their respective port; that was neglected but should not be omitted in the intended nominations

4th. Daniel Bissel, & not Russel is collector & inspector of Massac

---

Jehu Nichols is the officer at Tombstone—D. Duncan was commissioned as inspector for Michillimakinac of which port he had previously been appointed collector

It is presumed that the Commissions of Silas Crane as collector, of John Heard as collector, of B. Cheney & J. L. Shannonhouse as surveyors, were all dated 3d May, & that their nominations had been approved by the Senate; but, at all events, all four must be nominated as inspectors of the revenue, as the three last have received no commission for that office & that of Crane as inspector was temporary being dated 7th July.

Henry Bogert surveyor of Albany had resigned

W. Watson collector Little Egg harbor was removed

Joseph Hiller collector Salem did resign, but Mr Lee's commission was dated several days preceeding the date of his resignation—he was certainly removed A.G.

MS (DLC: TJ Papers, 128:22049); undated; in Gallatin's hand, with orders by TJ supplied in italics.

PRESIDENT'S LIST: Gallatin probably refers to a draft of TJ's list of interim appointments presented to the Senate on 11 Jan. 1803 for confirmation. The draft has not been found.

For the appointment of David DUNCAN as inspector at Michilimackinac, see TJ to the Senate, 27 Apr. 1802. Duncan was appointed collector in the summer of 1801 (Vol. 34:573n).

To Ephraim Kirby

DEAR SIR Washington Dec. 10. 1802

Immediately on the reciept of your favor of Nov. 30. I directed a commission to issue to mr Judd under the bankrupt law. mr Granger had before spoken to me on the subject but added that you would write. I am extremely happy when I can recieve recommendations for office from characters in whom I have such entire confidence; as nothing chagrins me so much as when I have been led to an injudicious appointment. this happens sometimes, not from any intentions in our friends, but their inexact or partial estimate of the character they recommend. the other duties of administration are easy in comparison with this. the appointment to office, where one cannot see but with the eyes of others, is far the most difficult of my duties. these observations are meant as proofs of the satisfaction I recieve when *you* are kind enough to tell me who is, & who is not, fit for office.—we are now in the 5th. day of the session & have no senate, nor any prospect of one for several days, but 12. members being as yet arrived. consequently I have not yet made the accustomary communication to Congress, and probably shall not till the 14th. the acts of the last session have so fully rectified what was going amiss that the quiet train in which things are flowing now, offers little to communicate: nor do I foresee a single question which ought to excite party contention. still every question will excite it, because it is sufficient that we propose a measure, to produce opposition to it from the other party. a little of this is not amiss, as it keeps up a wholesome censorship on our conduct; and the excess to which it is still carried is daily likely to lessen, as the elections in every part of the union evince. I pray you to accept assurances of my great esteem & respect.

TH: JEFFERSON

RC (Herbert R. Strauss, Chicago, Illinois, 1953); at foot of text: "Ephraim Kirby esq." PrC (DLC).

The second SESSION of the Seventh Congress convened on 6 Dec. The House achieved a quorum on the 7th, but the

Senate did not have the 17 members necessary to conduct business until Monday, the 13th. It took the Senate another day to obtain a Republican majority to elect Stephen R. Bradley, president pro tempore (JHR, 4:243-4; JS, 3:241-3).

From Robert Smith

Nav Dep
10 Decr 1802

SIR!

By the accompanying package, you will perceive, that the statements called for by the House of Representatives, in their resolution of the 5th. May, have been duly prepared, so far as the resolution respects this Department. Before I forward these statements to the Speaker, I deem it proper to submit them to you.

I have the Honor to be, with the greatest respect & esteem Sir, your mo ob st

RT SMITH

RC (DLC); in a clerk's hand, signed by Smith; at foot of text: "President of the United States"; endorsed by TJ as received from the Navy Department on 10 Dec. and "report of exp. in Navy deptmt by ord. H.R." and so recorded in SJL. FC in Lb (DNA: RG 45, LSP). Enclosures subsequently printed as a 569-page document entitled *Documents Accompanying a Message from the President of the United States, with Sundry Statements of Expenditures; Containing Detailed Accounts of the Expenditures of Public Monies, by Naval Agents; from the 1st January, 1797, to 31st December, 1801, Contingencies of the Navy Department, and Copies of Contracts for Cannon, Timber, and Other Military and Naval Stores, during the Same Period* (Washington, D.C., 1803; Shaw-Shoemaker, No. 5285).

Smith's PACKAGE included a second letter to the president dated 10 Dec.: "The accompanying papers, exhibiting detailed accounts of the expenditure of all public Monies which have passed through the Navy Agents, and an account of monies drawn out of the Treasury for the contingencies of the Naval Establishment, from the Establishment of the Department to the 31 Decr. 1801: also copies of contracts made by this department for the purchase of Timber and Stores, and the amount of monies paid under such contracts, have been prepared in obedience to a Resolution of the Honorable The House of Representatives, of the 5 May 1802" (FC in Lb in DNA: RG 45, LSP, not recorded in SJL).

RESOLUTION OF THE 5TH. MAY: that is, the 3 May resolution of the House of Representatives, requesting an account of certain expenditures by the War and Navy Departments (JHR, 4:237; TJ to Gallatin, Dearborn, and Smith, 5 May 1802).

To John Steele

DEAR SIR Washington Dec. 10. 1802.

Your favor of Sep. 30. found me here on the 17th. of October; since which the duplicate has been also recieved. I deferred answering until a new appointment should be made. this is at length done, and mr Duval's commission issues to day, which is consequently the termination of yours, a substitute having been appointed to act till now. I am really sorry that circumstances different from what you expected when you left us, should have changed your determination, and disappointed us in the expected society of yourself & family here. I regret it the more as I had hoped your agency here might have contributed to reconcile the opponents of the present authorities, if any thing could reconcile them short of retaining exclusive possession of office. but instead of conciliation their bitterness is got to that excess which forbids further attention to them. although in a former letter I expressed to you without disguise the satisfaction which your conduct in office since my coming into the administration had given me, yet I repeat it here with pleasure; and testify to you that setting just value on the able services you rendered the public in the discharge of your official duties, I should have seen your continuance in office with real pleasure & satisfaction: and I pray you to be assured that in the state of retirement you have preferred, you have my prayers for your happiness and prosperity, and my esteem & high consideration.

TH: JEFFERSON

RC (Nc-Ar: John Steele Papers); addressed: "John Steele esquire Salisbury N.C."; franked and postmarked; endorsed by Steele. PrC (DLC).

SUBSTITUTE: David Rawn, principal clerk in the comptroller's office (enclosure listed at Steele to TJ, 30 Sep.; Gallatin to TJ, 1 Nov., second letter).

From Marten Wanscher

MESTER TOMS JEFFERSON Alaxander—Decembere 10th. 1802

if you please to Let me have 30 thirty Dallors i have Sat op Shop in qeen Strith

yours morst obeden Servent

MARTEN WANSCHER

RC (MHi); addressed: "Tomos Jefferson president City Washington"; franked; postmarked 13 Dec.; endorsed by TJ as received 14 Dec. and so recorded in SJL.

German immigrant Marten Wanscher of Alexandria did plaster work at Monticello from 1801 to 1802, and again for several months in 1804. TJ had made several payments to Wanscher since the completion of his first term of employment in April 1802, including most recently a $30 payment on 4 Dec. A letter from Wanscher to TJ dated 2 Dec. 1802, recorded in SJL as received on 3 Dec. with the notation "30. D.," has not been found (MB, 2:1053, 1073, 1087, 1126, 1137; Vol. 35:49-51, 95-6; Vol. 38:676; TJ to Wanscher, 30 Nov. 1803, 10 Apr. 1804; RS, 5:352).

To John Barnes

Th: Jefferson must trouble Mr. Barnes for 40. Dollars more in five dollar bills.
Dec. 11. 1802.

RC (MHi); addressed: "Mr. Barnes"; endorsed by Barnes as paid to Joseph Dougherty on 12 Dec.

In his financial memoranda on 11 Dec. 1802, TJ recorded the receipt of $40 from Barnes. Later the same day, TJ gave $20 each to Martha Jefferson Randolph and Mary Jefferson Eppes (MB, 2:1088).

From Justus Erich Bollmann

Dear Sir, Philada December 11th 1802

I flatter myself from the known Kindness and Liberality of Your Character that You will excuse my taking the liberty of addressing You, though I am scarcely known to You, for the Purpose of saying a few Words in behalf of Mr. Jams Yard my particular Friend. You are no Doubt informed that He is a Man of distinguished Talents and of a very cultivated Mind; that He has been extensively engaged in Business; that He has been unfortunate and that He was obliged about a Twelve Months ago to stop Payment, principally on Account of the bad Result of Shipments to the Spanish Main.—His Character has rather gained than be impaired by his Misfortunes since they became an Opportunity of evincing that He had Principles and also Strength enough to remain true to them though pressed by Difficulties. In the Month of May last He went to Spain for the Purpose of endeavouring to recover some of his confiscated Property in lima and He is still engaged in that Pursuit.

It has occurred to some of his Friends that He would be eminently qualified, as well from his Talents generally as His Acquaintance with the Spanish language, to be appointed One of the Commissioners to defend the Claims of American Citizens on the Spanish Government and a Petition for that Purpose is now circulating in the City which has already been signed by a considerable Proportion of its most respectable Inhabitants.

As the Petition itself can not well be sent off[1] from hence before Tuesday next I have ventured to give You this previous Intelligence of it for fear that its Purpose might be defeated by an earlier Appointment.

Knowing that You will yield to the Wishes of the Petitioners if You should deem the Appointment an expedient and proper One I have only to add that I am

with great Respect Dear Sir Your obt. hble. St.

J. ERICH BOLLMANN

RC (DNA: RG 59, LAR), endorsed by TJ as received 15 Dec. and "Yard James to be Commr. to Spain" and so recorded in SJL.

Justus Erich Bollmann (1769-1821) was a German physician who gained renown for an attempted rescue of Lafayette from imprisonment in Olmütz in 1794. Two years later he settled in Philadelphia, where in partnership with a brother he became a merchant. In addition, he invested in a steam-powered rolling mill and served for a time as the Danish vice-consul in Philadelphia. After the failure of his business in 1803, Bollmann shifted his entrepreneurial activities to New York, maintaining the esteem of the president, who offered him at different times a consulship in Saint Domingue and the factorship in Natchitoches, Louisiana. Bollmann also became an associate of Aaron Burr, who in 1806 made him a party to his plans to lead a military force into Mexico. Bollmann was arrested in New Orleans as one of the principal conspirators and shipped to Washington, where he related everything he knew about Burr's plans to TJ and James Madison. Refusing a pardon, Bollmann was saved by Burr's acquittal. He then moved back to Philadelphia, where he attempted to gain a foothold in several manufacturing enterprises and published pamphlets on banking and international commerce. After returning to Europe in 1814, he worked as a chemical manufacturer and at various times as an agent for Baring Brothers, the British banking concern (DAB, 2:421-2; Kline, *Burr*, 2:870-1, 970, 973, 976-7, 980-2; Fritz Redlich, "The Business Activities of Eric Bollmann," *Bulletin of the Business Historical Society*, 17 [1943], 81-91, 103-12; Exequator for Bollmann, 2 Aug. 1802, FC in DNA: RG 59, Exequators).

For the efforts of Philadelphia merchant James YARD to seek redress from Spanish authorities for the seizure of a valuable shipment of goods to Peru, see Madison, *Papers*, *Sec. of State Ser.*, 3:48-9.

[1] MS: "of."

From J. P. P. Derieux

MONSIEUR Hampton Ce 11. Decem. 1802.

Les bontés de pere dont vous avés eu la bonté de m'honorer depuis que je suis dans ce pays, jointes encore a la derniere preuve que vous venés de m'en donner, me pénétrent d'une trop grande reconnaissance pour que la crainte de vous importuner puisse L'emporter sur mon empressement a satis faire ce sentiment. J'ai reçu ce matin les 25. $. que vous avés chargé Mr. G Jefferson de me faire remettre; et comme cette somme m'etoit plus que Suffisante, j'en ay envoyé la moitié à ma malheureuse famille en Greenbrier, qui en avoit autant bésoin que moi. Permettés moi, Monsieur d'esperer, en m'éloignant de tout ce que j'ai de plus cher au monde, que vous Lui accorderés toujours votre protection, vous priant d'etre persuadé que la reconnaissance de ma famille pour tant de Bontés ne finira qu'avec leur existance.

Le Pilote est actuellement a Bord et n'attend plus que Le premier bon vent pour nous mettre en Mer.

J'ai L'honneur d'être dans les sentiments les plus respectueux et La reconnaissance La plus étendue.

Monsieur Votre trés humble et trés obeissant Serviteur

P. Derieux

EDITORS' TRANSLATION

Sir — Hampton, 11 Dec. 1802

The fatherly kindnesses you have bestowed on me since my arrival in this country, followed by this latest gesture fill me with such deep gratitude that the fear of disturbing you cannot outweigh my eagerness to express my feelings. This morning I received the 25 dollars you entrusted to Mr. G. Jefferson for me, and since the sum was more than sufficient, I sent half to my unfortunate family in Greenbrier, whose need is as great as mine. As I sail away from those who are dearest to me in the world, allow me, Sir, to hope that you will always protect them and to assure you that my family's gratitude for so much goodness will last as long as they live.

The ship's captain is now on board and merely awaits the first good wind to set sail.

I have the honor of feeling the deepest respects and the most lasting gratitude.

I am your most humble and obedient servant. P. Derieux

RC (DLC); endorsed by TJ as received 21 Dec. and so recorded in SJL.

To John Wayles Eppes

Dear Sir — Washington Dec. 11. 1802.

As it gives room for federal clamour for me ever to say any thing about an election, what I am now to say is confidential. Genl. Mason arrived here yesterday. I spoke to him on the subject of the resignation which he had meditated. he expressed great anxiety to withdraw, but finally said that if re-elected he would serve again. you can therefore affirm as a thing known to you through a single hand that he has expressed that determination: but not saying that I am the person communicating it. he promised me to write on the subject to Colo. Monroe; but there is a possibility he may be gone. it would be a real loss were he to withdraw from the Senate as yet. he has some talents peculiar & necessary. we have not a Senate yet, nor expect one till the 13th. in which case the message will be delivered on the 14th. Maria & Francis are well. Martha's cold a great deal better, indeed almost gone.—the shutting up the port of N. Orleans, which gave alarm at first, turns out to have been an unauthorised freak of the Intendant, which will probably be corrected before any inconvenience arises from it. health & affectionate attachment. TH: JEFFERSON

RC (Jefferson National Expansion Memorial Association, St. Louis, 1946); addressed: "John W. Eppes now at Richmond"; franked and postmarked.

SUBJECT OF THE RESIGNATION: TJ had expressed concern about Stevens Thomson Mason's contemplated departure from the Senate (TJ to Mason, 3 Sep. 1802).

On 10 Dec., Mason wrote to James MONROE urging him to run in his place in the upcoming Senate election in Virginia. There is no evidence that Mason later wrote Monroe indicating that he would run again (Preston, *Catalogue*, 1:139).

To James Monroe

TH:J. TO COLO: MONROE Washington Dec. 11. 1802.

S. T. Mason arrived here yesterday. I had immediately a conversation with him on the resignation he had meditated. he finally promised to serve again if reelected, and that he would[1] write to you to say so for him. lest he should delay it, I drop you this line, but you must not name me as the channel because of the ground it furnishes our enemies for clamour. accept assurances of my constant & affectionate esteem.

RC (NN); addressed: "Governor Monroe Richmond"; franked and postmarked; endorsed. PrC (DLC); endorsed by TJ in ink on verso.

[1] TJ here canceled "author."

From S. & S. Myers

SIR Richmond Decr: 11. 1802

With your Esteem'd favor of the 7 Curt. we received your Draft at sight on Messrs. Gibson & Jefferson for One Hundred and fifty Dollars. which is to the Credit of Mr Samuel Dyer of Albemarle

Much obliged by your attention, We have the Honor to be with the highest respect

Sir Your mo ob Serts S. & S. MYERS

RC (MHi); at head of text: "Thomas Jefferson Esquire"; endorsed by TJ as received 16 Dec. and so recorded in SJL but as a letter of 14 Dec.

From Richard Claiborne

Sir Capitol Hill, 12. Decr. 1802.

In justice to the favor you rendered me towards prosecuting my invention for propelling boats, I take occasion to inform you, that, after deliberate and correct experiments—(done however with imperfect works, and yet intended to be improved, and altered, even as to *mode*) I find the effect by hand, with the single stroke only, to justify the expected utility of the highest power that can be applied. I have produced a simple and sufficient resistance, and it only requires an equable and adequate force to render the invention publicly useful. The steam engine is my aim—and tho' it has been objected to as applied to navigation, upon the principle of Boulton and Watts's engine, as racking the vessel, yet that very objection may be entitled to a credit when fairly considered. I rather suppose that the failures heretofore have arisen from the modes of applying that power rather than that the power should be condemned. Surely Force is the primary object, and as surely can the strength of works be created sufficiently to withstand injury from that power.—Besides—my invention possesses the advantage of the alternate or successive resistance, so as to counteract the shock occasioned by the vacuum in the Engine, and perhaps only a partial resistance to meet with.—Be it however as it may, as regards the piston engine, I hope that some late inventions in steam, and others that are in progress to be matured, shortly, will produce that easy flow of power so much to be desired.—By the single stroke I have produced from 5 Miles to 5 and a half per hour, according to wind and weather and other circumstances—and by the adoption of an equable and durable force, allowing for additional resistance arising from increased velocity (if it is to be admitted in this case) I make up my mind that I can go 9 miles per hour, if not more, which will be sufficient to surmount the most of our currents to advantage. Until I can get a steam Engine to work, I shall rest my experiments.

I should do injustice to Doctor Thornton were I not to express a firm hope that he will succeed in a late idea he has hit upon with respect to steam.

I am Sir, with gratitude and respect, Your most obedient and humble Servant

R Claiborne

RC (DLC); at foot of text: "The President of the United States"; endorsed by TJ as received 13 Dec. and so recorded in SJL.

For Claiborne's invention, see Vol. 38:271-2.

From George Rogers Clark

Sir — Falls of Ohio 12th. December 1802

I latterly had the pleasure of the perruseal of a letter from the Secretary of War to my brother on the Subject of the post of Fort Jefferson on the Mississippi. his Answer to that letter completely discribed the place—A Military post & Tradeing Town there, must be Obvious to every man of Observation that is acquainted with the Geography of the Countrey—I was the more pleased as I had Contemplated the importance of that spot from my earliest acquaintance with the Western Countrey.

When I was ordered fix the garrison at or near the mouth of the Ohio in the year 1780 I lay three weeks in the point, and explored the banks of the river and Countrey before I fixed on the spot to build a Fort—and if my Instructions had not have been to place the Garrison South of the Ohio I certainly should have raised a Fortress in the point. I marked the ground the annual inundations flooded, it is about *five* feet, and from that to *seven* feet is the depth of the water that Covers this butifull Tract of bottom, which may be raised for a City of any Size, by the earth thrown out of the Canals, cut through the City and those Canals may be kept pure by turning the Cash River throgh them—I thus drew the plan and have been improveing on it frequently to the present time—what caused me to view this ground with more attention was that the Spanish shore opposit so high that a small expence, would free two or three hundred Acres of Land.

This circumstance induced me to think that it would be necessary for us, at least to have a fortress in this point as a Key to the enterance of the Ohio—Those were my Ideas while on the ground I segest to you, Sir, if worthey your attention, any further information, and the best perhaps that can be Obtained of that Country, may be got from my brother William, who is now settled at Clarksville in the Indiana Territory—I have long since laid asside all Idea of Public affairs, by bad fortune, and ill health I have become incapable of persueing those enterpriseing & active persuits which I have been fond of from my youth—but I will with the greatest pleasure give my bro: William every information in my power, on this, or any other point which may be of Service to your Administration. he is well quallified almost for any business—If it should be in your power to Confur on him any post of Honor and profit, in this Countrey in which we live, it will exceedingly gratify me—I seem to have a right to expect such a gratification when asked for—but what will greatly highten it is, that I am sure it gives you pleasure to have it in your power to do me a service.

With the greatest assureance of your prosperity I have the honor to be your ever sincere G R CLARK

NB Mr. Hurst the gentleman whome will hand you this letter is a young Lawyer from Vincennes, a Man of integrity and a good republican whom I beg leave to recommend to you. GRC

RC (DLC); at foot of text: "Thomas Jefferson President of the United States"; endorsed by TJ as received 7 Jan. 1803 and so recorded in SJL.

Albemarle County native George Rogers Clark (1752-1818) gained lasting fame from his military achievements during the American Revolution, which secured Kentucky and the northwestern territories for the fledgling United States. TJ corresponded with him frequently during his governorship and held his "enterprizing and energetic genius" in high esteem. In 1783, TJ asked if Clark would be interested in leading an expedition to explore the lands between the Mississippi River and California but Clark declined, citing his financial situation. Following the war, Clark settled at Clarksville on the Ohio River opposite Louisville, where financial reverses and alcoholism left him destitute. It was his younger brother, William Clark, who joined Meriwether Lewis in 1803 for TJ's long-sought western expedition (ANB; Vol. 3:292; Vol. 6:371; Vol. 15:609-10; Vol. 19:521).

LETTER FROM THE SECRETARY OF WAR: in a 6 July 1802 letter to William Clark, Henry Dearborn wrote that it was the "desire of the President" that Clark provide a description of "the shore of the Mississippi at or near where your Brother General Clark erected a Fort in the course of our Revolutionary War." Clark had inspected the site in 1795 and took notes of the visit. Dearborn asked Clark "to be as particular as you can from recollection" as to the fort's distance below the mouth of the Ohio River and above the "Yellow or Iron Bank," the composition and elevation of the land three or four miles inland from the Mississippi, the location of nearby streams or springs, and the composition of the shore and flats. Clark was also to offer opinions on the healthiness of the site and its potential for settlement and commerce, and to compare the general healthiness of the eastern bank of the Mississippi from the mouth of the Ohio and the yellow or iron bank "with the several posts, which have lately been occupied by our troops near the mouth of the Ohio" (DNA: RG 107, MLS; Jackson, *Lewis and Clark*, 8n; Missouri Historical Society, *Bulletin*, 25 [1969], 283).

Named in TJ's honor, FORT JEFFERSON was located on the eastern shore of the Mississippi River about five miles south from the mouth of the Ohio at a site chosen by George Rogers Clark. Built in 1780, the fort was abandoned the following year due to Indian attacks, desertions, and supply difficulties. Meriwether Lewis and William Clark visited the site in November 1803 (Gary E. Moulton, ed., *Journals of the Lewis & Clark Expedition*, 13 vols. [Lincoln, Neb., 1983-2001], 2:93-4; Vol. 3:278-9, 354-5; Vol. 4:188, 319-21).

Vincennes attorney and Virginia native Henry HURST was clerk of the Indiana Territory's general court and a protégé of William Henry Harrison. He traveled to Washington in an unsuccessful attempt to secure appointment to the territorial judgeship vacated by the death of William Clarke, securing additional recommendations from Harry Innes and Benjamin Sebastian (Jackson, *Lewis and Clark*, 8n; Andrew R. L. Cayton, *Frontier Indiana* [Bloomington, 1996], 232-3, 244; Innes to TJ, 13 Dec. 1802).

To Albert Gallatin

TH:J TO MR GALLATIN Dec. 12. 1802.

Benjamin Cheney was approved by the Senate both as Surveyor & Inspector

James L. Shannonhouse was approved by them also both as Surveyor & Inspector.

therefore their commissions as Inspectors might have issued & may now.

Thomas Worthington was nominated to the Senate at the last session as Supervisor of the Northwestern district, & so approved by them. on recurring to mr Gallatin's note of Apr. 24. I find he named him to me as *Supervisor.* on this the nomination was grounded. yet the Commission I signed was, if I noted it right, as *Surveyor.* if the commission was wrong we can correct it. if the nomination was wrong, a new one must be made to the Senate.

The list preparing for the Senate is rectified in every other part agreeably to mr Gallatin's corrections. it will await his information as to Worthington. TH:J.

RC (NHi: Gallatin Papers); addressed: "Mr. Gallatin"; endorsed.

Worthington was correctly nominated as SUPERVISOR for the collection of internal revenues in the Northwest Territory, after Congress approved a salary for the position. In his ongoing list of appointments, TJ entered Worthington as "Supervisor in the N.W. district. new" (Vol. 33:679; Vol. 36:204; Vol. 37:211, 323-4, 349).

GALLATIN'S CORRECTIONS: see Gallatin to TJ, 10 Dec., and enclosures.

From William Jones

Philada. 12th. Decemr 1802

DEAR SIR Wm. Jones

Mr Guy Bryan Merchant of this City has made me acquainted with his intention of soliciting for his nephew Mr Morrison the appointment of Collector at Massac in the Indiana Territory. My particular respect for and knowledge of the character and circumstances of Mr. Bryan excite a wish that he may succeed if the office shall be vacant. Knowing as I do the scrupulous delicacy and integrity of Mr Bryan you may be assured he would not interest himself for a person who was not qualified by his capacity and principles and the guaranty of Mr Bryan will afford ample security for the fidelity of the officer

In the traits of Mr Bryan's character there is also to be found that of as uniform and decided a Republican as any in this City.

I expected ere this to have paid my personal respects, and to have had the pleasure of sincerely congratulating you on the enviable situation of our happy country, and the unequivocal approbation of its Administration, evinced in the late Elections.

I trust however the pleasure I anticipated will not be delayed longer than the latter part of this month when I expect to attend my duty in Congress. In the interem I remain

Dear Sir With the highest regard and respect yours—

WM JONES

RC (NHi: Gallatin Papers); at foot of text: "The President of the United States"; endorsed by TJ as received 15 Dec. and "Morrison to be Collector at Massac" and so recorded in SJL; also endorsed by TJ: "qu. 1. is the place vacant? 2. is Morrison a republican? 3. is he a resident within the territory?"

GUY BRYAN and his nephew, William MORRISON, were partners in a leading western mercantile operation, maintaining stores at Kaskaskia and Cahokia and trading in produce, lead, and peltry. In addition to their mercantile endeavors, in 1802 Bryan and Morrison received a contract to carry the U.S. mail from Vincennes to Kaskaskia and Cahokia. Morrison did not receive the Massac appointment, which had already gone to Daniel Bissell (Bryan to Albert Gallatin, 14 Dec. 1802, in NHi: Gallatin Papers; *Terr. Papers*, 7:80; John Leslie Tevebaugh, "Merchant on the Western Frontier: William Morrison of Kaskaskia, 1790-1837" [Ph.D. diss., University of Illinois, 1962]; Gallatin to TJ, 10 Dec. 1802).

From Charles Willson Peale

DEAR SIR Museum Decr. 12. 1802.

Mr. Hunter is returned from Kentucky and tells me that the account of the upper part of the Skull of the Mammoth being found at Barry's Salt lick in Kentucky, is altogather a fabrication, no such bone found there—A New Englander detailed to me the same account except the difference of 2 pounds of the weight, as was afterwards published in a Virginia paper.

I am infinitely obliged to you for the Interest you take to procure for me the bones found near the sweet springs, which I flatter myself will throw more light on the structure of the Megalonyx—The Skeleton belonging to the King of Spain, is certainly far less complete than my Skeleton of the Mammoth—altho' this is deficient in two very essential parts, the Skull & ends of the toes—I suspect my Skeleton is more complete than you have immagined by the accounts you have received—I will not cease my exertions to make it perfect, but I realy find amongst the numbers of Persons I have conversed with, very few that have any critical knowledge of the bones of such Animals, & I have only the chance of geting the few that is realy wanting, by collecting in a mass all I can procure of those dug up at different places—or by going myself again to New York and exploring one other spot from which two Ribs only have been taken.

I was extremely fortunate in getting of one Animal so many bones—It is only in difficult deep morasses that any sound bones can be had, I have gained much experience, and paid for it, yet I do not regret the labour or expence for the knowledge acquired. It is a part of the foundation of an Institution which I flatter myself will in the issue be an honour to my Country.

I have not yet heard the success of my Sons since they have opened their Exhibition—Rembrandt writes me that he is publishing a Pamphlet in which he describes the essential differences between the Mammoth & Elephant, if successful in this, then another Edition with several hansome plates.

I am with much respect your Obliged friend C W Peale

RC (DLC); endorsed by TJ as received 16 Dec. and so recorded in SJL. Dft (Lb in PPAmP: Peale-Sellers Papers).

Regarding the rumor of the skull of a MAMMOTH in Kentucky and the report of bones of the MEGALONYX in Virginia, see Peale's letter of 28 Oct.

The SKELETON BELONGING TO THE KING OF SPAIN was of a South American megatherium, which like the megalonyx was a prehistoric ground sloth (Vol. 36:548-9).

See Vol. 37:423 and Vol. 38:591-3 for the EXHIBITION of a mastodon skeleton in London by his sons Rembrandt and Rubens. Rembrandt Peale's tract on DIFFERENCES between the heads of mammoths and elephants appeared in the *Philosophical Magazine* (Peale, *Papers*, v. 2, pt. 1:471n).

From Jonathan Williams

Sir, West Point 12th. Decr. 1802.

The Gentlemen composing the Corps of Engineers thinking that, besides the Duties prescribed to them, as such, it would be the most acceptable Service they could at present render to their Country to collect and preserve, as far as possible, the military Science which must still exist, in a different State, among the Veterans of our revolutionary Contest, and those of our fellow Citizens who have gathered scientific Fruits in the Course of their Travels have formed a Society for the Purpose of establishing and perpetuating a Repository, as well for such Knowledge as may be furnished by past Experience, as for what our Citizens in any Walk of Life may in future acquire.

They feel themselves assured, Sir, that however feeble the Attempt may appear in this infant State of their own Institution, yet, to a Character distinguished in the Republic of Science, this very Circumstance will be an additional Inducement to honour it with the fostering Aid of your Countenance and Protection.

Before they presumed to enroll your Name among the Members of the Society, it was thought decorous to obtain (through their President) an Intimation of your Disposition so to honour them; and it would highly add to their Sense of this Honour, if you would permit them to consider the President of the United States as their perpetual Patron.

It would be gratifying to the Society if their Constitution could be made Part of an Act of Incorporation, with such additional Clauses as are incidental to, and requisite for, all corporate Bodies; but although the President of the Society has an implied Power to make such an Application to Congress, yet he has conceived it proper to desist, until another Year shall have added something to the Usefulness of the Institution, and given it, from that Cause, a better Claim to Success; unless, in the Judgment of those more versed in such Matters, it should be thought expedient to make the Attempt now.

An Answer, to meet me in Philadelphia, will be highly gratifying.

With perfect Consideration I have the Honour to be, Sir, Very respectfully Your most obedient and Very humble Servant,

Jona. Williams
President of the United States
Military Philosophical Society

RC (DLC); at foot of text: "Thomas Jefferson President of the United States"; endorsed by TJ as received 21 Dec. and so recorded in SJL. Enclosure: "Constitution of the United States Military Philosophical Society Established at West Point 1802," containing nine preliminary articles unanimously approved at a meeting of the Corps of Engineers held on 12 Nov. 1802, and 11 chapters delineated at a later meeting, outlining the process for membership and meetings, election and duties of officers, proceedings on literary performances, and funds for the society (MS in same; in Williams's hand and signed by him "True Copy from the Record").

Williams designed the United States Military Philosophical society, whose motto was "Scientia in Bello Pax" (science in war is the guarantee of peace), to supplement the educational and scientific mission of the Corps of Engineers and the military academy at West Point. The society promoted military science among the rank and file by sponsoring several publications, establishing a library and museum for military art, rewarding invention, studying natural philosophy and mathematical sciences, and fostering internal improvements, commerce, and industry (Arthur P. Wade, "A Military Offspring of the American Philosophical Society," *Military Affairs*, 38 [1974], 103-7; Sidney Forman, "The United States Military Philosophical Society, 1802-1813," wmq, 3d ser., 2 [1945], 273-85; Jonathan Williams to TJ, 30 June 1805).

From John Wayles Eppes

DEAR SIR, Richmond Dec: 13th. 1802.

Nothing of importance had occured since the meeting of the Legislature, until Saturday last—On that we elected Mr. Page Governor by a general vote no other person being nominated as his opponent. on the same we replaced three members of the Executive council, two of whom to wit Wood & White where removed by joint vote of the two houses & the third to wit Pendleton by resignation—Their vacancies are filled by George Hay, Brokenbough, & Grimes—all republicans & men of Talents.

So far as we have had an opportunity of Judging of the strength the feds it is in number about the same as in the last Legislature but diminished both in Tone & Talent—

A very intemperate Resolution has been offered to our house on the licentiousness of the Federal Presses by Colo. Smith our former Speaker—200 copies of it to our great mortification are ordered to be printed for the use of the members—It will of course go to the world in a gurl extremely exceptionable in every point of view & in which it certainly will not finally pass the legislature—

The session will I think be short and unimportant—

Accept for your health My warm wishes Yours Sincerely

JNO: W: EPPES

RC (MHi); endorsed by TJ as received 17 Dec. and so recorded in SJL.

On 11 Dec., the Virginia General Assembly elected John Page of Rosewell as GOVERNOR to succeed Monroe. By joint ballot, the assembly also named to the EXECUTIVE COUNCIL George Hay in place of John Pendleton, William Brockenbrough in place of John W. White, and Philip Grymes in place of James Wood (*Journal of the House of Delegates of the Commonwealth of Virginia*, Dec. 1802-Jan. 1803, 10).

Larkin Smith introduced in the House of Delegates on 10 Dec. a RESOLUTION responding to the "extreme licentiousness of the Federal Editors in their abuse of the President." Because any legal restraint of the press would be unconstitutional, he proposed "That the present Legislature, as a component part of the community, declare their entire disapprobation, of the gross, indecent, and unprincipled attacks made on the character of the President of the United States, and so fully and confidently are they assured of the uprightness, and purity of his motives, as well as a sincere and firm belief that his official duties have been discharged in such a manner as to promote the real interest, happiness and independence of their Country; that they are induced to give their unequivocal and decided approbation to every part of his conduct, as far as it has come within their knowledge, and they feel a pleasurable duty in declaring, that there is no man in America, who deserves more of the confidence and support of the People of the United States, than the enlightened, philosophic, benevolent, and patriotic Republican, THOMAS JEFFERSON." The House directed the resolution to be forwarded to the Senate and ordered the immediate printing of 250 copies (same, 9).

From Harry Innes

SIR, Kentucky Frankfort Decr 13th 1802

The office of Cheif Judge in the Indiana Territory being vacated by the death of Mr. Wm Clarke I take the liberty of soliciting the appointment, or more properly speaking your nomination in favor of James Blair Esqr. of this town.

Mr. Blair has officiated for several years in this State as Atto. General, which he is inclined to abandon on account of the too arduous duties imposed on the person holding that office by our legislature.

Mr. Blair's moral rectitude is unexceptionable, & he is well respected by those who have the pleasure of being acquainted with him.

I have lived a neighbour to Mr. Blair for five or six years, during which period he has always espoused the cause of republicanism.

With this Sketch of Mr. Blairs general character, he is recommended to your attention on the present occasion by him who is anxious for your happiness and prosperity, in both your public & private life & who has the honor to be with great respect & esteem

your mo. ob. Servt HARRY INNES

RC (DNA: RG 59, LAR); endorsed by TJ as received 4 Jan. 1803 and "James Blair to be Judge of Indiana" and so recorded in SJL.

JAMES BLAIR migrated from Virginia to Kentucky and had served as attorney general of the state since 1796 (*Register of the Kentucky State Historical Society*, 14 [1916], 37-8). He also secured recommendations from Benjamin Howard, Joseph Crockett, and Humphrey Marshall in his unsuccessful bid for the Indiana judgeship (Howard to St. George Tucker, 6 Dec. 1802, probably enclosed in Tucker to TJ, Williamsburg, 13 Jan. 1803, which is recorded in SJL as received 18 Jan. with the notation "Blair to be judge Indiana," but has not been found; Crockett to James Madison, 9 Dec. 1802, endorsed by TJ: "Blair James of Kentucky to be judge Indiana"; Marshall to Madison, 16 May 1803, endorsed by TJ: "Blair James to be judge of Indiana. v. Davies"; all in DNA: RG 59, LAR).

Innes also recommended Vincennes attorney Henry Hurst for the vacant Indiana judgeship. Writing James Madison on 14 Dec., Innes stated that Hurst was clerk of the territory's superior court and son-in-law to Judge Benjamin Sebastian of Kentucky. Innes has known Hurst for more than seven years and asserts that his "moral rectitude, (to my knowledge) has never been impeached." Citing his recommendation to the president of James Blair for the same office, Innes assures Madison that "neither that nor this letter is to be considered as giving by me a decided preference, on the contrary, merely containing a statement of character, as far as my knowledge extends" (DNA: RG 59, LAR; endorsed by TJ: "Innes Harry to mr Madison. Hurst to be judge Indiana"). His letter to Madison also enclosed a recommendation from Sebastian, dated 10 Dec., in which the Kentucky jurist describes Hurst as "unstained" by any vice, "inflexibly honest," and "rigidly temperate." In addition to his legal acumen, Hurst's politics "are purely republican, and he is firmly attached to the present administration" (same; endorsed by TJ: "Hurst to be judge of Indiana").

From George Jefferson

Dear Sir Richmond 13th. Decr. 1802

Your favor of the 7th. to G. & J. inclosing 350$ came duly to hand; the receipt of which from pure inattention *in myself*, was not in course acknowledged: it has been in part, and shall be in full, applied as you direct.

I am Dear Sir Your Very humble servt. Geo. Jefferson

RC (MHi); at foot of text: "Thos. Jefferson esqr."; endorsed by TJ as received 17 Dec. and so recorded in SJL.

To Levi Lincoln

Th: Jefferson to mr Lincoln. Dec. 13. 1802.

Will you be so good as to satisfy yourself and advise me on the following persons?

Samuel Whittermore Surveyor & Inspector of Gloster to be removed and Zachariah Stevens to be put in his place. he is recommended by Capt Crowninshield.

Nath. F. Fosdick Collector of Portland to be removed, and who to be put in his place?

Would it do good or harm at Boston for mr Bradford the marshal of Massachusets to be *indirectly* informed that the neutrality of his own conduct in the late election (which is all that is desired) is known and approved at Washington; but that his deputies, or some of them have been active in support of that party whose object is to overturn the present order of things? that it will not be permitted that the influence of the National offices shall be used to oppose the National will; & that it is expected from his candor that he will immediately remove such deputies as have done any thing more than give their own vote in support of the opposition at the late election, & appoint others who concur in sentiment with the government.

health & friendly salutations.

What sort of a lawyer is Genl. Lyman. there is a vacancy in Indiana.

PrC (DLC).

In December 1796, Washington appointed Samuel BRADFORD, a deputy marshal, "firm federalist," and "gentleman of education," marshal of the Massachusetts district. Adams renominated him for another four-year term in December 1800. He remained in office until the expiration of his second term, on 22 Dec. 1804 (JEP, 1:216, 217, 362, 476; Washington, *Papers, Pres. Ser.*, 8:424n; Madison, *Papers, Sec. of State Ser.*, 8:342-3).

For TJ's efforts to find a suitable position for William LYMAN, see Henry Dearborn to TJ, [12 July 1802].

From Levi Lincoln

Sir. Washington Decr 13th 1802.

It is to be feared, that I shall be too troublesome. But deeming it of importance tht. the feelings, spirit, and measures of the people, especially at the *head quarters of opposition principles*, should be seasonably and correctly known, I am induced to ask your perusal of the inclosed. I should have personally waited on you, but from an idea, that at the present time, it would have been impossible to have found you alone, and possessed of a leisure moment. The signature of the writer alluded to, is concealed, for a reason which will appear satisfactory on a future disclosure—

Permit me to add, as a supplement to the inclosed, & a partial confirmation thereof, that Mr. Story is considered, as among the first of his age, in point of ability & sound principles. That it was his, and a few others, with Carlton's, day & night, exertions, to arrest error & falshood, & to establish the truth, which defeated federalism in their late election. Besides a select meeting of leading characters from all parts of their district, personal private interviews with influential individuals, & a well written circular letter, sent to every considerable republican in the district. They caused for some time before the election, as many of Carlton's papers edited for the purpose to be printed and dispersed in every town in the district, free of expence, as there were individuals, who could be induced to take & read them. It had the desired effect. Similar exertions would have been successful every where—This, generally was & is known, especially to the judges of our respective courts—Their implacable hatred to the new order of things, to the administration, & to its friends, has & will continue to shew itself in a persecution of all who dare to be active. Judge Sewall at the Marblehead meeting, for the choice of the representative, descended to a most virulent invective against the administration. With it, the judges of our Courts, or at least some of them have placed themselves in a state of war. A favorite object, undoubtedly is, in the course of hostilities, to mark & bear down, every obnoxious individual, who can be reached.

Carlton is already seised. Story frowned upon, watched, & sought, as a desirable victim. He is considered as formidable, and if he can be depressed or driven from his post, an important victory will be gained. By Carlton's prosecution, it is meant, not only to humble him and his paper, but to damp the ardor, & render vapid & ineffective the other papers engaged in the support of Govt. There can be but little doubt, if times shall not be very much altered, before the trial, of his conviction. It will be easy, by sending the veniries for 30 jurors to federal towns, & by a second selection of twelve from these 30, to obtain one pannel of full blooded filtrated federalists and from them, the political verdict—But little can be expected from proceedings, where the unceasing variety of direct and virulent libels, against the general Govt. and every person connected with it yielding it support, are passed by, to notice a single query, implicating with suspicion, a federal individual. The fact is, opposition arrogance claims for itself, an inviobility of character, while it indulges to a most intolerable and wanton outrage on the reputations of its opponents. It will be perceived, that my wishes are, that you would consider the propriety of making Story the naval officer. Altho, I do not believe, that Pickman's conduct, has been so exceptionable as either Fosdick or Whettemore's, yet I am persuaded, that the appointment of Story, would be more promotive of the general good than the removal of them both—This kind of reprisal, on state violence will check the evil and give firmness to the friends of the Union—I fear if when violently pushed by the officers of particular states, on account of their attachment to the national Govt. if they do not receive some marked support & countenance from it, they will be born down, lose their spirits, & remit of their exertions—I think for myself, considering the measures & clamors of the federalists, that removals are become one of the most defensible measures of the present administration—

I am not personally acquainted with Mr Stevens but have frequently heard him mentioned as a respectable character, & have no doubt, of his making a good officer—

A Mr Boyd who is expected from sea every hour meets my judgment, the most agreeably of any one, I have heard mentioned, as a successor to Fosdick. He also is personally unknown to me. But beleive from information his appointment would give satisfaction, unless he has apostatized since he left this country—[1]

Mr Lyman read law late in life, and I beleive never regularly studied and practiced it—was, I think, never admitted to the bar; but, for a short time, did small business, appearing under special powers—I have a good opinion of his natural abilities & general information, and also of his political merit, but am satisfied he would not be equal to fill the place you mention, & that it would not be useful to him, or the Govt, to place him there—

On the last subject, I have my difficulties. The federalists in Boston & its neighbourhood, are intrenched in pride, power, wealth, and obstinate malignity to the present administration, and will impute every thing to it, which they can in any way distort & pervert to its injury. They can only be prostrated by a superior force. The Marshall's duty calls him into various parts of the Country, places him with the Court in their Sessions, he has the custody of the juries in their deliberations, and some times, on trials of great political expectation, selects talesmen from a crowd brought into the court for the purpose. From the two first circumstances, the beneficial influence of a Marshal of intelligence, independance and attachment to the Govt. would be very great; in the two last, an important security for justice & impartiality, especially if their should be an attempt to carry the federal common law doctrines into execution—I know of no such character, at the present moment, nor do I beleive it best, at present, to remove Bradford—But if opposition will continue its outrage, it may become necessary to seek such a character for the Marshal's office. By an extract from a thanksgiving sermon in the last centinel, which may be worth your perusal, we have a specimen of the spirit which Govt. has to contend with. A negative merit, or mere inaction, in its officers, will, I fear, be unequal to the conflict, A private citizen, much more an officer, ought to endeavour to check the abuse, & correct the misrepresentations which he is constantly hearing against the Govt—Ought the forbearing to influence the suffrages of others, tho, deserving of approbation, give to such a neutral officer any security for his being continued? If Bradford should remove his deputies, in pursuance of an indirect intimation from authority, would it not be considered as the compliance with a condition, which would render himself irremovable, however he might be deficient in his general duty to support the Govt.? ought not a difference to be taken betwixt the priviledge, of not voting, or voting for whom one pleases, in the choice of a representative, & the elective officers of Govt., & the subsequent duty, in reference to supporting or withholding that support from the Govt. which is the result of such a priviledge or choice?

Besides I am apprehensive if the change of the deputies should be made, & understood to be made, in compliance with a communicated sentiment of the administration, federal perversness would make every thing of it, but the right one, and would labour to load the measure with odium, for the sake of imputing it to the executive—

I have insensibly been betrayed into length in stating the ideas which have occured on this subject. and am inclined to think altho it is desirable, that *principal* officers should know that they are considered by Govt. as responsible for the political conduct of their *deputies*, it will be safest to leave them to collect this information from the measures of the administration, or from news paper paragraphs, and anonymous defences of removals, on the grounds of hostility to the Govt. in proof of which, the employing & continuing in office deputies, who unduly interfere in elections, may be adduced—

Permit me to offer the strong impressions on my mind, of the great support Govt would derive from able, spirited, & well disposed officers, in such bitter places, as Boston, Salem & Portland as an apology for the trouble, I now give you—

I am Sir with high esteem most respectfully your obt Svt

LEVI LINCOLN

RC (DNA: RG 59, LAR); at head of text: "President of the US"; with one comment by TJ in the margin (see note 1 below); endorsed by TJ as received 15 Dec. and so recorded in SJL; also endorsed by TJ: "Bradford Storer Boyd Lyman." Enclosure: probably Jacob Crowninshield to Levi Lincoln, Salem, 26 Nov., urging, out of a "sense of public duty," further removals in Essex County; not satisfied with "pouring out the most foul mouth'd abuse against the President" and scandalous invectives against the Treasury secretary and attorney general, the Essex Federalists have brought suit against William Carlton, the editor of the *Salem Register*, with the grand jury presenting a bill against him for the libel of Timothy Pickering, obliging the editor to give bonds, draining him of all his cash; he urges the appointment of Joseph Story, one of a very few Republican lawyers in Massachusetts, as naval officer at Salem in place of William Pickman; although Story received a commission as bankruptcy commissioner, "there does not two failures happen in a year in this Country, so that no pecuniary advantage can be derived from it"; unless Story receives an appointment that allows him to continue in his profession, it is feared he will go to one of the southern states; it is important for the Republican cause that he remain in Massachusetts; his political writings "have rendered the most essential service to the Government" and knowing this, Federalists have made him a target; the late conduct of the Federalists has convinced Crowninshield that it would have been "the better policy, at first, to have swept the whole board of officers at once; & not left a federalist standing"; he does not encourage the removal of every federal officer in Salem at this time, but he would recommend one other change, that is, the appointment of Francis Carr in place of Michael Hodge, the surveyor of Newburyport, who is violent against the administration "& keeps no bounds in his conduct" (RC in DNA: RG 59, LAR, incomplete, lacks inside address and signature, in Jacob Crowninshield's hand; Pasley, *Tyranny of Printers*, 277; Prince, *Federalists*, 33).

DEFEATED FEDERALISM: Jacob Crowninshield won a seat in the Eighth Congress by defeating Timothy Pickering (Vol. 36:120n).

WELL WRITTEN CIRCULAR LETTER: perhaps the broadside, dated Salem, 24 Sep. 1802, signed by John Hathorne and Joseph Story, chairman and secretary, respectively, of the convention of delegates, which met at Danvers, Massachusetts, on 22 Sep., and unanimously endorsed Crowninshield as the Republican congressional candidate. The address cited the accomplishments of the administration in Washington and contrasted successful Republican with failed Federalist policies. For "the purposes of giving information to the people" and counteracting false reports, convention delegates resolved to have extra copies of the *Salem Register* printed and distributed "GRATIS among the people by the committees of the various towns." All were encouraged to gain subscribers for the *Register*, "as a free and well conducted paper, devoted to the republican cause." Republicans of every town were to inspect the list of voters to see that no legal voters were excluded. The address concluded, "we hold that liberty is the birthright of mankind, and a Democracy its only sure preservative" (broadside in MWA; see Shaw-Shoemaker, No. 2628).

Samuel SEWALL, associate justice of the state supreme court, had practiced law in Marblehead before serving as congressman from 1796 to 1800. In June 1798, he introduced a sedition bill in the House (*Biog. Dir. Cong.*; Vol. 30:395n).

CARLTON'S PROSECUTION: the trial for libel was moved to Ipswich, a Federalist stronghold, where the jury quickly found the editor guilty. Carlton was sentenced to two months in prison, fined $100 and court costs, and ordered to produce $800 in bonds for two years to ensure his good behavior (Pasley, *Tyranny of Printers*, 211, 277; Clyde A. Duniway, *The Development of Freedom of the Press in Massachusetts* [Cambridge, Mass., 1906], 146).

Upon his return from France in 1803, Joseph C. BOYD tried to qualify for his appointment as bankruptcy commissioner, but found that during his absence John Mussey, a Portland merchant, had been appointed in his place (Madison, *Papers, Sec. of State Ser.*, 4:333; 5:346-7; Vol. 37:703, 707).

Extracts FROM A THANKSGIVING SERMON appeared in the 4 Dec. issue of the *Columbian Centinel.* The author chided the "chief magistrate" for inviting a foreigner and choosing as a confidant "the most inveterate hater of Christ and his religion"—that is, Thomas Paine; for dating public documents on Sunday "thereby exhibiting himself to the eyes of the nation as a non-observer of the Christian sabbath" (TJ's response to the New Haven Merchants was dated 12 July 1801, a Sunday); and for allowing the secretary of war to review fortifications and military stores on a Sunday "thereby obliging the officers and soldiers guarding those fortifications to attend him instead of their Maker on that day." The writer feared that "heavy judgments" would descend upon the nation after "such an awful departure from the religious principles and practices of our ancestors."

[1] In the left margin adjacent to this paragraph, TJ wrote: "I have very unfavble accts of Boyd."

To John Smith

TH: JEFFERSON TO GENERAL JOHN SMITH. Dec. 13. 1802.

Altho' the subject of the inclosed letter is at a distance from your local position, yet you may have opportunities of making enquiry from your colleagues & others, so indirectly as not to have it's drift observed, how far it is expedient to make the removals proposed. the present state of parties in New York increases much the difficulty of obtaining and estimating information as to characters. if the persons proposed to be removed have been guilty of official delinquencies, or have been active in electioneering in favor of those whose object is to overthrow the established order of things, or openly zealous to discredit the existing functionaries legislative or Executive, there would be no hesitation to remove. otherwise it should be avoided. health & friendly salutations.

RC (NNPM); addressed: "General John Smith of New York"; endorsed by Smith. PrC (DNA: RG 59, LAR, 10:0381-2); endorsed by TJ in ink on verso. Enclosure not identified, but see below.

John Smith (1755-1816), of Mastic, Long Island, began representing Suffolk County in the New York Assembly in 1784, and, except for six years, served continuously until 1800. He was among the 12 Antifederalists who voted in favor of the ratification of the Constitution at the New York Convention in 1788. Smith served as a Republican in the U.S. House of Representatives from February 1800 to 1804 and in the Senate from 1804 to 1813. In that year he became the U.S. marshal for the Southern District of New York, a position he held until 1815. Smith was also a major general in the state militia (Merrill Jensen, John P. Kaminski, Gaspare J. Saladino, and others, eds., *The Documentary History of the Ratification of the Constitution*, 24 vols. [Madison, Wis., 1976-], 21:1330n; 22:1676-7; 23:2498n).

For REMOVALS PROPOSED at the custom house at Hudson, New York, see Thomas Jenkins to TJ, 7 July; Jenkins, Ambrose Spencer, and Alexander Coffin to TJ, 16 Oct.; and Isaac Dayton to TJ, 19 Oct. In March 1803, TJ REMOVED John C. Ten Broeck, surveyor and inspector at Hudson, describing him as a "delinqt. of old" and categorizing him with others who were dismissed for "Misconduct or delinquency." Henry Malcolm, collector at the port, remained in office until 1814 (New York *Columbian*, 30 July 1814; Vol. 33:673).

Smith's 14 Dec. response to TJ, recorded in SJL as received the next day, has not been found.

From Timothy Bloodworth

DEAR SIR Wilmington December 14th 1802

Pardon the freedom of the appelation, which proceeds from the sincearity of my Heart. to me as an Individual, You are certainly Dear; but to Your Country eminently so. when I reflect on the precipice to which we were expos'd, & observe the Change that has already taken place by the Measures of Your Administration, my very Soul exults in the pleasing prospects of a Republican Government, once languishing under the pangs of desolution, but now restor'd to a flattering prospect of perfect recovery, the Blinded multitude bewildered in the dark error of delution, & ready to subscribe to their own destruction, appear to have discovered a ray of light, to direct their wandering steps from the Gloomy regions of Aristocracy, to the bright sunshine of Republican Government. Many are the prosolites, & More in the pangs of Conviction, some remain incorigible, & altho prick'd to the heart, Yet knash with their Teeth, & use every ungenerous Means to subvert the truth, injure Your Character, & bring your Administration into disrepute, but I flatter myself their efforts are as fruitless, as they[1] are unjust, & Scandelous.

Permit me to Mention the application of Mr: Larrance Dorcey for the appointment of Marshal of this State. it appears that Mr West proposes to resign that office, should that event take place, Mr. Dorcey is desirous to fill the Station. he is an Active Republican, & has supported a good Character as Deputy Marshal in this Town.

That Heaven may preserve Your Health, & Continue Your Administration for the happiness of Your Country, is the ardant wish of Dear Sir,

Your very Humble Servant TIMOTHY BLOODWORTH

RC (DLC); endorsed by TJ as received 26 Dec. and so recorded in SJL.

[1] MS: "the."

From Gabriel Duvall

DEAR SIR, Washington 14 Dec. 1802.

It was my wish, immediately on my return from this place in November last, to have furnished the information which I promised to procure, as to the probable result of a choice of Electors in Maryland by a general ticket, but I found some difficulty in obtaining correct information from the Counties represented by federal members, & my peculiar situation confined me pretty much at home: hence the delay.

The inclosed list contains the most correct information which I could obtain through different channels. In Dorchester, Somerset & Worcester, on the Eastern; & in St. Mary's & Charles Counties on the Western Shore, there has been no opportunity of trial. In these Counties a great majority of the people are so decidedly federal that there never has been a regular systematic opposition.

With equal industry I am persuaded that the Republican ticket would prevail, but I should deem it imprudent to adopt that mode of Election. In Maryland, it is unpopular; & in any rational division of the State, the Republican candidate will succeed in seven of the Eleven districts.

I am, with great respect, Your obedt. Servt. G. DUVALL

RC (DLC); at foot of text: "Thomas Jefferson, Esq. President U.S."; endorsed by TJ as received 17 Dec. and so recorded in SJL.

CHOICE OF ELECTORS IN MARYLAND: in 1800, Republicans defended the system of choosing electors by popular vote in the separate districts to thwart the Federalist plan to transfer the power of selection to the Federalist-dominated state legislature, where they would take all ten electoral votes. In the fall of 1800, Republicans campaigned aggressively and gained control of the lower state house, derailing the Federalist plan. Republican electors won in five districts in November 1800 (Frank A. Cassell, *Merchant Con-*

gressman in the Young Republic: Samuel Smith of Maryland, 1752-1839 [Madison, Wis., 1971], 91-3; Vol. 32:48-9, 100, 128-9, 208, 225-6).

TJ left an undated note describing George Dashiell, an applicant for office from SOMERSET County, Maryland. TJ wrote: "Dashiels Colo. George of Salisbury in Somerset cty. Maryld. a Lieutt. of Militia in 1779. father of a family, seems about 58. respectable modest deportment rendd. inactive by some personal infirmity republican. known to mr Duval asks a clerkship or any little office when a vacancy occurs" (MS in DNA: RG 59, LAR; entirely in TJ's hand; written on verso of a torn address sheet). There is no evidence that Dashiell received a federal appointment (Papenfuse, *Maryland Legislature*, 1:252-3).

ENCLOSURE

Distribution of Votes in Maryland

	Fed.	Rep.	
Harford County	50	1300	Estimated difference
Baltimore —	1000	2000	
Baltimore City	900	1800	
Anne Arundel Co.	463	986	State of the poles in 1800.
Annapolis	132	148	
prince George's Co.	680	747	in 1802.
Calvert —	240	340	Estimated difference
Charles —	1000	500	
St. Mary's —	700	150	
Frederick —	2007	2226	State of the poles in 1802.
Montgomery —	900	400	Estimated difference
Washington —	600	900	
Allegany —	300	250	
	8972	11,747	
		8,972	
		2775	Republican majority, Western Shore
Cecil County	700	800	Estimated difference
Kent —	500	600	
Queen Anne's —	480	920	State of the poles in 1798.—
Caroline —	233	570	
Talbot —	550	650	Estimated difference.
Dorchester —	1300	400	
Somerset —	1300	100	
Worcester —	1300	300	
	6363	4340	
	4340		
	2023	Federal majority Eastern Shore	
			2775
			2023
			752 Rep. majority in the *State*.

MS (DLC); undated; entirely in Gabriel Duvall's hand.

To Albert Gallatin

TH: JEFFERSON TO MR. GALLATIN Dec. 14. 1802.

Mr. Duval's nomination waits only for a Senate. it may be sent in tomorrow & confirmed the next day. I inclose you a copy of a letter from our agent at the Havanna stating reasons to believe a great number of slaves are smuggling and about to be smuggled into Georgia and S. Carolina. would it not be well to inclose a copy of it to the Collectors of those states, and to direct their revenue cutters to be aiding to the state laws in preventing this contraband, by seizing and informing, and for this purpose plying on the proper grounds for intercepting them? health & affectionate salutations.

RC (NHi: Gallatin Papers); addressed: "The Secretary of the Treasury." PrC (DLC). Recorded in SJL with notation "Duval. slave trade." Enclosure: Vincent Gray to Madison, 10 Nov. 1802, noting that the slave trade from Havana, Nassau, and St. Augustine to South Carolina and Georgia "is now carried on to a very great extent"; using small vessels, such as large pilot boats, the slaves are conveyed to the U.S. coast and "disposed of generally, to great advantage" (Madison, *Papers, Sec. of State Ser.*, 4:109-10).

On 20 Dec., the Treasury Department issued a circular letter to the customs COLLECTORS in Georgia and South Carolina, including Robert G. Guerard, the collector at Beaufort. A copy of the 10 Nov. letter from Vincent Gray was transmitted with the circular as "directed" by the president. Gallatin requested that Guerard and the other collectors "lend such aid as comes within the sphere of your official Powers, in detecting and informing the proper authority, of any attempts of the kind contemplated in the letter, which may contravene the laws of your State" (RC in Gallatin, *Papers*, 7:831; in a clerk's hand, signed by Gallatin; endorsed: "Circular to the Collectors of Georgia & South-Carolina"; also endorsed in another hand: "Letters respecting the bringing Negroes in Small Vessells"). REVENUE CUTTERS: a sentence was added to the circular sent to Thomas de Mattos Johnson, collector at Savannah, requesting that he communicate the information to the master of the cutter at the port "in order that he may assist in the same object" (FC in Lb in DNA: RG 56, CL; Vol. 33:220n). For Madison's circular letter to the governors of Georgia and South Carolina on the same subject, see Madison, *Papers, Sec. of State Ser.*, 4:189-90.

From Thomas Marston Green

SIR, Decer 14th 1802

I have the pleasure of enclosing a Letter which I received this day, from His Excellency William C. C. Claiborne, for your perusal

With great respect & esteem I am Sir, your mo: obt: Servt:

THOMAS M. GREEN

RC (DNA: RG 59, LAR); at foot of text: "His Excellency Thomas Jefferson"; endorsed by TJ as received 14 Dec. and so recorded in SJL; also endorsed by TJ:

"Cato West
David Ker
Abner Green
Capt. Claiborne } Govr. Claiborne recommends one of these to be Surveyor Genl of Missisipi, in a letter enclosed in this for my perusal & returned."

Enclosure not found.

Virginia native Thomas Marston Green (1758-1813) moved to the Natchez region in the early 1780s. A member of the Mississippi Territory's first general assembly, he served as the territorial delegate to Congress from December 1802 to March 1803, filling the vacancy caused by the death of Narsworthy Hunter (*Biog. Dir. Cong.*).

None of the men recommended by CLAIBORNE received the appointment to be surveyor of the lands south of Tennessee, which instead went to Isaac Briggs (Vol. 32:502n).

From Thomas Randall

SIR, City of Washington 14th December 1802

Persuaded, that in nomination to public employment, The President is inclined to prefer native citizens, who have formerly served their country in the civil and military departments; I solicit permission respectfully to observe, that during the revolutionary war, I served with the rank of Captain of Artillery, under the command of General Washington, with such reputation as induced him to give me an honorable certificate of approbation of my services; since which I have been honored by the Old Congress with their appointment to act as Vice Consul at Canton in China, which office, at that time, was unaccompanied with any emoluments, and my appointment expired with the dissolution of that form of administration: I have since lived in a private station, during which period, I have made several voyages to India and China, as Supercargo, and also as Commander of different India Ships, and have been happy in thereby adding to the revenues of my country, by having paid on my part to the amount of near two hundred thousand dollars import duties.—

The last seven years of my life have been spent in france, from which country I returned last february with my family consisting of my wife and three children.—

I now again, Sir, am induced to solicit public employment, by a wish to be useful to my country, as well as to enable me to rear with reputation an infant family of respectable republican connections.—I have friends that will give ample security for my faithfully fulfilling any employment of pecuniary trust to which I might be nominated, however, I should be happy to serve my country, either in the Naval or Civil departments, in such station, as it should please The President, considering the rank I have held in society, to nominate me for, either at home or abroad.—

Doctor Eustis, an ancient friend, who will do me the honor to deliver this letter to The President, can inform him, of any other particulars, he may Wish to know respecting me.—

Should I be deemed worthy to be honored by The Presidents notice, permit me to say, that to the respectful admiration I have of his high character, and the eminent station he so justly fills, will be added, the most grateful personal attachment to President Jefferson, through every eventful scene of life.—

I have the honor to be Most respectfully The Presidents Most obedient and faithful servant THO: RANDALL

My residence is in the City of New York

RC (DNA: RG 59, LAR); at head of text: "The President of the United States"; endorsed by TJ as received 17 Dec. and "for office" and so recorded in SJL. Enclosures: (1) Certificate by George Washington, 1 May 1779, attesting that Randall, of the Corps of Artillery, resigned his commission having served as an "attentive, active, intelligent and brave officer" (Tr in same; in Randall's hand). (2) Certificate by Henry Knox, 1 Feb. 1786, attesting Randall's military service and his promotion in 1777 to the rank of captain and his reputation as a "good officer and man of honor" (Tr in same; on same sheet as above; in Randall's hand).

Thomas Randall (d. 1811) of Boston resigned from the Continental Army in 1779 and pursued privateering and commercial enterprises in Philadelphia with Thomas Truxtun until 1783, when their partnership dissolved. With fellow artillery unit veteran Samuel Shaw, Randall became a supercargo on the *Empress of China*. In 1784, the ship became the first American vessel to trade with China, exchanging ginseng for teas and other Chinese manufactures. Congress commissioned Shaw as consul and Randall as vice consul of Canton in January 1786 (Philip Chadwick Foster Smith, *The* Empress of China [Philadelphia, 1984], 60; Kenneth Scott Latourette, "The History of Early Relations between the United States and China 1784-1844," *Transactions of the Connecticut Academy of Arts and Sciences*, 22 [1917], 10-26; Washington, *Papers, Rev. War Ser.*, 2:181-2; E. James Ferguson and others, eds., *Papers of Robert Morris*, 9 vols. [Pittsburgh, Pa., 1973-99], 9:67n; Syrett, *Hamilton*, 9:38-55; JCC, 30:28-9, 30-1; Vol. 16:40; Vol. 17:252).

From Caesar A. Rodney

HONORED & DEAR SIR, Wilmington Decr. 14th. 1802.

On my return yesterday from the Court at Dover, I had the pleasure of recieving your agreeable & acceptable favor of the 28th. ultimo. The intelligence which it contains on the flattering state of our finances must give satisfaction to every honest man, & is to me a subject of sincere joy.

The idle tale of your anxiety for my election originated here after

Senator White's return from Congress & I believe proceeded entirely from him, in consequence of the representations he gave of what fell from you in his presence & that of Dr. McCreery who differed substantially[1] with him about the business & he declined therefore a publication on the subject. Unless by accident at the post office they can not know of any correspondence between us.

Altho' personally speaking, as it relates to myself as an individual I wish to see no man turned out of office, yet I take the true line to be pursued & the proper course adopted is the public will. Every private feeling must be occasionally sacrificed on the shrine of the general welfare & general interest. Experience has evinced that firmness & decision, especially in those states where toryism has swayed with an "iron sceptre," are the best & most effectual remedy for that obstinate & malignant disease.

I am glad in a case, which had excited so much sensation in this State, the desired object is at length[2] to be attained in a way calculated to produce the least irritation. As to the important & as you truly observe "most difficult part of the subject" who is to be the Successor, permit me to recommend you on this point, to consult Col: Hall the Governor of the state who makes all appointments within the state & from his perfect acquaintance with the different characters, will be able to give you the best advice. He has long been engaged in active political life & has repeatedly since his appointment travelled thro' the State with a view to this subject of appointment as well as others & tho' I know it is a case where there may be rivals contending for the office, because of value, yet he will weigh their pretensions & merits, collect public opinion & be responsible for the selection. He not only knows what men *are*, but what they *were*. I have only to add that as it is a collector for the *port of Wilmington*, the person should be friendly to the commerce of this place, & this circumstance will be attended to by him.

Who our Senator is to be seems uncertain. Bayard they say will not accept. White some think will be continued for his *services* at the late election. I wish God, we had it in our power to send you a supporter of your Administration. However the idle empty sounds which may be uttered by any body they may send will only reverberate on themselves. With great personal & political esteem I remain Dr. Sir,

Yours Most Sincerely C. A. RODNEY

RC (DLC); endorsed by TJ as received 17 Dec. and so recorded in SJL.

IDLE TALE: see Rodney to TJ, [before 4 Nov. 1802]. DESIRED OBJECT: for the understanding that Allen McLane would resign as customs collector in 1803, see same.

The Delaware General Assembly CONTINUED Samuel White as senator (Rodney to TJ, 6 Oct.).

[1] Word interlined in place of "entirely."
[2] MS: "lenth."

From William Short

14. [Dec. 1802]

Jefferson—mention that of Minor—& to let me know if he hears from Lilly—desire to convert my land into money or ground rent at Alexia.—Barton—Bartram

FC (DLC: Short Papers); partially dated; entirely in Short's hand, consisting of an entry in his epistolary record. Recorded in SJL as received from Philadelphia on 17 Dec.

Earlier in the year, TJ had engaged John MINOR of Fredericksburg as an attorney to represent Short's interest in the government's suit against Edmund Randolph. Minor wrote Short early in December, noting that his services were no longer needed in consequence of the decision by Madison and Gallatin to pay Short's claim for back salary without waiting for the outcome of the suit (Minor to Short, 1 Dec., in DLC: Short Papers; Short to Minor, 13 Dec., entry in epistolary record, same; Vol. 37:50-1, 81-2; TJ to Gallatin, TJ to Short, and Gallatin to TJ, all 9 Oct.; TJ to Short, 18 Oct.).

Gabriel LILLY managed Short's land in Albemarle County (Vol. 37:472).

ALEXIA: Alexandria.

Annual Message to Congress

TO THE SENATE AND
HOUSE OF REPRESENTATIVES OF THE UNITED STATES.

When we assemble together, fellow-citizens, to consider the state of our beloved country, our just attentions are first drawn to those pleasing circumstances which mark the goodness of that being from whose favor they flow, and the large measure of thankfulness we owe for his bounty. another year has come around, and finds us still blessed with peace and friendship abroad, law, order and religion at home, good affection & harmony with our Indian neighbors, our burthens lightened, yet our income sufficient for the public wants, and the produce of the year great beyond example. these, fellow citizens, are the circumstances under which we meet: and we remark with special satisfaction those which, under the smiles of providence, result from the skill, industry & order of our citizens, managing their own affairs in their own way, & for their own use, unembarrassed by too much regulation, unoppressed by fiscal exactions.

Discriminating duties.

On the restoration of peace in Europe, that portion of the general[1] carrying trade, which had fallen to our share during the war, was abridged by the returning competition of the belligerent powers. this was to be expected and was just. but, in addition, we find, in some parts of Europe, monopolising discriminations, which, in the form of duties, tend effectually to prohibit the carrying thither our own produce in our own vessels. from existing amities, and a spirit of justice, it is hoped that friendly discussion will produce a fair & adequate reciprocity. but should false calculations of interest defeat our hope, it rests with the legislature to decide whether they will meet inequalities abroad with countervailing inequalities at home, or provide for the evil in any other way.

British Countervail.

It is with satisfaction I lay before you an act of the British parliament anticipating[2] this subject, so far as to authorise a mutual abolition of the duties and countervailing duties, permitted under the treaty of 1794. it shews on their part a spirit of justice and friendly accomodation, which it is our duty and our interest to cultivate with all nations. whether this would produce a due equality in the navigation between the two countries, is a subject for your consideration.

Seamen

Another circumstance which claims attention, as directly affecting the very source of our navigation, is the defect or the evasion of the law providing for the return of seamen, & particularly of those belonging to vessels sold abroad. numbers of them, discharged in foreign ports, have been thrown on the hands of our Consuls, who, to rescue them from the dangers into which their distresses might plunge them, & to save them to their country, have found it necessary in some cases, to return them at the public charge.

Louisiana.

The cession of the Spanish province of Louisiana to France, which took place in the course of the late war, will, if carried into effect, make a change in the aspect of our foreign relations, which will doubtless have just weight in any deliberations of the legislature connected with that subject.

Tripoli

There was reason, not long since, to apprehend that the warfare in which we were engaged with Tripoli might be taken up by some other of the Barbary powers. a reinforcement therefore was immediately ordered to the vessels already there. subsequent information however has removed these apprehensions for the present. to secure our commerce in that sea, with the smallest force competent, we have supposed it best to watch strictly the harbour of Tripoli. still however the shallowness of their coast, & the want of smaller vessels on our part, has permitted some cruisers to escape unobserved: and to one of these an American vessel unfortunately fell a prey. the Captain, one American seaman, & two others of colour, remain prisoners with them; unless exchanged under an agreement formerly made with the Bashaw, to whom, on the faith of that, some of his captive subjects had been restored.

Georgia.

The convention with the state of Georgia has been ratified by their legislature, and a repurchase from the Creeks has been consequently made, of a part of the Talassee[3] county. in this purchase has been also comprehended a part of the lands within the fork of Oconee and Oakmulgee rivers. the particulars of the contract will be laid before Congress so soon as they shall be in a state for communication.

Missipi territity

In order to remove every ground of difference possible with our Indian neighbors, I have proceeded in the work of settling[4] with them, and marking the boundaries between us. that with the Choctaw nation is fixed in one part, & will be through the whole within a short time. the country to which their title had been extinguished before the revolution is sufficient to recieve a very respectable population, which Congress will probably see the expediency of encouraging, so soon as the limits shall be declared. we are to view this position as an Outpost of the United States, surrounded by strong neighbors, and distant from it's support. and how far that monopoly, which prevents population, should here be guarded against, & actual habitation made a condition of the continuance of title, will be for your consideration. a prompt settlement too of all existing rights & claims within this territory, presents itself as a preliminary operation.

Indiana.

In that part of the Indiana territory which includes Vincennes, the lines settled with the neighboring tribes fix the extinction of their title at a breadth of twenty four leagues from East to West, and about the same length, parallel with & including the Wabash. they have also ceded a tract of four miles square including the Salt-springs near the mouth of that river.

Finance.

In the department of finance, it is with pleasure I inform you that the reciepts of external duties, for the last twelvemonth, have exceeded those of any former year, & that the ratio of increase has been also greater than usual. this has enabled us to answer all the regular exigencies of government, to pay from the treasury, within one year, upwards of eight millions of dollars, principal & interest, of the public debt, exclusive of upwards of one million paid by the sale of bank stock, and making in the whole a reduction of nearly five millions and an half of principal, and to have now in the treasury four millions and an half of dollars, which are in a course of application to the further discharge of debt, and of current demands. Experience too, so far, authorises us to believe, if no extraordinary event supervenes, and the expences which will be actually incurred shall not be greater than were contemplated by Congress at their last session, that we shall not be disappointed in the expectations then formed. but nevertheless as the effect of peace on the amount of duties is not yet fully ascertained, it is the more necessary to practise every useful economy, and to incur no expence which may be avoided without prejudice.

Housel. taxes

The collection of the internal taxes having been compleated in some of the states, the officers employed in it are of course out of commission. in others they will be so shortly. but in a few, where the arrangements for the direct tax had been retarded, it will still be some time before the system is closed. it has not yet been thought necessary to employ the agent authorised by an act of the last session, for transacting business in Europe relative to debts &

Reloans

loans. nor have we used the power, confided by the same act, of prolonging the foreign debt by reloans, and of redeeming, instead thereof, an equal sum of the Domestic debt. should however the difficulties of remittance on so large a scale, render it necessary at any time, the power shall be executed, and the money thus unemployed abroad shall, in conformity with that law, be faithfully applied here in an equivalent extinction of Domestic debt. When effects so salutary result from the plans you have already sanctioned, when, merely by avoiding false objects of expence, we are able, without a direct tax, without internal taxes, & without borrowing, to make large and effectual paiments towards the discharge of our public debt, & the emancipation of our posterity from that mortal canker, it is an encouragement, fellow citizens, of the highest order, to proceed as we have begun, in substituting economy for taxation, and in pursuing what is useful for a nation placed as we are, rather than what is practised by others under different circumstances. and whensoever we are destined to meet events which shall call forth all the energies of our countrymen, we have the firmest reliance on those energies, and the comfort of leaving for calls like these, the extraordinary resources of loans and internal taxes. in the mean time, by paiments of the[5] principal of our debt, we are liberating, annually, portions of the external taxes, & forming from them a growing fund, still further to lessen the necessity of recurring to extraordinary resources.

Estimates

The usual account of reciepts and expenditures for the last year, with an estimate of the expences of the ensuing one, will be laid before you by the Secretary of the treasury.

War deptmt

No change being deemed necessary in our military establishment, an estimate of it's expences for the ensuing year, on it's present footing, as also of the sums to be employed in fortifications, and other objects within that department, has been prepared by the Secretary at war, and will make a part of the general estimates which will be presented you.

Militia.

Considering that our regular troops are employed for local purposes, and that the militia is our general reliance for great and sudden emergencies, you will doubtless think this institution worthy of a review, & give it those improvements of which you find it susceptible.

Naval estimates

Estimates for the naval department, prepared by the Secretary of the navy for another year, will in like manner be communicated with the general estimates. a small force in the Mediterranean will still be necessary to restrain the Tripoline cruisers: and the uncertain tenure of peace with some other of the Barbary powers, may eventually[6] require that force to be augmented. the necessity of procuring some smaller vessels for that service, will raise the estimate: but the difference in their maintenance will soon make it a measure of economy.

Dry dock.

Presuming it will be deemed expedient to expend annually a convenient[7] sum towards providing the naval defence which our situation may require, I cannot but recommend that the first appropriations for that purpose, may go to the saving what we already possess. no cares, no attentions, can preserve vessels from rapid decay, which lie in water, & exposed to the sun. these decays require great and constant repairs, and will consume, if continued, a great portion of the monies destined to naval purposes. to avoid this waste of our resources, it is proposed to add to our Navy yard here a Dock, within which our present vessels may be laid up dry, & under cover from the sun. under these circumstances experience proves that works of wood will remain scarcely at all affected by time. the great abundance of running water which this situation possesses, at heights far above the level of the tide, if employed as is practised for lock navigation, furnishes the means for raising and laying up our vessels, on a dry and sheltered bed. and should the measure be found useful[8] here, similar depositories for laying up, as well as for building and repairing vessels, may hereafter be undertaken at other navy yards, offering the same means. the plans and estimates of the work, prepared by a person of skill and experience, will be[9] presented to you,[10] without delay, and from these will be seen that scarcely more than has been the cost[11] of one vessel is necessary to save the whole;[12] and that the annual sum to be employed towards it's completion may be adapted to the views of the legislature as to Naval expenditure.

Conclusion

To cultivate peace, & maintain commerce & navigation in all their lawful enterprises; to foster our fisheries as nurseries of navigation & for the nurture of man, and protect the manufactures adapted to our circumstances; to preserve the faith of the nation by[13] an exact discharge of it's debts and contracts, expend the public money with the same care and economy we would practise with our own, & impose on our citizens no unnecessary burthens; to keep in all things within the pale of our constitutional powers, & cherish the federal union, as the only rock of safety; these, fellow citizens, are the landmarks by which we are to guide ourselves in all our proceedings. by continuing to make these our rule of action, we shall endear to our countrymen the true principles of their constitution, and promote an union of sentiment and of action, equally auspicious to their happiness and safety. on my part you may count on a cordial concurrence in every measure for the public good; and on all the information I possess which may enable you to discharge to advantage the high functions with which you are invested by your country.

TH: JEFFERSON
Dec. 15. 1802.

MS (DLC: TJ Papers, 128:22071-3); entirely in TJ's hand. MS (DNA: RG 46, LPPM, 7th Cong., 2d sess.); in Meriwether Lewis's hand with emendations by TJ; signed and dated by TJ; lacks section headings; endorsed by Senate clerks. MS (DNA: RG 233, PM, 7th Cong., 2d sess.); in Lewis's hand with emendations by TJ; signed and dated by TJ; lacks section headings. Enclosures: (1) Act of Parliament of Great Britain, 24 Mch., enabling the crown to cease or suspend until March 1803 the countervailing duties on American goods imported in American ships and the tonnage duties on American vessels (MS in DNA: RG 46, LPPM; in a clerk's hand; endorsed). (2) Extracts of: William Eaton to the secretary of state, Tunis, 13 Dec. 1801, 3 Feb. 1802; James Simpson to the secretary of state, Tangier and Gibraltar, 8 Jan., 20 Feb., 19 Mch., 13 May, 5, 14, 17, 26 June, 3, 16 July (enclosing Simpson to Abd al-Rahman Ashash, governor of Tangier, 5 July), 27 July, 3, 12 Aug., 3 Sep.; Richard O'Brien to the secretary of state, Algiers, 1 Feb., 14 June; unidentified (Nicholas C. Nissen, Danish consul in Tripoli) to James Leander Cathcart, 12 Mch. to 30 Apr., 10 May; Cathcart to the secretary of state, Leghorn, 2, 4, 15 July; Andrew Morris to Cathcart, Tripoli, 22 July; Simpson to Mawlay Sulayman, Tetuan, 31 July; Sidi Mohammed ben Absalom Selawy to Simpson, Tangier, 6 Aug.; Simpson to Selawy, [Tangier, 1 Sep.]; Simpson to John Gavino, Tangier, 27 Sep. (Trs and PrCs in DNA: RG 233, PM, in various clerks' hands, endorsed; Trs in DNA: RG 46, EPFR, in various clerks' hands, endorsed; Madison, *Papers*, *Sec. of State Ser.*, 2:313-14, 378-80, 432-3, 438-9, 481-2; 3:49-51, 221-2, 278-9, 306-8, 319-20, 342-3, 369-71, 394-5, 398-9, 433, 452-3, 475, 542-5, 545n, 608; NDBW, 1:637-8; 2:148-9, 165, 176-8, 179, 185-7, 189-91, 204-6, 211, 221-2, 231, 264-6); portions printed as *Documents Accompanying the Communication of the President of the United States, to Both Houses of Congress, Made the 15th day of December, 1802* (Washington, D.C., 1802; Shaw-Shoemaker, No. 3280); other portions printed as *No. II. Communications from Morocco. Accompanying the President's Message, of 15th December, 1802* (Washington, D.C., 1802; Shaw-Shoemaker, No. 3377). (3) Josiah Tattnall, Jr., governor of Georgia, to Madison, 18 June 1802, transmitting an act of 16 June to ratify and confirm the articles of agreement of 24 Apr. between the state of Georgia and commissioners of the United States; with a copy of the act with attestations by Tattnall and Horatio Marbury, secretary of the state (MS in DNA: RG 233, PM, in a clerk's hand, endorsed; PrC in DNA: RG 46, LPPM, endorsed, incomplete; Madison, *Papers*, *Sec. of State Ser.*, 3:321); printed as *No. III. Ratification of the Agreement between the United States and Georgia. By the Legislature of the Latter. Accompanying the Message of the President of the United States* (Washington, D.C., 1802; Shaw-Shoemaker, No. 3378).

WHEN WE ASSEMBLE TOGETHER: Congress attempted to convene on Monday, 6 Dec., but the House of Representatives did not have a quorum until the next day and the Senate did not achieve a quorum until the 13th. Aaron Burr was not present, and the Senate failed in its first attempts to elect a president pro tem. On the 14th, the Senate elected Stephen R. Bradley to preside, and a joint committee, consisting of John Dawson, Thomas Lowndes, and John P. Van Ness from the House and Robert Wright and Theodore Foster from the Senate, called on TJ. He advised them that they would receive his message the next day (JHR, 4:243-4, 248, 249; JS, 3:241-3; *Annals*, 12:11). Meriwether Lewis delivered the signed copies of the message and the accompanying documents to the two chambers on 15 Dec. To convey his first annual message in December 1801, TJ had written cover letters to the presiding officers of the Senate and the House. He did not do that with the second annual message. Lewis's simple declaration to the speaker of the House, Nathaniel Macon, is recorded in the journal: "I am directed by the President of the United States to hand you a communication, in writing, from the President to the two Houses of Congress" (JHR, 4:249; JS, 3:244; Vol. 36:57).

DISCRIMINATING DUTIES: the section headings that TJ placed in the margin of the fair copy printed above, and which identified the sections of the message during the drafting process, do not appear in the message as the House and Senate received it.

Robert R. Livingston had reported that American shippers were subject to extra duties and fees in SOME PARTS OF EUROPE. France, which had not relaxed all of its wartime trade policies, charged higher import duties on goods such as tobacco and fish carried in American or other foreign ships. Foreign vessels also paid higher port duties. In the Batavian Republic, extra duties were charged on shipments from the United States (Madison, *Papers*, *Sec. of State Ser.*, 3:77-8, 367; 4:144-5; Livingston to TJ, 28 Oct., second letter). RESTS WITH THE LEGISLATURE TO DECIDE: Levi Lincoln suggested the language that concludes the paragraph on discriminating duties; see his remarks on the draft message, Document IX of the group of documents on the drafting of the message, printed at 18 Nov.

WHETHER THIS WOULD PRODUCE A DUE EQUALITY: see Gallatin's remarks, Document III at 18 Nov. For the countervailing duties charged by Great Britain, see Vol. 36:67-8.

EVASION OF THE LAW: according to a 1792 statute, when an American-owned ship was sold in a foreign country, the master of the vessel had to send the members of the crew back to the United States or give them means to return on their own, unless the sailors consented to be discharged in the foreign port or their contracts made them liable to it (U.S. Statutes at Large, 1:256-7). Regarding American seamen stranded in foreign ports and THROWN ON THE HANDS of U.S. consuls, see Gallatin to TJ, 17 Aug., and Notes on a Cabinet Meeting, 21 Oct.

WILL, IF CARRIED INTO EFFECT: see Gallatin's remarks, Document III at 18 Nov., for his suggestion of this language.

The merchant brig *Franklin* was the AMERICAN VESSEL captured by Tripolitan corsairs. TJ did not know yet that the brig's captain, Andrew Morris, and members of his crew were no longer PRISONERS in Tripoli (Joseph Yznardi, Sr., to TJ, 12 Aug.; Mustafa Baba, Dey of Algiers, to TJ, 17 Oct.). AGREEMENT FORMERLY MADE WITH THE BASHAW: Captain Richard Dale released some captured merchants to Yusuf Qaramanli, the pasha and bey of Tripoli, in August 1801, and proposed a prisoner exchange. Tripoli had no American captives at the time, so Dale took a pledge for the future release of seven Americans (NDBW, 1:564, 584; Madison, *Papers*, *Sec. of State Ser.*, 3:456, 466n, 547n).

For the CONVENTION WITH THE STATE OF GEORGIA, see Vol. 37:300-1, 343-5. TJ transmitted the PARTICULARS of the purchase to the Senate on 27 Dec.

Regarding the boundary with the CHOCTAW NATION, see Vol. 38:272-3, 299, 300n.

HOW FAR THAT MONOPOLY: TJ may have incorporated some of Lincoln's suggestions for this sentence (Document IX at 18 Nov.).

For the VINCENNES tract and the salt spring or saline on the Ohio River below the mouth of the WABASH, see Vol. 38:139-40n, 169-70, 250-2, 572-3.

In the section on FINANCE, TJ apparently revised the draft message in accordance with Gallatin's remarks to say that the RATIO OF INCREASE of revenue from customs duties was GREATER THAN USUAL rather than "greater than any former year." For the figures cited by TJ, including the balance in the Treasury of $4,500,000, see Gallatin's remarks and the statement of receipts and expenditures he gave TJ during the drafting process (Documents III and IV at 18 Nov.). TJ also modified his draft to use Gallatin's suggested phrasing about expenses CONTEMPLATED BY CONGRESS the previous year (Document III).

ACT OF THE LAST SESSION: the 29 Apr. statute for retirement of the public debt (see Document III at 18 Nov.).

For Lincoln's concern that the reference to FALSE OBJECTS of expense might have political consequences, see Document IX at 18 Nov.

WILL BE LAID BEFORE YOU BY THE SECRETARY OF THE TREASURY: the House of Representatives adjourned for the day after TJ's message was read on the 15th. The following day, the House received Gallatin's report on appropriations for 1803 and of receipts and expenditures from October 1801 through September 1802. The statements were dated 10 Dec.

and signed by Joseph Nourse, the register of the Treasury (MS in DNA: RG 233, RCSH, 7th Cong., 2d sess.; in a clerk's hand, with report on appropriations for 1803 signed by Gallatin; lacks estimates for appropriations, p. 9-64 of the printed report). The House referred Gallatin's report to the Committee of Ways and Means (JHR, 4:252). William Duane printed the papers as a *Letter from the Secretary of the Treasury, Accompanying a Report and Estimates of Appropriation for the Service of the Year 1803; also an Account of the Receipts and Expenditures at the Treasury of the United States, for One Year Preceding the First Day of October, 1802* (Washington, D.C., 1802; Shaw-Shoemaker, No. 3314).

PREPARED BY THE SECRETARY AT WAR: in Gallatin's report, the War Department estimates incorporated $619,767.60 for expenses of the army; $109,696.88 for fortifications, arsenals, magazines, and armories; and $73,500 for Indian affairs. The ESTIMATES FOR THE NAVAL DEPARTMENT totaled $900,000, plus $198,797.46 to cover deficiencies in previous appropriations. The estimates were based on an expectation that six frigates and one schooner would be in active service and seven frigates would be laid up in ordinary. An amount of $114,425 was included for completion of contracts for six 74-gun ships (*Letter from the Secretary of the Treasury*, 6, 55).

Dearborn prompted TJ to suggest that dry docks might be built AT OTHER NAVY YARDS; see Document VI at 18 Nov.

PERSON OF SKILL AND EXPERIENCE: Benjamin Latrobe.

HIGH FUNCTIONS WITH WHICH YOU ARE INVESTED: the Senate, after the message and accompanying papers were read on the 15th, ordered the printing of 500 copies of the message and 100 copies of the documents "for the use of the Senate" (JS, 3:246). The House of Representatives heard the message read and then referred it to the Committee of the Whole House on the State of the Union. On 17 Dec., the House passed a set of eight resolutions that assigned portions of the message to different committees. The question of Britain's countervailing duties went to the Committee of Commerce and Manufactures, while matters relating to finances went to the Committee of Ways and Means. Six topics were given to select committees created for the purpose: one committee to consider Indian relations "and the establishment of a new settlement"; another for navy yards and docks; one for "the return of American seamen discharged in foreign ports"; one for the war with Tripoli and relations with other Barbary Coast states; one for "the Militia Institution of the United States"; and one for "so much of the President's message as relates to the fostering of the fisheries" (JHR, 4:252-3).

Duane printed the text of the message, without the supplementary documents, in pamphlet form for the House (*Message from the President of the United States, to Both Houses of Congress. 15th December 1802* [Washington, D.C., 1802]; Shaw-Shoemaker, No. 3350). He also published a broadside version on a single sheet (DLC: Broadside Collection, Rare Book and Special Collections Division). The broadside is headed "To the Senate and House of Representatives of the United States," without any reference to the conveyance of the document to Congress, and the date of 15 Dec. may have been added after the body of the text was set in type. Those features may indicate that Duane set the message in type before the 15th—that TJ gave him early access to its contents, just as the president had allowed Samuel Harrison Smith to prepare the 1801 annual message for publication before Congress received it (Vol. 36:53-4). One of Duane's printings was likely the version of the message that was available to TJ on the 16th (see TJ to James Garrard, 16 Dec.). Smith's *National Intelligencer* published the message on the 17th.

[1] Word interlined by TJ in MS in RG 46. Word lacking in MS in RG 233.

[2] Word interlined by TJ in place of "on" in MS in RG 46.

[3] MS: "Talasssee," which Lewis rendered as "Talasscee" in the copies for the House and Senate.

[4] Word interlined in place of "agreeing."

[5] Word interlined by TJ in MS in RG 233.

[6] Word interlined.

[7] Word written over an illegibly erased word (also in MS in RG 46 and MS in RG 233).

[8] Preceding four words interlined in place of "expedient succeed."

[9] Preceding two words interlined in place of "are now."

[10] TJ originally ended the paragraph here, then continued by interlineation.

[11] TJ first wrote "and from these it will be seen that less than the cost" before reworking the passage to read as above.

[12] TJ originally ended the interlineation here, then added the remainder of the sentence as an insertion in the margin. Remainder of sentence interlined by Lewis in MS in RG 46 and MS in RG 233.

[13] TJ first wrote "preserve the public faith by" before reworking the passage to read as above.

To John Barnes

Th: Jefferson will thank mr Barnes for thirty dollars for mr Wanscher and thirty three and one third to be sent to Monticello.

Dec. 15. 1802.

RC (MHi); endorsed by Barnes as a $70 payment, $30 for Wanscher and $40 for Monticello.

In his financial memoranda under 15 Dec., TJ recorded the receipt of $70 from BARNES and payments of $30 to Marten WANSCHER and $35 to Gabriel Lilly, from which Lilly was to pay $33.33 "to Polly Carr for the hire of her negro, making with that ante Nov. 1. is for the whole year" (MB, 2:1088; TJ to William Bache, 11 Oct., 22 Nov. 1802). A letter from TJ to Lilly dated 15 Dec. 1802 is recorded in SJL with the notation "35. D. P. Carr," but has not been found.

To Jones & Howell

GENTLEMEN Washington Dec. 15. 1802.

Having occasion for a supply of rod & hoop-iron, according to the invitation of your mr Jones, I address myself to you for two tons of rods of the sizes hitherto furnished me, that is to say from 6 d. to 20 d. and of a quarter of a ton of 4 d. hoops, which be pleased to ship immediately before the closing of your river, to the address of messrs. Gibson & Jefferson in Richmond, notifying me at the time. Accept my respects & best wishes. TH: JEFFERSON

PrC (MHi); at foot of text: "Messr. Jones & Howell"; endorsed by TJ in ink on verso. Recorded in SJL with the notation "2 tons rod. $\frac{1}{4}$ ton hoop."

Jones & Howell was the partnership formed by Benjamin Jones and Samuel E. Howell upon the death of Joseph Roberts, Jones's previous partner. The firm sold mostly iron goods from its store on the South Wharves of Philadelphia and remained TJ's regular supplier of iron for about 10 years. Howell's father had supplied iron to TJ in 1796 (James Robinson, *The Philadelphia Directory for 1805. Containing the Names, Trades and*

Residence of the Inhabitants of the City, Southwark, Northern Liberties, and Kensington [Philadelphia, 1804]; *Poulson's American Daily Advertiser*, 18 June 1802, 10 Dec. 1811; Josiah Granville Leach, *Genealogical and Biographical Memorials of the Reading, Howell, Yerkes, Watts, Latham, and Elkins Families* [Philadelphia, 1898], 171-2, 179; RS, 1:423n; Vol. 29:89n).

From Benjamin H. Latrobe

DEAR SIR Philadelphia Decr. 15th. 1802.

Captain Dale, of the Un. State's Navy, called upon me this morning, and in conversation upon the Naval Arsenal or Dry Docks proposed by You to be erected at the Federal City, which he most warmly approved,—he informed me that the Swedish Government had lately conceived the idea of adopting the same means of preserving their Navy in times of peace. The Swedish Admiral Söderstrom described to him the situation of the Dock which was then in the progress of construction. It was intended to contain 8 Ships of 74 Guns, and another was projected to contain 12, in all making provision for 20 Ships of the line. The situation was remarkably favorable. Deep water close to a perpendicular rock which can be easily wrought, gives the opportunity of excavating the dock, the rock forms the Wall, and the roof is laid over, at such a higth that the ships go in with their lower Masts standing. Captain Dale did not exactly know how the Ships were worked into the dock,—but from his description of the situation I presume they are tide docks.—Admiral Söderstrom said, that the Vessels were to be washed with fresh Water, perfectly drained, & opened to a circulation of Air,—and that he had no doubt of their remaining in perfect repair in the dock for a Century, and gave many reasons for his opinion which were convincing.—

This *example* of Sweden, added to that of *Venice*, may perhaps outweigh, the argument with which our Philadelphian federalists hope to answer every thing that can be said in their favor,—"*the British have never erected them*,"—of course they cannot be worth erecting.—I hope you will excuse this intrusion on your time,—as perhaps you are already acquainted with the facts, I have related.—Should they however be new, they may be useful in the hands of those who have to combat objections, such as are made by party men, who consider nothing an improvement worth adopting, that has [not] the sanction of Europaean practice.

I am with the sincerest respect Your much obliged hble Sevt

B HENRY LATROBE.

RC (DLC); torn; addressed: "The President of the United States Washington"; franked and postmarked; endorsed by TJ as received 22 Dec. and so recorded in SJL. Tr (DNA: RG 233, PM); extract consisting of first paragraph only; in Meriwether Lewis's hand.

For the cooperation between the naval squadrons of Commodore Richard DALE and Swedish Admiral Olaf Rudolf Cederström (SÖDERSTROM) in the Mediterranean against Tripoli, see Vol. 36:667n; Vol. 38:189-90. The naval facility described by Cederström was at Karlskrona, on the Baltic Sea in southern Sweden. It contained some of the most technologically advanced drydock, construction, and storage facilities in Europe (Daniel G. Harris, *F H Chapman, The First Naval Architect and His Work* [London, 1989], 115-23; Lars Otto Berg, "The Swedish Navy, 1780-1820," in Fred Sandstedt, ed., *Between the Imperial Eagles: Swedens Armed Forces during the Revolutionary and the Napoleonic Wars 1780-1820* [Stockholm, 2000], 92-6; William S. Lind, "Preserved in Amber: The 18th-Century Dockyard at Karlskrona, Sweden," *Sea History*, 97 [2001], 20-3).

To Thomas Mann Randolph

DEAR SIR Washington Dec. 15. 1802.

Genl. Sumpter has arrived here and I have this morning had a conversaton with him on the subject of the law of S. Carolina against the transportation of slaves across that state. he says there would be no doubt of the success of an application to the legislature while in session for a special permission, & that he met large emigrations of slaves going on upon that assurance but the legislature will rise on the 20th. inst. however he says also there is no doubt they will revise & modify the law so as to permit the transportation: that this will be done before they rise, and that himself is to recieve immediate information of it, which he thinks he may expect before the last day of this month. I shall take care to keep you advised of whatever I may learn on this subject.

The two houses formed yesterday and the message is at this moment delivering to them (noon.) should it be printed before the departure of the post I will inclose you a copy. all are well here. accept assurances of my affectionate attachment. TH: JEFFERSON

P. S. the new legislature of S. Carolina is

	Fed		Rep.		
in the H. of Representatives	27	to	97	=	124
in the Senate	14	to	23	=	37
	41	to	120	=	161

RC (DLC); at foot of text: "T M Randolph"; endorsed by Randolph.

For an earlier communication from Thomas Sumter, Sr. on South Carolina's ban on the TRANSPORTATION OF SLAVES, see Vol. 38:607. In a letter of 5 Jan. 1803 to John Milledge, Randolph wrote of his continuing desire to settle his slaves on a plantation in Georgia but that TJ was "unwilling I should violate the South Carolina laws by attempting a passage tho' I understand it is done daily allmost, without notice." He waited "anxiously to hear" of any modifications of South Carolina's law (RC in NcD: Milledge Family Papers).

To the Senate

GENTLEMEN OF THE SENATE

I nominate Gabriel Duval of Maryland to be Comptroller of the treasury of the US. vice John Steele resigned.

William Peck of Rhodeisland whose office of Marshal of Rhode island expired on the 13th. instant to be reappointed Marshal of that district.

TH: JEFFERSON
Dec. 15. 1802.

RC (DNA: RG 46, EPEN, 7th Cong., 2d sess.); endorsed by a Senate clerk; also endorsed at foot of text: "The Senate advise & Consent to Wm. Peck Decr. 15." PrC (DLC). Recorded in SJL with notation "nomns. Duval. Peck."

Meriwether Lewis delivered these nominations to the Senate on 15 Dec. The Senate read the message, dispensed with the rule that nominations should lie for consideration, immediately approved both appointments, and sent the decision to the president. The commission for Gabriel Duvall (DUVAL) is dated 15 Dec. and that for WILLIAM PECK, marshal of Rhode Island since July 1790, is dated 13 Dec. 1802 (FCs of commissions in Lb in DNA: RG 59, MPTPC; JEP, 1:53, 164-5, 426; Washington, *Papers, Pres. Ser.*, 5:149).

From John Conrad & Co.

SIR Philada Decemb 16th 1802

Beleiving that it will afford you pleasure, to see that we may soon expect to rival any European nation in the elegance of one of our principal manufactures, and proud of what can be done in our country, we have taken the liberty of forwarding to you (as the person who has done most for the encouragement of our manufactures) a specimen in Mr Linns poems, of American Type foundery, Paper making, engraving & printing not inferior to the best English productions—

We hope you will not put yourself to the trouble of acknowledging this. it is sent by post & will undoubtedly reach you, which is all we wish for—

With the highest Respect We are Sir &c

JOHN CONRAD & CO.

RC (MHi); at foot of text: "President of the United States"; endorsed by TJ as received 20 Dec. and so recorded in SJL.

John Conrad (1777-1851), a Philadelphia publisher and bookseller, was in business by 1800 under the name John Conrad & Co. at 30 Chestnut Street. He was also a partner in the Washington, D.C., bookstore and printing office of Rapine, Conrad, and Co. In November 1803, he sent TJ "the first number of our American Magazine Review," to which the president subsequently subscribed. In the spring of 1807, he contracted with Meriwether Lewis to publish the journals of the Lewis and Clark expedition, but was unable to complete the project by 1812, when the firm, by then operating as C. & A. Conrad & Co., failed (Jackson, *Lewis and Clark*, 393-4n; RCHS, 25 [1923], 199; New York *Weekly Herald*, 31 Jan. 1852; RS, 1:412, 668-9; Vol. 35:489n; Conrad and Co. to TJ, 28 Nov. 1803 and TJ to Conrad and Co., 2 Dec.).

MR LINNS POEMS: John Blair Linn, a co-pastor of the First Presbyterian Church in Philadelphia, wrote *The Powers of Genius, A Poem, in Three Parts*, which was published in a second enlarged and corrected edition by John Conrad & Co. in 1802 (Sowerby, No. 4469).

From Thomas T. Davis

SIR Washington Decr. 16th 1802

Altho the Indiana Territory is entitled to the second grade of the ordinance—it depends on the voice of a majority of the freeholders—But no mode is pointed out by which this is to be ascertained—last session petitions came to me to reduce that Territory to its first grade. From the inclosd paper you find the people trying to come to the second grade—You will see Governor Harrisons letter to his friend on the subject with strictures by some person. Having no other Legislators but their Governor & Judges they may perhaps be entitled to Congressional aid.

I am Sir respectfuly your obt Set. THO T. DAVIS

RC (DLC); endorsed by TJ as received 16 Dec. and so recorded in SJL. Enclosures not found.

Since 1801, calls had been circulating within the INDIANA TERRITORY to advance to the SECOND GRADE of government and elect a territorial legislature. William Henry Harrison opposed the measure, however, warning of the additional expenses such a move would precipitate. An 1801 petition calling for the privilege of sending a delegate from the territory to Congress, but continuing under the first grade of government, was likewise unsuccessful. Harrison did not authorize Indiana's advancement to the second stage of government until December 1804, with the first territorial legislature convening in July 1805 (*Gazette of the United States*, 6 Mch. 1802; *Letters of Decius* [Louisville, Ky., 1805], 7-8; Smith, *St. Clair Papers*, 2:533-4; Andrew R. L. Cayton, *Frontier Indiana* [Bloomington, 1996], 238-40).

To Thomas T. Davis

Dec. 16. 1802.

Th: Jefferson presents his compliments to mr Davis & his thanks for the information respecting Indiana. he had wished to see the law on the subject of it's going into the 2d. grade of government, not knowing but it might have been rested on the President to do some act promotive of it, which he should willingly have done, as being a friend to the advancement of the territories to a freer state of self-government. he finds however that the law has confided to the personal discretion of the Governor to take the sense of his freeholders, without prescribing to him time or manner, and consequently that there is no ground[1] for the President to [direct] him in the exercise of his discretion, all the responsibility resting on himself.

PrC (DLC); blurred.

The LAW creating the Indiana Territory was passed by Congress on 7 May 1800. Its provisions were based on the Northwest Ordinance of 1787 (U.S. Statutes at Large, 2:58-9).

[1] Word interlined in place of "reason."

From John Wayles Eppes

DEAR SIR, Richmond Decr. 16th. 1802.

In my last I mentioned to you a Resolution which had been offered by Mr Smith & the probability of a substitute being adopted—I now enclose you a copy of the substitute passed yesterday with 25 dissenting voices only & those the most bitter of their party. It was not supposed by many members of the Legislature that we ought to have acted on this subject at all—Mr. Smith however placed us in a situation from which we could not recede—It was necessary either to adopt his *Resolution*; a substitute; or to give by rejecting it, additional force to the late shameful calumnies—

Leave has been given to Bring in a Bill to establish a state University—

accept for your health the best wishes of yours affectionately

JNO: W: EPPES

RC (MHi); endorsed by TJ as received 21 Dec. and so recorded in SJL. Enclosure: Resolution of the Virginia House of Delegates stating "that the confidence of the Legislature in the wisdom, patriotism, & private worth of the President of the United States, is not only undeminished but increased; and that the constitutional and just principles of his administration, and his undeviating rectitude in their execution, merit the entire approbation of his country" (Tr in same; in Eppes's hand; endorsed by Eppes: "Resolution adopted as a substitute for Smiths").

MY LAST: John Wayles Eppes to TJ, 13 Dec.

SUBSTITUTE PASSED YESTERDAY: on 15 Dec., the Virginia House of Delegates adopted the resolution "without a question," and recorded the names and votes of 124 delegates in favor and 26 opposed. The Senate approved the resolution on 18 Dec. (*Journal of the House of Delegates of the Commonwealth of Virginia*, Dec. 1802-Jan. 1803, 13-14; Shepherd, *Statutes*, 2:469).

BILL TO ESTABLISH A STATE UNIVERSITY: on 14 Dec., the House of Delegates charged a committee of 12 men to prepare a bill "To establish a State College." The resulting "Act to establish an academy in the county of Albemarle, and for other purposes," passed on 12 Jan. 1803, and named 14 trustees and authorized them to conduct lotteries to raise $3,000 for buildings of the academy (*Journal of the House of Delegates*, Dec. 1802-Jan. 1803, 13; Shepherd, *Statutes*, 2:427).

From Jesse Franklin

Dec. 16th 1802

J. Franklin returns compliments to Mr. Jefferson, and acknowledges the receit of his note of the 14th Instant.

J. Franklin has no personal acquantanc with Mr. West. But from the best information he is able to obtain, he is a man of good Charactor and demeanor in his office and a republican and no Doubt well qualified to Discharge the Duties of *Marshall.*

RC (DNA: RG 59, LAR); endorsed by TJ: "West John Spence to be contind Marshal N.C." and "mr Franklin's note."

Born in Orange County, Virginia, Jesse Franklin (1760-1823), third son of Bernard and Mary Cleveland Franklin, moved with his family to Surry County, North Carolina, at the beginning of the American Revolution and joined a regiment under the command of Benjamin Cleveland, his uncle. By the end of the war, he was a major in the North Carolina militia. In 1784, he began serving as a state legislator. Franklin served one term, from 1795 to 1797, as a Republican in the U.S. House of Representatives. In 1798, he was elected to the U.S. Senate, where he represented North Carolina from 1799 to 1805 and from 1807 to 1813. President Madison, in 1816, appointed Franklin a commissioner, along with Andrew Jackson and David Meriwether, to treat with the Chickasaw and Cherokee Indians. The treaty was signed later that year. In 1820, Franklin was elected governor of North Carolina, a position he held for one year. He refused to stand for reelection (DAB; William S. Powell, ed., *Dictionary of North Carolina Biography*, 6 vols. [Chapel Hill, 1979-96], 2:235-6; Manning J. Dauer, *The Adams Federalists* [Baltimore, 1953], 290-1, 294-5).

TJ's NOTE to Franklin of 14 Dec. is not recorded in SJL and has not been found.

To James Garrard

SIR Washington Dec. 16. 1802.

Your favor of Nov. 30. has been duly recieved. the occlusion of the port of N. Orleans by the Spaniards, which is the subject of it, was calculated to give great alarm through the US. and especially the Western parts. information of it was recieved here from N. Orleans on the 6th. inst. and on the 8th. measures were taken to have the proceeding rectified. we think the evidence tolerably conclusive that it was not the consequence of any order from Europe, but merely an irregularity of the Intendant. measures were immediately put in motion for duly impressing him with the consequences of perseverance, and the Spanish minister here, expressing his entire conviction that the prohibition was unauthorised, undertook immediately to remonstrate to him against it, and also to dispatch a letter to the Govr. General who resides at the Havanna, to interpose efficaciously and without delay. we trust therefore that it will be as promptly remedied as the distance permits. it has furnished however a proper occasion of urging on Spain the danger of leaving the peace of the two countries exposed to the caprice of any officer, and the importance of some arrangement which shall leave us independant of that caprice, and free to maintain this treaty right without crossing the Atlantic to seek redress. for the present it is the interest of every part of our republic to cherish peace, and await a friendly rectification of the injury: and I have no doubt that seeing our present situation in a true point of view, you will concur in inculcating a reliance that the government will not be wanting in a just interference to preserve the rights of the nation. the uncertainty with what power we may have to settle this matter adds to it's difficulties. I take the liberty of inclosing you a copy of my communication to Congress, & of tendering you assurances of my great respect and consideration.

TH: JEFFERSON

PrC (DLC); at foot of text: "Governor Garrard." Enclosure: printed copy of Annual Message to Congress, 15 Dec.

GOVR. GENERAL: in the administration of Spain's colonies, Louisiana and the Floridas were within a captaincy general that also included Cuba. Salvador de Muro y Salazar, the Marqués de Someruelos, was the captain general (Gilbert C. Din, ed., *The Spanish Presence in Louisiana, 1763-1803*, vol. 2 of *The Louisiana Purchase Bicentennial Series in Louisiana History* [Lafayette, La., 1996], 113-16; Madison, *Papers*, *Sec. of State Ser.*, 2:69n).

From Craven Peyton

DEAR SIR Stumpisland 16. Dcr. 1802.

I am sorry I was undar the necessity of giving Mr. D. Carr a Draft On you for Six Hundred Dollars, this I did One Month later then you named to me woud. be convenient for you in the last payment, Augt., is the term named to him, resptg. the two first payments. I made engagements to meet Demand On the tenth of February & the tenth of March & I used every exertion in my power to get furthar time but to no effect. This I did for your Own convenience.

With Much Respt Yr Mst. Obt. C PEYTON

RC (ViU); endorsed by TJ as received 21 Dec. and so recorded in SJL.

According to his financial memoranda, TJ did not record an order on Gibson & Jefferson for Dabney CARR in the amount of $600 until 6 Sep. 1803 (MB, 2:1107).

LATER THEN YOU NAMED TO ME: for the postponed payment plan TJ arranged in the purchase of the Henderson lands, see TJ to Peyton, 2 Nov. 1802.

From Léonard Honoré Gay de Vernon

paris Ce 26 frimaire an 11
MONSIEUR LE PRÉSIDENT [i.e. 17 Dec. 1802]

L'hommage que nous avons l'honneur de vous offrir est l'expression de notre cœur. vous êtes cher à tous les amis de l'humanité, et en vous faisant leurs légeres offrandes, ils s'acquittent bien foiblement de la réconnaissance qu'ils vous doivent.

nous nous trouverions très heureux, monsieur le président, Si notre établissement nous fournissait l'occasion de vous faire connaître combien nous sommes touchés de la maniere dont vous gouvernes les états unis de l'amerique, et quelle vénération vous nous inspirés.

Soyez Sur, monsieur le président, que si quelque citoien des etats unis était au nombre de nos élêves; nous nous rappellerions avec le plus grand intérêt qu'il est le Sujet de la loy que vous faites si paternellement et si glorieusement éxécuter, et que nous luy prodiguerions tous les soins qui dependraient de nous.

Agrées monsieur le président, l'assurance de mes profonds respects et de ma haute considération GAYVERNON AINÉ
administrateur de l'établissement

EDITORS' TRANSLATION

MISTER PRESIDENT, 26 Frimaire Year 11 [17 Dec. 1802]

The tribute we have the honor of paying you is the expression of our hearts. You are dear to all friends of humanity, and these modest offerings are but meager repayment of the gratitude you deserve.

We would be very happy, Mister President, if our school allowed us to demonstrate how much we are touched by the way you govern the United States of America, and the veneration you inspire in us.

You can be sure, Mister President, that if a citizen of the United States were among our students, we would be keenly mindful that he is a subject of the law you oversee in such a paternal and glorious way, and we would bestow upon him all the attention in our power.

Accept, Mister President, the assurance of my deep respect and high esteem.

GAYVERNON THE ELDER
Director of the School

RC (DLC); English date supplied; at foot of text: "rue de Seves n. 959"; endorsed by TJ as received 18 Mch. 1803 and so recorded in SJL.

Léonard Honoré Gay de Vernon (1748-1822) became a Catholic priest as a young man. In 1791, under the "civil constitution" of the previous year that governed religious affairs, he was elected bishop of the department of Haute-Vienne, with his episcopal see at Limoges. He became a legislative deputy, then a member of the Convention, and in 1793 renounced his priesthood in accordance with his republican political views. He served on the Council of Five Hundred, was secretary of the revolutionary consulate for the Roman Republic, and held administrative posts in France, but resigned after the Brumaire coup that brought Bonaparte to power in 1799. Gay de Vernon then established a boarding school on the Rue de Sèvres in Paris. He signed as *ainé* in the letter printed above to distinguish himself from his younger brother, Simon François Gay de Vernon, an army officer who, in 1802, taught at the École Polytechnique (*Dictionnaire*, 15:905-6; *Biographie universelle*, 16:89-91; John H. Stewart, *A Documentary Survey of the French Revolution* [New York, 1951], 170).

From "Jack A Dandy"

[ca. 17 Dec. 1802]

Pay attention to oriental Pride—

JACK A DANDY

RC (DLC); undated; addressed: "His Excellency Thomas Jefferson Esqr. City Washington"; franked; postmarked 17 Dec.; endorsed by TJ as received from "Anon." on 24 Dec. and so recorded in SJL with notation "oriental pride."

From James Monroe

Dear Sir. Richmond Decr. 17. 1802.

Genl. Scott having intimated to me his intention to visit the federal city, I take the liberty to introduce him to yr. acquaintance as a very deserving and respectable citizen of this State. Tho' not at present a member of the legislature, yet having been here several days he will be able to communicate to you such incidents of this place as merit attention. The reelection of General Mason to the Senate is a thing of course. It is only necessary to make it known that he will serve, to secure him a very genl. vote in both houses. I have hinted his assent to some & presume it will be attended to in due time. with great

respect & esteem yr. frnd. & servt. Jas. Monroe

RC (DLC); endorsed by TJ as received 25 Dec. and "by Genl. Scott" and so recorded in SJL.

genl. scott: probably John B. Scott, a brigadier general in the Virginia militia and representative from Halifax County in the House of Delegates from 1799 to 1802 (cvsp, 9:1; Leonard, *General Assembly*, 216, 220, 224).

To the Senate

Gentlemen of the Senate

I nominate John Spence West, whose term as Marshal of North Carolina expired on the 10th. inst. to be reappointed Marshal of North Carolina. Th: Jefferson

Dec. 17. 1802.

RC (DNA: RG 46, EPEN, 7th Cong., 2d sess.); endorsed by a Senate clerk. PrC (DLC). Recorded in SJL with notation "nomn of West marshl N.C."

Meriwether Lewis brought TJ's nomination of john spence west to the Senate on Monday, 20 Dec. The Senate read, confirmed, and sent notice of the renewal to the president the same day. West's new commission "for a term of four years" is dated 10 Dec., the day his old commission expired (FC in Lb in DNA: RG 59, MPTPC; jep, 1:426).

From Thomas Cooper

Dear Sir Wilkesbarre 18 December 1802

I have received (yesterday) the kind letter you addressed to me in answer to mine from Northumberland. I thank you for the intimation respecting my Son, who I hope will do no discredit to the appointment. He will remain here untill he receives information of his being actually commissioned.

Believe me, with sincere respect Dear Sir Your faithful friend

THOMAS COOPER

RC (DLC); endorsed by TJ as received 24 Dec. and so recorded in SJL.

LETTER YOU ADDRESSED TO ME IN ANSWER TO MINE: TJ to Cooper, 29 Nov., in response to Cooper to TJ, 25 Oct.

INTIMATION RESPECTING MY SON: an inquiry into the intemperate lifestyle of Thomas Cooper, Jr., had delayed his naval appointment. Robert Smith issued a midshipman's warrant to him on 6 Apr. 1803, but revoked it on 20 July 1804 because of the young man's ongoing insobriety (Robert Smith to Thomas Cooper, Jr., 6 Apr. 1803 and 20 July 1804, in DNA: RG 45, LSO; Cooper to TJ, 21 Mch. 1803; TJ to Cooper, 9 Apr. 1803; Smith to TJ, 23 July 1804).

From Albert Gallatin

Treasury Department
December 18th. 1802.

SIR:

I have the honor of transmitting detailed statements of the Expenditures in the Quarter Master General's department, and by the Naval Agents, from the 1st. January, 1797, to the 31st. December, 1801, so far as the same were made upon accounts settled at the Treasury.

Those statements have been prepared by the Register of the Treasury, pursuant to the directions you gave on the 5th. of last May, for the purpose of carrying into execution a resolution of the House of Representatives of the 3d day of May, 1802: they embrace, however, only that portion of the objects contemplated by the resolution, which will not be contained in the documents prepared by the Accountants of the War and Navy departments.

I have the honor to be, Very respectfully, Sir, Your obdeient servant.

ALBERT GALLATIN

FC (Lb in DNA: RG 56, MLS); in a clerk's hand; at head of text: "The President of the United States." Enclosures: (1) "A Statement of Expenditures in the Quarter Master General's Department. According to the Accounts Thereof, Adjusted at the Treasury. Commencing with the 1st of January, 1797, and ending with 31st December, 1801, Stated in Pursuance of a Resolution of the House of Representatives of the 3d May, 1802," signed by Joseph Nourse, Register, 16 Dec. 1802, for the settlement of accounts totaling $292,212,27, printed in *Message from the President of the United States, Accompanying a Statement of Expenditures from the 1st of January, 1797, by the Quarter Master General, and the Navy Agents, for the Contingencies of the Naval and Military Establishments, and the Navy Contracts for Timber and Stores. Transmitted in Pursuance of a Resolution of the House, of the 3d of May Last* (Washington, D.C., 1803, last section; Shaw-

Shoemaker, No. 5357). (2) "A Statement of the Monies advanced at the Treasury to Naval Agents, from 1st January, [1797], till 31st December, 1801, stated in compliance with an Order of the House of Representatives of 3d May, 1802," from the Treasury Department, being a table with the names of naval agents and account totals, with the final column stating the balance remaining to be accounted for on the Treasury books, amounting to over $310,000, printed in *Documents Accompanying a Message from the President of the United States, with Sundry Statements of Expenditures; Containing Detailed Accounts of the Expenditures of Public Monies, by Naval Agents; from the 1st of January, 1797, to 31st December, 1801, Contingencies of the Navy Department, and Copies of Contracts for Cannon, Timber, and Other Military and Naval Stores, during the Same Period* (Washington, D.C., 1803, 569; Shaw-Shoemaker, No. 5285).

From Rufus King

SIR, London December 18. 1802.

Mr Gore having during my absence acknowledged the receipt of your letter to me, and at the same time transmitted to you copies of the correspondence with the President of the Sierra Leone Company, I have only to resume the subject where he left it—

The idle and disorderly Character of the Negroes who deserted their masters and joined the Br: army in america, and who constitute the greater part of the Inhabitants of Sierra Leone, has produced an unfavourable Opinion of our Slaves in general, which it is not easy to correct, and which unfortunately operates against the adoption of the Plan we have offered to the African Company.

Hitherto the Colony has done but little towards defraying the Expence of its Protection, which is so considerable that the Company feels the Burthen, and is unwilling to consent to any measure that may chance to increase it. I have taken some pains, but hitherto without success, to do away what has appeared to me an unfounded Apprehension on this Subject, and to engage the Company to adopt our Proposition—I have not pressed for a Decision, having reason to beleive that it might be in the negative—At present I am recommending a modification of the Plan, to be tried in the first instance as an Experiment, & upon a small scale, and ultimately adopted upon a larger one, if found to be free from the Inconveniencies that are apprehended—

Though I dare not encourage the Expectation that the Company will agree to the Proposal upon any terms, I am not without hope that it may consent to receive a limited number of our Negroes by way of Experiment.

There is no prospect whatever of our being able to combine the

Transportation of these Slaves with any beneficial plan of Trade: it would be an important Point gained, could we obtain Permission to send them to Sierra Leone—:and the Expence of their Passage would be small in comparison with the advantage of their Banishment.

I cannot close this letter, without begging you to be assured that I am duly sensible of your obliging approbation of the manner in which I have performed the Duties of my Office in this Country: the like zeal and industry will continue to be employed during the residue of my mission, & I shall moreover be ready after my return home, to give to the Department of State any such information as it may be supposed my residence here has enabled me to acquire—

With distinguished Consideration I have the Honour to be Sir Your ob. & most Hbl Servant

Rufus King

RC (DLC); at foot of first page: "The President of the United States"; endorsed by TJ as received 4 Mch. 1803 and so recorded in SJL. FC (NHi: Rufus King Papers); dated 20 Dec.

Christopher gore, as acting chargé d'affaires while King was away, had written to TJ on 10 Oct. in response to TJ's letter to King of 13 July.

joined the br: army in america: many of the inhabitants of Sierra Leone were African Americans who escaped from slavery during the American Revolution and took up arms for the British. After the Revolution they lived in Nova Scotia, or in lesser numbers in London, until they migrated to the Sierra Leone colony (Wallace Brown, "The Black Loyalists in Sierra Leone," in John W. Pulis, ed., *Moving On: Black Loyalists in the Afro-Atlantic World* [New York, 1999], 103-34).

From Philippe Reibelt

George Town a la Taverne de Mr. Barneÿ le 18 Dec. 1802.

Monsieur le Président!

Dans la Supposition que la lettre que j'avais pris la liberté d'adresser à Votre Excellence le 30 Nov. de Norfolk Vous soit parvenûe, je prie Votre Excellence de Vouloir bien me faire savoir l'heure, à laquelle je puisse jouir du Bonheur de Vous presenter mes Respects, et de recevoir de vos mains tout ce que j'ai sollicité par ladite lettre.

Ne possedant pas encore la langue anglaise je dois Vous demander en même tems la permission de Vous parler ou en Français ou en Allemand, et n'yant pas trouvé dans le Port d'Alexandrie mes Effets qui m'y devoient avoir devancés, Vous voudriez bien m'excuser en Philosophe, si je ne puis paraitre qu'en habit de Voyageur.

J'ai l'honneur d'etre Votre Excellence très obeïssant Serviteur

Phil. Reibelt

EDITORS' TRANSLATION

Mr. Barney's tavern in Georgetown
18 Dec. 1802

Mister President!

Assuming that Your Excellency received the letter I took the liberty of sending from Norfolk on November 30, I beg Your Excellency to inform me of the time when I might have the pleasure of presenting my respects and receiving from your hands the documents I requested in that letter.

Not yet possessing the English language, I must also ask permission to speak to you in French or German. The belongings that were supposed to be forwarded to me did not arrive in Alexandria, so I beg you, as a philosopher, to excuse me if I visit you in traveling clothes.

I have the honor of being, Your Excellency, your very obedient servant.

Phil. Reibelt

RC (MHi); endorsed by TJ as received 18 Dec. and so recorded in SJL.

DE VOUS PRESENTER MES RESPECTS: John Dawson, with whom Tadeusz Kosciuszko was acquainted, introduced Reibelt to TJ (Vol. 30:196n, 314, 508; Vol. 33:288-9; Reibelt to TJ, 12 Dec. 1808, in DLC).

From Philip Pearson

Bunker Hill
19th. Decemr. 1802.

May it please your Excellency.

We the Trustees of Jefferson Monticello Society in Fairfield District and State of South Carolina at this distance beg leave to represent to your Excellency that the Society considering the general introduction of learning and Science in any free Country to be one great means of advancing and securing its national prosperity and happiness; and influenced solely by those motives which had for their object the public good, have with the aid of our benefactors the friends of literature, at a very considerable expense Erected a handsome and commodious building near Broad River in the District aforesaid, and there Established a School by the name of Jefferson Monticello Academy; That we have every reason to believe great and important advantages must result to this Country from the Establishment provided the design can be carried fully into effect; But the ability of the Society being unequal to their good intentions, their plan for carrying into Execution what they consider a laudable and beneficial undertaking must in some measure be frustrated or delayed for want of the means to accommodate the same with a Library and other Apparatus necessary for the instruction of youth in the more advanced branches of learning and Science, unless the Honorable the Legislature of this State to whom we have applied, or the Liberal and Affluent should patronize the Establishment so far as to give the Society the pecuniary aid they so essentially need.

The Society have engaged a Worthy able Tutor to the Academy and the Institution though embarrassed with difficulties appears to flourish. Our youth have been honoured with public Encomiums on their progress in Literature, on their compositions, and the propriety with which they have in public Exhibited their Scholastic Exercises: We are therefore the more Sollicitous to see the same compleatly acommodated and permanently Established, that not only our youth but those of succeeding Generations at Jefferson Monticello Academy may acquire the advantages of a virtuous and liberal Education; and that the worthy name (dear to all good Citizens) which it has received as a testimony of the high opinion we entertain of your Excellency's distinguished virtues, may be perpetuated to posterity: And this being the sum of our Wishes we are the less backward in making known our wants to the Patriotic and the Wealthy, the friends of Science and of Literature.

Our worthy benefactor General Richard Winn will convey and present this our humble Address, which we hope your Excellency's singular goodness will Excuse, as we are with Submission and sentiments of the highest esteem and Veneration, May it please your Excellency.

Your Excellency's most Obedient And most devoted Servants

PHIL.' PEARSON
in behalf of himself and James Davis
Trustees for the Society.

RC (DLC). Recorded in SJL as received from "Jefferson Monticello academy" on 26 Jan. 1803 with notation "by Phil. Pearson."

Philip Pearson (1746-1835) of Fairfield, South Carolina, furnished supplies for the state troops and Continental soldiers in 1781 during the Revolutionary War. An eminent surveyor who reputedly laid out the city of Columbia, he was the first clerk of court of Richland County, a justice of the peace, and a trustee of the Jefferson Monticello Academy. His son, Philip Edward Pearson, a prominent lawyer who was educated at the academy, also later became a trustee (Edwin L. Green, *A History of Richland County* [Columbia, S.C., 1932], 54-5, 101; John Belton O'Neall, *Biographical Sketches of the Bench and Bar of South Carolina*, 2 vols. [Charleston, S.C., 1859], 2:99).

The JEFFERSON MONTICELLO ACADEMY, built in 1800 in the village of Monticello in Fairfield, with the voluntary contributions of its citizens, opened its doors "for the reception and instruction of youth" in January 1801 under the direction of the Reverend James Rogers. In addition to Pearson, its trustees were William Cato and James Davis. The founders and trustees petitioned the South Carolina legislature on behalf of the Jefferson Monticello Society on 2 Nov. 1802, and gained its incorporation without financial assistance on 18 Dec.

(Thomas Cooper and David J. McCord, eds., *Statutes at Large of South Carolina*, 10 vols. [Columbia, S.C., 1836-41], 8:214; *Columbia South-Carolina State Gazette and Columbian Advertiser*, 26 June 1801; Fitz Hugh McMaster, *History of Fairfield County, South Carolina from "Before the White Man Came" to 1942* [Columbia, S.C., 1946], 62-5).

Richard WINN was a Republican congressman from Fairfield (*Biog. Dir. Cong.*).

From Caesar A. Rodney

HONORED & DEAR SIR, Wilmington Decr. 19th. 1802.

You were so good as to subscribe One hundred dollars to the Seminary at this place. I enclose you an advertisement on the subject.

Our *Feds* have not yet agreed on their Senator. Your message is read with great avidity. Our friends are delighted with the good news which it proclaims & our enemies I beleive consider it invulnerable, as they are yet silent as the grave about it. Bayard will not take his seat until the Courts are over & until I suspect his will & pleasure are known on the subject of senators. If he possesses any one quality of a statesman he will limit his indecorous language in the house this winter

I feel an inclination to visit Washington during the Session, in order to gather information & to collect that knowledge which may be beneficial to the general cause hereafter: To understand the characters of many with whom I have no acquaintance that I may not enter the house entirely ignorant of men & their real situation. I wish to brighten the chain with our friends whose experience will be of more use than a volume written on the subject. I fear I shall not be able to accomplish my wishes as my business call for all the attention my health will enable me to bestow. With affectionate regard I am Dr. Sir

Yours most Sincerely C. A. RODNEY

RC (DLC); endorsed by TJ as received 22 Dec. and so recorded in SJL. Enclosure: perhaps the advertisement placed by James Lea, secretary of the board of trustees of the Wilmington Academy, dated 10 Dec., calling on subscribers to pay the sums promised either to the gentlemen who took their subscriptions or to Henry Latimer, treasurer of the academy (printed in Wilmington *Mirror of the Times, & General Advertiser*, 18 Dec. 1802).

SEMINARY AT THIS PLACE: according to his financial records, TJ subscribed $100 to the Wilmington Academy on 11 July (MB, 2:1077). The academy, which was opened in 1766 and chartered in 1773, was closed for several years during the Revolutionary War, but reopened in 1781. It closed again in 1798 after the departure of the principal. An address to the public on behalf of the Wilmington Academy, dated 31 July 1802, and signed by Gunning Bedford, Jr., president of the board of trustees, and James Lea, secretary, called for the revival of the academy with a system of education "on a scale commensurate with every useful object" and with the "circle of the sciences" as complete as resources permitted. The trustees sought contributions not only from the citizens of Delaware, but from "all lovers of science and patrons of literature" in the United States (Wilmington *Mirror of the Times*, 4 Aug.; John A. Munroe, *Federalist Delaware, 1775-1815* [New Brunswick, N.J., 1954], 171-3; Anna T. Lincoln, *Wilmington, Delaware: Three Centuries under Four Flags, 1609-1937* [Rutland, Vt., 1937; repr. Port Washington, N.Y., 1972], 322-3).

From Johann Gotthilff Angerman

EDITORS' TRANSLATION

MOST GRACIOUS SIR! Lingen, 20 Dec. 1802

Your great and widely appreciated concern for the welfare of the noble American nation is so well known that there is little need for my pitiable praise. Nevertheless, the very encouragement you offer to foreigners and observers in the most distant locations emboldens me to present a piece of writing to Your Eminence. This writing has as its principal purpose guaranteeing the safety of the property of residents of this county, who have protection under the present system of surveillance, against devastating flames of major and destructive fires, as appropriate to their individual circumstances. So all the more I hope that this treatise of mine which has just left the press may gain a favorable reception since the publication protects the security of dwellings throughout my native land and, by extension, touches the true common welfare and benefit of every country. In the fondest hope that Your Excellency will deign to receive my well-meaning intentions favorably, I have the pleasure to remain, with the greatest respect

Your most humble and completely devoted servant, who esteems you highly,

J. G. ANGERMAN
Regional Master Builder for the Counties of Tecklenburg and Lingen in Westphalia

RC (DLC); original in German; at head of text: "Hochgebietender hoher Herr Präsident"; endorsed by TJ as received 28 June 1803 and so recorded in SJL. Enclosure: Johann Gotthilff Angerman, *Anweisung, wie das Holz zum Haus- und Schiffsbau so zubereitet werden könne, dass es vor Feuer, Faulniss und Wurmfrass . . . verwahrt bleibe: nebst einer Anweisung, wie Stroh-, Rohr- und Schindeldächer feuerfest . . . auszuführen, auch die Feueranstalten zu verbessern seyn* (Lingen, 1802).

Upon receiving Angerman's letter and pamphlet, TJ forwarded them for translation to Jacob Wagner at the State Department, who informed TJ that they were written by "Mr. Angerman of Lingen in Westphalia" (Wagner to TJ, 28 June 1803).

From Joseph Barnes

SIR, Livorno Decemr. 20th 1802.

On my Arrival from the north of Italy I had the pleasure of receiving my Commission for the Island of Sicily in the month of Novr. brought by Commodore Morris, and left in care of my friend Mr Appleton from whose hand I reced. it. I am well persuaded Mr Jefferson will excuse me for observing, that I did flatter myself I should have reced. the appointment for the *two Sicilies*, which include Naples; and, I am equally persuaded Mr Jefferson will believe me when I assure him that motives of interest never induc'd me to apply for the appointment.—I am not fond of boasting of my regard for my Country, tho' perfectly sensible no individual feels more *Amer Patria* than I do. Knowing the patriotism and integrity of Mr Jefferson's mind; and the independence of his sentiments, I take the liberty of communicating mine freely; first, foreigners can *never* feel what native Citizens feel; consequently a number of Evils occur from the want of natural interest; a more convincing proof cannot exist than the conduct of Mr Mathieu of Naples, of which I believe Mr Mazzei, Mr Jefferson's old friend, and others have fully inform'd Mr Jefferson, his inattention has universally been so detrimental to the interest of the United States, from his conduct relative to the Louisa of Philada., his appointment of Vice consuls of the worst of characters, and of whom they say he reced. money!! That foreigners Who are appointed by & under the *Comptrol of native Citizens of the U.S.* may probably in some instances be more useful than Natives is admissible, but those appointed by Mr Mathieu are of such an order of men that ought *not* to fill even a private situation much less a public one—The man he appointed at Messina was the Vice consul to the British who, from his *base* conduct in the sale of some prizes, was sent for on Board by the British Commodore Trowbridge, and when on Board, convinc'd by the commodore from the Accounts of infamy in Robbing the seamen, and forced to disgorge near 1000 £ Sterg. or he would have been hung up to the Yard arm, which circumstance is well known to every one in Messina; and, after this, is such a man to represent our Nation?—The character of the man in Palermo I believe I troubled Mr Jefferson with in a former letter, he almost confesses like a British Senator once did to his constituents, who wanted him to vote against the Ministry, who gave 2500 £ Sterg. for his Borough, that he bought them for 2500 £ Sterg. & he should sell them for as much profit as possible: The conduct of the man in question at Palermo to Capt. Sawyer of the Brig Fox of Boston was most shameful.

Other motives more powerful than the above induce me to trouble Mr Jefferson with further observations; not merely to remove grievances which exist, but by means of good arrangements with the Neapolitan Government to obtain future advantages, in commercial objects that would benefit my Country; this I am *deprived* of doing, as the King and Court have removed from Palermo to Naples, where I cannot consistently reside while my office is in Sicily about 150 Miles distant—In all these weak and despotic Governments, 'tis necessary to be on the spot, keep up a little parade of offices, & in fact; *Bribe* some of the officers about the court—Mr Jefferson being so well Acquainted with the political History of Most Nations, it would be presumption in me to take up his time by detail, shall therefore only observe that *no* commercial advantage is to be gain'd in these Countries, particularly Naples, except by the *force* of *Arms*, or *force of influence*—the British & French gain advantages by the first; we should try to keep up with them by the second means.—It is not[1] vanity in me to notice, that thro' some contracts I have had with the British Govt. in the Kingdom of Naples, I am well acquainted with some of the principal characters about the Court—should Mr Jefferson think it proper to make a change, and add it to my appointment, my exertions I flatter myself will be fully equal to his expectations, and to my promises; should he however think otherwise at this moment, I shall nevertheless, as far as my circumscribed situation will permit, in the Island of Sicily, promote the interest of my Countrymen & benefit of my country; and wait a more favorable[2] opportunity. One point Mr Jefferson must permit me to notice, which I am well persuaded has been done without his knowledge and I am equally persuaded when known to him, he will not approve of; being a thing contrary to the usage of all Nations in regard to their respective Consuls; and injuring them in the Esteem of the Governments in which they reside, to represent their own; it does not affect me alone; and Mr Jefferson will clearly perceive that it is not any pecuniary interest which prompts me to notice it; the British & French Vessels of War, and indeed Ships of War of all Nations, except ours; when they arrive in any Port apply naturally to the Consuls of their respective Nations for any Supplies necessary—Our Commanders Acting differently at Leghorn has surprized the People much, and indeed Occasion'd many remarks, consequently astonishment at Mr Appleton's not being applied to—And, when I arrive in

Sicily, the same remarks will naturally be made; and, by any jealous person making a bad use of this circumstance, they may very properly say, as their own Government has not confidence in them to supply their Vessels of War, of course the parties cannot have confidence in our Government.—Mr Smith, the secretary of the Navy, no doubt has done it without reflection, and, when convinced of the injury it may do, our Govt. I am sensible he will feel a pleasure in correcting it.—

I shall now submit to Mr Jefferson a few observations relative to our situation respecting the Barbary powers, and the means in my opinion best calculated to remove the Evil should the trade be consider'd of consequence; first, if a consul general, or a *charge d'affaires* was constituted to reside at Malta or in Sicily to comptrol, and with whom all the consuls of the coast of Barbary should corrispond, & he with the U.S. great good might result, as he could not be menaced, by the tyrany of those pittit powers; consequently act independently for the interest of his Country.

And, should the British keep Malta, which most likely they will, by proper management & a good understanding with them these frequent and unprovoked Wars with those pirates might easily be avoided; I am on such good terms with the present Governor Ball, of Malta, that I know I could do much good, & lay the foundation of *more*; notwithstanding the jealousy of the British in regard to our trade; and I am well satisfied that the freedom of the Mediterranean with about 20.000 £ Sterg. to the French Minister Taleyrand might easily be effected—The Swedes have procured their peace thro' the medium of the French; and, thro' the medium of the French & British we may always keep at peace—Knowing the independent spirit of Mr Jefferson, I am aware he will probably *not* approve, but tho' we dispise the means we may approve the effect; and indeed under our present circumstances we are at too great an expence; and shall I fear be obliged to come at least in part to their terms.—

The only mode I can perceive, should it be Mr Jefferson's determination *not* to submit to the impositions of these Barbarians; would be: by making an arrangement with the Neapolitan Govt. who are dreadfully oppress'd by those pirates; so much so; that along the whole south Coast of Sicily, the Turks venture on shore and carry away whole families!—And while they have plenty of Wheat & corn at Mamfredonia in the Adreatic, & even in the south of Sicily, they are much in want in Palermo, Messina and Naples, and obliged to buy foreign Wheat &c at great prices; indeed, at a place call'd Licata near Cape Passaro, in the south of Sicily tho only about 150 Miles from Messina the difference of the price of Wheat & corn will be nearly $\frac{1}{3}$d—as there are no Roads thro' great part of the Island of Sicily; And, the Turks will not permit their Vessels to Navigate; a small Vessel will remain some times two months in port before she will attempt to sail—On my return from Malta to Girgenti on the South coast of Sicily; I was surrounded at one time by four Turkish Vessels, and saw I suppose in the distance of 60 miles nearly twenty—

The object of my troubling Mr Jefferson with this Account is simply to show, that I think the Neapolitan Govt. would be very happy to pay for ten or twelve Vessels of War, "chiefly Schooners similar to the Enterprize answer best, as they sail quick & are[3] powerful enough for any of the Turks," to join them; &, fixing Sicily as the general rendivous—From thence to Malta, Sardinia, Gibralter, and on along the coast of Genoa, Leghorn & Naples, changing, & keeping continually the stations, our Vessels, would always have a convoy, as well as the Neapolitans—We should improve our Navy and render ourselves respected in this quarter, at little expence—however my Sentiments have never been in favor of a Navy nor Army, but if a Navy must be kept, tis as well to be thus employ'd with such force as to command respect for the Nation & itself—otherwise we must submit to similar measures to the Danes & Swedes.—

The Neapolitans are under such terror of the Turks; that a Kings Vessel of double force will scarcely attack them—and Arm'd Vessels of 10 Guns are often desert'd by the men in their Boats, when only pursued by a Row-Galley with 30 or 40 men without cannon; I am therefore well satisfied in my mind; that the Neapolitans would be happy to pay $\frac{2}{3}$rds of our expence for the consideration of a certain convoy & protection of their trade.—

Having troubled Mr Jefferson with a much longer letter than I first intended; I only wish any of my Ideas may, from his superior judgement, be put into such a shape as to be useful to my country; from whose, liberality, independence & perseverence I expect every good that can attend our common Country—and only wish all my countrymen were as sensible as myself of the favorable disposition, he would remain in the office of chief Magistrate 'till he should have accomplish'd the perfectionation of the great Machine of Government upon such unerring principles as to ensure the perpetuation of Liberty, Republicanism & Virtue in the United States, made them the model & envy of the World—in haste

I have the honor to be with the highest sentiment of respect Mr Jefferson—your obedt. Sert.— J: Barnes

P.S. in a few days I shall set out for Naples to get my commission acknowledged—shall then be under the necessity of returning to Genoa & Marseilles to close some matters of importance, which effected shall proceed to Sicily, make my arrangements & commence my office—mean while shall have a despatch there—

NB—much is said here, which circumstances seem to corroborate, of a new rupture between the French & English—at this moment the French Virtually govern all Italy,—their troops are in all the states except those of Rome & Naples—& such is the state of the finances of the Emperor of Germany, that his Bank paper especially at Venice is at 20 pr ct. discount—

RC (DLC); at head of text: "His Excellency Thomas Jefferson President of the United States"; addressed, portion missing: "[...]son [...] of the United States Washington"; postmarked and franked; endorsed by TJ as received 21 Mch. 1803 and so recorded in SJL.

Barnes's COMMISSION, which made him consul for the island of Sicily, was dated 10 Feb. (DNA: RG 59, PTCC).

Barnes had long been a critic of John S. M. MATHIEU, the consul at Naples, who stood in the way of Barnes's desired appointment as consul to the Two Sicilies and Naples. In May 1803, a group of Americans in Naples, joined later by others in Boston, appealed to Madison to remove Mathieu. Those memorials, however, made no mention of Barnes as a potential replacement for Mathieu. Stating that there was no American citizen established at Naples to do the job, they urged that the consulship be given to a well-informed Prussian merchant (Samuel Welles and others to Madison, 1 May 1803, in DNA: RG 59, CD, Naples; Madison, *Papers*, *Sec. of State Ser.*, 4:567; Vol. 32:174; Vol. 34:49).

Early in 1801, after a British blockade turned the LOUISA away from Leghorn, the ship went to Messina, where it was detained for a time on orders from Mathieu. Later, when the *Louisa* departed for Gibraltar and the United States, the captain left some of his crew behind, forcing Mathieu to arrange for the seamen's return to the U.S. (*Philadelphia Gazette*, 10 Feb.; *Alexandria Advertiser*, 18 Apr.; Salem, Mass., *Impartial Register*, 18 May; *Gazette of the United States*, 8 Oct.; New York *Daily Advertiser*, 17 Oct. 1801; Madison, *Papers*, *Sec. of State Ser.*, 2:79; NDBW, 1:543).

BRITISH COMMODORE: Sir Thomas Troubridge directed British naval forces around Naples and Sicily from the fall of 1798 to the spring of 1800 (DNB).

When the *Louisa* was detained, the brig FOX was also held for a time in Sicily by Mathieu's orders. Not long after that, David Sawyer, the captain of the *Fox*, aided Barnes's efforts to be named consul of the Two Sicilies (*Impartial Register*, 18 May 1801; *New-York Gazette*, 29 June 1801; Vol. 33:563n; Vol. 34:49, 133).

SOME CONTRACTS I HAVE HAD: Barnes sold supplies to the British on Malta (Madison, *Papers*, *Sec. of State Ser.*, 4:185-6).

MR APPLETON'S NOT BEING APPLIED TO: Thomas Appleton considered it a "disgrace" that he was not the U.S. naval agent at Leghorn as well as consul (Vol. 37:253).

THOSE PITTIT POWERS: that is, petty (petit) powers.

Sir Alexander John BALL, a British naval officer, was named governor of Malta in 1799 to serve as a liaison between the local population and blockading British forces. He remained after the French surrendered the island in 1800. Barnes was a close acquaintance by February 1801. Ball left Malta in April of that year. He returned in June 1802 as Britain's minister plenipotentiary to the Order of Knights of St. John, and became civil commissioner as British forces ceased their withdrawal from the island

(Desmond Gregory, *Malta, Britain, and the European Powers, 1793-1815* [Madison, N.J., 1996], 76, 158; DNB; Joseph Attard, *Malta: A History of Two Millennia* [Valletta, Malta, 2002], 166-7; Grainger, *Amiens Truce*, 120-1; Vol. 32:587).

THE SWEDES HAVE PROCURED THEIR PEACE: frustrated that the U.S. squadron was convoying merchant ships instead of attacking Tripoli, that coordination of policy with the United States was cumbersome, and that the war was too expensive, the Swedish government ceased hostilities with Tripoli by a treaty of 2 Oct. 1802. The truce required a large payment by Sweden to Tripoli, plus annuities thereafter. Tripoli was to release all Swedish prisoners. The treaty was the result of mediation by a French diplomat, Horace Sébastiani (Madison, *Papers, Sec. of State Ser.*, 4:8-9n, 162-3n, 452n; Parry, *Consolidated Treaty Series*, 56:407-10; Tulard, *Dictionnaire Napoléon*, 1554).

[1] Word interlined.

[2] Barnes here canceled "appointment."

[3] Barnes here canceled "equall."

To Francis Taliaferro Brooke

Washington Dec. 20. 1802.

Th: Jefferson presents his salutations to Mr. Brooke Speaker of the Senate of Virginia, and availing himself of the moment when the confidence of his country has placed him where the little volume accompanying this may be a convenience, he asks his acceptance of it as a testimony of the respect of the giver.

RC (Julian Goldman, New York City, 1947). Not recorded in SJL. Enclosure: TJ's *A Manual of Parliamentary Practice. For the Use of the Senate of the United States* (Washington, D.C., 1801).

A veteran of the Continental army and brother of former Virginia governor and attorney general Robert Brooke, Francis Taliaferro Brooke (1763-1851) was a lawyer from Fredericksburg, Virginia, first elected to the state senate in 1800. A supporter of the president, he was elected speaker on 7 Dec. 1802. He served a short tenure, after which he became a circuit court judge and eventually a judge on the Virginia Supreme Court of Appeals (DVB, 2:259-61).

From Thomas T. Davis

SIR Washington Decr 20th 1802

I dont know whether it is proper for me to make this application to you or not—if is not proper it is the effect of mis[take.] The Death of Mr. Clark Judge of the Indiana Terrory makes a vacancy there:

It would be a great acccomodation to me be appointed his successor. I live Convinent to the Territory—know the people and am known to them—Thire was not a Law Character on the Bench—My success as a Lawyer in a practice of two years can be easily known. Some persons (whither authorized by you not) have spoken to me about being the successor of Steel the Secretary to Govr. Claiborne—Some words of mine might be construed into a willingness to accept Tho it would not be a choice—Tis too far & it might be thot I had been instrumental in Steels removal. The Idea would injure me with independent men—my reletives are all in Kentucky—I dont want to leave them or the state far. I must quit Congress for I cant afford to loose my time from my private concerns.

I am Sir with sentiment of respect your Ob h s

THO. T. DAVIS

RC (DNA: RG 59, LAR); torn; endorsed by TJ as received 20 Dec. and "to be judge of Indiana" and so recorded in SJL.

Davis was appointed JUDGE OF THE INDIANA TERRITORY in Feb. 1803 (TJ to the Senate, 2 Feb. 1803). For his opposition to John Steele's continuation as SECRETARY of the Mississippi Territory, see William C. C. Claiborne to TJ, 4 Mch. 1802.

From Albert Gallatin

DEAR SIR 20th Decer. 1802

I enclose the proposals made for building the marine hospital; and also some objections made by Doctr. Eustis as to the site & plan. Are they sufficient to induce a postponement & inquiry. The consequence of the delay will probably be that the building cannot be completed till summer of 1804, instead of being done in the course of next year.

A. M'Clene has called on me, and on coming to an explanation of his letter, says that he never intended it as a resignation; but that he meant to convey the idea that *if* the President intends removing him, which he still hopes, will not be the case, the removal might not take place till next spring.

With respect & attachment Your's ALBERT GALLATIN

RC (DLC); endorsed by TJ as received from the Treasury Department on 20 Dec. and "Marine hospital Boston" and "Mc.lane" and so recorded in SJL. Enclosures not found.

BUILDING THE MARINE HOSPITAL: on 18 Dec., William Eustis wrote Gallatin that he had examined the proposals for the hospital and believed that Ward Jackson and Joseph Eaton, two Boston builders who had submitted the lowest bid, should receive the contract, though he feared the young men were making "a bad bargain for themselves." On 23 Dec., Gallatin returned the proposals to Benjamin Lincoln, the collector at Boston. Gallatin noted that, unless Lincoln had objections, he should employ the contractors who made the lowest offer (Gallatin, *Papers*, 7:828, 846; *The Boston Directory: Containing the Names of the Inhabitants, Their Occupations, Places of Business, and Dwelling-Houses* [Boston, 1803], 45, 73). For the hospital plan and the call for bids, see Gallatin to TJ (second letter) and TJ's response, both at 7 Oct.

From Thomas Munroe

Superintendants Office
Washington 20th December 1802

Sir,

Pursuant to the sixth section of the Act of Congress, of last Session, intituled "An Act to abolish the Board of Commissioners in the City of Washington, and for other purposes," and under your direction of the 16th June last, I proceeded with all possible diligence to prepare a Statement of all the Lots of the description in the said Section mentioned; and on the 19th. of that Month advertised the same for sale, on the 30th day of August, then next ensuing; which Advertisement was published according to Law, and on the day appointed the said Sale commenced, and was continued by Adjournment until the 29th day of October last, during which time the whole of the said Lots were sold, and produced the sum of $\$26,848\frac{10}{100}$ of which I paid away agreeably to the 4th section of the above recited Act of Congress, the sum of \$2,249.03 (together with \$2,563.85, which arose out of other funds of the City) for debts which had been contracted by the late Commissioners, in their Capacity as such, the payment whereof was not specially provided for, by the aforesaid Act of Congress; and the balance to wit, \$24,599.07 was applied as directed, by the Said Act of Congress, towards the payment of the Loan of \$50,000 by the State of Maryland.

It may not be improper, here, to mention, that very few, if any, of these Lots produced by the resale thereof, the amount of the original purchase money due thereon—that the deficiency is very considerable, and that it is not probable the debtors will be able to pay more than about \$10,000 thereof—

Some, however, who are deemed able to pay contend that they cannot be compelled to make payment, because they say the Act of the Maryland Legislature of 1793 Chapter 58 which authorises a resale, in case of default in payment, does not admit of reselling more than once; and that if the power of resale be exercised, the original purchaser is not bound for any deficiency, as the public or City Agent had a choice of two remedies, to wit, a Suit, or resale; and having elected to resell they have not a right to use both remedies, and to resort to a Suit for the deficiency. This Doctrine is particularly insisted on in the case of an Endorser of the Note of a deceased purchaser, at a resale, in which case a second resale has been made and a considerable deficiency has in consequence happened—The Endorser now says he is ready and willing to pay the amount due on the Lots as purchased by his principal upon the same being conveyed for his

Indemnity—Before I adopt any compulsory measure on this subject I have supposed it to be proper to submit the circumstances for the Consideration and opinion of the proper Law officer, and to pray the Instructions of the President in the premises.

The number of Lots which were thrown into the Market at the public Sale, directed by the Act of Congress before recited, being much greater than the demand, and the positive and unconditional obligation imposed by the Act of Congress to sell the whole of them, within a limited time, not only subjected those Lots to great sacrifices and disadvantages in the sale thereof, but has also materially injured the private Sales of all the other public Lots in the sale of which the President might exercise his discretion—of this Description of Lots, however, I have sold five which have produced $1,531.43 Cash:

In my accounts from 1st June last to the 1st Ultimo, prepared for the Treasury department, it appears that in addition to the receipts and Expenditures herein before stated I have received

From the late Board of Commissioners, being the balance which remained in their hands when the Commission ceased,—1 June last	$110.59
For Lots purchased prior to 6th May 1796, voluntarily paid by the purchasers before the public sale, on 30th August last	1274.28
For balance of purchase Money for Lots sold by the Commrs. since 6th May 1796	109.93

And from sundry persons, for small balances, which were due to the City on Accounts, other than for Lots sold $320.73 making $1815.53 which has been expended as follows viz $374.60 for expenses attending the aforesaid public sale of Lots and $408.51 for other expenses necessarily incurred in the Execution of the duties of the Office of Superintendant, the balance, to wit, $1032.42 is included in the sum of $2563.85 herein before stated to have been paid for Debts contracted by the Commissioners

The Receipts and Expenditures since 1st. Ulto. amount to $36.80 only.

The Debts now due to the City, and considered as good, exclusive of the Deficiencies on the Lots resold for default of payment, amount to upwards of $13,000. Of these deficiencies it is thought (as is before stated) the debtors will be able to pay about $10,000—The property of the City, (besides the debts,) as stated in the Representations of the late Commissioners to the President, on 28 January 1801, and 4th December 1801, estimating the Lots at the average prices of those previously sold under the Condition of Improvement (which were much lower than the unconditional Sales by Individuals) amounted to $884,819.88 out of which, Lots have been since sold, to the amount of $9,886.24 only; for about the prices at which they were estimated.

Besides the Debts, and Property before mentioned, there is due to the City (including Interest) upwards of $100,000—eighty thousand Dollars (principal) whereof, is for the 1000 Lots mentioned in the Commissioners' representations, to have been conveyed to Messrs. Morris and Greenleaf, under the Circumstances therein particularly detailed; and concerning which a Bill has been filed in the high Court of Chancery of the State of Maryland.—The balance, between four and five thousand Dollars principal, is due for valuable water Lots, originally bought by James Greenleaf, and resold in the usual manner for default of payment, and for which, the second purchaser has always been ready to pay the purchase Money, but has been prevented by an Injunction of the Chancellor of Maryland, on a Bill filed by Mr. Greenleaf's Trustee—This Bill, as well as that filed, with regard to the 1000 Lots, is still pending, and the Counsel for the City are of opinion, the Decisions in both Cases, will be favorable to the public Interest.—

The Debts due, and to become due, from the City (except for the advances from the Treasury of the United States, and the two Loans by the State of Maryland of $100,000 each) are very inconsiderable; And it is hoped that the large fund herein before stated (by the future Sales of the property, being made commensurate, only with the demand therefor, agreeably to the provision contained in the 5th Section of the before recited Act of Congress.) will not only be adequate to the indemnity of the Government, for its liberal patronage, but will also yeild a surplus for the uses of the City.

The State of the public buildings (directed to be reported) is the same as at the last session of Congress, or not materially changed—The private buildings then 735 in Number have since increased a few more than 100.

The before mentioned Representations of the late Commissioners in January and December 1801, and the Documents accompanying them, which were laid before Congress, being very full, and minute, on the affairs of the City, prior to their respective dates, I beg leave to refer to them; but if there be any thing which you, Sir, deem necessary, and which those Representations and the present do not embrace it will afford me much pleasure to communicate it.

I have the honor to be with sentiments of the greatest Respect Sir Your mo. Obdt. Servt. THOMAS MUNROE

RC (DNA: RG 233, PM, 7th Cong., 2d sess.); at foot of text: "President of the U.S."; endorsed by TJ as received from the Washington Superintendent on 22 Dec. and so recorded in SJL; endorsed by a House clerk. Tr (DNA: RG 46, LPPM); in Meriwether Lewis's hand. Dft (DNA: RG 42, LRDLS). Enclosed in TJ to the Senate and the House of Representatives, 24 Jan. 1803.

For the ACT OF CONGRESS of 1 May 1802 abolishing the Washington, D.C., board of commissioners and for Munroe's efforts regarding the sale of LOTS in the city, see TJ to Munroe, 16 June, 8 Aug. 1802 and Munroe to TJ, 19 June, 17 Sep. 1802.

For the REPRESENTATIONS OF THE LATE COMMISSIONERS TO THE PRESIDENT of 28 Jan. and 4 Dec. 1801, see Vol. 36:13-17.

From Robert Snelson

SIR New york 20th [Dec.] 1802

Pardon me for the liberty I have taken in addressing you on a Subject So Interesting to my self as the preasent one, vizt. by the hand of providence my little family the last Summer was cut off and is no more & am left my Self as it ware a Single man, in this place Soliciting your Survilities to give me aid as a Cleark in the House of Mr. Daniel Ludlow of this City or any Mercantile house that your Self or Mr Ludlow may think proper to appoint, my comeing here a Stranger labours under much Disadvantage in getting a birth—But your friends of New-york have advised & named Mr Ludlow whoe thay think might be a proper Person with a line from you to get Employ Either in the house of him Self or Else whare—

I am sorry to trouble you on this head at a time when Crouded with the good & wellfare of our Country, but as my welfare much depends upon this I rest my self with hopes of a line by Post Shortly or when convenient

I add with all respect to be your most Humble Srvt.

ROBERT SNELSON
from Milton

Stubility & Industery shall not be lacking in my self as a Cleark to which I have been bred RS

RC (DNA: RG 59, LAR); partially dated; at head of text: "Thomas Jefferson, his Excelency"; endorsed by TJ as received 25 Dec. and "wants employment" and so recorded in SJL.

Robert Snelson operated a store in Milton, Virginia, for Robert Rives & Co., where he sold nails from TJ's nailery in the mid-1790s. Snelson and TJ corresponded between 7 Mch. 1795 and 18 Feb. 1797, but the letters are missing (MB, 2:924, 926; Vol. 28:365-6, 409-10).

Recommended by Burr, New York City merchant DANIEL LUDLOW was appointed navy agent at New York early in TJ's presidency. TJ transacted business with Daniel Ludlow & Co., Van Staphorst & Hubbard's agents in New York (Kline, *Burr*, 1:530-1, 537-8; MB, 2:997; Vol. 31:55-6, 570-1; Vol. 33:308-9; Vol. 34:515n).

From Henry Voigt

SIR! Philadelphia Decembr 20th 1802

Having been employed as coiner of the mint of the United States for several years, and understanding that either a total abolishion, or a considerable alteration would be made in its Organization, I have reflected with a good deal of attention on the most Economical and advantagious plan of conducting that business, supposing it to be continued by an Act of Congress.

But as it is not my duty to communicate on that Subject with any member of the Administration, I deemed it proper in the first instance to ask permission to communicate my Observation; for it appears to me possible, that a mint can be conducted on such a plan, as that no expences would fall on the United States.

In the construction of the machinery, great improvements might be made, not only to facilitate the work and save labour; but also to give a more beautiful impression on the coin. But as some of these improvements ar not easily represented by drawings on papir so as to be understood, models would be necessary, and these again would be too expensive and of no use, if the mint were to be abolished.

Nevertheless should you think it worthy of your Attention or advantageous to the United States, it would give me pleasure to explain, as far as it could be done in writing, all my Ideas on the Subject. I hope this will not be considered as an Attempt to force myself into notice, by doing that, which perhaps ought to come from my superiores in his official capacity, but only as a communication from one Citizen to an other on the welfare of ouer common Country; and also as a mark of my Gratitude for the Assylum I have met with here; and the friendship I have experienced from yourself.

I am Sir, with great respect Your very Humble Servant

HENRY VOIGT

RC (DLC); endorsed by TJ as received 24 Dec. and so recorded in SJL.

For the debate over the continuation of the MINT, see Vol. 36:566 and Elias Boudinot to TJ, 1 Jan. 1803.

From Joshua Wingate, Jr.

War Department
SIR, 20th. December 1802.

I have been directed by the Secretary of War to transmit you "the detailed Statement of the expenditures and application of all the public monies which have passed through the Quarter Master Generals Department from the 1st. of January 1797 to the 31st. of December 1801, and a similar account of the Contingent Expences of the War Department"—Made agreeable to a resolution of the House of Representatives of the United States of the 3d. of May last.

I have the honor &ca. J. WINGATE JUR. Chief Clerk.

FC (Lb in DNA: RG 107, LSP). Enclosures: (1) "A Detailed Statement of the Expenditures Made By John Wilkins, Junior, Quarter Master General. Ascertained from his Accounts Rendered to the Office of the Accountant of the War Department," printed in *Message from the President of the United States, Accompanying a Statement of Expenditures from the 1st of January, 1797, by the Quarter Master General, and the Navy Agents, for the Contingencies of the Naval and Military Establishments, and the Navy Contracts for Timber and Stores. Transmitted in Pursuance of a Resolution of the House, of the 3d of May Last* (Washington, D.C., 1803; Shaw-Shoemaker, No. 5357). (2) "A Detailed Account of the Expenditure and Application of All Public Monies, Which Have Passed Through The Quarter Master General's Department, From the 1st January, 1797, to 31st December 1801. Ascertained from the Books of the Accountant of the War Department, and Furnished in Pursuance of a Resolution of the House of Representatives of the United States, Dated the Third May, 1802," printed in *Documents Accompanying a Message from the President of the United States, with Sundry Statements of Expenditures Containing the Following Statements: A Detailed Account of the Expenditure and Application of Public Monies in the Quarter Master General's Department, from the 1st of January 1797, to the 31st of December 1801; Abstract Expenditure and Application of Public Monies for the Contingent Expences of the War Department from the 1st of January 1797, to 31st of December 1801. A Statement of Expenditures in the Quarter Master General's Department, Commencing with 1st January 1797, and Ending 31st December 1801* (Washington, D.C., 1803; Shaw-Shoemaker, No. 5286, printed as part II of No. 5357). (3) "Abstract of the Expenditure and Application of Monies for the Contingent Expenses of the War Department, From the 1st January, 1797, to 31st December, 1801, Ascertained from the Books of the Accountant of the War Department, and Furnished in Pursuance of a Resolution of the House of Representatives of the United States, Dated the Third May, 1802" (printed in same).

To John Armstrong

SIR Washington Dec. 21. 1802.

I informed General Kosciuszko of your kind attention to the location of his lands, and of your refusal to accept of any thing for it, expressing a pleasure at the opportunity of rendering him a service, and he in answer desires you to be assured how sensible he is of this mark of recollection & friendship, and the pleasure he has recieved from this testimony of regard from an old brother souldier. Having sold the lands to Madame Louisa Francis Felix, who is now come over to settle on them with her family, and leaves this place in a few days for that purpose, I have, in pursuance of a power of Attorney from the general, given her a written power to enter into possession of the lands and to hold them according to the contract of conveyance from the general. should there be any difficulty in finding the lands, I trust that your good dispositions towards the General will lead you to render her any information necessary for that purpose. Accept my respects and good wishes. TH: JEFFERSON

RC (PHi); addressed: "John Armstrong esquire." PrC (MHi); endorsed by TJ in ink on verso.

I INFORMED: see Vol. 31:560. Tadeusz KOSCIUSZKO may have given an ANSWER to Armstrong's efforts in an undated letter, recorded in SJL as received 14 Dec. but not found. TJ received the letter from Philippe Reibelt, the agent for Louise Françoise FELIX (Reibelt to TJ, 30 Nov.).

From Therese Ceracchi

GÉNÉREUX PROTECTEUR
DES INFORTUNÉS, Rome, le 21: Xbre 1802.

La malheureuse famille du Sculpteur Ceracchi, pour le quel vous avez eu mille bontés pendant son séjour en Amérique, se trouve en proie aux horreurs de l'indigence la plus horrible et dans l'affreuse Circonstance de périr de misere à chaque instant.

Veuve, avec six enfans, hors d'état de gagner leur pain, je ne vis plus que de larmes amères, rongée par le plus noir chagrin. Ma situation empire chaque jour; trop souvent, hélas! le soleil se leve et se couche, sans que je sache où donner de la tête, où trouver de quoi appaiser les besoins qui nous tourmentent.

C'est après avoir goûté les aisances de la fortune que je suis réduite dans une chambre étroite, privée de meubles, de linge et autres objets de première nécessité, que je suis absorbée sous le poids énorme d'un désespoir concentré, que je n'ai plus d'autre ressource que celle qu'une main sensible laisse échapper en fuyant. Non, je ne me plaindrais pas, si je n'entendais point nuit et jour les cris de mes pauvres enfans qui manquent de tout et qui, par le vuide que firent la mort de leur père et la longue chaîne des infortunes qui, depuis trois ans, pèsent sur nous, sont privés des avantages de l'éducation. Ah! Vertueux Président, le récit de mes maux dévore l'ame; le spectacle en est plus monstrueux encore.

Comme vous le savez, Ceracchi avait été chargé de l'exécution d'un monument national pour perpétuer l'époque de l'heureuse fondation de la République Américaine. Il a fait tous ses modèles en terre cuite, et cet ouvrage ayant été suspendu, Ceracchi ne fut point payé de ses travaux. Ne pourriez-vous pas, sous ce prétexte, décider le Gouvernement des Etats Unis à m'accorder, à titre d'indemnité, un secours qui puisse m'aider à nous soulever de l'abyme affreux dans lequel nous sommes plongés?

Pardonnez, bienfaisant Jefferson, si je vous parle si librement, si je ne crains pas d'exciter trop vivement votre sensibilité, la pénible situation de mes enfans m'y force et la connaissance de votre bon cœur, le souvenir flatteur de la tendre amitié que vous témoignâtes à mon infortuné mari me donnent un droit puissant à votre indulgence.

J'ai l'honneur de vous saluer avec respect.

TERESA CERACCHI

EDITORS' TRANSLATION

GENEROUS PROTECTOR OF THE AFFLICTED, Rome, 21 Dec. 1802

The afflicted family of the sculptor Ceracchi, to whom you were so kind during his stay in America, is assailed by the horror of the most terrible indigence and is in the awful circumstance of being close to perishing from poverty at every moment.

Widowed, with six children and unable to earn bread for them, consumed by the darkest sorrow, I subsist on bitter tears. My situation grows worse every day. Too often, alas, the sun rises and sets without my knowing what to do, where to find ways to meet the needs that torment us.

After having tasted the comforts of wealth, I am reduced to one small room, with no furniture, linens or other basic necessities. I am caught under the enormous weight of intense despair. I have no resources but those some kind hand hastily lets fall. No, I would not complain if I was not hearing, day and night, the cries of my poor children, who lack everything and who are deprived of the advantages of education because of the absence left by their father's death and the long chain of misfortunes that have befallen us for the past three years. Ah, virtuous president, hearing about my misfortunates devours the soul. Seeing them is even more monstrous.

As you know, Ceracchi was entrusted with creating a national monument to perpetuate the period of the auspicious founding of the American republic. He made all the models in clay. When the project was suspended, he was not paid for his work. In light of this, could you not persuade the United States government to indemnify me with some assistance to help me raise my family from the awful abyss in which we are plunged?

Forgive me, beneficent Mr. Jefferson, for speaking so frankly to you, for daring to arouse your feelings. My children's desperate situation forces me to do so. The knowledge of your good heart and the gratifying memory of your warm friendship for my unfortunate husband give me a strong right to your indulgence.

I have the honor of greeting you with respect. TERESA CERACCHI

RC (DLC); at foot of text: "Teresa Ceracchi recapito al Sig. Gaetano Chiassi in piazza di Spagna"; endorsed by TJ as received 4 July 1803 and so recorded in SJL.

À TITRE D'INDEMNITÉ: for TJ's response to this letter and the one of 3 Dec., see TJ to Thomas Appleton, 5 July 1803.

To Albert Gallatin

TH:J. TO MR. GALLATIN. Dec. 21. 1802.

If there be any doubt about the position of the Marine hospital at Boston, we are hardly competent here to decide it. I should have supposed it might be decided by Genl. Lincoln as a military man as well as a citizen. would Doctr. Eustis think it better to join the Govr. or any other person or persons with the Genl. to fix on the best position? I suggest this for your consideration. With respect to Colo. Mc.lane his letter was fairly construed as a request to remain in office to a certain day only, & consequently a resignation, & has been the foundation of ulterior arrangements, no longer revocable. and in fact it must be so evident to himself that his continuance in office excites perpetual irritation, that I considered his letter as an evidence of his candor & attention to our peace as well as his own.

RC (NHi: Gallatin Papers); addressed: "Mr. Gallatin." Not recorded in SJL.

POSITION OF THE MARINE HOSPITAL: on 23 Dec., Gallatin instructed Benjamin Lincoln that when drawing up the construction contract, the hospital site laid out by the navy agent should "not be specifically and exclusively designated." Gallatin continued: "the contractors may be bound to erect the building on such spot, within the navy yard-ground, as *shall* be designated and laid out; it having been suggested that a spot nearer the water would be more convenient for the use of the hospital, and less in the way of any fortifications, which it may be found necessary hereafter to erect." Gallatin requested Lincoln's opinion on the issue. On 17 Feb., Gallatin authorized the site for the hospital recommended by the Boston collector (Gallatin, *Papers*, 7:846; 8:107).

From Peder Blicher Olsen

SIR Decembr. 22. 1802.

The emotion Your extraordinary goodness and offer have produced on me, is to strong to allow me, at the present moment any other expression, but that of admiration and gratitude.

I respectfully accept and thank—Sir Yours very humble and obedient servant

BLICHER OLSEN

RC (DLC); endorsed by TJ as received 22 Dec.

Peder Blicher Olsen (also Blicherolsen) arrived in the United States in July 1801 as consul general and resident minister of Denmark. He was previously the Danish consul in Morocco and had been on the staff of his country's legation in Berlin. He resided in Philadelphia, staying with the Madisons as their guest on his occasional visits to Washington. Blicher Olsen appointed vice consuls in locales from Massachusetts to Georgia. In poor health, he departed for Denmark on leave of absence in July 1803. He did not return to the United States, and at his request the Danish government recalled him from the post in 1805. Although Gallatin remarked, after first meeting him, that Blicher Olsen "does not appear extremely bright," Madison noted on the diplomat's departure that he "leaves this Country under good impressions" (Emil Marquand, *Danske Gesandter og Gesandtskabspersonale indtil 1914* [Copenhagen, 1952], 137, 450, 451, 459; Madison, *Papers*, *Sec. of State Ser.*, 1:452, 489; 2:206n, 400-1; 3:440, 499; 4:206; 5:52, 55, 62, 109-10, 118, 327; 8:349-50; Vol. 34:451n; Vol. 35:13, 163n; TJ to Christian VII, King of Denmark, 6 June 1803, 16 Oct. 1805, in DNA: RG 59, Credences).

OFFER: with information about Richmond and a letter of introduction to John Page, TJ assisted Blicher Olsen's preparations for an intended trip into Virginia; see TJ to Blicher Olsen, [21 Jan. 1803], and TJ to Page, 20 Jan., 18 Mch. 1803.

From Benjamin Gorton

RESPECTED FRIEND Troy December 22d. 1802.

I have taken the liberty to present you with a Scriptural account of the Millennium or Christs Reign on Earth a Thousand years, not that I Suppose you ignorant of that important event—but fearing you like many others may not have Sufficiently contemplated the Subject in all its parts—have as a friend to your never dying Soul thought propper to put you in remembrance More fully of that important day— I have long been impressed with the certainty of that event, not meerly as an opinion of mine, but as founded on holy writ (as you will find by perusing the Book in all its parts) and not Supposing with many that it is only to be Spiritual and in Some way which we Know not, but exactly as related litterally or more full and Compleat—as Gods power is not abated—and also believing that

that day is fast approaching—therefore calls for our more Serious attention—and being desirous of communicating this information fully to the Children of men generally—have thought propper to have a Number of those Books printed in order for circulation—and you are well aware that Books of a Serious Nature are not Soon received by the worldly minded as those of a more worldly Nature are—although of much more importance—as I believe you must on Mature reflection acknowledge—when Christ tells us to watch that that day does not come on us unawares

Seing this publication is not made from lucrative views as you will Se by the former part of the Book is Set forth. I have thought proper to make application to you beleiveing from information that you are not a Stranger to true benevolence—and that as God has placed you in an ellevated Sittuation wherein by your influence you may do much Good or harm as you may be disposed—I flatter my Self you will not think this matter unworthy your Notice and by your influence in Such way as you may think propper—be instrumental in giving them a circulation and asist in doing what Christ Said Should be done before the end come. Mathew XXIV—14th verse—God has done great things for you in a temporal Sence—and from whom Much has been Given Much will be required—the greater the blessings are we recieve from God the greater the obligation we are under to Serve him—We and all we have are Gods and at the hour of Death we Shall be as respects the flesh on a level—But Spiritually & eternally a [...] to our works or deeds done in the body when in[...] State of probation or trial—for God has made us free Morral agents—and wishes us to accept Salvation which is offered to all by humble obedience to his will—

If therefore on perusal of this Book you can Say any thing in its behalf Seperate from any advantage of mine please to do it and God will reward you if done to his Glory—and you will recieve the thanks and prayers of your Sincere friend and well wisher—

Benjn. Gorton

RC (DLC); torn; addressed: "Thomas Jefferson Esqr—President of the United States of America *Washington City*"; endorsed by TJ as received 7 Jan. and so recorded in SJL. Enclosure: Benjamin Gorton, *A Scriptural Account of the Millennium: Being a Selection from the Prophecies Concerning Christ's Second Coming, and Personal Glorious Reign on Earth A Thousand Years* (Troy, N.Y., 1802; Sowerby, No. 1609).

Benjamin Gorton (1757?-1836) from Norwich, Connecticut, saw military service with distinction during the American Revolution and later became a merchant involved in the China trade. In 1791, he settled in Troy, New York, where he became a trustee of the First Presbyterian Church, a charter member of the Apollo Lodge of freemasons, and a Troy trustee, president, and village clerk. He grew increasingly flamboyant in his dress and fanatic in his beliefs and wrote several nondenominational religious books promulgating an imminent millennium (Rutherford Hayner, *Troy and Rensselaer County New York: A History*, 3 vols. [New York, 1925], 1:323; Arthur James Weise, *Troy's One Hundred Years 1789-1889* [Troy, N.Y., 1891], 32, 45, 46, 81, 93, 322, 323).

GOD HAS DONE GREAT THINGS: Luke 8:39.

MUCH WILL BE REQUIRED: Luke 12:48.

To the House of Representatives

GENTLEMEN OF THE HOUSE OF REPRESENTATIVES

I now transmit a report from the Secretary of state with the information requested in your resolution of the 17th. instant.

In making this communication, I deem it proper to observe that I was led by the regard due to the rights and interests of the United States and to the just sensibility of the portion of our fellow citizens more immediately affected by the irregular proceeding at New Orleans, to lose not a moment in causing every step to be taken which the occasion claimed from me: being equally aware of the obligation to maintain in all cases the rights of the nation, and to employ for that purpose those just and honorable means, which belong to the character of the United States.

TH: JEFFERSON

Dec. 22. 1802.

RC (DNA: RG 233, PM, 7th Cong., 2d sess.); endorsed by a clerk. PrC (DLC).

The RESOLUTION, passed by the House on 17 Dec., stated: "That the President of the United States be requested to cause to be laid before this House, such information in possession of the Department of State, as relates to the violation, on the part of Spain, of the twenty-second article of the treaty of friendship, limits, and navigation, between the United States and the King of Spain" (JHR, 4:253).

After Meriwether Lewis delivered the COMMUNICATION and the papers were read, the House ordered that the materials lie on the table. William Duane printed the message and accompanying papers as *Message from the President of the United States, Transmitting a Report from the Secretary of State, with the Information Requested in a Resolution of the House, of the 17th Instant, Relative to the Violation on the Part of Spain, of the Twenty-second Article of the Treaty of Friendship, Limits and Navigation, between the United States and the King of Spain* (Washington, D.C., 1802).

ENCLOSURE

From James Madison

The Secretary of State, to whom the Resolution of the House of Representatives of the United States of the 17th inst, was referred by the President, has the honor to inclose to him, the letters and communications annexed from the Governor of the Mississippi Territory, the Governor of Kentucky and from Wm E. Hulings formerly appointed Vice Consul of the United States at New Orleans. In addition to this information on the subject of the Resolution, it is stated from other sources that on the 29th of October American vessels from Sea remained under the prohibition to land their cargoes; and that the American produce carried down the Mississippi could be landed only on paying a duty of 6 ℔ Cent with an intimation that this was a temporary permission. Whether in these violations of Treaty the Officer of Spain at New Orleans has proceeded with or without orders from his Government cannot as yet be decided by direct and positive testimony; but it ought not to be omitted in the statement here made, that other circumstances concur with the good faith and friendship otherwise observed by His Catholic Majesty, in favouring a belief that no such orders have been given.

James Madison
Department of State,
21st. Decr. 1802

RC (DNA: RG 233, PM, 7th Cong., 2d sess.); in a clerk's hand, signed by Madison. Tr (DLC); in Meriwether Lewis's hand, unsigned. FC (Lb in DNA: RG 59, DL); at head of text: "The President of the U. States." Enclosures: (1) William E. Hulings to Madison, 18 Oct., from New Orleans, sending an extract of "a decree this day published" by the intendant prohibiting Americans from depositing goods; the "difficulties and risks of property that will fall on the citizens of the United States, if deprived of their deposit, are incalculable," Hulings notes; "their boats being so frail, and so subject to be sunk by storms that they cannot be converted into floating stores, to wait the arrival of sea vessels to carry away their cargoes"; the port has also been closed to all foreign commerce, so that only trade by Spanish subjects using Spanish vessels is allowed (Tr in DNA: RG 233, PM; in Jacob Wagner's hand); enclosing an extract in English of Juan Ventura Morales's proclamation, 16 Oct. (Tr in same; in Wagner's hand, with his attestation that he translated the decree from Spanish). (2) William C. C. Claiborne to Madison, 29 Oct., from Natchez, enclosing a letter from Hulings and a translated extract from Morales's order; sending also a copy of a letter Claiborne wrote to "the Governor General of the Province of Louisiana" asking for clarification about whether a substitute place of deposit has been designated in accordance with the provisions of the treaty; Claiborne noting also that the intendant's action "has excited considerable agitation" in and around Natchez, having "inflicted a severe wound on the Agricultural and Commercial Interest of this Territory," and the event "will prove no less injurious to all the Western Country"; considering this matter to be of great importance, Claiborne is sending his letter by express to Nashville, where it can go into the mail (Tr in same); enclosing Hulings to Claiborne, 18 Oct., announcing the closure of New Orleans to foreign commerce and the termination of the right of deposit, without any mention in the public notices about a substitute site for the deposit (Tr in same; lacks a postscript that Hulings appended to the letter reporting that Morales had refused to allow U.S. government stores to pass through Spanish territory to Fort Stoddert without payment of duty; see Dunbar Rowland, ed., *Official Letter Books of W. C. C. Claiborne*,

1801-1816, 6 vols. [Jackson, Miss., 1917], 1:207, and Madison, *Papers*, *Sec. of State Ser.*, 4:68n); also enclosing a copy of Claiborne to Manuel de Salcedo, 28 Oct., saying that he has examined the treaty between Spain and the United States and finds Article 22 to be unambiguous with regard to the establishment of a substitute location for the deposit; Claiborne asks for "an *early answer*" due to the importance of the subject (Tr in DNA: RG 233, PM; in Wagner's hand). (3) James Garrard to TJ, 30 Nov. Enclosures collectively endorsed by a clerk.

Claiborne mentioned the six percent DUTY in a letter to Madison of 6 Nov. (Madison, *Papers*, *Sec. of State Ser.*, 4:99).

From Robert Snelson

SIR New York Decr. 22nd. 1802

Since my Request to you of 20th. Ulto.—have Observed in the Gazett of this place three Mercantile houses that ar in Want of a Cleark, but my beeing here a Stranger & not having no Letters to recommend me only prevents my getting a birth here If your address to Mr D Ludlow in my favour could be obtained so fare as your Knowledge of me Serves while doeing Business for Ro. Rives & Co Milton, thares not a doubt of my not getting Business Pardon me for troubling you in the maner to drop a line to me now in New York by as Early post as your Survilities think fit which Will Ever be acknowledged By your Most obedient & Houble Srvt. RO SNELSON

RC (DNA: RG 59, LAR); at head of text: "Mr. Jefferson"; endorsed by TJ as received 26 Dec. and so recorded in SJL.

From Thomas Worthington

SIR Washington Decr 22nd 1802

I have the honour to enclose to you a copy of the constitution of the state of Ohio together with a communication from the convention of that state

With sentiments of the highest respect I have the honour to be Your Obt St T. WORTHINGTON

RC (DLC); at foot of text: "The President of the United States"; endorsed by TJ. Recorded in SJL as received 22 Dec. Enclosures: (1) *Constitution of the State of Ohio* (Chillicothe, 1802; Shaw-Shoemaker, No. 2819). (2) Address from the "convention of the State of Ohio" to the president and both houses of Congress, 27 Nov. 1802, expressing gratitude to Congress "for the prompt and decisive measures taken at their last Session" to enable the inhabitants of the Northwest

Territory "to immerge from their colonial government and to assume a rank among the sister states," and adding their "unequivocal approbation of the measures" pursued by the president and Congress "in diminishing the public burthens, cultivating peace with all nations, and promoting the happiness and prosperity of our country" (RC in DNA: RG 46, LPRC, 7th Cong., 2d sess., signed by Edward Tiffin, President of the convention, and Thomas Scott, Secretary). (3) Probably Edward Tiffin to TJ, Chillicothe, 4 Dec. 1802 (recorded in SJL as received 22 Dec., but not found).

From John Wayles Eppes

DEAR SIR, Richmond Decr: 23.

We yesterday reelected Mr. Mason to the[1] Senate with an almost unanimous vote—I should have written to you last Evening but I was anxious to give You the issue of an affair between George Hay & Callender. An abusive piece appeared against Mr. Hay in the Recorder about ten days since—Hay accidentally meeting with Callender gave him very freely a good cudgel—Callender was very severely beat & his head so much cut as to require a physician to sew up the wound—In consequence of this Callender applied for a warrant and Mr. Hay after a discussion of some length was bound to appear at the next Court—A warrant has been issued against Callender to bind him to good behaviour on the ground of being a common disturber of the neighbourhood peace by being a constant publisher of libels—This warrant has been issued by a County Magistrate & will be tried tomorrow—Callender is sinking fast into that obscurity from which by infamy he has attempted to raise himself—That he will be totally deserted by the Federalists & again turned to infamy and beggary in a short time I have no doubt—The decided Tone of the present Legislature after his infamous attacks on the Republican party will cause the Federalist to feel that the importance attached by them to this scoundrel will give wings to; instead of retarding their ruin—I do not believe that even the Legislature of 98 was not more decided than the present—In every case where elections have taken place the Feds have marched out & I do not believe that a single man of that principle within the reach of the Legislature will continue to hold an office—The party having thrown the gauntlet & spurned the tender of reconciliation the general sentiment appears to be *out* with the whole—

The Message has struck a general panic in the party—To take off Taxes, honestly meet our engagements, & comply in substance with our oeconomical arrangements, & leave a surplus of 4 millions in the Treasury galls terribly & the more so because it is true—

accept for your health my warm wishes yours sincerely

JNO: W: EPPES

P.S. Mr. Page arrived in Town this Evening

RC (ViU: Edgehill-Randolph Papers); endorsed by TJ as received 28 Dec. and so recorded in SJL.

ABUSIVE PIECE: an anonymous article appeared under the title "Mr. George Hay" in the Richmond *Recorder* on 15 Dec. The author made disparaging comments about Hay, describing him as "one of the president's most devoted vassals," and accusing him of "ignorant and dastardly conduct." By late 1802, Hay came into direct conflict with James Thomson Callender, whom he had previously defended in a sedition trial in 1800 (Steven H. Hochman, "On the Liberty of the Press in Virginia," VMHB, 84 [1976], 437; Richmond *Virginia Gazette*, 29 Dec. 1802; Durey, *Callender*, 164-5; Vol. 31:589-90n).

LEGISLATURE OF 98: "An Act directing the mode of appointing the public printer, prescribing his duties, and for other purposes therein mentioned" was passed by the Virginia General Assembly on 22 Jan. 1798. It allowed Augustine Davis to continue as printer with annual compensation of $2,700. In November 1802, Callender and his Federalist partner Henry Pace proposed to assume the public printing for a lesser amount (Shepherd, *Statutes*, 2:118; Richmond *Recorder*, 1 Dec. 1802).

THE MESSAGE: TJ's Annual Message to Congress, 15 Dec. 1802.

[1] MS: "the the."

To the House of Representatives

GENTLEMEN OF THE HOUSE OF REPRESENTATIVES

In pursuance of the resolution of the House of Representatives of the 3d. of May last, desiring a statement of expenditures from Jan. 1. 1797. by the Quartermaster General and the Navy agents for the contingencies of the Naval & Military establishments and the Navy contracts for timber & stores, I now transmit such statements from the offices of the Secretaries of the Treasury, War, and Navy, where alone these expenditures are entered.

TH: JEFFERSON

Dec. 23. 1802.

PrC (DLC). Recorded in SJL with notation "expenditures Contingt from Jan. 1. 97." Enclosures: (1) Albert Gallatin to TJ, 18 Dec. 1802, and enclosures. (2) Joshua Wingate, Jr., to TJ, 20 Dec. 1802, and enclosures. (3) Robert Smith to TJ, 10 Dec. 1802, and enclosures.

Upon receiving TJ's message and its accompanying STATEMENT OF EXPENDITURES, the House of Representatives ordered them to lie on the table. On 25 Feb. 1803, the House ordered them printed, provided the cost did not exceed $5,200 (JHR, 4:257-8, 367-8).

Statement of Account with Jones & Kain, with Jefferson's Order

1802	His Excellency Thos. Jefferson Esqr. President UStates	
	Dr. To Jones & Kain	
Sepr. 13.	To Mending a pump Handle	$ 1 —
Octr. 6.	To 2 Removes	25
Decr. 23.	To a New Body to the pheaton Lined with Moroco	35 —
phaeton 35.	To 58 feet of molding and 6 Scrolls	32 —
32. *20*	To painting and Silvering the Carriage and Wheels	20 —
87 *harness 23.*	To a New Bridle with plated mounting a New Collar with Harness Tugs and Straps with plated Buckles a new pair of Shaft Tugs, a new pair of Traces mending the Butcher and Back band and 2 new loops	23 —
	To a piece of plated molding to the Sulkey	75
	To mending the Sulkey Harness	1 50
	To a Sett of wheels to the Markett Waggon	40 —
	To Repairing the Harness of Do.	50
		$154 —

[*Order by TJ*:]

Mr. Barnes will be pleased to pay the amount 154. Dollars.

Th: Jefferson
Jan. 4. 1803

MS (CSmH); in an unidentified hand, with words and figures in italics added by TJ in left margin; endorsed by TJ in ink on verso: "Jones & Kain."

TJ had previously enlisted the carriage repair services of Jones & Kain. According to TJ's financial records, on 4 Jan. 1803, he gave an order on John Barnes for $154 "for body & finishing phaeton, wheels to market waggon, & repairs of harness" (MB, 2:1048, 1089; Vol. 34:707, 708; Vol. 36:693).

From Francis Taliaferro Brooke

Senate Chamber
Richmond Virginia Decembr 24 1802

F Brooke Returns his thanks to Mr Jefferson for the Book Sent him—Such a Treatise on the Duties of a Situation of which he had little Experience and to which he was unexpectedly Called was very Desirable—he will endeavour to Evince his high respect for its author and the Value he Sets on it by his Constant Exertion to make it as usefull as possible to the respectable Body over which he has the honor to Preside

RC (DLC); endorsed by TJ as received 29 Dec. and so recorded in SJL.

BOOK SENT HIM: see TJ to Brooke, 20 Dec.

From Andrew Ellicott

SIR Lancaster December 24th. 1802

I beg leave to introduce to your acquaintance, and civilities, the bearer Mr. Levett Harriss:—he is a young Gentleman of talents, and education, and whose connexions are very respectable. He is well acquainted with merchantile transactions, and proposes settling in some commercial city in europe, where if a consulship should be vacant, I have no doubt but he would perform the duties of such an office with reputation to himself, and do credit to the appointment.

I have the honour to be with great esteem, your sincere friend, and Hbl. Servt.
ANDW; ELLICOTT

RC (DNA: RG 59, LAR); at foot of text: "President U.S."; endorsed by TJ as received 10 Jan. and "Harris Levitt. to be Consul" and so recorded in SJL; also endorsed by TJ: "Petersbg if does not accept." PrC (DLC: Ellicott Papers).

In March 1803, Madison asked Levett Harris to choose between the CONSULSHIP at Rotterdam and the one at St. Petersburg, Russia. Harris did not reply promptly, so Madison and TJ gave him the position at Rotterdam. When Harris, on receipt of the commission, expressed his preference for the other city, TJ signed a new commission appointing him consul at St. Petersburg (Madison, *Papers*, *Sec. of State Ser.*, 4:466).

From John Wayles Eppes

DEAR SIR, Richmond Decr. 24. 1802.

I have attended to day the trial of a warrant against Callender & Pace under the act of assembly authorising the justices of the peace to demand "security for the good behaviour of those who are not of good fame"—Various English precedents as to the extent & meaning of the words "*not of good fame*" were cited and it has been decided by the Magistrates who set in the trial that the common publisher of libels came under the phrase "not of good fame." Under this opinion of the magistrates Callender & Pace were sentenced to find surety for good behavior in a penal bond of 500 dollars the principals & 250 dollars the Securities—Callender has either refused or is unable to find surety and is committed to goal. Pace has given security—

I regret extremely that this kind of notice has been taken of the scoundrels as (even admitting that this novel doctrine that a man may be bound to his good behaviour for publishing a libel be correct) the imprisonment of Callender will retard the rapid progress he was making to complete infamy & contempt. This nefarious & infamous wretch devoid of feeling or decency appeared drunk before the Magistrates who tried him & his grim vissage was alternately distorted by Tears & the most hideous grimaces—

Adieu accept for your health the sincere & affectionate wishes of yours &c.

JNO: W: EPPES

RC (MHi); endorsed by TJ as received 29 Dec. and so recorded in SJL.

THE ACT OF ASSEMBLY: "An Act to reduce into one the several acts declaring who shall be conservators of the peace within this commonwealth" was passed by the Virginia General Assembly on 17 Oct. 1792 (Shepherd, *Statutes*, 1:10).

Writings of William Blackstone, Michael Dalton, and Richard Burn were among the ENGLISH PRECEDENTS on judges and justices cited by the prosecution in the case (Richmond *Virginia Argus*, 29 Dec.).

SURETY FOR GOOD BEHAVIOR: Henry Pace offered William Marshall and William Richardson as his sureties. Callender refused to provide his own and was sent to jail to await trial during the regular monthly session of the Henrico County court on 3 Jan. (Durey, *Callender*, 164-5; Steven H. Hochman, "On the Liberty of the Press in Virginia," VMHB, 84 [1976], 438).

To Albert Gallatin

TH:J. TO MR GALLATIN Dec. 24. 1802.

I recollect but slightly the within case: in general that the party appeared guilty: but I presume there can be no objection to the permitting his decision to be expedited, and our suggesting that to mr Hollingsworth.

RC (NHi: Gallatin Papers); addressed: "The Secretary of the Treasury"; endorsed. Not recorded in SJL. Enclosure not found, but see Gallatin to TJ, 3 Jan. 1803, for correspondence from Zebulon Hollingsworth, the Maryland district attorney.

From Thomas S. Cavender

Dear Sir Virg. Orange December 25. 1802

I still continue Traveling and preaching the unitarian doctrine in opposition to the Trinitarian System and all other political and Ecclesiastical impositions whatever. In all my public Orations I conclude in favour of your just administration teaching my Countrymen the necessity of Continuing you as their president so long as you Conduct our government as well as you have done and Sir notwithstanding all the political blood hounds, and ecclesiastical bulldogs that are barking at your political and religious economy and howling at the trcc of liberty I still believe and publickly declare that I think that you will end your days in peace and in honour to your family and country: Sir after my departure from Charlottsville last summer was a year, I had the honour of conversing with you a few minutes the October following in the presidents house and would have seen you this fall had you have been in the city when I came throug it on my way from Baltimore to this State. Sir as a republican I hope you will pardon me in the liberty I have taken in inclosing this letter to you, as I was afraid that mr paines enemys might open or distroy it, althoug now sir I rest satisfied that it will come to his hands with safety. I have some hopes of having the honour to see you before I return the next summer to the ohio river. And Sir if I should be so unfortunate as never to see you in time may heaven smile upon you with matchless and endless blessings.

I am your real friend & humble Servant

Thomas Stett Cavender

RC (MHi); addressed: "His Excellency Thomas Jefferson President of the US. Federal City"; franked; postmarked 27 Dec.; endorsed by TJ as received 31 Dec. and so recorded in SJL. Enclosure not found.

An itinerant Unitarian clergyman and Republican, Thomas S. Cavender wrote TJ several times during his first term. In his letters, Cavender claimed acquaintances with Thomas Paine and William Duane and asked TJ to forward pieces written under the pseudonym "Old Soldier" to Republican newspapers for publication. He suffered from a leg wound received during the Revolutionary War (Bardstown, Ky., *Western American*, 10 Nov. 1803; MB, 2:1095; Cavender to TJ, 22 Mch. 1803, 17 Nov., 6 Dec. 1804).

To Albert Gallatin

Th:J. to mr Gallatin Dec. 25. 1802.

The giving Sea letters to vessels is very troublesome, and extremely burthensome to the Post office: at the same time it is totally destitute of utility and contrary to usage. can the merchants shew us a sea letter given by the English government now when they, like us, are at peace with all the world? there is no reason for departing from universal practice, and therefore they may be informed that Sea letters[1] will not be given unless the war breaks out again. health & friendly salutations.

PrC (DLC).

sea letters: see TJ to Gallatin, 7 Dec.

[1] Interlined in place of "passports."

From Thomas Paine

[25 Dec. 1802]

I congratulate you on the *birth-day of the New Sun*, now called christmas day; and I make you a present of a[1] thought on Louisana—

T. P—

RC (DLC); undated, date supplied from contents and endorsement; addressed: "Mr. Jefferson"; endorsed by TJ as received 25 Dec. and so recorded in SJL.

[1] Preceding three words interlined.

ENCLOSURE

Paine's Memorandum on Louisiana

Of Louisana

Spain has ceded Louisana to france and france has excluded the americans from N. orleans and the navigation of the Mississipi—the people of the western territory have complained of it to their government, and the governt. is of consequence involved and interested in the affair. The question then is, What is the best step to be taken first.

The one is to begin by memorial and remonstrance against an infraction of a right. The other by accomodation, still keeping the right in view, but not making it a ground-work—

Suppose then the Governt. begin by making a proposal to france to repurchase the cession made to her by spain of Louisana, provided it be *with the consent of the people of Louisana or a majority thereof.*

By beginning on this ground any thing can be said without carrying the appearance of a threat—the growing power of the western territory can be stated as matter of information, and also the impossibility of restraining them from seizing upon New Orleans and the equal impossibility of france to prevent it.

Suppose the proposal attended to, the sum to be given comes next on the carpet. This, on the part of america will be estimated between the Value of the commerce and the quantity of revenue that Louisana will produce.

The french treasury is not only empty but the Government has consumed by anticipation a great part of the next year's revenue. A monied proposal will, I believe, be attended to; if it should, the claims upon france can be stipulated as part of the payment, and that sum can be paid here to the claimants.—

MS (DLC); undated; in Paine's hand.

WHAT IS THE BEST STEP: the notion that the United States should try to obtain Louisiana "occurred to me without knowing it had occurred to any other person," Paine later wrote to TJ about this document. Paine discussed the idea with Michael Leib, who lived in the boarding house where Paine was staying in Washington, and it was on Leib's suggestion that Paine put his thoughts down on paper and sent them to TJ. The next day, as Paine later recalled, TJ told him that "measures were already taken on that business." Learning that Leib had been aware that TJ had already given consideration to the matter, Paine asked Leib why he had encouraged him, under those circumstances, to send his memorandum to TJ. The congressman replied that "two opinions concurring on a case strengthen it" (Paine to TJ, 25 Jan. 1805, in DLC).

CONSENT OF THE PEOPLE: an unsigned memorandum in French, addressed to the president of the United States and purporting to speak for the inhabitants of Louisiana, protested the retrocession of the colony from Spain to France and advocated the joining of Louisiana to the United States. The document is in the records of the State Department but has no endorsement or notation by TJ to confirm that he ever saw it. The undated tract was probably written before the closing of the right of deposit at New Orleans, which the writer did not mention (MS in DNA: RG 59, MLR; 8 p. in an unidentified hand; at head of text: "Au Président des Etats-unis").

From John Vaughan

Dear Sir Philad: Dec. 25. 1802

Under present circumstances I do not concieve myself authorised not to send you an extract of a letter from a common & much respected friend—he wishes his name may not be used, because he thinks it probable "in the course of human Events, that the French may find it perfectly convenient to take possession of this quondam apendage to Louisiana," in which case the avowal of such sentiments might materially injure him—I do not concieve it improbable he may have written directly to yourself—but as an important fact was communicated, & as possibly some weight may be attached to his opinions with you, I have resolved to send it—I subjoin two other extracts not relative to this subject & remain with the greatest respect

Your friend & Servt. JN VAUGHAN

RC (DLC); at foot of text: "Thomas Jefferson Pt. of US"; endorsed by TJ as received 29 Dec. and so recorded in SJL. Enclosure: extracts of a letter from an unidentified correspondent (William Dunbar—see below), dated 8 Nov., reporting a widely held belief that the actions of the intendant at New Orleans foretell the treatment that Americans can expect once the French take control of Louisiana; a vessel arriving from Bordeaux two days before the intendant issued his proclamation brought news that "troops destined for Louisiana," reportedly 10,000 in number, were to embark in France in September; it is widely believed that the intendant's actions are "a french Machination" to deprive Americans of the right of deposit on the eve of the arrival of French soldiers; the United States will then no longer have recourse through the "pusilanimous Govt. of Spain," and the "imperious minions of Buoanaparte" will say that they are simply maintaining the policies that were in place when they took control of the colony; the U.S. will then have to negotiate for the right of deposit upon terms that "will divert the course" of our commerce "from a British into a French channel"; although some Americans will not consider this a matter of great importance, others "will always spurn the idea of bending the will to any Earthly foreign power"; it would be bad policy to do anything to strengthen the power of France at sea, for France is "the most powerful nation on Earth" by land, and the only limits on its "devouring ambition" are set by Great Britain at sea; in 100 years the United States will be powerful enough to defy France, but until then the best policy is to keep Britain and France in rivalry; a few years previously, "our Brethren of Kentucky were extremely partial to the French," and it seemed likely that Kentuckians would break away from the United States rather than go to war against France; such "is not the case now—They only wait the orders of Govt. & in the twinkling on an Eye New Orleans would be ours"; if the United States and France come into conflict, it will be of critical importance to send immediately a force of 4,000 to 5,000 men to protect the Mississippi Territory "& keep in awe the Savages who are still much attached to the French"; otherwise "this prosperous Colony would be cut up root & branch"; the "Spaniards do not yet presume to refuse us the navigation of the river," but without the right of deposit, loads must be transferred directly from river boats to ships (Tr in DLC: TJ Papers, 124:21504-5; in Vaughan's hand; at head of text: "Extracts"). For other enclosure, see below.

As is clear from the second set of extracts, the MUCH RESPECTED FRIEND was William Dunbar. For another occasion on which Vaughan sent TJ passages from Dunbar's communications, see Vol. 37:431, 434n. In this period, Dunbar refrained from commenting directly to TJ on political topics (Dunbar to TJ, 10 June 1803). QUONDAM APENDAGE TO LOUISIANA: the Natchez district where Dunbar resided.

TWO OTHER EXTRACTS: Vaughan enclosed, in addition to the passages from Dunbar's 8 Nov. letter relating to Louisiana, four paragraphs of extracts on scientific topics (Tr in DLC: TJ Papers, 124:21506; in Vaughan's hand). Vaughan took those extracts, which he did not date or identify, from a letter written by Dunbar at Natchez on 22 Oct., a fragmentary text of which appears in Mrs. Dunbar Rowland (Eron Rowland), ed., *Life, Letters and Papers of William Dunbar of Elgin, Morayshire, Scotland, and Natchez, Mississippi: Pioneer Scientist of the Southern United States* (Jackson, Miss., 1930), 117-18. A brief paragraph of comments by Vaughan separates the four paragraphs of extracted material into two sections. "Mr Michaux had not on 8 Novr. arrived at Natchez," Vaughan wrote—a reference to François André Michaux, the son of André Michaux. The younger Michaux made a journey through the western states collecting botanical specimens in 1802, but he traveled overland from Nashville to Charleston, South Carolina, and did not go to Natchez (Henry Savage, Jr., and Elizabeth J. Savage, *André and François André Michaux* [Charlottesville, 1986], 246-54; ANB). Vaughan continued his comments: "D Coxe has in Poulson of Fryday, has communicated a method of preserving the Vaccine Virus, from Soaking the Vaccine Crust of the Pock in Water—It will no Doubt be republished" (see John Redman Coxe to TJ, 5 Jan. 1803). In the first of the extracts, Dunbar—referring to a grant of £10,000 from Parliament to Edward Jenner (DNB)—expressed regret that the British had "conferred so paltry a recompence upon Dr Jenner for his noble discovery, published in the true Spirit of Philanthropy for the benefit of mankind." Dunbar hoped that other European nations and Congress would also recognize Jenner's achievement. In the next extract, Dunbar reported that the "portion of the Cranium & horn of an animal of the Ox kind" had passed through Natchez and down the Mississippi River before he could see it. From what he had learned of the horn he did not believe the animal was a mammoth, although it was "a most Stupendous animal" that must have weighed 40,000 pounds (see Vaughan to TJ, 21 July). In the first of the quoted extracts following Vaughan's comments, Dunbar stated that he had obtained "two tolerably complete Vocabularies of two Indian tongues from the west side of the Mississippi with some particulars of the history & religious Opinions of those Tribes," along with information on fossil bones from the same region, "all which I am preparing to Send to Mr Jefferson" (see Dunbar to TJ, 5 Jan. 1803). In the final extract copied by Vaughan, Dunbar commended the resolution of the Pennsylvania General Assembly that made the state's telescope available to Andrew Ellicott (see Vol. 37:446, 447n). He also reported that a telescope he had ordered for himself from London, "a Gregorian reflector of $5\frac{1}{2}$ or 6 feet length in the great Tube with 9 Inches aperture, possessing 6 magnifying powers from 100 to 525," would soon arrive, enabling him "to cooperate in the prosecution of objects so interesting to Science." The area where he lived, Dunbar observed, sometimes had "a Sky of such peculiar transparency as seems to have given additional Splendour to the Heavenly bodies."

To Jonathan Williams

SIR Washington Dec. 25. 1802.

I have duly recieved your favor of the 12th. inst. a friend to science in all it's useful branches, and believing that of the Engineer of great utility, I sincerely approve of the institution of a society for it's improvement. from the smallness of our establishment, it's numbers will be small for awhile but it's pursuits being directly in the line of their profession and entitled to all their time, they may render the society important & useful. altho' it is not probable that I may be able to render it any service, yet I accept thankfully the patronage you are pleased to propose, and the more justifiably as the perfect coincidence of it's objects with the legal duties of the members, will render the respects shewn to the society always consistent with the duties which I owe to their military institution. Wishing to the society the success which it merits, I pray you to accept for them & yourself assurances of my great respect and consideration. TH: JEFFERSON

RC (NHi); addressed: "Colo. Jonathan Williams now in Philadelphia" and "recommended to the care of mr Patton P.M."; franked and postmarked; endorsed by Williams. PrC (DLC).

INSTITUTION OF A SOCIETY: that is, the United States Military Philosophical Society.

From William Bache

DEAR SIR, George Town Decr. 26th. 1802.

I was desirous of speaking with you yesterday to request you to releive me from an embarrassment arrising from a bad calculation I made respecting the expences of my journey to Philaa. I left Albemarle with 130 dollars and the enormous expences of coach hire, with the stoppages occasioned by the necessities of the little children have nearly exhausted my fund. I will esteem it a great obligation if you will lend me one hundred dollars, which I will remit to you immediately upon my arrival at Philadelphia where I have funds. This will be an act of friendship added to many others which will be gratefully remembered by your sincere friend. WILLIAM BACHE

RC (MHi); with note by TJ at foot of text: "Dec. 26. 1802. gave him order on J. Barnes for 100. D."; endorsed by TJ as received 26 Dec. and so recorded in SJL.

I LEFT ALBEMARLE: prior to traveling to New Orleans to become director of the marine hospital, Bache leased his Franklin farm and property in Virginia and moved his family back to Philadelphia where his in-laws resided (Jane Flaherty Wells, "Thomas Jefferson's Neighbors: Hore Browse Trist of 'Birdwood' and Dr. William Bache of 'Franklin,'" *Magazine of Albemarle County History*, 47 [1989], 9-10; MB, 2:1089; Vol. 37:620n).

To the Senate

GENTLEMEN OF THE SENATE

I lay before you a treaty which has been concluded between the state of New York and the Oneida Indians, for the purchase of lands within that state:

One other between the same state and the Seneca Indians, for the purchase of other lands, within the same state:

One other between certain individuals, stiled the Holland company with the Senecas for the exchange of certain lands in the same state:

And one other between Oliver Phelps a citizen of the US. and the Senecas, for the exchange of lands in the same state: with sundry explanatory papers; all of them conducted under the superintendance of a commissioner on the part of the US. who reports that they have been adjusted with the fair and free consent & understanding of the parties. it is therefore submitted to your determination whether you will advise & consent to their respective ratifications.

TH: JEFFERSON
Dec. 27. 1802.

RC (DNA: RG 46, EPIR, 7th Cong., 2d sess.); endorsed by clerks; notations by a clerk alongside each of the first two paragraphs indicate that those treaties were received by the Senate "in Committee of the Whole." PrC (DLC). Enclosures: (1) Treaty between the state of New York and the Oneida nation, held at the Oneidas' town, 4 June; John Tayler attending as commissioner of the United States and Ezra L'Hommedieu and Simeon De Witt as agents of New York; completing a provisional agreement for the cession of two tracts of land by the Oneidas and payment by New York of $600 in addition to $300 already advanced, and an annuity of $300 (printed copy in DNA: RG 46, EPIR). (2) Treaty between the state of New York and the Seneca nation, 20 Aug., described as Enclosure No. 5, Dearborn to TJ, 3 Sep. (3) Indenture between the Senecas and the Holland Land Company, 30 June, described as Enclosure No. 7, same. (4) Treaty between the Seneca nation and Oliver Phelps, Isaac Bronson, and Horatio Jones, held at Buffalo Creek, 30 June, with Tayler present as commissioner of the U.S.; the Senecas conveying a two-square-mile tract known as Little Beard's Reservation to Phelps, Bronson, and Jones for the sum of $1,200 (printed copy in DNA: RG 46, EPIR). (5) Tayler to Dearborn, Albany, 19 July, conveying the treaty between the Oneidas and the state of New York and the treaties of the Senecas with the Holland Land Company and Oliver Phelps; Tayler noting that he would not have considered himself authorized to attend Phelps's negotiations with the Senecas had Phelps not assured him that Phelps and Dearborn had corresponded on the matter and it was considered to be within Tayler's commission; noting also the failure of Governor George Clinton's agents to effect an agreement with the Senecas for the sale of the tract on the Niagara River (RC in same). (6) Clinton to Dearborn, Albany, 21 Aug.; described as Enclosure No. 2, Dearborn to TJ, 3 Sep. (7) Act of the legislature of New York, 19 Mch. 1802, described as Enclosure No. 3, same. (8) Tayler to Dearborn, 23 Aug.; described as Enclosure No. 4, same. (9) Paul Busti to Dearborn, 9 Aug.; described as Enclosure No. 6, same. (10) Phelps to Dearborn, Albany, 24 July, explaining that the small Seneca reservation known as Little Beard's lay in the center of a tract owned by Phelps, and the Senecas desired to exchange it for land adjoining one of their other reservations; Phelps understood from George Clinton that the U.S. commissioner would be empowered to oversee this transaction, but he discovered that Tayler's commission contained "nothing explicit on the Subject"; Tayler, however, was present as Phelps and the Senecas reached an agreement, and Phelps hopes that the transaction will be approved (RC in DNA: RG 46, EPIR; endorsed by Dearborn: "refer to Judge Taylors report"). Message and enclosures printed in ASP, *Indian Affairs*, 1:663-8.

For the sale of land by the ONEIDA INDIANS, see Vol. 37:9.

For the negotiation between the SENECA nation and the state of New York for the strip of land along the Niagara River—a transaction that Red Jacket sought and Handsome Lake opposed—see Vol. 36:633, 634n; Vol. 37:9, 30;

Dearborn to TJ, 3 Sep.; TJ to Dearborn, 6 Sep.; and TJ to Handsome Lake, 3 Nov.

The HOLLAND Land Company had purchased rights to large tracts of land that Robert Morris acquired from the Senecas in 1797 (Vol. 36:342n; Vol. 37:37).

The Senate in March 1802 had confirmed TJ's nomination of John Tayler as the U.S. COMMISSIONER for the negotiations with the Oneidas and the Senecas (Vol. 37:23-4).

RESPECTIVE RATIFICATIONS: Meriwether Lewis delivered the message and documents on 28 Dec. On the 31st, the Senate unanimously approved the treaty between the Oneidas and the state of New York and the one between the Senecas and the state. The other two treaties required longer consideration as other matters intervened to take up the Senate's time. The Senate approved the one between the Senecas and the Holland Land Company on 10 Jan. 1803 in a split vote, with Robert Wright of Maryland casting a lone negative against 21 ayes. On 7 Jan., the Senate referred the agreement between Phelps and the Senecas to a committee consisting of De Witt Clinton, Wright, and Gouverneur Morris. On 17 Jan., the Senate removed the injunction of secrecy, which was usual with regard to pending ratifications, from that treaty. On 4 Feb., the committee recommended approval and the Senate unanimously ratified the treaty (JEP, 1:427-31, 437, 442).

To the Senate

GENTLEMEN OF THE SENATE

I lay before you a treaty which has been agreed to by Commissioners duly authorised on the part of the US. and the Creek nation of[1] Indians, for the extinguishment of the native title to lands in the Talassee county, and others between the forks of Oconee and Oakmulgee rivers in Georgia, in pursuance of the convention with that state; together with the documents explanatory thereof; and it is submitted to your determination whether you will advise and consent to the ratification thereof.

TH: JEFFERSON
Dec. 27. 1802.

RC (DNA: RG 46, EPIR, 7th Cong., 2d sess.); endorsed by clerks. PrC (DLC). Enclosures: (1) Treaty between the United States and the Creek nation, 16 June, made near Fort Wilkinson on the Oconee River, for the cession of a specified tract of land to the United States by the Creeks; the U.S. agreeing to pay the Creeks $3,000 annually; the U.S. also to pay $1,000 per year for ten years "to the chiefs who administer the government"; the U.S. also to pay $10,000 in goods, $10,000 toward certain debts at the government trading factory, and $5,000 to satisfy claims for property taken by the Creeks from U.S. citizens; the treaty also allowing for the establishment on the Creeks' land of one or more garrisons "for the protection of the frontiers"; in an added stipulation, the U.S. commissioners—James Wilkinson, Benjamin Hawkins, and Andrew Pickens—agree that ten chiefs of the Upper Towns and ten chiefs of the Lower Towns will share in the special $1,000 annuity to be paid to the Creeks' leaders for ten years, with "the speaker in the national council which has been established as a part of the plan of civilization, agreeably to the orders of government," to receive $150 per year, three "first chiefs" to receive $70 each, and the remaining 16 chiefs to have equal shares of the remainder of the $1,000 (printed copy in DNA: RG 46, EPIR). (2) Wilkinson and Hawkins to Dearborn, 15 July; reporting the distribution of $10,000 in goods according to the treaty, which took some time "amidst the distinct claims & pretensions of twenty-seven Towns & eight Villages"; reporting also that early in the negotiations, "difficulties & divisions" among the Creeks caused delays, the commissioners learning that "certain disaffected Tribes" that claimed some lands were not in attendance at the treaty conference and might "attack our frontier" if the lands were sold; the commissioners, finding that the citizens of Georgia "held those tracts in light Estimation," agreed to remove that land from consideration; the commissioners note that it was the Creeks' wish to have U.S. military garrisons "posted on their Lands, in front of our Settlements," to protect them from the Americans; the commissioners concur on that point, believing that by separating the army from the settlers, "the principles of subordination & discipline may be more effectually enforced, and those animosities, broils, & debaucheries, which are inseperable from a connexion between them, may be prevented"; such an arrangement will also "have a natural tendency to familiarize the Indians to the Idea" of giving up lands near the military establishment and will restrict interaction between the Indians and "our disorderly Citizens, from whom they derive naught but their vices & bad habits"; during the treaty negotiations, a Cherokee delegation arrived and complained to the commissioners about encroachments by whites, but the delegation's main purpose was to negotiate a boundary between the Cherokees and the Creeks, which was done in the commissioners' presence; the Creeks complain of trespassing in the area of the Tombigbee and Mobile Rivers, where whites have built houses and cleared fields; the Indians formerly made land concessions to the British in that zone, "but the precise bounds have not yet been discovered"; two incidents marred the negotiations, the theft of some of the Creeks' horses by whites and an altercation in which a young Indian warrior wounded a white man, but neither incident escalated to cause wider problems; overall the commissioners "believe a solid foundation has been laid, for a salutary reform in the Habits & manners of this People, and we have no doubt, that, by due perseverance in the Systems which have prevailed, the great work of their civilization may be accomplished" (RC in same, in Hawkins's hand, signed by him and Wilkinson). (3) "Journal of a Conference between The Commissioners of the United States & The Creek Nation of Indians held at Fort Wilkinson in the months of May & June 1802," a compilation dated 8 May to 30 June; includes transcriptions of the commissioners' correspondence with Dearborn and Governor Josiah Tattnall, Jr., of Georgia, and minutes of conferences with Creek leaders (Tr in same, with certification of Alexander Macomb, Jr., as the commissioners' secretary). Message and enclosures printed in ASP, *Indian Affairs*, 1:668-81.

EXTINGUISHMENT OF THE NATIVE TITLE: in an April 1802 agreement for the cession of lands by Georgia, the United States pledged to remove Indian claims to the Tallassee district and the area of the Oconee and Ocmulgee Rivers. Congress had previously appropriated funds for a treaty conference for that purpose (Vol. 36:191n; Vol. 37:344n).

The Senate received the message and accompanying papers from Meriwether Lewis on 28 Dec. and gave its consent by unanimous vote on 4 Jan. 1803 (JEP, 1:427, 429). TJ signed the RATIFICATION one week later, and the State Department later sent a copy of the treaty, certified by Madison on 1 Apr. 1803, to the state of Georgia (MS in G-Ar; Madison, *Papers*, *Sec. of State Ser.*, 4:472).

[1] Preceding two words interlined.

To the Senate and the House of Representatives

GENTLEMEN OF THE SENATE AND
OF THE HOUSE OF REPRESENTATIVES

In my message of the 15th. instant, I mentioned that plans and estimates of a Dry dock, for the preservation of our ships of war, prepared by a person of skill and experience, should be laid before you without delay. these are now transmitted; the report & estimate by duplicates; but the plans being single only, I must request an intercommunication of them between the houses, and their return when they shall no longer be wanting for their consideration.

TH: JEFFERSON
Dec. 27. 1802.

RC (DNA: RG 233, PM, 7th Cong., 2d sess.); endorsed by clerks. PrC (DLC). RC (DNA: RG 46, LPPM); endorsed by a clerk. Enclosures: (1) Robert Smith to TJ, 8 Dec. 1802, and enclosures. (2) Extract consisting of the first paragraph of Benjamin Henry Latrobe to TJ, 15 Dec. 1802 (Tr in DNA: RG 233, PM, in Meriwether Lewis's hand, endorsed by a clerk; Tr in RG 46, LPPM, in Meriwether Lewis's hand). Message and enclosures printed in ASP, *Naval Affairs*, 1:104-8.

TJ's MESSAGE and enclosures were presented to Congress on 28 Dec. The Senate ordered that the papers be printed for their use, while the House referred them to the committee appointed on 17 Dec. to consider the part of TJ's annual message of 15 Dec. relating to navy yards and docks (JS, 3:248; JHR, 4:253, 260). William Duane printed the papers as *Message from the President of the United States, Transmitting Plans and Estimates of a Dry Dock, for the Preservation of our Ships of War* (Washington, D.C., 1802; Shaw-Shoemaker, No. 3361).

From John Smith

SIR Near Cincinnati Decr. the 27th 1802

The removal of Governor St Clair from Office has produced much Joy & triumph among the Republicans of this new State; especially as the administration of the Government devolves on Charles W Byrd Esquire, with whom the Republicans are universally pleased with us And certainly would elect him for our first Governor, was it not that we are not well supplied with proper characters for the Judicial department of our State—It therefore would be very pleasing to see him appointed to the office of Federal Judge as I took the liberty to mention in a former letter

Mr Edward Tiffin is the Republican Candidate for Governor. I know not that any will oppose him, I am sure that none of the opposite party can with success—Tomorrow fortnight will be the day of Our election, and such is the spirit of the times that it will be deficult for an aristocrat to be elected even to the office of a constable. We are confident of a Republican Legislature as well as Governor & of course a Republican Representation in Congress We flatter ourselves that the aristocracy of this Country has got such a state that it will not be revived in the present generation

Be pleased again to pardon the freedom I have taken & accept the assurance of the high consideration & respect with which I am

Sir Your most obedt Servt JOHN SMITH

RC (DLC); at foot of text: "Thomas Jefferson President of the United States"; endorsed by TJ as received 1 Feb. 1803 and so recorded in SJL.

For the REMOVAL of Arthur St. Clair, see TJ to the Senate and the House of Representatives [on or after 22 Nov. 1802].

FORMER LETTER: Smith to TJ, 26 Nov. 1802.

From Indiana Territory Citizens

The Memorial and Petition of the Citizens of the Indiana Territory, by their Representatives in general Convention assembled, Respectfully sheweth

That your memorialists scattered over a remote and extensive Territory, have for a considerable time struggled with all those Difficulties and Dangers incident to a frontier Situation and a sparce population

Unrepresented and almost unknown in the national Councils, it was as much impossible that they should lay their Grievances before the Government, as it was for the Government to redress, without knowing the Causes which produced them.—Untill the formation of the Indiana Territory in the year 1800 not a Gleam of hope broke in upon their distressed situation—This measure, however, promised, and indeed produced much Relief to your memorialists—but from the Combination of a variety of Causes, the great object of our hopes, and to which our strongest solicitudes, are directed—self government, seems removed to a period so distant as to cause the most painful Reflections in the Breast of your memorialists.—The obstacles which have retarded the Improvement and population of this Country are detailed in the memorial to the Congress of the United States, a Duplicate of which is herewith transmitted to your Excellency.

In the Solicitude which you have always discovered, Sir, for the prosperity and happiness of our common Country and of the western parts of it in particular, your memorialists have a certain pledge that their Grievances, as far as they depend upon you will be amply redressed—As coming particularly under this Description, they take the liberty to mention the ascertaining and marking the Indian boundary Lines as a matter of much Importance—This Business, it is understood is progressing in the Neighbourhood of Vincennes, but in the other parts of the Territory, nothing of the kind has been attempted.

Accept the Thanks of the People of this Territory Sir, for the Attention with which you have pleased to honour their former Petitions—And their wishes that your life may be long, happy and prosperous.

Done in Convention at Vincennes in the Indiana Territory the twenty Eighth Day of December in the Year of our lord one thousand Eight hundred and two and of the Independence of the United States the twenty seventh.

By the unanimous order of the Convention,

WILLM HENRY HARRISON. President
& Delegate from the County of Knox

Teste
Jno Rice Jones
Secy.

RC (PHi: Daniel Parker Papers); in hand of John Rice Jones, signed by Harrison; at head of text: "To Thomas Jefferson President of the United States"; endorsed by TJ as received 23 Feb. and "Indiana Memorl & petn" and so recorded in SJL. Enclosure: "The Memorial and Petition of the Inhabitants of the Indiana Territory" to the Senate and House of Representatives, Vincennes, 28 Dec. 1802, stating that "nine tenths of your Memorialists" believe that the sixth section of the Northwest Ordinance, which prohibits slavery in the territory, has been "extremely prejudicial to their Interest and Welfare"; they therefore asked the governor to call a general convention at Vincennes to take measures to secure the repeal or suspension of the article by Congress, as well as the passage of "such other laws, as would in the opinion of the Convention, be conducive to the general welfare, population and happiness of this distant and unrepresented portion of the United States"; the convention claims that the sixth article has driven many citizens owning slaves to settle on the Spanish side of the Mississippi River; keeping the prohibition on slaves in force would oblige other potential immigrants "to seek an Asylum in that Country, where they can be permitted to enjoy their property"; the convention requests a ten-year suspension of article six, during which time slaves brought into the Indiana Territory, and their progeny, would continue in the same state of servitude as other parts of the country where slavery is permitted; the convention also requests that title to the Indian lands lying between the Illinois country, Clark's grant, and the Ohio and Wabash Rivers be extinguished, which would encourage "a speedy population of the Country," and that said lands be sold in smaller tracts and at less cost than allowed under existing laws; a preemption for those already settled on public lands is requested, along with a proviso that a portion of the public lands should be set aside for those who will actually settle and cultivate it; the convention also seeks land grants for schools and for persons willing to open good wagon roads and establish houses of entertainment, the vesting of the Wabash saline in the territorial government, alterations to the location and distribution of donation lands in the Illinois country, repeal of the property requirements for suffrage, and increased compensation for the attorney general of the territory; the memorialists hope that Congress will consider the "neglected and orphan like situation" of their territory and grant them "all the Indulgence and Attention necessary to secure to them the relief which is so essential to their welfare and happiness" (MS in same; in Jones's hand, signed by Harrison; attested by Jones).

On 22 and 24 Nov. 1802, William Henry Harrison, acting on petitions received from "a Considerable number" of Indiana Territory citizens, issued proclamations calling a GENERAL CONVENTION "for the purpose of taking into consideration the propriety of repealing the sixth article of Compact between the United States and the people of the Territory, and for other purposes." Convening at Vincennes on 20 Dec., the convention adopted a resolution on 25 Dec. calling for a ten-year suspension of article six of the Northwest Ordinance of 1787, which prohibited slavery in the territory, and prepared a MEMORIAL TO THE CONGRESS OF THE UNITED STATES on 28 Dec. The House of Representatives received the resolution and memorial on 8 Feb. 1803 and referred them to a committee consisting of John Randolph, Roger Griswold, Robert Williams, Lewis R. Morris, and William Hoge. Reporting on 2 Mch., the committee deemed it "inexpedient" to suspend the ban on slavery in the territory, stating their opinion that "the labor of slaves is not necessary to promote the growth and settlement of colonies in that region." The committee also denied the requests regarding land grants to encourage the establishment of roads and public houses, the vesting of the Wabash saline in the territorial government, and altering the existing rights of suffrage. The committee recommended that up to one thirty-sixth part of the public lands be set aside for the support of schools in the territory, that the right of preemption be granted to current settlers on public lands, and that compensation be made to the attorney general of the territory for services rendered on behalf of the United States. Recommendations were also made to clarify and make more equitable the location of donation lands in the Illinois country. The committee also noted that the authority to extinguish Indian land titles in the United States rested with the president, not Congress (Esarey, *William Henry Harrison*, 1:60-7; JHR, 4:326, 381; ASP, *Public Lands*, 1:160).

For the previous efforts to fix the INDIAN BOUNDARY LINES and extinguish Indian land titles in the Indiana Territory, see TJ's Annual Message to Congress, 15 Dec. 1802.

From Arnold Oelrichs

RIGHT HONORABLE SIR! Bremen 28th. decbr. 1802.

On the 14th. of September 1801. I had the Honor of addressing myself to your Excellency ℔r. the Ship Philadelphia Captn. Peter Yorcke duplicate whereof I send under Couver of Mr. James Zwisler of Baltimore and Triplicate ℔r. the ship Harmonie Captn. E: Hillers to all of which Letters, I have not been favor'd with an Answer from either your Excellency or your Secretary. all I Know is that the 3 Boxes I took the Liberty to Address to your Excellency arrived, and were forwarded by George Latimer Expr. Collector of the Customs at Philadelphia.

You will be pleased to pardon when I frankly declare, that I am under great Uneasiness on account of not being favored with a Line from Your Excellency or your Secretary by your directions.

I hope I have not incurred your Excellency's displeasure by my Proceedings but wish rather to Suppose that the Letters addressed to me, miscarried by some Accident or Other.

Being under much Apprehension that neither of my Letters has reached your hands, I use the freedom to send hereby Quadruplicate thereof as it is my sincere Wish to convince your Excellency that not even the smallest Inattention or Neglect can be laid to my charge.

Permit me on this Occasion the singular pleasure of paying my best Respects to your Excellency and flattering myself with the best hopes, of being very soon favored with agreable Intelligence from your Excellency.

I have the Honor to subscribe myself, Right Honorable Sir! your Excellency's! most devoted & most Obedient humble Servant—

Arnold Oelrichs

RC (DLC); at foot of first page: "His Excellency the Right Honorable T Jefferson President of the United States"; endorsed by TJ as received 6 Apr. 1803 and so recorded in SJL. Enclosure: quadruplicate of Oelrichs to TJ, 14 Sep. 1801 (see Vol. 35:294n).

According to the notification that TJ received from GEORGE LATIMER when the items sent by Oelrichs arrived in Philadelphia in November 1801, the ship was named *Pennsylvania*, not *Philadelphia*. The boxes contained sculptures (Vol. 35:292-5, 741).

From Jean François Perrey

Poste vincennes 28 Decembre 1802

J'ai L'honneur de vous adresser cy inclus une petition faites Entre tous Les membres de la Convention du teritoire indiana qui a pour But La recommandation En faveur de M john rice jones Comme un homme propre par ses talents a remplir L'office de premier juge du teritoire Vacant par la mort de William Clark.

M. jones D'aprés notre opinion, Est la personne Capable de remplir Cet office important. depuis nombre Dannées il reside parmi nous, possede notre Langue et nos Loix aussi bien que qui Ce soit parmi nous. J'ose donc vous prier de vouloir Bien prendre notre petition En Consideration, persuadés que nous sommes que vous ne voulez que notre Bonheur.

J'ai L'honneur d'etre avec le plus profond respect de Son Excellence Le trés humble Et trés obeissant Serviteur

Perrey
Membre de la Convention
de St Claire Comté

EDITORS' TRANSLATION

Post Vincennes 28 Dec. 1802

I have the honor of sending the enclosed petition from all the members of the convention of the Indiana Territory. Its goal is to recommend Mr. John Rice Jones as a man whose talents qualify him to fulfill the office of principal judge of the territory, vacated by the death of William Clarke.

In our opinion, Mr. Jones is the person capable of filling this important position. He has resided among us for many years and has mastered our language and laws as well as anyone among us. I therefore dare to beg you to consider our petition, since we are convinced that you seek only our well-being.

With the deepest respect for Your Excellency, I have the honor of being your very humble and obedient servant.

Perrey
Member of the Convention
from St. Clair County

RC (DNA: RG 59, LAR); at foot of text: "Son Excellence"; endorsed by TJ: "Jones John Rice. to be judge of Indiana. Harrison, Perrey & others" and as received 27 Jan. 1803, and so recorded in SJL.

Jean François (John Francis) Perrey (1766-1812) immigrated to the Illinois region from his native France in the early 1790s. His education included some legal training, and he became a territorial county judge of common pleas and of quarter sessions. He was engaged in the land trade and in milling. Perrey was one of a number of residents of the western part of Indiana Territory, a region that was predominantly French in origin, who feared that they would be dominated in the legislature by heavily populated eastern counties. They repeatedly appealed to Congress, beginning in 1803, asking that the western counties be separated from the territory and joined to a territorial government for Upper Louisiana. William Henry Harrison consequently depicted Perrey to TJ as someone who opposed the advancement of Indiana Territory to the legislative stage of government. Perrey was nominated to the legislative council in 1805, but Harrison favored another candidate and Perrey did not receive the appointment (Francis S. Philbrick, ed., *The Laws of Indiana Territory, 1801-1809*, vol. 21 of *Collections of the Illinois State Historical Library* [Springfield, Ill., 1930], lxxiv, cxxiv, ccxxix, cclvii-cclviii; *Terr. Papers*, 3:488; 7:140-5, 262n, 551-4; Harrison to TJ, 20 Nov. 1805).

ENCLOSURE

From William Henry Harrison and Others

To Thomas Jefferson President of the United States of America

The undersigned beg leave to recommend to the President of the United States John Rice Jones Esquire the present Attorney General as a proper person to fill the appointment of a Judge of the Territory. Mr Jones has been regularly bred to the Bar and has resided as a practising Attorney in the said Territory for many years which has given him an opportunity of being acquainted with the Local Laws and Customs of the Country—perhaps better than is possessed by any other Character—The undersigned will further add that Mr Jones has ably performed the duties of Attorney General to the Territory since the Establishment without any Salary, and as we believe without any Compensation whatever—

Dated Vincennes the 28. day of December 1802

Willm. H. Harrison

RC (DNA: RG 59, LAR); in a clerk's hand, signed by Harrison, Perrey, and ten others; the date 27 Dec. appears above Perrey's signature; endorsed.

Memorandum for Henry Dearborn on Indian Policy

Hints on the subject of Indian boundaries, suggested for consideration

An object, becoming now of great importance, is the establishment of a strong front on our Western boundary, the Missisipi, securing us on that side, as our front on the Atlantic does towards the East. our proceedings with the Indians should tend systematically to that object, leaving the extinguishment of title in the interior country to fall in as occasions may arise. the Indians being once closed in between strong settled countries on the Missisipi & Atlantic, will, for want of game, be forced to agriculture, will find that small portions of land well improved, will be worth more to them than extensive forests unemployed, and will be continually parting with portions of them, for money to buy stock, utensils & necessaries for their farms & families.

On the Missisipi we hold at present from our Southern boundary to the Yazoo. from the Yazoo to the Ohio is the property of the Chickasaws, a tribe the most friendly to us, & at the same time the most adverse to the diminution of their lands. the portion of their territory of first importance to us, would be the slip between the Missisipi on the

West, and on the East the Yazoo and the ridge dividing the waters of the Missisipi & Tenissee. their main settlements are Eastward of this. I believe they have few within this slip & towards the Missisipi. the methods by which we may advance towards our object will be 1. to press the encouragements to agriculture, by which they may see how little land will maintain them much better, and the advantage of exchanging useless deserts to improve their farms. 2. to establish among them a factory or factories for furnishing them with all the necessaries & comforts they may wish (spirituous liquors excepted) encouraging them, & especially their leading men, to run in debt for these beyond their individual means of paying; & whenever in that situation they will always cede lands to rid themselves of debt. a factory about the Chickasaw bluffs, would be tolerably central, and they might admit us to tend corn for feeding the factory & themselves when at it, and even to fix some persons there for the protection of the factory from the Indians West of the Missisipi & others. after a while we might purchase there, and add to it from time to time. 3. we should continue to nourish and increase their friendship & confidence, by every act of justice and of favor which we can possibly render them. what we do in favor of the other Indians, should not constitute the measure of what we do for these, our views as to these being so much more important. this tribe is very poor; they want necessaries with which we abound; we want lands with which they abound; & these mutual wants seem to offer fair ground of mutual supply.

The country between the Missisipi & Illinois on one side, & the Ohio & Wabash on the other, is also peculiarly desirable to us, and is in a situation at this moment which renders it particularly easy for us to acquire a considerable portion of it. it has belonged to the Kaskaskias, Cahokias and Piorias. the Cahokias (of whom the Michigamis were a part) have been extirpated by the Sacs, the Piorias driven off, & the Kaskaskias reduced to a few families. Governor Harrison, in his letter of Nov. 28. 1802. says the Pioria chief has offered the right of his nation to these lands for a trifle. we should not fail to purchase it immediately. the Cahokias being extirpated, we have a right to their land, in preference to any Indian tribe, in virtue of our paramount sovereignty over it. he also says that De Coigne, the Kaskaskia chief would make easy terms with us. I think we should be liberal in our offers to the Kaskaskians. they are now but a few families, exposed to numerous enemies, & unable to defend themselves, and would cede lands in exchange for protection. we might agree to their laying off 100. acres of the best soil for every person young & old of their tribe, we might inclose it well for them, in one general inclosure, give to every family utensils, & stock sufficient for their portion of it, & give them an annuity in necessaries, on their ceding to us their whole country, or retaining for themselves only a moderate range around their farms for their stock to range in; & we might undertake to protect them from their enemies. having thus established ourselves in the rights of the Kaskaskias, Cahokias & Piorias, we should have to settle the boundaries between them, & the Kickapoos, Poutawatamies and Weaws. we should first gain the good will of these tribes by friendly acts, & of their chiefs by largesses, and then propose to run the line between us, to claim whatever can be said to be doubtful, offering them a liberal price for their pretensions, and even endeavoring to obtain from them a cession of so much of their acknoleged territory as they can be induced to part with.

As to the country on the Missisipi above the mouth of the Illinois, it's acquisition is not pressing in the present state of things. it might be well to be enquiring into titles, and to claim whatever may have been abandoned or lost by it's native owners, so as to prevent usurpation by tribes having no right: as also to purchase such portions as may be found in the occupation of small remnants of tribes nearly extinct & disposed to emigrate.

For the present it is submitted to the consideration of the Secretary at war, whether instructions should not be immediately given to Governor Harrison to treat with the Pioria & Kaskaskia chiefs. as to the latter, which is most important, it would be easy to sollicit & bring over by presents every individual of mature age.

TH: JEFFERSON
Dec. 29. 1802.

PrC (DLC). Recorded in SJL as a communication to the War Department, with notation "Indian boundaries."

The KASKASKIAS, the Peorias, the Cahokias, and the Michigameas were tribes of what were collectively called the Illinois Indians. They had all been hard pressed by other Native American groups, and the Peorias had abandoned their traditional homelands to live west of the Mississippi. The SACS (Sauks) lived to the north of the Illinois tribes (Sturtevant, *Handbook*, 15:596, 648, 651, 673, 678-9).

LETTER OF NOV. 28: William Henry Harrison wrote to Dearborn from Vincennes on 28 Nov. regarding "Indian boundary lines, & the disposition of the Indians generally." The letter, received at the War Department on 23 or 24 Dec., has not been found (recorded in DNA: RG 107, RLRMS).

DE COIGNE, THE KASKASKIA CHIEF: Jean Baptiste Ducoigne, whose father was French Canadian and his mother a Kaskaskia, had allied his small tribe with U.S. interests in the Illinois country since the American Revolution. In 1802, he and Little Turtle of the Miamis assisted

Harrison by influencing leaders of other tribes to agree to Harrison's delimitation of the Vincennes tract. TJ and Ducoigne were acquainted, the latter—accompanied by his wife and an infant son, Louis Jefferson Ducoigne—having called at Monticello in the spring of 1781, when TJ was governor of Virginia. They exchanged gifts, and TJ deemed himself and his visitor to be "Americans, born in the same land, and having the same interests." TJ applauded Ducoigne's request for teachers to instruct the Kaskaskias, but said the endeavor must wait until the war with Britain was over. The two met again in the winter of 1792-93, when Ducoigne was the speaker for a delegation that traveled to Philadelphia to meet with George Washington. A few years later, TJ hoped that Volney would call on Ducoigne in the west (Robert M. Owens, "Jean Baptiste Ducoigne, the Kaskaskias, and the Limits of Thomas Jefferson's Friendship," *Journal of Illinois History*, 5 [2002], 109-36; Vol. 6:60; Vol. 24:806; Vol. 25:17-18, 112-19, 133-4; Vol. 29:131-2).

In February 1803, TJ appointed Harrison a commissioner to hold treaties with Indian nations. Dearborn then wrote to Harrison with INSTRUCTIONS to complete the surveys of tracts included in the 17 Sep. convention signed at Vincennes. The secretary of war also asked the governor to "take the earliest opportunity" to consult with "the Chiefs of the Nation or Nations" that claimed the area around Kaskaskia and "a tract bordering on the Mississippi and Ohio from their junction up each River a considerable distance." Once Harrison had information about the land and the "probable sum" necessary to acquire it, arrangements would be made for him to complete the transaction (Dearborn to Harrison, 21 Feb. 1803, in DNA: RG 75, LSIA; Notes on Bounds of the Vincennes Tract, [on or after 26 Oct. 1802]; TJ to the Senate, 2 Feb. 1803).

From John Condit

SIR Capitol Hill Decr. 30 1802

I had intended last evening to have done myself the Honor this morning of Waiting on the President for the purpose of communicating what I am now (from Indisposition) about to do in writing—Yesterday Arived a Vessel from New York, at George Town And landed, to the Care of Mr. John H Barney 52 Barels of NewArk Cyder, said to be of a fine Quality—I had in consequence of what the President had said to me on the Subject written to One of the Persons concerned in the Cyder, who informs me that it was Shipped before the receipt of my letter—but that he had taken the Liberty of marking two Barels with the Name of the President—

There are also 10 or 12 other Barels marked with the Names of certain gentlemen mostly Members of Congress who had requested Some Sent here for them, when On their way to this place—I informed Mr. Barney that the President must have as many Barels as he wished, that he had mentioned Six, and would perhaps wish more—And as there are about 30 Barels not yet engaged I would Suggest the Propriety of the Presidents causing a Selection in addition to the two already Marked of as many Barels as he may think proper to take to be made Immediately—I do not expect there is much Difference in the Quality, However there may be Some—I should Pick for that which is very Sweet, Clear, and high Coloured Especially if it is to be put into Bottles or otherwise kept Untill next Summer before it is Used—

I am Sir, with great respect your Obt. Servt. JOHN CONDIT

RC (MHi); at foot of text: "The President of the U.S."; endorsed by TJ as received 30 Dec. and so recorded in SJL.

Made from Harrison and Canfield apples grown at orchards in Essex County, New Jersey, NEWARK cider was celebrated for its quality and shipped especially to the South. In 1803, TJ again asked the New Jersey congressman to order the cider for him (*Proceedings of the New Jersey Historical Society: A Magazine of History, Biography and Genealogy*, new ser., 3 [1918], 25, 52; *National Intelligencer*, 9 Feb. 1807; TJ to Condit, 1 Oct. 1803).

From Edmund Harrison

Richmond 30 Decr. 1802

Edmund Harrison presents his respectful acknowledgments to Mr. Jefferson,—thanks him for the parliamentary Manual, which is enhanced in value from the polite and friendly manner in which it was presented.

Where the voice of Millions join in the wish that our present chief Magistrate may long fill the exalted station, which he has so much dignified, the single expression of an Individual conforming to that Wish, cannot be deemed intrusive.—

RC (DLC). Recorded in SJL as received 4 Jan. 1803.

Edmund Harrison (1764-1826) represented Prince George County in the Virginia House of Delegates in the late 1780s and early 1790s, and subsequently served on Virginia's Council of State. Having established an estate in Amelia County, he represented that county for seven consecutive terms as a delegate, and was speaker during the 1802-3 term. In 1806, he married Martha Wayles Skipwith, a niece of Martha Wayles Jefferson (E. Griffith Dodson, *Speakers and Clerks of the Virginia House of Delegates, 1776-1955* [Richmond, 1956], 39; CVSP, 5:190; 6:680; Leonard, *General Assembly*, 170, 177, 181, 185, 189, 192, 219, 223, 227, 231, 235, 239, 243).

To the House of Representatives

I. TO THE HOUSE OF REPRESENTATIVES, 30 DEC. 1802

II. TO THE SPEAKER OF THE HOUSE, 30 DEC. 1802

EDITORIAL NOTE

Among the papers that Jefferson sent to the House of Representatives on 22 Dec. was a copy of William C. C. Claiborne's letter of 28 Oct. to Manuel de Salcedo, the Spanish governor of Louisiana, questioning the suspension of the deposit at New Orleans. The State Department received a copy of Salcedo's reply to Claiborne by 30 Dec., and on that day Jefferson wrote a brief message to the House transmitting the document as an addendum to the materials sent on the 22d (Document I). The president took the unusual step of writing also to the speaker of the House (Nathaniel Macon) to suggest that publication of the full contents of Salcedo's letter might have undesirable consequences (Document II). The House received Jefferson's message and the letter to the speaker from Meriwether Lewis on 31 Dec. After all the papers were read, motions to refer the matter to a select committee and to print the documents "for the use of the members" failed. A third motion, to refer the papers received on the 22d and the 31st to the Committee of the Whole House on the State of the Union, then passed, 65 votes to 16 (*Annals*, 12:299-301; JHR, 4:395).

The House had not yet taken up the subject of the closure of the deposit when, on 4 Jan., Federalist Roger Griswold of Connecticut, observing that the president had referred to the cession of Louisiana from Spain to France in his annual message, introduced a resolution calling on the executive to furnish copies of documents on that subject, along with a report about the terms of the cession. After considerable debate, John Randolph succeeded in a motion to commit discussion of Griswold's proposed resolution, "which might embrace points nearly connected" with Jefferson's messages of 22 and 30 Dec., also to the Committee of the Whole House on the State of the Union, for consideration behind closed doors. The Republican members then blocked Griswold's attempt to bring his matter up before the committee, and would not allow it to be considered in open session. After discussions in closed sessions, the House on 7 Jan. approved a resolution expressing a willingness to "wait the issue of such measures" as the executive branch might take relative to the situation at New Orleans, particularly as the "breach of compact" appeared to be the result of "unauthorized misconduct of certain individuals" rather than "a want of good faith on the part of His Catholic Majesty." Immediately after passing the resolution, the House lifted the injunction of secrecy regarding its proceedings on the president's messages of 22 and 30 Dec. By the time Griswold, on 11 Jan., tried again to use Louisiana to bring the administration's actions into question, Randolph could allude to the appointment of James Monroe as an envoy to settle matters with Spain, arguing that the Federalists only wanted to make trouble by disrupting relations between Spain and the United States (*Annals*, 12:312, 314-43, 352-68; Malone, *Jefferson*, 4:268-9).

The resolution of 7 Jan. contained an assertion that the House was "relying, with perfect confidence, on the vigilance and wisdom of the Executive." Griswold and his colleagues in the House fought the inclusion of that clause, the Connecticut congressman later saying in debate that "I could not express a confidence which I did not feel." Randolph took pains to point out that Griswold and his allies had approved every other part of the resolve, but then voted against the measure as a whole because they objected to the passage that declared confidence in the administration. "There was a time, sir," Randolph asserted, "when such conduct would have been denounced by a portion of this House as the essence of Jacobinism and disorganization." Opponents of Jefferson's presidency, according to Randolph, could not abide contentment and prosperity—they must sow "war, confusion, and a consequent derangement of our finances" in hopes of regaining power (*Annals*, 12:336, 339, 354).

Due to the injunction of secrecy, the smooth journal of the House made no reference to the receipt of a message from the president on 31 Dec. The journal for that day was probably already in print when the House removed the secrecy requirement on 7 Jan. (The clerks sent the journals out to be set into type after only a short interval: on 11 Jan., for example, when Randolph wanted to refer to the official journal for debates of a few days earlier, probably 6-7 Jan., he could not do so because the record for those days was already "at the printer's"; same, 357.) Later, the clerks copied into the smooth journal, after the entry for the last day of the session, "A supplemental journal of such proceedings, as, during the time they were depending, were ordered to be kept secret, and respecting which the injunction of secrecy was afterwards taken off by order of the House." That addendum to the proceedings contained the record of what had transpired on 31 Dec. concerning the message, and of closed sessions on 5 and 6 Jan. (DNA: RG 233, journals, 7th Cong., 2d sess.; JHR, 4:263, 395-8).

I. To the House of Representatives

Gentlemen of the
House of Representatives

In addition to the information accompanying my message of the 22d. instant, I now transmit the copy of a letter on the same subject recently recieved.

Th: Jefferson
Dec. 30. 1802.

PrC (DLC). Tr (DNA: RG 233, journals, 7th Cong., 2d sess.); in the "supplemental journal" appended at the end of the session (see Editorial Note). Enclosures: (1) William C. C. Claiborne to Madison, Natchez, 25 Nov. 1802; he sends a copy, with translation, of a communication received this morning "from the Governor General of the Province of Louisiana" in reply to Claiborne's letter to him of 28 Oct. (Tr in DNA: RG 233, PM; PrC in DLC). (2) Manuel de

Salcedo to Claiborne, New Orleans, 15 Nov., a translation in English; the king, Salcedo writes, has not designated a new place of deposit; in response to royal instructions and to the peace in Europe, the intendant suspended neutral trading and also suspended the deposit to put an end to abuses and fraud; while it is true that adherence to the terms of treaties promotes good relations, if a treaty has a "defect" that brings unintended negative consequences, "it will be necessary to undo it"; the intendant did not feel, as he ended the trade of neutrals, that he could continue the right of deposit beyond the original term specified by the treaty without instructions from the royal government; "it is to be hoped" that the crown will restore the deposit either at New Orleans or at another location, and "it ought to be confided, that the Justice and generosity of the King will not refuse to afford to the American Citizens all the advantages they can desire"; "I ought at the same time," Salcedo writes, "to inform you that I myself opposed on my part, as far as I reasonably could, the measure of suspending the deposit," until the intendant persuaded him that, as not all events can be foreseen, "a just and rational interpretation is always necessary"; Salcedo sent an inquiry to the captain general, whose reply, when it arrives, will remove any doubt on the question; Salcedo will strive to preserve "the most perfect and constant good harmony" that has existed between the two countries, also "keeping it in view that the felicity and glory of Nations are deeply concerned in the advantages of a wise and prudently conducted Commerce" (Tr in DNA: RG 233, PM, endorsed by a clerk; PrC in DLC).

II. To the Speaker of the House

SIR — Washington Dec. 30. 1802.

Altho' an informal communication to the public, of the substance of the inclosed letter, may be proper for quieting the public mind, yet I refer to the consideration of the House of Representatives whether publication of it in form might not give dissatisfaction to the writer, and tend to discourage the freedom and confidence of communications between the agents of the two governments. Accept assurances of my high consideration and respect.

TH: JEFFERSON

RC (DNA: RG 233, PM, 7th Cong., 2d sess.); at foot of text: "The Speaker of the H. of Representatives"; endorsed by a clerk. PrC (DLC).

INCLOSED LETTER: Salcedo's communication to Claiborne (Enclosure No. 2 listed at Document I above).

From Carlos Martínez de Irujo

DEAR SIR — Capitol Hill this 30th. December 1802

To morrow morning I'll give myself the honor of waiting upon you with the congratulations of the *new* year; but to-day I take the liberty of sending to you, with this, a *new* supply of my excellent champaigne. This new remittance with the former one will compose the number of 200 botles half of my stock, which I can spare without inconvinience—Abusing perhaps of your indulgence, I must request the favor of another dozzen of your excellent Madeira which the bearer will take the charge of—May the new year render you as happy as you deserve for your important services in the present, & as it is the sincere wish of your

attach'd & respectful Servt— LE CHEVALIER D'IRUJO

RC (MoSHi: Jefferson Papers); at foot of text: "H Ex. Thomas Jefferson"; endorsed by TJ as a letter of 31 Dec.

200 BOTLES: in January, TJ paid Irujo $150 for the champagne, 100 bottles received early in December, and another 100 received in January. TJ also paid customs duties of $22.50 on the wine (MB, 2:1090, 1092, 1115).

From James Miller

Cincinnata
December. 30. 1802

DEEAR SIR

This Day I was in the Commissioners office where I saw the land Jobbers imposeing on the poore labouring people Charging them from $\frac{1}{4}$ to too Dollars per achree for their preemtions for which they never paid one Cent and now I find they are about to petetion for one year longer for to Speculate and for the Reserve Sections because they know that numbers of them are first Rate and will Sell high if it Could bee or would bee Convenient for the honoured Congress to Order it so as to Sell thease lands in Small quantitees they would find the benefit boath to them selves and the people Deear Sir if the land Jobers Do send their petetion I hope your honour will be kind anuf to Delay it Untill you have the voice of the people at large as I Do Expect their will be a petition Forwarded Relaiting their Situation and Expressing their wishes Deear Sir I am your most obedient and humble Servent JAMES MILLER

RC (ViW: Tucker-Coleman Collection); addressed: "To the honoured president of the United States Thomis Jefferson Washenton City Collumbia"; franked; postmarked 4 Jan. 1803; endorsed by TJ as received 1 Feb. 1803 and so recorded in SJL.

On 3 Feb. 1803, the House of Representatives received a petition from James Miller and others, "inhabitants and settlers on Mad river, in the State of Ohio," requesting the right to purchase "small portions" of public land in Ohio "on such terms and conditions as may be deemed reasonable and proper." Miller was apparently among those who had settled on the Miami Purchase lands claimed and sold by John Cleves Symmes, but which were later found to lay beyond the authorized boundary of his purchase. In 1801, Congress granted persons residing on these lands a right of preemption to purchase them from the United States at a fixed price of $2 per acre. The act also authorized the president to appoint two commissioners, who, in conjunction with the receiver of public monies at Cincinnati, would ascertain the rights of those claiming preemptions. Claims were to be made by 1 Jan. 1802, but Congress later extended the deadline to 1 Mch. 1803. Additional letters from Miller to TJ dated 28 Oct. and 6 Dec. 1804, and an undated letter received 8 Feb. 1805, are recorded in SJL, but have not been found (JHR, 4:320; U.S. Statutes at Large, 2:112-14, 179-80; Vol. 31:8n; Vol. 35:392n; Miller to TJ, 1 Feb. 1803).

To Timothy Bloodworth

DEAR SIR Washington Dec. 31. 1802.

Your letters of Nov. 30. & Dec. 14. have been duly recieved. commissions under the bankrupt act, in conformity with the former, were immediately issued. mr West having chosen to be continued as Marshal, his commission was renewed.

I feel with great sensibility the friendly expressions in your letter, and the sentiments of approbation as to the conduct of our affairs for their wisdom it would be presumption in me to argue: but that they are well intended I may say with conscious truth. if I know myself I have no passion adverse to the interests of man. I have no pleasure in the exercise of power, wishing that any body should have to dispose of favors, or to exercise severities rather than myself. therefore I shall not be seduced by that to set examples which may lead to abuse of power, or to draw to the executive the authorities more safely possessed by the legislature. to fortify the principles of free government, to fence them by every barrier practicable, and to establish in the government habits of economy, present the principal means by which I can render any permanent service: and if the pursuit of these should be found to acquire popularity, the love of popularity may induce some of those who come after me to practise what their natural dispositions might not otherwise lead them to. if a sense of correct principles can be established among our citizens, instead of the delusions by which our predecessors endeavored to lead them, they will be enabled to keep their governors in the right way. You will have seen by the message that little important is proposed to Congress. the settlement of the Missisipi territory I think the most so. I am in hopes the obstructions on the Missisipi will be amicably & immediately removed. accept assurances of my sincere esteem & friendly attachment. TH: JEFFERSON

PrC (DLC); at foot of text: "Timothy Bloodworth esq."

To Dwight Foster

Th: Jefferson requests the favour of *Mr. D. Foster* to dine with him *on Monday next, the 3rd. January* at half after three, or at whatever later hour the house may rise.

Friday Decr. 31st. 1802.

The favour of an answer is asked.

RC (MB); printed form, with blanks filled by Meriwether Lewis reproduced in italics.

To Heads of Departments

[31 Dec. 1802]

Th: Jefferson asks a consultation with the heads of departments to-morrow at 11. aclock, on the subject of N. Orleans & the Floridas. should we meet later, we may be prevented by the visits usual on the day. will mr Smith be so good as to send the inclosed over the way to mr Lincoln?

RC (MHi: Levi Lincoln Papers); undated or date clipped; endorsed by Levi Lincoln as 31 Dec. 1802; with unrelated notations by Lincoln on verso. Enclosure not found.

From John Joseph Rey

SIR George Town December 31st. 1802.

Though a blustering storm darkens the sunshine for a short space, yet it clears the atmosphere to radiate brighter the next day.

Thus your brilliant character & republican principles after being ignominiously & repeatedly aspersed with showers of calumny by Lewd, envious & injudicious adversary hosts, who wished to obscure its lustre, have at length displayed more luminous rays than ever.

In testimony thereof the good Citizens of these United States, induced with a high sense of gratitude for the important services you had rendered their country, have with cordial affection invited you with their suffrages to preside over them,—for the protection of their rights & liberties: & the overthrown party (not relishing the dish.) did not fail at the same time to exert the most atrocious vengeance on the unprotected individuals, who were not disposed to bewail with them their irretrievable fall.

May you long continue to govern the columbian republic, for the glory of God, & her prosperity.

My long desired Congratulation would have been humbly addressed to you—in due time, had I not been interrupted by reasons, closed in my bosom.

The inclosed chain made of seventeen links linked together, is metaphorical of the sixteen confederated states, & the district of Columbia, wherein their respective republicans defeated the Aristocrats at the last election, & as they carried you triumphant, they uttered alternatively the following victorious panegyric, which may be read round the outside of each link, namely. The largest link begins thus, IV March MDCCCI, felix Œra. (which records the event, figuring the district of Columbia)

"Victory or death, is our hue & Cry,
Tyrants, to Justice must ply;
all united in one voice,
great Jefferson is our choice;
in him, his foes will find address,
and his friends, get redress;
God bless, his pert administration,
as the Bulwark, of our Nation."

Please to observe the unity of the three colors with which every link of this chain is decorated, which affords the eye a flattering aspect; it is emblematical of the three branches of the administration, which when United together and Conducted by one spirit of wisdom, Virtue & justice, their toil presents their Country the happiest prospect.

Deign Sir, to accept of this frivolous matter (as a pledge of my respectful joy for your elevated dignity) not as an experiment of my genius; not as an object worthy of your notice; not as a present made with requital views: but as a tender I take the liberty to make you, in the name of all your friends the republicans of the Union, to bear record of their Justice in your behalf;—& to shew your enemies a queer typography.

Providence furnishes me with a seasonable opportunity to wish you a happy—new year, accompanied with precious gifts of gracious blessings.

I remain with great veneration Sir, Your most obedt. humb Servt

John Joseph Rey

RC (DLC); at foot of text: "Thomas Jefferson Esqre: President of the United States of America"; endorsed by TJ as received 31 Dec. and so recorded in SJL.

John Joseph Rey (d. 1811?), of Baltimore, wrote several letters to the president requesting employment, admission to the Library of Congress, and financial assistance. In October 1806, Rey advertised for pupils to attend his school at East Street and St. Paul's Lane in Baltimore. He proposed a day school with instruction in spelling, reading, writing, arithmetic, and bookkeeping, as well as an evening school for French and Spanish lessons (Baltimore *American and Commercial Daily Advertiser*, 20 Oct. 1806; Baltimore *Federal Gazette*, 30 Jan. 1811; Rey to TJ, 1 May, 31 Dec. 1805, 23 Jan. 1806).

To Caesar A. Rodney

DEAR SIR Washington Dec. 31. 1802.

I thank you for the mention you made in your's of the 19th. of my subscription to the academy. immediately after subscribing I had set it down on a list of paiments to be made by mr John Barnes of this place, who transacts all my pecuniary affairs. I supposed it paid, and he supposed it was to be called for, and thus it has laid and would have laid but for your letter which recalled my attention to it. mr Barnes will now immediately remit it to mr Latimer according to the printed advertisement.

Congress is not yet engaged in business of any note. we want men of business among them. I really wish you were here. I am convinced it is in the power of any man who understands business, and who will undertake to keep a file of the business before Congress & to press it as he would his own docket in a court, to shorten the sessions a month one year with another, & to save in that way 30,000. D. a year. an ill-judged modesty prevents those from undertaking it who are equal to it.

You will have seen by the message that there is little interesting proposed to be done. the settlement of the Missisipi territory is among the most important. so also, in my opinion, is the proposition for the preservation of our Navy, which otherwise will either be entirely rotten in 6. or 8. years, or will cost us 3. or 4. millions in repairs. whether the proposition will surmount the doubts of some, and false economy of others, I know not. Accept assurances of my great esteem & respect.

TH: JEFFERSON

RC (Robert Clark, Chairman, Board of Directors, The Corporation for Jefferson's Poplar Forest, 2011); addressed: "Caesar A. Rodney esqr Wilmington Delaware"; stamped and postmarked. PrC (DLC); endorsed by TJ in ink on verso.

From John Vaughan

DEAR SIR. Philad. Decr 31. 1802

I have just recieved the inclosed from M Dunbar, which I think it proper to forward to you although I doubt not you will have recieved official notice of the information.

I remain with respect D sir Your obt Servt JN VAUGHAN

RC (DLC); endorsed by TJ as received 3 Jan. 1803 and so recorded in SJL. Enclosure: William Dunbar to Vaughan, Natchez, 25 Nov. 1802, stating that with the post about to depart, he has time only to say that W. C. C. Claiborne "has received an answer to his remonstrance" to Manuel de Salcedo (see TJ to the House of Representatives, 30 Dec.), in which the closing of the deposit at New Orleans "is justified on the principle of mercantile fraud introduced into the port" and "it is asserted" that Juan Ventura Morales acted without orders from Madrid; Dunbar adds that "General Victor is hourly expected with 3000 french troops & 7000 more will follow" (RC in DLC).

From George Trisler

Office of the Triumph of Liberty,
RESPECTED SIR, Winchester, 1802

The enclosed will apprize you of my determination of conducting two newspapers in the Borough of Winchester, provided the encouragement will justify the attempt.

The immense advantages accrueing to society from the invention of PRINTING are not duly appreciated. How few, how very few, are sensible, that to the unrestrained exercise of this ART, we are indebted for the greater part of our private enjoyments; and by it, are enabled to communicate our ideas, from one extremity of the globe to the other.

No person, I am confident, can hold in greater abhorrance, than you, SIR, every attempt to restrain the exercise of an Art of such inexpressible utility.—Such attempts ought to be considered as open violations of the Rights of the American People, and the most flagrant injuries to society in general. The thoughts of elegant and judicious writers, contribute largely to enlighten and improve the mind, and are, in fact, the ESTATE of the public, which, by the advantages of the Press, create a common and continually increasing fund, for the pleasure and benefit of mankind.

The usefulness of the Press, when considered in a political point of view, is unbounded. It is the Centinel and Safe guard of CIVIL LIBERTY, and a source from whence the government of every free nation, may derive a most desirable assistance. It is to the Press, that we are in a great measure indebted for the GREAT and GLORIOUS CHANGE in favour of LIBERTY & EQUALITY, in this our beloved land; and to the talents and exertions of its REPUBLICAN CONDUCTORS, may we look for a continuation of those invaluable blessings, which your patriotism, I am assured, will never suffer to decrease, by withholding your patronage and support.

I cannot refrain from expressing my determination to urge a pacific and friendly disposition among the people. My best endeavors shall aim at a love of order and respect for the constituted authourities, nor shall I ever be backward in cultivating a spirit of submission and obedience to the laws: for it is an irrefragible truth, that the REPUBLIC can never have a firm existance unless all ranks of men co-operate in its preservation, with the utmost spirit and energy.

WITH MUCH ESTEEM, I REMAIN, RESPECTFULLY, YOUR OBEDIENT SERVANT, GEORGE TRISLER.

P.S. Should Mr. Jefferson be pleased to encourage this Press, any money subscribed shall be discharged by a regular [...] of [...] paper.

RC (DLC: TJ Papers, 128:22153); printed broadside; partially dated; at head of text: "Democratic Presses"; postscript, faint, in Trisler's hand.

George Trisler (1768-1845), from Fredericktown, Maryland, was a printer of German descent who assisted Matthias Bartgis and Henry Willcocks in the production of the Winchester *Virginia Gazette*. He published, alone or in partnership, the weekly *Winchester Triumph of Liberty*, established in 1799 and continued through November 1803. He also pursued the mercantile business and, in 1805, advertised groceries, patent medicines, porter, and glassware available for purchase from his store on Market Street in Fredericktown (J. Thomas Scharf, *History of Western Maryland*, 2 vols. [Philadelphia, 1882], 1:468-9; Brigham, *American Newspapers*, 2:1165-7; Fredericktown *Republican Advocate*, 26 Apr. 1805).

ENCLOSURE

Circular on the *Winchester Triumph of Liberty*

FOR THE ENLARGEMENT, ENCOURAGEMENT AND CONTINUATION OF THE

Winchester Triumph of Liberty

AND MORE PARTICULARLY FOR THE DESIRABLE PURPOSE of procuring a Quantity OF BEAUTIFUL LONG PRIMMER TYPE—WE, whose names are hereunto annexed, agree, to pay in advance the respective sums, by us subscribed, to accomplish the above laudable design.

The object of the Editor is, to raise the sum of *One Hundred and fifty dollars*, in addition to his collections, from his *Republican Friends*, to be re-imbursed in all manner of *Job-work, Hand-bills, Blanks, Advertiseing, Pamphlets or Newspapers*, individually, or collectively, to every one concerned—The editor also pledges himself, to conduct and publish a paper, the workmanship of which and the elegance of the type, shall exceed any Newspaper ever published in the Borough of Winchester, to the honor of its Patrons and the dignity of the cause. *Vive la Republique!!*

Out of the above raised fund, and the encouragement offered by my German Friends, A Newspaper, in the German Language, will immediately be published—This will be an undertaking worthy of public Patronage, as there is not a single German paper issued in the state of Virginia.

Broadside (DLC: TJ Papers, 128:22154); undated; at head of text: "Democratic Presses"; endorsed by TJ on verso: "Trisler, George."

From E. T. Hadwen

YOUR EXCELLENCY: Isle of Mann January 1st. 1803

Although I being an entire stranger to you; yet I do pray the Most High Almighty propitious God in Christ Jesus that we may become sincerly and perfectly acquainted. And now I must prepare the annexed subject as concise as possible because in the limits of a letter I cannot enlarge much. But I have to treat upon a variety of heads to give you necessary hints & Ideas entirely new to you: and I lament I cannot now speak to you Face to Face to explain. I am an Engineer in the mysterious art of Flax Spinning upon Water Engines vulgarly called Spinning Frames, by Machinery. or, an inventor a constructer & a builder of Engine spinning Frames, for Flax & Hemp and Tow Spinning. A new secret bussiness which I myself by God's Help have brought to astonishing perfection in 12 years. And should be happy to serve the Great Empire of America with this profitable art If I could come to America under your Auspices & be encouraged without defraud.

About October 28th. 1801 I recd. a letter from Mr. Geoe. Edkin at New York. An Englishman with Gen. Gates at Rose Hill,[1] formerly a distant acquaintance Wherein after encouraging me to come to America he says "You would be received with open arms; you would come not as a common, but as a Mechanick of the *first* Magnitude, and with the greatest respect due to your unequalled abilities." He strongly invited me to come, writing high encomiums upon the country and the government of America.

Well, I immediately wrote him two letters by different vessels, I paid

2s/14d carriage of one ℔ the packet, and waited above six Months without receiving his answer. Again in last May I sent him other two letters, but never once did I get his answer. His first letter was directed to the care of a person in Lancaster Old England: that person is dead, but the letter got into the hands of a Brother to me, who reprobated the Idea of my going to America. he indeed sent me the letter, but strongly disswauded me not to leave my native country. But I charged Mr George Edkin to be careful to direct the next letter to me at the Isle of Mann Old England Europe &c. G. Edkin said he had spoke of me to Genl. Gates who highly approved of my coming to New york. And I since wrote to the General first wishing to know if he could get me safe good employers who would be legally bound to secure me those advantages due to my merit; else I would not come. But I have not at all recd. any reply from either of them. I told Edkin my works far exceeded and answered better than any Idea he could easily form of the business, And that I had been exceeding ill used at several Mills by their base art of redily defrauding me out of my share & wages. by making me the most fine & fair but detestable false promises. And I had been so cheated and taken in by their getting knowledge from me to learn them and set their mills to Spinning, So that I now believed it a crime to trust mankind any longer. But I proposed to Mr Edkin & the General, if they would find for me any Able honourable & safe persons who would honestly be bound to secure me my share & decent wages, I would venture to come, and do better for them in spinning then they could believe till they saw: and according to the prices of spinning as mentioned by Edkin in America, I told them 100000£. might be annually cleared by the profits of the business. And I said I had been at such enormous expenses as well as labour and pains and hard study to accomplish the great end of good spinning that I had not money enough to pay for necessary articles to bring with me towards expediting a New Mill in America. & they must send me Cash to get the same. I enjoined them to lasting secrecy, *Never, Never* to betray me; nor mention I had proposed to come, least I was fined & imprisoned for it, which is both heavy severe & hard. Tho I think a man should do the best for himself, yet we are not allowed. However I never heard since from them, nor cannot tell their motive for Silence.

Now, Mr. Jefferson I will propose to you, But I first most solemnly charge you in the Name & by the power of that Blessed God & Christ Jesus, that you will never in any wise betray me nor let it be known to any English subject nor to any soul upon earth who would willfully or inadvertently tell of me, so that if it was known here, I should be fined which I never *never* could pay, & be imprisoned as an Engineer for attempting to leave my native Land. But May God & Christ Jesus who sees & will reward & punish all actions, keep your heart true to me & never let any one copy any part of this letter. *But burn it before* you die. And depending upon your honour friendship & veracity, I propose I would come to America under your Auspicious favour if you can engage me yourself or procure me Native Americans to employ me, in Flax Spinning &c. by Water Engines or spinning Thomas. perhaps I shall put 36 spindles in each spinning Frame to spin fine Flax yarn & 28 spindles to spin Hemp coarse yarn, & Tow, which is the waste from Flax & Hemp. Each Frame is managed [...] Children [...] And 36 spindles will spin as much as 40 good foot wheel spinners. We have some clever Children & women & a man to prepare & make ready the Flax Hemp or Tow for spinning. But the total expence is not $\frac{1}{4}$ part of what is paid for spinning it by the Hand. At this place we spin coarse yarn for sailcloth weft and warp, and each spinning Frame will pay its expences and clear 3£ ℔ week profit very easily. We can spin four five and 6 lbs weight of coarse yarn in a day upon each spindle for sailcloth weft, And about one pound weight of common flax yarn for double warps each spindle in each days work.

But when we come to spin fine yarn of a small quality we spin about half a pound weight of this fine yarn in a day on each spindle. And as we can get such an enormous quantity of yarn in so little a time with a few work people. So the profit is quite sure & very great.

According to G. Edkins account you pay more than double the price for foot wheel spinning to what they pay in old England. So your profits would be far greater by Water spinning

Above 9 years ago my Engine yarn was reckoned & was certainly the best of any that went to the manufactory. And 7 years ago I claimed the honour of being the Ablest Engineer on earth at Flax Spinning for I then built Some Machinery which did & could spin faster & smaller & better yarn than any spinning Mill in England could do. And I spun for a wager with another Mill, and I spun above two yards for there one yard, and I spun Seven Sizes of yarn smaller than their Engines would do.

I was greatly encouraged to build Machinery & set one Mill forward after another, But I still wanted to fix and abide by getting a share to make a small fortune, but their promises ended in deceit and actual roguery.

In the year 1799 I spun upon a new spinning Frame, Six thousand yards of the best Engine yarn ever then Seen. The Frame contained 24 spindles & in less than 12 hours they spun 144000 yards of yarn which is 6000 [yds] for each spindle. This was fairly attested and approved. And it was advertised as an extraordinary feat in the provincial Newspapers. And if you can get a London Newspaper called the "General Evening post" dated from June 25 to June 27th. 1799 you will find my name and the above account therein advertised in the 2nd. page of that London paper. That I spun six thousand yards of Engine yarn the best ever Seen, in 12 hours on each spindle at Newlands Flax Mill in Lancashire.

I was then immediately invited to this place; avoiding and refusing all other sollicitations I have waited 3½ years Staying in this poor Isle and at the same spinning Mill where I am quite certain no Mill on earth can spin so well. And till Providence can appoint me a better & a more certain place I am determined not to change to be defrauded out of my knowledge as I have been. I have been the chief & even the Sole Engineer at Seven Mills, & I do know the business to perfection. I have acted as head Engineer about 12 years. But I have been 28 years in the Flax business. I am near 40 years of Age, was never drunk nor intoxicated with any kind of Liquor in all my life; And I believe in the Grace of our Lord, Jesus Christ I never shall be. I am not married, nor ever was. *Others* have got more by my skill and industry than I have got myself. All the Machinery & all the Mills I set to spinning are all spinning well & are doing prosperously. And now Mr Jefferson, I must come to the point and say, I am an American in my heart & have no able friends to help me in Europe & I do wish to come. Therefore—Sr you can do your country the great and vast benefit of getting your own necessary yarn and cloth spun by Water, I will do this business for you, effectually & completely and perfectly. I can & have spun 30 different sizes of yarn as perfect good yarn *as needs be*, & better than women generally spin. And I will engage for a term of 12 years if I can be legally secure to have my common wages and a third share of all the clear profits. I ought to have half the profits. for my *knowledge* which *gets* the profits must be quite equal in value to the money which sets the business to getting profit: But I will be content with one third of the profit and least you should think I need not be careful how much money is expended, I say I will allow legal intrest for one third of the Cash necessary to be employed, out of my third share of the profits. My wages shall be only Three Guineas ℘ week till we get to spinning upon Seventy two spindles. I am sure you cannot but reasonably think half a Guinea ℘ day very

low wages for a person acting [in] my capacity, & possessed of my long proved abilities. But after we get to spinning upon One hundred and Eight spindles, my wages to be four Guineas ℔ week. And after we get to spinning upon One hundred & forty four spindles & upwards my wages to be five guineas ℔ week.
I omitted above to say. after we get to spinning upon 72 spindles my wages to be three and a half Guineas & wait till we get to spinning upon Three Engines say [100?] Spindles & then to rise to four Guineas & then to five &c &c [...] have with reason and justice [stated] [...] the business.
And if you will set your heart & your hands & your Back, to my heart & hands and Head I can make you to be the Richest man of wealth in all America. Edkin urged me to come hastily to obtain & get a patent from Congress. But I cannot do thesse things myself for want of money. I have not been able to save money! I have been at heavy charges many ways to bring this business to the most profitable perfection. & it is now high time for the business to pay me But if you engage me or can get me engaged, I wish we could get a patent which I ought to have, unless you can find another that can spin as well so me. I lately say 9 weeks since sent a challenge to a boasting Mill to spin them for a good Wages either flax or Tow what sort and size they choose. They refused fairly.
you will want to know the expense. As for me I have about 130£ worth of sand Models plans patterns & things, some of them very usefull & for which I should not charge any thing but carriage for the use of them & which could facilitate a new Mill. Every good spinning Frame made to spin 30 sizes of different yarn & give any twine will cost about Two Guineas ℔ spindle—So 36 spindles will cost about—£75–12–
Preparing Engines to prepare the [Length] of Flax or Hemp for spinning will cost (each set to serve for four spin'g Frames) 96£. Observe the preparing Engines to serve for Two spinning Frames to spin Tow will be £84. Now observe well our profits are so certain and quick, if as much money is at forth come as will set 72 spindles [to work] Thesse will earn & clear money very fast to pay for & build more Engines to fill a whole Mill.
A Mill in America will require a Cutting Engine of a great size to cut [tooth] & space pinion Wheels. cost 24–0–0
A Fluting Engine to Flute our Greatest Iron Engine Rollers 3 feet 6 inch long for prepareing 18–0–0
A Double Laith or Turning [Throw calibrating] a Great spindle & bead Centers—18–0–0

Our various & curious Work Tools £20. Those to be renewed as when occasion required &c.
The above would serve continually [for to build] for a whole Mill. And here is 80£ sunk for no working Machinery. Then Two spinning Frames 72 spindles would *be* not above 151.£–4. & Flax preparing Engines which would serve for 144 spindle, but must be had if we had but one spindle, & cost 96£.
Here the expense is 96 + 80 + 151 = £327. Also some new [...] and Wood Hand Models 60£.=£387. for all the [matters] necessary to begin.
If we spin Tow which is *most exceeding* profitable we should want a preparing Engine to cost £84 more.
A Mill 45 feet Long within & 36 feet wide within wd. contain 12 spinning Frames, to be 3 floors high with [...]
Any rivulet discharging 5 Ton of Water (& 1[0] foot fall) in a minute of time will work 12 Spin'g Frames.
I did offer to engage with General Gates for [5] Guineas ℔ week & a fourth share. But since that time I have discovered the most wonderful Astonishing & beneficial way of dressing or heckling or preparing the Flax or Hemp by Water. Viz. formerly the Flax was dressed or heckled fine by Flax dressers And upon an average we used to get about 56 lbs of spun yarn out of 112 lbs of undressed or Raw unheckled Flax. I mean the Hecklers after dressing 1 Cwt. say 112 lbs Raw Flax, on an average got 56 lbs of dressed Flax or 60 lbs. The rest was Tow and waste. So that we on an average got only about 56 lbs of Flax yarn produced from 112 lbs of Raw Flax before it was heckled
But by a most glorious discovery I can upon an average heckle the Flax by Engine work & get 84 lbs of better Flax yarn out of 112 lbs of Flax. This is 28 lbs more of Flax yarn out of 1 Cwt. than they can get the old way. And if the Flax is good I can out of 112 lbs of Raw Flax, get 96 lbs to 100 lbs of fine yarn. The rest is Tow & Waste. This unequalled profitable discovery I hold a secret *yet* to myself. They know I can do it but I have kept it as secret as possible. And I will not divulge it for six months longer in Hopes to Hear from you. This profitable method alone would clear thousands a year. because every hundred weight will clear at least 15 lbs more than the common way. And The Flax yarn is better & stronger. Indeed all my yarn is as good as needs be. But this new way cannot fail to yield plenty of profit. And if you conclude to join me to receive the benefit of my Engineering business you must send me at least 160£ to buy the above Engines and to purchase Brass works, Steel & Iron works. Tow

Cards, & a many other needful articles cheaper here than in America. I do declare in the name of the Blessed God I will keep as honest account as is possible, & not[2] defraud you no not the fortieth part of a farthing! for it is not my way to do so neither to defraud [...]

Januy. 19th. 1803

As it is now near 15 months since I wrote G. Edkin without getting his reply that he can get me employers within the United States And as it is above 8 months since I made proposals to his Excelly. Gen. Gates, without receiving any reply. So if my honest reasonable & fair proposals meet your hearty approbation, I will now abide by this offer exactly & honestly. and if they raise me friends I mean if they procure me employers I will return them every penny of their money if they send any to me, on the proposal I made by their first encouragement.

Therefore if you can agree with my offer & enable me to come under your auspices I will be very honest & faithfull to theese proposals, & think [myself] excusable from their concern. Because I have not heard at all from them as I requested & expected in due course And I beg your Excellency to be so Great & Generous as give me an early reply. And if I be to come I could not an American [...] nor [...] call for me here! And [...]

RC (DLC); torn and blurred; authorship determined from TJ's endorsement and Hadwen's letter of 3 Jan.; addressed: "To His Excellency Mr. Jefferson President of the United States of America at the City of *Washington*; or Elsewhere in America. ℘ the kind favour of a Captain of an American Ship"; also on address sheet in Hadwen's hand: "January 21st. 1803 Sent this away" and "To be forwared unto His Excellency. Mr. T. Jefferson President of the United Sates of America as Early & as Soon as Possible by the kind Captain of some American ship"; franked; postmarked New York, 26 Mch.; endorsed by TJ as received from "Elama." Hadwen on 4 Apr. and so recorded in SJL. Enclosures: (1) Hadwen to TJ, 3 Jan. (2) Hadwen to TJ, 17 Jan.

E. T. Hadwen may have been the engineer identified as "Mr. Hadwen" in accounts of technological advances in the spinning of flax thread in Ulverston, Lancashire, in 1799, and in Liverpool in 1807. Writing from Wales in 1809, "E. T. Hadwen, Engineer, &c." requested that copies of a London newspaper be sent to a family of his acquaintance on the Isle of Man (London *General Evening Post*, 25 to 27 June 1799; *Lancaster Gazette and General Advertiser*, 4 July 1807; William Hone, *The Year Book, of Daily Recreation and Information: Concerning Remarkable Men, Manners, Times, Seasons, Solemnities, Merry-Makings, Antiquities and Novelties, Forming a Complete History of the Year; and a Perpetual Key to the Almanac* [London, 1832], 102).

George EDKIN managed the nursery of Horatio Gates and likely acted as an intermediary in some of Gates's transactions (George Edkin to Horatio Gates, 2 Apr. 1799, RC in NHi: Gates Papers; John F. Meginness, ed., *History of Lycoming County, Pennsylvania* [Chicago, 1892], 425, 1033-4; George Streby, *History of Eagles Mere Borough and Shrewsbury Township, Including the Early Settlements*

Together with Biographical Sketches and Statistics and Matters of General Interest [Dushore, Pa., 1905], 19).

Praising the "very great perfection" of the "spinning of flaxtow brought upon water-machinery" at Newland's (NEWLANDS) Flax Mills in Ulverston, England, an account appearing in London's *General Evening Post* of 25 to 27 June 1799 singled out the 24-spindle spinning frame built by "Mr. Hadwen, the engineer," which had spun 144,000 yards of tow yarn in 12 hours.

[1] Preceding six words interlined.
[2] MS: "not not."

From David Humphreys

SIR George Town Jany. 1st. 1803

In referring to that part of the letter addressed by me, on the 28th. of June last, to the President of the U.S., which relates to the measures I took to avoid recieving without the consent of Congress the Royal Present usually offered to Ambassadors & Ministers who had resided near H.C.M.; I now hasten to give information that Mr. Codman has brought from Europe to this Country a small Package (unaccompanied by any letter or Note) simply addressed on the cover to Mrs. Humphreys. It will be perceived, by inspecting the Ornaments contained in it, that they were designed, by their quality & form, for female use. My Wife will solicit the honour of delivering them into the hands of the President, to be remitted or otherwise disposed of as shall be judged most proper.

I shall only add, that, whatsoever Order shall be given respecting the destination of these Objects in question, will doubtless be applied in its principle to the disposal of the Sabre & Belt mounted in gold, which were sent to me in the Year 1795, as a Present by the Dey of Algiers, after having concluded the negociation for Peace with him; also which are in possession of the Department of State.

With Sentiments of perfect consideration and high esteem,

I have the honour to be, Sir, Your Mo. ob: & Mo. hble. Servt

D. HUMPHREYS

RC (DNA: RG 59, DD, Spain); at foot of text: "Thomas Jefferson President of the U.S. of America"; endorsed by TJ as received 3 Jan. and so recorded in SJL; also endorsed by TJ: "refd. to Secy. of State Th: J."; endorsed for the State Department.

H.C.M.: "His Catholic Majesty," King Carlos of Spain.

American merchant Richard CODMAN carried official dispatches and other items on a voyage from Spain to the United States (Madison, *Papers*, *Sec. of State Ser.*, 3:481, 483, 486, 560, 561; 4:19, 89, 98).

Madison wrote to Humphreys on 5 Jan. returning the PACKAGE, which was a case of jewelry sent to Ann Humphreys by the queen of Spain. The president, Madison explained, "thought it most proper" that the gift should be returned to Humphreys and his wife "without deciding how far the Constitution," which gave Congress the authority to allow officeholders to receive presents from foreign governments, "may or may not be applicable to this particular case." Humphreys refused to take back the jewelry without approval from Congress (same, 4:239).

For the gift to Humphreys from the DEY OF ALGIERS, see Vol. 37:671, 675n.

From Joseph Coppinger

Pittsburgh 3d January 1803

The obliging and ready condecension with which your Excellency has been pleased to answer the letter I addressed to you in October last, on the subject of a Patent, and how such may be procured, demands, and always will have, my grateful acknowledgments. On turning to the act of Congress you direct, I find but one serious impedimt to my taking out a patent at the present, and that is that I am not more than six months, an inhabitant of the United States. If your Excellency has the power, of removing this obsticle, in order to promote what I conceive will be found a great National good and that individual character has any weight in the scale I beg leave to refer you for mine to your neighbour the Rigt. Revd. Doctor Carroll to whom the inclosed is addressed and which your Excellency will Please to have fowarded to him. In it I pray him to forward you two letters which were addressed to me by Mr. Nehemiah Bartley secretary to the Bath, and West of England agriculturel society, being part of a correspondance had with that Gentleman, before leaving Ireland on different subjects some of which have been favourably received. His treatise on Potatoe cultivation (which possesses great merit) I hope to have it in my Power to forward your Excellency before long. the two letters after perusal you will please to direct being forwarded to me here. If I am obliged to run out the time prescribed by law to constitute[1] Citizenship before a Patent can be procured. It is more than Probable I shall have passed away, my health in general being very delicate, and my circumstances so limitted, as not to leave me the option I would wish of at once giving it to the Publick, and a better legacy I shall never have it in my power to leave them, entreating your Excellency to execuse the freedom of this communication which the importance of the subject I treat of, can alone on my part Justify—

I am with real sentiments of respect Your Excellencys most Obt. And very humble Servant

Joseph Coppinger

RC (DLC); endorsed by TJ as received 11 Jan. and so recorded in SJL. Enclosure not found.

TJ's ANSWER to Coppinger of 23 Oct. 1802 was written in response to Coppinger's LETTER of the 17th on the SUBJECT OF A PATENT for preserving animal and vegetable substances.

NEHEMIAH BARTLEY, secretary and honorary member of the Bath Agricultural Society, wrote *Some Interesting Hints on the Utility of Applying the Potatoe as Food for Sheep, Particularly at the Present Juncture; From Practical Observations*, which was printed in *Some Cursory Observations on the Conversion of Pasture Land into Tillage*, published in London in 1802.

FORWARDED TO ME: see TJ to John Carroll, 25 Feb. 1803.

[1] MS: "constitue."

From William Dean

HONOR'D SIR— Philada. 3rd. January 1803

By a letter addressed to you by Isaac Williams Junr. War chief of the Wyandot Nation, you will observe that I am to pay attention to his buisiness at the seat of Government, the document relating to which, will be laid before you herewith by the Secretary at War: in two weeks I will be at the city of Washington, when I will do myself the hono'r of waiting on you, and be Govern'd by your advice in pursuing the interest of Mr. Williams whose situation at present requires all that can be done for him—

I have the hono'r to subscribe myself your very obedt. Servt.

WM. DEAN

RC (DLC); in a clerk's hand, signed by Dean; at head of text: "To His Excellency Thomas Jefferson President of the U-States"; endorsed by TJ as received 11 Jan. and so recorded in SJL.

The writer may have been William Dean (1741-1807) of Montgomery County, Pennsylvania, who as early as 1758 had connections to the trans-Appalachian region (PMHB, 38 [1914], 458; 45 [1921], 287; *United States Gazette*, 12 Oct. 1807).

The LETTER from Isaac Williams, Jr., has not been found, is not recorded in SJL, and does not appear in the correspondence registers of the War Department in DNA: RG 107, RLRMS.

Dean was probably in WASHINGTON on 9 Feb. Writing to him on that date in answer to an inquiry from earlier in the day, Dearborn stated that any purchase of land by citizens of the United States from Indian nations or individual Indians must be overseen by agents appointed by the president. Concerning the possibility that lands claimed by Williams fell within "the tract commonly called the Connecticut reserve," Dearborn wrote that the answer "can only be known with certainty by the lines being run under the direction of an Agent appointed for this purpose, by the President of the United States" (DNA: RG 75, LSIA).

To James Dinsmore

Dear Sir Washington, Jan. 3, 1803.

I conclude absolutely to cover my terras with sheet iron, and have accordingly written to Philadelphia to see if I can procure sheets 15. I. wide and 9½ f. long.—The method of doing it is shewn below Fig. 1. it consists in forming gutters across the terras declining from the ridge pole to the eaves, the gutters being 21. I. horizontal measure each. We shall take off the present shingling, and form our work on the sheeting plank, by taking new planks 12. I. wide and 9½ f. long, and laying them across the terras in ridges & gutters so that a single plank forms the side of the gutter or ridge. ab. in Fig. 1 is the upper course of sheeting c. c. c. c. c. c. & c. are the gutter planks, seen end wise, d. d. are sheets of iron 15. I. wide & 9½ feet long, hollowed to the gutter and nailed at their upper edges to the gutter plank. e. e. are similar sheets of iron bent over the ridges, and overlapping the gutter sheets so that the water is conveyed by them into the gutter.

I am so well satisfied of the efficacy of this covering that I think to adopt it for my offices, the roofs of which are so offensive to the eye. as Mr. Perry has not yet got on the roof of the N.W. offices I would have him stop immediately where he is, and let it lie till I come home. He may put a shelter of slabs over the ice house so as to keep out the rain. The method I think of for the offices is seen in Fig. 2. below. ab is the plate or horizontal wall on which the joists c. c. c. & c. rest. These joists are bevelled at top to a ridge, half way between them are guttered joists d. d. d. & c all these joists are 6 I. wider in the middle (at the ridge pole) than at the eves. Sheeting plank is nailed, one edge to the ridged joist, & the other edge to the guttered joist as e. e. e. e. & e. Then gutter sheets of iron i. i. i. i. & c and ridge sheets as o. o. o. o. & c are put on so in the former case of the terras all the stuff which Mr. Perry has got for these offices will still do for them, or for the mill. in both cases we shall lay a flat floor of plan across the ridges to walk on. I shall be glad to know the exact state of Mr. Perry's progress towards the compleating the roof of the offices, when he is stopped. Accept my best wishes. Th. Jefferson

Tr (ViC-M: Milton L. Grigg Papers); typescript and drawing in ink by Fiske Kimball, 1938.

The TERRAS was the low-hipped roof at the top of Monticello, behind the Chinese railing. TJ wrote notes on and sketched the framing of the terras in the remodeling notebook that he compiled during the 1790s, but in February 1803, added to these notes that "a much stronger form may be contrived on the principles of the geometrical bridge." The principal problem confronting TJ was that the roof's low pitch allowed water to get under the shingles. His solution was to lay SHEET IRON over a system of RIDGES & GUTTERS, which he later termed "rooflets" and which were intended to allow water to run off as easily as on a high-pitched roof. A set of notes in TJ's hand, likely executed around this time, included two sketches and detailed instructions on a method of constructing the rooflets, as well as on laying and securing the sheet iron. TJ obtained the iron from Benjamin Henry Latrobe, who was a partner in a Philadelphia rolling mill. A letter to Latrobe, recorded in SJL as sent 25 Dec. 1802, has not been found, nor has one from Latrobe, recorded as a letter of 29 Dec. received from Philadelphia on 1 Jan. Latrobe referred to the system as "the Presidents zigzag" roof and, in adopting it for the north wing of the Capitol, praised it as a "species of roof uniting all the good qualities of the pantile, without its bad ones" (William L. Beiswanger, "Jefferson and the Art of Roofing," *The Chronicle of the Early American Industries Association*, 58 [2005], 18-25, 36; Latrobe, *Correspondence*, 1:325; "Monticello: Notebook for Remodelling," [1794-1797], in MHi, Nichols, *Architectural Drawings*, No. 146; "Monticello: Notebook of Improvements," [1804-1807], in MHi, Nichols, *Architectural Drawings*, No. 171; MB, 2:1113n; TJ to Ferdinand R. Hassler, 3 Dec. 1825).

It is uncertain whether TJ adopted the variant plan of ridges and gutters for the OFFICES, or dependencies, described and sketched above. It is more likely that he preferred the design he worked out in his contemporaneous notebook of improvements and that the roofing of Monticello's wings was similar to that adopted for the top of the house. A restoration of the wings carried out between 1938 and 1941, nevertheless, adopted the plan as copied by Fiske Kimball (Beiswanger, "Jefferson and the Art of Roofing," 21-2).

From Albert Gallatin

DEAR SIR Jany. 3d 1803

I enclose the following papers vizt.

a letter from the district attorney of Maryland on the subject of the suit against De Butts whom I think very unworthy, & likely through his council L Martin, to give us some trouble by instituting a suit against the Collector of Nottingham for damages on account of the seizure of the vessel suspected of having been intended for the slave trade.—

a letter from Peter Audrain, a frenchman by birth, but settled these 25 years in the United States & now prothonotary of the County of Wayne. I am apt to think that his information concerning Detroit may be more depended upon than that of our other officers there.

and a letter from Eli Elmer collector of Bridgetown in New Jersey.

His confession that he is a defaulter may entitle him to some credit for candor; for the fact had not been discovered at the treasury: the sum being but small (1200 Dollars) had appeared to remain in his hands only from the 30th June last and it was supposed that the reason was the difficulty of making remittances. On the other hand, his cousin Mr Elmer of Congress to whom I applied on receipt of the letter says that he is in debt, addicted to intemperate habits & had been a most violent federal partisan. He did not say that he wished him removed, but that, if he must be removed, he could recommend a very proper successor.

With respect & attachment Your obedt. Servt.

ALBERT GALLATIN

RC (DLC); endorsed by TJ as received from the Treasury Department on 4 Jan. and so recorded in SJL with notation "Debutts' vessel. Eli Elmer defaulter. Audrain on Detroit"; also endorsed by TJ: "Debutts's vessel. Hollinguer's lre on it Eli Elmer Collector of Bridgetown N.J. defaulter Peter Audrain's lre on affairs at Detroit." Enclosures: (1) probably Peter Audrain to John Cleves Symmes, Detroit, December 1802, recalling that he lives in a county where news comes almost entirely from Federalist sources; Audrain and a few others recently defended TJ against charges in the newspaper that he had "displaced all the officers appointed by Mr. Adams"; Audrain argued that the continuation of Matthew Ernest as collector at Detroit, the most lucrative federal office "in this Country," refutes the charge and gives "unquestionable proof of the liberality of the President"; he also describes the collector at Michilimackinac, a TJ appointee, as "perhaps one of the warmest advocates for Adams's administration"; Audrain applauds the appointment of Charles Jouett, agent for Indian Affairs, as a man of knowledge and information, "attentive to public duty, and generally beloved & respected," with political principles in agreement with his own; as far as statehood is concerned, Audrain declares "there is not one man in this County capable of understanding the duties of a member of the legislature"; he continues, "it is to be wished, for the good of these people, that they may remain a Colony for ten years to come; untill their children may get instructed and become fit for public business"; Audrain urges Symmes to support the petition for land grants for schools in the files of the House of Representatives and to engage the support of others, especially Madison and Gallatin; he has already written Gallatin on the subject; "I rely upon your benevolence," Audrain concludes, "and your Zeal in promoting public learning, and upon your local Knowledge of our people & Country" (RC in NHi: Gallatin Papers, postmarked Detroit, 15 Dec.; for the petition from Detroit, Wayne County, dated 2 Sep. 1800, relating to the establishment of a seminary of learning, see *Terr. Papers*, 3:103-8). (2) Eli Elmer to Gallatin, collector's office, Bridgeton, New Jersey, 15 Dec. 1802, noting that it is apparent from the current accounts that he might "with propriety" be dismissed at any time; if he is allowed to remain in office, he writes, "with Six or Nine month from 1st January next I will positively discharge all the Monies that may be due at the Close this year, with Interest" (RC in DNA: RG 59, LAR; endorsed by TJ: "Elmer Eli to mr Gallatin"). Other enclosure not found.

DISTRICT ATTORNEY OF MARYLAND: Zebulon Hollingsworth. William Coombs, an owner of the *Sally*, may have brought SUIT AGAINST Elias DE BUTTS, who commanded the schooner at the time it was seized on suspicion of being outfitted for the slave trade. Coombs noted that the intended voyage to Africa had commenced without his knowledge and contrary to his wishes. He failed to gain possession of the schooner after it was released by the court. De Butts took the vessel to Baltimore, where it was libelled and sold. On 26 Jan. 1802, Coombs signed a statement exonerating the Nottingham customs house officers from any damages that might arise in consequence of the seizure (Gallatin, *Papers*, 15:805; 16:223-5). For Nottingham collector George Briscoe and the case against the *Sally*, see Vol. 35:711, 738-40, 741-3.

From E. T. Hadwen

[*Isle of Man*], *3 Jan. 1803.* Confined within the limits of a letter, he cannot say as much as he should. He looks upon America as superior to Europe, "as the Sun is better than the Moon." He believes that many engineers and mechanics have emigrated to America, but few or none have been clever and able. As for himself, he does not lack a situation; he "could get 50 in 40 days." There are so many engineers in England, however, that "a clever person cannot have the advantages due to merit." Yet if the price of spinning yarn in America be equal to the rates quoted to him by George Edkin, then he sees great opportunities to bring his technological innovations to the United States. Having borne the expenses of "bringing to real perfection" the spinning of flax, hemp, and tow yarn with water-powered engines, he lacks money to buy the necessary equipment. He praises the "Grand effect" and "Noble appearance" of his engines and the "neat profit" that each engine guarantees. British customs laws and concerns that information about his plans might reach his employer mandate that he take great care in obtaining and exporting cards, lathes, metal fixtures, and other necessary equipment. They should be packed in separate boxes and directed either to TJ or to some other trustworthy person. He must sail from a port where he is not known. TJ might easily remit £160 to the American consul in Liverpool, with orders for him to pay Hadwen, or TJ might send the funds by an American ship's captain. Hadwen begs that the president not reveal the secret to anyone, for he risks a fine of £500 and a 12-month imprisonment. If TJ legally engages him and sends him, say, £700, he will work for a one-third share of the profits and the aforementioned wages. He will not come for less. He hopes that TJ will relieve his mind by writing to him. It would be best to write by an American captain with instructions to put the letter into an English post office. If TJ sends the letter directly, the president should be careful not to "set the word Engineer" on the letter, lest his employer spot it, but simply to "direct for E T Hadwen at Ballasalla. Isle of Mann. old England Europe." If the two reach an agreement, he pledges to make TJ the "richest man in America." He hopes that the president can inform him about the presence of brass and iron foundries in the United States, as these are necessary in making the smaller parts of his engines. It has been about eight months since he wrote to Horatio Gates, and as the general has been silent and as his recent advances in "Heckling Flax by water" have greatly increased his output, he thought he would offer his skills to TJ instead. He signs himself with deference and respect, "Verily the Ablest Engineer on Earth at Flax & Hemp and Tow Spinning."

RC (DLC); 2 p.; signed "Elama. T Hadwen." Enclosed in Hadwen to TJ, 1 Jan.

From Ephraim Kirby

Dear Sir Litchfield January 3rd. 1803

Accept my grateful acknowledgement of the letter which you did me the honor to write on the 10th. ulto.—The appointment of Mr Judd under the Bankrupt Law will not be condemned as injudicious or unfit, even by those who are in the constant habit of condemning every act of the present administration. His age, experience, and respectable rank in society placed him on uncontested ground.

The official communication at the opening of Congress is read with approbation and pleasure by every friend of the government in this vicinity. Even the most clamorous opposers are struck with a temporary *locked jaw*, and yeild a kind of tacit approbation. This however will not continue. The leaders of the party will discover in it many faults, for with them no executive act can pass without censure.

Mr. Abraham Bishop of New Haven has frequently communicated with me on the subject of a reform in the Collection Laws of the United States. I have given attention to the subject, and am fully persuaded that the present system is susceptible of great improvement. Every thing hitherto, on this subject has been a course of experiment. Twelve years has furnished a stock of experience sufficient for a permanent foundation. Perhaps a better time for the perfection of our system of revenue laws will never occur. We are at peace with all nations; and the nations of Europe are at peace with each other; our commercial relations are established, the republican sentiments which gave us a national existence are in full operation, and the people are earnestly looking forward with expectations of governmental reform and improvement. The present laws which respect the external revenues have been passed at different times, are intermingled with the other laws throughout the five volumes of Statutes; to these may be added a cumbrous mass of Treasury instructions, frequently furnished on the spur of the occasion, without concert or digestion, forming in the whole a system too complicated to be easily understood by those most conversant with all its parts, and altogether uninteligible to a great portion of our fellow citizens whose interests are most materially affected by it.—Hence the frequent complaints of penalties being incurred and petitions for redress, &c. I will convey to you the outlines of Mr. Bishops plan in his own words.—

"1. Supposing all the laws on the collection of the external revenues, including registering &c. to be as good as they can be made; it is proposed that they be printed in one volume, and all additions to be made in the same, as is done in Statute law books, this to be entitled "Collection law of the United States." The advantage of this would be that the officers could more easily refer to them, Merchants, Owners & Masters of Vessels could have them, which they never will have, provided they must purchase all the laws in order to know the collection laws. Now from the circumstance of not having them, they are frequently subjected to penalties, and commerce which you would encourage is injured. Penalties are undesirable; they are like public whippings, and they would seldom be incurred, if no vessel was allowed to be cleared without having one of the collection laws. The expence of the United States would be defrayed by the purchases of Merchants and Masters of Vessels, and Collectors would be supplied for that purpose on a plan hereafter to be proposed.—This is the simplest of Improvements, yet of great consequence to a permanent system of revenue.

"2nd. Supposing the principles and provisions of the Collection Law, and the language and arrangement to be the best, yet that the law is made obscure by reason of its length. I propose that the forms of oaths, bonds &c. be excluded—in fact that all forms of doing the business shall be refered to the Secretary to be by him communicated in a mode to be noted hereafter (and sanctioned by Congress if necessary). Thus the things to be done, and the things which are prohibited will constitute the law. Reference to the Collection law of 1799, will show that the detachment of the forms will greatly abridge the law—and a reference to other laws establishing Courts &c will shew that the mode of doing business is not necessary to be enacted.—The shortening of the laws, leaving all its principles & provisions entire, will be found a great improvement.

"3rd. Supposing as before (except that the laws are in one volume, the forms excluded) the arrangement to be incorrect. this can be corrected by retaining all the words, yet reducing each distinct subject to a distinct chapter.—if the language is tedious or obscure, it can be altered by the mere application of plain english and the introduction of inteligible law terms. In the first pages in which the districts &c are defined The repetition[1] of words may be saved, and under the head of each State may be placed each collection district in one column, the officers in a second, ports of entry in a third &c.—fees, penalties rates of duties should form so many distinct tables. Under this head I propose no alteration which shall affect the principles or provisions of the collection law, but such mere mechanical alterations as would be obviously convenient.

"4th. Supposing any alterations to be necessary in the principles or provisions of the Law, the knowledge necessary to do this to any extent must be in the officers of the Treasury, as they are in possession of all the letters which have been written and have seen every difficulty which attended the operation of collecting—It must occur to them that the coasting Act is extremely obscure in its provisions, multiplied and severe in its penalties. The Coasters are very reluctant at paying hospital money, because they employ landsmen, and change them often and seldom collect it, and the hospital lists from this circumstance are very uncertain.—I would propose that no papers issue for Coasters, except in January of each year—then the Officers and Coasters are most at leisure & the business issuing annually in a certain month would not be forgotten—if there was any change of owners in the interim, they should be endorsed—& each Coaster should pay on receiving new papers, in lieu of hospital & tonnage money 20 Cents ℔r. Ton, and give bond in 20 Dollars ℔r. ton. The definition of what a Coaster may not carry without clearance and entry is more abstruse than fluxions.—The registering act is in much the same way exceptionable, but I forbear to comment on improvements on the structure of the laws.

"5th. Supposing the foregoing improvements to be made, the mode of doing business safely and perspicuously next deserves consideration. The Secretary will prepare a printed book of forms of every kind of business under distinct heads—that is—supposing the registering forms to be good, let these be printed of every class—so of the forms of all returns to the Comptroler—to the Secretary &c. and in the preface to these let instructions be given as to the manner in which the whole is to be transacted between the officers and the Treasury department—each paper to have the title headings and columns printed. This will make the weekly and all other returns to the Treasury alike—and the instructions would be headed as the Blanks—thus under the head of drawbacks every instruction on that subject would be given, so of fisheries, debentures, tonage, hospital &c.—These forms should be well considered, and when done there should be no additional columns. Any instructions distinct from these, afterwards wanted, must be given without abstract. The multiplication of abstracts &c since the begining has been great and the bias has been towards burthening instead of lightening it.—The Secretary will also prepare another Book of forms, continuing all the forms of entries, oaths, bonds, clearances, &c. each headed with the business alluded to—and in order to reduce to a smaller number the forms, let all the oaths belonging to an entry be printed in small type at the foot of it—also the entries for bounty &c Forms on forms are now attached by wafers, which is inconvenient.

"As another improvement under this head, I propose that of the forms thus prepared, a sufficient number be struck off to form a supply for all the offices. This would produce the Books in the offices all of each kind of a length—the returns from the offices all similar in form to the Books and to each other, and an immense saving of labor to the officers. This mode may appear at first expensive and difficult in practice, but it will be profitable to the United States and highly convenient to the officers.—At present each Collector has a small stock of blanks, which he will deliver over to his successor, if he approves of him. He has a small set of Books, of which he will sell the blank part, if he is suceeded or superceeded. From the want of printed or precise forms, the mode of keeping the Books will be various; and the whole business being of very uncertain tenor and duration, the calculations are accordingly.—Any individual would take on himself the whole expence if he might have such emoluments as the saveings to the Collectors could afford—And the conveyance of a stock for all the eastern offices to Boston, of the middle to New York and Philadelphia, of the Southern to Petersburgh and Charlestown could not be difficult.

"Mechanical uniformity can be attained in all the offices and if one person were to contract for all the printing of law books, registers, sea letters, enrollments, blanks, and every thing belonging to the external revenue, he could supply all the unofficial papers according to any demand

"I have spoken of an uniformity of new books Of these the actual state of the registering business &c should be brought forward on the   day of   and thence continued, and all returns would be merely copying, without the labor of ruling, heading, and hazard of mistakes—and even if the first arrangement of the business should cost the United States as much as half the expence of a frigate at the outfit, the emolument to the government, would in the course of a few years be greater than the value of a navy.

"As the business is now done in every port in the United States, it is not probable that the Registers Office can ascertain within two hundred thousand Tons the amount of actual tonage in the United States—This is oweing to the complication of the System;—Exports are subject to all manner of uncertainties, and indeed all that part of the external revenue system which can be discerned by a collector is obscured.—It must be the worth of some time & of several men to place this business in a situation, which shall require few alterations or letters of explanation."

Thus far I have given the very words of Mr Bishop. Believing that even imperfect hints toward improvement on a subject of that importance, would not be unacceptable, I have presumed to submit the foregoing observations, and am

with the highest respect Your Obedt. Servt EPHM KIRBY

RC (NHi: Gallatin Papers); at foot of text: "The President of the U. States"; endorsed by TJ as received 10 Jan. and so recorded in SJL with notation "T." Enclosed in TJ to Gallatin, on or after 10 Jan. 1803, with the message: "Th:J sends the inclosed to mr Gallatin for consideration. he has always believed the Collection law capable of more simplificn" (RC in same; undated; addressed: "The Secretary of the Treasury"; endorsed; not recorded in SJL).

FIVE VOLUMES OF STATUTES: the fifth volume of *The Laws of the United States of America*, published "by Authority" in Philadelphia in 1803, included acts passed during the two sessions of the Sixth Congress (Shaw-Shoemaker, No. 5321). The first three volumes were published as a set in Philadelphia in 1796 and included acts passed through the Fourth Congress. Acts passed during the Fifth Congress made up the fourth volume published in 1799 in Philadelphia (see Evans, Nos. 31356, 32973, 36523).

In response to a 1797 House resolution requesting that the Treasury secretary compile a report to be used by the House to combine into one law the various acts for the collection of duties on imports and tonnage, Oliver Wolcott prepared and submitted a plan that led to the COLLECTION LAW OF 1799. To "obviate inconveniencies," Wolcott introduced into the proposed law official forms to be used by government officers. Scattered throughout the act were 16 forms for oaths and 8 for bonds; numerous forms of certificates; forms for manifests, entry of goods, and drawbacks; clearance forms; verification forms; forms for the report of spirits, wines, and teas; forms for the coastal trade; forms for the entry of fish and provisions for bounty; and forms for returns to be prepared by inspectors, weighers, gaugers, and measurers. The 1799 law included 112 sections (*Letter and Report of the Secretary of the Treasury, Accompanying a Plan, for Regulating the Collection of Duties on Imports and Tonnage, Prepared in Pursuance of a Resolution of This House, of the Second of February Last* [Philadelphia, 1798; Evans, No. 34856]; JHR, 2:677; U.S. Statutes at Large, 1:627-704).

The COASTING ACT of 18 Feb. 1793 included 37 sections for enrolling, licensing, and regulating fishing vessels and ships in the coastal trade. The 1798 "Act for the relief of sick and disabled Seamen" required that masters of coasting vessels provide custom collectors with information on the number of seamen engaged by them. Before a license could be renewed, the master had to pay 20 cents per month for every month each seaman was employed during the continuance of the license. A master was fined $100 for a false account of those hired (same, 305-18, 605-6). REGISTERING ACT: the "Act concerning the registering and recording of ships and vessels," of 31 Dec. 1792, included 30 sections (same, 287-99).

[1] MS: "repetion."

From John Reich

Philadelphia
January 3d. 1803.

MAY IT PLEASE YOUR EXCELLENCY!

I beg your Excellencie's pardon for troubling you again. The appearance of a reformed establishment of the mint of the United States induces me to do so; I flatter myself that I possess abilities sufficient

to make myself useful in such an establishment. Some Medals of my engraving have been favorably received by the judicious part of the public; I have lately executed another of the masonic kind; but not altogether in that stile respectg. to emblems as are required here; it did not turn out to my advantage; but I hope nevertheless you will permit me to offer to you the homage of the inclosed—
If your Excellency should think proper to make use of my services in the establishment of the Mint which may take place, my endeavours shall not be wanting to discharge with faith to the public and honor to myself the duties incumbent on me.

I have the honor to be with the greatest respect

Your Excellency! most obedient humble Servant,

John Reich

RC (ViW: Tucker-Coleman Collection); at foot of text: "His Excellency the President of the U. *States*"; endorsed by TJ as received 6 Jan. and "to be engraver at the mint." Enclosure not found.

TROUBLING YOU AGAIN: Reich last wrote TJ on 4 May 1801. For his medals and TJ's high opinion of his engraving skills, see Vol. 34:71-5, 167-8; Vol. 36:239-40, 386; Vol. 37:175.

From John Wayles Eppes

Dear Sir, Richmond January 4. 1803.

Callender has been this day discharged from his recognizance by the County Court of Henerico—6 magistrates in favor of his discharge & 1 against it—The trial took up two days & the cause has been fully and ably argued—As I had not an opportunity of getting into the Court House from the concourse who attended I can give you no sketch of the arguments—

Accept for your health &c My friendly wishes Yours &c

Jno: W: Eppes

RC (ViU: Edgehill-Randolph Papers); endorsed by TJ as received 8 Jan. and so recorded in SJL.

The legal proceedings in the case of Henry Pace and James Thomson CALLENDER against George Hay finally concluded when six out of seven Henrico County magistrates voted to discharge Callender from custody and Pace from his obligation. Hay was required to keep the peace for one year. The court also ruled that it was a violation of the Bill of Rights to confine the defendants and that liberty of the press was more properly a legislative than a judicial matter (Durey, *Callender*, 167-8; Richmond *Virginia Gazette*, 5, 8, 12 Jan. 1803; Richmond *Virginia Argus*, 5 Jan. 1803; *Alexandria Advertiser*, 11 Jan. 1803; John Wayles Eppes to TJ, 23 and 24 Dec. 1802).

Petition of William Connor, with Jefferson's Order

To the President of the United States—
William Conner of the County of Washington, and District of Columbia, petitioning, States—That at the late races, near the City of Washington, he was in a Booth, where a gaming table was kept by one—Mordacai—that permission was granted him to keep said table a few minutes, whilst some emergency called off said Mordacai to some other part of the race ground, which he did for the space of ten or fifteen minutes only, when said owner returned and again took possession of it—in which time nothing considerable was won or lost, the bets being the small sum of five pence half penny a time only, and the persons playing, but two or three—that the Grand Jury were notified of this by a Constable, and presented your petitioner therefor, and that during the present Circuit Court of the County aforesaid, he hath been fined the sum of fifty pounds under the statute of Maryland against excessive gaming passed in the year 1797—and Costs of prosecution—for which fine and fees he is now in close confinement in the Common Jail of said County—Your petitioner solemnly avers that he was ignorant of the Law prohibiting the act which he committed—that he is a young man just released from his apprenticeship, extremely poor and has no other means of support, than by hiring himself as a journeyman Hair-dresser, and is besides under the necessity of applying part of his wages, to the support of an aged Mother—notwithstanding the inauspicious aspect exhibited by said prosecution, on account of his recent unfortunate conduct; yet the general tenor of his life has been that of honesty and industry; and this unfortunate instance is rather attributable to the inexperience and ignorance of youth, than to a wanton propensity to vice, or idle dissoluteness of manners—that his present unfortunate condition shall serve as a memento against similar imprudence in future, and stimulate to the honest & industrious pursuit of his said trade—He therefore implores the humanity of the president, and prays a remission of the fine & fees aforesaid—

William Connor

William Conner the Petitioner this day made oath on the Holy Evangels of Almighty God that the facts stated in the aforegoing petition are substantially true as stated—

Sworn before me a Justice of the peace for the County of Washington this Fifth day of January 1803— BENJAMIN MORE

[*Order by TJ:*]
Let a pardon issue

TH: JEFFERSON
Jan. 7. 1802. [i.e. 1803]

MS (DNA: RG 59, GPR); petition and attestation in an unidentified hand, signed by Connor and More; TJ's order written below affidavits signed by William Kilty, James Marshall, and William Cranch, 5 Jan. 1803, recommending the remission of Connor's fine, and by John Thomson Mason, undated, stating that he has known Connor for several years and believes him to be well behaved, that he is just out of his apprenticeship and probably still underage, and that Connor had no interest or property in the gaming table and that his exhibiting the same "happened accidentally." Enclosure: Affidavit of Robert McClan, 5 Jan. 1803, stating that he has known Connor for nearly six years, describing him as "a very young man scarcely twenty one years of age"; Connor is just out of his hairdresser's apprenticeship and has maintained "the character of an honest industrious person" for the time that McClan has known him; Connor's mother, "a Widow extremely poor," receives much of her support from her son's labor and McClan believes that Connor "is worth nothing more than what he has made by hiring himself as a journeyman Hair dresser" (same; attested by Uriah Forrest).

According to the record of his trial, William Connor of Washington County was indicted for operating a "Fair play table" on 4 Dec. 1802. Appearing before the December 1802 session of the U.S. Circuit Court of the District of Columbia, he was found guilty and fined $\$133.33\frac{1}{3}$ plus court costs (Tr in same; attested by Uriah Forrest). TJ issued a pardon and remission of Connor's fines and charges on 8 Jan. 1803 (FC in Lb in same).

LATE RACES: the annual meeting of the Washington Jockey Club commenced on 30 Nov. 1802 with three days of horse racing held at an oval track west of the President's House. TJ attended the first two days, recording a total expenditure of $2.25 at the event in his financial memoranda (MB, 2:1087; *Washington Federalist*, 8 Nov., 1 Dec. 1802).

STATUTE OF MARYLAND AGAINST EXCESSIVE GAMING: the Maryland legislature passed "An Act to prevent excessive gaming" on 20 Jan. 1798. The act authorized a fine of £50 upon persons found guilty of keeping gaming tables or other devices in any dwelling house, out house, or any place occupied by a tavern keeper or retailer of wine, liquor, beer, or cider (*Laws of Maryland, Made and Passed at a Session of Assembly, Begun and Held at the City of Annapolis on Monday the sixth of November, in the Year of our Lord One Thousand Seven Hundred and Ninety-Seven* [Annapolis, Md., 1798], chap. 110).

From John Redman Coxe

SIR Philada. Jany. 5th. 1803

I have this morning procured a small quantity of Vaccine Infection, taken the 9th day of the disease, which I hope may succeed with Dr. Gantt.—I should have forwarded some before, but the opposition to

Inoculation at this Season is so great, that I have not been able to procure even in the Dispensary, an opportunity to continue it.—

I inserted a few days past in Mr. Paulsons Gazette, a valuable fact from a late treatise on Vaccination, relative to the mode of preserving the infection,—viz. by securing the *Scab* produced by the genuine disease, which is regarded by the Author as the most active Virus in a state of dryness.—He asserts that he has succeeded with it *six* weeks & *two* Months after taking it. A small portion broke off—and dissolved, is to be employed as recent—Virus. Though this is of such importance to the Community, I have not seen it copied from Paulson. I hope the Printers elsewhere, will be more attentive.—

I inclose for Mr. Vaughan two letters on behalf of the Philosophical Society the objects of which you will perceive on perusing them. We are ignorant of the address of the Gentlemen to whom they are written—and are in hopes You may possibly know—Should this be the Case, we trust you will forgive the trouble we put you to, in requesting you to forward them.

I am Sir with great respect Yr much obliged & very humble Servt.

John Redman Coxe

RC (DLC); at foot of text: "Ths. Jefferson"; endorsed by TJ as received 8 Jan. and so recorded in SJL. Enclosures not identified.

On 24 Dec. 1802, *Poulson's American Daily Advertiser* published an analysis by Coxe of the 1802 TREATISE of Edinburgh physician James Bryce, *Practical Observations on the Inoculation of Cowpox.* Bryce had discovered a better means of preserving active cultures of the cowpox vaccine. If dried matter from a pustule formed from the vaccine was protected from exposure to the air, it remained "perfectly effectual at two months distance of time" as a source for subsequent vaccinations. Soaking a portion of the scab in water would reactivate the virus and facilitate successful vaccinations. Disappointed that PRINTERS ELSEWHERE did not publish his letter, Coxe wrote to *Poulson's* about two months later to share his success in "producing a most perfect disease, with a dry scab, of *seven* weeks old;—of which no particular care had been taken, except wrapping it loosely in paper" (*Poulson's American Daily Advertiser*, 10 Mch. 1803).

From William Dunbar

Dear Sir — Natchez 5th. January 1803

A series of bad health which has endured above twelve months has withdrawn much of my attention from Philosophic objects, a favorable change having lately taken place, I perceive with satisfaction that my Mind & body are both recovering their former tone, and now again enjoy the pleasing prospect of dedicating my leisure hours to my favorite amusements; which however must for a time be suspended, in consequence of a Call (which I knew not how to refuse) to the Infant Legislature of this Territory.

I have now the pleasure to enclose a letter addressed to me from a french Gentleman of considerable merit and talents; he acts in the Capacity of Civil Commandant over the Oppelousas Country to the West of the Missisippi: his letter contains some particularities of his Country and is accompanied by two pretty full vocabularies of the tongues of two indian nations of that country to which is added a sketch of the religion, or superstition of those peoples; which I hope may afford you and the Society some small entertainment. From several other quarters I have used some efforts to draw similar information but am hitherto disappointed. Should you be of opinion that Mr. Duralde merits the distinction of an honorary Member of your Society, I have no doubt that such mark of your Approbation will operate as a strong incentive for this Gentleman to exercize his talents in promoting the views of the Society.

My sketch of a history of the Missisippi has been long delayed from the cause above assigned, but shall be prepared and forwarded as soon as it can be completed.

I have lately been honored by a letter from Sir Joseph Banks with an Extract from the transactions of the Royal Society on the subject of stones supposed to have fallen from the Clouds—I do not recollect to have heard of any such phenomenon having been observed upon the continent of America.

By a letter with which I was favored from my much esteemed friend Mrs. Trist by her son lately arrived, she says that you had informed her, it was my intention to remove shortly from this Country; I beg leave to remove this impression. Since the Country has been united to the American federation I have never ceased to consider it as my own Country, which I hope never to be under the necessity of abandoning.

With high consideration I remain Your most Obedient Servant

William Dunbar

RC (DLC); endorsed by TJ as received 9 Feb. and so recorded in SJL. Enclosures: (1) Martin Duralde to Dunbar, Opelousas, Louisiana, 24 Apr. 1802; he sends two Native American vocabularies; one is from the Atakapa tribe, recorded by Duralde; the other, from the Chitimachas, was prepared by another person; he had expected to get vocabularies of the Opelousas and the Conchatis (probably the Koasatis; Sturtevant, *Handbook*, 14:408, 413); those groups, however, communicate with outsiders through the Mobilian trade idiom (see below), and he has not found anyone who can directly translate their languages; he reports that people digging wells in the Opelousas district have found bones, layers of shell, and artifacts; in more than one location, skeletal remains that look like those of elephants have been found; Duralde has not been able to collect more information from those sites (RC in PPAmP; in French). Enclosed in TJ to Caspar Wistar, 28 Feb. (2) Vocabulary of the Atakapas' language, giving the equivalents of almost 300 French words and terms and 30 sentences; with an explanation of Atakapa pronunciation; the vocabulary is followed by a narrative, headed "tradition," of the Atakapas' origin story and religious beliefs, including stories of a universal creator and a great flood; a tradition holds that the women of the tribe provided the labor to build its burial mounds; one legend, regarding a very large animal, predates the discovery of the carcass of an elephant in the region; most of the remains of that animal washed away, but in 1765, Duralde was shown one or two of the teeth; he states that this is an accurate copy of the vocabulary, traditions, and beliefs of the Atakapas that he wrote down from their testimony (MS in same; in Duralde's hand and signed by him, 23 Apr.; in French and Atakapa). (3) Vocabulary of the Chitimachas' language, giving the equivalents of approximately 350 French words and terms; as Duralde does not understand the Chitimacha language and did not record the vocabulary himself, he cannot provide any guidance regarding pronunciation; the vocabulary is followed by a narrative, headed "Croyance des Chetimachas" ("Belief of the Chitimachas"), that describes the bestowal of laws and tools by a creator, the Chitimachas' religious beliefs, their customs regarding marriage and death, and the social stratification that gives special status to a nobility of chiefs; Duralde states that this is an accurate copy of the vocabulary and the substance of the history and beliefs of the Chitimachas sent to him at his request (MS in same; in Duralde's hand and signed by him, 23 Apr.; in French and Chitimacha).

In 1803, Dunbar was a member of the house of representatives in the LEGISLATURE of Mississippi Territory (*Terr. Papers*, 5:267, 298).

PARTICULARITIES OF HIS COUNTRY: on 28 Feb., TJ sent Martin Duralde's letter to Caspar Wistar for the American Philosophical Society, which received the document at a meeting of 4 Mch., gave it to John Vaughan for translation, and on 18 Mch. referred it to Benjamin Smith Barton and Caspar Wistar. On their recommendation, the society published an abstract in English. Dunbar had included some information from Duralde in a letter to TJ in August 1801. The APS did not make Duralde a member (APS, *Proceedings*, 22, pt. 3 [1884], 334, 335, 339; APS, *Transactions*, 6 [1809], 55-8; MS of translation, PPAmP; Jack D. L. Holmes, "Martin Duralde Observes Louisiana in 1802," *Revue de Louisiane*, 9 [1980], 69-84; Vol. 35:121-2, 124n).

TWO INDIAN NATIONS: the Chitimachas lived west of the Mississippi River, along the Gulf Coast and inland. The Atakapas were farther west, from Vermillion Bay to Galveston Bay. Albert Gallatin later used the vocabularies from Duralde in his research on American Indians. The Mobilian trade language that Duralde mentioned in his letter to Dunbar was a pidgin language that developed from Choctaw and other sources and was used as a lingua franca in the lower Mississippi Valley (Sturtevant, *Handbook*, 14:45, 79, 80, 174, 642-52, 659-63, 690; 17:124-7).

SKETCH OF A HISTORY: Dunbar was working on a description of the lower Mississippi River and the lands along it (APS, *Transactions*, 6 [1809], 165-87; Vol. 32:55n).

Joseph BANKS had probably sent Dunbar an extract from a presentation to the ROYAL SOCIETY of London in February 1802. The paper, of which Edward Howard was the primary author, compiled information about observed meteorite impacts and reported the analysis of "stony and metalline Substances, which at different Times are said to have fallen on the Earth." Banks asked Dunbar about an impact near Baton Rouge in the spring of 1800. Dunbar did not witness the event, but had obtained information about it that he forwarded to the APS through TJ. Dunbar informed Banks that he would try to find out if pieces of the meteorite could be recovered (Royal Society of London, *Philosophical Transactions*, 92 [1802], 168-212; Neil Chambers, ed., *Scientific Correspondence of Sir Joseph Banks, 1765-1820*, 6 vols. [London, 2007], 5:259-60; Vol. 32:55n).

HER SON LATELY ARRIVED: for Hore Browse Trist's plan to relocate to Mississippi Territory, see Vol. 36:389 and Vol. 37:98, 619. Correspondence of James Wilkinson to Henry Dearborn had given TJ the IMPRESSION that Dunbar intended to go to Europe (Vol. 37:661).

To the House of Representatives

GENTLEMEN OF THE HOUSE OF REPRESENTATIVES

Agreeably to the request of the House of Representatives I now transmit a statement of the militia of those states from which any returns have been made to the War-office. they are, as you will percieve, but a small proportion of the whole. I send you also the copy of a circular letter written some time since for the purpose of obtaining returns from all the states. should any others, in consequence of this be made during the session of Congress, they shall be immediately communicated.

TH: JEFFERSON
Jan. 5. 1803.

RC (DNA: RG 233, PM, 7th Cong., 2d sess.); endorsed by a House clerk. PrC (DLC). Recorded in SJL with notation "statement of Militia." Enclosures: (1) "Return of the Militia of the respective States in the Union, rendered agreeably to the resolution of the Honorable the House of Representatives of the United States, of the 20th day of December, 1802," dated War Department, 29 Dec. 1802, and signed by Henry Dearborn, compiling into tables returns made by each state and territory for general and field staff, field officers and regimental staff, artillery, cavalry, grenadiers, infantry, light infantry, riflemen, and arms, ammunition, and accoutrements; returns for New Hampshire, Rhode Island, Vermont, New York, New Jersey, Delaware, Maryland, North Carolina, Kentucky, and Tennessee are blank; the report also includes a note stating: "Those States which are left blank in the above return, have failed to furnish this department with the annual statement, required by the Act of the 8th of May, 1792. It may be proper further to remark, that the returns from some of the States comprised in the above, from the want of regular Regimental returns, do not exhibit the whole military strength of the State. Others are defective in not designating the different species of troops, of which the Militia of the State is composed, the whole being embraced in the column headed 'Infantry.'" (2) Circular letter from the War Department to the governors of the states and territories, calling their attention to section ten of the 8 May 1792 act of Congress that requires the submission of annual militia returns to the president; the letter adds that it would be "very desirable" and "highly important" to receive this information and asks the governors to give the necessary directions for carrying the law into effect; a form is also enclosed "for the purpose of introducing and preserving uniformity in the returns" (both printed in *Message from the President of the United States, Transmitting a Statement of the Militia of Those States from which Any Returns Have Been Made to the War Office* [Washington, D.C., 1803], Shaw-Shoemaker, No. 5369).

REQUEST OF THE HOUSE: on 20 Dec. 1802, the House of Representatives passed a resolution calling on the president "to direct the proper officer to lay before this House a statement of the militia, according to the returns last received from the respective States" (JHR, 4:255).

The House received TJ's message and its accompanying papers on 5 Jan. and referred them to the committee appointed on 17 Dec. 1802 to consider the portions of TJ's annual message relating to the militia. TJ forwarded additional militia returns to the House on 1 Mch. (JHR, 4:267; TJ to the House of Representatives, 1 Mch. 1803).

To John Smith

Th: Jefferson requests the favour of *Genl. John Smith of N.Y.* to dine with him *on Friday next, the 7th. Inst.* at half after three, or at whatever later hour the house may rise.

Wednesday Jany 5th. 1803.

The favour of an answer is asked.

RC (NNPM), printed form, with blanks filled by Meriwether Lewis reproduced in italics; addressed by Lewis: "The Honble. Genl. John Smith of N. York."

From Joseph Anderson, William Cocke, and William Dickson

SIR 6th January 1803

We beg leave to recommend the following Gentlemen, as proper Characters to act as Commissioners of Bankruptcy within the State of Tennessee—

Edward Scott Esqr atty at Law, Mr John Crozier Merchant, Moses Fisk Esqr Atty at Law—and Mr. George M Deaderick Merchant—The two former of Knoxville—the two latter of Nashville—

with Sentiments of Very great respect—

JOS: ANDERSON
WM. COCKE
WM. DICKSON

RC (DNA: RG 59, LAR); in Anderson's hand, signed by all; endorsed by TJ as a letter of 7 Jan. received the same day and "Commrs bkrptcy" and so recorded in SJL; also endorsed by TJ: "Edward Scott John Crozier}Knoxville" and "Moses Fish—George Mc.Deaderick}Nashville."

Born in North Carolina, William Dickson (1770-1816) moved to Tennessee in 1790. He studied and practiced medicine in Nashville for many years. A Republican, Dickson served as speaker of the state house of representatives from 1799 to 1801 and as a Tennessee congressman from 1801 to 1807 (*Biog. Dir. Cong.*; Harold D. Moser and others, eds., *The Papers of Andrew Jackson*, 8 vols. [Knoxville, 1980-], 1:259n).

For an earlier recommendation and the appointment of bankruptcy commissioners for Tennessee, see Joseph Anderson's letter to TJ of 10 Oct. 1802. At that time, Anderson recommended Samuel Donelson, not MOSES FISK; the other candidates were the same as above. TJ did not receive Anderson's letter of 10 Oct. until 17 Nov. According to SJL, TJ wrote separate letters, now missing, to Anderson, Cocke, and Dickson on 18 Oct., requesting recommendations for bankruptcy commissioners (see TJ to Nathaniel Macon, 18 Oct.). The commissions for the Tennessee candidates were dated 28 Mch. (see Appendix I).

To John Barnes

Th: Jefferson will be obliged to mr Barnes for 20. or 30. D. in small bills.

Jan. 6. 1802. [i.e. 1803]

RC (ViU: Edgehill-Randolph Papers); addressed: "Mr. Barnes"; notation by Barnes: "sent $30—pr Mr Dougherty"; endorsed by Barnes as a letter of 6 Jan. 1803. Not recorded in SJL.

In his financial memoranda, TJ recorded the receipt of $30 from Barnes on 6 Jan. 1803 (MB, 2:1090).

From Abijah Hart

SIR, New York Jany 6th. 1803

Possessing but little self confidence, it is with great diffidence that I address you, with an offer of my services to the Public.—Some eight or nine years ago, I was solicited to accept a Consulate Office at some important Port among our commercial relations in foreign Countries—my engagements in Commercial pursuits then were such, that self-interest forbade my acceptance—but I have since been unfortunate—the depredations committed by beligerent Powers on our Commerce in 1794 @ 1796 bore heavy on me,* and the sudden peace of 1801 has completed my ruin—I am now disengaged, & have so far overcome my natural modesty, as to solicit an appointment as commercial Agent for the U.S. at some Port which is, or soon may be vacant.

Perhaps it is unfortunate for me, that my particular friends at the seat of Government, are of the "Old Connecticut School"—but

* In those years I lost three Vessels & Cargoes & many smaller adventures.—From the Abstracts of Custom-House returns, it may be seen that in those years I paid more than $76,000 Import Duties—& since, under the firm of Vanderbilt, Hart & Hicks $28,000. more—

Were I permitted to name places of preference, I should mention Liverpool, Bordeaux, *Lisbon*, *Madeira*, *Cadiz*, Barcallonia, Marseilles, Naples, Leghorn &c.—Some of these I believe are Vacant—some are represented by Foreigners.—

they are honest men & I presume will candidly answer any enquiries after my character or ability—I refer to the Honl. Messrs. Hillhouse, Dana, &c.

My Politics are free from prejudices against any Nation, while it ever has been my pride to contribute towards the Independent support of our national Character & Government.

My commercial pursuits having been extended to all Countries, I feel much the Seaman's friend, as I have known much of his toils & perils.—

Should you think proper to clothe me with a skirt of Presidential favor, my Countrymen may depend on all that vigilence & honest intentions can effect for them, either as an Agent of our Government or as a Citizen of the United States.—

I am with high consideration Your most obedient Humble Servant

Abijah Hart

RC (DNA: RG 59, LAR); addressed: "Thomas Jefferson. President of the United States Washington ℔. favor of Dr. Mitchill"; endorsed by TJ as received 10 Jan. and "to be Consul" and so recorded in SJL.

Abijah Hart (1764-1829), a Connecticut-born merchant, had engaged in trade with Portugal as a partner in the New York City firm of Hicks, Vanderbilt & Hart. When his commercial endeavors failed as a result of French spoliations, he sought a government appointment as treasurer of the national mint or as consul, but to no avail. Hart wrote Madison in July 1804, lamenting that he had heard nothing from TJ since his initial inquiry and repeating his request for a foreign commercial agency. He maintained political connections with Connecticut Federalists James Hillhouse and Samuel Dana. In 1808, Hart returned to his paternal roots in New Britain to become a farmer (Hart to James Madison, 30 July 1804, in DNA: RG 59, LAR, endorsed by TJ: "to be Consul at Guadaloupe, Martinique, Palermo or elsewhere"; Washington, *Papers, Pres. Ser.*, 10:297-8; Madison, *Papers, Sec. of State Ser.*, 7:544n).

From Anthony Van Mannierck

Most respect'd Sir Antwerpen Jany 6h 1803.

Last March was a Year since[1] I have made Application for the Consulship of Belgium without Success, altho I had every flattering hope before my Departure from Philadelphia where I am naturaliz'd and remain'd for about twenty Years always strongly attach'd to your present Administration, testes Andrew Ellicott, General Muhlenbergh, Wm. Jones, Member of Congress &c &c the place of Consul or Agent, is become vacant by the Death of a Mr. Thigh, in Ostende; if you think me that place Worthy, I beg leave to recommand myself: my Certificates from Baron de Beelen Bertholff and my Recommandation from several Gentlemen Known to your Excellency, remain in your Possession since March 1801, I beg the favor you would cause them to be return'd.

I crave your Pardon, Sir, if I take the Liberty in thus addressing you, not knowing a surer Way, tis through my unbounded Admiration for your greatness, I have taken that Confidence of writing you with Offer of my best Services I remain with Respects the most profound

your Excellency's Most Humble Servt.

ANTHY M: VAN MANNIERCK

RC (DNA: RG 59, LAR); at head of text: "Thomas Jefferson Esqr."; endorsed by TJ as received 1 Mch. and "to be Consul at Ostend" and so recorded in SJL.

Anthony Van Mannierck, a Philadelphia-based merchant, sold imported goods including textiles, coffee, glass, and metal from his wholesale stores at 91 Race Street and 171 South Third Street. He was a native of Belgium, but had been a citizen of the U.S. for 18 years. In June 1802, he announced in the Philadelphia press his recent move back to Belgium and the establishment of a commercial house in Antwerp under the firm of Anthony Mannier Van Mannierck (Philadelphia *Federal Gazette*, 30 July 1793; *Philadelphia Gazette*, 1 July 1796, 12 June 1802; Van Mannierck to Secretary of State, 2 Mch. 1801 [RC in DNA: RG 59, LAR]).

APPLICATION: Van Mannierck applied to the secretary of state for a consulship on 2 Mch. 1801. Baron de Beelen Bertholf recommended him (Vol. 33:667, 668n).

PLACE OF CONSUL OR AGENT: TJ commissioned Francis L. Taney of Maryland as commercial agent for Ostend on 23 July 1801. Taney's departure for Belgium was delayed and he died in Georgetown in September 1802 after having contracted yellow fever. On 9 Dec. 1803, TJ nominated Henry Wilson of Maryland to fill his vacancy (Madison, *Papers, Sec. of State Ser.*, 1:363, 2:295, 3:596; JEP, 1:459; Vol. 34:614n, Vol. 36:333).

[1] MS: "since since."

From Horatio Gates

DEAR SIR Rose Hill 7th: January, 1803.

Feeling an irresistable impulse for the Glory of your Administration; & convinced your Friendship will Pardon the Intrusion; I cannot forbear addressing you upon the present Political Crisis.—The Governour, & the Intendant of New Orleans, in shutting that Port, & refusing a depot for our Produce down the River; Strikes me as a preconcerted Measure between the Ministers of France & Spain; but principally of France; who Dictates what she pleases to her pittifull Neighbour; I presume therefore to think, that the Wisest Conduct on our part would be to feel the Pulse of the French Rulers upon that Subject. In the mean time order Strong hold to be taken of the Natches, and particularly of the Post where Fort Rosalie formerly Stood; See what Charlevoix wrote so long ago upon that Subject; you have a person here, or in France, to whom you can give your confidence, to Sound the Rulers of that Nation, upon this most interesting National Subject; for I would not commit it to the Formality of going through the Organ of our Ambassador at that Court; The person might also be charged, to know if the Rulers would be Inclined to Sell the Right of France to Louisiana! The Government of France must at the present Moment be under many Embarrasments, such as, Raising a Fleet, St: Domingo, The Indemnities, The Mediterranean, & above all The Greedy Eye she casts upon The English Possessions in the East Indies;—If for the sake of Money, The Government of France could be induced to part with Their Right to Louisiana, & Possession of *so much of it*, as will Answer our purpose, can be Obtain'd; Ten Millions of Dollars would be a cheap Purchase for the U. States. This Purchase, would put all Future Contention with France, or Spain, to so remote a distance, that all attempts thereafter to Wrest the possession from The US, would be utterly impracticable. The following is what Charlevoix says with regard to the post at The Natches;

"Fort Rosalie in the Country of The Natches, was at first pitched upon for the Metropolis of this Colony; but though it be necessary to begin by a settlement near the Sea; yet, if ever Louisiana comes to be in a Flourishing Condition, as it may well be; it appears to me, that the Capital of it cannot be better Situated than at this place; it is not Subject to Inundations of The River; the Air is pure, The Country very extensive; The Land, fit for everything, & well watered; it is not at too great a distance from the Sea, and nothing hinders Vessels to go up to it; In fine, it is within reach of every place intended to be Settled. Charlevoix His: de la N: France III Vol: 415."

After The Natches, Our Fort upon the Tom Bec Bee, should have our Secondary Attention; & be well Secured; These Posts, with the Strength of the Settlements to protect them, in a very few Years would become Hors D'insulte, which is Obtaining every thing for The UStates.

As you have no time to throw away, I only request to know that you receive this in due course by The Post, and that you are yet disposed to Honour the Writer with your regard. with the most disinterested, and Sincere Attachment to You; He remains your Faithfull, & Obedient Servant,

Horatio Gates

RC (DLC); endorsed by TJ as received 13 Jan. and so recorded in SJL.

The *Histoire et description générale de la Nouvelle France* of Pierre François Xavier de CHARLEVOIX was first published in 1744. Charlevoix had seen the Natchez area in 1722, on a journey from

Quebec through the Great Lakes region, the Illinois settlements, and down the Mississippi. TJ owned the book and recommended it to others. No English translation of the work was published until the third quarter of the nineteenth century (Charles E. O'Neill, ed., *Charlevoix's Louisiana: Selections from the History and the Journal* [Baton Rouge, La., 1977], xviii, xxiv, xxv; Vol. 8:411; Vol. 12:137; Sowerby, No. 4004).

INDEMNITIES: spoliation claims against France by American citizens (Vol. 37:419n).

OUR FORT UPON THE TOM BEC BEE: after the survey of the boundary between the United States and Spanish territory, the United States took possession of a small Spanish military post at St. Stephens on the Tombigbee River, but did not garrison it with troops. The American fort in that region was Fort Stoddert, approximately 20 miles from St. Stephens, on the Mobile River below the confluence of Tombigbee and Alabama Rivers. By September 1802, TJ and Dearborn expected to locate a trading house on the Tombigbee and considered moving the military post there (Powell A. Casey, "Military Roads in the Florida Parishes of Louisiana," *Louisiana History*, 15 [1974], 230; Gilbert C. Din, "The Spanish Fort on the Arkansas, 1763-1803," *Arkansas Historical Quarterly*, 42 [1983], 284; Vol. 35:561; Enclosure No. 4 listed at TJ to the Senate, 7 Jan.).

HORS D'INSULTE: too strong to fear an attack.

From George Meade

DEAR SIR [...] 7th. January 1802. [i.e. 1803]

I beg [...] request You would Give me an appointment, [if it could?] be, for this City, it would be more agreeable: if not, for Alexandria, Baltimore, New York, or Boston, tho' I own to You I would prefer this place, where I have always lived. from our long acquaintance, I take the liberty of addressing You freely.

Commissioners are going to Madrid one is not Yet appointed (as I am Informd) I wish You would give it to my Son, Richard W. Meade, he is a Master of the French language, & understands a little of the Spanish, & would You may rely on it (tho' my Son) do your appointment honor.

I wish You the Compliments of the Season, & many happy returns there of. I request You would be so obliging as to favor me with [...] You, I am with great Respect, & Reg[ard]

[...] & most Obedt. hble Servt. GEO: MEADE

RC (DNA: RG 59, LAR); damaged; at foot of text: "President, United States, City of Washington"; endorsed by TJ as received 9 Jan. and so recorded in SJL with notation "Philada."; also endorsed by TJ: "office" and "[...] a commr. to Spain."

THIS CITY: Philadelphia.

OUR LONG ACQUAINTANCE: Meade, a Federalist, began corresponding with TJ in December 1791, when both were in Philadelphia (ANB; Vol. 23:63).

From Caesar A. Rodney

HONORED & DEAR SIR, Wilmington Jany. 7. 1803.

I have received your favor of the 31. ulto. & thank you most sincerely for your attention & liberality to our Seminary. I trust our exertions to revive it will be crowned with success. It is matter of real concern, that those places which have acquired celebrity, on the score of education should unfortunately be under the influence of false principles. Every honest mind must feel afflicted, when the situation of the institutions, in New-England Princeton & Caroline become the subjects of reflection. To behold at the head of those seminaries men opposed to the theory & practice of those principles which have cost so much blood & treasure, excites serious apprehensions. I trust this badge of Federalism will in time be destroyed.

Your late message has operated like an electric shock on our Opponents. It has paralised them so much that they have not yet, so far recovered, as to make an attack. It is unfortunate for them, that it is so securely mailed as to be invulnerable by their weapons. The little mist which their idle stories may have raised has vanished before the light of truth, & I beleive most firmly that the day star of Federalism has set to rise no more in this country.

It would be a great object to shorten the session of congress as much as possible, by dispatching business as speedily as the nature of the case will admit. It would render a seat, less inconvenient & save much time for those who cannot well afford it, & much expense to the Public. The Speaker must always have a good deal in his power on this head. I recollect the late Govr. Mifflin in his better days, when Speaker of the house of Rep: of Pena. used to press the business pending before them on the attention of that body. Mr. Macon possessing the same authority, & added to it, a knowledge of business ought I should suppose to urge on the business, especially when the modest merit of those on the floor prevents them assuming a task, to which I know so many of them are competent. With great esteem & sincere respect I remain Dr. Sir Yours affy. C. A. RODNEY

RC (DLC); endorsed by TJ as received 9 Jan. and so recorded in SJL.

EXERTIONS TO REVIVE IT: on 18 Jan., a memorial by Rodney and others on behalf of the trustees of the Wilmington Academy was presented to the Delaware House of Representatives, requesting that the charter for the academy be enlarged "to embrace the whole of a collegiate education." They also requested financial support from the legislature to evince "the importance of education, & the diffusion of knowledge in a republican government." During the session, the state legislature revoked the academy's charter and established instead "The College of Wilmington, in the State of

Delaware." Thirty trustees, prominent Republicans and Federalists, were appointed to govern the new college, including Rodney, David Hall, Gunning Bedford, Jr., John Dickinson, Henry Latimer, and James A. Bayard. No public funds were designated for the new institution (*Laws of the State of Delaware, Passed at a Session of the General Assembly, which was Begun and Holden at Dover, on Tuesday the Fourth Day, and Ended on Friday the Twenty-Eighth Day of January, in the Year of Our Lord One Thousand Eight Hundred and Three* [Wilmington, Del., 1803], 292-8; *Journal of the House of Representatives of the State of Delaware, at a Session of the General Assembly, Commenced and Held at Dover, on Tuesday, the Fourth Day of January, in the Year of Our Lord One Thousand Eight Hundred and Three* [Dover, Del., 1803], 36-7; John A. Munroe, *Federalist Delaware, 1775-1815* [New Brunswick, N.J., 1954], 216-17).

To the Senate

Gentlemen of the Senate

I submit for your approbation and consent a Convention entered into with the Choctaw nation of Indians, for ascertaining and marking the limits of the territory ceded to our nation, while under it's former government, and lying between the Tombigby and Mobile rivers on the East, and the Chickasawhay river on the West.

We are now engaged in ascertaining and marking in like manner the limits of the former cessions of the Choctaws from the river Yazoo to our Southern boundary; which will be the subject of another convention; and we expect to obtain from the same nation a new cession of[1] lands of considerable extent between the Tombigbee and Alabama rivers.

These several tracts of country will compose that portion of the Missisipi territory, which, so soon as certain individual claims are arranged, the United states will be free to sell & settle immediately.

Th: Jefferson
Jan. 7. 1803.

RC (DNA: RG 46, EPIR, 7th Cong., 2d sess.); endorsed by clerks. PrC (DLC). Recorded in SJL with notation "Choctaw convention." Enclosures: (1) Convention between James Wilkinson, as commissioner on behalf of the United States, and the Choctaw nation, 17 Oct. 1802, on the Tombigbee River; agreeing that the president may appoint commissioners to resurvey the old boundary line once agreed to by the Choctaws and Great Britain (see Dearborn to TJ, 22 Aug. 1802); the Choctaws will appoint two commissioners to attend the survey at the expense of the United States; the line shall become part of the boundary between the United States and the Choctaws, and for the consideration of one dollar, the Choctaws release their claim to the tract enclosed by that boundary on the north, the Chickasawhay River on the west, the Tombigbee and Mobile Rivers on the east, and the U.S. boundary with Spain on the south; leaders of the Choctaws' upper towns may alter the location of the line near the mouth of the Yazoo River; this convention to become effective upon ratification by the president and the Senate (printed copy in DNA: RG 46, EPIR). (2) Wilkinson to Dearborn, 17 Oct., enclosing the convention; the decision to let the chiefs of the upper towns decide about one part of the line is to correct a "defect" that Wilkinson found in the old line; believing that the cession of the tract bounded by the Chickasawhay, the Tombigbee, and the Mobile, "which includes one and an half Million of Acres, might prove interesting to Government at an early period, (it is certainly so at this moment to our Citizens settled on that tract)," Wilkinson applied his "feeble faculties" to the attainment of that goal "and with much difficulty effected it"; he thought it "essential" to distribute the Choctaws' annuity at his conference with them, and saw that it was done, although he has been ill with a fever; more than 1,800 Indians attended the conference, yet their subsistence costs will total less than $300; in two days Wilkinson will mount his horse, "tho' illy able to keep the seat," and set out for the mouth of the Yazoo River (Tr in same). (3) Dearborn to Wilkinson, 7 Sep., authorizing him to reach an agreement with the Choctaws concerning the old boundary between them and the British and asking his opinion concerning the site for a trading house for the Choctaws (Tr in same; see TJ to Dearborn, 27 Aug. 1802). (4) Dearborn to Wilkinson, 14 Sep., stating that the trading house will likely be located on the Tombigbee and asking Wilkinson's opinion about establishing a guard at the store or perhaps moving the army's garrison there from the Mobile River; there is reason for concern about the influence of the Panton firm and others, but should they do anything "hostile to the benevolent intentions of the government, we shall have it in our power to confine their trade within the Spanish boundaries"; when Wilkinson is in New Orleans, he might be able to discuss with the government there the prospect of the trading house on the Tombigbee and the need of the United States to have passage along the Mobile River through Spanish territory; it "should be taken for granted, that those rivers which empty themselves out of the United States into the Ocean, through a small part of the Spanish territory, are common highways"; if Wilkinson finds this subject to be "delicate" he need not press it, but can communicate to Spanish officials that the United States expects no interruption in the supply of its posts and trading houses until the two governments can make an arrangement on that subject; "all that is wished at present is, that the disposition of the Spanish Officers may be so far known as to prevent any difficulties" until an agreement is reached; Dearborn also reports the news of the disaffection of the Chickasaw leader Ugulayacabe from the Spanish interest (see TJ to Dearborn, 30 Aug., and TJ to Madison, same day); it "may be proper to take advantage" of that situation in an effort to ally Ugulayacabe to the United States (Tr in DNA: RG 46, EPIR). Message and enclosures printed in ASP, *Indian Affairs*, 1:681-3.

APPROBATION AND CONSENT: the Senate received the message and documents from Meriwether Lewis on 7 Jan. and unanimously approved the convention with the Choctaws on the 12th (JEP, 1:430, 435-6).

[1] TJ here canceled "all the."

From Albert Gallatin

DEAR SIR [8 Jan. 1803]

The Constitution of the State of Ohio requiring that a man to be eligible to the Legislature should not hold any office under the United States, and the election taking place on Tuesday next, Colo. Worthington who is a candidate has been obliged to resign his two offices. He wishes the resignation may be accepted on Monday.

Mr Ellicot claims compensation for the service mentioned in the within Letter. This cannot be done without your approbation & is on the whole rather embarrassing. If you think, however, that on his own declaration it is just that the expence should be reimbursed, I will try to find some mode in which it can legally be done, though I apprehend a specific appropriation will be necessary.

With perfect respect and attachment Your obdt. Servt

ALBERT GALLATIN

RC (DLC); endorsed by TJ as received from the Treasury Department on 8 Jan. and "Ellicot Worthington" and so recorded in SJL. Enclosure: perhaps Thomas Worthington to Gallatin, 7 Jan. 1803 (not found, but see below). Other enclosure printed below.

According to Article 1, Section 26 of the CONSTITUTION OF THE STATE OF OHIO, no person "holding any office under the authority of the United States" was eligible to take a seat in the general assembly (*Constitution of the State of Ohio* [Chillicothe, 1802], 3, 9). In a letter dated MONDAY, 10 Jan., Gallatin wrote Worthington: "Your letter of the 7th. instant, in which you resigned the Offices of Register of the land Office for the District of Chillicothe, and Supervisor of the internal Revenue for the North west District, was laid before the President of the united States, who has accepted the resignation on *this* day" (Gallatin, *Papers*, 7:920; see also TJ to Gallatin, 13 Jan.).

ENCLOSURE

Andrew Ellicott to Albert Gallatin

DEAR SIR Lancaster December 27th. 1802

I wish you to give me credit for the map, and observations that accompanied it, which I furnished last year.—In the construction, and delineation of the map, and drawing up the observations, I was constantly engaged more than forty days.—

The map has cost me about forty dollars, which arose from the following circumstance.—When I began the work, I had to purchase a pentagraph, to reduce my original charts, to a smaller, and, to the same scale.—This instrument cost me thirty three dollars; and is now of no use whatever to me, and was never used but on the work above mentioned.—This, or a similar instrument, was much wanted in the Office at Washington when I was there, and if one has not been procured since that time, this may be had for what I gave for it. For the writing on the map, I paid Samuel Lewis six dollars,—the paper, and other expenses, I suppose amounted to at least one dollar, exclusive of my own time, which I have already stated at upwards of forty days.—

If I stand charged on the books of the U.S. with a Telescope, it is erronious:—the U.S. were paid for it by me in the year 1796.

With this, you will receive a statement of some small sums of money expended by me, for certain purposes interesting to the U.S. and which have not been repaid, or covered by any charge, or introduced into any other account.—As those sums were paid under the administration of Mr. Adams, I intended speaking to him upon the subject, but was never able to obtain an interview with him after my return from our southern boundary.—This statement you will easily percieve is strictly confidential, and not intended to go beyond the President, and heads of departments—

I now have a work of considerable magnitude with the printer relative to our southern country, and which would be published in a few weeks; but for want of the engravings of the maps, charts, and figures.—

I am sir with great esteem your friend and Hble. Servt.—

ANDW; ELLICOTT

RC (DNA: RG 217, MTA); at foot of text: "Honble. Albert Galiten Secretary of the Treasury of the U.S." Enclosure not found, but see below.

For the MAP of the Mississippi and OBSERVATIONS THAT ACCOMPANIED IT, see Ellicott to TJ, 10 Oct. and 2 Nov. 1801. Gallatin authorized $127 as compensation for Ellicott's "labour & expense in preparing the map & observations" and $33 for the pentagraph. "The work was done at the request of the Secretary," Gallatin noted, and it "has been & continues to be of great utility." The credit of $160 was approved by the comptroller's office on 15 Jan. 1803 (MSS in DNA: RG 217, MTA). James Monroe requested that Ellicott's map and remarks be included in the State Department packet for his mission to France (Madison, *Papers, Sec. of State Ser.*, 4:388).

On 7 Aug., Ellicott provided Gallatin with a statement and affidavit verifying his payment for the TELESCOPE (Gallatin, *Papers*, 8:585).

STATEMENT OF SOME SMALL SUMS: that is, the expenses Gallatin questioned in his cover letter to TJ, above, noting that such expenditures required the approval of the president. On 12 Jan., Ellicott informed Madison that while working on the southern boundary he used his own money to procure private information, which he could not "conscientiously cover by a fictitious charge," even if it meant he would "lose the whole" (Madison, *Papers, Sec. of State Ser.*, 4:251-2). On 4 June, TJ issued a certificate declaring that representations by the secretary of state indicated that Ellicott had dispersed $350 "for objects in relation to the duties of the said Department and to promote the interest of the United States, the specification of which disbursement at this time" was "deemed inexpedient." The certificate served as Ellicott's voucher for $350 to be paid out of the funds for foreign intercourse (MS in DNA: RG 217, MTA, signed by TJ and countersigned by Madison; FC in Lb in DNA: RG 59, DL). On 13 June, the auditor's office credited Ellicott's account, noting it covered sums "disbursed by him in the years 1797, 1798 and 1799 for objects in relation to the duties of the Department of State and to promote the Interest of the United States" (MS in DNA: RG 217, MTA).

WORK OF CONSIDERABLE MAGNITUDE: *The Journal of Andrew Ellicott, Late Commissioner on Behalf of the United States during Part of the Year 1796, the Years 1797, 1798, 1799, and Part of the Year 1800*, published later in 1803 (see Vol. 35:106-7).

From George Jefferson

DEAR SIR Richmond 8th Janr. 1803

As I do not know where Mr. Short is at present, I take the liberty of inclosing you a letter for him, which you will much oblige him, as well as myself by forwarding.

I am Dear Sir Your Very humble servt. GEO JEFFERSON

RC (MHi); at foot of text: "Thomas Jefferson esqr."; endorsed by TJ as received 13 Jan. and so recorded in SJL. Enclosure not found.

From James Lovell

TO THE PRESIDENT
OF THE UNITED STATES Boston January 8th. 1803.

Self Interest once forced me to intrude upon the busy moments of your Excellency, for the purpose of showing how much it was my own choice to hold a Commission "during the Pleasure of the President of the United-States for the time being." A more generous motive leads me to intrude a second time, for the purpose of proving how much I am convinced that my watchful concern for my own official-Integrity is, in fact, a just tribute due to the Reputation of Him who continues to me the same Patronage which I enjoyed under the two former Persons of a Trinity of Presidents.

I have exhibited to the Comptroller of the Treasury my annual-account of Fees, according to two Laws, and *his* particular Instructions. It differs, in a single Item, from any of *my* former accounts, tho' it resembles those of all other Officers in the same line of employment, and is as solemnly true. I shall not condescend to point out and explain the difference to any one but my Patron; and no one else, perhaps, will happen to perceive it. The inclosed memoranda will suffice to elucidate it, after one additional declaration that "I am conscientiously free to take credit for *less* than my actual Expenditures, tho' I shall ever scorn to insert *more*, be the provocation to do it ever so great."

In amusing myself with "canonical" books and making observations upon real-life I have found that "the most subtle of all the Beasts of the field," tho' he eats eggs & flesh in common with Foxes and Monkies, yet picks his Dessert among Flowers of the "best-characters," just as another kind of Glutton culls a whole garden bed to find his peculiar "best-sort" of Lettuce. If it was that Beast's

"Taste" for fruits in-general or "apples" in-particular which in "good old times" procured him the Crown of "Subtlety," yet, it is funfull to guess why, in later times, he should be quoted as a "wise"-model for Men's imitation, and be recommended jointly with the "harmless"-Dove.

When Legislators in Massachusetts, not long ago, borrowed Shears from the Parcæ to cut the Fees of the naval-office of Boston alone, the glaring-Injustice of the action bewildered all search after the Wisdom of their motives: But, when the Legislators of the United-States borrowed those same Shears last April, from laudable motives, doubtless, tho' inscrutable by my small mental-abilities, They handled the instruments with so many appearances of Impartiality, and with such demonstrations of some rule of equity, within their own minds, that the principal-Officers in some of the principal-Districts will, naturally, correct any past too-niggardly Propensities, towards their Deputies and other necessary-assistants, in the expenditure of their own lawful & righteous Earnings.

Whoever boasts of living under "a government of Laws" ought to know that the "liberty of the press" is most intimately connected with his *Ground* of boasting.

At present, the "Licentiousness" of the press is so fully engaged against the executive-part of our Governments that the legislative-parts cannot be complimented with any due Specimens of its "Liberty"-from want of spare-types and impartial-printers.

Thus, from some Charity to myself and much Devotion to your Excellency, I have penned a few additional-traits of the principles the conduct and the conscience of an obedient Fellow-citizen, who is also

Your obliged and very humble Servant JAMES LOVELL
Navl. Off

RC (DLC); endorsed by TJ as received 19 Jan. and so recorded in SJL. Enclosures: (1) Lovell to Secretary of the Treasury Alexander Hamilton, dated Boston, October 1792, acknowledging the directions contained in his circular letter of 31 Aug. regarding an order of the United States Senate of 7 May and enclosing the demanded account; Lovell hopes "that *my* statements may not prove injurious to such Officers as have had *usual & necessary* Assistance of Clerks, without being driven to devote their own Nights as well as days to their Offices. Adversity has formed but few such callous Drudges as myself in a similar-Line of life." (2) "Notes to the Comptroller" accompanying Lovell's account of 1795, "the sentiments of which have governed all my after Exhibits until July 1st of the past year"; Lovell's notes maintain that the "voluntary assistance of Sons whom I maintain" cannot be considered as hired clerks, nor can "Douceurs-ad-libitum" be considered as "other official expences" according to the Treasury Department forms used to make his returns (Trs in same, in Lovell's hand; Syrett, *Hamilton*, 12:303-4).

James Lovell (1737-1814) of Boston

was a Harvard graduate and prominent patriot during the American Revolution. He served continuously in the Continental Congress from 1777 to 1782, becoming one of its most active members, particularly as part of the Committee for Foreign Affairs. He was also known for his outspoken and sarcastic manner and his convoluted style of correspondence. He was appointed naval officer for the port of Boston by George Washington in 1789 and served in that office until his death (ANB; John L. Sibley and Clifford K. Shipton, *Sibley's Harvard Graduates: Biographical Sketches of Those Who Attended Harvard College*, 18 vols. [Cambridge, Mass., 1873-], 14:31-48; JEP, 1:9, 2:534).

FORCED ME TO INTRUDE: a letter from Lovell, dated 12 Aug. 1802, is recorded in SJL as received 22 Aug. from Boston, but has not been found.

TWO LAWS: as part of the 2 Mch. 1799 act of Congress to establish compensations for customs officers, all collectors, naval officers, and surveyors were required to keep accounts of all fees and official emoluments received and all expenditures for rent, fuel, stationery, and clerk hire. Accounts were to be submitted annually to the comptroller of the Treasury within forty days after 31 Dec. An amendment to the act passed on 30 Apr. 1802 limited annual emoluments, after deducting expenditures, to $5,000 for collectors, $3,500 for naval officers, and $3,000 for surveyors. Any surplus above these amounts was to be paid to the Treasury. The terms of the act did not extend to fines, forfeitures, and penalties under federal revenue laws (U.S. Statutes at Large, 1:704-9, 2:172-3).

HARMLESS-DOVE: "Be as wise as serpents and harmless as doves" (Matthew 10:16).

The PARCÆ, or Parcae, were the Roman equivalent of the Fates (Simon Hornblower and Antony Spawforth, eds., *The Oxford Classical Dictionary*, 3d ed. [Oxford, 1996], 589-90).

From Thomas Munroe

Superintendants Office, Washington
8th January 1803

SIR,

I yesterday received the enclosed Letter from the Treasurer of the Western Shore of the State of Maryland together with the Account of a quarters Interest due 1t. Instant to the said State on the Loans of $200,000 in the Treasurers Letter mentioned—

The funds of the City do not at present enable me to make the payment as required, nor do I beleive a sufficient sum for the purpose could be raised by a sale of the public Lots in the City at prices not unwarrantably low—.

I am with sentiments of the greatest respect Sir Yr mo Obt. Servt

THOMAS MUNROE

RC (DLC); at foot of text: "President of the U.S"; endorsed by TJ as received 8 Jan. and so recorded in SJL. Enclosure not found.

On 12 Jan., Munroe wrote Thomas Harwood, TREASURER OF THE WESTERN SHORE of Maryland, and enclosed a draft on the Office of Discount and Deposit at Baltimore for the $3,000 in quarterly interest due the state (Dft in DNA: RG 42, LRDLS). For the previous payment, see Munroe to TJ, 9 Nov. 1802 (first letter).

To Owl and Others

Brothers Miamis and Delawares.

I am happy to see you here, to take you by the hand, & to renew the assurances of our friendship. the journey which you have taken is long: but if it leads to a right understanding of what either of us may have misunderstood it will be useful for all. for, living in the same land, it is best for us all that we should live together in peace, friendship and good neighborhood.

I have taken into serious consideration the several subjects on which you spoke to me the other day, & will now proceed to answer them severally.

You know, brothers, that, in antient times, your former fathers the French settled at Vincennes, and lived and traded with your ancestors, and that those ancestors ceded to the French a tract of country, on the Wabash river, seventy leagues broad, & extending in length from Point coupée to the mouth of White river. the French, at the close of a war, between them and the English, ceded this country to the English; who, at the close of a war between them & us, ceded it to us. the remembrance of these transactions is well preserved among the White people; they have been acknoleged in a deed signed by your fathers, and you also, we suppose, must have heard it from them. sincerely desirous to live in peace & brotherhood with you, and that the hatchet of war may never again be lifted, we thought it prudent to remove from between us whatever might at any time produce misunderstanding. the unmarked state of our boundaries, & mutual trespasses on each others lands, for want of their being known to all our people, have at times threatened our peace. we therefore instructed Governor Harrison to call a meeting of the chiefs of all the Indian nations around Vincennes, & to propose that we should settle and mark the boundary between us. the chiefs of these nations met. they appeared to think hard that we should claim the whole of what their ancestors had ceded and sold to the whitemen, and proposed to mark off for us from Point coupée to the mouth of White river, a breadth of twenty four leagues only, instead of seventy. this offer was of little more than a third of our right. but the desire of being in peace and friendship with you, and of doing nothing which should distress you, prevailed in our minds, and we agreed to it. this was the act of the several nations, original owners of the soil, and by men duly authorised by the body of those nations. you brothers seem not to have been satisfied with it. but it is a rule in all countries that what is done by the body of a nation must be submitted to by all it's members. we have no right to alter, on a partial deputation, what we have settled by treaty with the body of the nations concerned. the lines too which are agreed on, are to be run and marked in the presence of your chiefs, who will see that they are fairly run. your nations were so sensible of the moderation of our conduct towards them. but they voluntarily offered to lend us for ever the salt springs, & four miles square of land near the mouth of the Wabash, without price. but we wish nothing without price: and we propose to make a reasonable addition to the annuity we pay to the owners.

You complain that our people buy your lands individually, & settle or hunt on them without leave. to convince you of the care we have taken to guard you against the injuries and arts of interested individuals, I now give you a copy of a law, of our great council the Congress, forbidding individuals to buy lands from you, or to settle or hunt on your lands; & making them liable to severe punishment: and if you will at any time sieze such individuals, and deliver them to any officer of the United States, they will be punished according to the law.

We have long been sensible, brothers, of the great injury you recieve from an immoderate use of spirituous liquors. and altho' it be profitable to us to make and sell those liquors, yet we value more the preservation of your health and happiness. heretofore we apprehended you would be displeased, were we to withold them from you. but learning it to be your desire, we have taken measures to prevent their being carried into your country: and we sincerely rejoice at this proof of your wisdom. instead of spending the produce of your hunting in purchasing this pernicious drink, which produces poverty, broils and murders, it will now be employed in procuring food & cloathing for your families, and increasing instead of diminishing your numbers.

You have proposed, brothers, that we should deduct from your next year's annuity, the expences of your journey here. but this would be an exactness we do not practise with our red brethren. we will bear with satisfaction the expences of your journey, and of whatever is necessary for your personal comfort; and will not, by deducting them, lessen the amount of the necessaries which your women and children are to recieve the next year.

From the same good will towards you, we shall be pleased to see you making progress in raising stock and grain, and making clothes for yourselves. a little labour in this way, performed at home & at ease, will go further towards feeding and cloathing you, than a great deal of labour in hunting wild beasts.

In answer to your request of a smith to be stationed in some place convenient to you, I can inform you that mr Wells, our agent, is authorised to make such establishments, and also to furnish you with implements of husbandry, & manufacture, whenever you shall be determined to use them. the particulars on this subject, as well as of some others mentioned in your speech, and in the written speech you brought me from Buckangelah & others, will be communicated and settled with you by the Secretary at war. And I shall pray you on your return, to be the bearers to your countrymen and friends of assurances of my sincere friendship: and that our nation wishes to befriend them in every thing useful, and to protect them against all injuries committed by lawless persons from among our citizens, either on their lands, their lives or their property.

TH: JEFFERSON
Jan. 8. 1803.

PrC (DLC). Recorded in SJL as "Long-beard for Miamis & Delawares."

Owl (also Hibou; also Meshingomesia) was a chief of the Miami Indians by 1778. TJ and Dearborn knew him as Long Beard when he met with them in Washington in January 1803. He was a political rival of Little Turtle, and after his visit to the capital, William Henry Harrison called him "an artful fellow." Owl did not sign any treaties with the United States until 1804. Thereafter he was on friendly terms with the U.S. government, although on at least one occasion he contradicted Harrison during negotiations over land cessions (Stewart Rafert, *The Miami Indians of Indiana: A Persistent People, 1654-1994* [Indianapolis, 1996], 38, 60, 70, 72, 73, 76; Esarey, *William Henry Harrison*, 1:77, 82-3, 142, 370-1, 479, 684; Richard White, *The Middle Ground: Indians, Empires, and Republics in the Great Lakes Region, 1650-1815* [Cambridge, 1991], 495, 501; Robert M. Owens, *Mr. Jefferson's Hammer: William Henry Harrison and the Origins of American Indian Policy* [Norman, Okla., 2007], 201).

BROTHERS MIAMIS AND DELAWARES: Dearborn called the document printed above a "talk" delivered by the president on 8 Jan. The delegation that TJ met spoke for a council that had convened on the White River in Indiana Territory. Several groups, including Miamis, Delawares, Munsees, and Nanticokes, had been represented at that gathering. Two members of Owl's deputation were George White Eyes, a Delaware who had attended school in New Jersey, and Beaver, who had recently become the leading member of the Delaware national council (Dearborn to Buckongahelas and others, 10 Jan., in DNA: RG 75, LSIA; Dearborn to John W. Brownson, 12 Jan., in same; Lawrence Henry Gipson, ed., Harry E. Stocker, Herman T. Frueauff, and Samuel C. Zeller, trans., *The Moravian Indian Mission on White River: Diaries and Letters, May 15, 1799, to November 12, 1806* [Indianapolis, 1938], 32, 193-4, 247, 387n; C. A. Weslager, *The Delaware Indian Westward Migration* [Wallingford, Pa., 1978], 62; Vol. 37:584, 585n).

HAPPY TO SEE YOU HERE: the delegation, consisting of a dozen people, passed through Moravian settlements on the Tuscarawas River in mid-November and arrived unexpectedly at Pittsburgh in the latter part of that month. The assistant military agent at Pittsburgh, John W. Brownson, had standing instructions from Dearborn that Indians without passports "must not come on" to Washington, and he wrote the War Department for orders. Dearborn replied that Brownson could help these travelers make a written communication to the president, but then, after giving them some clothing and supplies, he must send them all home.

Visits to the capital could only be made "in conformity to the regulations." Probably before Dearborn's orders got to Pittsburgh, however, Brownson allowed six of the deputation to continue on to Washington and advanced them money for their expenses (Dearborn to Brownson, 19 Apr., 7 Dec. 1802, 13 Jan. 1803, in DNA: RG 75, LSIA; Brownson to War Department, 27 Nov., 10, 15 Dec. 1802, recorded in DNA: RG 107, RLRMS; Gipson, *Moravian Indian Mission*, 194n).

The War Department did not make a record of what Owl said to the president and the secretary of war about the SEVERAL SUBJECTS of concern to the delegation. From what the Moravian missionaries learned as the travelers passed through Ohio, the delegation wanted to call attention to the easy availability of liquor, which they held to be the cause of 20 murders during the previous year in the Indian towns of the White River region. Other complaints centered on Harrison's negotiations in September to obtain the VINCENNES tract and the SALT SPRINGS of the Wabash saline. Those concerns were compounded by rumors that White River lands were being sold away by tribes that had no claim to them (Gipson, *Moravian Indian Mission*, 194n, 214-15; Notes on Bounds of the Vincennes Tract, [on or after 26 Oct. 1802]).

COPY OF A LAW: an act of Congress of 30 Mch. 1802 regulated the acquisition of land from Indians. It also allowed the president to restrict or stop the sale of spiritous LIQUORS. A few days after TJ addressed Owl, Dearborn sent extracts from the statute to territorial governors and Indian agents, asking them to inform the Indians in their areas of the law's provisions (Dearborn to W. C. C. Claiborne and others, and to Silas Dinsmoor and others, both 13 Jan. 1803, in DNA: RG 75, LSIA; TJ to Handsome Lake, 3 Nov.).

Dearborn promised to send a SMITH "as soon as a suitable man can be obtained, who can mend your Axes, hoes, and Guns," and he indicated that the government would also send plows and other implements (Dearborn to Buckongahelas and others, 10 Jan., in DNA: RG 75, LSIA). William WELLS, who was Little Turtle's son-in-law and had, with him, assisted Harrison in the recent negotiations over land boundaries, was the Indian agent at Fort Wayne (Vol. 36:285n; Notes on Bounds of the Vincennes Tract, [on or after 26 Oct. 1802]).

WRITTEN SPEECH YOU BROUGHT ME: the Delaware leader Buckongahelas, who had been to Washington with Black Hoof's delegation of Shawnees and Delawares the previous winter, lived on the upper part of the West Fork of the White River. At the council before the departure of Owl's delegation to Washington, Buckongahelas, who was retiring from the Delaware council, and other speakers made addresses directed to the U.S. government. John Conner, who accompanied Owl's party as a translator—see his letter to TJ at 10 Jan. below—made notes of those addresses, and when the deputation passed through the Moravian towns in Ohio, one of the missionaries put Conner's notes into fuller form. That manuscript has not been found, but Dearborn's reply, in a written message of 10 Jan., indicates that Buckongahelas, who was wary of a close relationship with the United States, objected to Harrison's transactions in September. Buckongahelas and others from the White River must be "mistaken or deceived" if they thought their tribes had any say regarding the Vincennes tract or the saline, Dearborn declared. They had "no reason to complain" of the agreements reached with Harrison. Buckongahelas and his colleagues apparently also brought up crimes committed against Indians. "The President your father," Dearborn answered, "will never fail to punish any white Man, who shall be wicked enough to kill or in any manner injure any of his red Children"—provided, of course, the wrongdoer could be apprehended. To Harrison, Dearborn wrote in February that the "deputation of Delawares and Miamis, who visited the seat of Government the present winter complain loudly of the unfair means used for obtaining the assent of some of the Chiefs to the proposed boundaries, and they state that the loan of the Salt Spring was only for one year." The government "ought not to deviate from the principles of strict integrity in any of our dealings with the Indian Nations," Dearborn advised. He also informed Harrison that Owl and Conner had reported French or Spanish agents might be attempting to influence the Indians against the United States (Dearborn to Buckongahelas and others, 10 Jan., in DNA: RG 75, LSIA; *Terr. Papers*, 7:86-7; Gipson, *Moravian Indian Mission*, 194n; Weslager, *Delaware Indian Westward Migration*, 54, 57, 62; Vol. 36:514, 516).

David Redick, who wrote to Gallatin from Washington, Pennsylvania, in December, understood that the delegation then on its way to the nation's capital represented eleven tribes who "go to speake of grievances they suffer at the hands of Governor Harrison as they say." There were also reports that Conner was "at much pains to abuse the British" for intriguing to alienate the Indians from the United States, yet "at the same time it is some how or other believed that he is a British Subject if not a British agent." Redick, whose information about the delegation was secondhand, particularly wanted to inform TJ, through Gallatin, that someone traveling with the group was claiming to be Logan, the Mingo Indian whose famous 1773 address to Lord Dunmore TJ had published in *Notes on the State of Virginia* (and which became a controversial issue in 1797, leading to TJ's preparation of his *Appendix to the Notes on Virginia*). "I have many strong reasons for believing that the Genuine Logan has been long dead," Redick wrote. He hoped to arrange for the imposter to be brought before someone who remembered Logan. Redick also thought it a "Suspicious circumstance" that George White Eyes was in the deputation bound for Washington. It was George White Eyes, Redick wrote, who the previous year had spread a story, damaging to Moravian and Presbyterian missionary endeavors, that TJ "had advised the Indians not to embrace the Christian Religion." Redick wanted the president to know that after he received TJ's June 1802 letter denying the rumor, a group of missionaries confronted White Eyes in Wheeling and got him to retract what he had said (Redick to Gallatin, 17 Dec., RC in ViW: Tucker-Coleman Collection, endorsed by TJ with notation "Logan"; Vol. 29:452-5; Vol. 30:285-8; Vol. 31:373n, 551-4; Vol. 37:584-5, 627-8).

From Samuel A. Ruddock

[on or after 8 Jan. 1803]

Your Excellency will be pleased when you see that I am the son of John Ruddock Esq. of Boston, who was the only man that stood forth to defend the Liberty of The United States by the side of Saml. Adams Esq. Late governor there—These two men were the first opposers of the British Government in finuel Hall in Boston—They risked their lives & property for the liberty of their Country which has since been obtained, and which is now enjoyed undisturbed by all our free born sons—It will give you further satisfaction when I inform you that I have by my own industry obtained a good Education and am well versed in all kinds of Military tactics, as well as Mathematics, Philosophy, Astronomy, and all Political Creeds—I have travelled throughout seven different kingdoms—My writings are very extensive but few of which are in print: my constant experiments in different branches of Science have entitled me to respect—when I was in Jamaica a Petition was signed by above twenty masters of American Vessels in the year 1799 and sent to the then President of the United States in order to obtain an appointment for me as American Agent for Commercial affairs in that Island, as 273 american vessels had then been condemned most of which was owing to the negligence of the American agent there—I am not personally acquainted with Mr. Savage, the american there and of course cannot impeach him with any misdemeanor from hear say—which if all true would disqualify him for the Office he now holds under our Government—Doctor Jarvis & Doctor Wm. Eustis were well acquainted with me when I left Boston and with my political principles but I have had the greatest test put to them in foreign countries, as one time I was taken by a band of his majesties soldiers in the night and striped then laid on the floor with a block under my head and an executioner placed by my side under the pretence of saying that I was a Spy. because I had a large collection of Mathematical & Philosophical Instruments & Books and an Invoice of about ten ton of Powder in my pocket book which I bought for the State of Massachusetts in Septr. 1798—But when they saw that I was willing to die for my republican principles they did not wish to deprive me of my life but used every means in their power to deprive me of my reason and if possible to render me useless to Society—But the God of my life has brought me once more to my native shore, which I shall never again leave unless your Excellency may see fit for to appoint me to some foreign agency after you have obtained sufficient satisfaction with respect to my respectibility talants and Commercial information—No man now in america has been nearer death for the liberty of his country then myself—and no one requires more protection.

Should an opening offer and your Excellency feel satisfied with my abilities I should have no objections to serve my country as a foreign agent—But I do not solicit the office I can by my industry obtain a handsome living here and support my little family—But I only give a hint here that when it calls for the united exertions of the natives of this country to use their efforts to maintain their liberty as such a one I must support it at the risk of my life—

with profound respect for Your Excellency I remain your most devoted servant—

Saml. A. Ruddock

RC (ViW); written below printed circular for newspaper subscribers; undated, with date supplied from circular; addressed: "His Excellency Thos. Jefferson President of the United States at Washington City" and "Pr. Post"; franked;

endorsed by TJ as received from Charleston, S.C., on 26 Jan. and so recorded in SJL.

Samuel A. Ruddock (d. 1828) trained as a surveyor and accountant. He wrote several works related to these subjects during the 1790s, and in 1797 advertised his services in Boston as an instructor of bookkeeping. After a short-lived partnership with a Boston merchant dissolved in 1798, Ruddock moved to Jamaica, encouraged perhaps by a lawsuit initiated by his former partner. He had settled in Charleston by December 1802, where he published a price current list for the *Charleston Courier*, taught school, worked as a surveyor, and contributed astronomical information to regional almanacs. At different times, he served as a justice of the peace and as secretary of the Charleston Marine Society. About 1820, he left Charleston with the intent of mapping the Americas. He returned to the East Coast by 1825, when he published his broadside *Statistical and Geographical Atlas of North America, Showing the Latitude and Longitude of the Capital Cities, Their Distances from Each Other in Every Direction, from Quebec to Panama*. Although unsuccessful in an 1826 petition to Congress for funds to publish his maps, Ruddock contributed to a congressional report on establishing a military post in the Pacific Northwest. He informed Congress that he had been part of an exploring party that in 1821 had traveled from Council Bluffs to Santa Fe and from there to the mouth of the Columbia River, becoming along the route the first white explorers to reach the Great Salt Lake. No contemporaneous evidence for the expedition has been identified, and historians have doubted Ruddock's claims. Ruddock remained in Washington, where he worked as a clerk in the Post Office Department (Boston *Massachusetts Mercury*, 10 Feb. 1797, 5 June 1798; Boston *Russell's Gazette*, 8 Oct. 1798; New York *Commercial Advertiser*, 26 Feb. 1799; *Charleston Courier*, 29 Dec. 1802, 15 Apr., 23 July 1803; Charleston *City Gazette*, 17 May 1825; Joseph Folker, *A Directory of the City and District of Charleston; and Stranger's Guide: Containing Considerable Subjoined Matter on Different Subjects* [Charleston, 1813], 70, 103; "Samuel A. Ruddock," 19th Cong., 1st sess., H. Report 178, Ser. 142; "Northwest Coast of America," 19th Cong., 1st sess., H. Report 213, Ser. 142; "Letter from the Postmaster General," 20th Cong., 2d sess., H. Doc. 62, Ser. 185; Frederick V. Holman, "Oregon Counties: Their Creations and the Origins of Their Names," *The Quarterly of the Oregon Historical Society*, 11 [1910], 45-6; J. Cecil Alter, *James Bridger, Trapper, Frontiersman, Scout and Guide; A Historical Narrative* [Salt Lake City, 1925], 51-3).

JOHN RUDDOCK, a political leader in Boston before the American Revolution, did have a son named Samuel, who died in 1773 (*Boston News-Letter*, 7 Jan. 1773; Robert J. Taylor and others, eds., *The Papers of John Adams*, 16 vols. [Cambridge, Mass., 1977-], 1:238).

From William Wirt

DEAR SIR WmsBurg. Jany. 8. 1802. [i.e. 1803]

I understand that the office of a judge for the Indiana Territory is vacant by the death of Mr. Clarke, and that Mr Ninian Edwards of Kentucky has been proposed for that appointment. I hope that I am not presuming too far on my acquaintance with you in certifying my opinion of Mr. Edwards.

Having known him from youth to manhood, I feel a pleasure in having it in my power to declare, with certainty, my opinion that few judgments are more clear and sound, no heart more scrupulously upright & honorable than Mr. Edwards'. He has, I am told, practised the law in Kentucky with great reputation; but of his legal acquirements, the discontinuance of my intercourse with him for several years disqualifies me for expressing an opinion—I am, Dr. Sir, Yr. frd, & dev. Sev.

WM. WIRT

RC (DNA: RG 59, LAR); endorsed by TJ. Recorded in SJL as received 8 Feb. 1803 with notation "Ninian Edwards to be judge of Indiana."

NINIAN EDWARDS, a former classmate of Wirt's, served as a judge in Kentucky until 1809, when James Madison appointed him territorial governor of Illinois (ANB; Madison, *Papers*, *Pres. Ser.*, 1:137-8).

From Carlos Martínez de Irujo

DEAR SIR Capitol Hill Sunday morn. [9 Jan. 1803]

Last night on my return home I had the pleasure to see by some letters from my court that the King my Master had had the goodness to grant to me my children & successors a *Title Castille* under the denomination of Marquis of Casa-Irujo as a public testimony of his aprobation of my services. As I Know by experience the friendly part you are so good as to take in what may promotte my interest & satisfaction, I take the liberty to impart to you this information & to assure you that the same sentiments of affection & respect which the Chevalier d'Irujo has always entertain'd towards you will be Kept alive in

Your most obt. & devoted Servt.

EL MARQUES DE CASA DE IRUJO

P.S. I'll have the pleasure to dine with you on Tuesday next.

RC (MoSHi: Jefferson Papers); partially dated; at head of text: "His Exc. Thomas Jefferson"; endorsed by TJ as received 9 Jan. and so recorded in SJL.

By a decree of 26 Dec. 1802 followed by a royal order of 6 Mch. 1803, Carlos IV of Spain created the hereditary title of marqués of CASA-IRUJO (Eric Beerman, "Spanish Envoy to the United States [1796-1809]: Marques de Casa Irujo and his Philadelphia Wife Sally McKean," *The Americas*, 37 [1981], 452).

From James Jackson

SIR, Washington, Jany 9h, 1803.

Relying on your goodness to excuse this intrusion on your time, I beg leave to interest myself in behalf of Brigadier General Wilkinson—That Gentleman by his conduct on the Frontiers of Georgia and at the late Creek treaty, has won the affections of I may almost say, all the Citizens of that State—Had the other Commissioners acted with the same Zeal and candor which guided the General, there is little doubt, but that the whole of the Talassee County, and the Okmulgee fork, agreeably to the intentions of the General administration, would have been ceded to the United States, instead of a slip of land, which it is impossible to form into any shape for a County; and which when settled, if the boundary remains as fixed by that treaty, will continually embroil the United States with those tribes—I mention this as a reason for his having interested me and I add my Fellow Citizens in his favor.

A land Office under the mutual Cession between the United States and Georgia, is to be soon opened—a Surveyor General for the territory will, it is presumed, be appointed—Shall I be permitted to mention General Wilkinson as a proper character to fill this Office.—He is getting old in the service of his Country—has a Family to support; and he is by no means in affluent circumstances—I have seen some Gentlemen from the Mississipi & from what I can gather they are also in that Quarter Friendly to the General—and from his conduct in Tenessee, I am led to believe it would be gratifying to the Citizens of that State—and from Tenessee, and Georgia, in a considerable degree, will that territory be peopled—To have the confidence of the Whites and Reds, it strikes me, would be a necessary, qualification for that Office, and if This be correct—placing his long services out of view—in no one person in the United States, so far as my information goes, is this confidence so well established as in General Wilkinson.

I have had the pleasure of a particular intimacy with the General this last Year, and know that his attachment to the present administration is unlimited.

I am Sir with the sincerest respect & veneration Your Obedt Servt

JAS JACKSON

RC (DNA: RG 59, LAR); at foot of text: "The President of the United States"; endorsed by TJ as received 10 Jan. and "Wilkinson Genl. to be Surveyr. Missi. territory" and so recorded in SJL.

According to the April 1802 "Articles of Agreement and Cession" between the United States and Georgia, a LAND OFFICE would open within one year after the agreement became effective (Vol. 37:344n).

From James Monroe

DEAR SIR Richmond Jany 9,[1] 1803

I should have acknowledged the rect. of your favor containing a copy of yr. message to the congress before this had I not expected[2] to have done it in person. It was my intention after remaining here as long, from the expiration of my late office, as was sufficient to make it known unequivocally to the publick that I was sincere in returning to the bar, to pass thro' the federal city on my way to N. York & to have halted a day with my friends there. I contemplated that visit previous to one which I must make to the westward to look after some property which I possess in that quarter. But I find that the exertion necessary to carry me through the whole route is greater than I have reason to think I shall be able to make in the present state of my health. On that idea I decline for the present my visit to N. York with a view to attend to my interest to the westward whither I shall sit out in a few days by Albermarle. If my health permits me my return, and I have time to proceed to N. York & be back to the courts, I shall certainly do it. My present pursuits which are commanded by imperious considerations, will absorb much of the time and labour—which under other circumstances would be bestowed on publick subjects: but they will not diminish the interest which I have always taken in those subjects and in the success and welfare of my friend, to whom they are entrusted. That your future life may continue to be highly useful & honorable to your country & prosperous & happy to yourself is the wish of yr. sincere friend & servant JAS. MONROE

11. since writing the above a professional incident has occurr'd wch. may probably draw me to Washington immediately, that is early next week

RC (DLC); endorsed by TJ as received 15 Jan. and so recorded in SJL. Dft (DLC: Monroe Papers); dated 7 Jan.; lacks postscript.

A FAVOR from TJ to Monroe CONTAINING A COPY of his annual message of 15 Dec. 1802 has not been found.

[1] Date reworked from "7" to "9."

[2] MS: "expeted."

From Joseph Anderson

Senate Chamber

SIR 10th January 1803

Unwilling to tresspass, upon one moment of your time, which I know is devoted to the best interests of our Country—I trust the cause of the *war worn Veteran*—will never with the *Philanthropic* mind—be considered Obtrusion, or require apology. Thus impress'd and thus believeing, Permit me to recommend to your patronage—Brigadier General Wilkinson, as a candidate, for the appointment of Surveyor Genl. within the Mississipi Territory—(Shou'd such an Officer be appointed)—I have reason to believe, it wou'd be acceptable to him, and his situation and *that* of *his family*, woud be much benefited thereby—I can with pleasure Say that the General is among those Officers, who hath not forgotten to blend the Character of Citizen, with that of Soldier—and that his appointment to the Office Solicited—woud be highly acceptable, to the Citizens of Tennessee whose confidence the General in a Very high degree acquird, by his Conduct as a Commissioner, and his Deportment as a Gentleman—

with Sentiments of Very high consideration I am Most Respectfully

JOS: ANDERSON

RC (DNA: RG 59, LAR); addressed: "The President of the *United States*"; endorsed by TJ as received 10 Jan. and "Genl. Wilkinson to be Survr. Missi territory" and so recorded in SJL.

From John Conner

PRESIDENT OF THE UNITED STATES— 10 January 1803— Washington Sitty

in Consyquence of the misunderstanding among the Indin Nations agrebly to what they have laid before the president I felt my Self Interrested in behalf of the United States as well as of the Indins—and by their earnast Request was endused to Come forword as thir Interpertar, but not from pecuniery motives—I am not able to Judge whether ther atention at the seat of Gaverment is Cunsiderred of much Consyquence here, but am Shure the Indins are Very much Interestd—When I Considerred to Come with theme they Required of me their Subsistanc on the Way, which I have given them as fare as pitsburgh, but my Acct is Rejectted at this place—they also Require mony to eneble them to Return, it apieres that Some mony has been advanced for that purpose to a person withhoom they are not a quented & who knows not their Lenguage, or is Even going to their Cuntry—while I am left to find my way back to the Nations as I Can, after having bourn their Expences mostly to this place—I do not present this to Your Excellency with an Intintion to prove my Right to Claime eny thing from the Gavernment, but leave it to your Consderetion with which I Shall be Satisfied—

I am Sir Your Obet. Servant JOHN CONNOR

RC (PHi); endorsed by TJ as received 10 Jan. and so recorded in SJL; endorsed by Dearborn.

John Conner or Connor (1775-1826), a trader, resided on the upper White River in Indiana Territory. He was born in a Moravian mission settlement on the Tuscarawas River. Neither of his parents was an Indian, but his mother, who had been captured on the Pennsylvania frontier as a young child, grew up among the Shawnees. Conner spoke several Native American languages and married a Delaware Indian woman. In the winter of 1802-3, Conner accompanied the Miami chief Owl and the delegation from the White River tribes on their visit to Washington. He acted as a translator at treaty conferences and maintained good relations with Moravian missionaries. In 1816, he was elected to the state senate of Indiana (Charles N. Thompson, *Sons of the Wilderness: John and William Conner* [Indianapolis, 1937], 9-12, 15-17, 40, 42-3, 89, 156; John Lauritz Larson and David G. Vanderstel, "Agent of Empire: William Conner on the Indiana Frontier, 1800-1855," *Indiana Magazine of History*, 80 [1984], 301-28; Lawrence Henry Gipson, ed., Harry E. Stocker, Herman T. Frueauff, and Samuel C. Zeller, trans., *The Moravian Indian Mission on White River: Diaries and Letters, May 15, 1799, to November 12, 1806* [Indianapolis, 1938], 99, 194, 273-4, 329n, 332-3, 350, 379, 605, 614; Esarey, *William Henry Harrison*, 1:118, 123, 242, 248, 291; C. A. Weslager, *The Delaware Indians: A History* [New Brunswick, N.J., 1972], 333-4, 346-7).

LAID BEFORE THE PRESIDENT: see TJ to Owl and Others, 8 Jan.

When the War Department ADVANCED funds for the delegation's return journey, Dearborn arranged for some of the money to go to Conner, who intended to escort part of the delegation home by way of Philadelphia (Dearborn to J. W. Brownson, 12 Jan., and to Mr. Larwill, 12, 13 Jan., in DNA: RG 75, LSIA).

From Henry Dearborn

War Department
10th. January 1803

SIR,

I have the honor to transmit you a list of the appointments, promotions and Transfers which have taken place in the Army, during the last recess of Congress, together with a nomination of sundry persons to supply certain vacancies now existing.

Accept, Sir, assurances of my high respect and consideration.

H. DEARBORN

RC (DLC); in a clerk's hand, signed by Dearborn; at foot of text: "The President of the United States"; endorsed by TJ as received from the War Department on 10 Jan. and "Military nominations" and so recorded in SJL. FC (Lb in DNA: RG 107, LSP).

E N C L O S U R E

List of Army Appointments

War Department
10th. January 1803

List of appointments in the Army of the United States, made during the last recess of Congress

A. William King to be	Surgeons mate,		10th. June 1802.
Joseph West	Ditto. Ditto.		10. June 1802.
John F. Heilaman	Ditto. Ditto.		2. July 1802.
G. W. Maupire	Ditto. Ditto.		5. Nov. 1802.
Alexander McComb Junr. to be	lst. Lieut: in the Corps of Engineers to take rank from		12. Oct. 1802.
Joseph G. Swift	2d Lieut: " " " " Engineers to take rank from		12. Oct. 1802.
Simon Levy	2d Lieut: " " " " Engineers to take rank from		12. Oct. 1802.
Ephraim Emmory	2d Lieut: in the Regiment of Artillerists to take rank from		12. Oct. 1802.
Henry Brevoort	Ensign in the 2d. Regt. of Infantry to take rank from		7. May 1802.[1]
Peyton Gay	Ensign in the 2d. Regt. of Infantry, to take rank from		12. Oct. 1802.
Josiah Taylor	Ensign in the 2d. Regt. of Infantry, to take rank from		12. Oct. 1802.
William L. Chew	Ensign in the 2d. Regt. of Infantry, to take rank from		12. Oct. 1802.
William Simmons	Ensign in the 2d. Regt. of Infantry, to take rank from		12. Oct. 1802.

Promotions and Transfers

Jonathan Williams to be Lieut: Colonel in the Corps of Engineers to take rank from 8th. July 1802.

Decius Wadsworth of the Regt. of Artillerists to be Major in the Corps of Engineers, to take rank from 9th. Jany. 1800.

Capt. George Ingersoll to be Major in the Regt. of Artillerists, vice Wadsworth transfered to take rank from 8th. July 1802.

lst. Lieut: Peter Tallman to be Capt. in the Regiment of Artillerists, vice Ingersoll, promoted, to take rank from 8th. July 1802.

lst Lieut: Thomas Swaine to be Capt. in the 2d Regt. of Infantry, vice, Vance, resigned, to take rank from lst. July 1802.

2d. Lieut: Edward P. Gaines to be lst Lieut: in the 2d. Regt. of Infantry, vice, Erwine, resigned, to take rank from 27. April 1802.[2]

Ensign George T. Ross to be 2d. Lieut: in the 2d. Regt. of Infantry, vice, Gaines, promoted, to take rank from 27th. April 1802.

Ensign Henry B. Brevoort to be 2d. Lieut: in the 2d. Regt. of Infantry, vice Barde, promoted to take rank from lst. July 1802.

B. The following persons are respectfully nominated for the appointments, to their names respectively annexed.

Cary Clark, of Rhode Island, to be 2d. Lieut: in the Regt. of Artillerists.
Francis Newman, of Maryland, to be 2d. Lieut: in the Regt. of Artillerists.
James S. Swearingin, of Ohio, to be 2d. Lieut: in the Regt. of Artillerists.
W. S. Graham of Vermont to be 2d. Lieut: in the Regt. of Artillerists.
Thomas Coit Jr. of Connecticut to be Surgeon's Mate in the Army of the United States. H. DEARBORN

MS (DNA: RG 46, EPEN, 7th Cong., 2d sess.); in a clerk's hand, signed by Dearborn; endorsed by a Senate clerk. FC (Lb in DNA: RG 107, LSP). Enclosed in TJ to the Senate, 11 Jan. 1803 (third letter).

For background on the army appointments, promotions, and transfers approved by TJ DURING THE LAST RECESS OF CONGRESS, see Dearborn to TJ, 31 May, 10 June, 2, 8, 9 July, 7, 8 Oct., and 3 Nov. 1802.

[1] Clerk here canceled "Henry Irvine Ensign in the 2d Regt of Infantry to take rank from 12 Oct. 1802."

[2] Clerk here canceled "2d. Lieut: Robert G. Barde to be 1st Lieut: in the 2d. Regt. of Infantry, vice Swaine, promoted, to take rank from 1st. July 1802."

From Henry Dearborn

War Department
10th. January 1803

The Secretary of War has the honor of proposing to the President of the United States, that, Hannibal Montisure Allen, be appointed a Cadet in the Corps of Engineers, and that John Doyle be appointed a Cadet in the Regiment of Artillerists.

FC (Lb in DNA: RG 107, LSP).

On 14 Jan., Dearborn sent letters to Hannibal M. ALLEN and John DOYLE informing them that the president had approved their appointments (FC in Lb in DNA: RG 107, LSMA). Allen was a son of Ethan Allen (John J. Duffy and others, eds., *Ethan Allen and His Kin: Correspondence, 1772-1819*, 2 vols. [Hanover, N.H., 1998], 1:253; 2:727).

From William Edgar

SIR New York 10th Jany 1803

I shall ever gratefully Remember your appointing me a Commissioner of Bankruptcey; And I hope you will Belive a sense of duty only, induce's me to give in my Resignation—

I Reside in the Country during the Summer season—this prevents My giving due attendance to the Buisness; and I cannot think of holding any office without performing the duty's—

May you long priside over The Affairs of Our Nation is most Sincerely Wished, by Your Excellencys Much Obliged Hble Servt

William Edgar

RC (DNA: RG 59, LAR); at head of text: "His Excellency the President of the United States"; endorsed by TJ as received 27 Jan. and "Charles Ludlow to be appd." and so recorded in SJL; also endorsed by TJ: "resigns as Commr. bkrptcy." Enclosed in Edgar to DeWitt Clinton, New York, 10 Jan., with the request that the New York senator seal and deliver the letter if he thinks it proper, but "If it requires any Correction; I beg you will correct it, and, if necessary Return it to me"; Edgar notes that the appointment of Charles Ludlow in his place "will give me and Your friends much pleasure, and the sooner this is done the better" (RC in same).

William Edgar (1736-1820), a wealthy New York City merchant of Irish descent, was chosen by Burr to serve as one of the initial directors of the Manhattan Company when it was chartered in 1799. Burr consulted him during his financial difficulties in 1801 and 1802. DeWitt Clinton recommended Edgar as bankruptcy commissioner in May 1802, and during the New York elections of 1804, Edgar was clearly allied with the Clintonian Republicans. The Irish merchant also served as a governor of the New-York Hospital, a director of the United Insurance Company, and an officer of the Society of the Friendly Sons of St. Patrick (Kline, *Burr*, 1:413; 2:643, 723-4, 838; *An Act of Incorporation of the Manhattan Company* [New York, 1799], 7; Beatrice G. Reubens, "Burr, Hamilton and the Manhattan Company: Part I: Gaining the Charter," *Political Science Quarterly*, 72 [1957], 594-6; Alfred F. Young, *The Democratic Republicans of New York: The Origins, 1763-1797* [Chapel Hill, 1967], 80; New York *Minerva, & Mercantile Evening Advertiser*, 17 May 1797; New York *Daily Advertiser*, 16 Feb. 1803; Vol. 37:516).

TJ accepted Edgar's RESIGNATION and appointed Charles Ludlow in his place, as recommended by Edgar in his 10 Jan. letter to Clinton (see descriptive note above). Ludlow, who served as John Barnes's correspondent in New York, began handling business transactions for TJ as well. Ludlow's bankruptcy commission is dated 1 Mch. 1803 (list of commissions in Lb in DNA: RG 59, MPTPC; Vol. 37:308, 708; TJ to Charles Ludlow, 17 June 1803).

To George Jefferson

Dear Sir Washington Jan. 10. 1803.

Not knowing whether Colo. Monroe is in Richmond, Albemarle or where, & it being important the inclosed letter should go to him, without delay, by post, if he be absent, I ask the favor of you to deliver it to him immediately if in Richmond, or to direct it to him by post wherever he is. Accept my affectionate salutations.

Th: Jefferson

PrC (MHi); at foot of text: "Mr. George Jefferson." Recorded in SJL with notation "Colo. Monroe." Enclosure: TJ to James Monroe, 10 Jan.

From Robert Leslie

Sir Philadelphia January 10th 1803

As the subject of dry Docks, is now under consideration, I take the liberty of intruding a few observation on that subject,

Mr Latrobe call'd on me a few days after his return from your City, and gave me a verbal description of what he had plan'd, it struck me at the time, that he had not fully considered the subject. as a matter of great importence seemed to be left out, yet as I could not be certain without seeing some drawing or scetch of the plans &c, I did not venture to say any thing to him on the subject, I have since seen a detailed account of it, in the Aurora, which if it is corect, confirms my opinion,

I am well convinced that nothing is so offensive to such a man as Mr Latrobe, as to have any defect pointed out in any of their planns, I therefore do not wish to say any thing to him on the subject, at present, as I think he will certainly discover it himself, as it is of considerable importence, and if not remedy'd will in a great measure counteract the adventages expected from the Docks, and be a continuel source of vexation and expence. if the plan is as I suspect, I have no doubt but you will readily discover it yourself, by a revew of the drawings, and if so, you can with propriety point it out to Mr L, which would have much more weight than any thing I could say,

In Mr Latrobes letter I was very much surprised to find, the following.

"Should the works be undertaken immediately, while the very numerous skilful and experienced workmen, who have been colected and in part educated, in the execution of large and difficult works, at the Pennsylvania Bank, and the works for supplying the City of Philada. with water, are within reach, I have not the smallest Doubt &c &c."

From what motive Mr L recommends those workmen, I shall not pretend to say. but am very certain that they are the most improper of any set of men in the United States. I have attended to their performence, ocasionly, ever since my return from England and have no hesitation to say, they are the most lazey, indolent set of men I ever saw, and as to skill I have seen nothing like it in any of them,

Mr L has generally had a Pr Centag on the money laid out, for his superintendence, and has always treted with the utmost contempt, every Idea of Oconomy. these men, have found it their intrest to support him in every expensive measure, as it made more work for them, and frequently of such a nature, that gave them an oppertunity of charging any price they chose, by which means the Engine house, and the Pennsylvania Bank, can only be vewed as lasting monuments of useless extravigance, the expence of the Bank, has so far exceeded Mr L first estimate, that the director are ashamed to publish an accompt of it, tho call'd on by the legislature to do it, twelve months ago, I belive I have seen nearly as maney dry Docks as Mr L, and am certain that I have investigated their constructions as menutely as ever he did, and am of opinion, that in any Circle of twenty miles, in the inhabited parts of the United States, thare can be found as good workmen both in Stone and Wood, when used for the building of dry or wet Docks, as those in Philada, and much cheaper, and more active, tho perhaps not so well *Educated* in the arts of extravigence and useless expence,

I am afrade you will think me impertinate in attempting to find fault with the performence of a man who stands so high in the public opinion, I certainly should not have done it, did I not think it a dutie I owe you, and the public, as the mater of greate magnitude and should be examined [with?] caution previous to being acted uppon,

I shall only farther observe, that if the defect I suspect does realy exist, and Mr L discovers it himself, and applys the best remedy, it will produce a wet Dock, to contain six or eight Ships, without[1] one dollar of additional expence, and render the filing and emptying the docks, and Locks, mouch more expeditious, and with less water from the Springs or Streams, intended for that purpose,

I am with respect your very Humble Servt ROBERT LESLIE

RC (DLC); torn; addressed: "The President of the United States"; franked and postmarked; endorsed by TJ as received 14 Jan. and so recorded in SJL.

The 7 Jan. 1803 edition of the Philadelphia AURORA printed TJ's message to Congress of 27 Dec. 1802 and its sundry enclosures regarding Benjamin Henry Latrobe's plans and estimates for a dry dock at Washington.

[1] MS: "withou."

From Levi Lincoln

SIR Washington Jany. 10. 1803—

I ought to dismiss all scruples, and apprehensions respecting the constitutionality of the proposed bargain with France, when Gentlemen much more capable of viewing the transaction in all its various bearings have satisfied themselves on the subject. The importance of New Orleans and the Floridas, with the unimpeded navigation of the Mississippi to the U.S., to their peace and prosperity, is, in my opinion so great, as to justify, almost any risque for their attainment.—A mode, differing in shape and in principle, but to all the purposes for which the acquisition is of moment, precisely the same with the proposed one, has occured to me, which, I wish you to look at. My idea if a practical one, by giving a new aspect to the contemplated negotiation, while it substantially secures the object of pursuit, will, perhaps, free it from some formidable difficulties. The idea is,—that for the common advantage of having great, fixed, and natural boundaries, between the territory of France and of the United States, and to secure to the latter, the full and unimpeded enjoyment of the navigation, maritime & commercial[1] rights important, and naturally appurtenant to a country bordering on navigable rivers, in the neighbourhood of a sea-coast, and from the interior of which country, navigable rivers empty themselves into a neighboring sea, France agrees to extend the boundaries of the Mississippi Territory, and of the State of Georgia, respectively, so that the former shall be bounded on the middle of the channel or bed of the river Mississippi from the 31.° of N. Lat: to its mouth, on the Gulf of Mexico on the South, and on the middle of the river Appalachicola on the East, including the Island of New Orleans, and all the Islands bays & harbors on its southern boundary, and the latter shall be bounded by the middle of the sd Appalachicola on the west, by the sd Gulf on the South, & by the Atlantic on the east, including all the Islands bays and harbors on & belonging to the sd. Coast—

By this indirect mode, if it is feasible, would not the general Govt. avoid some constitutional, and some political embarrassments, which a direct acquisition of a foreign territory by the Govt. of the United States might occasion?—

For instance, would not the territory added to the respective states by the enlargement of their boundaries, as an incident immediately by the art of accretion, assimilate to the principal, and merging in them, be subject to their authority, and of course to the authority of the United States?

If the proposed acquired property, or territory, can be thus melted down, and consolidated, instead of being federated with the States already united, their laws would extend to it, in common with other parts of the enlarged States, without risking the doubtful attempt, so to amend the constitution, as to embrace the object; or hazarding the ratification of the treaty, from an opposition to such an amendment;—or being exposed to the consequences of such an amendment's being refused—The Inhabitants thus added, and who would have been citizens of the enlarged State, had the acquired territory originally been a part of such State, would, of course be considered as citizens; and others get naturalized under the existing laws. This mode of naturalization would keep one door closed against future controversy, and dangerous divisions, in our country, and on a principle, somewhat similar to the one sanctioned by jay's treaty—

If the opinion is correct, that the Genl. Govt. when formed, was predicated on the then existing *united* States, and such as could grow out of *them*, & out of *them* only, and that its authority, is, constitutionally, limited to the people composing the several political state Societies in that union, & such as might be formed out of them; would not a direct independent purchase, be extending the executive power further, and be more alarming and improveable by the opposition and the Eastern States, than the proposed indirect mode?—Is there not danger, that, the Eastern States, including even Rhod Island & Vermont, if not New-York, & other States further South, would object to the ratification of a treaty directly introducing a state of things, involving the idea of adding to the weight of the southern States in one branch of the Govt. of which there is already too great a jealousy & dread, while they would acquiese in that increase of the other branch consequent on the enlargement of the boundaries of a State?—

It is foreseen,[2] that the opposition, and the eastern States will take a distinction, between securing the free navigation of the Mississippi, with a convenient deposit for merchendize, and a measure and the principles of a measure, which may add one or more States to the Union, and thereby change that relative influence between different parts of the united States, on which the general Govt was predecated. No plea of necessity; of commercial utility, or national security, will have weight with a violent party, or be any security against their hostile efforts & opposition clamor. It is recollected that the sending a squadron, to the defence of our Commerce as necessary & useful as the measure appeared to be, was arraigned by some, as a usurpation of power, calling for investigation & impeachment—

The principles, and the precedent, of an independent purchase of territory, it will be said, may be extended to the east or west Indies, and that some future executive, will extend them, to the purchase of Louissiania, or still further south, & become the Executive of the United State of North & South America—

The mode of acquiring new territory by extending the boundaries of existing States, will foreclose those objections, as well as supersede the necessity of amend the constitution, and perhaps prevent the rejection of the acquisition treaty, if such a one should be made—

The consequences deducible, from the principles & the precedent, in the present case, if predicated on the advantages & necessity of having great natural boundaries for national ones, and the river navigation naturally belonging to the country; would necessarily be limited by the object, and if extended, to the utmost could never be injuriously applied in future. The only case, in which the principle could possibly be applied hereafter, would be in extending the boundaries of some of the northern States to the river St. Lawrance.

This mode of acquiring property by the U.S. in adding to the territory of particular States, would require their consent. In the proposed instance they would not object. Georgia ought to give the money we owe her, on account of her late cession for this acquisition. New Orleans & W Florida being a part of the territory of Mississippi, may in future be made a State, if it shall be found to be useful, without altering the constitution. From this accession of inhabitants to the territorial Govt. it would, soon arrive to its second grade, and increase the value & the sale of lands belonging to the U.S.—

These ideas have occured to me in reflecting on the subject; From a fear that I should appear to be too squeamish, visionary, or apprehensive of difficulties, I have rather prevailed on myself, than gratified an inclination, in asking you to look at them—

I am Sir most respectfully your obedient Sert

LEVI LINCOLN

RC (DLC); addressed: "To the President of the United States"; endorsed by TJ as received 10 Jan. and so recorded in SJL with notation "treaty France."

No notes of the cabinet meeting "on the subject of N. Orleans & the Floridas," called by TJ for the morning of 1 Jan., have been found (see TJ to Heads of Departments, 31 Dec.), nor any documentation of the details of the PROPOSED BARGAIN WITH FRANCE or cabinet members' opinions of it.

SANCTIONED BY JAY'S TREATY: Article 2 of the treaty with Great Britain concerned the evacuation of posts that had been occupied by the British within the boundaries of the United States. People living in the vicinity of such posts could remain where they were and would not be compelled to become citizens of the United States. After one year, those who remained and had not declared an intention of remaining subjects of Great Britain "shall be considered as having elected to become Citizens of the United States" (Miller, *Treaties*, 2:246).

On the same day, TJ apparently wrote a note to Lincoln, which reads: "Th: Jefferson asks the favor of the Attorney General to attend a consultation to-day at 12. oclock" (Tr in Sotheby's Catalogue, Item No. 74, New York City, 29 Oct. 1986; not recorded in SJL).

[1] Lincoln here canceled "advantages."

[2] Lincoln here canceled "I am sure of it."

To James Monroe

Dear Sir Washington Jan. 10. 1803.

I have but a moment to inform you that the fever into which the Western mind is thrown by the affair at N. Orleans[1] stimulated by the mercantile, & generally the federal interest, threatens to overbear our peace. in this situation we are obliged to call on you for a temporary sacrifice of yourself, to prevent this greatest of evils in the present prosperous tide of our affairs. I shall tomorrow nominate you to the Senate for an extraordinary mission to France, & the circumstances are such as to render it impossible to decline; because the whole public hope will be rested on you. I wish you to be either in Richmd or Albemarle till you recieve another letter from me, which will be written two days hence if the Senate decide immediately, or later according to the time they will take to decide. in the mean time pray work night & day to arrange your affairs for a temporary absence; perhaps for a long one. accept affectionate salutations.

Th: Jefferson

RC (DLC: Monroe Papers); at foot of text: "Colo. Monroe." PrC (DLC). Enclosed in TJ to George Jefferson, 10 Jan.

[1] TJ interlined the preceding phrase beginning with "by."

From Charles Willson Peale

Dear Sir Museum Jany 10th. 1803.

I have received letters from my Sons dated Octr 14th, about two weeks after they had opened their exhibition of the Skeleton of the Mammoth. They inform me, although but little company had visited the Room yet they were respectable and seemed pleased. my Sons had not then published in the news papers, and probably not known to the Public. they had only thrown out a few hand-bills

Enclosed I send you Rembrandt's Pamphlet, the next edition probably will have plates. he was just beginning a view of our last days work at Mastens in which he introduces an American thunder-storm it was in reallity the most dreadful in appearance I had ever seen, yet passed away with wind only, I dont know whether an exact representation will be credited by Englishmen that had not been in America.

I also enclose a few profiles taken by the Physiognotrace in the Museum, invented by Mr. Hawkins. another engenious invention of his, promises to be very useful. I have written to Mr. Maddison, who will I presume will shew the Letters to you.

Mr. Hawkins has a prospect of making money by selling Patent rights for improving Rum & whiskey—His engenious Mechanical powers will be of great[1] advantage to America if we can keep him—but I fear he will not return if he goes to England as he proposses in the Spring. though he tells me he intends to settle finally with us—but his republicanism is our only securiety for possessing of him. My progress to improvements and dress of the Museum goes on faster than I had expected—the utility of it will be rendered more conspicuous with this winters labour. ?May I hope the favour of your visit the insueing spring or Summer? it will be highly gratifying to

Dear Sir your much obliged friend C W PEALE

RC (DLC); at foot of text: "His Excellency Thos. Jefferson Esqr."; endorsed by TJ and recorded in SJL as received 13 Jan. PoC (PPAmP: Peale-Sellers Papers). Enclosure: Rembrandt Peale, *Account of the Skeleton of the Mammoth, A Non-Descript Carnivorous Animal of Immense Size, Found in America* (London, 1802). Other enclosures not found, but see below.

VIEW OF OUR LAST DAYS WORK AT MASTENS: Rembrandt Peale apparently did not complete his painting of the excavation of mastodon remains at John Masten's farm in Shawangunk, New York. Charles Willson Peale later painted his own version of the scene and incorporated the thunderstorm (Peale, *Papers*, v. 2, pt. 1:482n; Vol. 35:xlviii, 382 [illus.], 435n).

John Isaac Hawkins designed a PHYSIOGNOTRACE, a device for making silhouettes of people's faces, and supervised the construction of a prototype that Peale installed in his museum in Philadelphia. Visitors to the museum could use the machine to take their own profiles. Peale sent TJ various examples of silhouettes made with the physiognotrace. The other INVENTION, which Peale discussed in a letter of 9 Jan. to Madison, was Hawkins's design for a multiple-pen copying device that he called the polygraph. Hawkins was afraid that someone might steal his concept, and Peale's letter to Madison was meant as notice of Hawkins's intention to file a patent application. He patented his design in May 1803 as an "Improvement in the pentagraph and parallel ruler" and obtained a British patent later in the year (Silvio A. Bedini, *Thomas Jefferson and His Copying Machines* [Charlottesville, 1984], 40-8; Susan R. Stein, *The Worlds of Thomas Jefferson at Monticello* [New York, 1993], 208-9; *List of Patents*, 34; Madison, *Papers*, *Sec. of State Ser.*, 4:245).

IMPROVING RUM & WHISKEY: Hawkins and the Reverend Burgess Allison worked together in the development of several inventions and industrial processes, including an "Improvement in the application of the principle of rectifying or improving spirits" that was patented in Allison's name in the spring of 1803 (Bedini, *Thomas Jefferson and His Copying Machines*, 40; *List of Patents*, 34; Vol. 33:104n).

[1] Peale here canceled "service."

Petition of John Baker, with Jefferson's Order

To the President of the United States
the petition of John Baker respectfully represents, that your petitioner is an extremely young man, of the age of sixteen years, entirely inexperienced, and unacquainted with matters of law. He came from Baltimore to the City of Washington to seek for work; and finding there was horse-racing in the said city or it's neighborhood in november last, amusement and curiosity led him to be a spectator of it. While there he was unfortunately requested by a certain Greenberry Willson, with whom he had been acquainted slightly in Baltimore, and accidentally met with at the races, to keep a certain game for him during a few minutes. He did so, but he has since learnt that the game was unlawful, being what is usually called an equality table, and which is prohibited by the laws of Maryland. This unadvised and incautious compliance, with a request of which your petitioner did not apprehend the danger, being entirely ignorant of any law against it, has subjected him to presentment and conviction for the offence, and to a sentence of a fine of fifty pounds, which the court have not power to lessen, and which he is totally unable to pay. He therefore submissively prays the humane interposition of the President of the United States for it's remission.

John Baker
his × Mark

District of Columbia, county of Washington, to wit. This day John Baker the above petitioner appeared before me a justice of the peace for the said county and made oath that the matters of fact stated in the above petition are true. At the same time appeared Robert Mc.Clan Jailer and made oath that John Baker is a young man apparently of the age of sixteen and has demeaned himself well since he has been in prison. Given under my hand this 11th. day of January one thousand eight hundred three.

Corn. Coningham

[*Order by TJ*:]

Let a pardon issue

Th: Jefferson
Jan. 23. 1803.

MS (DNA: RG 59, GPR); in a clerk's hand, with Baker's mark; day of month inserted in attestation and signed by Cornelius Coningham; TJ's order written on same sheet below an affidavit signed by William Kilty and William Cranch, 19 Jan. 1803, recommending a remission of Baker's fine; endorsed by TJ as received 22 Jan. and so recorded in SJL with notation "petn. pardon.

gaming" and as received from "jail"; also endorsed by TJ: "Petition."

According to the record of his trial, John Baker of Washington County, a laborer, was indicted for operating a "Fair play table" on 4 Dec. 1802. Appearing before the December 1802 session of the U.S. Circuit Court for the District of Columbia, he was found guilty and fined \$133.33$\frac{1}{3}$ plus court costs (Tr in same, attested by Uriah Forrest, 20 Jan. 1803). TJ issued a pardon and remission of Baker's fines and charges on 24 Jan. 1803 (FC in Lb in same).

LAWS OF MARYLAND: see William Connor to TJ, 5 Jan. 1803.

From Mary Jefferson Eppes

DEAR PAPA Edgehill january 11th [1803]

We arrived here safe yesterday after a most disastrous journey sufficiently distressing in itself but more so at the time from the depression of spirits felt on leaving you, the pain of seeing you turn back alone after having experienc'd so many happy hours with you My dear Papa in the little room to us endear'd by your sitting in it allways, & the recollection of the heavy expense this journey has been to you for indeed it must be in all immense, made my heart ache I must confess in no slight degree. suffer me to dwell upon it a moment My dear Papa to mention partly in excuse for myself that inexperience in some respects was greatly the cause on my own part[1] of the great abuse of your indulgence towards us.

The horses have been so much fatigued as to render it necessary for them to rest a day, they will set off tomorrow with John, whom I fear you have miss'd very much in the dining room. I found Martin here waiting for me, but as there is a possibility of the childs having taken the measles I shall remain here 'till the time is past in which it would appear if taken, & shall not leave this if he escapes it 'till the first of next week. Mrs Trist is here & desires to be particularly remember'd to you, she has at last recieved a letter from her son dated from the Natches, they are themselves living at Pen Park & will remain there I believe while here.

You will hear soon I imagine from Aunt Marks it is said here that H. Marks is dead or dying & the report is supposed to be true. Adieu dear Papa My Sister is well & desires me to give her love to you, Virginia would not recognise her till she changed her dress for one that she remember'd from its being a calico. Adieu once more, how much do I think of you at the hours which we have been accustom'd to be with you alone My dear Papa, & how much pain it gives me to think of the unsafe & solitary manner in which you sleep up stairs. Adieu dearest & Most beloved of fathers I feel my inability to express how much I love & revere you but you are the first & dearest to my heart

yours with sincere affection M E

RC (MHi); partially dated; endorsed by TJ as received 16 Jan. and so recorded in SJL.

WE ARRIVED HERE: at the outset of their journey on 5 Jan., TJ personally escorted his family to the Georgetown ferry where he paid $2.83 for their passage across the Potomac River as well as $.50 for his own return. Thomas Mann Randolph, who came to Washington expressly to accompany his family home, escorted them the rest of the way to Edgehill. They arrived on 10 Jan. (MB, 2:1090; Thomas Mann Randolph to John Milledge, 5 Jan. 1803, in NcD: Milledge Family Papers).

JOHN Freeman, a domestic servant, received $6 from TJ on 5 Jan. for his traveling expenses (Lucia Stanton " 'A Well-Ordered Household': Domestic Servants in Jefferson's White House" *White House History*, 17 [2006], 9; MB, 2:1090; Vol. 37:341n).

MARTIN: a slave and wagoner in TJ's employ as of April 1801. In 1805, TJ purchased him from Thomas Eston Randolph (MB, 2:1039, 1162).

CHILDS HAVING TAKEN THE MEASLES: for the ailments of Francis Wayles Eppes, see John Wayles Eppes to TJ, 10 Feb.

Elizabeth TRIST and her family had been in residence at PEN PARK, the estate just north of Charlottesville that had belonged to TJ's doctor, George Gilmer (MB, 1:72-3n).

H. MARKS IS DEAD OR DYING: Hastings Marks, the husband of TJ's youngest sister, Anne Scott Jefferson Marks, lived until 1811 (RS, 4:416n).

VIRGINIA: Martha Jefferson Randolph's youngest daughter remained behind when other members of the family visited TJ in Washington (TJ to John Wayles Eppes, 22 Nov.).

[1] Preceding four words interlined.

Petition of John Henderson

To the President of the United States

the petition of John Henderson respectfully represents, that your petitioner is not a common gambler nor given to an idle and dissolute life, but happening from misfortune inadvertently to undertake at the late races in the City of Washington the keeping of a kind of gaming table, frequently called an equality table, in entire ignorance of the prohibition of that species of game, by some ancient statute of the State of Maryland, he has been presented convicted and sentenced to a fine of fifty pounds, which the court have not power to lessen, and which he is utterly unable to pay; and of which he therefore submissively prays the humane remission by the President of the United States. John Henderson

District of Columbia, county of Washington, to wit; This day appeared before me a justice of the peace for the said county John Henderson the above petitioner, and made oath that the matters of fact therein stated are true. At the same time appeared Robert Mc.Clan jailer and made oath that the petitioner has demeaned himself well since he has been in prison. Given under my hand this 11th. day of Janry. 1803 CORN. CONINGHAM

MS (DNA: RG 59, GPR); in a clerk's hand, signed by Henderson, and dated and signed by Cornelius Coningham; endorsed by TJ as received 22 Jan. and so recorded in SJL with notation "petn pardon gaming" and as received from "jail"; also endorsed by TJ: "Petition."

STATUTE OF THE STATE OF MARYLAND: see William Connor to TJ, 5 Jan.

For the REMISSION of Henderson's fine, see Augustus B. Woodward and others to TJ, 18 Jan.

To George Jefferson

DEAR SIR Washington Jan. 11. 1803.

I inclose you the sum of three hundred and thirty Dollars to cover an order drawn on you this day in favor of Joseph Moran 200. D and of another drawn this day also in favor of Joseph Bran

for	124.25
which be pleased to honor on account of	324.25

Your friend & sevt. TH: JEFFERSON

P.S. I should have noted that an order of T M Randolph on mr Brown makes 60. D. of the above sum.

PrC (MHi); at foot of text: "Mr. George Jefferson." Recorded in SJL with notation "324.25. Bran & Moran."

On this day, TJ recorded in SJL sending a letter to JOSEPH MORAN with the notation "200" and a letter to Joseph Brand (BRAN) with the notation "124.25." Neither letter has been found.

To John Langdon

DEAR SIR Washington Jan. 11. 1803.

We learn by the public papers that a great calamity by fire has happened to Portsmouth, and that yourself and some others are appointed to recieve contributions for the distressed sufferers and to distribute them. I take the liberty of inclosing to yourself an hundred dollars for this purpose. I observe the trustees say in the papers that they will make a record of the donations. I pray that in my case it may be of the sum only, without the name. the former I suppose is necessary in making up your accounts. Accept assurances of my constant & affectionate esteem & respect. TH: JEFFERSON

RC (NhPoS: John Langdon Papers); addressed: "John Langdon esquire Portsmouth N.H."; franked; endorsed by Langdon: "Ansd." PrC (MHi); endorsed by TJ in ink on verso.

PUBLIC PAPERS throughout the country reprinted accounts of a FIRE that broke out in Portsmouth, New Hampshire, on 26 Dec. 1802. The conflagration originated in the building occupied by the state bank and spread to about 100 surrounding structures, resulting in an estimated $200,000 in damages. Langdon was among those appointed to a committee to receive CONTRIBUTIONS. In a national effort to solicit aid, the committee commissioned three people to travel to different regions (Nathaniel Adams, *Annals of Portsmouth* [Portsmouth, N.H., 1825], 324-5; *National Intelligencer*, 10 Jan. 1803; *Alexandria Advertiser and Commerical Intelligencer,* 10 Jan. 1803; *Alexandria Expositor*, 10 Jan. 1803; *United States Oracle, and Portsmouth Advertiser*, 1 Jan. 1803; Amherst, N.H., *Farmer's Cabinet*, 30 Dec. 1802, 13 Jan. 1803; Georgetown *Olio*, 21 Jan. 1803).

According to his financial memoranda, TJ made two anonymous DONATIONS of $100 each in "charity for Portsmouth," including one on 11 Jan. and one on 12 Feb. to "Mr. Willard." Joseph Willard, a former Harvard president and Congregational clergyman whose in-laws were the Sheafes of Portsmouth, had been sent by the committee to cities south of New York (*New-York Gazette and General Advertiser*, 17 Jan. 1803; ANB, s.v. "Willard, Joseph"; MB, 2:1090, 1092).

To the Senate

GENTLEMEN OF THE SENATE

The cession of the Spanish province of Louisiana to France, and perhaps of the Floridas, and the late suspension of our right of deposit at New Orleans, are events of primary interest to the United States. on both occasions, such measures were promptly taken as were thought most likely amicably to remove the present, & to prevent future causes of inquietude. the objects of these measures were to obtain the territory on the left bank of the Missisipi and Eastward of that, if practicable, on conditions to which the proper authorities of our country would agree; or, at least, to prevent any changes which might lessen the secure exercise of our rights. While my confidence in our Minister Plenipotentiary at Paris is entire and undiminished, I still think that these objects might be promoted by joining with him a person sent from hence directly, carrying with him the feelings & sentiments of the nation excited on the late occurrence, impressed by full communications of all the views we entertain on this interesting subject, & thus prepared to meet & to improve to an useful result, the counterpropositions of the other contracting party, whatsoever form their interests may give to them, and to secure to us the ultimate accomplishment of our object.

I therefore nominate Robert R. Livingston to be Minister Plenipotentiary, and James Monroe to be Minister extraordinary & plenipotentiary, with full powers to both jointly, or to either on the death of the other, to enter into a treaty or convention with the First Consul of France, for the purpose of enlarging, and more effectually securing, our rights and interests in the river Missisipi, and in the territories Eastward thereof.

But as the possession of these provinces is still in Spain, and the course of events may retard or prevent the cession to France being carried into effect, to secure our object, it will be expedient to address equal powers to the government of Spain also, to be used only in the event of it's being necessary.

I therefore nominate Charles Pinckney to be Minister plenipotentiary, and James Monroe of Virginia to be Minister extraordinary and plenipotentiary, with full powers to both jointly, or to either on the death of the other, to enter into a treaty or convention with his Catholic majesty for the purpose of enlarging and more effectually securing our rights and interests in the river Missisipi, and in the territories Eastward thereof. TH: JEFFERSON

Jan. 11. 1803.

RC (DNA: RG 46, EPEN, 7th Cong., 2d sess.); endorsed by clerks.

Meriwether Lewis delivered the message on 11 Jan., and the Senate approved the nominations in executive session on the 12th. On the appointment of MONROE to join Robert R. Livingston in France, the vote was 15 to 12. The votes on the other appointments were not recorded (JEP, 1:431, 436).

To the Senate

GENTLEMEN OF THE SENATE

During the late recess of the Senate, I have granted commissions for the following persons and offices, which commissions will expire at the end of the present session of the Senate. I therefore nominate the same persons to the same offices for reappointment: to wit

Rufus King who is Minister Plenipotentiary of the US. at London, to be a Commissioner for the settlement of boundaries between the US. and the British territories East, North, and North-West of the US.

George Wentworth of New-Hampshire to be Surveyor for the district of Portsmouth in New Hampshire, & Inspector of the revenue for the same, vice Samuel Adams deceased.

William R. Lee of Massachusets, to be Collector for Salem and Beverley in Massachusets, vice Joseph Hiller resigned.

Joseph Farley of Massachusets, to be Collector for the district of Waldoborough in Massachusets & Inspector of the revenue for the same, vice Joshua Head removed.

John Gibaut of Massachusets to be Collector for the district of Gloucester in Massachusets vice William Tuck removed.

Joseph Wilson of Massachusets, to be Collector for the district of Marblehead in Massachusets, & Inspector of the revenue for the same, vice Samuel R. Gerry removed.

Ralph Cross of Massachusets to be Collector for Newbury port in Massachusets vice Dudley A. Tyng removed.

John Swartwout, who was marshal of the former limited district of New York, to be Marshal of the present district of New York.

Abraham Bloodgood of New York to be Surveyor for the port of Albany in New York & Inspector of the revenue for the same, vice Henry Bogert resigned.

Silas Crane of New Jersey who is Collector for the district of Little egg harbour in New Jersey, to be Inspector of the revenue for the same.

Oliver Barnet of New Jersey to be Marshal of New Jersey, vice John Heard transferrd

John Smith of Pensylvania, who was Marshal of the Eastern district of Pensylvania to be Marshal of Pensylvania.

Peter Muhlenburg of Pensylvania to be Collector for the district of Pensylvania, vice George Latimer resigned.

Tenche Coxe of Pensylvania, to be Supervisor of the revenue for the district of Pensylvania, vice Peter Muhlenberg transferred.

Alexander Scott of Maryland to be Collector for the district of Nanjemoy in Maryland & Inspector of the revenue for the same, vice John C. Jones deceased.

William White of Virginia, to be Surveyor for the port of East river in Virginia, and Inspector of the revenue for the same.

Francis Armistead of Virginia to be Collector of East river in Virginia.

Joseph Scott of Virginia, who was Marshal of the Eastern district of Virginia to be Marshal of Virginia.

John Shore of Virginia to be Collector for Petersburg in Virginia, vice Wm. Heth, removed.

Thomas Archer of Virginia to be Collector of Yorktown in Virginia & Inspector of the revenue for the same, vice William Reynolds deceased.

John Easson of Virginia to be Surveyor of Smithfield in Virginia, & Inspector of the revenue for the same, vice Thomas Blow resigned.

John Rowan of N. Carolina, to be Surveyor of Windsor in North Carolina & Inspector of the revenue for the same, vice William Benson deceased.

Jehu Nichols of North Carolina to be Surveyor of Tombstone in N. Carolina and Inspector of the revenue for the same.

Henry Tooley of North Carolina to be Surveyor of Slade's creek in N. Carolina and Inspector of the revenue for the same.

Robert Elliott Cockran of South Carolina to be Marshal of South Carolina vice Charles B. Cockran resigned.

Thomas Stuart of Tenissee to be Attorney for the US. in the West district of Tenissee vice William P. Anderson resigned.

Robert Anderson New of Kentucky to be Collector of Louisville in Kentucky, and Inspector of the revenue for the same, vice James Mc.Connel removed.

Griffin Greene of the NorthWestern territory, to be Collector for the district of Marietta in the N. Western territory, & Inspector of the revenue for the same.

Joseph Wood of the North-Western territory, to be Register of the land office at Marietta in the said territory vice Peregrine Foster resigned.

John Selman of the NorthWestern territory to be Commissioner on Symes's land-claims vice William Goforth resigned.

Daniel Bissell of the Indiana territory to be Collector for Massac in the said territory and Inspector of the revenue for the same, vice William Chribs removed.

David Ker of the Missisipi territory, to be third judge of the Missisipi territory, vice Daniel Tilton resigned.

James Anderson of South Carolina to be Commercial Agent at Cette in France.

Isaac Coxe Barnet of New Jersey to be Commercial Agent at Antwerp.

Th: Jefferson
Jan. 11. 1803

RC (DNA: RG 46, EPEN, 7th Cong., 2d sess.); with clerk's notation "passd" added in ink in left margin by nominees confirmed on 17 Jan. and "passed" written in pencil by those confirmed a few days later (see below); endorsed by a Senate clerk. PrC (DLC); TJ added a check mark in ink next to each name and noted at the foot of the first page: "√ mark means approved by the Senate." Recorded in SJL with notation "renominations."

Meriwether Lewis delivered the interim appointments to the Senate on 11 Jan., along with three other messages. The Senate read this message the same day and ordered it to lie for consideration. They considered the nominations on 14 Jan. and on the 17th confirmed all but Farley, Wilson, Cross, Alexander Scott, White, Armistead, Tuley (Tooley), Archer, Easson, and James Anderson. These were referred to DeWitt Clinton,

Wilson Cary Nicholas, and David Stone for consideration. On 21 Jan., Clinton recommended and the Senate consented to all the remaining nominees, except that of Scott as collector at Nanjemoy. The Senate confirmed his appointment on 25 Jan. (JEP, 1:431-3, 436-7, 440).

To the Senate

GENTLEMEN OF THE SENATE

During the late recess of the Senate I granted commissions for the Promotions, transfers, and appointments in the army of the US. which are under the mark A. in the inclosed Schedule signed by the Secretary at war, which will expire at the end of the present session of the Senate. I therefore nominate the same persons for the same commissions for reappointment.

I also nominate the persons named in the same schedule under the mark of the letter B. to be appointed to the grades of command affixed to their names respectively.

TH: JEFFERSON
Jan. 11. 1803.

RC (DNA: RG 46, EPEN, 7th Cong., 2d sess.); endorsed by a Senate clerk. PrC (DLC). Recorded in SJL with notation "renominations & nominations Military." Enclosures: see Henry Dearborn to TJ, 10 Jan. 1803 (first letter).

The Senate received TJ's list of army PROMOTIONS, TRANSFERS, AND APPOINTMENTS on 11 Jan. The following day, the nominations were referred to a committee consisting of Joseph Anderson, Uriah Tracy, and Jonathan Dayton. Acting on the committee's recommendations, on 25 Jan. the Senate consented to all of the nominations except those of Ephraim Emery and Peyton Gay, which were postponed and subsequently rejected on 22 Feb. (JEP, 1:433-5, 436, 440, 445). For opposition to Emery's nomination, see William Wingate to TJ, 7 Feb. 1803.

To the Senate

GENTLEMEN OF THE SENATE

The Spoliations and irregularities committed on our commerce during the late war by subjects of Spain, or by others deemed within her responsibility, having called for attention, instructions were accordingly given to our minister at Madrid to urge our right to just indemnifications, and to propose a convention for adjusting them. the Spanish government listened to our proposition with an honorable readiness, and agreed to a Convention, which I now submit for your advice and consent. It does not go to the satisfaction of all our claims: but the express reservation of our right to press the validity of the residue has been made the ground of further instructions to our minister, on the subject of an additional article, which it is to be hoped will not be without effect.

TH: JEFFERSON
Jan. 11. 1803.

RC (DNA: RG 46, EPFR, 7th Cong., 2d sess.); endorsed by clerks. PrC (DLC). Tr (NNC); entirely in TJ's hand and signed by him, with his signed attestation dated 1 Jan. 1824: "The above is truly copied from the press-copy retained of the original sent to the Senate"; enclosed in TJ to John Hollins, 1 Jan. 1824. Recorded in SJL with notation "Spanish convention." Enclosures: (1) Convention signed at Madrid, 11 Aug. 1802, by Pedro Cevallos for Spain and Charles Pinckney for the United States, providing for the creation of a five-member commission to examine claims by subjects of Spain or citizens of the United States and determine compensation; the commission to assemble in Madrid and conclude its work within 18 months of its first meeting; the negotiators being unable to agree on a means by which the bilateral commission could arbitrate claims stemming from acts of foreign vessels or agents, each government reserves the right to pursue that category of claims at a later time (printed copy in DNA: RG 46, EPFR, endorsed by a clerk; Miller, *Treaties*, 2:492-7). (2) Extracts of letters of the secretary of state to Pinckney, 9 June, 25 Oct. 1801, 5 Feb., 25 Oct. 1802; extracts of memorandum from Pinckney to Cevallos, 24 Mch. 1802; extracts of Pinckney's dispatches to the secretary of state, 1, 6, 8 July, 15, 30 Aug. 1802; in his letters of 15 and 30 Aug., Pinckney reports that Cevallos refuses to include any provision in the convention for the settlement of claims relating to seizures by privateers operating under French authority or to condemnations by French consuls (Trs and PrCs in same; in various hands; endorsed by Jacob Wagner: "Mr. Pinckney's correspondence. Note. The enclosures referred to in this correspondence have been only partially received. Such as are material have been selected from those received, and accompany this, in original"; endorsed by a Senate clerk). Message and enclosures printed in ASP, *Foreign Relations*, 2:475-83.

For the INSTRUCTIONS to Charles Pinckney that resulted in the convention with Spain, see Joseph Yznardi, Sr., to TJ, 12 Aug. 1802.

ADVICE AND CONSENT: Meriwether Lewis delivered the message and the accompanying papers to the Senate on 11 Jan. On the 18th, a resolution to ratify the convention passed, with 18 votes in favor and only one senator, Gouverneur Morris, voting in opposition. Immediately, however, the Senate approved a motion to reconsider that resolution. Beginning on 25 Jan., the chamber took up the matter several times in executive session. On 3 Mch., the last day of the Seventh Congress, the Senate voted again. The tally on that occasion, 13 in favor and 9 opposed, did not meet the requirement for approval by a two-thirds majority. Once again the senators agreed to reconsider their vote, but they had to postpone further action on the issue. During the Eighth Congress, in January 1804, they finally ratified the convention with the required majority. Spain, however, did not ratify the instrument until 1818 (JEP, 1:435, 436, 437, 440, 441, 442, 443, 445, 447-8; Miller, *Treaties*, 2:496-7).

TO PRESS THE VALIDITY OF THE RESIDUE: under instructions from Madison dated 25 Oct., Pinckney was to keep negotiating on the issue of settling claims for seizures that had been made under French authority with Spanish complicity (Madison, *Papers*, *Sec. of State Ser.*, 4:53-6).

To the Senate and the House of Representatives

GENTLEMEN OF THE SENATE AND OF
THE HOUSE OF REPRESENTATIVES

I transmit you a report recieved[1] from the Director of the Mint on the subject of that institution.

TH: JEFFERSON
Jan. 11. 1803.

RC (DNA: RG 46, LPPM, 7th Cong., 2d sess.); endorsed by a Senate clerk.

[1] Word interlined.

E N C L O S U R E

From Elias Boudinot

TO THE PRESIDENT OF
THE UNITED STATES

Mint of the United States
1st. January 1803

The Director of the Mint of the United States begs leave respectfully to make his annual report on the Issues and State of the Mint.

He is happy to inform the President, that the Bullion deposited in the Mint during the past year, has far exceeded, what was expected, at the beginning of it; notwithstanding the considerable cheque given to deposits for some time, by frequent reports from the Seat of Government, during the last Session of Congress, that the Mint would be abolished.

Since the 1st day of January 1802, there has been issued from the Mint a Sum, amounting in the whole, to Five hundred and sixteen thousand one hundred and fifteen Dollars, eighty three Cents, as will appear, in detail, by Schedule No. 1, hereunto annexed, which have been added to the Current Coin of the Union.—Of this Sum, One Hundred and twenty nine thousand seven hundred and thirty Dollars and ninety one Cents, in Value, in Gold, have been coined from Bullion and Gold dust imported into the United States, and collected to the Mint, as a Center, from the different parts of the Union. The Ballance of the Gold Coinage, has been coined from clipped, plugged, and otherwise spoiled Foreign Coins, which have been sent to the Mint as Bullion.—Had not this whole Sum been coined in the United States, it must have been remitted to the European Marketts, in which case the Freight, Insurance, and Commissions, with the profits on the Cents[1] would have amounted to a Sum nearly equal to the Current Expenditures of the Mint.

All these Deposits were private property, the Certificates for which, were sold, generally, as soon as given, to the Banks in this City, at a Fourth and an half pr.C: Discount for the delay of Coinage.—The Banks are fond of keeping the Coin in their Vaults, as part of their Capitals, on account of the ease with which they are counted, without the trouble of weighing.—The Bank of the United States, indeed, having a considerable part of their Specie in this Coin, have been enabled, for some time past, to cancel their Five Dollars

Notes, and to substitute the payment of half Eagles, by which our Coins begin to be more generally dispersed among the People.

There have never been any of the precious Metals coined on Account of the Government of the United States.—

Comparative Issues from the Mint, for several Years past, will appear by Schedule No. 2, also, hereunto annexed.—The Current Expences of the Mint, for the past year, have amounted to Seventeen thousand four hundred and sixty two Dollars and sixty five Cents, as will appear from Schedule No. 3, from which the Profits on the Copper Coinage amounting to 5,644.$\frac{33}{100}$ Dollars should be deducted.—Besides the Cents on hand, we have near Twenty four Tons of Copper Planchetts ready for striking; the Coinage of which are in daily operation, at the rate of Fifteen thousand Cents a day.—

It is a duty incumbent on the Director of the Mint, respectfully to call the President's attention to the expiration of the Law of the United States for continuing the Mint at Philadelphia, on the 4th of March next, by its own limitation. It therefore becomes absolutely necessary, that the subject should be brought before Congress, so early, that provision may be made for the Contingency.—If Congress should rise without doing any thing therein, the Mint could not be continued in Philadelphia with propriety; neither could it be removed to the Seat of Government for want of a Law to authorise it.—

It is but doing justice to merit, to say, that the Officers of the Mint, concerned in the Coinage, and the Workmen, have greatly increased in their professional knowledge, and have acquitted themselves with strict integrity, and particular attention to their several departments for many years past; so that not a Dollar has been lost, except in one solitary instance, when the Culprit was detected by their assiduity and care, prosecuted and punished, and it was by their exertions, that the Mint was kept open during the late distress of the City, by the Fever of last Summer.

If the Mint should remain in its present situation, there will be a necessity of, at least, two additional Horses, and some repairs to the Machinery, part of it having been repaired the past year from necessity. At least Five hundred Dollars will be necessary in that case, to be added to the usual Estimate, to be appropriated for the purchase of Horses and further repairs to the present Machinery.—

All which is respectfully submitted to the President by his very obedient and humble Servant, Elias Boudinot, Director

RC (DNA: RG 46, LPPM, 7th Cong., 2d sess.); in a clerk's hand, signed by Boudinot; endorsed by a Senate clerk. FC (Lb in DNA: RG 104, DL). Enclosures: (1) "An Abstract of the Coins struck at the Mint of the U States from 1st Jany. to 31 Decb: 1802," recording $423,350 in gold coins, including 15,090 eagles, 53,176 half eagles, and 2,612 quarter eagles; $58,343 in silver coins, including 41,650 dollars, 29,890 half dollars, 10,975 dimes, and 13,010 half dimes; and $34,422.83 in copper coins, including 3,435,100 cents and 14,366 half cents; making an aggregate total of $516,115.83. (2) "Comparative statement of the coins issued by the Mint of the United States from the years 1798 to 1802 inclusive," recording $545,698 in gold, silver, and copper coins issued in 1798, $645,906.68 issued in 1799, $571,335.40 issued in 1800, $510,956.37 issued in 1801, and $516,115.83 issued in 1802, making an aggregate total of $2,790,012.28. (3) "An Abstract of the Expenditures of the Mint of the United States from 1st January to 31st December 1802 inclusive," recording a total of $4,251.69 expended on salaries, wages, and incidental charges during the quarter ending March 1802, $4,276.64 for the quarter ending in June, $4,384.25 for the quarter ending in September, and $4,550.07 for the quarter ending in December, making an aggregate total of $17,462.65. (4) "A Statement of the Gain on Copper coined at the Mint of the United States, from the 1st January to the 31st December 1802," recording a profit of $5,644.32 on the $34,422.83 in copper coins issued by the Mint for the year 1802 (all in DNA: RG 46, LPPM, attested to by G. Ehrenzeller, 31 Dec. 1802, for Benjamin Rush, treasurer of the Mint, endorsed by a Senate clerk; DNA: RG 233, PM, same attestation, endorsed by a House clerk; printed in ASP, *Finance*, 2:18-21).

EXPIRATION OF THE LAW: on 3 Mch. 1801, Congress passed an act authorizing the continuation of the Mint at Philadelphia until 4 Mch. 1803. Congress extended the act on 3 Mch. 1803, continuing the Mint for an additional five years (U.S. Statutes at Large, 2:111, 242; Vol. 36:566n).

FEVER OF LAST SUMMER: see Vol. 38:95, 96-7.

[1] Preceding six words interlined.

Commission for James Monroe and Robert R. Livingston

TO ALL WHOM THESE PRESENTS SHALL CONCERN, GREETING:

Know Ye, That reposing special Trust and confidence in the Integrity, Prudence and Abilities of James Monroe, late Governor of the State of Virginia, and of Robert R. Livingston, at present the Minister Plenipotentiary of the United States to the French Republic, I have nominated, and by and with the advice and consent of the Senate, appointed them the said Robert R. Livingston to be Minister Plenopotentiary, and the said James Monroe to be Envoy Extraordinary and Minister Plenipotentiary, with full power and authority to them both jointly or to either of them separately in case of the death of the other, for and in the name of the United States to confer, treat and negotiate with any person or persons duly authorized by the Government of the said Republic, of and concerning the enlargement and more effectual security of the rights and interests of the United States in the River Mississippi and in the Territories Eastward thereof, and to conclude and sign a Treaty, or Treaties, convention or Conventions thereon, transmitting the same to the President of the United States for his ratification by and with the advice and consent of the Senate.

In Testimony whereof, I have caused these Letters to be made Patent, and the Seal of the United States to be hereunto affixed.

Given under my Hand at the City of Washington, the Twelfth day of January in the year of our Lord one thousand Eight hundred and three, and of the Independence of the United States of America, the Twenty Seventh. TH: JEFFERSON

RC (Archives Nationales, Paris: AE/III/222); in a clerk's hand, signed by TJ; at head of text: "Thomas Jefferson President of the United States of America"; at foot of text: "By the President," signed by Madison as secretary of state; sealed. FC (Lb in DNA: RG 59, Credences); at foot of text: "A Commission similar to the foregoing, joining with Mr Monroe, Charles Pinckney Esq now Minr. Pleny. in Spain, to treat if necessary with the Spanish Govt.; was issued at the same time with the above, & of which Mr. Monroe was the bearer."

WITH FULL POWER AND AUTHORITY: Madison sent the joint commissions—the one printed above, for Livingston and Monroe for negotiations with France, and one for Charles Pinckney and Monroe for negotiations with Spain—to Monroe at New York on 2 Mch. with other documents for Monroe to take with him to Europe (Madison, *Papers*, *Sec. of State Ser.*, 4:364, 379, 381, 395).

To George Jefferson

DEAR SIR Washington Jan. 12. 1803

Will you be so good as to deliver or send the inclosed to Colo. Monroe.

Yours affectionately TH: JEFFERSON

PrC (MHi); at foot of text: "Mr. George Jefferson." Recorded in SJL with notation "Colo. Monroe." Enclosure: TJ to James Monroe, 12 Jan. and enclosure.

To George Jefferson

DEAR SIR Washington Jan. 12. 1803

Messrs. Jones and Howell have forwarded to you for me [190.] bundles of nail rod and 8. do. of hoop iron: & messrs. Smith & Buchanan of Baltimore are desired to send to your address two half pipes of wine recieved for me from Lisbon. the former be so good as to forward to Monticello by any early water conveyance; but the wine I would wish to be [trusted?] but to the most trustworthy of the Milton boatmen as it's immediate passage is not so important as the other. Accept assurances of my affectionate attachment

TH: JEFFERSON

PrC (MHi); faint; at foot of text: "Mr. George Jefferson"; endorsed by TJ in ink on verso.

A letter of 4 Jan. from JONES AND HOWELL, recorded in SJL as received 8 Jan., has not been found.

To James Monroe

Dear Sir Washington Jan. 12. 1803

The mail is closing just as the inclosed is put into my hands. to-morrow we shall write to you fully. Adieu. Th: Jefferson

PrC (MHi); at foot of text: "James Monroe"; endorsed by TJ in ink on verso. Enclosure: Resolutions of the Senate, 12 Jan., agreeing to Monroe's appointments as minister extraordinary and plenipotentiary to France and Spain (see TJ to Monroe, 13 Jan.; JEP, 1:436). Enclosed in TJ to George Jefferson, 12 Jan. (first letter).

From Thomas Paine

Jany. 12 1803

I will be obliged to you to send back the Models, as I am packing up to set off for Philadelphia and NYork. My intention in bringing them here in preference to sending them from Baltimore to Philadelphia, was, to have some Conversation with you on those Matters and others I have not informed you of. But you have not only shewn no disposition towards it, but have, in some measure, by a sort of shyness, as if you stood in fear of federal observation, precluded it. I am not the only one, who makes observations of this kind.

Thomas Paine

RC (DLC); endorsed by TJ as received 13 Jan. and so recorded in SJL.

send back the models: upon his arrival in Washington in November, Paine loaned TJ some of his models of bridges and carriage wheels. He planned to ship them to Philadelphia for display in Charles Willson Peale's museum (Foner, *Thomas Paine*, 2:1051; Paine to TJ, on or before 3 Nov. 1802).

sort of shyness: although Paine had dined with TJ and other heads of department in early December, invitations may have been less frequent after Congress was in session. TJ remained silent on the subject of Paine, despite both the ongoing efforts of the Federalist press to link the two and the appearance of a series of letters by Paine, "To the Citizens of the United States," beginning in late November in the *National Intelligencer*. James Cheetham observed that Paine's "reception at Washington was cold and forbidding. Even Mr. Jefferson received him with politick circumspection; and such of the members of congress as suffered him to approach them, did so from motives of curiosity. *Policy* dictated this course" (*New-York Evening Post*, 10 Jan. 1803; Jerry W. Knudson, *Jefferson and the Press: Crucible of Liberty* [Columbia, S.C., 2006], 77, 81; Malone, *Jefferson*, 4:197-9; James Cheetham, *Life of Thomas Paine* [New York, 1809], 227).

Port of New-Orleans SHUT.

By an Expreſs arrived this evening from New-Orleans, we have received the following important intelligence, which we haſten to give to our readers.—

Extract of a Letter from a gentleman in New-Orleans to his friend in this place, dated Oct. 19, 1802.

"Yeſterday the Intendant iſſued orders, not only for ſhutting the port of New-Orleans againſt American veſſels coming with cargoes to ſell, which was expected; but even totally to prevent the depoſit—a ſtep that muſt produce infinite embarraſſment, as well as much loſs to many of the citizens of the United States. Two boats that arrived from above yeſterday, with flour, were not allowed to land it; conſequently cotton, &c. coming from Natchez will be in the ſame predicament."

PROCLAMATION OF THE INTENDANT:

AS long as it was neceſſary to tolerate the trade of neutrals which is now aboliſhed, it would have been prejudicial to this colony, that the Intendant complying with his duty ſhould have prevented the depoſit in this city of the property of Americans as granted to them by the 22 article of the Treaty of Friendſhip, Limits and Navigation of the 27th October, 1795, at the expiration of the three years prefixed; but now that with the publication of the Treaty of Amiens and the re-eſtabliſhment of the communication between the Engliſh and Spaniſh ſubjects that inconvenience has ceaſed, conſidering that the 22d article of the ſaid treaty prevents my continuing this toleration, which neceſſity required after the fulfillment of the ſtipulated time this miniſtry can no longer conſent to it without an expreſs order of the King's. Therefore without prejudice to the exportation of what has been admitted in proper time, I order that from this date ſhall *ceaſe the previlege which the Americans had of bringing and depoſiting their goods in this capitol.* And that the foregoing may be publicly known, and that no body may plead ignorance, I order it to be publiſhed in the accuſtomed places, copies to be poſted up in public; and that the neceſſary notice to be given of it to the departments of Finance, Royal Cuſtom-houſe, and others that may be thought proper.

DONE at the Intendancy, ſigned with my hand, and counterſigned by the Notary Public of Finance, at New-Orleans, 16th October, 1802.

(Signed)

JUAN VENTURA MORALES.

By order of the Intendant,

PETER PEDESCLAUX.

Herald Office, Natchez, Thurſday Night, October 28, 1802.

Leg. 95

Broadside from the *Mississippi Herald*

N° II
Fig. I. Plan of the principal Dry Dock or Naval Arsenal, to contain
Frigates in three tier of four ships each.
B. Henry Latrobe Engineer
Decr 4th 1802.

Dry Dock

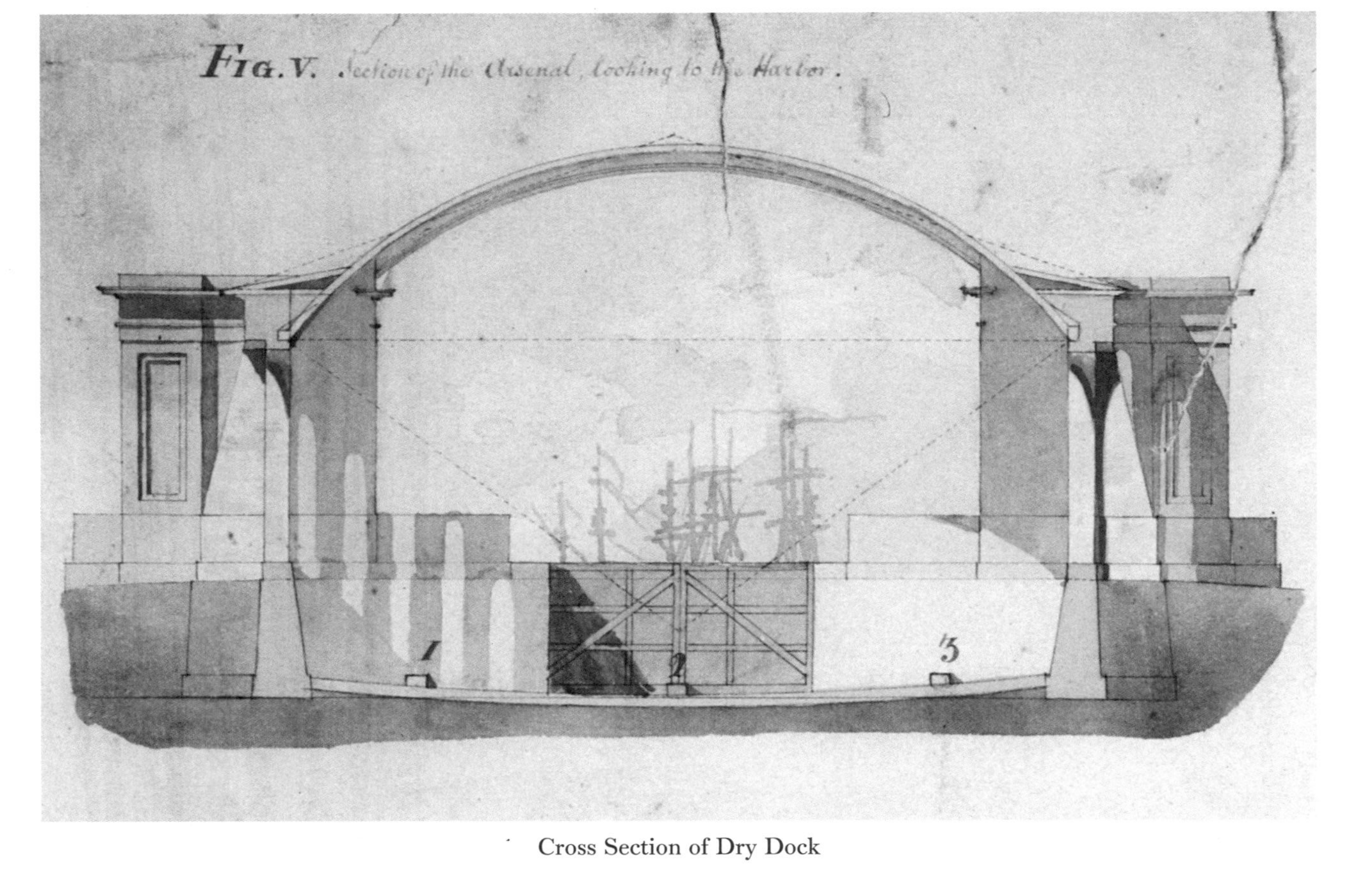

Cross Section of Dry Dock

View of Washington

Dear Grand Papa

We have been expecting the measles but have escaped it as yet. Virginia has learnt to speak very well. Ellen is learning french. Cornelia sends her love to you I would be very much obliged to you if you would bring me a book of geography adieu Dear Grand Papa your affectionate Grand son Thomas Jefferson R

Letter from Thomas Jefferson Randolph

Seneca Mother and Child

"Sauvage de Balston Spring"

"Mad Tom in a Rage"

To Christopher Smith

Sir — Washington Jan. 12. 1803

You gave me leave the last year to deposit in Richmond the money then due you for negro hire. as it would be very difficult for me to find the means of conveying it to your residence, I will take the liberty of depositing what is now due, about the 10th. of the ensuing month in the hands of Messrs. Gibson & Jefferson in Richmond, to wit, 400. Dollars with directions to pay it to your order. as also $66\frac{2}{3}$ Dollars for mr Charles Smith payable to his order; of which if you will be so good as to give him notice you will oblige me. Accept my respects and best wishes. Th: Jefferson

PrC (MHi); at foot of text: "Mr. Christopher Smith Louisa"; endorsed by TJ in ink on verso.

gave me leave: see Vol. 36:21.

To S. Smith & Buchanan

Gentlemen — Washington Jan. 12. 1803.

Mr. Jarvis of Lisbon informs me of his having addressed to your house for me two half pipes of Oeyras wine, and Genl. Smith tells me they are arrived. I must ask the favor of you to forward them to Richmond to the care of Messrs. Gibson & Jefferson. mr Jarvis has said nothing of the price, nor to whom I am to pay it for him. should it be to yourselves, and you will be so good as to inform me of the sum, it shall be remitted without delay. Accept assurances of my respect and best wishes. Th: Jefferson

PrC (MHi); at foot of text: "Messrs. Smith & Buchanan"; endorsed by TJ in ink on verso. Recorded in SJL with notation "Oeyras wine."

S. Smith & Buchanan was the Baltimore mercantile firm of Samuel Smith and his cousin James Buchanan. Reorganized in the early 1790s from earlier firms operated by Smith and/or his father, it was perhaps the most important commercial house in Baltimore until its collapse during the economic panic of 1819. Buchanan was the more active of the two partners, allowing Smith to pursue his political career (Frank A. Cassell, *Merchant Congressman in the Young Republic: Samuel Smith of Maryland, 1752-1839* [Madison, Wis., 1971], 44, 222-4).

jarvis of lisbon: William Jarvis to TJ, 25 Oct. 1802.

From Albert Gallatin

Dear Sir [13 Jan. 1803]

You have not returned any answer in the case of Colo. Worthington's resignation. He recommends Jesse Spencer of Chilicothe as a proper successor for the place of Register of the land office.

I enclose a recommendation for keeper of the light house at old Point Comfort.

The enclosed letter from the Collector of Michillimakinac (which you will be good enough to return) deserves consideration. It will not do to run the risk of an Indian war, and yet if it shall be once known that we dare not enforce the collection law, it will be perpetually evaded. Perhaps the best mode will be at first to confine the operation of the law to Michillimakinac & the entrance of Lake Michigan which commands the whole trade to the Indians South of the Lake and to the Mississipi & Missouri countries; and not to attempt doing any thing at the falls and straights of St Mary's which form the entrance into Lake Superior, until it shall be found convenient to have a military post there, at which time a surveyor of the revenue may also be appointed, and the law carried into effect as I believe without difficulty. It must be, however, observed that there being [no][1] positive reservation or grant to the United States, along the straights of St Mary or any where in Lake Superior, made by the Indians in the Greenville treaty, they may object to the establishment of either a military post or a revenue officer.

I have read Mr Lincoln's observations and cannot distinguish the difference between a power to acquire territory for the United States, and a power to extend by treaty the territory of the United States: yet he contends that the first is unconstitutional, & supposes that we may acquire East[2] Louisiana & West Florida by annexing them to the Mississipi territory. Nor do I think his other idea, that of annexation to a State, that for instance of East Florida to Georgia as proposed by him, to Stand on a better foundation. If the acquisition of territory is not warranted by the constitution, it is not more legal to acquire for one State than for the United States: if the Legislature and Executive established by the constitution are not the proper organs for the acquirement of new territory for the use of the Union, still less can they be so for the acquirement of new[3] territory for the use of One State: if they have no power to acquire territory, it is because the constitution has confined its views to the then existing territory of the Union, and *that* excludes a possibility of enlargement of one State as well as that of territory common to the United States. As to the danger resulting from the exercise of such power, it is as great on his plan as on the other. What could on his construction, prevent the Presidt. & Senate, by treaty annexing Cuba to Massachussets or Bengal to Rhode Island; if ever the acquirement of colonies shall become a favorite object with Government and colonies shall be acquired.

But does any constitutional objection really exist?

The 3d Sect. of the 4th Art. of the Constitution provides

1st. that new States may be admitted by Congress into this Union.

2dly. that Congress shall have power to dispose of and make all needful rules and regulations respecting the territory or other property belonging to the United States.

Mr Lincoln, in order to support his objection is compelled to *suppose* 1st that the new States therein alluded to must be carved either out of other States, or out of the territory belonging to the United States and 2dly that the power given to Congress of making regulations respecting the territory belonging to the U.S. is expressly confined to the territory *then* belonging to the Union.

A general and perhaps sufficient answer is that the whole rests on a supposition, there being no words, in the section, which confines the authority given to Congress to those specific objects; whilst, on the contrary, the existence of the United States as a nation presupposes the power enjoyed by every nation of extending their territory by treaties, and the general power given to the President & Senate of making treaties[4] designates the organs through which the acquisition may be made, whilst this Section provides the proper authority (vizt. Congress) for either admitting in the Union or governing as subjects the territory thus acquired.

It may be further observed in relation to the power of admitting new States in the Union, that this section was substituted to the 11th Art. of confederation which was in these words "Canada acceding &a. shall be admitted into &a. this Union: but no other colony shall be admitted into the same, unless such admission be agreed to by nine states." As the power was there explicitly given to nine States, and as all the other powers given in the articles of confederation to nine States were by the Constitution transferred to Congress, there is no reason to believe, as the words relative to the power of admission are, in the Constitution, general, that it was not the true intention of that Constitution to give the power generally & without restriction.

As to the other clause, that which gives the power of governing the territory of the United States, the limited construction of Mr Lincoln is still less tenable: for if that power is limited to the territory belonging to the United States at the time when the constitution was adopted, it would have precluded the United States from governing any territory acquired, since the adoption of the constitution, by cession of one of the States; which, however, has been done in the case of the cessions of North Carolina & Georgia: and, as the words "other property" follow and must be embraced by the same construction which will apply to the new territory, it would result from Mr L.'s opinion, that the United States could not after the constitution, either acquire or dispose of any personal property.

To me it would appear

1st. That the United States as a Nation have an inherent right to acquire territory

2d. That whenever that acquisition is by treaty, the same constituted authorities in whom the treaty making power is vested have a constitutional right to sanction the acquisition

3d. That whenever the territory has been acquired, Congress have the[5] power either of admitting into the Union as a new State, or of annexing to a State with the consent of that State, or of making regulations for the government of, Such territory.

The only possible objection must be derived from the 10th[6] amendment which declares that powers not delegated to the United States, nor prohibited by it to the States are reserved to the States or to the people.

As the States are expressly prohibited from making treaties, it is evident that, if the power of acquiring territory by treaty is not considered within the meaning of the amendment as delegated to the United States, it must be reserved to the people. If that be the true construction of the Constitution it substantially amounts to this—that the United States are precluded from, and renounce altogether the enlargement[7] of territory; a provision sufficiently important and singular to have deserved to be expressly enacted. Is it not a more natural construction to say that the power of acquiring territory is delegated to the United States by the several provisions which authorize the several branches of Government to make war—to make treaties—& to govern the territory of the Union.

I must, however, confess that after all, I do not feel myself perfectly satisfied: the subject must be thoroughly examined; and the above observations must be considered as hasty & incomplete.

With respect Your affecte. servt. ALBERT GALLATIN

RC (DLC); undated; endorsed by TJ as received from the Treasury Department on 13 Jan. and "Latimer Pt. Comfort. Collector Michillimacinac. Lincoln's proposn" and so recorded in SJL. Enclosures not found.

TJ appointed JESSE SPENCER register of the land office at Chillicothe, with a commission dated 8 Feb. 1803. Spencer remained in office until replaced during the Jackson administration (FC of commission in Lb in DNA: RG 59, MPTPC; Malcolm J. Rohrbough, *The Land Office Business: The Settlement and Administration of American Public Lands, 1789-1837* [New York, 1968], 273).

COLLECTOR OF MICHILLIMAKINAC: David Duncan. The collection district included Michilimakinac Island and lands ceded to the U.S. by the Indian nations at the Treaty of Greenville, including waters, inlets, and shores to the west and north of lakes Michigan and Superior (U.S. Statutes at Large, 1:638; Gallatin to TJ, 10 Dec., Enclosure No. 2).

LINCOLN'S OBSERVATIONS: see Levi Lincoln to TJ, 10 Jan.

Article 11 of the Articles of CONFEDERATION reads, "Canada acceding to this Confederation, and joining in the measures of the United States, shall be admitted into, and entitled to all the advantages of this Union; but no other colony shall be admitted into the same, unless such admission be agreed to by nine States" (*Articles of Confederation and Perpetual Union* [Williamsburg, Va., 1778], 13).

[1] Written over one or two illegible words.

[2] Word interlined.

[3] Word added in left margin.

[4] Gallatin here canceled "implies."

[5] Gallatin here canceled "exclusive."

[6] Figure interlined.

[7] Word interlined in place of "acquirement."

To Albert Gallatin

TH:J. TO MR GALLATIN [13 Jan. 1803]

I happened to be extraordinarily pressed by business which prevented my answering on the subject of Worthington's resignation. but I observed to him yesterday that as he had a right to resign, his act of resignation was final, and did not need an acceptance to validate it. if he apprehends any question, he might be furnished with an acceptance of the same date with his resignation. Spencer shall be nominated Register. but as to the place of light-house keeper at Old Point Comfort sollicited by Latimer, you may recollect that long ago I had the most powerful recommendations in favor of Capt Samuel Eddins, a revolutionary officer of great merit, the officer who in the days of terror saved M. Jones's press in Richmond from being pulled down by a mob of Federalists, and a good republican. these recommendations have been lying by me eighteen[1] months. by the bye I do not know whether the appointment is by you or me; & if the latter, whether it must go to the Senate. I have given mr Ellicot's letter to mr Madison for enquiry & consideration. this should have been settled by him with our predecessors, who alone could estimate the secret service and his authority to engage in it. I think with you on the subject of the smuggling at Michilimackinac: that we must not get into disagreement with the Indians, that without openly relinquishing the right of collection, the officer should wink at things at a distance, and go on as he has done. in time we shall get rid of those traders by underselling them, and engage the Indians themselves in watching for us against smuglers.—you are right in my opinion as to mr L's proposition. there is no constitutional difficulty as to the acquisition of territory: and whether, when acquired, it may be taken into the union by the constn as it now stands, will become a question of expediency. I think it will be safer not to permit the enlargement of the Union but by amendment of the constitution. Accept affectionate salutations. TH: JEFFERSON

RC (NHi: Gallatin Papers); undated; at foot of text: "The Secretary of the Treasury"; endorsed. PrC (DLC). Recorded in SJL as a letter to the Treasury Department of 13 Jan. with notation "Worthington. Eddins. Ellicot. Michillimac. Lincoln's opn."

For the written ACCEPTANCE of Thomas Worthington's resignation, dated 10 Jan., see note to Gallatin to TJ, printed at 8 Jan.

TJ received recommendations for SAMUEL EDDINS in July and August 1801, including one from Meriwether Jones, editor of the Richmond *Examiner* (see Vol. 35:112). For the defense of JONES'S PRESS by armed Republican sympathizers, see Vol. 31:165n. TJ wrote the Treasury secretary on 3 Aug. 1802 that he had "irresistable recommendations" for Eddins as lighthouse keeper at Old Point Comfort. WHETHER THE APPOINTMENT IS BY YOU OR ME: the president had the legal authority to appoint the lighthouse keeper without Senate approval (U.S. Statutes at Large, 1:125, 553).

ELLICOT'S LETTER: see enclosure printed at Gallatin to TJ, 8 Jan.

MR L'S: for Gallatin's reaction to Levi Lincoln's proposition, see Gallatin to TJ, of this date.

[1] Word interlined in place of "[...] twelve."

To James Monroe

DEAR SIR Washington Jan. 13. 1803.

I dropped you a line on the 10th. informing you of a nomination I had made of you to the Senate, and yesterday I inclosed you their approbation not then having time to write. the agitation of the public mind on occasion of the late suspension of our right of deposit at N. Orleans is extreme. in the Western country it is natural and grounded on honest motives. in the seaports it proceeds from a desire for war which increases the mercantile lottery; in the federalists generally & especially those of Congress the object is to force us into war if possible, in order to derange our finances, or if this cannot be done, to attach the Western country to them, as their best friends, and thus get again into power. remonstrances, memorials &c. are now circulating thro' the whole of the Western country & signing by the body of the people. the measures we have been pursuing being invisible, do not satisfy their minds. something sensible therefore was become necessary; and indeed our object of purchasing N. Orleans & the Floridas is a measure liable to assume so many shapes, that no instructions could be squared to fit them. it was essential then to send a Minister extraordinary, to be joined with the ordinary one, with discretionary powers, first however well impressed with all our views and therefore qualified to meet and modify to these every form of proposition which could come from the other party. this could be done only in full & frequent oral communications. having determined on this, there could not be two opinions among the republicans as to the person. you possessed the unlimited confidence of the administration & of the Western people; & generally of the republicans every where; and were you to refuse to go, no other man can be found who does this. the measure has already silenced the feds here. Congress will no longer be agitated by them: and the country will become calm as fast as the information extends over it. all eyes, all hopes are now fixed on you; and were you to decline, the chagrin would be universal, and would shake under your feet the high ground on which you stand with the public. indeed I know nothing which would produce such a shock. for on the event of this mission depends the future destinies of this republic. if we cannot by a purchase of the country ensure to ourselves a course of perpetual peace & friendship with all nations, then as war cannot be distant, it behoves us immediately to be preparing for that course, without however hastening it, and it may be necessary (on your failure on the continent) to cross the channel. we shall get entangled in European politics, and figuring more, be much less happy & prosperous. this can only be prevented by a succesful issue to your present mission. I am sensible after the measures you have taken for getting into a different line of business, that it will be a great sacrifice on your part, and presents from the season & other circumstances serious difficulties. but some men are born for the public. nature by fitting them for the service of the human race on a broad scale, has stamped them with the evidences of her destination & their duty.

But I am particularly concerned that in the present case you have more than one sacrifice to make. to reform the prodigalities of our predecessors is understood to be peculiarly our duty, & to bring the government to a simple & economical course. they, in order to increase expence, debt, taxation & patronage tried always how much they could give. the outfit given to ministers resident to enable them to furnish their house, but given by no nation to a temporary minister, who is never expected to take a house or to entertain, but considered on the footing of a voyageur, they gave to their extraordinary missionaries by wholesale. in the beginning of our administration, among other articles of reformation in expence, it was determined not to give an outfit to missionaries extraordinary, and not to incur the expence with any minister of sending a frigate to carry him or bring him. the Boston happened to be going to the Mediterranean, & was permitted therefore to take up mr Livingston[1] and touch in a port of France. a frigate was denied to Charles Pinckney, & has been refused to mr King for his return. mr Madison's friendship & mine to you being so well known the public will have eagle eyes to watch if we grant you any indulgencies out of the general rule; and on the other hand, the example set in your case will be more cogent on future ones, and produce greater approbation to our conduct. the allowance therefore will be in this & all similar cases, all the expences of your journey and voiage, taking a ship's cabin to yourself, 9000. D. a year, from your leaving home, till the proceedings of your mission are terminated, & then the quarter's salary for the expences of your return as prescribed by law.—as to the time of your going, you cannot too much hasten it, as the moment in France is critical. St. Domingo delays their taking possession of Louisiana, and they are in the last distress for money for current purposes. you should arrange your affairs for an absence of a year at least, perhaps for a long one. it will be necessary for you to stay here some days on your way to New York. you will recieve here what advance you chuse. Accept assurances of my constant & affectionate attachment.

TH: JEFFERSON

RC (DLC: Monroe Papers); at foot of first page: "Colo. Monroe"; endorsed by Monroe. PrC (DLC). Tr (NN); consists of an extract in TJ's hand, including the dateline, salutation, and beginning of the first paragraph through the phrase "for on the event," TJ there noting in square brackets: "&c. to the end of the paragraph, to wit, at the words 'evidence of her destination & their duty' "; the extract then continues in an unidentified hand to conclude the first paragraph; at foot of text in Monroe's hand: "Mr Jefferson"; endorsed.

For Robert R. Livingston's travel to France on the BOSTON, see Vol. 35:125, 187, 188n, 216-17, 292n. In 1801, when CHARLES PINCKNEY was preparing to leave for Spain, Madison informed him that he would have to arrange for his own passage across the Atlantic, to be paid from his allowance for costs. Rufus KING, when he requested permission to resign as minister to Great Britain, inquired if it would be possible for him, his family, and their possessions to return to the United States aboard a public ship. King noted that traveling on a frigate would let him carry more baggage than would be possible on a commercial ship, enabling him to transport his carriage horses and some sheep that could improve American breeding stock. He suggested that a frigate could convey his successor to Britain, then take him on its return voyage to the United States, or a ship returning from the Mediterranean squadron could stop in England to get him. As he acknowledged, however, a ship entering a British port from the Mediterranean would probably have to undergo quarantine, "which would occasion a long detention, as well as great Expense." Madison cited the problem of the quarantine when he informed King, in October 1802, that he would need to make private arrangements for his voyage (Madison, *Papers*, *Sec. of State Ser.*, 1:278; 3:457-8, 499; 4:5-6).

QUARTER'S SALARY: it was a long-established practice to grant a minister plenipotentiary one quarter of the amount of his annual salary to cover the expenses of his return to the United States at the conclusion of his service overseas (same, 1:278, 333-4; 2:321; Vol. 17:229; Vol. 24:188).

[1] TJ here canceled "& set him down."

To Thomas Paine

TH:J. TO MR PAINE. Jan. 13. 1803.

The bearer brings your models. you have certainly misconcieved what you deem shyness. of that I have not had a thought towards you, but on the contrary have openly maintained in conversation the duty of shewing our respect to you and of defying federal calumny in this as in other cases, by doing what is right. as to fearing it, if I ever could have been weak enough for that, they have taken care to cure me of it thoroughly. the fact is that I am so pressed with business till 1. or 2. aclock, & then to get a little exercise before I am engaged again with company to dine, from which I am not disengaged till night, that I have only the evening in which I can indulge in the society of my friends. and as to mechanics, mathematics, philosophy &c. I am obliged to give one answer to the many communications on those subjects, that I am obliged to abandon them entirely, as I have not a moment to give to them which would not be taken from some pressing duty.—I thank you for the sight of the models. they are all interesting to the public; the one for planing is most so to me personally. I imagine somebody at your new establishment will set up the trade of making them; and when that is the case I will apply to him for a pair. accept my friendly salutations & respects.

PrC (DLC); endorsed by TJ in ink on verso.

WHAT YOU DEEM SHYNESS: see Paine to TJ, 12 Jan.

DEFYING FEDERAL CALUMNY: James Thomson Callender and other Federalist editors charged that TJ shared Paine's religious views and brought him back from France to serve as his partisan writer. Callender also insinuated that Paine sought the companionship of Sally Hemings (see Jerry W. Knudson, *Jefferson and the Press: Crucible of Liberty* [Columbia, S.C., 2006], 78-80).

INTERESTING TO THE PUBLIC: Paine's essay on "The Construction of Iron Bridges," dated 3 Jan. 1803, sought to foster public interest in a bridge over the Schuylkill River. His later efforts to convince Congress to appropriate funds for its construction received no response (Foner, *Thomas Paine*, 2:1051-7; Jack Fruchtman, Jr., *Thomas Paine: Apostle of Freedom* [New York, 1994], 400).

From Henry Dearborn

SIR January 14th. 1803

I herewith enclose a rough draught of a report on Indian affairs. will you please to make such amendments and alterations as it may require, and a form for the heading or preamble.

I am Sir with sentiments of respectfull consideration your Humb Servt. H. DEARBORN

RC (DLC); at head of text: "To the President of the United States"; endorsed by TJ as received from the War Department on 14 Jan. and "Indian affairs" and so recorded in SJL. Enclosure: Dft, not found, of the enclosure to TJ to the Senate and the House of Representatives, 18 Jan. (second message).

Perhaps in preparation of the report submitted to Congress on 18 Jan., Dearborn gave TJ a "List of Factories or Trading Houses established with the Indian Nations." Dearborn listed Detroit, Fort Wayne, Chickasaw Bluffs, the Choctaw nation, the Tennessee frontier, and the Georgia frontier as locations of the trading houses (MS in DLC: TJ Papers, 128:22215; entirely in Dearborn's hand; at head of text: "for the President of the U.S.").

From Harry Innes

SIR, Kentucky Frankfort Jany. 14th. 1803

The inclosed copy of the proceedings in the suit Robert Morris assee. of Humphry Marshall against George Rogers Clark & myself exhibits a case which in my opinion merits Congressional interference, because being the sole Judge in this District no decision can ever take place so long as the present system of the Judicial Courts of the United States continue & my continuance in Office.

This communication should have been long since made if I had not been induced to beleive that the suit so far as it related to me had been discontinued, & this misconception existed until the last Term in November.

The cause of making me a party is obvious to those acquainted with the history of the transaction—A discussion of the subject would be improper, I conceive it sufficient to obviate the mischeif to state that the suit exists & to prove it by the inclosed documents.

The Constitution making it the duty of the President to see that the laws be duly executed, I have thought it my duty to make this communication to shew that a legal obstruction exists in the administration of Justice, & that the evil may be remedied if you think it an object worthy of attention, of which I have no doubt, such a representation will be made to the present Congress as may induce them to provide for the present case as also to guard against any case of a similar kind in future.

Pardon me Sir if this mode of communication be improper, I have been induced to do it for two reasons 1st. from the injunction contained in the Constitution. 2dly. that if a representation was made by you it wou'd be duly considered

With considerations of great esteem & respect I am Sir your mo. ob. Servt.

HARRY INNES

RC (DLC); addressed: "His Excy. The President of the United States City of Washington"; endorsed by TJ as received 8 Feb. and so recorded in SJL. Enclosures not found, but see TJ to John Breckinridge, 17 Feb. 1803.

The PROCEEDINGS IN THE SUIT mentioned above are not known, but were undoubtedly colored by the unremitting political feud between Innes and Humphrey MARSHALL, Kentucky's leading Federalist and the cousin and brother-in-law of Chief Justice John Marshall (Mary K. Bonsteel Tachau, *Federal Courts in the Early Republic: Kentucky 1789-1816* [Princeton, 1978], 35-6, 42-3; Vol. 32:569-70). During the 1790s, Marshall was involved in land speculations with Robert Morris and George Rogers Clark. In 1796, Morris conveyed more than 150,000 acres of Kentucky land to Marshall and authorized him to sell part of it in order to settle his $20,000 debt to Marshall. Two years later, Marshall assigned Morris his 1795 contract with Clark for the purchase of 74,000 acres of land near the mouth of the Tennessee River. Morris agreed to pay Clark 50 cents per acre if he secured the land from all Indian and military claims. Morris later assigned the land in the Clark contract to Thomas FitzSimons (Barbara Ann Chernow, *Robert Morris: Land Speculator, 1790-1801* [New York, 1978], 206-7).

PRESENT SYSTEM OF JUDICIAL COURTS: the Judiciary Act of 1802 removed Kentucky from the jurisdiction of any United States circuit court and left Innes, the United States district judge, as the sole federal judge in the state (U.S. Statutes at Large, 2:157; Tachau, *Federal Courts*, 25, 57).

From Thomas S. Kennedy

SIR, Baltimore 14th January 1803

I have just seen your Excellency's nomination of Mr. Monroe to the appointment of Minister to France &c announc'd in the public prints. If this information be correct, there is no doubt of the Senate's Concurrence, in which event 'tis probable Mr. Monroe will shortly be at Washington

Should the office of Secretary to the Embassy be vacant upon his arrival there, and this be the first application you have had, or there is no other person for whom your Excellency is particularly interested, I would beg leave to solicit the favour of your Interest in my behalf for that Birth— I can if necessary procure the most satisfactory recommendations, and your Excellency cannot in the *present case* I am sure do a greater good than promoting my advancement to that place. My Constitution is very much impaired, by two years close confinement in prosecuting the study of the Law, which would render a Voyage across the Atlantic very desirable if I could conveniently accomplish it, and besides it might be a step of incalculable advantage, in facilitating my future fortune in Life— These Sir are the reasons for wishing to obtain your Excellency's patronage on the present occasion— I have written to several Gentlemen High in office, to the same effect, with some of whom I have the Honour to be slightly aquainted

I am Sir with profound Respect your Excellency's most Obd H St

THOMAS SEILLES KENNEDY

RC (DNA: RG 59, LAR); endorsed by TJ as received 17 Jan. and so recorded in SJL; also endorsed by TJ: "to be Secy of legn to Colo. Monroe."

Thomas Seilles Kennedy, a native of Maryland, served as a clerk to William C. C. Claiborne in the Mississippi Territory from July 1804 until May 1805, when he became clerk of court. He was reappointed clerk of the court in the spring of 1807 and in 1809 (Jared William Bradley, ed., *Interim Appointment: W.C.C. Claiborne Letter Book, 1804-1805* [Baton Rouge, 2002], 146-7n; *Terr. Papers*, 9:375-6, 598, 749, 836).

An announcement of Monroe's NOMINATION appeared in the Baltimore *Republican; or Anti-Democrat*, 14 Jan. 1803.

From Benjamin Hawkins

Creek agency 15 January 1803

The bearer Mr. William Hill is an assistant in this agency as I have known him for five years and believe him to be a very honest and useful man I have thought him worthy of an introduction to you, that you may hear from such a man a detail of occurrences in this quarter. The object of his Visit to the seat of government is to carry the accounts and Vouchers in this department to the War office.

I have the honour to be with the highest regard my dear Sir, your obediant servant

BENJAMIN HAWKINS

RC (DLC); at foot of text: "Mr. Jefferson"; endorsed by TJ as received 9 Feb. and so recorded in SJL.

Hawkins also sent a letter of introduction for WILLIAM HILL to James Madison, dated 13 Jan. 1803. Hill was appointed agent to the Chickasaw Indians in January 1806, but he committed suicide before assuming his duties (Madison, *Papers, Sec. of State Ser.*, 4:254; Henry Dearborn to Hill, 7 Jan. 1806, in DNA: RG 75, LSIA; Savannah *Georgia Republican*, 18 Mch. 1806; James R. Atkinson, *Splendid Land, Splendid People: The Chickasaw Indians to Removal* [Tuscaloosa, Ala., 2004], 198).

From George Jefferson

DEAR SIR Richmond 15th. Janr. 1803

I have this instant returned from Williamsburg where I have been for some days, and find your favor of the 12th. inclosing a letter for Colo. Monroe. Mr. Gibson informs me that the one inclosed in your letter of the 10th. he forwarded on to N. York whither Colo. M. had gone the day previous to its receipt.

As I think it probable however that he may make some stay in Washington, or at any rate that you will know how to forward it, I return you the last inclosed.

The 330$ inclosed in your favor of the 11th. are received, and are of course entered to your credit.

I am Dear Sir Your Very humble servt. GEO. JEFFERSON

RC (MHi); at foot of text: "Thos. Jefferson esqr."; endorsed by TJ as received 20 Jan. and so recorded in SJL. Enclosure: TJ to James Monroe, 12 Jan., and enclosures.

Proclamation Extending Building Regulations in the City of Washington

BY THE PRESIDENT OF THE UNITED STATES.

Whereas by the first Article of the Terms and Conditions declared by the President of the United States on the seventeenth day of October 1791 for regulating the Materials and manner of Buildings and Improvements on the Lots in the City of Washington, it is provided "that the outer and party walls of all Houses in the said City, shall be built of Brick or Stone," and by the third Article of the same terms and Conditions it is declared, that the wall of no house shall be higher than 40 feet to the roof in any part of the City, nor shall any be lower than 35 feet on any of the Avenues; And Whereas the above recited Articles were found to impede the settlement in the City of Mechanicks and others whose Circumstances did not admit of erecting houses authorized by the said Regulations, for which cause the operation of the said Articles has been suspended by several Acts of the President of the United States from the fifth day of June 1796 to the first day of January 1803[1] and the beneficial effects arising from such suspensions having been experienced—it is deemed proper to revive the same, with the exception hereafter mentioned—Wherefore

I Thomas Jefferson President of the United States do declare that the first and third Articles above recited shall be, and the same are hereby suspended until the first day of January 1804, and that all Houses which shall be erected in the said City of Washington previous to the said first day of January 1804 conformable in other respects to the regulations aforesaid shall be considered as lawfully erected, except that no wooden house covering more than 320 square feet or higher than twelve feet from the Sill to the Eve shall be erected—nor shall such house be placed within 24 feet of any brick or Stone house.

Given under my hand this 15th January 1803

TH: JEFFERSON

MS (DLC: District of Columbia Papers); in Thomas Munroe's hand, signed by TJ; instructions by Munroe on a separate sheet: "Mr. Smith, Please insert once a week for six weeks successively & let me have the Original again. T Munroe 15 Jany 1803"; endorsed by Smith: "For Ths. Munroe"; endorsed by Munroe.

For TJ's previous approval of temporarily suspending certain building regulations in the CITY OF WASHINGTON, see Vol. 33:154-5; Vol. 36:415-16.

Samuel Harrison Smith published TJ's proclamation in the *National Intelligencer* on 17 Jan. 1803.

[1] Year altered from 1802 to 1803.

From John Smith

SIR Near Cincinnati Jany the 15th 1803

The next Post will announc the result of our Election of Governor & Representatives for this new State—which took place last tuesday. I have not yet seen the return of votes from the different Counties, but we have no shadow of doubt of the election of Mr Tiffin to the Office of Governor—and sufficient ground to believe, that our first Legislature will be Republican—Nothing could exceed the intrigues, the calumies and the machinations of the party attatched to old Mr St Clair Their number was too small to take the open field to oppose us, but with all their artifices attempted to divide us—However, in that they were defeated—And thank God that Republicanism rides in triumph over the aristocricy of this Country—The People are much pleased with their change of government, insomuch that nothing could be more unpopular with us then to find fault with it—

I expect in a few days to embark for New Orleans, where I have some private business to transact and hope to sale for Baltimore in may—I would not have troubled you Sir, with another letter but to inform you of the great & universal satisfaction which the people of the

Western Country express with the steps you have taken for having the port of N Orleans opened again. Large numbers of the people[1] here, have been heard to declare "that your regards are not confined to the Eastern states alone, but extended to the western states also" That you are the friend & the true patriot of your Country

I am Sir with high consideration and respect your most Obedt Servt.

John Smith

RC (DLC); at foot of text: "The Hon T. Gefferson President of the U States"; endorsed by TJ as received 8 Feb. and so recorded in SJL.

Edward TIFFIN won election as governor of Ohio by an overwhelming margin, securing at least 90 percent of the vote. Republicans also won decisively in the elections for the new state legislature (Donald J. Ratcliffe, *Party Spirit in a Frontier Republic: Democratic Politics in Ohio, 1793-1821* [Columbus, Ohio, 1998], 75-6).

[1] MS: "peo."

From William Hamilton

The Woodllds. 16th. January. 1803.

Mr. Hamilton presents his respectful compliments to the President, & with great pleasure, sends him a few seeds of the mimosa farnesiana, being all he saved during the last year.

Lest these should not vegetate, Mr. H. will, as soon as they ripen, forward some of the present years growth to the president, who will confer a favor on him, in naming any seeds or plants he may wish to have from the Woodlands collection.

RC (DLC); endorsed by TJ as received from the Woodlands on 27 Jan. and so recorded in SJL.

TJ shipped some specimens of the sweetly fragrant MIMOSA FARNESIANA from France in 1789 and described the plant as "the most delicious flowering shrub in the world." On three separate occasions, in the spring of 1800, July 1806, and March 1808, TJ requested its seeds from Hamilton, a Philadelphia horticulturalist and owner of the Woodlands estate (Betts, *Garden Book*, 322, 366; Vol. 15:376; Vol. 23:355; Vol. 31:535).

From Peter Carr

Dear Sir

Richmond. Janry 17th. 1803

The appointment of Colo. Monroe as Envoy to the courts of France and Spain was communicated to us here, through the gazettes, two days ago. It is thought probable that no person has yet been selected as Secretary to the embassy. Under this impression, Mr. Lewis

Harvie has requested, that I would mention him to you as wishing to fill that place. He appears, to feel very great anxiety for the success of this application, and I believe, some of his friends have written to Colo. Monroe on the subject. There is no man who would be farther from what is termed office-hunting, from the knowledge I have of him, than Mr. Harvie. But as he does not suppose there is any thing lucrative attached to this appointment, he hopes you will not consider this solicitation in that point of view, which might injure him, in your good opinion. You are too well acquainted with this young gentleman, to make it necessary for me to say a word to you, with respect to his talents and character. He requests that this application may not be made known; because if unsuccessful he might be placed in a point of view, which would be disagreeable. Mr. Harvie, is desirous to know your determination upon this subject, as early as possible. The nomination of Mr. Monroe meets with the most unqualified approbation of all parties here. His conduct whilst Governor, has extorted the applause of the Federalists in this place. We expect, to rise in the course of ten days, but hope, we shall before that time, adopt some resolution upon the subject of the Mississipi, of which Mr. Randolph's will be the basis. Accept assurances Dear Sir of my affectionate attachment—

P: CARR

RC (DLC); endorsed by TJ as received 22 Jan. and so recorded in SJL.

For John RANDOLPH's resolution on the Spanish suspension of the right of deposit at New Orleans, see TJ to the House of Representatives, 30 Dec. 1802.

To John Wayles Eppes

DEAR SIR Washington Jan. 17. 1803.

Yesterday morning I recieved information of Maria's safe arrival at Edgehill. some apprehension that Francis had recieved the infection of the measles on the road had determined her to await there the usual term of it's appearance. I have to acknolege several letters from you. Colo. Monroe arrived here[1] the night before last, not having previously heard of his appointment to Paris & Madrid to settle our affairs relative to the Missisipi. this measure has suppressed all further inflammatory proceedings meditated by the Federalists for instigating the Western country to force on a war between us & the owners of New Orleans. their confidence in Monroe will satisfy them that their rights will be safe in his hands.—I expect to be at Monticello about the 10th. of March for the residue of that month only. accept assurances of my affectionate attachment—

TH: JEFFERSON

PrC (CSmH); at foot of text: "J. W. Eppes"; endorsed by TJ in ink on verso.

SEVERAL LETTERS FROM YOU: TJ had not yet acknowledged Eppes's six letters to him of December 1802 as well as that of 4 Jan. 1803.

EXPECT TO BE AT MONTICELLO: TJ left Washington on 7 Mch. and arrived at Monticello on the 11th (MB, 2:1094).

[1] TJ here canceled "yesterda."

From E. T. Hadwen

MR. JEFFERSON. January 17th. 1803.

Because I have inclosed for you a within Copy of our Lord, Christ Jesus His Letter,

Ergo I believe God, Elshaddai. Shall bear *this* as on Eagles wings and bring it to your self. Exodus 19. Chap. 4th. ver. But I am not a Papist but a Baptized Baptist. And A True Believer in the Holy only Son of God Christ Jesus.

And that JESUS CHRIST is now in Heaven, and is the SON of GOD with POWER, and that Christ has All power in Heaven and in Earth now at this time, I can convince you by a Miracle I can do in His name; and which I can teach you to do the same miracle if ever I see you alive in this world to your astonishment joy and peace.

RC (DLC). Enclosed in Hadwen to TJ, 1 Jan.

ENCLOSURE

Religious Testimony of E. T. Hadwen

A Copy of the letter of our Lord Jesus Christ found under a Stone, and carried to the City of Iconium, and published by a person belonging to the Lady Cuba, whereon was written the Commands of Our Lord Jesus Christ the Blessed Son of God. And signed by the Holy Elect Angel called Gabriel, Ninety Eight years after the Birth of our blessed Saviour Christ.

The Letter &c.

"Whosoever worketh on the Sabbath Day shall be accursed."

"I Command you to go to God's House of Prayer, and Keep the Lords Day Holy, without doing any manner of work thereon. You shall not idle nor misspend your time in dressing yourselves with superfluities of costly array of apparel and vain cloathing: for I will have that Day Kept Holy that your sins may be forgiven you. You shall Not break my Commandments, but observe

and keep. I write them with My own Hand; so write them in your hearts. Study and observe they were written with my own Hand and Spoken by My own Mouth. You must not go alone to my Houses of Prayer, but make your servants of both sexes go with you, or any other person that is well disposed: And there learn My Commandments. You shall finish your work every Saturday by Four or Six O Clock in the evening, and then prepare for the Sabbath; which prepareation then begins.
I advise you to Fast Five Fridays in the year; beginning at with Good Friday, and the four Fridays next after in memory of the Five Bloody and cruel wounds I received for all Mine Elect. Two through either Hand, two through either Leg, and One through my side to My Heart.
You shall diligently and peaceably labour in your respective callings, in which God hath been Pleased to place you. You shall Love one another with Brotherly Love, for I Loved you, and gave myself for you.
And cause them who are not Christians to come to my Ministers and receive Baptism and the Lords supper; Which are my two Holy Sacraments, and be made Members thereof. In so doing I will give you prosperity and Saveing Grace and Deliverance from Sin, with all Needfull Blessings, and Comfort and Keep you with all needfull Blessings from the temptations of every devil and infernal enemies. But surely he that doth not Keep My words shall be accursed and unprofitable to his own precious soul. I will also send hardness of heart upon them, till I have destroyed them; but especially upon hardned and impenitent unbelievers. He that giveth to the poor, Shall for the sake of Christ be rewarded. And Remember to keep Holy the Sabbath Day: For I arose from the dead on the Lords Day: and thereby have made it Holy, and to be kept Holy by My servants. And he that hath a Copy of this Letter written with my own Hand and which I spoke with my Mouth, if they sincerely and truly Keep it, not boasting of it to others, Shall be Blessed of Me: and if his sins be in number as the Stars of the sky, on his truly forsaking all and every of his evil deeds, and believing in Me shall be pardoned.
But if believes not my words, I will send the plagues of destruction upon them and consume them, their Children and Cattle. And whoever shall have a Copy of this Letter, Keeping it in their Houses and with them, Nothing shall hurt them, Not pestilence lightning nor Thunder, if they truly and humbly put their Trust in the Father Son and Holy Ghost. And if a Woman be with Child or in labour, if a Copy of this be about her, and she humbly put her Trust in Me the Almighty God Jesus Christ, she shall be safely delivered of the Child.

You shall have no news of Me, but by the Holy Scriptures, which only is the true Word of Me the Blessed God till the day of Judgment. All Mens Peace and Salvation shall be with them, and My Angels I will Commission to guard them who treasure up My precious Gospel in their hearts inwardly, lives outwardly and Houses openly: and make My Lovely Commands to Guide and Rule by Saveing Faith, their whole lives and conversation." Finshed &c.

MS (DLC: TJ Papers, 128:22159); on verso of letter above; entirely in Hadwen's hand.

This LETTER was an early example of a popular piece of invented apocrypha that was occasionally reprinted in newspapers or sent as chain mail in Great Britain and the United States during the nineteenth and twentieth centuries (Edgar J. Goodspeed, *Strange New Gospels* [Chicago, 1931; repr. Freeport, N.Y., 1971], 100-7; *The Christian Intelligencer and Eastern Chronicle*, 4 [1830], 101; Mrs. Wirt Johnson Carrington, "Bacon Family," WMQ, 2d ser., 5 [1925], 188-90).

To Thomas Mann Randolph

DEAR SIR Washington Jan. 17. 1803.

Your's from Gordon's did not reach me till the 15th. and was the first information which relieved us from the state of anxious suspense into which we had been thrown by reports of the difficulties & delays you met with at Bullrun. yesterday morning[1] John & the carriage got back. I rejoice that the journey has been accomplished without any sinister accident; for a journey with a family in winter is always to be set down as a calamity. I concur with pleasure in Fitch's undertaking the service you desire; and to me it will be of no inconvenience, as he is employed in nothing pressing. the S. Carolina assembly have amended their law so as to permit negroes to be carried through their state. yours therefore will meet with no difficulty. I inclose you a reciept from mr Duane put into my hands by Capt Lewis. Colo. Monroe arrived here yesterday without previous knowlege of his appointment to Paris & Madrid for settling our Missisipi affairs. this measure has suppressed all further inflammatory proceedings meditated by the Federalists for[2] instigating the Western country to force on a war between us & the owners of New Orleans. their confidence in Monroe will tranquilise them on that subject. in the mean time we have the best grounded presumptions that the suspension of the right of deposit will be immediately removed. my tenderest love to Martha and the children. sincere & affectionate attachments to yourself.

TH: JEFFERSON

P.S. your dirk was found in your room and delivered to Abrams, who will be at[3] Milton with this letter.

RC (DLC); at foot of text: "T M Randolph"; endorsed by Randolph as received 24 Jan. Enclosure not found.

YOUR'S FROM GORDON'S: a letter of 10 Jan., recorded in SJL but not found.

South Carolina's General ASSEMBLY rescinded the ban on transporting slaves through the state in an act of 18 Dec. 1802. All the state now required was an oath precluding persons transporting slaves from selling their property within the state's borders (*Acts and Resolutions of the General Assembly of the State of South-Carolina. Passed in December, 1802* [Columbia, S.C., 1803], 36-9).

[1] Word interlined.

[2] TJ here canceled "blowing."

[3] TJ here canceled "Charlottesville."

From Markes Vandewall

SIR Richmond Post Office January 17th. 1803.

I have inclosed to you the letter directed to Col. Monroe, who I am informed left this place three days past for Washington City. also. inclosed one from Mr. Madison to Col. Monroe:

I am Sir Yours with great respt MARKES VANDEWALL

RC (DLC); endorsed by TJ as received 22 Jan. and so recorded in SJL. Enclosure: TJ to James Monroe, 13 Jan. Other enclosure not found.

Markes Vandewall (ca. 1754-1808) enlisted as a second lieutenant in one of the Virginia infantry regiments of the Continental Army in October 1777. Promoted to first lieutenant several months later, he served until retiring at the beginning of 1783. He was taken prisoner by the British at Charleston in 1780. After the war, he went into business as an auctioneer and commission merchant in Richmond. A "republican in practice" and "in principle, heart and soul," he was appointed the city's postmaster early in 1802 and served in that position until his death (Richmond *Virginia Argus*, 1 Nov. 1799; Richmond *Enquirer*, 14 June 1808; Heitman, *Register*, 555-6; Stets, *Postmasters*, 269).

Meriwether Lewis: Estimated Costs of Missouri River Expedition

[before 18 Jan. 1803]

Recapitulation of an estimate of the sum necessary to carry into effect the Missie. expedicion.—

Mathematical Instruments	$217.–
Arms & Accoutrements extraordinary	81.–
Camp Ecquipage	255.–
Medecine & packing	55.–
Means of transportation	430.–
Indian presents	696.–
Provisions extraordinary	224.–
Materials for making up the various articles into portable packs	55.–
For the pay of hunters guides & Interpreters	300.–
In silver coin to defray the expences of the party from Nashville to the last white settlement on the Missisourie	100.–
Contingencies	87.–
Total	$2,500.–

MS (DLC: TJ Papers, 116:19946); entirely in Lewis's hand; undated; endorsed by TJ: "Lewis Meriwether. Estimate Missouri." Not recorded in SJL.

TOTAL: it is likely that Lewis prepared these figures before 18 Jan., when TJ requested an appropriation of $2,500 in his confidential message to Congress about the proposed western expedition. In the spring of 1803, Lewis got some equipment for the expedition at the Harpers Ferry armory, obtained supplies from the government stores at Philadelphia, and had the purveyor of public goods there purchase items that he could not obtain by other means. The purveyor's office recorded $412.95 spent for mathematical instruments; $182.08 for arms, ammunition, and accoutrements; $116.68 for camp equipage; $94.49 for medicines; $669.50 for presents for Indians; $366.70 for provisions; and $317.73 for clothing (Jackson, *Lewis and Clark*, 1:8-9, 93; TJ to the Senate and the House of Representatives, 18 Jan., first message; Lewis to TJ, 20 Apr.).

To Mary Jefferson Eppes

MY DEAR MARIA Washington Jan. 18. 1803.

Your's by John came safely to hand, and informs me of your ultimate arrival at Edgehill. mr Randolph's letter from Gordon's recieved the night before gave me the first certain intelligence I had recieved since your departure. a rumor had come here of your having been stopped two or three days at Bull run and in a miserable hovel; so that I had passed ten days in anxious uncertainty about you. your apologies my dear Maria on the article of expence, are quite without necessity. you did not here indulge yourselves as much as I wished, and nothing prevented my supplying your backwardness but my total ignorance in articles, which might suit you. mr Eppes's election will I am in hopes secure me your company next winter, and perhaps you may find it convenient to accompany your sister in the spring. mr Giles's aid indeed in Congress, in support of our administration, considering his long knoledge of the affairs of the Union, his talents, and the high ground on which he stands through the United States, had rendered his continuance here an object of anxious desire to those who compose the administration: but every information we recieve states that prospect to be desperate from his ill health, and will relieve me from the imputation of being willing to lose to the public so strong a supporter, for the personal gratification of having yourself & mr Eppes with me. I inclose you Lemaire's reciepts. the orthography will be puzzling and amusing; but the reciepts are valuable. present my tender love to your sister, kisses to the young ones, and my affection to mr Randolph & mr Eppes whom I suppose you will see soon. be assured of my unceasing & anxious love for yourself.

TH: JEFFERSON

RC (Gabriel Wells, New York City, 1946); at foot of text: "Mrs. Eppes." PrC (CSmH); endorsed by TJ in ink on verso. Enclosure not found, but see below.

YOUR'S BY JOHN: Mary Jefferson Eppes to TJ, 11 Jan.

MR RANDOLPH'S LETTER: see TJ to Thomas Mann Randolph, 17 Jan.

MR EPPES'S ELECTION: after his term as a member of the Virginia House of Delegates from Chesterfield ended on 29 Jan. 1803, John Wayles Eppes was elected in April as a representative to the Eighth Congress. He began his term with the fall 1803 session (*Biog. Dir. Cong.*; Leonard, *General Assembly*, 227; Richmond *Virginia Argus*, 30 Apr. 1803).

ILL HEALTH prompted the retirement of William Branch Giles, whom some speculated had plans to run for governor. He complained to Madison of an "inflexible perseverance" of rheumatic symptoms and observed that TJ's message to Congress had so clearly marked the path to be followed that there would be no occasion for his services (*New-York Herald*, 25 Dec. 1802; *Charleston Courier*, 16 June 1803; Giles to Madison, 6 Jan. 1803, in DLC: Madison Papers; Vol. 38:81).

For Étienne LEMAIRE'S recipes, see TJ to Martha Jefferson Randolph, 27 Jan.

From Albert Gallatin

DEAR SIR Washington Jany. 18th 1803

As the appropriation bill for the navy is ready to be reported, it is necessary to know in what manner the provisional authorization for six frigates should be introduced.

I would propose that exclusively of the appropriations for the deficiencies of 1802 & of those for the 74s, vessels in ordinary, navy yards & general contingencies, the other naval appropriations amounting for estimate to 476,874.$\frac{86}{100}$ should be voted in manner following to wit.

$\frac{3}{5}$ of the whole *certain* for the frigates & other vessels[1] in actual service	286,000
for the purchase of smaller vessels— say	70,000
certain	356,000
and for such[2] expenses as, with the approbation of the President, may be incurred during the recess of Congress, on account of any vessels which he may think necessary to put in commission (or to employ in actual service) if any war should break out (or, if any hostilities should be committed) between the United States and any of the Barbary powers other than Tripoli—the remaining	120,000
	476,000

The manner in which this should be expressed is wanted[3]

You will be pleased to notice that those 476,000 dollars are the estimate of keeping in actual service, for the whole of the year 1803, six frigates & one schooner—and that there is an additional appropriation of 180,00 dollars which covers all the deficiencies of 1802, including the pay provisions & all other expences of the whole Mediterranean Squadron to the 31st Decer. last. I think, therefore, that $\frac{3}{5}$ths of that estimate will be sufficient to support the intended establishment in the Mediterranean for 1803 if only Tripoli shall continue at war.

In order to bring the whole subject before you, I will from the estimates recapitulate the naval appropriations ordered for this year vizt.

1.	Six frigates & 1 schooner in commission, including repairs & contingencies	476,874.86
2.	7 Frigates in ordinary including repairs & contingencies	100,042.34
3.	Half pay to officers not in service	14,136.—
4.	Stores, military & naval, ordnance &—.	15,000.—
5.	General contingencies (*exclusively* of those for vessels) vizt. store rent, commissions, freight, travelling expences of officers	40,000.—
6.	74-Gun ships	114,425.—
7.	Navy yards, docks,	48,741.37
8.	Marine corps	90,780.43
		900,000.—

exclusively of 181,849.09. for deficiencies of 1802

The appropriations marked 1. 2. 3. & 5. amount to 631,053.20 which, the Secretary of the navy requests may be arranged under following heads vizt.

a.	—Pay of officers & seamen & subsistance of officers		283,993
b.	—Provisions		157,360.20
c.	—Hospital & medical account		7,700.—
d.	Contingent account vizt.		
	repairs & contingencies of vessels in commission—	79,000	
	do—do—of 7 vessels in ordinary	63,000	182,000.—
	general contingencies as pr. No. 5 above	40,000	
			631,053.20

To those two last items of contingencies—63,000 & 40,000 dollars I object as much beyond what is really necessary for those objects: it is incredible that the annual repairs of the frigates in ordinary should amount to 9,000 dollars per frigate; and with no great economy, ten thousand dollars ought to suffice (instead of 40,000) for the general contingencies of commission, rent & travelling expences; since there are appropriations, exclusively of that of 40,000 dollars, for the contingencies of vessels, for repairs, for the contingencies of the marine corps[4] and for stores. What those 40,000 dollars, therefore are for, I am totally at a loss to know: only 16,000 are asked for the military establishment: indeed, I cannot discover any approach towards reform in that department, (the navy) and I hope that you will pardon my stating my opinion on that subject, when you recollect with what zeal & perseverance I opposed for a number of years, whilst in Congress, similar loose demands for money: my opinions on that subject have been confirmed since you have called me in the administration and although I am sensible that in the opinion of many wise & good men, my ideas of expenditures are considered as too contracted; yet I feel a strong confidence that on this particular point I am right. Indeed the possibility of wanting 600,000 dollars more a year, without additional taxes must at this time, be a sufficient apology for urging every practicable economy.

I enclose a letter from Mr Bradley, and one from Mr Wadsworth of Congress. To the last I do not know what answer to make. This cold weather affects me so much that I remained here to day & have troubled you with this letter, instead of waiting on you.

With sincere respect & attachment Your obedt. Servt.

Albert Gallatin

RC (DLC). Recorded in SJL as received from the Treasury Department on 19 Jan. and "navy apprprn. Fosdyck. Russel." Enclosures: (1) Stephen R. Bradley to Gallatin, 17 Jan. 1803, noting that both he and Congressman Israel Smith have informed the president that Republican friends of the administration in Vermont expect the removal of David Russell, collector on Lake Champlain, who is very bitter against the present government; Doctor Jabez Penniman, who wishes to obtain the appointment, is a good Republican of fine reputation who would "discharge the duties of the office to the satisfaction of the Government"; he encloses two letters to be laid before the president, one from James Witherell, judge of the Rutland County Court, the other from Eben W. Judd, the state land officer (RC in DNA: RG 59, LAR; endorsed by TJ: "Genl. Bradley to mr Gallatin. Penniman Jabez v. Russell Collectr. of Alburgh on L. Champlain"). (2) Witherell to Bradley, Burlington, 8 Nov. 1802, relating the wishes of Penniman to be appointed collector and observing "the Public would be well served, and his friends highly Pleased in his obtaining the Office" (RC in same; endorsed by TJ: "Doctr. Witherell to Stephen R. Bradley Doctr. Pennyman to be Collector Alburgh"). (3) Judd to Bradley, 1 Jan. 1803, noting complaints by "some of our Republican friends" that Russell "does not attend at the place appointed by Law" and entrusts a clerk with all of the collector's business; no "man is more bitter nor more officious in his observations & conduct against all those who wish to support our government"; his place should be given to Penniman "or some other person who would use his influance to support the government and friends to the present administration" (RC in same; endorsed by TJ: "Judd to Genl. Bradley. Russell to be removd"). (4) Peleg Wadsworth to Gallatin, Capitol, 15 Jan. 1803, defending Nathaniel F. Fosdick, collector at Portland, as punctual and impartial and noting that if he has displeased anyone it is for his rigid adherence to the letter of the law; the collector is a Federalist but "his Federalism is of that Sort that can give offence to no Man, unless it is an Offence for a mere difference of Opinion"; Wadsworth encloses a letter Fosdick wrote him, dated Portland, 1 Jan. 1803, in which the collector declares that he has attended to the duties of his office with "punctuality & strict attention" and has shown "the most perfect respect for the present administration"; recently "violent prepossessions" have been made against him; as a friend, Fosdick requests that Wadsworth inquire and inform him as soon as possible "if any of the suggestions or insinuations" have been heard in Washington "that I may have an opportunity to justify myself and character to those to whom I am responsible" (RCs in NHi: Gallatin Papers; with a note on Fosdick's letter directed by Gallatin to "Mr Jefferson": "What answer should be given to this? A.G.").

On 15 Feb., John Randolph, chairman of the Committee of Ways and Means, presented the 1803 APPROPRIATION BILL FOR THE NAVY to the House. Four days later the Committee of the Whole House considered the bill and agreed on several amendments. Without further debate, the bill was passed and sent, on 21 Feb., to the Senate. A week later the Senate approved it without amendment (JHR, 4:342, 355-6; JS, 3:269, 277; *Annals*, 12:566). The act signed by TJ on 2 Mch. differed only in the arrangement of the subtotals, above, with Gallatin's A., B., C. categories of $283,993, $157,360.20, and $7,700, respectively, appearing first in the act, followed by No. 4, $15,000 for the "purchase of ordnance and other military stores." The contingent account (D., above) appears next but is not subdivided. The $182,000 is designated for the "repairs of vessels, store rent, and other contingent expenses." Numbers 6, 7, and 8, above, appear next in the act. The $90,780.43 appropriation for the marine corps is subdivided into four categories, but the final sum remains the same. The $900,000 total, excluding the deficiencies for 1802, was the same figure that Gallatin used in his estimates for 1803, submitted to the House on 16 Dec. 1802. In the estimate and in the act of 2 Mch., $198,797.46 was designated to cover the 1802 deficiencies, for a total appropriation of $1,098,797.46. Gallatin's total, above, of $181,849.09 for previous deficiencies, does not include the payment of $16,948.37 to the estate of John Habersham, former collector at Savannah, for naval supplies (U.S. Statutes at Large, 2:208-9; *Letter from the Secretary of the Treasury, Accompanying a Report and Estimates of Appropriation for the Service of the Year 1803; also an Account of the Receipts and Expenditures at the Treasury of the United States, for One Year Preceding the First Day of October, 1802* [Washington, D.C., 1802], 6; note to Annual Message to Congress, 15 Dec.).

OTHER NAVAL APPROPRIATIONS: for Robert Smith's breakdown of the estimate of $476,874.86, see enclosure printed at Gallatin to TJ, 22 Jan.

[1] Preceding two words and ampersand interlined.

[2] Gallatin here canceled "additional."

[3] Preceding sentence written in left margin perpendicular to preceding text.

[4] Preceding seven words interlined.

To James Garrard

SIR Washington Jan. 18. 1803.

Soon after the date of my letter to you of Dec. 16. the Memorial of the Senate & House of Representatives of Kentucky to the President of the US. and the Senate & House of Representatives of Congress came to hand. in that letter I informed you that we had reason to believe that the suspension of the right of deposit at New Orleans was an act merely of the Intendant, unauthorised by his government; that immediately on information of it we had taken measures to have it rectified & that we had been seconded in these by the cordial interposition of the Minister of his Catholic majesty residing here. further information shewing that this act of the Intendant was unauthorised, has strengthened our expectation that it will be corrected.

In order however to provide against the hazards which beset our interests & peace in that quarter, I have determined, with the approbation of the Senate, to send James Monroe, late Governor of Virginia, with full powers to him & our ministers in France & Spain to enter with those governments into such arrangements as may effectually secure our rights and interest in the Missisipi, and in the country Eastward of that. he is now here & will depart immediately. in the mean time knowing how important it is that the obstructions shall be removed in time for the produce which will begin to descend the river in February, the Spanish minister has, at our request, reiterated his interposition with the Intendant of New Orleans.

I inclose you a resolution of the House of Representatives on this subject, which with the measures taken by the Executive, will I hope furnish new grounds for the confidence which the legislature of Kentucky is pleased to express in the government of the US. and evince to them that that government is equally and impartially alive to the interests of every portion of the union.

I pray you to accept assurances of my high respect & consideration.

TH: JEFFERSON

PrC (DLC); at foot of text: "The Governor of Kentucky." Enclosure: Resolution of the House of Representatives, 7 Jan. (see the Editorial Note to TJ to the House of Representatives, 30 Dec.).

See the MEMORIAL of the Kentucky legislature at 1 Dec.

CORDIAL INTERPOSITION: although he had no power over Spanish officials in New Orleans, Carlos Martínez de Irujo had agreed in November to write to Juan Ventura Morales and Manuel de Salcedo about the withdrawal of the right of deposit. Irujo REITERATED his concerns in a second letter to Morales (Madison, *Papers*, *Sec. of State Ser.*, 4:147, 148-9, 153, 154n, 159; Madison to TJ, 10 Mch.).

Notes on Navy Appropriations for 1803

[on or after 18 Jan. 1803]

6. frigates & 1. schooner in commission including repairs & contingencies	476,874.86
7. frigates in ordinary (includ. rep. & conting.)	100,042.34.
half pay to officers not in service	14,136.

Genl. contingencies (*exclusive* of those for vessels) viz. store rent, commissions, freight, travelg. exp. of officers.		40,000
		631,053.20
Stores, military & naval ordnance		15,000.
74. gun ships		114,425.
Navy yards, docks		48,741.37
Marine corps		90,780.43
		900,000.
exclusive of deficiencies of 1802		181,849.09
Pay of officers & seamen & subsistence of officers		283,993.
Provisions		157,360.20
Hospital & medical account		7,700.
Contingt acct. viz	D	
repairs & contingens. of vessels in commn	79,000.	
do. of 7. vessels in ordinary	63,000	
general contingencies as @ contra	40,000	182,000
		631,053.20[1]

		D
2. frigates in commn.	4. months (@75,000 pr. ann.)	50,000
2. do.	6.	75,000
1. do.	1. year	75,000
the Enterprise	1. year	30,000
3. others of 16. guns.	building	72,000
	8 months in commn. (@ 30,000)	60,000
		362,000
7. frigates in ordinary (includg. repairs & contingencies)		100,042.34
half pay of officers not in service		14,136.
Genl. contingencies, viz store rent, commns, freight, travellg		10,000.
		486,178.34

	631,053.20
Saving	144,874.86
Marine corps	90,780.43
	235,655.29

for other expences in the event of war, or danger of it, with any of the Barbary powers, other than Tripoli [2. frigates]6 mo.]	75,000
	561,178.34

Stores and ordnance	15,000–	114,425	
the 74. gun ships	114,425	48,741.37	
Navy yards, docks	48,741.37		178,166.37
			739,344.71
Deficiencies of 1802.	181,849.09		

MS (DLC: TJ Papers, 128:22142); undated, but apparently prepared after receipt of Gallatin to TJ, 18 Jan. (see note 1); entirely in TJ's hand; with notes written on recto and verso; brackets in original.

FRIGATES IN COMMN.: with this entry, TJ begins his notes on the verso in which he calculates savings in several categories for the navy. TJ's notes on the recto are taken from Gallatin's letter to him of 18 Jan.

[1] TJ's notes to this point are based on Gallatin's 18 Jan. letter.

To the Senate and the House of Representatives

CONFIDENTIAL.

GENTLEMEN OF THE SENATE AND OF THE HOUSE OF REPRESENTATIVES.

As the continuance of the Act for establishing trading houses with the Indian tribes will be under the consideration of the legislature at it's present session, I think it my duty to communicate the views which have guided me in the execution of that act; in order that you may decide on the policy of continuing it, in the present or any other form, or discontinue it altogether if that shall, on the whole, seem most for the public good.

The Indian tribes residing within the limits of the US. have for a considerable time been growing more & more uneasy at the constant diminution of the territory they occupy, altho' effected by their own voluntary sales: and the policy has long been gaining strength with them of refusing absolutely all further sale on any conditions. insomuch that, at this time, it hazards their friendship, and excites dangerous jealouses & perturbations in their minds to make any overture for the purchase of the smallest portions of their land. a very few tribes only are not yet obstinately in these dispositions. In order peaceably to counteract this policy of theirs, and to provide an extension of territory which the rapid increase of our numbers will call for, two measures are deemed expedient. First,[1] to encourage them to abandon hunting, to apply to the raising stock, to agriculture and domestic manufacture, and thereby prove to themselves that less land & labour will maintain them in this, better than in their former mode of living. the extensive forests necessary in the hunting life, will then become useless, & they will see advantage in exchanging them for the means of improving their farms, & of increasing their domestic comforts. Secondly[2] to multiply trading houses among them, & place within their reach those things which will contribute more to their domestic comfort than the possession of extensive, but uncultivated wilds. experience & reflection will develope to them the wisdom of exchanging what they can spare & we want, for what we can spare and they want. in leading them thus to agriculture, to manufactures & civilization, in bringing together their & our settlements, & in preparing them ultimately to participate in the benefits of our government, I trust and believe we are acting for their greatest good. At these trading houses we have pursued the principles of the act of Congress, which directs that the commerce shall be carried on liberally, & requires only that the capital stock shall not be diminished. we consequently undersell private traders, foreign & domestic, drive them from the competition, & thus, with the good will of the Indians, rid ourselves of a description of men who are constantly endeavoring to excite in the Indian mind suspicions, fears & irritation towards us. a letter now inclosed shews the effect of our competition on the operations of the traders, while the Indians, percieving the advantage of purchasing from us, are solliciting generally our establishment of trading houses among them. In one quarter this is particularly interesting. the legislature, reflecting on the late occurrences on the Missisipi, must be sensible how desireable it is to possess a respectable breadth of country on that river, from our Southern limit to the Illinois at least; so that we may present as firm a front on that as on our Eastern border. we possess what is below the Yazoo, & can probably acquire a certain breadth from the Illinois & Wabash to the Ohio. but between the Ohio and Yazoo, the country all belongs to the Chickasaws, the most friendly tribe within our limits, but the most decided against the alienation of lands. the portion of their country most important for us is exactly that which they do not inhabit. their settlements are not on the Missisipi, but in the interior country. they have lately shewn a desire to become agricultural, and this leads to the desire of buying implements & comforts. in the strengthening and gratifying of these wants, I see the only prospect of planting on the Missisipi itself the means of it's own safety. Duty has required me to submit these views to the judgment of the legislature, but as their disclosure might embarras & defeat their effect, they are committed to the special confidence of the two houses.

While the extension of the public commerce among the Indian tribes may deprive of that source of profit such of our citizens as are engaged in it, it might be worthy the attention of Congress, in their care of individual as well as of the general interest to point in another direction the enterprise of these citizens, as profitably for themselves, and more usefully for the public. the river Missouri, & the Indians inhabiting it, are not as well known as is rendered desireable by their connection with the Missisipi, & consequently with us. it is however understood that the country on that river is inhabited by various tribes, who furnish great supplies of furs & peltry to the trade of another nation carried on in a high latitude, through an infinite number of portages and lakes, shut up by ice through a long season. the commerce on that line could bear no competition with that of the Missouri, traversing a moderate climate, offering, according to the best accounts, a continued navigation from it's source, and, possibly[3] with a single portage, from the Western ocean, and finding to the Atlantic a choice of channels through the Illinois or Wabash, the lakes and Hudson, through the Ohio and Susquehanna or Potomac or James rivers, and through the Tennissee and Savanna rivers. an intelligent officer with ten or twelve chosen men, fit for the enterprize and willing to undertake it, taken from our posts, where they may be spared without inconvenience, might explore the whole line, even to the Western ocean, have conferences with the natives on the subject of commercial intercourse, get admission among them for our traders as others are admitted, agree on convenient deposits for an interchange of articles, and return with the information acquired in the course of two summers. their arms & accoutrements, some instruments of observation, & light & cheap presents for the Indians, would be all the apparatus they could carry, and with an expectation of souldier's portion of land on their return, would constitute the whole expence. their pay would be going on, whether here or there. While other civilized nations have encountered great expence to enlarge the boundaries of knowledge, by undertaking voyages of discovery, & for other literary purposes, in various parts and directions, our nation seems to owe to the same object, as well as to it's own interests, to explore this, the only line of easy communication across the continent, and so directly traversing our own part of it. the interests of commerce place the principal object within the constitutional powers and care of Congress, and that it should incidentally advance the geographical knowledge of our own continent,[4] cannot but be an additional gratification. the nation claiming the territory, regarding this as a literary pursuit which it is in the habit of permitting within it's dominions, would not be disposed to view it with jealousy, even if the expiring state of it's interests there did not render it a matter of indifference. The appropriation of two thousand five hundred dollars 'for the purpose of extending the external commerce of the US,' while understood and considered by the Executive as giving the legislative sanction, would cover the undertaking from notice, and prevent the obstructions which interested individuals might otherwise previously prepare in it's way. TH: JEFFERSON

Jan. 18. 1803.

RC (DNA: RG 233, PM, 7th Cong., 2d sess.); entirely in TJ's hand; endorsed by clerks as "Confidential" and "Message from the President of the United States, inclosing a letter relative to the concerns of the United States with the Indian tribes, and the establishment of a new settlement"; also endorsed as read in the House on 18 Jan. "and referred to the Committee appointed on so much of the President's message of the 15th. ultimo, as relates to the same objects," and endorsed that the committee reported on 31 Jan. PrC (DLC). RC (DNA: RG 46, LPPM, 7th Cong., 2d sess.); in Meriwether Lewis's hand, signed and dated by TJ; endorsed by clerks. Recorded in SJL with notation "Indian affairs. Missouri. confidential." Enclosure: Extract of Matthew Ernest, collector of customs at Detroit, to Gallatin, 1 Nov., reporting that British merchants who have traded with the Indians through Detroit intend to close their operations because the reduced price of goods offered by the United States trading house "must effectually ruin them, as well as the American traders"; reporting too that the merchants approve of the prohibition on sale of spiritous liquors to the Indians (Tr in DNA: RG 233, PM; in Joshua Wingate, Jr.'s hand, attested by him on 17 Jan.).

In April 1802, Congress revived and extended an expired ACT FOR ESTABLISHING TRADING HOUSES. The law, first passed in April 1796, authorized the president to establish facilities for trade with Indian nations and to appoint agents to run them. The act also appropriated funds for the enterprise. The revived act was due to expire on 4 Mch. 1803 (U.S. Statutes at Large, 1:452-3; 2:173; Vol. 36:440-3).

CARRIED ON LIBERALLY: according to the 1796 statute, the president could establish trading operations at such places "as he shall judge most convenient for the purpose of carrying on a liberal trade with the several Indian nations." Prices at the stores would be regulated to ensure that the CAPITAL STOCK invested by the United States would not be DIMINISHED (U.S. Statutes at Large, 1:452, 453).

TRADE OF ANOTHER NATION: that is, Great Britain. Employees of the Hudson's Bay and North West companies, as well as some independent traders, traveled through Canada to reach the Mandan and Hidatsa Indians on the Missouri River (W. Raymond Wood and Thomas D. Thiessen, eds., *Early Fur Trade on the Northern Plains: Canadian Traders Among the Mandan and Hidatsa Indians, 1738-1818* [Norman, Okla., 1985], 2, 24-30, [299-308]).

NATION CLAIMING THE TERRITORY: Spain. In the latter part of November or very early in December, TJ had a conversation with Carlos Martínez de Irujo to sound out the possible reaction of the Spanish government to an exploration by the United States of the course of the Missouri River. The nominal objective of the expedition would be the advancement of commerce, TJ explained, since Congress could not appropriate funds for the actual purpose of the undertaking, which was the advancement of geographical knowledge. Irujo replied that he did not believe Spain would approve of the undertaking. TJ, according to Irujo's report to his government, then stated that he could not see why there would be any objection to learning more about the territories lying between 40 and 60 degrees north latitude. New information, he urged, in conjunction with the discoveries of Alexander Mackenzie, might establish a route to and from the Pacific. Irujo countered by naming several explorations of the Pacific Coast that confirmed there was no Northwest Passage, and he pointed out that Mackenzie had reached the sea only by traveling much of the way by land. The Spanish minister thought his arguments dampened TJ's enthusiasm for the venture, but he cautioned his government that he did not know what the president's decision would be on the matter. TJ, Irujo reported, might be motivated to extend the influence of the United States to the shores of the Pacific. Irujo learned by late January that TJ had brought the subject to the Senate's attention. Apparently unaware that the House of Representatives had also received the president's message, Irujo thought the Senate would probably quash the expedition (A. P. Nasatir, ed., *Before Lewis and Clark: Documents Illustrating the History of the Missouri, 1785-1804*, 2 vols., [St. Louis, 1952], 2:712-16).

A one-sentence act of Congress approved on 28 Feb. made an APPROPRIATION of $2,500 "for the purpose of extending the external commerce of the United States" (U.S. Statutes at Large, 2:206).

COVER THE UNDERTAKING FROM NOTICE: the House of Representatives put an injunction of secrecy on this communication from the president, and the journals of the House's proceedings on 18 Jan. made no reference to the receipt of the message. The injunction was lifted on 26 Feb. To keep its actions confidential, the Senate went into executive session when Meriwether Lewis delivered the message on 18 Jan. (JHR, 4:291-3, 369; JEP, 1:437-9).

[1] TJ wrote this word in a larger and more ornate hand. Lewis wrote it in a larger hand in RC in RG 46.

[2] TJ wrote this word in a larger hand.

[3] Word interlined in place of "perhaps."

[4] Preceding seven words interlined in place of "the interests of science."

To the Senate and the House of Representatives

GENTLEMEN OF THE SENATE AND OF THE HOUSE OF REPRESENTATIVES

I inclose a report of the Secretary at War, stating the Trading-houses established in the Indian territories, the progress which has been made in the course of the last year, in settling and marking boundaries with the different tribes, the purchases of lands recently made from them, and the prospect of further progress in marking boundaries, and in new extinguishments of title in the year to come; for which some appropriations of money will be wanting.

To this I have to add that when the Indians ceded to us the salt-springs on the Wabash, they expressed a hope that we would so employ them as to enable them to procure there the necessary supplies of salt. indeed it would be the most proper and acceptable form in which the annuity could be paid which we propose to give them for the cession. these springs might at the same time be rendered eminently serviceable to our Western inhabitants, by using them as the means of counteracting the monopolies of the supplies of salt, and of reducing the price in that country to a just level. for these purposes a small appropriation would be necessary to meet the first expences, after which they should support themselves & repay those advances. these springs are said to possess the advantage of being accompanied with a bed of coal.

TH: JEFFERSON
Jan. 18. 1803.

RC (DNA: RG 233, PM, 7th Cong., 2d sess.); endorsed by a clerk. PrC (DLC). RC (DNA: RG 46, LPPM, 7th Cong., 2d sess.); endorsed by a clerk. Recorded in SJL with notation "Indian affairs. public."

Following an assertion by Black Hoof, in February 1802, that the Shawnees had rights to the SALT springs near the mouth of the Wabash River, Dearborn had asked William Henry Harrison to lease the springs for the Indians' benefit. Harrison, however, dismissed the Shawnees' claim to the spot and obtained title to the springs for the United States (Vol. 36:517, 524, 525n; Vol. 38:140, 250-2, 572-3).

TO MEET THE FIRST EXPENCES: an act of Congress of 3 Mch. appropriated $3,000 for the establishment of a salt works at the springs. The law authorized the president to have the works operated at the expense of the United States or to lease out the facility for up to three years "on such conditions as will insure the working the same most extensively, and to the most advantage to the United States" (U.S. Statutes at Large, 2:235).

ENCLOSURE

Henry Dearborn: Report on Indian Affairs

War Department
January 17th. 1803

SIR,

By Treaties held with the Creek and Chocktaw nations of Indians in the course of the last year, considerable tracts of land have been obtained, and there is reason to believe that additional cessions, may be obtained on reasonable terms from the aforementioned and other Indian Nations in the course of the present year.—

The boundary line between the State of North Carolina and the Cherokees has been completed, and the line between the Natchez Territory and the Chocktaws, is probably by this time established and marked in a manner, which it is presumed will be satisfactory to the United States and to the Chocktaw Nation.—

A boundary line has also been agreed on to the tract of land on the Wabash river including Vincennes, which will soon be run and marked, and likewise the lines around the two tracts on the portage between the head Waters of the Wabash and the Miami of the Lake, including Fort Wayne.— Some measures have been taken for ascertaining the boundaries between the Indians and the white People on the Mississippi commonly called the

Kaskaskia settlements, below the Mouth of the Illinois river, but for want of authentic documents, it will probably be necessary to resort to a new Convention with the Indian Nation for establishing said boundaries and for procuring some additional Cessions, for the purpose of affording means for increasing and strengthing that distant & exposed frontier.—

In addition to the Two Factories or Indian Trading houses, heretofore established, it has been considered as advisable to establish four others, (Viz) One at Detroit—One at Fort Wayne—One at Chickasaw Bluffs, and One with the Chocktaws.—The surplus of One hundred and fifty thousand Dollars appropriated by an act of Congress of the 16th. of April 1796 and which had not been applied to the two factories heretofore established on the frontiers of Georgia and Tennessee, has been applied to the four other establishments recently made.—From an investigation of the accounts made and reported to Congress at its last session, it was satisfactorily evident, that the funds employed prior to that period had not been diminished and it is confidently believed that the sum appropriated to that object may be employed not only without diminution, but with great advantage to the public, not in point of commercial profits, but by attatching and securing the friendship and confidence of the Natives, which cannot be sufficiently relied on, while their Towns and hunting Camps are constantly the resort of unprincipled foreign traders, who make every exertion in their power to withdraw the confidence of the Natives from the United States and to inspire them with jealousies and unfriendly dispositions towards our frontier settlers, our public Agents and the Government—The greatest caution has been observed in selecting the Agents for managing the several factories, and in the course of another year, it is presumed that a satisfactory statement may be made of the State of the funds, and of the effects of their application.—

An appropriation of Ten Thousand Dollars* to enable the Executive to embrace any favorable opportunity for obtaining any further cession of land from the Natives, and a renewal of the Act authorising the establishment of trading houses with the Indians, with a renewal of the appropriation for that object is submitted to the consideration of Congress.—

With respectful consideration, I am Sir your Hume. Sert.

H. Dearborn

* This sum is in addition to the *sum* in the general Estimate—

RC (DNA: RG 46, LPPM, 7th Cong., 2d sess.); in a clerk's hand, signed by Dearborn; at head of text: "The President of the United States"; endorsed by a clerk. RC (DNA: RG 233, PM, 7th Cong., 2d sess.); in a clerk's hand, signed by Dearborn; endorsed by a clerk. FC (Lb in DNA: RG 107, LSP).

The act of congress for the establishment of the trading houses, which received approval on 18 (not 16) Apr. 1796, appropriated $150,000 "for the purpose of carrying on trade and intercourse with the Indian nations" (U.S. Statutes at Large, 1:452-3).

Meriwether Lewis delivered the message and enclosure to the House and the Senate on 18 Jan. The House referred the matter to a committee established on 17 Dec. to deal with Indian affairs and the opening of lands to settlement as boundaries between Mississippi Territory and the Choctaws were resolved. John Dawson reported for that committee on 31 Jan., and on 10 Feb. the House agreed that bills should be prepared to meet needs suggested by TJ's message and

Dearborn's report. One of the statutes that resulted was an act of 3 Mch. for the disposition of lands in Mississippi Territory. The APPROPRIATION of $10,000 for further land acquisitions from Indians was included in a general funding act approved on 2 Mch. Another act, of 28 Feb., provided for the RENEWAL of the law on trading houses for two years beginning 4 Mch., and then to the end of the next session of Congress (JS, 3:253-4; JHR, 4:253, 292, 314, 333-4; U.S. Statutes at Large, 2:207, 215, 229-35; Annual Message to Congress, 15 Dec., and note).

To the Senate and the House of Representatives

GENTLEMEN OF THE SENATE AND OF THE HOUSE OF REPRESENTATIVES

I now lay before Congress the annual account of the fund established for defraying the contingent charges of government. a single article of 1440. Dollars, paid for bringing home 72. seamen discharged in foreign ports from vessels sold abroad, is the only expenditure from that fund, leaving an unexpended balance of 18,560. Dollars in the treasury.

TH: JEFFERSON
[Jan. 18. 1803.]

RC (DNA: RG 46, LPPM, 7th Cong., 2d sess.); undated, with date supplied from PrC; endorsed by a Senate clerk as received 19 Jan. PrC (DLC) of letter, now missing, to the House of Representatives; date added by TJ in ink. Recorded in SJL as letters to the Senate and the House of Representatives of 18 Jan. with notation "Contingent account." Enclosure: "Account of the Grant of Twenty thousand Dollars for the Contingent Charges of Government by 'An Act making Appropriations for the support of Government for the year 1802,'" dated Register's Office, 17 Jan. 1803, stating the single payment of $1,440 on 26 Oct. 1802, by order of the president, to "Daniel Cutter & Brothers, Owners of the ship Jefferson, being for the passage of 72 American Seamen in the said ship from Bourdeaux to Norfolk, ℔ Treasury Settlement No. 13,876—and Warrant No. 3859," leaving an unexpended balance on 31 Dec. 1802 of $18,560, to be accounted for in the next annual statement (MS in DNA: RG 233, PM, 7th Cong., 2d sess., in a clerk's hand, signed by Joseph Nourse, endorsed by a House clerk; MS in DNA: RG 46, LPPM, 7th Cong., 2d sess., in same clerk's hand, signed by Nourse, endorsed by a Senate clerk).

Gallatin had forwarded the ACCOUNT from the register's office to the president on 17 Jan., stating: "The Secretary of the Treasury, has the honor to transmit to the President of the United States, triplicates of a statement of Expenditures, upon the Funds heretofore appropriated for defraying the Contingent expenses of Government, up to the 31:st of December last. All which is respectfully submitted" (RC in DLC; in a clerk's hand, signed by Gallatin; at foot of text: "The President of the United States"; endorsed by TJ as received from the Treasury Department on 18 Jan. and "Contingent account" and so recorded in SJL). Regarding the payment for BRINGING HOME discharged seamen, see Vol. 38:531, 564.

The document printed above is recorded in the House and Senate journals as a letter of 19 Jan., the date Meriwether Lewis delivered it to the two chambers.

The letter to the House (now missing) was presumably undated, as was the one to the Senate. The Senate read the letter and accompanying statement on the 19th and referred it to Gouverneur Morris, Stevens Thomson Mason, and Jonathan Dayton. On 19 Jan., the House read and ordered the message and statement to lie on the table (JS, 3:254; JHR, 4:293-4).

From the Town Committee at York, Massachusetts, with Jefferson's Notes

SIR York January 18th. 1803.

The Inclosed Papers presented to your Excellency by the Undersigned Committee appointed in behalf of the Town of York are in the Vindication of the Character of Joseph Tucker Esq. Collector of the Customs for their District and Subscribe ourselves with the Highest Consideration.

Sir. Very respectfully Your Obedient Servants.

MOSES LYMAN
JOSEPH BRAGDON
THEODORE WEBBER
ELIHU BRAGDON
} Selectmen and Committee in behalf of the Town of York.

[*Notes by TJ*:]

Tucker is represented to be constantly drunk and incapable of business, and a violent federalist. the writers of the within are of the same party.

to lie till mr Cutts enquires into facts.

1803. mr Cutts sais Majr. Darby shd be appd.

must say in writing[1]

Darby Saml. to be Collector at York Mass.[2]

RC (DNA: RG 59, LAR); in Lyman's hand, signed by all; at head of text: "To His Excellency Thomas Jefferson Esquire President of the United States of America"; with TJ's notes written on verso above and below endorsement at a later date in two or more sittings; endorsed by TJ as received 28 Jan. and "Tucker Joseph. Collector of York not to be removd" and so recorded in SJL.

A colonel of the militia, Moses Lyman served as town clerk of York from 1802 to 1808 and later as a justice of the peace for York County. Joseph and Elihu Bragdon served terms as representatives from York in the Massachusetts General Court. Both were elected to the town's first school committee in 1800, and Theodore Webber was elected in 1801. Elihu Bragdon was a founding member of the York Cotton Factory Company, the first cotton mill in Maine, incorporated in 1811. He represented York at the 1819 Maine constitutional convention (Charles Edward Banks, *History of York, Maine*, 2 vols. [Baltimore, 1967], 2:217, 263, 280, 354, 358-9; Boston *New-England Palladium*, 21 May 1805; Portland *Freeman's Friend*, 18 June 1808; Kennebunk

Weekly Visitor, 14 Feb. 1818; Boston *Columbian Centinel*, 15 May 1819; Bangor *Weekly Register*, 28 Oct. 1819).

INCLOSED PAPERS: memorial printed below, with the certified summary of the 17 Jan. York town meeting described in the explanatory note.

President Washington appointed JOSEPH TUCKER, a Revolutionary War veteran, collector at York in 1793. He served as town clerk there from 1795 to 1801 (Washington, *Papers, Pres. Ser.*, 13:232-4).

For the recommendation by Richard CUTTS, see his letter to TJ of 25 Nov. Samuel Derby (DARBY) replaced Tucker in Dec. 1803 (TJ to the Senate, 9 Dec.).

[1] Preceding four words possibly written in pencil.

[2] TJ wrote the preceding line above his endorsement, probably after he received the letter from Richard Cutts of 25 Nov. 1803.

ENCLOSURE

Memorial from the Town Committee at York, Massachusetts

The Undersigned a Committe appointed by the Unanimous voice of the Legal Voters assembled in the Town of York in the State of Massachusetts, at a Legal Town Meeting duly notifyed and called by the Selectmen, for the Special purpose of making known

the following facts. That Joseph Tucker Esq. a Collector in the District of York in said State, Was an Officer in the revolutionary War, and as such was highly esteemed, That He was a Member of the Legislature of this State when appointed to the Office of Collector which He now holds, That He has since held every Office in the Town of which He would accept That he is now an amiable Citizen and possesses every qualification, for the proper discharge of the duties of his Office. That no complaint intitled to Credit or belief has, or can now be made against him. That so far as punctual attention and a Strict regard to the Interest of the Goverment, as well as to accomodation of the People doing business at his Office entitle him to your approbation, so far We feel secure in his safety: but knowing as We do—that misrepresentations calculated to deceive are about being made, We cannot but fear their effect. We in behalf of said Town, do assure The President that such misrepresentations are untrue, and that they originate with a Man who is endeavouring to remove the present Collector from his Office that he may thereby be appointed in his Stead. We would further beg leave to suggest that He has always been firmly attached to True Republican principles, which forms our excellent Republican Goverment and We are well assured that He came very near being dismised from his Office by our late President Mr. Addams, only on account of his political principles. for the above and many other reasons We solicit the continuance of the present Collector in his Office, and in duty bound will ever pray your Memorialist.

York January 17th. 1803.

JOSEPH BRAGDON
THEODORE WEBBER
MOSES LYMAN
ELIHU BRAGDON } Committee In behalf of the Town of York.

MS (DNA:RG 59, LAR); in Lyman's hand, signed by all; at head of text: "To the President of the United States."

Joseph Bragdon was chosen "Moderator" of the town meeting held in York on 17 Jan. to respond to efforts to remove JOSEPH TUCKER as collector. MISREPRESENTATIONS CALCULATED TO DECEIVE: the town had learned of Congressman Richard Cutts's letter to Daniel Sewall, court clerk and postmaster at York, informing him that Tucker was to be removed and requesting that he "collect the minds of the Republicans in York" and recommend a replacement. According to the minutes of the town meeting, Sewall, "without consulting the Republicans of this Town, and for interesting motives," recommended Jeremiah Clarke. The meeting noted that Sewall "had not a Republican spirit, in so doing" and in their opinion Clarke was "in no Respect capable" of filling the office. All 106 townspeople present voted in favor of continuing Tucker in the collector's office, declaring that they were "fully satisfyed" with his honesty and integrity and that it would not be in the interest of the United States to remove him. They voted to have the selectmen transmit minutes of the meeting to Cutts and the treasurer of the U.S. and to forward the facts in favor of Tucker to the president (MS of Notes on 17 Jan. Town Meeting in same, in Lyman's hand and certified by him on 18 Jan.; Boston *Columbian Centinel*, 3 June 1795, 13 Feb. 1799; Boston *New-England Palladium*, 21 June 1803; Stets, *Postmasters*, 133).

Petition of Augustus B. Woodward and Others, with Jefferson's Order

Washington January 18. 1803.

The Subscribers beg leave to represent to the President that a man by the name of John Henderson was tryed and Convicted before the Circuit Court of the District of Columbia for the County of Washington during their present Term for keeping a gaming table and fined agreeable to Our Laws One hundred thirty three dollars thirty three and one third Cents which together with the Costs of the Prosecution Amounts to a sum which he is intirely unable to pay. We are informed that this is a poor but honest man who owes his Misfortune rather to an unfortunate aquaintance than a disposition to violate the laws of his Country, and that his wife and Several Small Children are in a Situation truly distressing as their only Support is derived from his personal labour and that his confinement has thrown them on the Charity of their Neighbours. Supposing that his confinement has Attoned for his Offence and that a Continuation of it will only be a Continuation of expence on the part of the United States, We feel it Our duty to recommend him to the Clemency of the President

AUGUSTUS B. WOODWARD

[*Order by TJ*:]

a pardon to be issued TH: JEFFERSON

MS (DNA: RG 59, GPR); in a clerk's hand, signed on verso by Woodward, George Hadfield, Benjamin More, and eleven others; at head of text: "To the President of the United States of America"; statement at foot of text in U.S. Attorney John Thomson Mason's hand and signed by him, declaring "I believe the above is a correct statement"; statements of concurrence with Mason's declaration in the hands of Uriah Forrest, Daniel Carroll Brent, and William Cranch and signed by them; with TJ's order written below signed statements.

On 25 Jan., TJ issued a pardon to JOHN HENDERSON, remitting his fines and the cost of his prosecution and ordering all other proceedings against him to be stayed and discharged (FC in Lb in same).

From John Wayles Eppes

DEAR SIR, Richmond Jan: 19. 1803.

Mr Lewis Harvey of this place is anxious to accompany Colo. Monroe as Secretary to the embassy to which he has been lately appointed—He has requested me to convey to you his wishes with which I the more readily comply, as I am aquainted with no man of his age whose claims are better on the ground of Talent of private worth and of principle—

accept for your health & happiness my warm wishes.

Yours sincerely JNO. W. EPPES

P.S. I take the liberty of enclosing a letter for Colo. Monroe which you will be kind enough to forward wherever he may be—

RC (ViU: Edgehill-Randolph Papers); endorsed by TJ as received 23 Jan. and so recorded in SJL. Enclosure not found.

From Lewis Harvie

SIR [19 Jan. 1803]

I avail myself of that acquaintance which it is my happiness to enjoy to address to you a letter on the application which has been made to you through the agency of my friends. A sentiment of delicacy induced me in the first instance to be silent; but maturer, I hope more just reflections have determined me to explain to you my motives in requesting the post of Secretary in the mission which the folly of foreign nations has rendered necessary. If I considered this as a post of profit I should feel degraded by the conduct which I have pursued: I shudder at the suspicion that my political character could be influenced by hopes of personal emolument. It is unnecessary I flatter myself to call to your recollection that my principles were avowed in the most explicit language, at a period when Republicanism offered to its votarys as a reward only the danger of Martyrdom. In a pecuniary point of view this appointment would be probably injurious; for it will abstract me from a profession which gives to Industry and Integrity ample remuneration for the exertions it compels; And whatever the salary may be, although I should not imitate the philosopher who impatient of delay threw away his treasure in the *desert*, I beleive my accumulated riches would very little retard my progress homeward. A visit to Europe has long been the object of my fondest desire, of my most anxious solicitude. An opportunity of examining the governments of the old World, of witnessing the manners of its Inhabitants & of tracing more accurately the causes which have checked their *moral* improvement appears to me calculated to energize and adorn any mind; and I will not deny that an infantine desire of amusement, of viewing their architecture, their paintings and their sculpture may have given the acmé to a passion which I feel in every pulsation of my frame. No moment of my life could be more favourable to the indulgence of this wish than the present. I have within a few months obtained a licence to practise law; but not having hitherto attended any court, I am free from ingagements which might retard my departure. Should my return from Europe be immediate, I could resume the profession I abandon; if prolonged, I have the prospect of a patrimonial estate which insures to me an honorable independence. Prompted by those considerations, I induced those gentlemen who have communicated my wishes to you, to request for me an appointment which will enable me to view European Society in its most polished form. An application has also been made to Mr Monroe, as I have understood it is customary to consult the wishes of the minister. The personal intercourse which has passed between Mr Monroe & myself has been but slight; It is not impossible that unfavourable impressions may be entertained by him towards me; if they are not removed by the inform[ation] which I hope it is in your power to afford, and to [...] which those gentlemen whom I am proud to call my friends have given to my pretensions, I shall have cause to regret that the calumnies with which my enemies have assailed me should have found their way to the breast of one who ought to know from his own experience, that the Voice of Federalism is not the Oracle of Truth. I have conveyed my sentiments not in the formal language I should assume to a stranger, but in that candid and plain manner, which an acquaintance is supposed to justify. I have only to observe that the rejection of this application can excite but feeble emotions, compared with those which swell within my breast at the recollection of those favours which I received at the most critical moment of my life. LEWIS HARVIE

RC (DLC); undated; torn; addressed: "Thomas Jefferson esqre. President of the United States City of Washington"; franked; postmarked Richmond, 19 Jan.; endorsed by TJ as received 23 Jan. and so recorded in SJL.

The son of John Harvie of Belvidere, Lewis Harvie (1782-1807) attended William and Mary in 1798. He offered his services as TJ's secretary sometime after the latter's election as president. Harvie began a course of study under John Thomson Mason in Georgetown, with the intention of setting up a legal practice in Baltimore, but he gave up this idea when the president asked him to succeed Meriwether Lewis as secretary. He served in this post, while still pursuing his studies, for about a year. Having established a practice in Richmond, Harvie was elected to represent the city in the House of Delegates in 1805, developing a reputation as a stirring, if perhaps overheated, orator. He was elected again the following year but resigned the seat after his colleagues elevated him to the Council of State. Ill for about the last 18 months of his life, he died in April 1807 in Norfolk, "on his way to France, for the benefit of his health" (Richmond *Enquirer*, 9 Dec. 1806, 21 Apr. 1807; Leonard, *General Assembly*, 241, 245; Gerard W. Gawalt, "'Strict Truth': The Narrative of William Armistead Burwell," VMHB, 101 [1993], 116-17; Harvie to TJ, [before 12 Mch. 1803]; TJ to William A. Burwell, 26 Mch. 1804).

From Edward Livingston

SIR New York Jany 19. 1803.

I take the liberty of enclosing for your perusal the outline of a plan lately formed in this city for promoting the cultivation of the fine arts. having seen and admired the master pieces they have produced abroad I am sure it will be gratifying to your love of country that an attempt should be made to improve them at home. under this impression no apology I believe is necessary for asking your patronage and advice in the progress of the undertaking

I have added to it the project of another plan which tho entirely local may perhaps not be wholly void of interest, if you should find liesure for its perusal—I am with the greatest Respect Sir Your Mo Obd Ser EDWARD LIVINGSTON

RC (DLC); at foot of text: "The President of the US"; endorsed by TJ as received 26 Jan. and so recorded in SJL. Enclosures not found, but see below.

PLAN LATELY FORMED: at the urging of his brother Edward, Robert R. Livingston, while minister to France, agreed to procure and send to New York casts "of all the finest antique statues" to serve as the foundation of a gallery and school of sculpture. A subscription of $50 shares, in the summer of 1802, raised about $3,000 to purchase the models, and it was proposed that a society be formed to establish an adequate fund to continue the acquisitions. On 4 Dec., the *Morning Chronicle* printed the minutes of the first official meeting of the New-York Academy of the Fine Arts, with Edward Livingston elected president and Peter Irving, editor of the *Chronicle*, secretary. On 22 Jan., the newspaper included an article signed by Livingston outlining the goals of the new society. An increase in the number of shares to 500 would raise $25,000 to complete the collection of casts and to procure good copies of the best masters of painting, "together with a few originals," as well as a selection of architectural models and plans. They would be exhibited at a gallery open to the public for an admission fee. Livingston envisioned using the collection as the foundation of the first school for the fine arts in the United States (New York *Daily Advertiser*, 30 June 1802; New York *Morning Chronicle*, 27 Oct. 1802, 22 Jan. 1803; Kline, *Burr*, 2:744n; Richard A. Harrison, *Princetonians, 1776-1783: A Biographical Dictionary* [Princeton, 1981], 331-2). In 1808, the New York state legislature incorporated the society as "The American Academy of the Arts" (*The Charter and By-Laws of the American Academy of the Arts. With an Account of the Statues, Busts, Paintings, Prints, Books, and Other Property Belonging to the Academy* [New York, 1817], 3).

From "A Merchant of Charleston"

Charleston South Carolina
19th January 1803

SIR/

I take the liberty of addressing you on a subject which I conceive of consequence; a certain Mr Campbell lately imported into this port a Quantity of Dry Goods from Europe and according to the custom House Rules at this place, lodged his Entry, but with *false* Invoices to amount of about 3 or 4 thousand pounds Sterling instead of 7 or 8 Thousand pounds with intent to defraud the Revenue of about ½ the Duty thereon which would probably have amountingd to 6 or 7 thousand Dollars, on one of the Clerks mentioning this matter to the Collector he gave directions to have the Goods brought to the Custom House, in consequence of which the importer withdrew his Entry & false invoices, without having taken the oath thereon which is usually done the next day; the collector afterwards commenced an action against him—but at trial he was discharged as there was no proof against him—had the Collector done his Duty by not informing the importer of his suspicions, but suffered him to swear to his Entry & invoices which he would have done, then the proof would have been enough to have forfeited the Goods; instead of which the Collector put him in the way of escaping the Law, and even went so far as to send his own Son to a Lawyer with Campbell the importer to take advice from him as defendant & also said *publicly* in his office that he would pay the Lawyers fee himself—as Campbell said he had not money to do it, this transaction is well known in this City. I have therefore thought proper to communicate the matter to you *secretly*, though it could be publicly proved if necessary—this while an officer is placed by Government to execute the Laws and detect & punish Rogues who attempt to defraud the Revenue he puts him in the Road to escape justice & encourages him to continue his malpractices, & at the same time discourages honest men from paying the *full* Duties on the Goods which they may import—This Mr Campbell has since made another entry of these Goods and lodged other Invoices to calculate the Duty on, which amount to nearly if not quite double the amount of the false ones first lodged & afterwards taken away—

There are several other transactions of this Collector which require correction—the Drawback Business is done by his Son a Lad lately from College, who is not acquainted with the Quality of Goods & rates of the Duties which he calculates frequently before the impost Entry is calculated, & these entries are certified by persons in the Naval office equally as ignorant as himself—the cancelling of Exportation Bonds has been neglected for several months past, most of the Entries for goods imported in October last are yet uncalculated as he has discharged a number of his Clerks within a few months wishing to make as much from his office as possible; in consequence of which the Business since 1st Oct last has not been kept up as before, which is a great inconvenience to the Merchant and no doubt must be so to Government provided he does not send on all his Accounts & Returns within the times prescribed by Law—As I have had frequent occasions to transact Business at the Custom House, these facts have come within my knowledge and can be proved in case an enquiry is made into them—I therefore hope you will be pleased to take them into your serious consideration. I am decidedly of opinion that the interest & economy of the Government would be promoted greatly if Congress or yourself would appoint a proper person to visit & examine the manner of executing the different Departments of the Custom House Business in the Custom Houses of the United States, as it is impossible at present for the different blunders & negligences of all the officers to be Known to Government—In this port the naval officer is governed by the Collector in allmost every instance of his official Duty, instead of his being a check on the Collector—in fact several other instances of neglect & improper conduct could be produced, but those before mentioned are in my opinion sufficient at present to induce you to consider whether some correction ought or ought not to take place—

You will no doubt keep this communication *secret*, from this collector as my object is not to be considered as an informer, but to have Custom House transactions executed properly, which is very far from being the Case at present in the united States—

with Sentiments of consideration, I remain Your Humble Servant

A MERCHANT OF CHARLESTON

RC (NHi: Gallatin Papers); at foot of text: "Thomas Jefferson Esqr."; addressed in another hand: "Mr. Gallatin Secy of the Treasury Washington"; endorsed by TJ as received from "Anon." on 2 Feb. and so recorded in SJL; also endorsed by TJ: "Collector of Charleston."

For other anonymous letters critical of the collector at Charleston, James Simons, see Vol. 35:713-14 and Vol. 36:91-3, 266-8.

HIS OWN SON: probably Charles Dewar Simons (*S.C. Biographical Directory, House of Representatives*, 3:648-50; Charleston *City Gazette and Daily Advertiser*, 6 Oct. 1802).

For a previous complaint on the cancellation of EXPORTATION BONDS, see "A. B." to TJ, 2 Jan. 1802. In 1802, Simons reported $11,039 in fees and commissions, with a note that the income from commissions on bonds was incomplete pending a decision in the Treasury Department. He paid almost $7,000 for the hire of CLERKS. Only the Boston and New York collectors paid more, $7,262.50 and $10,153.07, respectively. Simons reported an income of $3,518.26, after the payment of salaries and other expenses (*Letter from the Secretary of the Treasury, Transmitting a Letter from the Comptroller to Him, Dated the 23d Instant, Accompanied with a Statement of the Emoluments of the Officers, Employed in the Collection of the Customs, for the Year 1802* [Washington, D.C., 1803]).

NAVAL OFFICER: Thomas Waring (same; Vol. 33:513).

From Robert Smith, with Jefferson's Note

Nav: Dep:

SIR! 19th Jany 1803

The enclosed Letter, to Mr Eustis is proposed in answer to a Letter received from him some time since. I have mentioned *four small vessels* instead of *three*—that if it shall be deemed proper to purchase a Zebec, the purchase may be made out of the money that may be appropriated, in pursuance of my Recommendation to Mr. Eustis—

I have the honor to be with the greatest respect & esteem, Sir, your mo: ob: St

RT SMITH

[*Note by TJ*:]

	D		
building a 14.	20,000.	a 16.	24,000
annual exp.	27,000		30,000

RC (DLC); in a clerk's hand, signed by Smith; at foot of text: "President U States"; endorsed by TJ as received from the Navy Department on 19 Jan. and "small vessels" and so recorded in SJL. FC (Lb in DNA: RG 45, LSP). Enclosure: Smith to William Eustis, 18 Jan. 1803, replying to a letter from Eustis dated 23 Dec. 1802; to better protect American seamen and commerce in the Mediterranean and elsewhere, Smith recommends that Congress authorize the construction or purchase of four small vessels of war not exceeding 16 guns each, leaving the means of acquisition to the president's discretion; Smith subjoins a cost estimate for building a vessel of 14 or 16 guns, calculating an average cost of $24,000 per vessel; if Congress authorizes the procurement of these vessels, Smith believes that an appropriation of $96,000 would be adequate; Smith also encloses an estimate of the annual expense of maintaining a vessel of 14 and 16 guns, respectively (NDBW, 2:346).

Congressman William EUSTIS was a member of the House committee appointed 17 Dec. 1802 to consider the part of TJ's annual message relating to Tripoli and the other Barbary states. The committee presented its report on 25 Jan., which the House considered the following day. After debate, the House agreed to a resolution that "provision ought to be made, by law, for building or purchasing four vessels of war, to carry not exceeding sixteen guns each" and ordered a bill brought in on the subject. On 28 Feb. 1803, Congress passed "An Act to provide an additional armament for the protection of the seamen and commerce of the United States," appropriating $96,000 for the purpose and an additional $50,000 for the construction of up to 15 gunboats (JHR, 4:253, 301, 304; U.S. Statutes at Large, 2:206).

From Dr. John Vaughan

Wilmington Jany. 19th 1803.

Will Mr. Jefferson be so obliging as to accept the little pamphlet on fever, per mail of the day. The importance of the subject is the best apology the writer can offer for submiting his[1] observations to the better judgements of others. The origin & nature of the malignant disease which has afflicted various parts of our Country for some years, is a common object of interest & inquiry.

Be pleased, also, to accept the respectful tender of esteem & veneration, from your devoted hbl Servt. JNO. VAUGHAN

RC (DLC); endorsed by TJ as received 22 Jan. and so recorded in SJL.

LITTLE PAMPHLET ON FEVER: *A Concise History of the Autumnal Fever, which prevailed in the Borough of Wilmington in the Year 1802* (Vol. 32:269n).

[1] Vaughan here canceled "[hearty]."

From William Helms

Thursday, 20th Jany 1803

Helms, informs the President of the United States, *he cannot* accept his invitation, contained in his note of yesterday, to dine on friday.

RC (MHi); addressed: "The President of the United States"; endorsed by TJ: "Helms J."

TJ's NOTE OF YESTERDAY to the New Jersey congressman is not recorded in SJL and has not been found.

From John Langdon

SR. Portsmouth Jany 20th. 1803

I am informed that a statement of the conduct of our Destrict Judge Mr. Pickering has been transmitted to government, by which it will be seen, by intemperence and other causes, it would be highly improper he should be continued a moment longer in his important office, if he is removed and it should be your pleasure to appoint John Sam. Sherburne Esq who is now the Destrict attorney who I think would fill the office of Judge to your Approbation; in which case I beg leave to Name John Steel Esq of Durham near this Town a gentleman of the Law, and now Clerk of the Destrict Court, as well qualified to take the place of Mr. Sherburne as Destrict Attorney, and who, no doubt would give general satisfaction.

I have the honor to be with the highest consideration and respect. Sr. your Oblig'd Hbl. Servt JOHN LANGDON

RC (DNA: RG 59, LAR); at foot of text: "President of the United States"; endorsed by TJ as received 29 Jan. and so recorded in SJL with notation "Shelburne & Steel to office"; also endorsed by TJ: "Sherburne John Sam. to be distr. judge v. Pickering Steel John. to be District atty v. Sherburne."

For the CONDUCT of federal judge John PICKERING of New Hampshire, and his subsequent impeachment and removal by Congress, see Langdon to TJ, 14 May 1802, and TJ to the House of Representatives, 3 Feb. 1803. Following Pickering's removal in 1804, TJ appointed John S. SHERBURNE to the U.S. district judgeship and Jonathan Steele (STEEL) in place of Sherburne as U.S. attorney for New Hampshire. Steele, however, declined the appointment, stating that "I was unwillingly made a contributory instrument in creating vacancies; and a due regard to my own reputation forbids me to profit by that achievement" (JEP, 1:466; Madison, *Papers, Sec. of State Ser.*, 7:108-9).

In an undated note, TJ recorded additional recommendations for the position of U.S. attorney in New Hampshire made by William Eustis: "Henry Langdon son of Woodbury to be atty of N.H. by Dr. Eustis his bror in law. Jacob Eustis bror of the Dr. he prays he may have no office yet very fit for it" (MS in DNA: RG 59, LAR, 7:0055; entirely in TJ's hand).

From John Lithgow

SIR Philada Jany. 20th 1803

although you never Subscribed for the "Temple of Reason" we thought proper to send it forward to you for about 2. years. the Second Vol. is nearly complete and we intend at that period to decline it—

We have no claim upon you, & never intended to make any: but as we shall be considerable losers by the undertaking and are determined to fullfil our obligations that the Christians may have nothing wherewith to reproach us, we beg leave to let you know how the two Vols. may be paid for which is 6. Dol. if you think them worth viz *To Henry Voigt—Coiner of the Mint*

I am with due respect, yr ms. obt. Servt.

J LITHGOW
for the proprietors of the
Temple of Reason

RC (DLC); endorsed by TJ as received 24 Jan. and so recorded in SJL.

A former Scottish loom builder who was associated with an unsuccessful manufacturing venture in the 1790s, John Lithgow (d. 1834?) wrote anonymously or pseudonymously for several publications. He claimed authorship of *The Collected Wisdom of Ages, the Most Stupendous Fabric of Human Invention, the English Constitution*, written as "Timothy Telltruth" and published in Philadelphia in 1799. A serialized utopian tract, *Equality—A Political Romance*, published in 1802, and *An Essay on the Manufacturing Interest of the United States*, published in Philadelphia in 1804, are also attributed to him (Sowerby, No. 3309; PMHB, 106 [1982], 344, 346, 361-2; *Baltimore Gazette and Daily Advertiser*, 1 Oct. 1834; Lithgow to TJ, 24 Dec. 1804). For Lithgow's background, see Vol. 37:318n.

TEMPLE OF REASON: according to his financial records, on 16 Feb. TJ had George Logan pay Henry Voigt $6 for the two volumes of the weekly deistic publication. The final issue of the newspaper was apparently that of 19 Feb. 1803 (MB, 2:1092; Brigham, *American Newspapers*, 2:953-4).

To John Page

DEAR SIR Washington Jan. 20. 1803.

I take the liberty of introducing to your notice the bearer hereof, mr Olsen, minister of his Danish majesty residing here. his public and diplomatic character would of course mark him to you as an object of deserved respect and attention wheresoever he may present himself; but his personal character authorises me to assure you you will find him a person entitled to more than formal civilities. honesty, candor and simplicity have claims on us all independant of public station, and no one I am sure will be more ready than yourself, to meet them with cordiality. in your attentions therefore to this gentleman, besides the respect to merit which your own dispositions always lead you to render, you will have the further inducement of obliging an ancient and constant friend, who takes this opportunity of renewing to you assurances of his affectionate attachment and high consideration.

TH: JEFFERSON

PrC (DLC); at foot of text: "Governor Page." Enclosed in TJ to Peder Blicher Olsen, [21 Jan.].

To Peder Blicher Olsen

[21 Jan. 1803]

Th: Jefferson presents his friendly salutations to mr Olsen and incloses him a letter for the Governor of Virginia of which he prays him to be the bearer. as a traveller wishes to know what is most worth seeing at any place which he visits, Th:J. informs mr Olsen that at Richmond the objects to be seen, are the Capitol, & it's model kept at the Governor's house the Penitentiary, the Manufactory of arms, and the James river canal of about 6. miles in length. the whole may be seen between breakfast & dinner.

Th:J. has recieved by the stage from Baltimore a box containing a dozen bottles of wine, with this stamp on the bottle.  no letter or explanation accompanied it, but he suspects it to be the Tokay of which mr Olsen was so kind as to undertake to direct the person who had it, to send him a small quantity. is he right in his conjecture?

Th:J. is still going through the little book of French Neology which he finds very amusing. he will be ready to return it when mr Olsen gets back from Richmond. he advises him much against setting out on his journey until the weather becomes milder, which cannot according to our experience, be more than a few days.

PrC (DLC); undated. Recorded in SJL as a letter of 21 Jan. Enclosure: TJ to John Page, 20 Jan.

The BOOK OF FRENCH NEOLOGY to which TJ was referring may have been the 1801 work by Louis Sébastien Mercier, *La Néologie, ou vocabulaire de mots nouveaux, à renouveler, ou pris dans les acceptions nouvelles*. Mercier structured the work according to the many French lexicons of new words that appeared during the Revolution, but far from a dictionary, *La Néologie* operated as humorous social criticism and as a celebration of the creativity inherent to all language formation (Daniel Rosenberg, "Louis-Sébastien Mercier's New Words," *Eighteenth-Century Studies*, 36 [2003], 367-86). Although TJ owned several works by Mercier, there is no record of his owning *La Néologie*. He did own a 1795 French lexicon, *Nouveau Dictionnaire Français, contenant les expressions de nouvelle création du Peuple Français*, by Leonhard Wilhelm Snetlage, a professor at the University of Göttingen (Sowerby, No. 4828). Snetlage's dictionary is mostly notable for having inspired in 1797 a critical response by Giacomo Casanova. It was the Italian adventurer and scholar's last publication (*Ma voisine, la postérité: à Leonard Snetlage, docteur en droit de l'université de Goettingue* [Paris, 1998]).

From Daniel Carroll Brent

SIR, Washington, January 21st. 1803

I now enclose you the account and copies of the Contract and Bill of particulars respecting the Jail directed at the last Session of Congress, to be built in this City.

Although every effort was made to complete the Plan adopted for the Sum appropriated, it could not be done:—it was then determined to finish only certain parts of the Building, and to keep the amount for such as should be finished within the appropriation—Messrs. Huddlestone & Nesmith contracted to complete all the Building except the interior of the west wing and the Iron grated Doors which were at first contemplated to be put in, for the Sum of Dollars 7,426. and Mr. George Hadfield, whose Plan was adopted was appointed to superintend the erection of the Building.—An Estimate of the Sum necessary to complete the west wing in the same manner as the east wing, is herewith transmitted which amounts to the Sum of two thousand five hundred & seventy seven Dollars leaving out all the iron grated Doors—if a Kitchen should be built, and one is absolutely necessary, the further Sum of about three hundred Dollars will be wanted—

The Contractors have completed their Work, except a few articles which will be done.—In the 6th Article of the Contract, it is stipulated that such alterations or additions to the mode of building the Jail as could not be adjusted by the Parties, was to be left to reference—Some alterations were considered as proper and directed by the Superintendent, and one respecting the cell Doors was directed by me. The Contractors claim for extra Work, the Sum of one thousand and ninety eight Dollars:—on this subject however, there is a considerable difference between the Superintendent and them.—They claim for many things as extra work—which he does not admit to be extra. There is also a difference of opinion between them on the amount of the deduction that ought to be made in the Iron work—If he is correct in his opinion, there remains the Sum of Dollars $449. for extra work only to be examined, which will be seen by a reference to his Letter to me a copy of which is sent. The Contractors under the 5th Article of the Contract, claim a right of reference upon those subjects. If all these claims should be established & congress determine to finish the Jail and build the Kitchen, the Sum of Dollars 3,702$\frac{66}{100}$ in addition to the Sum of Dollars 272$\frac{34}{100}$ of the Sum appropriated which is in hand, will be requisite.—

When I appointed Mr. Hadfield the Superintendent, I agreed to give him for his services the Sum of two hundred Dollars, and this is the amount of his claim against me; but he states that he thinks this Sum too small a compensation for his trouble—he has, in drawing Plans, making out Bills of particulars & Estimates and superintending the work, been closely engaged for seven months, and that two Dollars per day for his services cannot be thought unreasonable—and I must do Mr. Hadfield the Justice to say, that I think the Sum of $200 is not a sufficient compensation for his trouble, and I believe he has been very attentive—If it should be thought proper to come up to Mr. Hadfield's idea, the Sum of $220 more will be wanted on his account.

with sentiments of the highest respect I am Sir yr. obt sert

Daniel C. Brent

RC (DNA: RG 233, PM, 7th Cong., 2d sess.); in a clerk's hand, closing and signature in Brent's hand; addressed: "The President"; endorsed by TJ as received 22 Jan. and so recorded in SJL; endorsed by a House clerk. Tr (DNA: RG 46, LPPM); in Meriwether Lewis's hand. Enclosures: (1) Statement of account between the United States and Brent, 21 Jan. 1803, listing payments made by Brent from 26 July 1802 to 20 Jan. 1803, recording a balance of $272.34 remaining in Brent's hands, and a list of warrants drawn on the Treasury Department from 20 Aug. to 12 Oct. 1802 from the appropriation of $8,000 for the Washington jail, recording a balance of $2,200 not yet drawn (MS in DNA: RG 233, PM, in a clerk's hand, signed by Brent; Tr in DNA: RG 46, LPPM, in Lewis's hand). (2) George Hadfield to Brent, Washington, 19 Jan. 1803, informing Brent that the new jail is finished except for a few items that may be completed at a later time; Hadfield believes the work has been done "with fidelity to the Contract" and describes the structure as "plain but the work is strong substantial and firm"; some extra expenses have unavoidably arisen, either for work deemed "greatly advantageous to the Building" or other unforeseen contingencies; in consequence of these additional articles, the contractors have brought $962 in extra claims, of which Hadfield rejected $253 as unfounded; the remaining $709 is for iron work and "other Articles ordered for reasons as above mentioned"; Hadfield deducts an additional $260 for the omission of the iron frames, leaving a remaining sum of $449 for "extras to be examined"; Hadfield presumes that if Brent approves of the building, he will receive it and close the contract with the undertakers without delay, leaving the business of the extra claims to be settled at a later time; in a postscript, Hadfield adds a list of "Articles to be completed by agreement," which includes painting the cornice of the north side and two ends, pointing in slating, finishing painting the inside and outside bars, fixing the grate in the jailer's room, and repairing any plaster damaged by frost; Hadfield closes by stating that another claim by James Maitland amounting to £52.4 "is positively inadmissable" (Tr in DNA: RG 233, PM, endorsed by a House clerk; Tr in DNA: RG 46, LPPM, in Lewis's hand). (3) George Hadfield, "Estimate of the expence necessary for finishing the interior of the West side of the new Jail in the City of Washington," dated Washington, 18 Jan. 1803, estimating a total cost of $2,577 for labor and materials, with a notation in Brent's hand at the foot of text, "Iron Grated Door in this Estimate is not included, or is the Kitchen, which if built will cost about 300$" (MS in DNA: RG 233, PM, endorsed by a House clerk; Tr in DNA: RG 46, LPPM, in Lewis's hand). Printed in *Message from the President of the United States, Transmitting Sundry Documents, Relative to the Affairs of the City of Washington, in the District of Columbia* (Washington, D.C., 1803), 13-17. Other enclosures not found. All enclosed in TJ to the Senate and the House of Representatives, 24 Jan. 1803.

For the construction on the new JAIL in Washington, D.C., see Vol. 37:138-40, 665-6, 694-6; Vol. 38:155-6, 164-5. Congress appropriated $8,000 for the purpose on 3 May 1802.

To Thomas C. James

SIR Washington Jan. 21. 1803

A pressure of business for some days past has prevented my acknoleging the reciept of your favor of the 7th. inst. informing me that at the last annual election of officers of the American Philosophical society, they had been pleased unanimously to re-elect me their President. I beg leave through you, Sir, to express my thankfulness to the society for the reiterated proofs of their good will to me, & to assure them of my sincere devotion to the society itself, as well as of my attachment to it's members individually. entirely engrossed by the duties of another office, I feel with pain my inability to render those services which the kindness of my colleagues ought to command from me: and can only repeat assurances that my zeal for the interests of science is unabated, and my disposition to be useful to our institution, whenever occasions arise, will continue always the same. I pray you to accept for the society and for yourself assurances of my high consideration and respect. TH: JEFFERSON

RC (PPAmP); addressed: "Thomas C. James esq. Secretary of the Amern. Philos. society Philadelphia"; endorsed for the APS. PrC (DLC).

Thomas C. James (1766-1835), a Philadelphia physician, specialized in obstetrics. Educated at the University of Pennsylvania, he received additional medical training in London and at the University of Edinburgh. In 1803, he served as one of the secretaries of the American Philosophical Society, a position that he had held on earlier occasions as well (ANB; APS, *Proceedings*, 22, pt. 3 [1884], 320, 330; Vol. 30:273n).

FAVOR OF THE 7TH. INST.: James wrote to TJ from Philadelphia on 7 Jan. to report that TJ had been unanimously reelected president of the American Philosophical Society on that day. James enclosed a list of the officers selected in the annual election, including Robert Patterson, Caspar Wistar, and Benjamin Smith Barton as vice presidents, James and three others as secretaries, and John Vaughan as treasurer (RC in DLC, at foot of text: "Thomas Jefferson Esqr.," endorsed by TJ as received 10 Jan. and so recorded in SJL; enclosure: list of officers, 7 Jan., MS in same, entirely in James's hand). ASSURE THEM OF MY SINCERE DEVOTION: the society received TJ's acknowledgment of his election at a meeting held on 4 Feb. (APS, *Proceedings*, 22, pt. 3 [1884], 332).

From James A. Stewart

DEAR SIR New York Jany. 21st. 1803

Inclosed I send you for Convinence, the Report of the Commitee of Congress, on Countervaling Dutys, on Vessells, & Raw Materials of the United States, this Paper was Printed Yesterday, and its Contents hurt my feelings very much, finding on perusial that a Dedly blow, was struck by the British and French Nations, on the Navigation of the United States.

Bred a Mercht. which Occupation I have followed for thirty Six years, and a true Patriot for my Country, having during the Revenational Warr, with Great Britain, I was Concerned in 4th. 5th. 6th. & 8ths. in thirty two arm'd Vessells, each Carrying a Commission and Carrying from Twenty four Guns, down to Eight, am now Retired from Bussiness, have leasure time on hands, to peruse the Politicks of the World,—I am Intimately acquainted, with the Vice President, and Mr. Dewint Clinton, of Either of them your may Know my Character if you think it worth your while to ask them Respecting it.

I beg Sir you will pardon the Freedom I have taken in addressing you, but Knowing my Intention flows from a good Hart, and in a good Cause for the love of my Country, I could not Refrain from Droping you my Oppinion upon this Inclosed Report.

On perusing the text of the Treaty of amity, Commerce & Navigation Dated London 19th Novemr. 1794, which the Commitee of Congress builds heavily on, the plan I am about to Propose, is perfectly Clear of any Breach of Faith, pledged by the United States, respecting said Treaty, and in my Opinion Nither Britain nor France can take it amiss and the United States come of with Honor, and Stear Clear for ever, of haveing any more of there Countervailing Dutys, or Obstructions to our Navigation—

Please Notice the Commitees Report on a Ship of 250 Tons, carrying 250 Tons of Oil in Time of Peace the British Ship will receive full Freight, when the American Ship will receive only £171.5 Sterling, which will not pay her Double light money & other Expenses in London, by which means the whole Freight & more is sunk to Owners—the same remark on Tobacco, & other Raw Materials, of the United States, paying Countervailing Dutys.

Now for my Plan, Sir, which I hope will meet your approbation. & will not Interfere with any Treaty now Subsisting between the Nations of Great Britian France & the *United* States of America—lay a Duty on All Articles of Raw Meterials of the United States, Shipt in a British or French Ship, the Exact sum, or sums on Each Article, Numerated by the Countervailing Dutys, laid on Goods, by American Ships, Carried to Either Nation, by which means American Ships will have the Same Chance with Ships of England or France—there Ships will have the advantage of ours by a Difference in the Wages of Seamen—to Ballance that, we build our Ships for much less, then Either of them, & Victual for about the half the British do—provided this Sketch or plan, meets your approbation, or my Writing to you is not found Disagreeable, when I Know this by a line from a Friend, will give you my Sentiments on the Banckrupt Law, which coud be amended so as to be Agreeable to all the Merchents of the United States—

I have the Honor to be Your Devoted, Hble. Servt.

James A. Stewart

RC (MoSHi: Jefferson Papers); at head of text: "Thomas Jefferson Esqr."; endorsed by TJ as received 27 Jan. and so recorded in SJL. Enclosure: *Report from the Committee of Commerce and Manufactures, To Whom was Referred so Much of the Message of the President of the United States as Relates to Discriminating and Countervailing Duties, and the Act of the British Parliament, on that Subject* (Washington, D.C., 1803), presented 10 Jan. 1803, details the adverse impact on American shipping and commerce by the discriminating and countervailing duties imposed by Great Britain, France, and other foreign nations; in order to "obviate the disadvantages resulting to the carrying trade of the United States" from these actions, the committee recommends the repeal of discriminating duties on tonnage imposed by the United States, "so far as the same respects the produce or manufacture of the nation to which such foreign ships or vessels may belong—such repeal to take effect in favor of any foreign nation, whenever the President shall be satisfied that the discriminating or countervailing duties of such foreign nation so far as they operate to the disadvantage of the United States, have been abolished."

James A. Stewart (ca. 1743-1813) was formerly a partner in the mercantile firm of Randall, Son, and Stewarts in New York City, which dissolved in 1795. He was also a member of the city's chamber of commerce, the Saint Andrew's Society, and served as an inspector of elections (William M. MacBean, *Biographical Register of Saint Andrew's Society of the State of New York*, 2 vols. [New York, 1922-5], 1:221; New York *Daily Advertiser*, 8 May 1795, 15 Sep. 1797; *New York Gazette and General Advertiser*, 19 Apr. 1799; New York *Mercantile Advertiser*, 7 Apr. 1803; New York *Olio*, 13 Feb. 1813).

From Albert Gallatin

DEAR SIR 22d Jany. 1803

I enclose a modification of the navy estimates in conformity to the ideas you suggested on the subject of my letter of the 18th instt.—It is extremely desirable that before the subject shall be taken up in the house, every part should be fully agreed on between the heads of the Departments; and I wish you would return the proposed modifications with such alterations as, after conversing with the Secretary of the Navy, you shall think proper.

Respectfully Your obedt. Servt. ALBERT GALLATIN

Please to let me know whether you wish to confer again with me on this subject before you decide—

RC (DLC); endorsed by TJ as received from the Treasury Department on 22 Jan. and "Naval approprn" and so recorded in SJL.

ENCLOSURE

Estimate of Navy Appropriations for 1803

Estimate of the Secretary of the Navy

Proposed

Specific appropriations	*Objects*				Amount of specific appropriations
	Vessels in commission six frigates & a schooner	Vessels in ordinary seven frigates	Half pay to officers	General contingencies Store rent commissions, freight travelling expenses	*Total*
Pay of officers & seamen and subsistence of officers	246,669.—.	23,188.—.	14,136.—.		283,993
Provisions	143,855.86	13,534.34.[1]			157,360.20
Medical & hospital	7,350.—.	350.—.			7,700.—
Contingencies	79,000.—.	63,000.—.		40,000.—.	182,000.—
	476,874.86	100,042.34.	14,136.	40,000	
Seventy four gun ships					114,425.—
Navy yards					48,741.37
Marine corps (subdivided under several distinct heads)					90,780.43
					900,000. [2]
		deficiencies of 1802			181,849.09
					1,081,849.09

The above estimate is calculated on the supposition that 6 frigates shall be kept in actual service the whole year; but it is understood that a part of the appropriations is to be made conditionally and not to take place unless with the consent of the President, and in case war should break out with some other Barbary powers. It is also intended that an appropriation should be made for purchasing some small vessels, and finally that the whole expenditure must not, under any circumstances, exceed, (exclusively of the deficiencies of 1802) the sum of 900,000 dollars.

The President proposes that	2 frigates should be kept in commission	for 4 months	estimated at 75,000 drs. per annum	50,000
	2 do	for 6 do.	do do	75,000
	1 do	for 12 do.	do do	75,000
	1 schooner (Enterprize)	" 12 do.	do 22,000	22,000
	3 small vessels	" [. . .] do.	do 30,000	60,000
	making for the vessels in commission			282,000

which sum is 4000 dollars *less* than the three fifths of the estimate sum of 476,874.86 for the same object and leaves the other two fifths applicable to the case of war with any other Barbary power. As to the sum of 72,000 dollars wanted for the purchase of vessels, it may be taken out of those two fifths, or out of the appropriation for seventy-fours, which last is preferable, because that appropriation will be rich enough when the deficiencies of 1802 shall have been made up, & because it will leave us a greater fund in case of war with Morocco &a.

Modifications proposed on the preceding plan

	Vessels in commission	Vessels in ordinary	Half pay to officers	General contingencies	Total
Pay of officers & seamen & subsistence of officers	148,001.40	23,188.—.	14,136 —		185,325.40
Provisions	86,313.52	13,534.34[3]			99,847.86
Medical & hospital	4,410.—.	350.—			4,760.
Contingencies	47,400.—	63,000		10,000—(*a*)	120,400.—
	286,124.92	100,042.34			
For such expences as may with the approbation of the President be incurred for the maintenance of the navy in case of war[4] with any other powers than Tripoli	190,749.94			30,000 (*c*)	220,749.94
	476,874.86				
Seventy four gun ships & purchase of small vessels				(b)	114,425.—
Navy-yards				(b)	48,741.3
Marine corps				(*d*)	90,780.4
					900,000.—

Notes

a it is proposed to reduce this item from 40 to 10 thd. dollars & to throw the other 30 thd. in the contingent appropriation in case of war with any other Barbary powers

b—If either of these appropriations is supposed not large enough, the increase will be deducted from the appropriation (*c*) so as to leave the whole sum the same

d—This may be diminished, if Congress shall amend the law respecting marines—

MS (DLC); undated; in Gallatin's hand, with emendation by TJ (see note 4 below).

In the 1803 navy appropriations act, the sum of $90,780.43 for the MARINE CORPS was SUBDIVIDED into $64,095.60 for pay and subsistence, "including provisions for those on shore, and forage for the staff"; $16,223.83 for clothing and military stores; $1,000 for medicines and other expenses for care of the sick; and $9,461 for "quartermaster's and barrack-master's stores," traveling expenses, and other contingencies (U.S. Statutes at Large, 2:208-9). ABOVE ESTIMATE: the total for the sums listed by Gallatin for specific appropriations is $885,000, not $900,000. In the estimate enclosed with his letter to TJ of 18 Jan., Gallatin included $15,000 for ordnance and other military and naval stores. The addition of this sum brings the total to $900,000.

For the APPROPRIATION for SMALL VESSELS, see Robert Smith to TJ, 19 Jan.

PRESIDENT PROPOSES: see Notes on Navy Appropriations for 1803 printed at 18 Jan. In that proposal, TJ estimated $30,000 in expenses for the *Enterprize* for one year. TJ also included $72,000 for building three vessels, bringing his total to $362,000, compared to the total here of $282,000.

[1] For totals, this figure should be 13,504.34.

[2] The sum is actually $885,000.

[3] Gallatin again means 13,504.34 (see note 1), but here the sum as written gives a total of "99,847.46" as in MS.

[4] TJ emended the remainder of this sentence to read "or imminent danger of war with any of the Barbary powers other than Tripoli."

[5] That is, 885,030 (see notes 2 and 3).

Memorandum for Henry Dearborn

Observations on mr Hawkins's letter of Dec. 22. 1802.[1]

Our proceedings on the subject of the deed by the Speaker of the Creeks to mrs Darant should be decisive, prompt and exemplary. if she be an Indian (which I should not expect as she is the sister of Mc.Gillivray) we cannot punish her. if she be an American citizen, the Attorney of the US. in the Missisipi territory might be instructed to avail himself of any opportunity of having her arrested and punished as provided by the Indian intercourse law; and if mr Hawkins can give us a clue to obtain evidence against the clerk or lawyers of Washington county (Georgia) or any others concerned in the intrigue, the Attorney of the US. in Georgia might be directed to prosecute them. In the mean time the Creeks should be assured of our protection, and that none of their lands shall ever be permitted to be sold or settled without the consent of the nation regularly given, and under our ratification. and if we have any settlers on their lands we ought to remove them if we can, or get them to remove them. as to the boundary between them & us, if it be any where undefined, we should join in defining it; but between them & Spain we can do nothing.   I imagine there will always be great difficulty in preventing our cattle & horses from ranging on the Indian lands, and the Indians should be prepared to allow a reasonable indulgence & laxity in this particular.

As to the pressure for lands from the frontier of Georgia mentioned by Colo. Hawkins & the land speculations of a private company there, the Creeks should understand that we will oppose it as well as they do: and as to the demand of Panton & Leslie, we might say that tho' we have no right to interfere between them & British creditors as to debts, yet if they determine to pay in lands, we will not suffer British subjects to own lands within the limits of the US. but would not object to take the lands and pay money to their creditors as far as we should think their value.

TH: JEFFERSON
Jan. 22. 1803

PrC (DLC); at foot of text: "The Secretary at War." Recorded in SJL as to the War Department with notation "incroachmts. on Creeks."

MR HAWKINS'S LETTER: on 21 Jan., the War Department received a communication written by Benjamin Hawkins at Tuckabatchee on 22 Dec. The document, which has not been found, related to "a tract of Land conveyed by the Indians to Mrs. Durant and the general uneasiness occasioned thereby" (DNA: RG 107, RLRMS).

IF SHE BE AN INDIAN: Sophia Durant was a sister of Alexander McGillivray, the trader and leader of the Creeks until his death in 1793. The family was of Scottish, French, and Native American ancestry. Their maternal grandmother was a Creek, which by matrilineal descent made them members of the politically important Wind clan. As a female member of the clan, Sophia had rights to property, and she owned or controlled land, slaves, and livestock. Hawkins came away from a visit to her homestead in 1796 with a negative impression, which perhaps influenced the information he provided to the War Department in December 1802. He had been surprised to find her living in "a small hut," and he thought that by "bad management" she failed to utilize the potential of her property and several dozen slaves (Edward J. Cashin, *Lachlan McGillivray, Indian Trader: The Shaping of the Southern Colonial Frontier* [Athens, Ga., 1992], 71-3, 75-6, 257, 307-8; Thomas Foster, ed., *The Collected Works of Benjamin Hawkins, 1796-1810* [Tuscaloosa, Ala., 2003], 43; ANB; Vol. 36:154n, 157n).

INDIAN INTERCOURSE LAW: by an "Act to regulate trade and intercourse with the Indian tribes, and to preserve peace on the frontiers," approved 30 Mch. 1802, it was "a misdemeanor in any person, not employed under the authority of the United States," to negotiate with Indians for land. The offense was punishable by a fine of up to $1,000 and imprisonment of up to twelve months (U.S. Statutes at Large, 2:139, 143).

SHOULD BE ASSURED OF OUR PROTECTION: Dearborn used this memorandum from TJ to compose a letter to Hawkins dated 24 Jan. Dearborn, at TJ's direction, asked Hawkins "to assure the Indians" that they could rely on the president's "friendship and on every exertion in his power, to prevent any improper measures which may be in contemplation for obtaining their lands." He added that "no purchase made of their lands will be considered as valid unless made under the immediate direction of the President." Hawkins was to give William Claiborne any information he could about the recent land transaction and Sophia Durant's citizenship. If she was a U.S. citizen, she would be arrested and prosecuted, and the government would also take action against a lawyer who, according to the information from Hawkins, had assisted her. SETTLERS on Indian lands without permission were to be evicted, except for the settlement under the leadership of William Wofford, as there were pending issues in that case (see Josiah Tattnall, Jr., to TJ, 20 July). The government, Dearborn continued, would try to resolve any problems regarding the BOUNDARY between the Creeks "and the white people of the United States." However, the U.S. could not intervene in disputes between the Creeks and subjects of SPAIN unless the matter in question fell within the limits of the United States, and the Indians must learn "to view with indulgence such petty intrusions" as settlers' CATTLE ranging on their land (Dearborn to Hawkins, 24 Jan., Lb in DNA: RG 75, LSIA).

The trading firm of PANTON, Leslie & Co. pressed the Creeks to give up some of their assets—land or annuities—to pay off a large collective and cumulative debt to the company. Beginning in the late 1790s, the firm attempted to obtain the assistance of the federal government in that endeavor. The company's partners were natives of Scotland who entered the Indian trade in Georgia and South Carolina but moved their operations to East Florida during the American Revolution and afterward based their commerce with the Creeks at Pensacola, in Spanish West Florida. In his letter to Hawkins, Dearborn stated that neither the Panton firm "nor any other foreigners" could acquire land within the United States "except in cases provided for by some particular States." If the Creeks took the initiative to cede territory to the U.S. in exchange for payment of the company's claim by the government, "perhaps such an arrangement might be acceded to," Dearborn wrote, "but we cannot consider ourselves under any obligation to interfere in the business" (same; William S. Coker and Thomas D. Watson, *Indian Traders of the Southeastern Spanish Borderlands: Panton, Leslie & Company and John Forbes & Company, 1783-1847* [Pensacola, Fla., 1986], 15-17, 26, 31-2, 229-31, 240; Robbie Ethridge, *Creek Country: The Creek Indians and Their World* [Chapel Hill, 2003], 11, 203-4).

[1] MS: "1803."

To John Avery

SIR Washington Jan. 23. 1803.

General Varnum has delivered to me your letter of Nov. 20. together with the maps which the Legislature of Massachusets has been pleased to destine for me. I pray you to deliver my respectful acknolegements to them for this mark of their attention, and to accept my thanks to yourself for the trouble you have been so good as to take, as well as assurances of my respect and consideration.

TH: JEFFERSON

PrC (DLC); at foot of text: "John Avery esq."; endorsed by TJ in ink on verso.

From Peder Blicher Olsen

Sir. Sunday morning [23 Jan. 1803]

Not being able to leave my room I am reduced by necessity to returning you in writing my humble thanks for Your Note of yesterday and for the letter to the Governor of Virginia.

The box that has been delivered, contains 12 bottles of Hungarian Wine—three large, with a piece of white tape tied round the neck are a *dry wine*, From upper Hungaria of very superior quality—three other large, without tape—a wine from the same country as commonly drank at table—and 6 small ones with *two kinds* of Tokay—perhaps two rich and luscious for the taste of the country in general.—Whatever kind you may approve most of, Mr. Bollmann will be happy to procure in future on command: He has an uncommon opportunity for that purpose in the country, and from my personal knowledge of Bollmanns character, and his attachment and veneration for You, I am satisfied, he will do it from no views unworthy of such feelings.—

I am fully aware of the obligation I am under to You Sir, for not having disdained to accept of this box, intruded upon You in so abrupt and incautious a manner, owing entirely to my illness—However, Your name has certainly not been exposed otherwise than just was advisable in order to secure the good services of the intermediate post.masters—As to the meaness of the offer I quote Moliere, who says some where:

"Le present n'est pas grand, mais la divinité
Ne jette le regard que sur la volonté."

The little book of *French Neology*, when offered, was intended for the library at Monticello with Your kind permission.

Should my wretched state of health interfere with my journey to Richmond, Your letter Sir for Mr. J: Page shall be faithfully returned to You.

Sir Your most obedient and humble servant

Blicher Olsen

RC (DLC); partially dated; endorsed by TJ as received 23 Jan. and so recorded in SJL.

The reference to moliere came from the uncompleted pastoral comedy, *Mélicerte*, 2.3, "Le présent n'est pas grand, mais les divinités Ne jettent leurs regards que sur les volontés," or, "The gift is not great, but the gods regard only the will" (*Oeuvres de Molière, avec des notes de divers commentateurs* [Paris, 1835], 332).

To Peter Carr

Dear Sir Washington Jan. 23. 1803.

Yours of the 17th. is recieved. certainly mr Harvie would have needed no advocate with me, for the appointment suggested, had such an one been to be made: but you will have seen Colo: Monroe, and learnt that as he is joined to the legations at Paris & Madrid to each of which secretaries are attached, none has been thought necessary for him. indeed it seems likely that we shall be obliged to revert to the former plan of private secretaries to be appointed by their principals. I had thought it desireable to send secretaries of legation selected from young men of talents and of such situations in life as might mark them out for future employ. but it does not seem to be acceptable to the ministers to fix in their families persons not of their own selection. we have not however decided to relinquish it, & should do it with reluctance. be so good as to present my sincere esteem to mr Harvie and to accept yourself assurances of my constant affection. Th: Jefferson

P.S. I shall be in Albemarle for 3. weeks during the month of March

PrC (DLC); at foot of text: "P. Carr"; endorsed by TJ in ink on verso.

To Charles Willson Peale

Dear Sir Washington Jan. 23. 1803.

I thank you for mr Rembrandt Peale's pamphlet on the Mammoth, and feeling a strong interest in his succesful exhibition of the Skeleton, shall be very happy to hear he has the great run of visitants which I expect he will have.

I was struck with the notice in the papers of mr Hawkins's physiognotrace, of the work of which you send me some specimens, which I percieve must have been taken from Houdon's bust. when you shall have nothing else to do, I would thank you for an explanation of the principle of it, for I presume no secret is made of it as it is placed in the Museum.

I rejoice at the progress of your collection. it is an immense work for an individual. that I must see the Mammoth is certain. but the time when, by no means so. probably I shall not know it myself till 24. hours before my departure, whether that may be this or the next year. Accept my sincere good wishes and respects.

Th: Jefferson

RC (Albert E. Lownes, Providence, Rhode Island, 1951); at foot of text: "C. W. Peale." PrC (DLC); endorsed by TJ in ink on verso.

THANK YOU: see Peale to TJ, 10 Jan.

A brief NOTICE of the physiognotrace devised by John Isaac Hawkins that was on display at Peale's museum appeared in Philadelphia newspapers on 28 Dec. "This curious machine," the item declared, produced perhaps "the truest outlines" of any such mechanism. It was of "so simple a construction, that any person without the aid of another, can in less than a minute take their own likeness in profile." Washington newspapers reprinted the notice early in January (Peale, *Papers*, v. 2, pt. 1:478; *Washington Federalist*, 3 Jan.; Georgetown *Olio*, 6 Jan.).

To make silhouettes of TJ with the physiognotrace, Peale apparently used a plaster copy of HOUDON'S BUST that TJ had given to David Rittenhouse (Peale, *Papers*, v. 2, pt. 1:483n).

To the President of the Senate

SIR — Washington Jan. 23. 1803.

As the files of the Senate seem to be the proper depository for the inclosed papers, I take the liberty of handing them on to you and of assuring you of my high consideration and respect.

TH: JEFFERSON

RC (CtY). PrC (DLC); at foot of text: "The President of the Senate." Recorded in SJL as a letter of 22 Jan. Enclosure: John Caldwell, clerk of the Delaware House of Representatives, to the President of the Senate of the United States, Dover, 17 Jan. 1803, transmitting credentials certifying the election of Samuel White to the United States Senate; the letter had been inadvertently delivered to TJ (RC in DNA: RG 46, LP, Reports and Communications Submitted to the Senate, 7th Cong., 2d sess.; addressed: "The Honourable The President of the Senate of the United States"; franked and postmarked; endorsed by TJ as received 22 Jan. and so recorded in SJL; endorsed by a Senate clerk).

On 24 Jan., Vice President Aaron Burr presented John Caldwell's letter and Samuel White's credentials to the Senate, which ordered that they lie on file (JS, 3:255).

To John Reich

Washington Jan. 23. 1803.

Th: Jefferson presents his salutations & thanks to mr Reich for the Masonic medal he was so kind as to send him, and which is another proof of the superior talents of mr Reich in that art. what may be the destinies of the Mint is yet unknown: but he will be very happy to see mr Reich's skill find full emploiment either privately or publicly in the US.

PrC (ViW: Tucker-Coleman Collection); endorsed by TJ in ink on verso.

MASONIC MEDAL: see Reich to TJ, 3 Jan. 1803.

From Robert Smith

Nav Dep
Sir! 23rd Jany 1803

I enclose a copy of a letter written by me to Cap Tingey on the 21st ins—and a letter from him in reply thereto—which I have the honor respectfully to submit.

I am with the greatest respect & esteem, Sir, your mo ob sr

Rt Smith

RC (DLC); in a clerk's hand, signed by Smith; at foot of text: "President of the United States"; endorsed by TJ as received from the Navy Department on 24 Jan. and "Tingey. naval magazines" and so recorded in SJL. FC (Lb in DNA: RG 45, LSP); dated 24 Jan. Enclosures: Smith to Thomas Tingey, 21 Jan. 1803, informing Tingey that it is "the determination of the President" that all navy vessels to be laid up in ordinary shall be brought to the Washington Navy Yard, and that all vessels now in service shall return there and be fitted out there as well; Smith instructs Tingey to state the number of warehouses and other improvements he deems necessary at the navy yard, and their probable expense, "having in view the perfect security and entire preservation of the public property of every description now in your care, and that may hereafter be committed to your care, under this arrangement" (DNA: RG 45, MLS). Other enclosure not found.

To William Tazewell

Washington Jan. 23. 1803.

Th: Jefferson returns his thanks to Doctor Tazewell for his Medical Vademecum. it has really brought the whole science of diseases & remedies within the shortest compass possible, and, not meddling with the details of the science himself, it presents exactly such a general view of every part of it, as he often wishes to take. he presents to Doctr. Tazewell his respectful salutations.

PrC (MHi); endorsed by TJ in ink on verso.

William Tazewell (d. 1832), a Virginia-born physician who completed his medical training at Edinburgh, was author of *Vade-Mecum Medicum in duas Partes divisum, quarum Prior, Nosologiam Cullinæam, Posterior, Compendium Materiæ Medicæ et Pharmacopœiæ, Exhibet*, printed in Paris, Edinburgh, and Philadelphia in 1798. From 1797 to 1798, Tazewell served as the Paris-London messenger for American envoy to France, Elbridge Gerry. Captured by a French privateer and imprisoned in his first attempted return passage to the United States in 1799, he successfully petitioned Congress in May 1800 for reimbursement of travel expenses. He practiced medicine in Williamsburg in 1800 and later moved to Richmond and became a member of the Virginia Medical Society (Madison, *Papers, Sec. of State Ser.*, 1:54; Washington, *Papers, Ret. Ser.*, 4:253-5; Sowerby, No. 898).

To Dr. John Vaughan

Washington Jan. 23. 1803.

Th: Jefferson presents his compliments and thanks to Doctr Vaughan for the treatise on fever he has been so obliging as to send him, and which he shall peruse at the first leisure moment with pleasure.

PrC (DLC); endorsed by TJ in ink on verso.

TREATISE ON FEVER: see Vaughan to TJ, 19 Jan.

From H. Bredaugh

Philada. January 24th 1802 [i.e. 1803]

Mr. Jefferson I thing that you are not acting wright about Orleans the Cittizens would certainly all love & esteam you much more If you wold only give them leave to take that place because if the French Comes there and takes possesion the will always be sparing with us but only give us leave and we will take it without the least Hesitation only think the Back Countries will become[1] fit for nothing all those fine objects will become waste the Kiantuckians have often said that only give them leave and the will go down and take it without reserve

H Bredaugh

RC (DLC); endorsed by TJ as a letter of 24 Jan. 1803 received 27 Jan. and so recorded in SJL.

[1] MS: "bcome."

From Albert Gallatin

[24 Jan. 1803]

It appears to me that a compliance with this request would amount to a fraud on the Govt. of that country to which the vessel was bound. If a Collector of Natchez is permitted to clear a vessel lying at N. Orleans as if she was sailing from Natchez, he may with equal propriety clear for London a vessel lying at Havannah giving her papers as if she had sailed from the american territory. Will the President be pleased to communicate his opinion. A. G.

RC (DLC); undated; endorsed by TJ as received from the Treasury Department on 24 Jan. and "clearances at N. Orleans" and so recorded in SJL.

THIS REQUEST: not identified, but for the 1802 effort by those in the Mississippi trade to gain authorization for the collector at Natchez to grant clearances for vessels loading at New Orleans and bound for British ports, see enclosures described at TJ to Gallatin, 13 Oct. and Gallatin's response printed at 14 Oct. (second letter).

To Albert Gallatin

TH:J. TO MR GALLATIN Jan. 24. 1803.

If we can do any thing ourselves in the case of the [...] from the Missisipi, let us do it. but if any thing has to be done by Congress I think the merchants had better be left to get it brought forward in their own way, and leave us free to modify. it is a question of some nicety whether in the seasons when exportations are strong, we might moor a [...] in the river opposite or near N. Orleans, and keep a Custom house deputy on board it to clear vessels.

PrC (DLC); faint. Recorded in SJL as a letter to the Treasury Department with notation "Missisipi."

From Samuel McFetrich

SIR, Philadelphia, Jan. 24 1803

With diffidence and respect I address a gentleman far superior in rank and understanding, well knowing that the person[1] I write to is not fond of being flattered not wanting the applause of an individual, or a few, but to prove by his actions that he is worthy of the exalted situation which the true friends of the people have placed him in.

As the revilers of Republicanism, have hitherto held you as a non-promoter of Religion, you have here an opportunity of giving the *Lie* direct, to all their base insinuations, or assertions.

Should you have leisure, to give this scrawl a perusal and the work meet your approbation you will confer an honor by forwarding it in the course of a month; if otherwise, it will not have the *least tendency* to *lessen*, you in my esteem.

Accept Dear Sir, the assurance of my respect, And believe me to be Your friend & Serv't, SAML. H. MCFETRICH

RC (MHi); at foot of text: "Thos. Jefferson Esq."; endorsed by TJ as received 27 Jan. and so recorded in SJL.

GIVE THIS SCRAWL A PERUSAL: McFetrich perhaps enclosed his 10 Jan. 1803 proposal to print, by subscription, "Tracts, or A Preservative against Unsettled Notions in Religion" by John Wesley, which included "The *advantages* of the members of the Church of England over those of the Church of Rome"; "The Scripture Doctrine on *Predestination*, *Election*, and *Reprobation*"; "Reasons against a separation from the Church of England"; the 1747 "letter to a person lately joined with the people denominated Quakers"; and nine other titles. The names of subscribers would be annexed to the work "as promoters of Christianity and Literature" (*Kline's Carlisle Weekly Gazette*, 16 Mch. 1803). The same collection of tracts was published in Bristol, England, in 1758 and 1770, as Wesley's *A Preservative against Unsettled Notions in Religion.*

[1] MS: "peron."

To the Senate and the House of Representatives

Gentlemen of the Senate and
of the House of Representatives.

I transmit a report by the Superintendant of the city of Washington, on the affairs of the city committed to his care. by this you will percieve that the re-sales of lots prescribed by an act of the last session of Congress, did not produce a sufficiency to pay the debt to Maryland to which they were appropriated: and as it was evident that the sums necessary for the interest and instalments due to that state could not be produced by a sale of the other public lots, without an unwarrantable sacrifice of the property, the deficiencies were of necessity drawn from the treasury of the US.

The office of Surveyor for the city, created during the former establishment, being of indispensable necessity, it has been continued: and to that of the Superintendant, substituted instead of the board of Commissioners, at the last session of Congress, no salary was annexed by law. these offices being permanent, I have supposed it more agreeable to principle that their salaries should be fixed by the legislature, and therefore have assigned them none. their services to be compensated are from the 1st. day of June last.

The Marshal of the district of Columbia, has, as directed by law, caused a jail to be built in the city of Washington. I inclose his statements of the expences already incurred, and of what remains to be finished. the portion actually compleated has rendered the situation of the persons confined much more comfortable & secure than it has been heretofore.

Th: Jefferson
Jan. 24. 1803.

RC (DNA: RG 233, PM, 7th Cong., 2d sess.); endorsed by a House clerk. PrC (DLC). RC (DNA: RG 46, LPPM, 7th Cong., 2d sess.); endorsed by Senate clerks. Recorded in SJL with notation "Columbia. Washington." Enclosures:

(1) Thomas Munroe to TJ, 20 Dec. 1802. (2) Daniel Carroll Brent to TJ, 21 Jan., and enclosures.

Meriwether Lewis delivered this message, the REPORT of Thomas Munroe, and the letter of Daniel Carroll Brent to the House and Senate on 25 Jan. The House referred the documents to the Committee of Ways and Means, which reported back on 28 Feb. a bill establishing SALARIES of $1,800 for the superintendent and $1,000 for the surveyor of the city of Washington. The bill passed the House the following day and received the Senate's concurrence on 3 Mch. (JHR, 4:300, 373-4, 377; JS, 3:285; U.S. Statutes at Large, 2:235-6).

From William H. Beaumont

SIR. Maysville, Kentucky, Janry. 25th 1803.

During the presidency of Mr. Washington, I commenced a Newspaper in the interior of Pennsylvania—Its tendency was by no means pleasing to the adherents of his successor Mr. Adams—The persecution of such Editors as dared to profess principles hostile to their views, became general throughout the United States. I among the rest, being pointed at as a disorganiser and consequently a dangerous person became one of the proscribed, and was destined to become the Victim of a formidable party.

Judge Addison, to whom, after repeated solicitations and threats, alternately made use of, I refused to become a tool in his nefarious pursuits, exerted himself to the utmost to accomplish my ruin. Scarcely established in business, and burthened as I was, with a large family, he was but too successful. I removed to the State of Kentucky, but the effects of the Malevolence I had experienced, followed me. I was, prior to the auspicious change in the Affairs of the United States, obliged to relinquish my employment, and have been for some time out of business, without the means of resuming it, or providing for my Children.

To the Secretary of the Treasury and several Gentlemen in Congress, I am personally known—they can vouch for the truth of what I have asserted, and also that I have ever demeaned myself as a good Citizen and a tried Republican.

The object, Sir, of my troubling you with this simple narrative, is to interest you so far in my behalf as to induce you to confer on me some appointment, if any should occur, that would enable me to rescue a promising family from indigence.—Messrs. Hoge, Smilie, Lucas and Fowler of the House of Representatives, will inform you if I may be confided in. To those Gentlemen I refer you.

Should I be deemed an object worthy your Attention, either at the present or a future day, I shall do my utmost to repay your confidence by a faithful discharge of the duties entrusted to me.

Convinced as I am of your Attention to the interest of all your fellow citizens, and knowing that you take a pleasure in relieving the oppressions of the former Administration I shall not attempt an Apology for this intrusion but subscribe myself

with the greatest Respect Your Obedt. W. H. BEAUMONT

RC (DNA: RG 59, LAR); at foot of text: "His Excellency the President"; endorsed by TJ as received 8 Feb. and "for office" and so recorded in SJL.

In addition to soliciting a federal office, William Henry Beaumont entertained the possibility of starting a Republican newspaper in Mississippi Territory. Although the paper never got off the ground, Beaumont did eventually settle in Natchez. He may have been the Henry Beaumont recommended by Albert Gallatin as a suitable candidate for the territory's land office in 1805. His devotion to the Republican cause was finally rewarded in 1809 when he became surveyor and inspector of the revenue for the port of Natchez (JEP, 2:131, 133; Robert V. Haynes, *The Mississippi Territory and the Southwest Frontier, 1795-1817* [Lexington, Ky., 2010], 63, 361n; Henry R. Graham to TJ, 10 July 1802; Albert Gallatin to TJ, 25 Feb. 1805).

From Nicolas Gouin Dufief

MONSIEUR, 25th of January. 1803

Je viens enfin de recevoir une partie de mes livres. quelques uns de ceux que vous m'aviez demandés s'y trouvent—

La riviere qui est prise, ne me permettant pas de vous les expédier par eau, Je me vois forcé, pour le faire, d'attendre que la Navigation soit libre—En attendant je vous envoye les trois seuls volumes des moralistes qui me sont parvenus; il parait que cette Interessante collection n'a pas été poussée plus loin, quoique l'éditeur nous en ait promis d'autres volumes—

Le poids leger de ces 3 petits formats m'a permis de [vous] les adresser directement par la Poste—Mon Catalogue pour l'an 1803 qui s'imprime en ce moment vous sera rendu aussitôt qu'il paraîtra—

Je vous salue avec tout le respect qui vous est du

NICHOLAS GOUIN DUFIEF

EDITORS' TRANSLATION

SIR,

I have just received, at last, a partial order of my books. Among them are some of those you requested.

Since the river is frozen and I cannot send them to you by boat, I have no choice but to wait until navigation once again becomes possible. In the meantime, I am mailing you all three volumes of moralists that I received. Apparently this interesting collection has not been continued, although the publisher promised other volumes.

Since these three small books are light, I can send them by post. My catalogue for 1803, which is now in press, will be delivered to you as soon as it is printed.

I send you greetings with all the respect you deserve.

NICHOLAS GOUIN DUFIEF

RC (DLC); torn; at foot of text: "Thomas Jefferson, Président des Etats-Unis"; endorsed by TJ as received 28 Jan. and so recorded in SJL.

VOLUMES DES MORALISTES: in March 1802, TJ asked Dufief for volumes in a series by Pierre Charles Lévesque, the *Collection des moralistes anciens* (Vol. 37:113, 114n).

To Samuel Hanway

SIR — Washington Jan. 25. 1803.

Your favor of Dec. 23. covering an address on the subject of the suspension of our right of deposit at N. Orleans was recieved on the 8th. inst. before that event took place I had taken measures for placing our rights on that river on a more secure footing, and immediately on hearing of the suspension, we set on foot such other measures as were most likely to remove it amicably and without delay; and my expectation is that this will be effected before the usual season of produce descending from the Ohio. and in order to preserve ourselves against the like risk in future, I have sent a Minister extraordinary, to Paris and Madrid, whose exertions joined with those of our ministers there, will we trust effect the desired object. these things you will have seen stated in the public papers, and they are repeated here only as a particular assurance to the inhabitants of Monongalia, in whose name the address is presented, that the interests of that country will be not less assiduously cherished than those of every other part. I may add with truth that in every form in which this subject has been brought before the legislature, they have shewn an equal sensibility to it. I pray you to accept assurances of my respect and consideration.

TH: JEFFERSON

PrC (DLC); at foot of text: "Samuel Hanway esq."

Samuel Hanway (1743-1834) settled in Monongalia County, in western Virginia, after the American Revolution. He became county surveyor and a justice of the peace in the 1780s, owned a mill and an iron furnace, and was one of the original trustees of Morgantown (Donald Jackson and Dorothy Twohig, eds., *The Diaries of George Washington*, 6 vols.

[Charlottesville, 1976-79], 4:38; Earl L. Core, *The Monongalia Story: A Bicentennial History*, 5 vols. [Parsons, W.Va., 1974-84], 1:254; 2:102, 120, 123, 268, 331, 360-1; 3:111).

Hanway's FAVOR of 23 Dec. has not been found, but is recorded in SJL as received on 8 Jan.

To Lewis Harvie

DEAR SIR Washington Jan. 25. 1803.

Your favor on the subject of Colo. Monroe's mission came to hand the day before yesterday. I had, that day answered P. Carr on the same subject, which doubtless he has communicated to you, and you will also in the mean time have seen Colo. Monroe. as he was joined to the missions of Paris & Madrid, to each of which a secretary was already attached, the giving none to him specially was considered as a proper economy. I have no doubt myself that the naming Secretaries of legation to the permanent missions is a wise policy. it was always practised by the old Congress, and was discontinued by the two preceding administrations. besides the propriety of having the papers of a mission delivered, in case of death, to the hands of some person known to, & confided in by the government, it furnishes an opportunity of selecting young men of talents and respectability, and of placing them in a station of improvement, which may prepare them for becoming useful administrators of the public affairs. this was my view in renewing the practice in such new diplomatic appointments as I have made. but it has not proved altogether without difficulties. gentlemen are not always satisfied to recieve into their families persons not of their own selection: a too great sense of independance on one side, & a too great suspicion of it on the other, easily engender jealousies, and mutual uneasiness. whether therefore we can continue the practice seems doubtful. that a trip of a year or two to Europe would be of service to you I am satisfied. but a longer one, at your time of life, probably would not; inasmuch as it would alienate the mind from application, and extinguish the habits of business, without which a man cannot succeed in this country. a certain course of practice at the bar, even where it is not meant to be permanently followed, is useful as it produces readiness & arrangement of ideas, correctness of reasoning, and a familiarity in public speaking. entering at the same time into our own H. of delegates, one is placed on the best stage for commencing a political career, & for rising on their own strength, the best of all foundations to rest on. thence after a proper initiation, the floor of Congress (of the H. of R. I mean) is the next step, from which the high offices of the government become attainable. you will pardon these hints from one who having run the career of political life from it's first to it's ultimate point, looks back on the ground he has passed over, and is glad to communicate the result of his experience to one just entering on the same course. they are given from a high sense of your capacity to pursue a tract splendid to yourself & useful to your country, and from a sincere wish that you may have all the success which your qualifications have a right to command. with a heart disposed to do whatever is honest and honorable, and a head able to decide by calculation that what is not right can under no possible circumstances be useful; you will be at no loss, under whatever embarassments you may at any time be placed, in whatsoever labyrinth of difficulties apparently inextricable you may find yourself, to decide that by going strait forward and doing exactly what is just and moral, the way will open before you, and the mountains of difficulty subside: when by resorting to head-work and contrivence, one only gets more & more entangled in the mazes of their own cunning, and finally enveloped in a self-woven web of disgrace. but I catch myself sermonizing again, & have again to seek my apology in assurances of my sincere concern for your welfare, and of my great esteem and respect. TH: JEFFERSON

PrC (DLC); at foot of first page in ink: "Lewis Harvie esq."

While on his MISSION to Paris, James Monroe employed John Mercer as his unofficial private secretary (John Mercer to TJ, 21 Sep. 1802).

From John Langdon

DEAR SR. Portsmouth Jany 26th. 1803

I am honor'd with your favor of the 12th. Inst with one hundred dollars inclosed for the distressed sufferers by the late fire in this Town, this sum has been enter'd on our books from a friend, your name has been omitted, agreably to your directions; I pray you Sr. to Accept of my thanks in behalf of the sufferers for this generous donation, which shall be faithfully appropriated, to the benevolent purpose, intended. The Calamity has been great indeed, but it would have been much more felt, had the fire happen'd in any other part of the Town, many of the sufferers are still wealthy. I have lost one house, my Son in law, another, my Brother a warehouse, which were rented, we consider ourselves small sufferers, the lots remain we must double our deligence and build new houses. We are experiencing the great sympathy of our fellow Citizens, in our misfortune, not only in our own state, but thro' the United States, the very generous donations made by the Citys of Philada. & New York with other Cities and Towns also by individuals, cannot fail to call forth our greatful Acknowledgements. Permit me Sr. to congratulate you on the flattering prospect of our Public affairs, the proceedings of our Government, cannot fail to give compleat satisfaction to every Republican and at the same time to silence, in some measure, the calumnies of the Federalists, who "sicken" at the sight of our prosperity, and are perpetually endeavouring to bring us into confusion, or into war with any Nation or Nations whatever they care not who or which, but thank God their attempts are vain. Peace will be our Glory, war would be our distruction; in my opinion even to meet Great Britain in our Commercial relations, on the ground of reciprocity for the present untill Negociation could take place, would be of Advantage. But these important affairs, I submit to superiour Judgemt. not doubting you'll be good enough to pardon me for the liberty I have taken,

I have the honor to be Dear Sr. with the highest possable respect and consideration Your Obligd Hbl. Servt JOHN LANGDON

RC (DLC); addressed: "Thomas Jefferson President of the United States. City of Washington"; franked and postmarked; endorsed by TJ as received 5 Feb. and so recorded in SJL.

YOUR FAVOR OF THE 12TH.: that is, TJ's letter of 11 Jan.

Langdon's SON IN LAW was Thomas Elwyn and his BROTHER, Woodbury Langdon.

VERY GENEROUS DONATIONS in response to the Portsmouth fire poured in from civic groups and churches around the country. In Philadelphia, a bookseller opened a subscription campaign. In New York, merchants and businesses, including a coffeehouse, raised funds. In addition to these regional efforts, TJ signed into law on 19 Feb. 1803, "An Act for the relief of the sufferers by fire, in the town of Portsmouth," allowing residents additional time to discharge their custom house bonds (*Gazette of the United States*, 7 Jan. 1803; New York *Commercial Advertiser*, 7 Jan. 1803; U.S. Statutes at Large, 2:201).

From Robert Leslie

SIR Philada. January 26th 1803

On the 10th inst. I took the liberty of troubling you with a few observations on the proposed dry Docks, at your City, at which time I was not certain, but suspected what I supposed a considerable defect in the plan offered by Mr Latrobe. I have since been informed that my conjecture was right, which was that all the twelve ships ware to be in one Dock, which I supposed to be a great inconvenience for the folowing reasons,

1st It will be impossible to take any one ship out, or in, without floating all the rest, some of which may be in a condition which would render such a measure very injurious, such as those which might have some of their planks striped off, for the purpose of admitting air as recommended in the report,

2d such as ware tight would have all their props, stanchans, and shores loosened, and displaced, and require great care and attention to get them secured in their places agane,

3d it would never be prudent to attempt to Build a Ship in such a Dock, as she might perhaps be subject to an inundation every month during the time of her being on the stocks,

4th the greate quantity of water that would be necessary to fill such a Dock would make the filling very tedious &c

I should not have troubled you so soon on the subject, had I not seen in this morning paper, that Congress had hisitated to grant the Sum Mr Latrobe had stated as nessary to compleat the Works, and that it had been proposed to pospone it till next Session, I tharefore consider it as my duty to offer any information that may be likely to do away the objections ariseing from the great expence any of the members may have in view, from Mr Latrobes estimate.

I have tharefore made a hasty scetch of a Plan which if you should approve of it, I flatter myself, will answer a better purpose than the one reported and if 200,000 Dollars (which is not the half of Mr Ls estimate) ware granted, and apply'd with judgment and Oconemy, in carrying it into effect, if it should not compleat the whole work required, would make so respectable an appearence that the leguslator would chearfully grant a sufficent addition at the next Session.

The plan I have inclosed represents twelve Dry Docks, all separate from each other, and in the centre of them, is one wet Dock. but as it is not likely that twelve ships will be ready to lay up in one place next year, it will not be nessary to begin all the Docks at first. four may be made this year. four next year, and four the year after, which will not require a large advance of money, nor a greater number of hands than can be procured with ease.

As for the kind of meterials I should propose, and the manner of executing the work, time will not permit me to enter into it at present, I am also well aware that a man who offers his opinion, and one who is askeed for it, stands on very different grounds, as thare is always a prepossession in favour of the one, and frequently against the other, under this consideration I should not have offerd my opinion on the above subject as I have done, either to Mr Washington, or Mr Adams, ware either of them now President of the U.S. as I am well convinced that Mr Latrobes eloquence, both in speaking, and write-ing, so far exceads mine, that with either of those gentlemen his plan would be prefer'd, wheather right or wrong.

But you Sir I know are capable of forming a correct opinion, and will without partiality adopt the best.

I am with the highest respect your Humble Servt

Robert Leslie

RC (DLC); addressed: "The President of the United States"; franked and postmarked; endorsed by TJ as received 29 Jan. and so recorded in SJL.

CONGRESS HAD HISITATED: the committee appointed to consider TJ's dry dock proposal presented its report to the House of Representatives on 10 Jan., which was thereafter considered by the Committee of the Whole House on 19 and 20 Jan. The report favored the plan, and committee chairman Samuel L. Mitchill suggested a $500,000 appropriation for the purpose. But several representatives, including William Eustis and John Bacon of Massachusetts and Roger Griswold of Connecticut, voiced concerns over its costs and practicality, and also questioned the wisdom of constructing a single, large dry dock at Washington in lieu of several smaller facilities elsewhere. After further discussion, the House adopted a resolution appointing a new committee to examine "the usefulness and propriety of constructing a dock or docks, at either of the public navy yards, or elsewhere, within the United States, for the building and repair of ships of war" (ASP, *Naval Affairs*, 1:109; *Gazette of the United States*, 25 Jan. 1803; *Aurora*, 26 Jan. 1803; JHR, 4:277, 294-6; *Annals*, 12:401-11).

ENCLOSURE

Plan of a Dry Dock

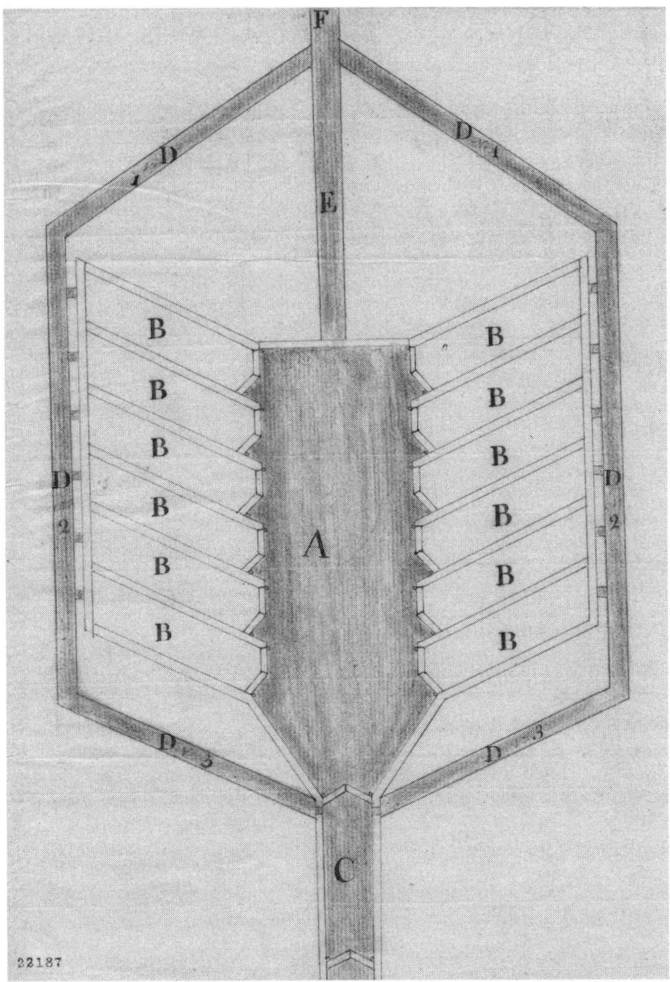

Discription of the Drawing

A The wet Dock, B twelve dry Docks, each to contain one Ship, C the upper Lock, by which the Ships are to pass in and out of the wet Dock, F the Canel to supply the Docks with water, E a branch of it leading into the wet Dock, D two other branches which surrounds the dry Docks and by gates opening into each, any one of them can be filled without the others.

The water in the wet Dock may always be kept to the same hight by the Canel E. and when the water in the dry Dock, in which the ship is to be let in or out, raises by means of the Canels D. to the same level with that in the wet Dock. the gates of that dock only are to be opened, and when the ship has passed out or in, the gates are to be shut, and a sluce opened from the back end of the Dock into a tunnel which cannot be seen in the drawing, but which is supposed to lay under D No 2, and a little below the bed of the Dock, and communicating with the river, by which means the water in the Dock will be soon discharged, the water in the Lock is supply'd by the Canels D No 3.

MS (DLC: TJ Papers, 128:22186-7); undated; in Leslie's hand.

TJ's papers also contain a series of four undated dry dock plans prepared in an unidentified hand. Drawn on a scale of 60 feet to one inch, they appear to relate to the dry dock for Washington, D.C., proposed by TJ. Simply rendered and lacking significant detail, the drawings show a series of plans for partitioning a single dry dock into smaller docks, with some capable of being flooded and drained independent of each other. The fourth and most detailed plan shows four docks measuring 100 feet by 175 feet designed to hold two ships each, a single dock measuring 150 feet by 175 feet designed to hold three ships, and a single dock measuring 80 feet by 180 feet. Additional notations describe gates of 48 feet each in width and partition walls 10 feet thick at the base, 5 feet thick at the top, and 24 feet in height (DLC: TJ Papers, 127:22029-35; endorsed by TJ: "Docks").

To William Hill Wells

Th: Jefferson requests the favour of *The Honble. Mr. Wells.* to dine with him on *Friday next, the 28th. Instant* at half after three, or at whatever later hour the house may rise.

Wednesday January 26th. 1803.

The favour of an answer is asked.

RC (PHC); printed form, with blanks filled by Meriwether Lewis reproduced in italics; addressed by Lewis: "The Honble. Mr. Wells"; endorsed by Wells.

William Hill Wells (1769-1829), a Federalist attorney in Delaware, was elected to the United States Senate in 1799 after the death of Joshua Clayton. Wells resigned in 1804 but was reelected to the Senate in 1813 to fill James A. Bayard's vacated seat (*Biog. Dir. Cong.*).

From Christopher Ellery

Jan. 27th. 1803

C. Ellery has the honor to present to the President of the United States the petition of Nathaniel Ingraham—to which he begs the attention of the President—C. Ellery will be happy to furnish every information in his power, at any moment; confident that the petitioner is a real object for mercy—

RC (DLC); endorsed by TJ as received 27 Jan. and "Ingraham's petn."

For earlier correspondence regarding NATHANIEL INGRAHAM, a Rhode Island mariner convicted by a federal court of engaging in the slave trade, see Vol. 37:199-200, 648; Vol. 38:606.

ENCLOSURE

Petition of Nathaniel Ingraham

[on or before 27 Jan. 1803]

The humble petition of Nathaniel Ingraham Mariner of Bristol in the County of Bristol in the State of Rhode Island & Providence Plantations, Sheweth

That in January in the Year of our Lord 1801, an action was brought against your Petitioner in the District Court for Rhode Island District by John W. Leonard, who sued as well for the United States as for himself, to recover certain penalties incurred by the Petitioner as Master of a certain vessel called the Fanney, under the acts of Congress against carrying on the Slave trade. That at November turm of said Court following the cause was tried and a verdict given by the jury against your Petitioner for the sum of Fourteen Thousand &   Dollars, and Judgment rendered accordingly for that sum with costs; that on the sixth Day of April AD. 1802 Execution having issued against your Petitioner upon said Judgment, he was thereupon committed to Jail in Bristol in said District. That on the voyage in which your Petitioner violated the Law as above stated the vessell was taken by the British, and together with the Cargo and your Petitioners adventure being all the Property he possessed, was condemned at New Providence, and totally lost. Now your Petitioner would humbly represent that he is so far from possessing means to discharge the amount of said Execution that he is utterly destitute of property for the support of himself and family from day to day. That in this his indigent situation and confined upon said Execution to Jail, his family would suffer the miseries of the most extreme poverty and the want even of food for the sustentation of life, but for the charity of friends and the scanty relief afforded by their own labour. That his family consists of a wife and five Children and an aged Mother who looked up to your Petitioner as their only hope and support, and have now no other prospect of relief from their distresses but in his liberation, But tho his own sufferings may be considered as the necessary consequence of his violation of the Laws. Yet theirs, tho they are innocent are not less severe, that for him & them there is yet hope in the clemency of the President of the United States, to whom your Petitioner emboldened by misfortune applies himself for Mercy and humbly supplicates for himself and his wretched family, that the President would be pleased to commiserate his condition, pardon his offence, and release that part of said penalty which is due to the United States. And your Petitioner as in Duty bound will ever pray— NATHANL INGRAHAM

We the Subscribers, whose names are hereunder written, certify that the Facts stated in the within Petition, are correct. We deplore the unhappy circumstances under which the Petitioner labours, and sincerely join with him in his Prayer for relief. We are certain that it is absolutely impossible for him ever to pay the fine imposed upon him; and there remains but the alternative, either to remit his fine, and restore to his distressed family their only support, and to the community an active and useful Citizen; or enforce the rigor of law against the unhappy delinquent, and oblige him to waste away an useful life in the depth of solitude and misery and plunge a virtuous and unoffending family into distress.

JOSEPH REYNOLDS. Justice S. Court.
JOHN D'WOLF. Just. Inf. Court.
AMOS HAIL Do. Do.
JOS. WHITMARSH. H. Sheriff Co. Bristol.
WILLIAM BRADFORD. Late Senator Congress.
SAMUEL ALLEN. Just. Inf. Court.
JOHN BROWN. Late Repr. Congress.
JOSEPH RAWSON. Justice Peace
BARNARD SMITH. Ditto
JOHN CHAMPLIN. Merchant.
DANIEL BRADFORD JUR. Justice Peace.
THO. CHURCH Merchant
WILLIAM HUNTER. Counsel. at Law
NICHO PECK Merchant.
ISAAC MANCHESTER Merchant
JEREMIAH DIMAN 2D Do.
CHARLES COLLINS Do.
CHARLES D'WOLFE Do.
JAMES ALLEN Do.
HERSEY BRADFORD Do.
BENJ BOSWORTH 2D Do.
JOHN W. BOURN Do.
JOSEPH SMITH, JUNR. Do.
WILLIAM GARDNER. } Do.
CALEB GARDNER } Newport

I know not the Petitioner but am well informd. he is a proper object of Clemency
CONSTANT TABER

MS (DLC: TJ Papers, 122:21038); undated; in an unidentified hand, signed by Ingraham; certificate on verso signed by all; at head of text: "To the President of the United States." Recorded in SJL as received 27 Jan. 1803 and "petn. fine for negro trade."

ACTS OF CONGRESS AGAINST CARRYING ON THE SLAVE TRADE: in 1794, Congress passed "An Act to prohibit the carrying on the Slave Trade from the United States to any foreign place or country." The act made any vessel built or outfitted in the United States that engaged in the international slave trade subject to seizure, prosecution, and condemnation in any federal circuit or district court. Persons owning or abetting such ventures were subject to fines of $2,000 and any United States citizen taking persons on board their vessels to be sold as slaves were liable to a fine of $200 for each slave received. Monies received as a result of the act were to be divided between the United States and the person or persons bringing the suit against the accused. The act was strengthened in 1800, subjecting owners of condemned slave ships to fines equal to double the amount of their share in the vessel, while citizens voluntarily serving on such vessels were liable for up to $2,000 in fines and two years imprisonment. Vessels commissioned by the United States were authorized to seize ships found in violation of the act, with the proceeds from the sale of condemned vessels to be divided among the officers and crew of the vessel making the seizure. Federal district and circuit courts also received specific cognizance "of all acts and offences against the prohibitions" contained within the act. An additional act, passed 28 Feb. 1803, prohibited the importation of "any negro, mulatto, or other person of colour, not being a native, a citizen, or a registered seaman of the United States" into ports where state laws prohibited such importations, thus making violations of the state law a violation of federal law as well. Federal customs and revenue officers were "enjoined vigilantly to carry into effect the said laws of said states, conformably to the provisions of this act" (U.S. Statutes at Large, 1:347-9; 2:70-1, 205-6; D. Kurt Graham, *To Bring Law Home: The Federal Judiciary in Early National Rhode Island* [DeKalb, Ill., 2010], 116-20).

Many of the SUBSCRIBERS above had a direct or indirect interest in the Rhode Island slave trade. As state and federal representatives, William Bradford and John Brown were active supporters of the trade, and Bradford's sons-in-law, Charles Collins and James D'Wolf, were among the state's leading participants. The D'Wolf, Champlin, and Gardner families had long and substantial involvement in slave trading. Nine of the subscribers were also directors of the Bristol Insurance Company, a firm incorporated in 1800 that supplied marine insurance on many slave vessels and their cargoes (Peter J. Coleman, *The Transformation of Rhode Island, 1790-1860* [Providence, 1963], 51-7, 211-12; Jay Coughtry, *The Notorious Triangle: Rhode Island and the African Slave Trade, 1700-1807* [Philadelphia, 1981], 37, 45-9, 94, 205, 209-10, 225-6, 262-85; Warren, R.I., *Herald of the United States*, 8 Jan. 1802).

To Horatio Gates

DEAR GENERAL Washington Jan. 27. 1803.

Nothing is so pleasing as to find that what we have done is so exactly what is approved by the friends whose judgment we esteem. not a tittle of what you recommend has been omitted; and it has been in train from June last. one article only varies. the situation of fort Rosalie, now the Natchez, being less favorable for a fort, one of the best on the Missisipi,[1] which happened to be very near our Southern boundary, was taken possession of, and a fort built by the former administration, under the name of fort Adams. it is an eminence on the river, commanding the river completely, & hors d'insulte itself: and it's harbour excellent. here we have been silently making a place d'armes, commensurate with the force of men in it's neighborhood. except as to the place, your ideas have been exactly & in every particular those on which we have acted. exclusive of these measures, the most important one now to be attended to is the opening a land office for the fine country we have lately got from the Choctaws, extending from the Missisipi to the Mobile & Alabama rivers, tho' nearly cut in two at the Pascagoula: our line running from the Yazoo S. Eastwardly to the Pascagoula, & thence N. Eastwardly to the Tombigbee, and including all the country between this last & the Alabama. if the lands be granted in small lots of $\frac{1}{4}$ of a mile each, making residence a condition of the continuance of the title, we shall have that country filled rapidly with a hardy yeomanry capable of defending it. if this speck in our horison blows over kindly I see nothing but smooth water before us. Monroe will be with you probably in a fortnight to take his immediate departure.—I hear with great pleasure from our friends, of whom I make frequent enquiries about you, that you preserve your health well. may it so continue to the end of the chapter, and that be as long a one as yourself shall desire. my respects attend mrs Gates, and to yourself I tender my affectionate & constant friendship.

TH: JEFFERSON

RC (NN); addressed: "General Gates New York"; franked and postmarked. PrC (DLC).

WHAT YOU RECOMMEND: see Gates to TJ, 7 Jan.

[1] MS: "Missipi," TJ having omitted a syllable when he hyphenated the word at a line break.

To Robert Leslie

DEAR SIR Washington Jan. 27. 1803.

Your favor of the 10th. came to hand in due time. the construction of the dry dock is laid aside for the present, from a cautious prudence not to undertake new expences, till experience fully establishes the state of our finances. I had contemplated the subject a great deal without foreseeing any thing which I thought could defeat it's effect. my curiosity therefore, as well as my concern, is excited by your observation that if the best remedy be applied to the defect of the plan, it may produce a wet dock? this I should consider as a total failure in our object; because in my eye a wet dock is not of much value. I presume from the tenor of your letter that you do not wish to make a secret of the particular defect you suppose to exist, and therefore take the liberty of asking a communication of it; as it is incumbent on me to guard the public against such a disappointment, should the object be returned at another session. Accept my best wishes & respects.

TH: JEFFERSON

PrC (DLC); at foot of text: "Mr. Robert Leslie"; endorsed by TJ in ink on verso.

DRY DOCK IS LAID ASIDE: see Leslie to TJ, 26 Jan. 1803.

Petititon of William Mattox, with Jefferson's Order

To the President of the United States

Washington City 27th. Jany. 1803

The Humble Petition of William Mattox Shewith that your Petitioner was convicted at the last Court held for the County of Washington in the district of Columbia—of Gambling for which he was fined to the amount of Fifty pounds Maryland Currency & cost. and is tharfore Committed to Jauil that your petitioner is a young Man and altho without any Family is unable to pay his fine and fees. that he is not in the habit of gambling that he was led into the Act for which he was Convicted from a want of Proper reflection that he has always sepperted a Good Character. that Josias M Speake and Samuel Speake his Brother both residents at this time in the City of Washington are both of them well acquainted with the said Petitioner and his Family have resided near to them from his Infancy untill a late period—and they do declare they never Knew of any misconduct of any one of his family untill the present and do believe he the said Petitioner being a young Man and Ignorent of the Laws was led into this by others. and being extreamly poor and now imprisoned. we think him a proper Object of the Clemancy of the President of the United States that as this is an act which he has not been in the habit of committing he tharefore hopes and prays that the President will remit his fine & fees and direct his discharge—his Statement is Supported by the papers herewith Sent—And the Petitioner will as in duty Bound ever pray

The Court while in session refused to recommend Mattox to the mercy of the President, as there did not appear on his trial any circumstances of extenuation. On the other hand, I do not recollect any of peculiar aggravation. It is stated to me that he has been in prison eight weeks. If the President should deem this imprisonment sufficient to answer the purposes of punishment for his offence, I feel confident that a remission of his fine would meet the approbation of the Court.—

W. Cranch, assistant Judge &c.
January 29. 1803.

I refused during the Session of the Court to recommend the remission of the fine imposed on Maddox or that imposed on Henderson, as I did not perceive any Sufficient Grounds for an active interference in their favour—But I am Willing to Concur in the Sentiments which

Mr Cranch has expressed, and think that, if they Should have any effect they ought to extend to Henderson as Well as Maddox

W KILTY
Jany 31 1803

I agree in opinion with Mr. Kilty— J MARSHALL

As attending Physician at the jail I have considered the case of the within petitioner Maddox.—His health appears to me to suffer much by confinement, & a large wen which he has under his ear is aggravated— FRED: MAY

[*Order by TJ:*]
A pardon to be issued April 21 1803.
TH: JEFFERSON

MS (DNA: RG 59, GPR); petition in an unidentified hand; statements on verso written and signed by William Cranch, William Kilty, James Marshall, and Frederick May. Enclosures: (1) Statement of Daniel C. Brent, undated, acknowledging his acquaintance with Josias and Samuel Speake and declaring that "neither of them wou'd *certify* any thing but what is correct." (2) Statement of John Thomson Mason, 28 Jan. 1803, declaring that there is no reason to doubt the correctness of the verdict against Mattox; Mason knows nothing of Mattox's "character or general deportment. He is from his appearance a young Man and a very poor one" (MSS in same). (3) Statement by William Kilty, 10 Feb. 1803, noting that his previous observations on Mattox's petition, in addition to those made by Cranch, were applicable to Mattox only, "but I also stated that Henderson was equally entitled to relief, leaving Maddox's case to depend on the recommendation which he had obtained" (MS in same; written at foot of Tr).

According to the record of his trial, laborer William Mattox (Maddox) of Washington County was indicted for operating a "Fair play Table" at the city race course on 4 Dec. 1802. Appearing before the December 1802 session of the U.S. Circuit Court for the District of Columbia, Mattox's attorney, Augustus B. Woodward, entered a plea of not guilty. The jury, however, found against the defendant and fined Mattox $133.33\frac{1}{3}$ plus court costs (Tr in same, attested by Uriah Forrest, 28 Jan. 1803). TJ issued a pardon and remission of Mattox's fines and charges on 22 Apr. 1803 (FC in Lb in same).

JOSIAS M. SPEAKE was a navy lieutenant stationed at the Washington Navy Yard (NDBW, *Register*, 51). His brother, SAMUEL SPEAKE, would be recommended to TJ as a candidate for justice of the peace in Washington, D.C. (Robert Brent to TJ, 4 Feb. 1803).

To Martha Jefferson Randolph

MY DEAR MARTHA Washington Jan. 27. 1803.

The last post-days have slipt away from me without adverting to them till too late. I learnt by a letter from Maria that you all got home safe, after a very disagreeable journey. indeed I suffered for you in imagination beyond any thing I had long felt. I found the road, in the short distance I went with you, so much worse than I expected, that I augured a dreadful journey, and sincerely lamented you did not await a better time. I felt my solitude too after your departure very severely.—your acquaintances here are well, except mrs Brent & mrs Burrowes. I find mr Lilly was to begin filling his icehouse the 21st. we have had no thaw here since that till yesterday, & the river is still entirely blocked up; so that if the weather has corresponded there, I am in hopes he will have got his house full. I must pray you to press on the making my shirts, so that I may have them on my arrival, which will probably be the 9th. of March. Edy has a son, & is doing well.—I inclose poetry for Anne's book. I must pray her to become my correspondent. it will be useful to her, and very satisfactory to me. Jefferson promised to write to me from Orange court house but was not as good as his word. I presume you were amused with the reciepts for making panne-quaiques and other good things. present my affectionate respects to mr Randolph, kisses to the young ones, and be assured of my tenderest love to yourself. TH: JEFFERSON

RC (NNPM); at foot of text: "Mrs. Randolph." PrC (CSmH); endorsed by TJ in ink on verso. Enclosure not identified.

LETTER FROM MARIA: Mary Jefferson Eppes to TJ, 11 Jan.

MRS BRENT: probably Anne Fenton Brent, wife of Daniel Carroll Brent (*National Intelligencer*, 27 Apr. 1803; Vol. 33:345n). Mary Bond Burrows was married to William Ward Burrows, commandant of the Marine Corps (*Washington Federalist*, 7 Feb. 1803; ANB, s.v., "Burrows, William Ward"). Both women died from their illnesses.

A letter of 9 Jan. by Gabriel LILLY was recorded in SJL as received 13 Jan. but has not been found. A letter by James Dinsmore of 13 Jan., recorded as received 21 Jan., has also not been found.

Edith (EDY) Hern trained in the White House kitchen and eventually became the head cook at Monticello. Although her first child likely did not live long, she and her husband Joseph Fossett had at least ten other children together (Stanton, *Free Some Day*, 60, Hern Family Tree).

For Lemaire's recipes for PANNE-QUAIQUES AND OTHER GOOD THINGS, see Marie Kimball, *Thomas Jefferson's Cook Book* (Charlottesville, 1976), 61, 62, 64, 104.

To John Campbell White

Washington Jan. 27. 1803.

Th: Jefferson presents his compliments to mr White. he has read with satisfaction the plan of Doctr. Kirwan; and does not doubt it's excellence for the country under his contemplation, or any other, under a single sovereignty. but the complicated form of our government would not admit of it. the constitution of the US. has not given to the general government the powers over the soil, nor the applications of money, which that would require. these powers remain with the ordinary legislature of every state, who alone could carry such a plan into effect, each within their own limits. he prays mr White to accept his thanks for the communication and his salutations.

PrC (DLC).

John Campbell White (1757-1847) was an Irish doctor and merchant who immigrated to Baltimore in 1798 and immediately established himself as a prominent member of the city's medical and business communities. He and his sons, many of whom also rose to commercial prominence, operated a merchant house and a successful gin distillery. White also served as president of the city's Benevolent Hibernian Society. He wrote TJ again in 1816 to forward some melon seeds from Persia (Baltimore *American and Commercial Daily Advertiser*, 12 July 1802, 20 Mch. 1809; Baltimore *Republican, or Anti-Democrat*, 12 Dec. 1803; biographical information in MdHi: John Campbell White Papers; Vol. 29:45n; White to TJ, 13 Aug. 1816).

White apparently enclosed the PLAN OF DOCTR. KIRWAN in a letter of 22 Jan., recorded in SJL as received from Baltimore on 24 Jan. but not found.

From John Conrad Lange

New York 28 January 1803

Hitherto I have hoped in vain for an answer respecting my deceased uncle, the merchant Adam Lange in Charleston, South Carolina. As my circumstances oblige me to return to Europe, I have given a regular power of attorney to Mr. Caspar Semler, near the 3 mile-stone, for the further prosecution of the business. I have therefore humbly to beg your Excellency to send the ultimatum, or at least the papers I lodged, to the said gentleman. In expectation of my petition being complied with I remain &c.

JOH: CONRAD LANGE

Tr (MHi); translation in Jacob Wagner's hand; dateline and signature supplied from RC. RC (same); in German; endorsed by TJ as received 8 Feb. and so recorded in SJL.

THE PAPERS I LODGED: aside from the letter printed above, the Editors have found no evidence of any correspondence or contact between Lange and TJ.

From Charles Willson Peale

DEAR SIR Museum Jany. 28th. 1803.

The Physiognotrace invented by Mr. Hawkins is made strong, because subject to be handled by all sorts of People that visit the Museum—The enclosed drawing and explanation of it, is rough, but correct—and I hope will give you a perfect Idea of all the essential parts of it. Mr. Hawkins has also contrived another Index, which is designed to give the lines of a $\frac{3}{4}$ face; the lines of the hair, eyes, eyebrows &c. The index of this is formed thus to let the head pass within the square & the point or side of it to moove & trace the subject, exactly corrisponding to the center of the joint of the Pentegraph

This kind of Index would require handling and therefore not fitted for a public Museum. It may be made equally correct to take the outer lines as well as the lines within—but the point to be mooved projecting so far from the joint, makes it so much of a lever to strain it, that such a movement unless carefully handled would soon be deranged.

His invention of the Polygraph, appears to me to possess many advantages over the copying-press—common Ink, and common paper, without any preparation, such as weting &c—Several originals may be wrote at once, without any considerable labour or restraint on the fingers. The machine patented before, is I beleive perfectly useless—Monsr. Chaudron (watch maker 3d Street) who possesses one, is of the same opinion. As soon as Mr. Hawkins returns and obtains his Patent, he will I beleive find it his interest to promote a manufactory of them.

I am in daily expectation of hearing again from my Sons, every interresting occurance I shall take the liberty to communicate, knowing your hearty wishes for their success—The Daily advertizer New York of the 24th Instant, gives a Sketch of an academy of Arts—such may be highly useful to America, and well conducted, may not be costly. In Philada. publick spirit is wanting for such incouragements—We were particularly unfortunate in some of our Members, when we attempted a like Institution. I endeavoured for some time to hold it up as a tender beautiful plant that if cherished would in future produce good fruit! Although my motives then for giving all the aid in my power, were actuated by a desire to promote a public benefit—yet I[1] was abused by writers, whom I never dained to make reply.

Altho' fond of the fine arts & desireous to promote a true taste in our Country—yet I see so many other objects that enter into the concern of every one; to encrease the comforts of life, that when possessed of leisure, will rather engage my attention—

I have wrote an essay on the means of preserving health and long life, which will be put to the press shortly. it may do good by opening the Eyes of some, who appear blind, or heedless of themselves—If some good is thereby promoted, I shall be satisfied.

I wish you every happiness and am with much respect your friend

C W Peale

RC (DLC); at foot of text: "The Honble Mr. Jefferson"; endorsed by TJ as received 31 Jan. and so recorded in SJL. PoC (PPAmP: Peale-Sellers Papers).

MACHINE PATENTED BEFORE: Marc Isambard Brunel received a U.S. patent in January 1799 for a device for writing with two pens. He manufactured his invention in England and marketed it there and in the United States (Silvio A. Bedini, *Thomas Jefferson and His Copying Machines* [Charlottesville, 1984], 36-9).

For the ACADEMY OF ARTS in New York, see Edward Livingston to TJ, 19 Jan. A few years earlier, Peale was involved in an effort to establish an arts academy called the Columbianum (Peale, *Papers*, v. 2, pt. 1:109-13).

For Peale's ESSAY, see his letter of 14 Feb.

[1] Peale here canceled "suffered."

ENCLOSURE

Description of the Physiognotrace

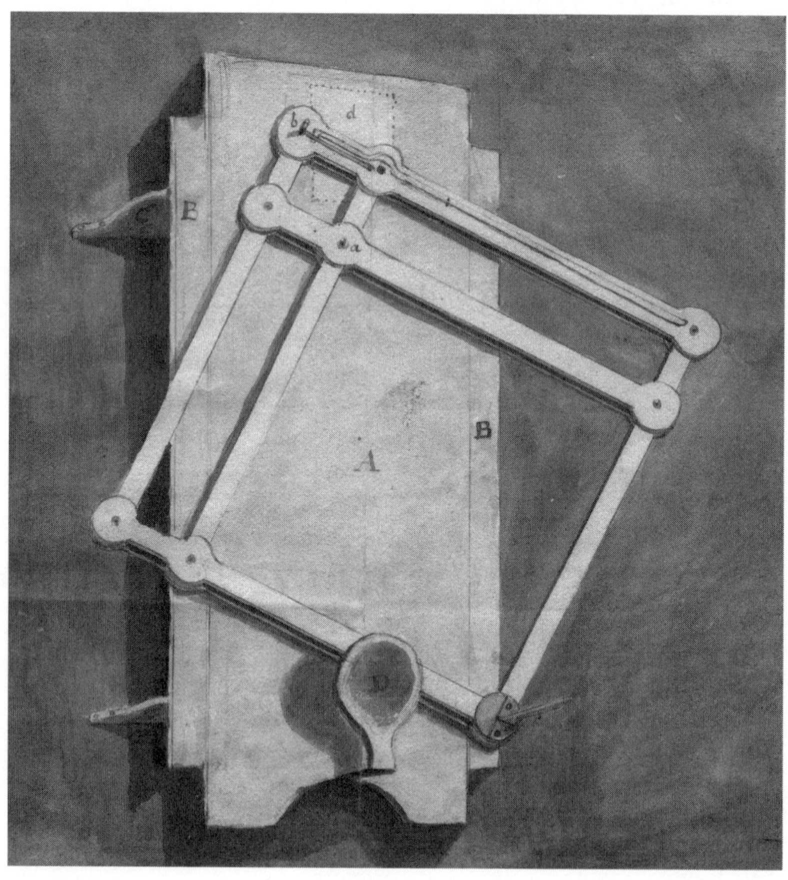

Explanation of Mr. Jno. I. Hawkins Physiognotrace

A is a board that mooves up and down in the frame B, B. which is fastened to the wall with brackets C, C,— This moovement is convenient to suit the heigth of different persons, and it is secured to its place by means of a screw on the back part,—D, is a hollowed board projecting 2½ Inches, to allow the Pentagraph to moove behind it. The person to be traced, setting in a Chair, rests their head on the concave part, & the hollow of the board below imbraces the shoulder—The Physiognotrace is fixed to the board A at a, and in the center of the joint b, is a conic Steel point with a spring to press it against the paper, represented by the doted lines, the Steel point is taken off the paper by means of a lever; having the upper end turned at a right angle under the spring in a wedged form, and the other end extended to the joint on the right to be in reach.

c, is an Index made of brass, the joint of which has plates on each side connected by a Center pin—to the out plate, is screwed a piece of brass 5 Inches long, with a thin edge, which edge is exactly perpendicular to the center of the joint.

This Index mooving round to trace any subject that the edge is keept too, as it mooves, the steel point in the center of the upper joint, gives a diminished size a perfectly correct representation. The paper to be traced is fixed on a square board by means of an Iron rim, and it is then placed on a door hinged to the back part of the Machine, & shut into a rabet made to receive & keep it at a proper distance from the Steel point.

MS (DLC: TJ Papers, 128:22193); in Peale's hand.

From Peter Carr

DEAR SIR Richmond. Janry. 29th. 1803

This will be presented by Mr William Brockenbrough, who is on a visit to Washington for a few weeks. A member of the Executive Council of Virginia, you will find in him, a man of real talents, and very great worth. This will be a sufficient recommendation, to your civilities and attention. Your letter of the 21st. was duely received. I communicated the contents of it to Mr. Harvie, and he appeared to be perfectly satisfied. We passed yesterday a resolution Upon the subject of The Missisipi, with but one dissenting voice. Accept assurances of my sincere attachment— P: CARR

RC (DLC); at foot of text: "President of U States"; endorsed by TJ as received 4 Feb. and so recorded in SJL.

WILLIAM BROCKENBROUGH was a lawyer and later a judge. Identified as a member of the so-called Richmond Junto, which wielded great influence over the state's Republican Party, he also helped shape arguments against John Marshall's nationalistic judicial philosophy. In 1818, he served on the commission that selected Charlottesville as the location for the University of Virginia (DVB, 2:255-6).

The RESOLUTION of Virginia's General Assembly expressed support for the national government in its efforts to secure the right of deposit at New Orleans and hoped that, if needed, "such measures will be adopted as become a free and independent nation, who know their rights, and are able to defend them" (Richmond *Virginia Argus*, 2 Feb. 1803).

From Albert Gallatin

DEAR SIR 29th Jany. 1803

I enclose a recommendation for the office of "Surveyor of the port of Nixinton in the district of Camden" (N.Ca.) and of "inspector of the revenue for the same port."

The office has long been vacant; but we had waited, for the meeting of Congress, for better information. Both Mr Stone and Mr Wynnes concur in approving Mr Brewer. [The] last gentleman lives not far from the [port]

The corrected navy estimates are much wanted. Whatever you will decide shall be recommended to the Committee of Ways & Means.

With great respect Your obedt. Servt. ALBERT GALLATIN

RC (DLC); torn; addressed: "The President of the United States"; endorsed by TJ as received from the Treasury Department on 29 Jan. and "nomn Wm. Brewer" and so recorded in SJL; also endorsed by TJ: "navy approprn." Enclosure: Enoch Sawyer to Gallatin, Collectors Office, District of Camden, 1 Sep. 1802, informing the Treasury secretary that upon the resignation of Hugh Knox, he designated William Brewer to perform the duties of surveyor of the port of Nixonton; Sawyer does not know a person better qualified for the appointment than Brewer, who is a gentleman of "property & integrity," resides at Nixonton, and "has some knowledge of the revenue laws having for some considerable time transacted the business there as Mr. Knox's deputy" (RC in DNA: RG 59, LAR; endorsed by TJ: "Brewer Wm. to be Collector & Inspector Nixonton v. Hugh Knox").

Republican Thomas Wynns (WYNNES), a planter from Hertford County, North Carolina, took his seat in the House of Representatives on 7 Dec. 1802, filling the vacancy caused by the death of Charles Johnson. He was reelected to the Eighth and Ninth Congresses and served until 3 Mch. 1807 (*Biog. Dir. Cong.*; William S. Powell, ed., *Dictionary of North Carolina Biography*, 6 vols. [Chapel Hill, 1979-96], 6:285; Vol. 37:343n).

For the appointment of William BREWER, see TJ to the Senate, 2 Feb.

From Robert Smith

SIR Navy Dep. Jan. 29. 1803

I some time since wrote to the Navy Agent at New York respecting Danl Baldwin. The result shall be Communicated to you when received.

I did not understand from Mr Gallatin that I was to send to him an additional Estimate of Navy appropriations. I will however see him this morning.

Respectfully H S RT. SMITH

RC (DLC); endorsed by TJ as received from the Navy Department on 31 Jan. and "navy approprns" and so recorded in SJL.

Disabled veteran Daniel BALDWIN and his wife, Phebe, sent letters to TJ in 1802 and early 1803 seeking employment, none of which have been found. Daniel wrote TJ from New York on 12 Apr. 1802, which SJL records as received 14 Apr. and forwarded to the War Department (Vol. 37:716). Phebe Baldwin's letters to TJ of 27 Dec. 1802 and 25 Jan. 1803 from Paterson, New Jersey, are recorded in SJL as received 18 and 29 Jan., respectively, the latter of which was forwarded to the Navy Department. On 27 Jan. 1803, Smith wrote Daniel Ludlow, the navy agent at New York City, enclosing a letter from Mrs. Baldwin soliciting employment for her husband, "who is represented as having lost his Leg in the Battle of Germantown," and requested that Baldwin be given "any employment for which he may be able and fit" (DNA: RG 45, MLS; see also Kline, *Burr*, 2:705).

For Albert Gallatin's revised ESTIMATE OF NAVY APPROPRIATIONS, see Gallatin to TJ, 18, 22, and 29 Jan. 1803.

From William Adamson

ESTEEMED FRIEND Philadelphia the 30th. of Jany. 1803

When I had the pleasure of seeing thee last year at Washington, I promised to send thee a copy of Rufs: King's Lettr. to my friend Henry Jackson granting him permission to come to America, & on going to Carlisle, I accordingly applied to my said frd. for a Copy, who replied that he wd. shortly go on to Washington & hand thee the original!—He did go there soon after, but his diffidence got the better of his strong desire to enjoy the pleasure of thy acquaintance; & on his return home he wrote me that seeing the base lengths wch. the Federal papers went in foul abuse of thy hospitable attentions to some individuals obnoxious to the malice of that maligning faction, he thought it best to avoid the possibility of their vilifying thee on his account, he being proscribed by the British government, for his attachment to free representative government, & abhorrence of that wch is corrupt & oppressive, as theirs is become: & knowing that their partizans in this Country are full as vindictive as themselves, he thought it most prudent for that time to decline his intended visit to thee!—An occasion has however recently occurr'd, for calling upon him for Rufus King's letter! Subsequent to the late peace in Europe, the British government relax'd in it's rigours towards the Irish state prisoners, & I believe all or most of them are now liberated: & some of them are come to this Country: these have united with the Aliens before resident here, in a Memorial to the present Congress for an amelioration of the late naturalization Law, enacted by that body: in which they took occasion to advert to the hostility of the late administration to Aliens of known republican principles, particularly the Irish, as evinced by the interference of the American Minister at the Court of St. James, with the British Government, to prevent their being allowed to emigrate to the United States; by which many respectable, industrious & opulent republicans, & some of first rate literary talents, were detain'd in dungeons near four years longer!—lest this should be cavill'd at, or it's authenticity disputed, by the friends of that administration, my friend Edwd: Hudson, one of the late prisoners of Fort George, wrote to our frd. Hen: Jackson for the Lettr., in order to send a copy of it to the friendly member who presents the Memorial to Congress, & received the original copy of wch. & of the memorial, as well as of E: Hudson's Lettr. & H: Jackson's answer, I now take the liberty of inclosing to thee, in order that thou mayest have a view of the whole ground: and knowing thee to be friendly to virtuous republican Aliens, I have great pleasure in assuring thee, on this occasion, that all my Countrymen who have taken asylum in this Country, from British Tyranny, are to a man strongly attach'd to the constitution of the united states, & inexpressibly happy in the present administration of this Government, in so much that I declare I believe they appreciate it more highly than the native patriots; from the glaring contrast of former missery, & Present happiness—of slavery and liberty! oppression & freedom! and tho this experience excited their jealousy against the venal measures of the late administration; it strengthens their confidence in the present, whose measures promise permanency to the blessings they enjoy under its mild & equal government:—a proof, I trust, sufficient, of the injustice of the charge that the Irish cannot be satisfied under any governmt: as Wm. Pitt & Rufus King, & all the enemies of real (not nominal) free government wd. have it.

I have the happiness now to call thee my fellow Citizen, having been enfranchized under the five years act of naturalization; & am with great esteem & regard

Thy respectful friend Wm Adamson

RC (DLC); at head of text: "Thomas Jefferson Esqr:"; endorsed by TJ as received 2 Feb. and so recorded in SJL. Enclosures: (1) Rufus King to Henry Jackson, Brighton, 28 Aug. 1799, replying to Jackson's letter of 22 July requesting permission to emigrate to America; King explains that Congress had recently given him "an assurance, that a particular description of persons in Ireland" would not be permitted to leave for the United States without that nation's consent; this restriction, King assumes, would be lifted on individuals "against whose emigration I should not object"; examining the political situation in America, King and others believe that a portion of their countrymen has "erroniously supposed" that America's civil and political institutions would be improved "by a close imitation of the Models of France"; this has created considerable divisions among Americans and "required a greater watchfullness and activity from the Government"; in particular, King states that a large proportion of Irish immigrants, especially in the middle states, has "arranged itself on the side of the Malcontents"; King excepts a few "enlightened & well educated Irishmen who reside among us," and largely confines his comments to the "indigent and illiterate, who entertaining an attachment to freedom are unable justly to appreciate those salutary restraints without which it degenerates into anarchy"; King worries that the Irish in America may enlist in "mischievous combinations against our Government"; he does not object in general to the emigration of persons of capital and skill, but such persons may become "tenfold more dangerous" if their opinions align them with the malcontents; "the motives which lead me to interfere with your Government to restrain the emigration of the persons above alluded to," King explains, "oblige me to observe a due caution on the present occasion"; the recommendation in Jackson's favor that he received from Joseph Wilson, the United States consul at Dublin, has led King to "*withdraw every objection* that may be supposed to stand in the way of your being permitted to go to the United States"; King urges Jackson to carry an "unbiassed mind" to America and hopes that he may find the country favorable to his future business endeavors "& its Government deserving your attachment" (Tr in same; King, *Life*, 2:645-7; JEP, 1:158). (2) Edward Hudson to Henry Jackson, Philadelphia, 20 Jan. 1803, restraining himself from giving full vent to his feelings on the betrayal of his country and the victimization of its people "to a mercantile, relentless policy"; Hudson has no desire to become "an American politician," but as an Irishman, Hudson must always feel as such; many of his countrymen in Philadelphia have resolved to send a memorial to Congress, praying an alteration of the naturalization laws; the memorial will also assert that because of the American minister's refusal to allow Irish political prisoners to reside in the United States, the British government made this the pretext for "detaining them in dungeons for the space of four years, in open violation of a solemn compact"; the aliens wish to support this statement with every document possible; while imprisoned, Hudson was present when Mr. Marsden, one of the secretaries of the Irish government, informed the prisoners that they would not be allowed to emigrate to America because of objections by the American minister in London; Hudson and his fellow prisoners, including Jackson, initially believed this was a lie concocted by the British to keep them imprisoned; Hudson recollects that Jackson wrote Rufus King on the subject, and received a reply establishing the fact "*that he did interfere against us*" and the "imprecations" by the prisoners against King as a result of his letter were unanimous; King's letter to Jackson would confirm the statement of the aliens in their memorial to Congress, and Hudson asks Jackson for a copy of it, or, preferably, the original; it may not be necessary to make use of the letter, but if a partisan of King should call for proof of the accusations made against him by the memorialists, the use of the letter would prevent the tables from being turned against the memorialists; anything brought before the public must not only be grounded in fact, but able to be proven as well; the accusations against King "cannot be questioned *by us*," but may be by others and the difficulty lies in proving them; "Without the letter in your possession," Hudson concludes, "we cannot—With it we can: and to the conviction of the most willfully incredulous" (Tr in DLC). (3) Henry Jackson to Edward Hudson, Carlisle, 24 Jan. 1803, forwarding Rufus King's letter to him, "full proof of his interfering, and I have little doubt of his doing as the English Government directed him"; Jackson also encloses "that Scoundrel Castlereagh's letter to me returning it, having sent it to him to remove the only objection the Irish Government said they had to my leaving Ireland"; King's delay in answering Jackson cost him £500; "*somebody* got that sum for procuring an order for leave for me to go to America," Jackson claims, although he did not learn this until a year after he arrived; "this same influence" now offers to procure leave for Jackson to return for a "few hundred pounds—*What a virtuous Government*"; Jackson asks Hudson to take care of the letters, since he may have occasion to make use of them at another day, and hopes to see some of Hudson's committee in Washington, "if the weather is tolerable, all depends on that" (RC in same). (4) "Memorial of the Aliens, Inhabitants of the City and County of Philadelphia" to the Senate and the House of Representatives, undated, stating that they had petitioned Congress during their previous session for a repeal of the existing naturalization law; describing the experiences of those memorialists residing in America from the summer of 1798 to the spring of 1801, the petition claims "Every *Alien* distinguished for his attachment to the principles of Liberty, was incessantly abused" by the Federalist press, that the American minister in London stated in the name of his government that Irish state prisoners would not be allowed to reside in the United States, that the British government made this a pretext for detaining them "in dungeons" for four years, that the president at that time was "notoriously hostile to Aliens of Republican principles," and that he was authorized by law to banish any alien at his pleasure; under these circumstances, few resident aliens declared an intention of becoming a United States citizen, "For by so doing, he placed his name on a list of proscription, and subjected himself to banishment, at the arbitrary will of an Individual"; the memorialists argue that even the poorest immigrant arriving in America "has a property in his life, in his liberty, and in his labour; and is as liable to the laws as the richest Citizen"; to tax, imprison, or execute him by laws that were framed without his representation "is to exercise against him an act of tyranny"; society would benefit by enfranchising aliens that have demonstrated good character, paid taxes, showed their attachment to American government, and declared their wish to reside permanently in the United States; they rest their case not only on rights, but on justice and policy as well; the majority of the memorialists are natives of Ireland and retain a love and appreciation for freedom; Congress acknowledged the services of Irish patriots to the cause of "*Humanity and America*" and invited them to partake of the United States and of their success, "and the countrymen of *Montgomery*, have never by their conduct in war, or their votes in peace, proved unworthy of the Blessing"; those who have sacrificed their country "for the Principles on which your Constitution is founded" deserve the trust and functions of citizenship; states like Pennsylvania and others, where the laws regarding foreigners are most liberal, "are not inferior in attachment to the American Union, in Morals, in Freedom, in Arts, Industry or Prosperity to any of their Sister States"; such states are foremost in population increase, affording strength and security to the nation, and by their constitutions the "Stranger of good Conduct" may become a citizen after two years residence; Spain and France suffered by expelling foreigners from their lands, and the memorialists urge Congress to "Encourage your Aliens, you will have the Arts and Manufactures of Europe;—neglect us, we suffer, but you are not served"; they therefore pray that Congress admit to citizenship those aliens who are now excluded on account of not having made a declaration of their intention three years previously, and to restore the time of two years' residence specified in the original naturalization law (printed copy in same).

SEEING THEE LAST YEAR AT WASHINGTON: no information regarding Adamson's meeting with TJ has been found. Adamson mentioned this meeting in his letter to TJ of 28 Dec. 1801, in which he detailed the travails of United Irish refugee Henry Jackson as well as Rufus King's efforts to thwart the emigration of Irish political prisoners to the United States in 1798 (Vol. 36:220-4).

MEMORIAL TO THE PRESENT CONGRESS: the petition from the aliens of the city and county of Philadelphia, seeking a revision to the naturalization act of 1802, was presented to the House of Representatives on 16 Feb. 1803 and referred to a select committee formed two days earlier. Committee member Michael Leib reported a bill on 17 Feb. that would allow any free white alien, who resided continually in the United States between 18 June 1798 and 14 April 1802, to become a citizen without complying with the portion of the naturalization law of 1802 that required an alien to declare in court his intention at least three years before his admission to citizenship. After much debate, in which opponents questioned the necessity of the act and objected to the indecorous language of the petition, the bill was rejected by the House (JHR, 4:339-40, 345-6, 347, 357-8; *Annals*, 12:570-81). George Logan presented memorials from sundry aliens in Pennsylvania to the Senate on 16 Feb., remarking that they "contained some expressions not so respectful and decorous as he could wish." After debate, the memorials were ordered to lie on the table (JS, 3:266; *Annals*, 12:97-9).

Dentist Edward HUDSON was among the United Irishmen arrested by British authorities in 1798 and subsequently imprisoned at Fort George in Scotland. Released in 1802, he emigrated to Philadelphia the following year, where he became a leading dental practitioner (DAB).

From Levi Lincoln

Jany 30th. 1803

Mr Lincoln's best respects to the President. he has no doubt of the propriety & utility, as it respects Stevens for Whittemore, & Story, for Pickman—but as to the successor of Fosdick, he is unable to determine—Mr Lincoln will have the honor of dining with the President on tuesday next—

RC (DLC); endorsed by TJ as received 30 Jan. and "nomns. Stevens Story Illsley" and so recorded in SJL.

SUCCESSOR OF FOSDICK: TJ saw a letter addressed to Madison by James Deering and five others dated 21 Jan. recommending Isaac Ilsley as collector at Portland and Falmouth if the president removed Nathaniel F. Fosdick. Ilsley was noted for his "good sense, integrity and abilities" as well as "his firm and avowed attachment to the present administration." The signers were careful to stipulate that they had "no idea of suggesting any thing against the abilities of Mr. Fosdick." While a "very few" might be against his removal, they observed, the appointment of Ilsley would give "general satisfaction" (RC in DNA: RG 59, LAR; signed by Deering, James Jewitt, Albert Newhall, Henry Sitcomb, Enoch Preble, and Salmon Chase; endorsed by TJ: "Isaac Ilsley to be collector v. Fosdyck"). TJ also viewed a letter that was critical of Fosdick. On 18 Oct. 1802, William Wilson wrote Robert Smith from Portland advocating Fosdick's removal, noting that in political debates he was "the most vociferous in his personal invectives" and made "scandulous remarks on the private and public conduct of the President." Wilson recommended Richard Hunewell for the collectorship, but he was already surveyor and inspector, having been appointed by Adams in December 1800 (RC in same, endorsed by TJ: "Wilson wm. to Robert Smith

Hunniwell Richard Collector of Portland. v. Fosdyck"; JEP, 1:357; ASP, *Miscellaneous*, 1:265). For Lincoln's view on the removal of Fosdick and other Federalists in Massachusetts, see his letters to TJ of 6 and 13 Dec.

To Madame de Tessé

DEAR MADAM Washington Jan. 30. 1803.

Mr. Short delivered me your favor of the 1st. Praireal an. 10. and gave me the welcome news of your good health. it has recalled to my mind recollections very dear to it. for the friendship with which you honoured me in Paris was among the circumstances which most contributed to my happiness there. when I left you at the close of 1790. I thought your situation in it's best possible state. at the end of 1791. I saw it was pressed, and in the course of 1792. that all was desperate. in the gloomy years which then followed my anxieties attended my friends personally, and particularly yourself of whom I could seldom hear. after such a shipwreck it is fortunate indeed that you can resume the interest you take in planting trees: and I shall be very happy in contributing to aliment it. to this however my present situation is not favorable, partly from my constant occupations, but more from my geographical position. not a single person in this quarter has attended to botanical subjects beyond the ordinary produce of the kitchen garden: nor are there, scarcely ever, any means of conveyance from hence to France. I have therefore selected from the catalogue you put into mr Short's hands those articles only which the forests of this neighborhood, or it's few gardens can furnish. these are

Liriodendron tulipifera.
Juglans nigra.
Juniperus Virginiana.
des glands de plusieurs especes.
Laurus Sassafras.
Magnolia glauca.
Magnolia tripetala (Umbrella)
Cornus florida.
fraxinus alba. doubtful if here.
Catalpa.

these are in my power. by undertaking more, I might have prevented mr Short's engaging for them a more certain agent. it was late in September when I recieved the catalogue. I was then at Monticello. the Sassafras had already lost it's seeds, and those of the others were still in a milky unripe state. on my return here I engaged an old Scotch gardener of the neighborhood, who had formerly lived some years in my family, to undertake this collection. he called on me a few days ago, and informed me that the season for collecting some of the articles had escaped him, but that he had collected a part, & would bring them in a few days. my difficulty will then be to find a conveyance; but no exertions will be spared to overcome this so that they may reach you in March. they will probably be addressed to mr La Motte, Vice consul of the US. in Havre. I will continue to lay my shoulder to these articles annually till you are fully supplied with them.

I own, my dear Madam, that I cannot but admire your courage in undertaking now to plant *trees*. it has always been my passion; insomuch that I scarcely ever planted a *flower* in my life. but when I return to live at Monticello, which may be in 1805. but will be in 1809. at the latest (because then, at any rate, I am determined to draw the curtain between the political world and myself,) I believe I shall become a florist. the labours of the year, in that line, are repaid within the year, and death, which will be at my door, shall find me unembarrassed in long-lived undertakings. but I acknolege there is more of the disinterested & magnanimous in your purpose.

This goes by mr Monroe, my eleve, my best friend, & the honestest man on earth, lately governor of Virginia, and now charged with a special mission to the governments of France & Spain. he will be the safest channel through which you can convey me any further orders. be so good as to present my respectful attachment to M. de Tessé, and accept yourself assurances of my constant & affectionate friendship & high consideration.

TH: JEFFERSON

PrC (DLC); at foot of first page: "Madame de Tessé."

YOUR FAVOR OF THE 1ST. PRAIREAL AN. 10: that is, 21 May 1802 (Vol. 37:480-1).

When he wrote to Robert Bailey on 9 Dec. about trees for Madame de Tessé's garden, TJ used English names for the tulip poplar (LIRIODENDRON TULIPIFERA), black walnut (JUGLANS NIGRA), and cedar (JUNIPERUS VIRGINIANA). TJ asked the horticulturalist to supply a variety of acorns (DES GLANDS DE PLUSIEURS ESPECES) and the SASSAFRAS, but not the two types of MAGNOLIA. His request to Bailey included dogwood (CORNUS FLORIDA), white ash (FRAXINUS ALBA), and CATALPA.

OLD SCOTCH GARDENER: Bailey.

MR LA MOTTE: F. C. A. Delamotte.

To Madame de Corny

Washington Jan. 31. 1803

So good an opportunity, my dear friend, offers of getting a letter safely to you by Colo. Monroe, that I cannot let it pass by, altho' I have nothing new to entertain you with: for it is not new to you for me to repeat assurances of my sincere and constant friendship. I often look back with regret on the days I passed so happily with my friends in Paris, and with none more than yourself. your subsequent adversities have never been known to me until they were over, which has saved me much pain. after seeing that your revolution took a turn which promised nothing good, my anxieties were fixed on my friends alone: and such were the times both here & there that little could be known of them. your government seems now strong enough to protect it's members against one another, and to ensure that degree of safety to person & property. our friends mrs Church and mrs Cruger are well. I have never seen them since their return to America. they are very distant from this place. it happens that all their connections are of a party opposed to the present order of things, and Colo. Hamilton, who married mrs Church's sister, is at the head of that party: and altho the body is absolutely reduced to nothing, the head and principal members keep up an appearance of opposition. I have no reason to believe that these circumstances have in the least affected the friendship of mrs Church or mrs Cruger towards me; and it certainly has not mine to them. you will have the pleasure of seeing mrs Monroe at Paris for a time, who will be able to give you more recent accounts of our friends of N. York. it will give me great pleasure to learn that you retain your health & chearfulness, and that you do not exclude yourself from society. you would do your friends great injustice and deprive them of a great enjoiment, in withdrawing yourself from their intercourse. cherish therefore, my dear friend, your health & hilarity; preserve for me always a place in your affection, & continue to assure me of it at times, and accept the homage of my constant and sincere attachment and respect. TH: JEFFERSON

PrC (DLC); at foot of text: "Mde. de Corny."

To Maria Cosway

MY DEAR FRIEND Washington Jan. 31. 1803.

I have to acknolege the reciept of your favor of July 20. 1801. from London, and of Feb. 25. 1802. from Paris. that I am so late in answering them arises from my incessant occupations which deprive me of the happiness of satisfying the affections of my heart by expressions of them on paper to my friends: to none would they be more warmly expressed, my esteemed friend, than to yourself, with whom the first interview produced an attachment which has never been diminished. and you are now at Paris, enjoying the remains of our friends there, basking in all the varieties of happiness which that place yields, indulging your taste & talents for painting and preparing to treat the world with a representation of the splendid works you are feasting on yourself. a splendid work yours will be, I am sure, and I wished long ago to have said so to you, and to have asked you to set me down as a subscriber. I see by the prospectus that the numbers are to be delivered & paid for in London, and shall take measures accordingly. this will be carried by my best friend mr Monroe, who is sent to Paris on an occasional diplomatic mission. he is the honestest man alive, and carries with him, in mrs Monroe, a specimen of our American beauties. any letter you may at any time confide to him for me will be safely forwarded; and besides wishing to learn the progress you make in your work, I am always wishing to hear of your health and happiness. you express anxieties for the catholic religion here. all religions here are equally free, and equally protected by the laws, and left to be supported by their own respective votaries. in some places the Catholic is better off than other sects, as they possess valuable endowments of land. your brother is well. he has lately superintended the erection of a public building with entire approbation. cherish on your part the friendship of our former days, and be assured of my constant and sincere affection & respect.

TH: JEFFERSON

PrC (DLC); at foot of text: "Mrs. Cosway."

FIRST INTERVIEW: TJ first met Maria Cosway in Paris in early August or September 1786 through an introduction from the artist John Trumbull (Helen Duprey Bullock, *My Head and My Heart: A Little History of Thomas Jefferson and Maria Cosway* [New York, 1945], 13, 21; MB, 1:637-8; Vol. 10:2).

THE PROSPECTUS: the Proposal to Publish Etchings of Pictures in the Louvre was enclosed with Cosway's letter of 25 Feb. 1802 (see Vol. 36:637).

YOUR BROTHER: George Hadfield, who designed and oversaw construction of the public jail in Washington (Vol. 37:694-6).

From Nicolas Gouin Dufief

MONSIEUR, Le 31 de Janvier, 1803—

Je vous envoie le catalogue des livres qui me restent de la Bibliothèque du Dr Franklin. Lorsque vous l'aurez parcouru, je vous prie de le faire remettre au Bibiothécaire du Congrés à qui je propose, dans la croyance qu'il pourrait être autorisé à le faire, l'achat de la

Collection, en tout, ou en partie. On m'a Suggeré cette idée à laquelle j'aurais sans doute pensé, si je m'étais rappellé que le Congrès avait destiné une certaine somme pour l'acquisition d'une bibliothéque.

Quel plus digne usage de cet argent, Monsieur, que de l'employer à racheter les livres d'un des Fondateurs de la Republique Américaine & d'un grand homme! Ce n'est point un esprit de Spéculatïon qui me fait tenir ce langage, car outre que ces livres conviennent à une bibliothèque nationale, étant en grande partie sur la *politique*, la *législation* & les affaires d'*Amèrique*, je les laisserais à un prix si raisonnable qu'on ne pourrait nullement m'accuser d'une chose pareille—

Si je ne réussissais pas dans une *Négociation* dont je désire ardemment le Succès, il me resterait une ressource pour m'en défaire; ce serait de les vendre à l'encan, votre choix fait de ceux qui pourraient vous convenir. Je suis pleinement convaincu que l'enthousiasme de nos concitoyens & le nom de Franklin, ne rendissent cette maniere d'en disposer avantageuse pour moi; cependant pour vous parler avec franchise, je me sens une grande repugnance à le faire; elle ne pourrait ceder qu'a une nécessité impérieuse & à l'embarras oû me jettent ces livres dans le petit local très resserré que j'habite—

Non, Monsieur quoique Libraire, je ne vendrais jamais publiquement que malgré moi les livres de *Gallilée*, de *Newton* & de *Franklin.*

J'ai cru vous faire plaisir & vous donner une preuve non équivoque de ma profonde estime en joignant au Catalogue deux petits ouvrages sur la Revolution américaine, rendus inestimables par les notes posthumes de votre illustre coopérateur dans le grand & glorieux œuvre de l'indépendance. Lisez-les, communiquez-les, si vous le désirez, à vos amis, & ensuite renvoyez-moi le volume qui les contient, par la même voie dont je me sers pour vous le faire parvenir—

Adieu, Monsieur, puissiez vous Jouir d'une santé égale à votre amour pour la chose publique, & aux sentimens que vous dois—

Votre très dévoué Serviteur N. G. DUFIEF

EDITORS' TRANSLATION

SIR, 31 Jan. 1803

I am sending you the catalogue of books that remain from the library of Dr. Franklin. After you have looked at it, would you be good enough to forward it to the librarian of Congress? I am offering him the opportunity to purchase all or part of the collection, assuming he is authorized to do so. Someone suggested this idea which I would undoubtedly have thought of had I remembered that Congress earmarked a certain sum for the acquisition of a library.

What more worthy use of this money, Sir, than to re-acquire books belonging to one of the founders of the American Republic and a great man! In using such language, I am not at all prompted by a spirit of speculation. These books are appropriate for a national library, since they deal mainly with politics, legislation, and American affairs. And I would let them go at such a reasonable price that no one could accuse me of such a thing.

If I do not succeed in a negotiation whose success I ardently desire, my only alternative for disposing of the books would be to sell them at auction where you could choose the ones you wished. I am fully convinced that the enthusiasm of our fellow citizens and the name of Franklin would make this manner of disposing of the books advantageous for me. Nevertheless, to speak frankly to you, I feel a great repugnance to do this. I would give in to this repugnance only out of imperious necessity and the problems these books create in the very small space I inhabit.

No, Sir, although I am a bookseller, I would never sell the works of Galileo, Newton and Franklin to the general public unless obliged to do so.

As an unequivocal sign of my high esteem, I thought you would appreciate receiving, along with the catalogue, two small works about the American revolution, rendered priceless by the posthumous notes of your illustrious partner in the great and glorious work of independence. Read them; share them with your friends, if you wish, and then return the volume by the same kind of mail I am using to send it to you.

Farewell, Sir. May you enjoy health equal to your love of the republic and to the sentiments I owe you.

Your very devoted servant N. G. DUFIEF

RC (DLC); at foot of first page: "Ths Jefferson, President of the United States"; endorsed by TJ as received 3 Feb. and so recorded in SJL. Enclosures: see below.

Dufief's manuscript CATALOGUE of approximately 2,000 books from Benjamin Franklin's library has not been found. TJ returned the list after the committee overseeing acquisitions for the congressional library declined to buy any of the works (see TJ to Abraham Baldwin, 4 Feb., and to Dufief, 1 Mch.). Dufief reluctantly sold Franklin's books at public auction—LES VENDRE À L'ENCAN—on the evening of 12 Mch. 1803 (Madeleine B. Stern, *Nicholas Gouin Dufief of Philadelphia: Franco-American Bookseller, 1776-1834* [Philadelphia, 1988], 26-32).

DEUX PETITS OUVRAGES: Dufief enclosed two pamphlets, Matthew Wheelock's *Reflections Moral and Political on Great Britain and her Colonies* (London, 1770) and Allen Ramsay's *Thoughts on the Origin and Nature of Government* (London, 1769), which had been bound together and contained extensive marginal NOTES by Franklin (Sowerby, No. 3073; TJ to Dufief, 4 Feb., 5 May 1803; Dufief to TJ, 14 Feb.).

From Augustine Eastin

SIR, Bourbon County, Kentucky. January 31st. 1803.

I have son Zechariah Eastin,[1] who offers for a certain office in the Indianna Territory; if his recommendations are sufficient to intitle him to your confidence, and the office he solicits, is not filled up; I offer a fathers wish, who has been at the expence of fitting a son for buisness in his favour: and ask only for that justice, to which an early adventurer to the Western country is intitled.

I am, with all due respect, Sir, Your mo obdt Sevt.

AUGUSTINE EASTIN

RC (DNA: RG 59, LAR); endorsed by TJ as received 17 Feb. and "his son for office" and so recorded in SJL.

Baptist minister Augustine Eastin (1750-1833) emigrated from Goochland County, Virginia, to Kentucky in 1784, eventually settling in Bourbon County. A co-founder of the church at Cooper's (Cowper's) Run along with future governor James Garrard, Eastin's standing and influence among state Baptists declined after he embraced Arianism. He published a pamphlet in defense of the doctrine in 1804, entitled *Letters on the Divine Unity*. His son Zachariah served with distinction as an officer at the Battle of Tippecanoe and during the War of 1812 (Phyllis Eastin Clendaniel, *The Eastins of Virginia & Kentucky and Allied Families of Bohannon, Johnson, Knox* [Louisa, Va., 1999], Section II; J. H. Spencer, *A History of Kentucky Baptists. From 1769 to 1885*, 2 vols. [Cincinnati, 1885], 1:131-2).

[1] Name and comma interlined.

From Albert Gallatin

Treasury Department
January 31st: 1803

SIR,

It having been represented that the District Judge of New-Hampshire had, in a suit where the revenue was concerned, acted in a manner which showed a total unfitness for the office; the District Attorney was requested to collect evidence on that subject. A copy of his letter and the original affidavits he has transmitted, are now enclosed—

The unfortunate situation of the Judge seems to render some legislative interference absolutely necessary—

I have the honor to be, with great respect, Sir, Your mo: obedt. Servt.

ALBERT GALLATIN

RC (DNA: RG 233, PM, 7th Cong., 2d sess.); in a clerk's hand, signed by Gallatin; at foot of text: "The President of the United States"; endorsed by a House clerk. Enclosures: (1) John S. Sherburne to Gallatin, Portsmouth, New Hampshire, 15 Jan., noting the seizure of the ship *Eliza* by the collector in October 1802 for unloading a cargo of cables contrary to law, which caused John Pickering, the district judge, to issue a libel against the ship and order the marshal to take both ship and cables into custody, with a trial date set for 11 Nov.; on 21 Oct., without the knowledge of the marshal or district attorney, Pickering appointed three persons to appraise the ship and cables; after the appraisal, without any documentation from the collector and naval officer that duties had been paid, the judge issued an order and directed the marshal to "deliver the ship and cables to a person" who later appeared at the trial as the claimant; on 11 Nov., the court convened but adjourned for the day for "obvious irregularities" in the judge's conduct; upon the continuance of the trial the next morning, before any of the waiting witnesses for the prosecution were called, "the judge abruptly declared that the ship & cables should be restored to the claimant, and ordered the court to be adjourned"; attempts to induce the judge to suspend his judgment and allow the trial to proceed were ineffectual; Sherburne concludes that while Pickering had been "universally respected" for his "philanthropy, probity & talents," several years of ill health have impaired his bodily strength and "had an unhappy influence on the powers of his mind" (Tr in same; endorsed by a House clerk). (2) Deposition by Jonathan Steele, clerk of the New Hampshire district court, Portsmouth, 12 Jan. 1803, describing the 11 Nov. trial for libels against the ship *Eliza* and the cables "alledged to be of foreign growth & manufacture" and unlawfully imported and landed from the vessel, as filed by the Portsmouth collector; instead of reading the libels, Judge Pickering remarked that he had "heard enough of the damn'd libels," and in profane language declared that he would "decide the whole business in four minutes"; he then invited several court officers and private gentlemen to sit with him on the bench, prompting the attorneys to move for an adjournment until the next day; on 12 Nov., the claimant introduced several witnesses, but before the government's case was heard "to my utter astonishment," the judge abruptly "decreed restoration of the Ship and Cables libelled, and ordered me to record the same, & declared that he would not sit to eternity to decide on the damn'd paltry matters"; upon the remonstrance of the district attorney, the judge "said he would hear everything, and swear every damn'd scoundrel that could be produced," but he rejected the government witnesses, ordered the court adjourned, refused to hear an appeal after an objection by the claimant's counsel or to allow the filing of a bill of exceptions; while attending the 7 Dec. special district court for a naturalization case, Steele again observed Pickering's "helpless condition" (MS in same; in a clerk's hand, signed by Steele; attested by Richard Cutts Shannon, justice of the peace and notary public; endorsed by a House clerk). (3) Deposition of Daniel Humphreys, Portsmouth, 14 Jan. 1803, describing the courtroom during the 11 Nov. trial as Judge Pickering called persons to come up to the bench and take a seat with him: "The manner of his doing this, his profane language, hasty loud boisterous way of speaking, & whole manner shewed him to be at that time quite incapable of supporting the character, or exercising the functions of a Judge of the District Court"; the next morning found the judge in a "no less wild and confused" state; "after hearing the causes in part, & saying a great deal himself, he abruptly ordered a restoration of the Ship & goods to the Claimants"; under protest, the judge continued in a "confused way to hear a little, & then stop & decide, & then hear again"; he displayed, Humphreys concludes, "a mind to a great degree deranged or subverted, either from nervous disorders, or intemperance, or both together" (MS in same; in a clerk's hand, signed by Humphreys; attested by Shannon; endorsed by House clerks). (4) Deposition of Thomas Chadbourn, deputy marshal, Portsmouth, 15 Jan., noting that on 11 Nov. 1802, when he was assigned to escort Judge Pickering to the court house for the trial of the ship *Eliza* and sundry merchandise, he found the judge "much intoxicated," but he came to the court house "& with difficulty reached the bench"; at the opening of the court, he ordered a number of people, including the deputy and strangers, "to come up, and sit with him on the bench"; the deputy refused until the judge exclaimed "damn you, won't you obey the Court"; shortly after the proceedings had begun, the judge "said he had heard enough of the damn'd libels, & would decide the business in four minutes"; persuaded to adjourn until the next morning, Pickering noted he would be sober then, but he appeared the next day "equally deranged or intoxicated" and declared the ship and cables "should be restored"; the district attorney unsuccessfully argued that the witnesses should be heard, but Pickering adjourned the court; when Sherburne pointed out the "mischiefs" the decision would "produce in the collection of the Revenue," Pickering exclaimed, "damn the revenue, I get but a thousand Dollars of it" and again adjourned the court; the district attorney was thwarted from seeking an appeal or filing a bill of exception with the judge's rebuke, " 'file what you please and be damn'd' "; Chadbourn concludes by testifying that during the past two years, he has seen Pickering about once a week, at which times he has appeared "greatly deranged and generally intoxicated" (MS in same; in a clerk's hand, signed by Chadbourn; attested by Samuel Penhallow, justice of the peace; endorsed by a House clerk). (5) Deposition of John Wentworth, Portsmouth, 15 Jan., reporting that when he took his place at the bar on 11 Nov. at the trial of "certain libels against a ship and sundry merchandize" for breach of the revenue laws, Judge Pickering swore "If I did not come up, and sit with him, he would come down and give me a damn'd Caning"; the judge issued the same invitation to the deputy marshal and others, causing great anxiety in some and "much Laughter in others," creating great confusion in the courtroom and a postponement of the trial; appearing "equally deranged, and incapable of business" the next morning, the judge, "without hearing either party through," over and over again declared "that the Ship & Cables, libelled, should be restored"; when the district attorney remonstrated against the abrupt proceedings and begged that his cause might be heard, the judge declared several times, in language to the same effect, that "he would sit to the day of Judgment, but if he sat four Thousand years he would be damn'd if the Ship should not be restored" and more than once ordered the court adjourned; the conduct of the judge both days indicated "he was greatly deranged by intoxication, or some other causes, which from their long prevalence" have rendered him incapable of business (MS in same; in a clerk's hand, signed by Wentworth; attested by Shannon; endorsed by House clerks). (6) Deposition of Joseph Whipple, Portsmouth, 15 Jan. 1803, noting his attendance at the 11 Nov. trial for libels, where the judge "appeared much intoxicated, deprived of his reason & Judgment and altogether unfit for business"; he answered the request for an adjournment with " 'Yes, adjourn the Court I shall be sober in the Morning I am now damned drunk' "; on 12 Nov., the judge was in the "same deranged & intoxicated condition"; proceedings of the court were "irregular & confused," government witnesses were refused a hearing, and "without attending to any evidence or reasoning in the Case," the judge ordered the seized property to be returned to the claimant; when the district attorney urged the case to be heard because it much affected the revenue, the judge exclaimed, " 'Damn the Revenue' " (MS in same; in a clerk's hand, signed by Whipple; attested by Shannon; endorsed by House clerks). (7) Deposition by Richard Cutts Shannon, Portsmouth, 17 Jan. 1803, detailing the events of the 11 Nov. trial and providing the same information as that in the depositions of Steele, the court clerk, and others, above, including Judge Pickering's response to the observation that the proceedings would have a detrimental impact on the revenue: "damn the revenue, 'I get but a Thousand Dollars of it' "; Shannon concludes: "I have had frequent opportunities of seeing, and conversing with Judge Pickering for more than three years past, during the whole of which time, he has appeared to me greatly deranged in his mind, which I believe has been much increased, if not altogether occasioned by habits of intemperance" (MS in same; in a clerk's hand, signed by Shannon; attested by Penhallow; endorsed by House clerks). All enclosed in TJ to the House of Representatives, 3 Feb.

SUIT WHERE THE REVENUE WAS CONCERNED: in October 1802, George Wentworth, surveyor of customs at Portsmouth, seized the ship *Eliza* along with cables that he charged were unloaded contrary to the law. Eliphalet Ladd, Federalist merchant and owner of *Eliza*, applied to Judge John Pickering and obtained the vessel's release without producing the proper documentation that duties had been paid. Joseph Whipple, collector of customs, had libels issued against the ship and the cables. A trial date was set for 11 Nov. Ladd obtained prominent Federalist Edward St. Loe Livermore as attorney for the defense (Lynn W. Turner, "The Impeachment of John Pickering," *American Historical Review*, 54 [1949], 489). For TJ's appointment of John S. Sherburne as U.S. attorney, Michael McClary as marshal, and Wentworth and Whipple, see Vol. 33:219, 559-61, 668-70, 672, 675-6; Vol. 34:129, 131n; Vol. 37:324, 326n.

For an earlier assertion of Judge John Pickering's TOTAL UNFITNESS for office, see John Langdon to TJ, 14 May 1802, and note.

From Levi Lincoln

SIR Jany 31. 1803

On the reception of your note yesterday, I waited on Mr Gallatin with the inclosed. He was so unwell, as to think, he should not be able to be out this day, but wishes to see you, before you give in your nominations. If you should judge it expedient to remove Watson, Warren is generally thought of as his successor—

I am Sir most respectfully yours LEVI LINCOLN

RC (DLC); at foot of text: "President of the U.S."; endorsed by TJ as received 31 Jan. and "removal of Watson" and so recorded in SJL. Enclosure not identified.

GIVE IN YOUR NOMINATIONS: see TJ to the Senate, 2 Feb. For the removal of William WATSON and the appointment of Henry WARREN as collector at Plymouth, see Vol. 37:555-6n.

From John Washington Scott

SIR Philada. Jany. 31st. 1803.

I take the liberty of a Citizen of a free & independent Republic of addressing to you my proposal for Publishing a small work, to which, should it meet your approbation, I request your patronage.—Although your exalted situation may furnish you with business of greater magnitude, I am induced to believe you will relax a moment from the arduous toil of governmental affairs to consider the request of a private Citizen just embarking on the sea of life, in a profession which is dependant on public patronage for Support—and your favour will be remembered with gratitude, by, Your fellow Citizen,

JOHN WASHINGTON SCOTT.

RC (DLC); at head of text: "To Tho: Jefferson, President of the United States"; endorsed by TJ as received 5 Feb. and so recorded in SJL.

John Washington Scott, possibly the assumed name of John Welwood Scott (1777?-1842), was a Philadelphia printer and publisher of both secular and religious material. Probably a native of Nova Scotia, he published the *Philadelphia Repository and Weekly Register* for 1804 at his shop on Bank Street. In 1809, he solicited subscribers, including TJ, for a proposed publication of a volume of Joseph McCoy's poetry. Scott later ran a bookstore at 147 Chestnut Street where, in 1813, he published *Scott's Philadelphia Price Current and Commercial Remembrancer* as well as *The Religious Remembrancer*, reputedly the first weekly religious newspaper in the United States (Brigham, *American Newspapers*, 2:950, 1479; Gaylord P. Albaugh, *History and Annotated Bibliography of American Religious Periodicals and Newspapers*, 2 vols. [Worcester, Mass., 1994], 2:839-40; John Welwood Scott, *A Discourse Delivered before the Provident Society of Philadelphia* [Philadelphia, 1811; Shaw-Shoemaker, No. 23879]; *The Poetical Recreations of John W. Scott* [Philadelphia, 1809; Shaw-Shoemaker, No. 18575], 33, 60; RS, 1:504n).

From William Canby

1st of 2nd. mo. 1803—

Esteemed friend Thomas Jefferson—

having cause to acknowledg thy friendly disposition freedom of access, & excellent Natural Capacity, I have a desire to salute thee in this way—wishing thy increas of Spiritual or Divine Life, which is only to be attained thr'o inward Communion with that which is Divine, as like communicates with its like, & seeing "no Man knoweth the Father but the Son & he to whom the Son will Reveal him" it is therefore Necessary to submit to that inward manifestation of the Truth which, as sure as there is a divine Being or Prinicple, must wait upon & be communicated to his Offspring, if they will but wait upon & Nourish it. obedience to whose operation wou'd Reduce Nature in the day of his power to great a child like simplicity, so as thankfully to receive the Truth in the love of it. farewell

WM. CANBY

RC (DLC); endorsed by TJ as received 27 Feb. and "postmark Baltimore" and so recorded in SJL.

FREEDOM OF ACCESS: Canby and Dorothy Ripley met with TJ at the President's House in May 1802 to seek his approval of a proposal to institute a school for African American girls in the capital (Vol. 37:506-7).

From Henry Dearborn

[1 Feb. 1803]

Genl. Wilkinson, to be appointed Commissioner to treat with the Chocktaws, Creeks, Chickasaws &c—
Govr. Harrison to be appointed Commissioner to treat with the Indians Northwest of the Ohio.

RC (DLC: TJ Papers, 129:22285); undated; entirely in Dearborn's hand; endorsed by TJ as received from the War Department on 1 Feb. and "Nominations."

GOVR. HARRISON: see TJ to the Senate, 2 Feb.

From Henry Dearborn

War Department
1st. February 1803.

The Secretary of War has the honor to propose to the President of the United States, that Joseph Doyle of the district of Columbia, and John Miller of the State of Maryland, be respectively appointed Ensigns in the 2d. Regiment of Infantry—That Pallus P. Stuart, of the North Western Territory, and William Lee of the State of Vermont, be respectively appointed Ensigns in the 1st. Regiment of Infantry; And that Joseph Goodhue of the State of Vermont be appointed a surgeon's Mate in the Army of the United States.

Also that William C. Smith nominated as Surgeons Mate in the last recess of Congress, be submitted to the senate of the United States, for confirmation.

RC (DLC); in a clerk's hand; endorsed by TJ as received from the War Department on 1 Feb. and "Nominns" and so recorded in SJL. FC (Lb in DNA: RG 107, LSP).

The above nominations proposed by the SECRETARY OF WAR were included in TJ's message to the Senate of 2 Feb. For the earlier nomination of WILLIAM C. SMITH, see Vol. 38:9.

From Nicolas Gouin Dufief

MONSIEUR, Le 1er de Février. 1803

Vous trouverez-ci inclus plusieurs exemplaires de mon Catalogue imprimé—J'ai joint au petit pacquet une lettre adressée à Mr. Beckley touchant les livres du Dr. Franklin. Dans le doute ou J'etais si ce Monsieur avoit ses ports francs, j'ai pris la liberté de profiter de votre couvert pour la lui faire passer, avec un Catalogue. L'objet de cette lettre me servira j'espère d'excuse, auprès de vous.

Monsieur le Lieutenant Colonel Williams qui connait parfaitement tous les livres du Dr. Franklin (de l'amitie & de la confiance duquel il Jouissait pendant sa vie) s'est offert de constater, en cas d'acquisition de la part du Committé, que tous ceux qui seraient envoyés à Washington, fesaient partie de Sa Bibliothèque—

Je Suis avec un profond respect, Monsieur, Votre très dévoué Serviteur N. G. Dufief

EDITORS' TRANSLATION

Sir, 1 Feb. 1803

In this small package you will find several copies of my printed catalogue. I have also enclosed a letter addressed to Mr. Beckley concerning Dr. Franklin's books. Since I was not sure whether he had free postage when receiving letters, I took the liberty of using this mailing to transmit it to him, with a catalogue. The message in this letter will, I hope, justify my doing so.

Should the committee acquire Dr. Franklin's books, Lieutenant Colonel Williams, who is entirely familiar with all of them (because of the friendship and confidence he enjoyed with Dr. Franklin during his lifetime), has offered to certify that all those sent to Washington come from his library.

With deep respect, I am, Sir, your very devoted servant.

N. G. Dufief

RC (DLC); at foot of text: "Le Président des Etats-Unis"; endorsed by TJ as received 4 Feb. and so recorded in SJL. Enclosures not found.

catalogue imprimé: that is, Dufief's printed catalogue of his current offerings, which was distinct from the list of books from Benjamin Franklin's library (see Dufief to TJ, 25, 31 Jan.).

To Pierre Samuel Du Pont de Nemours

Dear Sir Washington Feb. 1. 1803.

I have to acknolege the reciept of your favors of Aug. 16. and Oct. 4. and the latter I recieved with peculiar satisfaction; because while it holds up terms which cannot be entirely yielded, it proposes such as a mutual spirit of accomodation and sacrifice of opinion, may bring to some point of union. while we were preparing on this subject such modifications of the propositions of your letter of Oct. 4. as we could assent to, an event happened which obliged us to adopt measures of urgency. the suspension of the right of deposit at New Orleans, ceded to us by our treaty with Spain, threw our whole country into such a ferment as imminently threatened it's peace. this however was believed to be the act of the Intendant unauthorised by his government. but it shewed the necessity of making effectual arrangements to secure the peace of the two countries against the indiscreet acts of subordinate agents. the urgency of the case, as well as the public spirit therefore induced us to make a more solemn appeal to the justice and judgment of our neighbors, by sending a minister extraordinary to impress them with the necessity of some arrangement. Mr. Monroe has been selected; his good dispositions cannot be doubted. multiplied conversations with him, and views of the subject taken in all the shapes in which it can present itself, have possessed him with our estimates of every thing relating to it, with a minuteness which no written communication to mr Livingston could ever have attained. those will prepare them to meet & decide on every form of proposition which can occur, without awaiting new instructions from hence, which might draw to an indefinite length a discussion where circumstances imperiously oblige us to a prompt decision: for the occlusion of the Missisipi is a state of things in which we cannot exist. he goes therefore, joined with Chancellor Livingston, to aid in the issue of a crisis the most important the US. have ever met since their independence, & which is to decide their future character & career. the confidence which the government of France reposes in you will undoubtedly give great weight to your information. an equal confidence on our part, founded on your knolege of the subject, your just views of it, your good dispositions towards this country, and my long experience of your personal faith and[1] friendship, assures me that you will render between us all the good offices in your power. the interests of the two countries being absolutely the same as to this matter, your aid may be conscientiously given. it will often perhaps be possible for you, having a freedom of communication, omnibus horis, which diplomatic gentlemen will be excluded from by form, to smooth difficulties by representations & reasonings which would be recieved with more suspicion from them. you will thereby render great good to both countries. for our circumstances are so imperious as to admit of no delay as to our course: and the use of the Missisipi so indispensable that we cannot hesitate one moment to hazard our existence for it's maintenance. if we fail in this effort to put it beyond the reach of accident, we see the destinies we [have to] run, and prepare at once for them. not but that we shall still endeavor to go on in peace and friendship with our neighbors as long as we can, *if our rights of navigation & deposit are respected*; but as we foresee that the caprices of the local officer, and the abuse of those rights by our boatmen & navigators, which neither government can prevent, will keep up a state of irritation, which cannot long be kept inactive, we should be criminally improvident not to take at once eventual measures for strengthening ourselves for the contest. it may be said, if this object be so all-important to us, why do we not offer[2] such a sum as would ensure it's purchase? the answer is simple. we are an agricultural people, poor in money, and owing past debts.[3] these will be falling due by instalments for 15. years to come, & require from us the practice of a rigorous economy to accomplish their paiment: and it is our principle to pay to a moment whatever we have engaged, and never to engage what we cannot, and mean not faithfully to pay. we have calculated our resources and found the sum to be moderate which they would enable us to pay, and we know from late trials that little can be added to it by borrowing. the country too which we wish to purchase, except the part already granted, and which must be confirmed to the private holders is a barren sand, 600 miles from East to West & from 30. to 40. & 50. miles from North to South, formed by deposition of the sands by the gulph stream in it's circular course round the Mexican gulph, and which being spent after performing a semicircle, has made from it's last depositions the sand-bank of East Florida. in West Florida indeed, there are on the borders of the rivers some rich bottoms formed by the mud brought from the upper country. these bottoms are all possessed by individuals. but the spaces between river & river are mere banks of sand: and in East Florida there are neither rivers nor consequently any bottoms. we cannot then make any thing by a sale of the land to individuals: so that it is peace alone which makes it an object with us, and which ought to make the cession of it desireable to France. whatever power, other than ourselves, holds the country East of the Missisipi[4] becomes our natural enemy. will such a possession do France as much good, as such an enemy may do her harm? and how long would it be her's, were such an enemy, situated at it's door, added to G. Britain? I confess that it appears to me as essential to France to keep at peace with us, as it is to us to keep at peace with her: and that if this cannot be secured without some compromise as to the territory in question, it will be useful for both to make sacrifices to effect the compromise.

You see, my good friend, with what frankness I communicate with you on this subject, that I hide nothing from you, and that I am endeavoring to turn our private friendship to the good of our respective countries. and can private friendship ever answer a nobler end than by keeping two nations at peace, who, if this new position which one of them is taking, were rendered innocent, have more points of common interest, and fervor of collision than any two on earth; who become natural friends, instead of natural enemies which this change of position would make them. my letters of Apr. 25. May 5. and this present one have been written, without any disguise, in this view and while safe in your hands they can never do any thing but good. but you and I are now at that time of life when our call to another state of being cannot be distant, and may be near. besides, your government is in the habit of siesing papers without notice. these letters might thus get into hands like the hornet which extracts poison from the same flower which yields honey to the bee, might make them the ground of throwing up a flame between our two countries, and make our friendship & confidence in each other effect exactly the reverse of what we are aiming at. being yourself thoroughly possessed of every idea in them, let me ask from your friendship an immediate consignment of them to the flames. that alone can make all safe, and ourselves secure.

I intended to have answered you here on the subject of your agency in the [transacting] what money matters we may have at Paris, and for that purpose meant to have conferred with mr Gallatin. but he has for 2. or 3. days been confined to his room, and is not yet able to do business. if he is out before Mr. Monroe's departure, I will write an additional letter on that subject. be assured that it will be a great additional satisfaction to me to render services to yourself & sons by the same acts which shall at the same time promote the public service. be so good as to present my respectful salutations to Made. Dupont & to accept yourself assurances of my constant and affectionate friendship and great respect.

TH: JEFFERSON

PrC (DLC); blurred; at foot of first page: "M. Dupont."

OMNIBUS HORIS: at all hours.

MONEY MATTERS WE MAY HAVE AT PARIS: for Du Pont's proposal that his family's firms could handle financial transactions between the United States and Europe, see his letters of 16 Aug. and 4 Oct. 1802.

[1] Preceding two words interlined.

[2] Word interlined in place of "[give]."

[3] TJ first wrote "and in debt" before altering the phrase to read as above.

[4] TJ changed "that" to "the" country and interlined the preceding four words in ink.

From James Miller and Others

State of Ohio
Febuary. 1st 1803

HONOURED SIR

we are in Duty Bound To give you all The honour That a humain person can bee Worthy of For your by past prisedeings in the Behalf of the poore deear Sir we Still hope to find you Zealous in our Cause. Theirfore we Send Forth our petitian hopeing you will put it in to the hands of some worthy Friend that will speak For us you will find that those speculateors has sent on a petitian presenting that it will Benifit the poore But you may Believe us that not one twentieth person on the land ivver saw their petitian for it was Wrote in Cincinnata Betwene Chrismass and new year: and was Carryed a Bout By Gorge Turner and handed To Every person in the taverns and we will leave it to your honour to Judge what Capasity Men must bee in to Sighn a petitian or to Judge of it Deeare Sir we hope you will Speake to the honourable house and Mentian to them to give us an Eaquel Chance that is to Cease these petitians and Let us have have too others to Sirculate amongst us and let the moste in number take it Deear Sir you may believe us their is a grait Deale of advantage is taken in this State and we will mention one in particular that of Wm Ward Concerning Ic zeans to lay his warrents on Reserve Sectians Deear Sir all we want is to bee Fair and honest and bee permited to get land as Far as our moneys will get so that we May Bee yousfull both to our Famileys and the State we live in and not bee Impossed on by those Land Jobbers Deear Sir we Remain your Friends and Cityzens

JAS MILLER

NB Deear Sir I understand that Robert [Rannax?] is about to Make application for the land in the Forks of Mad River but how Could he Clame it as his Bargin when I have the Surveyors Certificate Certyfying that it was No. 16 thease from me. JAS MILLER

RC (ViW: Tucker-Coleman Collection); smudged; in James Miller's hand and signed by him and six others; addressed: "To Mr Thomis Jefferson President of the United States Washenton city"; franked; postmarked Cincinnati, 15 Feb.; endorsed by TJ as received 3 Mch. and so recorded in SJL. Enclosure: Petition of James Miller and 64 others to the Senate and the House of Representatives, dated state of Ohio, 20 Jan. 1803, thanking Congress for relieving them from excise and stamp taxes and for procuring peace to the states, and presenting their cause again; the petitioners are much aggrieved by the preemption rights granted to some persons "Because They have Imposeed on us Setlars From $\frac{1}{4}$ to 1 doll per achree which Makes us think hard that we have underwent So much hardships to Settle a Cuntery and to bee imposeed on by those Speculateors"; these speculators have sent their own petition "praying For longer time presenting that they Could not Enter their lands on the account it was not Surveyed"; the petitioners claim that William Ward and others have entered lands in the eleventh range "by the new lines" and that Judge George Turner has sold land on the "Extreeme part of his Township"; the petitioners question whether Ward and Turner are acting under the authority of John Cleves Symmes; they ask Congress to stop this land speculating "and to keepe those land Jobbers From imposeing on poore people," that the land may hereafter "Bee Sold in Small quantitees So that the poore Man May get land as well as the Rich," and that preemption rights may cease; "we Think we have an Eaquel Rite To The publick lands Because we have To bee an Eaquel part in Defending The Cuntery Boath by our lives and property Theirefore if we have little money let us have little land if we have Much Money let us have Much land" (same; entirely in Miller's hand).

OUR CAUSE: see Miller to TJ, 30 Dec. 1802.

George TURNER was appointed a judge of the Northwest Territory in 1789 and elected to the American Philosophical Society in 1790. He resigned his judgeship in 1797 following allegations of misconduct in office, and was forced to quit the society in 1800 after he was found to have diverted one of its funds to his own use (Mark Grossman, *Political Corruption in America: An Encyclopedia of Scandals, Power, and Greed*, 2d ed., 2 vols. [Millerton, N.Y., 2008], 2:446-8; Vol. 24:604n; Vol. 30:39-40n).

IC ZEANS: that is, Indian interpreter Isaac Zane. In April 1802, Congress authorized the conveyance of three sections of land, of one square mile each, in the Northwest Territory to Zane (U.S. Statutes at Large, 6:46; Vol. 36:515, 520n).

From William Bache

DEAR SIR. Philadelphia Feby. 2d. 1803.

Your prediction of the state of Navigation has been verified, our Journey from Washington was in slush, which I bore without repining as I had a prospect of an open river, but before the vesell was in readiness the Ice secured her. Today there is some prospect for tomorrow as it is warm and rains.

Yesterday I received remittances from Jersey. Inclosed you will find $100 which you so kindly lent me at Washington, and for which you have my grateful remembrances.

I am very anxious about the fate of Mr Trist, not having heard of him or his family since we left Albemarle. If you know anything of him and can spare time from your public duties, you will add to the many obligations to Mrs Bache & myself by communicating his fate to her.—Believe me with sincere respect & friendship to be your much obliged.— WILLIAM BACHE

RC (MHi); endorsed by TJ as received 12 Feb. Enclosure not found, but see below.

OUR JOURNEY: Bache was taking the Philadelphia route, rather than the Norfolk, to New Orleans to serve as physician for the proposed marine hospital there (Vol. 38:3-4, 29-30; George Jefferson to TJ, 1 Dec. 1802).

INCLOSED: on 12 Feb. 1803, TJ recorded in his financial memoranda the receipt of $100 from Bache for the loan "ante Dec. 26." (MB, 2:1092; Bache to TJ, 26 Dec. 1802).

From John Daly Burk

SIR Petersburg February 2d: 1803

I am employed in writing an history of Virginia. My contract is made; the subscription fills beyond my expectations and I shall doubtless receive the stipulated sum, whether the work be excellent or otherwise: but my pride and my principles instruct me that something more is expected from me; that it is my duty to make my book, as far as my opportunities will admit, correct and interesting. In the commencement of an undertaking so arduous and important, I naturally turn my eyes to you, for aid and advice: you must, Judging from the habits of your life & your particular pursuits, possess many valuable materials for such a work; and you, above all men, know how to appreciate a faithfull history of your own state. I ask, in full confidence of receiving it, the aid of your experience & information & solicit your permission to send you a copy of the work previous to its publication

I remain Sir With great respect your fellow Citizen

JOHN D. BURK

RC (DLC); at foot of text: "Thomas Jefferson. President of the United States"; endorsed by TJ as received 9 Feb. and so recorded in SJL.

Burk needed 500 subscribers before he could publish his proposed two-volume HISTORY OF VIRGINIA. An advertisement for the work pledged unbiased portrayals of wartime civil or military movements and impartial reflections on religious opinion in the state. In preparing the history, he relied heavily on TJ's *Notes on the State of Virginia* as well as the president's collections of newspapers and Virginia laws. In 1804, Burk dedicated the work to TJ, its "guardian and patron" and "the first and most useful citizen in the republic." Although his history, extending to three volumes, covered through 1775, a fourth volume continuing to 1781 was begun by Skelton Jones and completed by Louis H. Girardin in 1816 (*The History of Virginia, From Its First Settlement to the Present Day*, 4 vols. [Petersburg, 1804-16], 1:i-ii; Sowerby, No. 464; Richmond *Virginia Argus*, 12 Dec. 1802; DVB, 2:400-2; Vol. 34:388-9n; Burk to TJ, 26 May 1805; TJ to Burk, 1 June 1805).

From James Currie

Dr Sir Richmond February 2d. 1803

In compliance with your friendly request when I was at Monticello last fall I have taken the liberty of stating our account & hope youll find it Correct There is one payment you made Mr Burr as a fee in my unfortunate matter w Mr R Morris its amount I have forgot youll please take credit for it w interest on whatever it was till the 1st. of April next & state it when you are at leisure & if the ballce. can be paid by the time the act is stated up to, it will add to the many obligations & attentions I have had the honor to receive. with sentiments of the most unfeigned & respectfull regard & Esteem, I Ever am

Dr Sir—your much Obliged & very Devoted Hble Servt.

James Currie

RC (MHi); address clipped; in Currie's hand: "fav[or] T M Randolph Esqr."; endorsed by TJ as received 13 Mch. and so recorded in SJL.

In 1798, TJ paid Aaron burr $50 to perform legal services for Currie, who was trying to recover a debt owed him by Robert morris (mb, 2:984; Vol. 30:171-2, 356-7, 366-7).

From Philadelphia Merchants and Others

Philadelphia February 2d. 1803

The Memorial of the subscribers, Merchants and others of the City of Philadelphia Respectfully sheweth—

That they have heard with concern that applications have been made for the removal from Office of Allen McLane Esquire Collector of the Port or District of Wilmington in the State of Delaware—

That your Memorialists have been for many years, well acquainted with the said Allen McLane, and are most of them (from the nature of our Health Laws, and the occasional obstruction of the Navigation of the River Delaware) interested in, or have concerns with the Trade of Delaware State, particularly at the Port of Wilmington:—

That the said Allen McLane from his well known meritorious services during the Revolutionary War, was highly deserving of the Appointments which he received, and in the execution of the office which he now holds, We can, either from personal knowledge, or from well founded information, Certify, that he has given the utmost satisfaction to those who have had occasion to transact business with him; having uniformly facilitated the Mercantile interest by every possible accommodation not inconsistent with the Public Good.

That charges were made against him for supposed Misconduct in Office, but on a full Enquiry & Investigation made by order of the Secretary of the Treasury a Report was made favorable to the said Allen McLane, which we are informed was layed before your Excellency and approved, and further, that he has conducted himself in his office with such punctuality and Attention to his Duty to the United States as to have received the approbation of the Department under which he Acts—

And as the said McLane has for some years past withdrawn from other business, and applied himself solely to the Public Service, and having a large family to support, would be greatly injured by removal from his present office; We therefore beg leave respectfully to recommend him to the President to be continued in his said Office of Collector of the said Port or District of Wilmington—

THOMAS LEIPER
WM MCFADEN
MOSES NATHAN
MAHLON HUTCHINSON
CHA BIDDLE

RC (DLC); in an unidentified hand, signed by all; at head of text: "To His Excellency Thomas Jefferson Esquire President of the United States." Probably enclosed in "Muhlenberg Philip," that is, J. P. G. Muhlenberg to TJ, 4 Feb., recorded in SJL as received on the 8th with the notation "Mc.Lane to remain in office," but not found.

William McFaden (1751-1839), a sea captain and privateersman during the Revolutionary War, became a director, in 1803, of the newly established Delaware Insurance Company of Philadelphia. Moses Nathan and Mahlon Hutchinson were Philadelphia merchants on South Second Street and North Third Street, respectively. A successful merchant and political leader, Charles Biddle served as prothonotary of the Philadelphia County Court of Common Pleas in 1803, a position he obtained in 1791 (*Metropolitan Museum of Art Bulletin*, new ser., 9 [1951], 147, 155; *Aurora*, 14 Nov. 1803; James Robinson, *The Philadelphia Directory, City and County Register, for 1803* [Philadelphia, 1802], 29, 128, 185; Kline, *Burr*, 1:152n).

ENQUIRY & INVESTIGATION: see Vol. 34:170-1. For the REPORT, see Vol. 36:182-3.

To the Senate

GENTLEMEN OF THE SENATE

I nominate John Martin Baker of New York to be Consul for the islands of Minorca, Majorca, and Yvica.

Marien Lemar of Maryland to be Consul for Madeira.

William Patterson of New York to Commercial Agent of the US. at Nantes in the place of Francis L. Taney deceased.

<*Vale of New York to be Commercial Agent at Lorient instead of William Patterson transferred to Nantes.*>

William Henry Harrison to be Governor of the Indiana territory from the 13th. day of May next, when his present commission as Governor will expire.

Thomas T. Davis of Kentucky to be a judge of the territory of Indiana, in the place of William Clarke deceased.

Jesse Spencer of Ohio to be Register of the land office for the district of Chillicothe, instead of Thomas Worthington resigned.

William Henry Harrison of Indiana, to be a Commissioner to[1] enter into any treaty or treaties which may be necessary with any Indian tribes North West of the Ohio[2] & within the territory of the US. on the subject of their boundaries or lands.

Isaac[3] Illsley junr. of Massachusets to be Collector of Portland in Massachusets instead of Nathaniel F. Fosdick removed.

Zachariah Stevens of Massachusets to be Surveyor & Inspector of Gloucester in Massachusets instead of Samuel Whittermore removed.

Joseph Story of Massachusets to be Naval officer for Salem & Beverley in Massachusets instead of William Pickman removed.

Jabez Pennyman of Vermont to be Collector and Inspector[4] of Allburgh on Lake Champlain instead of David Russell removed.

John Heard of New Jersey, who is Collector for the District of Perth Amboy in N. Jersey to be Inspector of the revenue for the same.

William Brewer of North Carolina to be Surveyor and Inspector of revenue for the port of Nixinton in the district of Cambden in N. Carolina in the place of Hugh Knox resigned.

Joseph Doyle of Columbia to be an ensign in the 2d. regiment of infantry.

John Miller of Maryland to be an ensign in the 2d. regiment of infantry.

Pallus P. Stuart of Ohio to be an ensign in the 1st. regiment of infantry.

William Lee of Vermont to be an ensign in the 1st. regiment of infantry.

William C. Smith of   to be a surgeon's mate in the army of the US.

Joseph Goodhue of Vermont to be a surgeon's mate in the army of the US.

TH: JEFFERSON
Feb 2. 1803

RC (DNA: RG 46, EPEN, 7th Cong., 2d sess.); endorsed by Senate clerks. PrC (DLC); lacks one emendation (see Note 3); TJ added check marks in the left margin at the 11 nominees approved by the Senate on 8 Feb. (see below). Recorded in SJL with notation "nominations genl."

JOHN MARTIN BAKER: for his qualifications and recommendations, see Madison to TJ, 20 Aug. 1802, and enclosures.

CONSUL FOR MADEIRA: Marien Lamar, partner in a mercantile firm in Madeira where he settled about 1790, competed for the consulship with Lewis Searle Pintard, cousin of John Marsden Pintard, consul at Madeira since 1790 (see Kline, *Burr*, 1:546-7; JEP, 1:47, 49). John M. Pintard wrote Madison from Richmond on 3 Dec. that he had hoped to remain consul, "unless It was thought Proper" to appoint his kinsman Lewis S. Pintard. Understanding that the president planned to appoint someone else, Pintard recommended Lamar as a Republican who was well qualified to fill the office. Pintard also applied for the position of commissioner under the convention with Spain (RC in DNA: RG 59, LAR, endorsed by TJ: "Pintard John M. to mr Madison to be commr. to Spain"; Madison, *Papers, Sec. of State Ser.*, 4:176). On 14 Dec., Pintard once again wrote Madison offering James Monroe and Pierce Butler as character references who would convince the administration that he merited some mark of confidence, either to "receive the appointment I ask for, or be continued in the one I at present hold" (RC in DNA: RG 59, LAR; endorsed by TJ: "Pintard John Marsden to mr Madison to be commr to Spain"). For earlier recommendations for Lamar as consul, see Vol. 33:667-8n.

Robert R. Livingston supported the transfer of WILLIAM PATTERSON to Nantes. Thomas T. Gantt resigned as commercial agent there in October 1802. FRANCIS L. TANEY, whom TJ had appointed commercial agent at Ostend or Dunkirk in 1801, died of yellow fever in Georgetown in September 1802. Patterson's move allowed TJ to appoint Aaron Vail as consul at L'Orient, a position he had sought for more than a decade (Madison, *Papers, Sec. of State Ser.*, 3:596; Vol. 37:527n; Madison to TJ, [on or before 9 Sep. 1802]). For Vail's separate nomination, see TJ to the Senate, 14 Feb.

Meriwether Lewis delivered this message to the Senate on 3 Feb., where it was read the next day and ordered to lie for consideration. On 8 Feb., the Senate consented to all of the appointments except Baker, Patterson, Ilsley, Stevens, Story, Miller, Stuart, and Smith. Their nominations were referred to Uriah Tracy, Robert Wright, and Dwight Foster for consideration. Tracy brought in a report on 1 Mch. and the same day the Senate approved the remainder of the list (JEP, 1:440-2, 446).

[1] TJ here canceled "treat" and wrote "enter" over partially erased "with."

[2] Entry from this point to "US." interlined.

[3] Interlined in place of "Daniel." PrC not altered.

[4] Preceding two words interlined.

From "A. B."

DEAR SIR. [on or before 3 Feb. 1803]

I am not ignorant of the epithet that a Solicitation of this kind is intitled to, and that it ought to be treated accordingly, except the instance is Sufficiently Sympathetick with necessary quallifications to render it admisable. Which I trust when elucidated will in part if not in whole be an apoligy for this. I am a Single Citizen aged about 35 years whose family & Character I trust if necessary can be made appear little infereor to any, except my present State of indigence, after possessing a Small estate to the ammount of a bout 2000$ which my Father left me, which I shall hereafter acct. for, and for which I thank god under our present administration is no objection or Stigma, to a pure and Virtuous principle. My Father died when I was about 14 years of age and left a Relict with ten Small Children to bewail his death, of whom I was the eldest except one Sister. His estate being Somewhat involv'd and his named Extor in his will and Freind as he thought them, refused to quallify My Mother was obliged to administer, and like most other Women ignorant of the laws & her duty as an admtr., what little Estate there was except the real, which was left to myself & a younger Brother Soon fell a Sacrifice to intreaguing Villians before it was in my power to prevent it, and by the time I became of age they were dependent on Some freind for a further or additional Support to what little was left. I was the only one then to whom they could with propriety look up to. I hisitated not to Sacrifise the principle as well as the fruits of my labour in Supporting them as long as my little funds & health continued, which thank god was Sufficient to See them all well provided for by marriages & otherwise. at which period I was left with an emaciated constitution and only as much as paid my board & Cloathed me three years during which time I was Studeously imploy'd in the Study of medicine under two as good Physicians as any on the continent; at the end of which time, with which my money ended also I hoped, as I had Some opulent freinds when not dependant that some of them would assist me in Spending a Season on the lectures in Philadelphia & to get me a Small Shop to begin the world once again a new for myself. But alas I was mistaken No freind in need which would have been one indeed, and for what cause I am at a loss to Say, except a differance in our political principles might have had any influence, but whether or not, so it is they refuse to throw me a straw to keep me from Sinking till I could reach the Shore & return it again, and am Sorry to Say that they are the relicks of democracy deginerated into aristocracy.—

You cannot be ignorant thou Philanthropist of the impression and effect produced from So long antisipating the ultimate event of my benevelince, Indigence, dependance and disgrace, together with the afflicting hand of providence has render'd me incapable of laboreous excercise or Should disdain an application of this kind as it behoves every person who is able that has no other means to precure it to earn their bread by the Sweat of their brow. I have Stated to you facts which I hope your Sympathetic benevelence will give its due weight and Snatch me from the Jaws of distruction & render the ballance of my life happy by appointing me to Some little post of emolument after first acquainting yourself with my person Charactor family &c that will Support me, or if that is out of your power to be So friendly & good as to lend me a Small Sum of money to purchas a little medicine to commence practice with untill it is in my power to refund it. Pray my worthy Sir, Since your decision and answer to this is my last recourse provided you will condesend to answer me, which I trust you will, give it its due reflection & I trust I yet have a freind. a letter directed to A.B. to the care of the postmaster at Paris Fauquier County Virginia Shall be duly Attended to from your dependant & and most Obdt. Hbl. Servt. A. B.

RC (DLC); addressed: "Thomas Jefferson Esqr. President united States City Washington"; franked; postmarked "Goshen," Loudoun County, Virginia, 3 Feb.; endorsed by TJ as received from "Anon." on 4 Feb. and "office or money" and so recorded in SJL.

From Susana Carter

RESPECTED SIR Richmond Feby. 3rd 1803

I hope I shall escape the charge of presumption while I adress you on a Subject not less disagreable to myself than to you, I hope also that you will regard this rather as a compulsory measure on my part than agreable. I do assure you most pointedly that nothing is more Irckesome to me than the task of petitioning any Gentleman (particularly the chief Magistrate of this country who ought at all times to remain far from corespondencys like this) for money or on any other Subject, and nothing short of extreme nessesity could induce me to take the liberty of adressing you, however I know that minds enlightened as yours is will forgive an intrusion where excessive want compels me to be the Author. my property is now under distraint for House rent to amt of 50$ and I have no other way to pay it than by selling my beds. my Husband having by his imprudence disposses'd me of the tolerable quantity of furniture which I had in former days, when I was in a vastly better situation in life. he is now on the bed where In a very few days will draw his last breath and leave me destitute of his assistance and on the 27th. of this month of a bed, You may perhaps ask why I do not ask assistance of the citizens of Richmond I will Ansr. I have on a former Ocasion experience'd from them the most unlimited friendship, and am assham'd to solicit them a second time. I never have ask'd a favr. of them in my life but when nessesity compeld me and to their humanity and unbounded goodness do I acknowledge my self much indebted. I hope therefore when I Inform you of this, you will assist me letting me have the sum before mention'd, and should any of my children ever have it in their power which no doubt they will, they, will certainly return it with Interest, I would ask of the citzens of this place a little more of their assistance was it not for the reason Just mentiond, After this debt is discharged I will retire from a place where living is so expensive and money so hard to be had, and confine myself to some country place, pray Consider my situation before you Ansr. this which I hope will be as soon as convenient, and if possible assist me to the amt of 50$ or any sum which you may think proper I rely fully on yr. Goodness and discretion, and as in duty bound will ever pray for the prosperty and happiness of you and family in private and public life and the Happiness of the people of America under yr. Virtuous administration and for a continual Succession of heart felt self aprobation and shall

Always remain yr. Ob st. SUSANA CARTER

please to write me in Ansr. before the 27th. Instant please excuse me

RC (MHi); endorsed by TJ as received 8 Feb. and so recorded in SJL.

From Joseph Eaker

State of Ohio
Lancaster Feby 3d 1803

HONOURED SIR—

Pardon me for requesting for a few moments your attention (though devoted to more important concerns) to my private affairs that I may lay before you my past misfortunes and present distress—It is at all times painful to relate untoward changes of fortune and still more painful to be compelled to apply to the benevolence of Strangers for releif but it is sometimes the Lot of Humanity to be reduced to that necessity—It is, therefore, that I state to you that I served as a Surgeon during the whole of the late Revolutionary War in the American service and I trust without discredit either to my Country or myself since which I have by an unfortunate occurrence been deprived of the benefit of my vouchers for my services and thereby been barred from obtaining a large part of my pay—In the year 1789 I determined to move with my Family to this Country, and in November of that year was frozen up in the Ohio out of which we with difficulty escaped with our lives having lost almost all of our Goods and a valuable Stock of Medicine—I was thus deprived of all my property all my money and the means of earning more for a severe stroke of the Palzy had rendered me unable to labour—Let me add that I had a wife and seven small Children depending on me for their Bread—This is not a fiction but a reality the most of which is well known to Mr. Andrew Gregg who can inform you if you will enquire of him—

Thus circumstanced my family and myself can only rely on Divine Protection and the beneficence of our Fellow Creatures To your well known benevolence—to your desire to extend happiness to all mankind to your disposition to do good both in private and public capacities I take the liberty of humbly applying for some redress—In adressing a Person who though filling the most dignified Office on Earth is yet alive to the miseries of the unfortunate it is unnecessary to make any comments on my situation—to crave more of your time would be impertinent, further than to assure you with the most profound respect that for whatever assistence your bountiful hand may extend the most cordial gratitude shall be entertained and the most fervent prayers for your health and happiness be offered by

Your Most Ob. Sert. JOSEPH EAKER

RC (DLC); at foot of text: "The President of the U. States"; endorsed by TJ as received 1 Mch. and so recorded in SJL.

A former resident of Northumberland County, Pennsylvania, Joseph Eaker served as a surgeon's mate and second surgeon in the hospital department from 1777 to 1780 and later suffered several months of confinement aboard a prison ship in New York harbor. His petition for back pay and rations met a favorable reception from Congress in 1781, but subsequent requests to readjust his accounts were all denied (Eaker to the President of Congress, 24 Apr. 1781, 18 Feb. 1782 and Eaker to Congress, 26 Feb. 1782, in DNA: RG 360, PCC; Eaker to Congress, undated, received 9 Dec. 1801, in DNA: RG 233, PMRSL, 7th Cong., 1st sess.; JCC, 20:485, 544-5; 22:81; JHR, 1:458-9, 482; 2:98; 4:12, 17; Syrett, *Hamilton*, 10:471-2; 16:90-2).

From Thomas Marston Green

SIR, Washington City February 3rd 1803

In looking over the Acts of Congress passed last Session, I discovered the following, which in my opinion, will supersede the necessity of my resolution—It is, "An Act to provide for the establishment of certain districts, and therein to amend, "An Act to regulate the collection of duties on imports and tonnages"; and for other purposes.—See page 145, Sect. 5. And be it further enacted, That it shall be lawful for the President of the United States to establish, when it shall appear to him to be proper, in addition to the port of entry & delivery already established on the Mississippi, &c.

Should this provision, in your opinion, be sufficient for the establishing a port of delivery at Natchez I shall withdraw my resolution, if not, it will be my duty to endeavor to have one made to that effect—

With respect and consideration I am Sir, your obt. servt.

THOMAS M. GREEN

RC (DLC); endorsed by TJ as received 3 Feb. and so recorded in SJL.

The act FOR THE ESTABLISHMENT OF CERTAIN DISTRICTS cited by Green was passed by Congress on 1 May 1802. Section 5 authorized the president to establish a second port of entry and delivery on the Mississippi River (U.S. Statutes at Large, 2:181-2).

PORT OF ENTRY & DELIVERY ALREADY ESTABLISHED: John F. Carmichael was appointed collector for the Mississippi Territory in January 1800, to reside at Fort Adams (Vol. 38:255n; Vol. 39: Appendix I).

MY RESOLUTION: on 10 Feb., Green presented the House of Representatives a memorial and resolutions from the Mississippi Territory General Assembly, which detailed the inconveniences suffered in consequence of the closing of the port of New Orleans and the lack of an alternate place of deposit on the Mississippi River. After being read, the papers were referred to the Committee of the Whole House on the state of the Union (JHR, 4:332).

To the House of Representatives

GENTLEMEN OF THE HOUSE OF REPRESENTATIVES

The inclosed letters and affidavits exhibiting matter of complaint against John Pickering District judge of New Hampshire which is not within executive cognisance, I transmit them to the House of Representatives, to whom the constitution has confided a power of instituting proceedings of redress, if they shall be of opinion that the case calls for them.

TH: JEFFERSON
Feb. 3. 1803.

RC (DNA: RG 233, PM, 7th Cong., 2d sess.); endorsed by House clerks. PrC (DLC). Recorded in SJL with notation "judge Pickering." Enclosures: see Gallatin to TJ, 31 Jan., and enclosures. All are printed in *Message from the President of the United States, Enclosing Sundry Documents, Relative to John Pickering, District Judge of the District of New Hampshire* (Washington, D.C., 1803); Shaw-Shoemaker, No. 5360.

The House received TJ's message and the enclosed papers on 3 Feb. The next day they read the materials and referred them to Joseph H. Nicholson, James A. Bayard, John Randolph, Samuel Tenney, a New Hampshire Federalist, and Lucas C. Elmendorf, a New York Republican, to "examine the matter" and prepare a report offering their opinion. The report, presented by Nicholson on 18 Feb., was read and ordered to be considered on the 23d. Not until 2 Mch., the evening before adjournment, did the whole House consider the committee's resolve, "That John Pickering, Judge of the District Court of the district of New Hampshire, be impeached of high crimes and misdemeanors." Federalists Benjamin Huger of South Carolina and Calvin Goddard of Connecticut proposed delaying action on the matter until the next session of Congress, but their motion was defeated by a wide margin. The House then passed the resolution by a 45 to 8 vote. Tenney and Goddard were among those who voted against it. The next day Nicholson and Randolph notified the Senate of their action, promised that the House would, in due time, "exhibit particular articles of impeachment against him, and make good the same," and demanded that the Senate order the appearance of Pickering "to answer to the said impeachment." The Senate responded affirmatively later that day (*Biog. Dir. Cong.*; JHR, 4:322, 351, 383-4, 387, 392; *Annals*, 12:640-2, 645).

To Robert R. Livingston

DEAR SIR Washington Feb. 3. 1803.

My last to you was by mr Dupont. since that I have recieved yours of May 22. mr Madison supposes you have written a subsequent one which has never come to hand. A late suspension by the Intendant of N. Orleans of our right of deposit there, without which the right of navigation is impracticable has thrown this country into such a flame of hostile disposition as can scarcely be described. the Western country was peculiarly sensible to it as you may suppose. our business was to take the most effectual pacific measures in our power to remove the suspension, and at the same time to persuade our countrymen that pacific measures would be the most effectual and the most speedily so. the opposition caught it as a plank in a shipwreck, hoping it would enable them to tack the Western people to them. they raised the cry of war, were intriguing in all quarters to exasperate the Western inhabitants to arm & go down on their own authority & possess themselves of New Orleans, and in the mean time were daily reiterating, in new shapes, inflammatory resolutions for the adoption of the House. as a remedy to all this we determined to name a minister extraordinary to go immediately to Paris & Madrid to settle this matter. this measure being a visible one, and the person named peculiarly popular with the Western country, crushed at once & put an end to all further attempts on the legislature. from that moment all has become quiet; and the more readily in the Western country, as the sudden alliance of these new federal friends had of itself already began to make them suspect the wisdom of their own course. the measure was moreover proper from another cause. we must know at once whether we can acquire N. Orleans or not. we are satisfied nothing else will secure us against a war at no distant period: and we cannot pass this season without beginning those arrangements which will be necessary if war is hereafter to result. for this purpose it was necessary that the negotiators should be fully possessed of every idea we have on the subject, so as to meet the propositions of the opposite party, in whatsoever form they may be offered, and give them a shape admissible by us, without being obliged to await new instructions hence. with this view we have joined mr Monroe to yourself at Paris, & to mr Pinkney at Madrid, altho' we believe it will hardly be necessary for him to go to this last place. should we fail in this object of the mission, a further one will be superadded for the other side of the channel. on this subject you will be informed by the Secretary of State, and mr Monroe will be able also to inform you of all our views and purposes. by him I send another letter to Dupont, whose aid may be of the greater service as it will be divested of the shackles of form. the letter is left open for your perusal, after which I wish a wafer stuck in it before it be delivered. the official and the verbal communications to you by mr Monroe will be so full and minute, that I need not trouble you with an inofficial repetition of them. the future destinies of our country hang on the event of this negotiation, and I am sure they could not be placed in more able or more zealous hands. on our parts we shall be satisfied that what you do not effect cannot be effected. Accept therefore assurances of my sincere & constant affection and high respect. TH: JEFFERSON

P.S. Feb. 10. your letters of May 4. & Oct. 28. never came to my hands till last night. I am sincerely sorry for the misunderstanding therein explained. as mr Sumpter has long since asked and recieved permission to retire from his office, it cannot be necessary for me to say any thing on the subject but that I hope the dispositions to conciliate therein manifested, will be cherished and carried into effect by both.

RC (NNMus); at foot of first page: "Chancellr. Livingston"; endorsed by Livingston. PrC (DLC).

MY LAST TO YOU WAS BY MR DUPONT: the letter carried by Pierre Samuel Du Pont de Nemours was dated 5 May 1802. TJ had written to Livingston twice since then: once on 10 Oct., conveyed by Louise d'Egremont Brongniart, and again on 20 Nov. regarding books for the congressional library. TJ received Livingston's letter of 22 May on 5 Aug. (Vol. 37:484n).

INFLAMMATORY RESOLUTIONS: see the Editorial Note to TJ to the House of Representatives, 30 Dec.

Madison wrote to Livingston about Monroe's mission on 23 Feb. "The negotiation to be opened will bring the disposition and views of the French Government to a test," the SECRETARY OF STATE declared in that dispatch. Madison also drew up detailed instructions for Livingston and Monroe jointly. He signed that document on 2 Mch. but evidently had composed it by 31 Jan. The instructions included a plan for a treaty by which France would cede all territory east of the Mississippi River to the United States in return for a payment of 30 million livres tournois. The proposal, framed in the form of seven articles, incorporated some of the points of the projected treaty of four articles that Du Pont had sent to TJ on 4 Oct. The "overtures committed to you," Madison informed Livingston and Monroe, "coincide in great measure with the ideas of the person thro' whom the letter from the President of April 30th. 1802 was conveyed to Mr. Livingston, and who is presumed to have gained some insight into the present sentiments of the French cabinet." TJ had written to Du Pont on 30 Apr. and 5 May about the possible purchase of New Orleans and the Floridas, asking Du Pont to share the information with Livingston (Madison, *Papers, Sec. of State Ser.*, 4:343-5, 364-79; Vol. 37:365-7, 418-19, 421-2).

ANOTHER LETTER TO DUPONT: 1 Feb. Livingston wrote on 4 May 1802 about the MISUNDERSTANDING between him and Thomas Sumter, Jr., but, thinking the matter would be resolved by Sumter's resignation, he did not send that letter and its several enclosures to TJ until October (Vol. 37:410-16; Livingston to TJ, 28 Oct., first letter).

From Joseph Stokes

HONERED FRIEND Feby: 3rd: 1803

I have taken the Liberty to write a few Lines to thee[1] on a subject that would Perhaps be of great importance to the United States "and thinking that it would be better to Acquaint thee while Congress is Setting" this is to inform thy honer as the first Gentleman in America and wishing the wellfare of thy Country men I have the vanity to think that I have invented a machine that Can work a boat up against the Currant in Rivers that I think would carry twenty tons Burthan up the Common Currants and also with an additional machinery will work them up a falls or strong Rappids in Rivers and it will require but two men in this Boat and it may be Decked all over if Required and there may be ten or twelve or fifteen oars on Each side working all at once and the oars Not to touch the water as they go back and the oars shall make No holes in the sides of the Boat & they Can be Raised or Lowered answerable to the water & the Boat will Not be very much Cumbered with the machinery:—

the uncertainty of a Pattent in such a Case as this is but Little inducement for me to make a modle in order to Procure one that No one would Buy a Prevelage without an Experiment was made on the water though the modle might appear as though it would answer Every porpose it was intended for: though a modle I think might Be made for 20 Dollars or perhaps some Little more though Not willing to go into it on account of the uncertainty of the Privelage of a Pattent therefore I have wrote to thee on the subject & if thee in thy Great wisdom should think it worth thy notice as it will be of Great importance to America if it should answer the Porpose intended is that thee in thy Greatness would send me such word as thee may so mete & I will indeavour better to inform thee about it though fearfull when writeing this that it would Not be accepted as knowing that a man in thy Great station should know No stranger But haveing a Pitty that shuch Great usefullness should Lay Dormant therefore Please to Pardon thy sincere friend and wellwisher in harford County maryland Ten miles from belaire JOSEPH STOKES

P.S. if thy honer should think the above worth thy attention & would be willing to send anything about it shall thank thee to send as soon as Convenent &c: as I follow a mechanical Branch and the modle may be made in my shop and so I remain &c— J. S.

RC (MoSHi: Jefferson Papers); endorsed by TJ as received 23 Feb. and so recorded in SJL.

Joseph Stokes may have been the person of that name who in 1775 paid a fee assessed against Harford County citizens choosing not to associate with the patriot cause and who in 1783 appeared on the rolls of the county's Deer Creek Middle Hundred tax assessment area (Walter W. Preston, *History of Harford County Maryland from 1608 (the Year of Smith's Expedition) to the Close of the War of 1812* [Baltimore, 1901], 350; *Harford County 1783 Maryland Tax List from the Collection of the Maryland Historical Society* [Philadelphia, 1970], 95).

[1] MS: "the." Here and in seven subsequent appearances, the Editors have corrected "the" to "thee."

To Abraham Baldwin

DEAR SIR Washington Feb. 4. 1803.

Mr. Dufief a bookseller of Philadelphia who possesses Dr. Franklin's library, has inclosed me the catalogue with a desire that I would put it into the hands of the Committee charged with procuring a library for Congress, with an offer of the whole or any part of it at what he says shall be moderate prices. my dealings with him give me confidence that his prices would be moderate. without presuming on the answer of the committee to this proposition I have ventured to mark with a pencil a few particular books which I imagine are worthy of their acquisition if they are not already in the library. a return of the catalogue is asked when you have made of it the use which you may desire. Accept my friendly salutations & respect.

TH: JEFFERSON

PrC (DLC); at foot of text: "Mr. Baldwin"; endorsed by TJ in ink on verso. Recorded in SJL with notation "library." Enclosure not found, but see Nicolas Gouin Dufief to TJ, 31 Jan.

From Robert Brent

Sir, Feby 4th 1803

I take the liberty of enclosing a Memorial which has this day been presented me Soliciting my recommendation of Mr. Samuel Speake as a Justice of the peace, for the reasons therein stated—

I will add nothing to what has been stated in the memorial—which I am sure will have its full weight with you—when ever you may enter upon further appointments then those in Commission—

With Sentiments of Esteem & respect I have the honor to be Sir Your Mo Ob Sert.,

Robert Brent

RC (DNA: RG 59, LAR); endorsed by TJ as received 4 Feb. and "Speake to be justice of Columbia" and so recorded in SJL. Enclosure: Thomas B. Morriss and others to Robert Brent, Washington, D.C., 29 Jan. 1803, stating that although there are already several justices of the peace commissioned in the city, experience has found that it is "often very inconvenient to them to attend to the various Plaints and numerous Causes in this City"; this has led to frequent delays and inconvenience to suitors, "particularly so to the Poorer Class of Citizens"; the petitioners therefore ask Brent to recommend Samuel Speake's appointment as a justice of the peace to the president, believing that Speake will be able to carry out his official duties "without material injury to his Domestic Concerns" (same; signed by Morriss and ten others).

Samuel Speake did not receive an appointment from TJ. A member of the Washington, D.C., militia, Speake later worked as an auctioneer and operated a boarding house patronized by members of Congress. He died in 1817 (Perry M. Goldman and James S. Young, eds., *The United States Congressional Directories, 1789-1840* [New York, 1973], 42, 46, 49; *Washington Federalist*, 20 June 1803; *National Intelligencer*, 29 May, 27 Nov. 1807; Washington, D.C., *Monitor*, 19 Nov. 1808; *City of Washington Gazette*, 26 Dec. 1817).

To Nicolas Gouin Dufief

Sir Washington Feb. 4. 1803.

I recieved from you some days ago the three volumes of les Moralistes Anciennes, and last night your letter of Jan. 31. with Doctr. Franklin's catalogue, which I have this morning sent to the chairman of the library-committee of Congress. I observe in it the following books

Athenaei Deipnosophistorum &c. fol.
Philostratus works from the Greek. fol.
Durham's Physico and Astrotheology 8vo.

which I will ask the favor of you to send me with those you are about forwarding me. to this I should certainly add the volume inclosed in your letter, containing two small pamphlets with copious marginal notes by Dr. Franklin[1] but that from the binding, and the desire expressed to have it returned, I conclude you wish to preserve it for yourself as a relict of a saint. Colo. Monroe will soon be passing thro' Philadelphia on his way to France. I wish to send by him our last volume of Philosophical transactions to mr Volney. it is not to be had here. I will ask the favor of you therefore to get this volume, and inclose it under cover to mr Volney and put it into the hands of Colo. Monroe on his arrival in Philadelphia. you will certainly hear of his arrival immediately; and I will moreover ask of him to send to you for the book. it is only for fear he should forget to do this that I pray you to send it, on his arrival, without waiting for an application from him. Accept my salutations & respects. TH: JEFFERSON

RC (CtY); addressed: "Mr. Dufief Bookseller Philadelphia"; franked and postmarked. PrC (DLC); at foot of text in ink: "Dufief"; endorsed by TJ in ink on verso.

CHAIRMAN: Abraham Baldwin.

The BOOKS that TJ wanted from Franklin's collection were: *Athenaei Dipnosophistarum, sive, Coenae Sapientum Libri XV*, a 1556 edition of a work by the Greek scholar Athenaeus, a version of which TJ had sought to acquire a few years earlier (Sowerby, No. 42; Vol. 28:358); Charles Blount, *The Two First Books, of Philostratus, Concerning the Life of Apollonius Tyaneus*, published in London in 1680 (Sowerby, No. 1336); and *Derham's Physico and Astro Theology: or, A Demonstration of the Being and Attributes of God*, a two-volume edition published in London in 1786 that contained lectures by William Derham originally printed in 1713 and 1715 (Sowerby, No. 3727).

The fifth volume of TRANSACTIONS of the American Philosophical Society appeared in 1802.

[1] Preceding three words interlined.

From William Hoge and Joseph Hiester

SIR Thursday Feby. 4—1803

Having understood from conversation with Dr. Leib that it is his intention to withdraw from Congress by declining a reelection, we take the liberty of suggesting the propriety of assigning to him a place under the government, should any vacancies take place in Pennsylvania—To You, Sir, Who are well acquainted with the pretensions, qualifications and services of Dr Leib—it will be considered as a work of supererogation to enter into a detail of them; We will only remark, that in our opinion such an appointment would be acceptable to the people, and would conduce to the interest of the republican cause—As we know no one in our State better entitled to the attention of the administration—Feeling a deep interest in, and anxious to promote, the democratic cause in our State by the appointment of fit and approved men to office, we have been thus free in suggesting our spontaneous sentiments—We take the liberty of requesting, that this letter may be considered confidential, that no mortification may arise to our friend from having this unsolicited interposition attributed to him, in the event of our recommendation failing in its object

We are with sentiments of sincere consideration and respect—
Your fellow Citizens

W. Hoge
Jos: Hiester

RC (DNA: RG 59, LAR); in Hoge's hand, signed by Hoge and Hiester; at foot of text: "The President of U. States"; endorsed by TJ as received 4 Feb. and "Leib Michael to office" and so recorded in SJL.

Born in Cumberland County, Pennsylvania, William Hoge (1762-1814) moved to the western part of the state in 1782, where he founded the town of Washington with his older brother, John. In 1794, he was an officer of the Democratic Society of Pennsylvania in Washington County. He served in the state house of representatives in 1796 and 1797 and was elected to fill the congressional seat vacated by Gallatin in 1801. He served as a Pennsylvania congressman until October 1804 and again from 1807 to 1809 (Harry Marlin Tinkcom, *The Republicans and Federalists in Pennsylvania, 1790-1801: A Study in National Stimulus and Local Response* [Harrisburg, 1950], 257; Philip S. Foner, ed., *The Democratic-Republican Societies, 1790-1800* [Westport, Conn., 1976], 129-30; *Biog. Dir. Cong.*).

Born in Berks County, Pennsylvania, Joseph Hiester (1752-1832) grew up on a farm, became a clerk at a store in Reading, and in 1771, having married Elizabeth Whitman, the proprietor's daughter, became a partner in the business. He became sole owner in 1780. Hiester was an enthusiastic supporter of the American Revolution, serving as a delegate to the provincial congress at Philadelphia in 1776. As captain of the Berks County militia, he fought in the battle of Long Island in August 1776 and was captured by the British. After his release in a prisoner exchange, he recovered his health and as a lieutenant colonel in 1777 took part in the battle of Germantown. He served five terms in the Pennsylvania assembly between 1780 and 1790 where he represented the predominantly German population. In 1787, Hiester was among the 23 Antifederalists who voted against ratification of the Constitution. He was an influential participant at the convention that drew up the Pennsylvania Constitution of 1790. During the 1790s, Hiester served several terms in the state senate, before being elected to fill a vacated seat in Congress. He served as the Republican representative from Berks County from 1797 to 1805 and again from 1815 to December 1820, when he resigned, having been elected governor. As Pennsylvania's chief executive, Hiester advocated state-supported education and internal improvements. Noted for making appointments according to merit rather than along party lines, Hiester also believed in rotation of office and refused to stand for reelection (ANB; DAB; Higginbotham, *Pennsylvania Politics*, 87-8; Vol. 33:73n).

On 23 July 1801, in a letter now missing, Hiester and Peter Muhlenberg, writing from Philadelphia, recommended Michael LEIB for the office of inspector or surveyor (Vol. 34:704). For Hiester's advice on appointments and support for other Pennsylvania Republicans, see Vol. 33:29n, 247n; Vol. 34:355n, 470-1n, 523-5.

To William Jones

Th: Jefferson requests the favour of *The Honble. Capt. Jones* to dine with him *on Monday next, the 7th. Instant* at half after three, or at whatever later hour the house may rise.

Friday Febr: 4th. 1803.

The favour of an answer is asked.

RC (PHi); printed form, with blanks filled by Meriwether Lewis reproduced in italics; addressed by Lewis: "The Honble. Capt. Jones"; also on address sheet in another hand: "Thomas Truxton" and "Hugh G Campbell."

To Pierre Auguste Adet

DEAR SIR Washington Feb. 5. 1803.

It is long since I ought to have acknoleged the reciept of your favor congratulating me on my advancement to the post I now occupy. the constant demand of attention to cases which admit no delay has forced me to long postponements of those of a less urgent character. that my own happiness, & probably my reputation, will not gain by this [advance]ment is more than probable. you know too well yourself the delights of Study, and of literary pursuit to place those of a political character in any competition with them; and no one is better able to decide this question than yourself, whose services to your country have been so eminent in both lines.

You saw this country in the most unfavorable moment which it's history has ever presented. I will not develope to you the causes of this. you were an eye-witness to them. the delusions which led our countrymen astray from themselves were continual & even strengthened after your departure. but they were so much out of nature that they could not continue. the people awakened from the phrensy into which they had been caught, and restored things to their natural course. the extravagancies of various kinds which had been introduced are discontinued, & our citizens again consolidated in the genuine principles of their government. not so the leaders, who figured so highly when you were here. they were committed beyond retraction. but they are left almost without followers; are loud indeed in the newspapers; but are a vox et praeterea nihil. had your mission fallen in this period of time, I am persuaded it would have been much more satisfactory to yourself, and you would certainly have seen a more genuine representation of the character of our country. I thought myself peculiarly unfortunate that you should have been with our government exactly during the time which I was absent from it. I avail myself of the mission of mr Monroe to Paris to convey to you my sense of the obliging sentiments expressed in your letter. he comes to propose arrangements for ensuring the continuance of the peace & friendship between our two nations, which our expected neighborhood on the Missisipi renders the more urgent. we are induced to these measures of precaution by our strong desire to run a course of peace, friendship & commerce with all mankind, & to remove every occasion which might tend to commit us in the broils of Europe. deeply impressed with a sense of your personal merit and good dispositions, I with satisfaction tender you assurances of my great and sincere esteem, & very high consideration & respect.

TH: JEFFERSON

PrC (DLC); blurred; at foot of first page: "M. Adet."

Adet had written in June 1801 CONGRATULATING TJ on his election to the presidency (Vol. 34:421-3).

VOX ET PRAETEREA NIHIL: an empty threat; Caesar A. Rodney had used a variant of the expression a few months earlier (Vol. 38:638, 639n).

From Henry Dearborn

SIR Februy. 5th. 1803

I herewith enclose a statement of what I consider as a just, or at lest, an equitable claim on the United States. You will probably think the narative connected with this statement tedious, but I have considered it necessary exhibit a full view of the subject—when I ingaged in this unfortunate contract, I was not in debt, nor[1] was the Gentleman who has assisted me; within a few months of the time of my entering into this contract, I had sold a tract of land for near three Thousand dollars with a view of purchasing other real estate nearer home, which money,—except about eight hundred dollars, has been expended for the maintainence of my family while my whole attention was occupied in the fullfilment of my contract with the public,—having no other money concerns at the time, & not contemplating so unfortunate an issue, I did not consider it necessary to keep an account of my expenditures, knowing that by an exact attention to the application of the money received on account of the contract, I should at the close of the business know precisely what would be the ballance.—

with sentiments of respectfull consideration I am Sir Your Huml. Servt. H. DEARBORN

RC (DLC); at head of text: "To the President of the United States."

[1] MS: "no."

ENCLOSURE

From Henry Dearborn

SIR, Washington Februy. 5th. 1803

I take the liberty of presenting the following statement, as the grounds of what I concider a fair & equitable claim on the United States.

In the year 1798 I was applied to by the Treasury Department to undertake the erection of a stone lighthouse at Cape Hatteras, and a wooden one on a stone foundation at Shell castle, with dwelling houses, &c—after making what I considered the necessary enquiries and calculations, I entered into a contract to erect said buildings, and to compleat them for the sum of $38450–as soon as practicable. it had been understood by Congress at the time the act passed authorising the erection of those lights, and by the Executive & myself at the time the contract was made, that what was called shell castle Island, was really an Island, and all the enquiries I made of Masters of vessells who had frequently been there, and of Col Thos. Blount who I understood was interested in said Island, were answered in such manner as to confirm my belief of its being really an Island, but I since found that Beacon Island which is about two miles from shell castle, and which had been purchased by the United States for the purpose of erecting a fortification, had been concidered as the object of my enquiries—Immediately after I had entered into the contract, I made every excertion in my power in procuring materials and workmen for commencing the erection of the buildings early in 1799. finding that the principle materials could be obtained on better terms in New England, and freighted to the place, than they could else where, I had the frames of the wooden buildings, with all the materials for compleeting them prepared in the course of the winter of 98. 99. ready to put up. I had likewise engaged several vessels in Rhode Island to freight stone from there, where I had the principle part of the stone prepared for the object.—on the last of May 1799, a vessell of my own sailed from Kennebeck with the whole of the materials for the three wooden buildings, provisions stores & workmen, under the direction of Mr. Hobart who had agreed to assist me.—on the fifth of June, I sailed in an other vessell of my own for Rhode Island, there to take in a load of stone & proceed to Shell castle. after a short passage[1] to Rhode Island, I was about begining to load the vessell, when Mr. Hobart arrived from Boston and informed me that the vessell in which he sailed, had on the 8th. of June been over set in a gale of wind between Nantucket & Georges bank, was dismasted filled with water and a great part of the cargo lost or dammaged, and two men lost, that after much suffering they had got the wreck into Boston. I then ordered the vessell I had sailed in back to Kennebeck for the purpos of taking a cargo similar to the one which had been shiped in the other vessell. Mr. Hobart & myself returnd to Boston & from thence to Kennebeck and procured an other cargo, and on the 7th. of August 1799, I arrived in the vessell at shell castle with the workmen & materials ready to commence the erection of the wooden light house & dwelling house, but to my great disappointment & mortification, I found what had been called shell castle Island, two feet under water with a common tide, and no place where I could land my materials & workmen except on a wharf at about one hundred rods distance from the place where the light house & dwelling house were to be erected. by permission of the owner of the wharf I with great difficulty found means to land my cargo.—on enquirey I found that at low water the flats would be dry, and that the masons might probably work two or three hours each day on the foundations, but on further enquirey I was informed that Mr. Tredwell of Edenton who had been appointed to survey the flats purchased by the public, and to designate the scite for the buildings, had not yet arrived for that purpose. I immediately sent an express for Mr. Tredwell, but contrary winds & other obsticles prevented his arrival until about the last of the month, and by the time the survey was made & the scite designated, some of my workmen began to be unwell, being with my self & Mr. Hobart confined to a small shed & obliged to drink very impure water.—when the weather & tide admitted, every excertion was made, in laying the foundations, but in the course of the month of Septemr every workman, together with Mr. Hobart & my self were confined by sickness. by medical aid, we wer so far restored, that in the course of Octobr. & Novemr. with great expence & risque the buildings were put up and covered including the dwelling house at Cape Hatteras. but from the frequent relapses which attended the workmen, I was obliged to suspend the business until an other year, and every preperation was made for compleeting the whole in the course of the year 1800. workmen were procured at Philadelphia with a hope that they would be less effected by the climate than men from further North. in April 1800, I arrived with the workmen at Cape Hatteras and after waiting ten days for Mr. Tredwell to decide on the depth of the foundation, the Mason work of the Stone Light house was commenced and progressed until the walls were about twenty feet above the surface, when 13 of the workmen were taken sick & one died; it was then found necessary to suspend the prosecution of the business until an other year, and to transport the workmen back to Philadelphia at a great expence. in March 1801 workmen were again procured and arrived with Mr. Hobart at Cape Hatteras with a hope of compleeting the whole before they should be obliged to retire again, but the workmen & Mr. Hobart became sickley earlier than usual, and were under the necessaty of again returning home before the business was compleeted, and in the Spring of 1802 Mr. Hobart returned with the workmen & compleeted the buildings &c.—from my enquiries I had been induced to believe that the scite for the light-house at Cape Hatteras would be healthy, from its immediate vicinity to the sea & to Pamlico sound, it being on a narrow strip of land exposed to the sea breeses, but unfortunately the scite for the buildings was surrounded with fresh marshes, which are over flowed by every rain, and when the water drains off produce great quantities of very unhealthy exhalations, and to add to the other misfortune, there is no water to be had but what is extreemly impure and unhealthy.—the loss of the vessell & cargo before mentioned & the loss of an other vessell in the course of the business, althoug principally insured, were on account of the derangement of my plans of opperations, and the extra expenses resulting from those misfortunes, opperated as a serious misfortune, but those misfortunes wer small when compaired to what I experienced from other circumstances which I have enumerated, and especially the unexpected unhealthyness of the places,—from the foregoing unfortunate & unforeseen circumstances, notwithstanding every possible excertion on my part to accomplish the business with the least possible expence, I have actually been obliged to expend $4379—over and above the sum stipulated in the contract, which sum I am unable to loose without distressing my self & family, and I humbly concieve that the public ought in this case to do what would be, by all honest men, thought proper in a similar case between two individuals.

I declare in the most unequivocal manner, that the whole of the money received on account of the before mentioned contract, has been faithfully and exclusively applied to fullfilment of the contract, and that the sum of $4,379–is the fair & real ballance which has been expended (exclusive of any compensation for my own time & trouble) in the performence of the stipulations of the contract between the United States and myself, over and above the sum stipulated in said contract.

all which I submit to the concideration of the President of the United States with the most perfect confidence that he will do what ever Justice & equity shall require in the premise.—

with sentiments of respect I am Sir Your Huml Servt

H. DEARBORN

RC (DLC); at head of text: "To the President of the United States"; endorsed by TJ as received 12 Feb. and so recorded in SJL with notation "his own case."

FAIR & EQUITABLE CLAIM: TJ referred Dearborn's claim to Albert Gallatin, who was hesitant to support it, opposing the principle of altering contracts and believing that Congress would reject the demand. Dearborn subsequently reduced his request to $2,000 and Gallatin unsuccessfully requested an appropriation for that purpose in his expenditure estimates to Congress in 1804 and 1805. TJ, however, continued to back Dearborn's claim, believing it "a fair subject of additional compensation." In February 1808, Congress appropriated $1,145.44 in addition to the sums previously appropriated for erecting the Cape Hatteras lighthouse and Shell Castle Island beacon (Richard Alton Erney, *The Public Life of Henry Dearborn* [New York, 1979], 23-4; U.S. Statutes at Large, 2:465; Gallatin to TJ, 15 Feb., 19 Dec. 1803, 13 Dec. 1805; TJ to Gallatin, 7 Nov. 1806).

ACT PASSED AUTHORISING THE ERECTION OF THOSE LIGHTS: on 13 May 1794, Congress passed an act authorizing the erection of a lighthouse on the headland of Cape Hatteras, North Carolina, and a beacon on Shell Castle Island, near the

Ocracoke Island harbor (U.S. Statutes at Large, 1:368).

Thomas BLOUNT of North Carolina and Dearborn served together in Congress from 1793 to 1797 (*Biog. Dir. Cong.*).

Dudley B. HOBART was Dearborn's son-in-law (Vol. 36:200n).

Samuel TREDWELL had been appointed collector and inspector of the revenue for Edenton in 1793 (JEP, 1:129).

In TJ's papers, an undated, unsigned list in Dearborn's hand with the heading "Ballances due" records the following names and amounts:

Capt. Grant	$60
W. Hall	174
S. Wheler	1247
E. Hilyard	51
I. Whelen	59
J. Bowen	850
A. McCurry	100
D. B. Hobart	1838
	4379

(MS in DLC: TJ Papers, 129:22317).

[1] MS: "passade."

To Marc Auguste Pictet

DEAR SIR Washington Feb. 5. 1803.

It is long since I ought to have acknoleged your favor of May 20. 1801 which however I did not recieve till January 1802. my incessant occupations on matters which will not bear delay occasion those which can be put off to lie often for a considerable time. I rejoice that the opinion which I gave you on the removal hither proved useful. I knew it was not safe for you to take such a step until it could be done on sure ground. I hoped at that time that some canal shares which were at the disposal of Genl. Washington might have been applied towards the establishment of a good seminary of learning: but he had already proceeded too far on another plan to change their direction. I have still had constantly in view to propose to the legislature of Virginia the establishment of one on as large a scale as our present circumstances would require or bear. but as yet no favorable moment has occurred. in the mean while I am endeavoring to procure materials for a good plan. with this view I am to ask the favor of you to give me a sketch of the branches of science taught in your college, how they are distributed among the professors, that is to say how many professors there are, and what branches of science are allotted to each professor, and the days and hours assigned to each branch. your successful experience in the distribution of business will be a valuable guide to us, who are without experience. I am sensible I am imposing on your goodness a troublesome task: but I believe that every son of science feels a strong & disinterested desire of promoting it in every part of the earth, and it is the consciousness as well as confidence in this which emboldens me to make the present request. in the line of science we have little new here. our citizens almost all follow some industrious[1] occupation, and therefore have little time to devote to abstract science. in the arts, & especially the mechanical arts many ingenious improvements are made in consequence of the patent-right giving an exclusive use of them for 14. years. but the great mass of our people are agricultural; and the commercial cities, tho' by the command of newspapers they make a great deal of noise, yet they have little effect in the direction of the government. they are as different in sentiment & character from the country people as any two distinct nations, and are clamorous against the order of things established by the agricultural interest. under this order our citizens generally are enjoying a very great degree of liberty and security in the most temperate manner. every man being at his ease, feels an interest in the preservation of order, and comes forth to preserve it at the first call of the magistrate. we are endeavoring too to reduce the government to the practice of a rigorous economy, to avoid burthening the people, and arming the magistrate with a patronage of money and office which might be used to corrupt & undermine the principles of our government. I state these general outlines to you, because I believe you take some interest in our fortune, and because our newspapers for the most part, present only the caricatures of disaffected minds. indeed the abuses of the freedom of the press here have been carried to a length never before known or borne by any civilized nation. but it is so difficult to draw a clear line of separation between the abuse and the wholesome use [...] of the press, that as yet we have found it better to trust the public judgment, rather than the magistrate, with the discrimination between truth & falsehood. and hitherto the public judgment has performed that office with wonderful correctness. should you favor me with a letter, the safest channel of conveyance will be the American minister at Paris or London. I pray you to accept assurances of my great esteem & high respect and consideration. TH: JEFFERSON

PrC (DLC); faint; at foot of first page: "M. Pictet."

TJ and Pictet had corresponded in 1795 about the possible REMOVAL of the Academy of Geneva to the United States. TJ asked George WASHINGTON if he would be willing to use his shares in the Potomac and James River canal companies, which Washington wanted to apply to some educational purpose, to bring the highly respected Genevan institution to America. Washington, however, preferred to endow a new educational institution in the Federal District. In his letter of May 1801, Pictet indicated that TJ's counsel had done much to convince him to stay in Geneva (Vol. 28:239-40, 275-8, 306-9, 505; Vol. 34:152-4).

[1] Word interlined in place of "useful."

To Charles Pougens

SIR Washington Feb. 5. 1803.

I have to acknolege the reciept of several letters from yourself and mr Short making a friendly tender of your services as a bookseller. but the fact is that my collection of books is now so extensive, & myself so far advanced in life that I have little occasion to add to it. being charged with procuring some books for Congress, and observing you had established a correspondence with mr Duane, I put into his hands a catalogue, and at the same time wrote to mr Livingston our minister at Paris to advise in the execution of the commission and to pay for the books. I desired they might not be shipped till April, having experienced great damage to books in winter passages.

I am a subscriber to the Encyclopedie Methodique, and possess about 90. whole volumes of text and about as much of the plates as will make 16. or 17. volumes, and I am desirous of getting the parts since published. to do this I know no method so certain as to give you a state of what I possess, and you will hence be able to take up the sequel at the proper point and to send it to me. and if you will note the additional parts that you send me, you will be able hereafter to send what further comes out, which I should be glad you would do annually in the month of April. our minister at Paris can advise the channel of conveyance, but if you will send them to M. de la Motte our Vice-consul at Havre, no surer conveyance can be recommended. as I am utterly uninformed of the extent of the parts published subsequent to what I possess, I cannot conjecture the amount of cost, and therefore have imagined it might not be inconvenient, on the reciept of your bill to permit me either to pay the money into the hands of mr Duane, or to remit you a bill on Paris, Amsterdam or London as you should prefer. the books may come in any vessel bound to New York, Philadelphia, or any port of the Chesapeake. Accept my salutations and respects. TH: JEFFERSON

PrC (DLC); at foot of text: "M. Pougens." Recorded in SJL with notation "Encycl. Buffon. Aeschylus."

Marie Charles Joseph Pougens (1755-1833), born in Paris, received an exemplary education in a variety of subjects and began his career with diplomatic missions in Rome and Great Britain. In the libraries of the Vatican and the British Museum he researched the origins of languages, and in Rome he also studied art. He lost his eyesight to smallpox at the age of 24. As a chevalier of the Knights of Malta he received revenues from estates, but he lost that source of income during the French Revolution. Sentenced to death in 1794, he survived when the execution of Robespierre brought an end to the Reign of Terror. The National Convention awarded him a pension, and in 1795 he opened a business in Paris selling books on commission. He attempted without success to develop a market in the

United States for sets of books published in France. By 1803 he suffered financial losses, but Napoleon Bonaparte authorized a loan from the national treasury and later forgave half the debt. Pougens's marriage in 1805 to an Englishwoman of means enabled him to retire from business three years later. He was a scholar and writer who translated travel accounts, compiled dictionaries, wrote books on philosophy, science, language, and antiquities, and authored a historical drama. In 1799, he became a member of the section on ancient languages in the class of literature and fine arts of the National Institute of France. He was also honored by other learned societies, and the American Philosophical Society elected him to membership in 1829. After his death the APS memorialized him with a formal obituary. As a young man, Pougens was a protégé of Madame de Tessé. That bond ended after Pougens and Sophie Ernestine de Tott, whom Madame de Tessé treated like a daughter, fell in love and Madame de Tessé forbade the relationship (A. V. Arnault and others, *Biographie nouvelle des contemporains, ou dictionnaire historique et raisonné de tous les hommes qui, depuis la Révolution Française, ont acquis de la célébrité*, 20 vols. [Paris, 1820-25], 17:49-55; *Biographie universelle*, 34:210-11; J. C. F. Hoefer, *Nouvelle biographie générale depuis les temps les plus reculés jusqu'a nos jours*, 46 vols. [Paris, 1855-66], 40:916-18; *Mémoires et Souvenirs de Charles de Pougens . . . commencés par lui et continués par Mme Louise B. de Saint-Léon* [Paris, 1834], 156-7, 179, 188, 240-2; Amable Charles, Comte de Franqueville, *Le premier siècle de l'Institut de France, 25 Octobre 1795-25 Octobre 1895*, 2 vols. [Paris, 1895-96], 1:133; APS, *Proceedings*, 22, pt. 3 [1884], 596, 648, 656, 670; Vol. 10:158-9n; Vol. 29:597; Vol. 30:319, 482n; Vol. 38:135).

SEVERAL LETTERS: Pougens wrote to TJ in December 1797, a few months after William Short first recommended him to TJ. Pougens's letter reached TJ in March 1798, but has not been found. Short continued to mention him in correspondence to TJ (Vol. 29:333, 597, 598n; Vol. 30:481; Vol. 32:147, 158; Vol. 34:287, 292).

On 16 July 1802, TJ sent William DUANE the list of books wanted from Paris for the Library of Congress, and Duane indicated on 18 Oct. that Pougens would be handling those purchases. LIVINGSTON: see TJ to Robert R. Livingston, 20 Nov.

ENCLOSURE

Jefferson's Volumes of the Encyclopédie Méthodique

the following are the Dictionaries of the Encyclopedie Methodique which I possess, and the last article to which each [. . .]. the sequel to that article is wanting. to be unbound, that is to say in boards.
Agriculture. Ceteree.
Amusemens des Sciences. Geometrie page 583
Antiquités. Ogulnia.
Architecture. Coloris des fleurs.
Art Militaire. Zigs Zags.
Arts et Metiers. Zinc. Discours. Table Alphabetique
Assemblée nationale. Tome 1st. wanting.
I have Tome 2d. Absens.—[Auteurs] dramatiques.
Beaux arts. Sculpteurs. Damophon.
Botanique. Mauve.
Chirurgie. Tete.
Chymie. Airelle.

Commerce. Zoroche.
Econom. Polit. & diplom. Zwifalten & Supplement.
Encyclopediana. Zeuxis. [. . .] of 2. the remaining [becomes last].
Equitation. Tombé. l'art de nager.
Finances. Yvetot.
Forêts et bois. Utricules.
Geographie ancienne. Trachonitæ
Geographie. Zaara.
Grammaire. Strophe.
Histoire. Triumvirat.
Histoire Naturelle. Quadrupedes. Zurnapa.
Oiseaux. Zoucet.
Serpens. Umbre.
Poissons. Zingel.
Insectes. Gyrin.
Vers. Cone.
Jurisprudence. Zewerp.
Jurisprudence. Police. Voitures.
Logique. Systeme.
Logique morales: Voyages.
Manufactures et arts. Toileries.
do. Pelleterie. Recherches. Vocabulaire &c. 760. [. . .] & 28 pages
Marine. Zones et Supplement.
Mathematiques. Zubenel-Chemali. & supp. tab. de [lecture]
Medecine. Capillaire.
Musique. Cytharisterienne.
Philosophie ancienne et moderne. Fetichisme. but the [demi volume] Condillac—Fetichisme is so much injured, that I would wish to recieve a new copy of it. to wit after Collins.
Theologie. Zwingliens.

Planches

Atlas. Terre de Kerguelen.
Planches. Recueil. Tomes 1. 2. 3. 4. 5. 6. 7. 8.
Histoire naturelle. Poissons.
Discours. 215. pages.
Planches 100.
Hist. Nat. Cetacees / Reptiles / Serpens } Discours 7[1] pages. Planches 35.
Hist. Nat. Serpens. / Papillons / Oiseaux } pl. 36—42 / pl. 1—32. / pl. 1—77
Hist. Nat. Oiseaux. Discours lxxx. pages.
pl. 178—230.
Quadrups. pl. 1.—18.
a>
Hist. Nat. Ornithologie. Disc. pa. 193—220
Insectes pl. 66—165.
Hist. Nat. Vers. Discours. 84. pages
pl. 1.—95.

Hist. Nat. Vers. Discours. 85—132
pl. 96—189.
Botanique Discours. 440. pages
pl. 1—[308].
a> omitted. Hist. Nat. Ornithologie. Disc. 192. pages.
Papillons. pl. 33—65
Quadrup. pl. 49—112

I have les Oiseaux de Buffon [avec des] planches [enluminées]. 5. vols of [text] & 5 vols of plate [to the 646. plate.] Quarto [. . .]. I wish the sequel. When at Strasburg in April 1788, I bought a copy of [Aeschyle' qua. supr. sunt.] commentario, scholiis et lexico Schutz. 8vo. as far as it was then published. I should be glad to get the residue of the same

I have 4. vols 12mo. of Cepede's histoire naturelle des Quadrupeds ovipares, et des Serpens. if any more have been published I shall be glad to recieve them of the same [. . .]

PrC (DLC); faint and blurred; endorsed as sent to Charles Pougens by TJ in ink on verso.

TJ was an original subscriber to Charles-Joseph Panckoucke's *Encyclopédie méthodique* (Sowerby, No. 4889), the topical successor to the more famous *Encyclopédie* of Diderot and d'Alembert, and had last tried to update his collection in 1795 and 1796. The ambitious project had a complicated publication history. Between 1782 and 1832, three different publishers brought out over 155 volumes, as well as about 6,000 illustrative plates. Divided into more than 30 subject areas, unbound installments, or livraisons, were distributed to subscribers when completed. TJ's list above pairs each subject area with the last entry appearing in the livraisons in his possession and indicates that he had acquired most of the volumes published up through 1792 but, with a few possible exceptions, none published after that date. Of the volumes published by 1792, TJ appears to have lacked only the second volume on chemistry, the fourth volume on insects, and the fifth volume on medicine. In a couple of cases, however, he is reporting an incomplete volume. TJ's edition of AMUSEMENS DES SCIENCES (*Dictionnaire encyclopedique des amusemens des sciences mathématiques et physiques*) extending only to the entry on geometry, lacked about 300 pages. Ending with STROPHE, an entry on metered pairs of poetic lines, his collection of the encyclopedia's grammar and literature section was missing the third and final volume's last 320 or so pages. Incomplete volumes for ancient geography, TJ's last reported entry being that for TRACHONITÆ, music (last reported entry, CYTHARISTERIENNE), and philosophy (last reported entry, FETICHISME, or superstitions), resulted from their staggered publication, with demivolumes arriving after 1792. In addition, no first volume on France's National Assembly ever appeared, thus accounting for TJ's acquisition of only the second volume, or tome. Plates (PLANCHES) were distributed separately from the other volumes. The list indicates that TJ had received both volumes of the ATLAS, as well as the eight volumes of plates published between 1783 and 1790 as *Recueil des planches*, which related to Art Militaire, Mechanical Arts, Manufactures, History, Mathematics, nautical concerns (Marine), and the volume *Arts académiques, équitation, escrime, danse, et art de nager*. Plates connected to the natural history division were also published about this time and eventually appeared under the collective title *Histoire naturelle des trois règnes de la nature*. It is more difficult to assess the comprehensiveness of TJ's collection of these plates, as he seems to have classified them differently than did the publishers. Publication dates for volumes of plates, as well as the above list, leave little doubt, nevertheless, that TJ possessed plates that appeared in the volumes related to ichthyology, marine mammals (CETACEES), herpetology and ophiology

(REPTILES and SERPENS), and ornithology, all of which were published by 1790. He also had collected plates related to botany and insects, even though the volumes in which those plates appeared were published in 1793 and 1797, respectively. The volume of plates on quadrupeds, also represented in this list, has not been dated, and a volume including plates of invertebrates, represented on this list as VERS, was not published until the 1820s. When TJ sold his books to the Library of Congress in 1815, his collection of the *Encyclopédie méthodique* was catalogued as 136½ volumes, quite possibly a complete set up to that point (George B. Watts, "The Encyclopedie Methodique," *PMLA*, 73 [1958], 348-66; Christabel P. Braunot and Kathleen Hardesty Doig, "The *Encyclopédie méthodique*: an introduction," *Studies on Voltaire and the eighteenth century*, 327 [1995], 1-152; Vol. 28:357-9; Vol. 29:4).

To Justus Erich Bollmann

SIR Washington Feb. 6 1803.

Mr. Olsen, the Danish minister here, was so kind as to send me some specimens of Hungarian wines for [trial?]. among these were two kinds in long necked quart bottles, one of which was quite a sweet wine; the other he called a dry wine, but I considered it as rather sweetish, or what we call silky. the bottle in which this was is stamped [symbol] he informed me he recieved them from you, and that you had a correspondence by which you could procure any of them which should be desired and that such an undertaking would not be entirely foreign to your occupations. it is on his assurances I presume to ground a request to you to import for me some of the wine last described a dry wine as he called it[1] and to avoid any mistake as to the kind I have had a bottle of it packed in a box, and will send it to you by the stage as soon as I can meet with any person who will take it under his care & deliver it to you. on your being so kind as to inform me you can undertake this, I will take the liberty of informing you of the quantity desired, which would be governed in some degree by the price at which you suppose it will come. Accept assurances of my esteem & respect.

TH: JEFFERSON

PrC (DLC); faint and blurred; at foot of text: "Doctr. Bollmann"; endorsed by TJ in ink on verso.

For descriptions of the HUNGARIAN WINE sent to TJ, see Peder Blicher Olsen to TJ, [23 Jan. 1803].

[1] Preceding seven words interlined.

To Jones & Howell

Gentlemen Washington Feb. 6. 1803.

Be pleased by the first conveyance to Richmond to forward to the address of Messrs. Gibson & Jefferson of that place for me the bar iron below stated, on account of

Your very humble servt Th: Jefferson

$2\frac{1}{2}$ ~~Cwt~~ of iron of the highest quality in flat bars, for making hinges.
5 ~~Cwt~~ in $\frac{3}{4}$ I. square bars of a harder quality.

PrC (MHi); endorsed by TJ in ink on verso. Recorded in SJL with notation "$7\frac{1}{2}$ ~~Cwt~~ bar iron."

List of Groceries for Monticello

Coffee 50 lb.
100. lb white powdered sugar
6. loaves loaf do. single refined
6. lb. young hyson.
10. lb pearl barley
25. lb rice
25. lb crackers
2. gross of porter.
Feb. 6. 1803. desired mr Barnes to forward the above to Monticello

Th: Jefferson

MS (ViU: Edgehill-Randolph Papers); in TJ's hand; on scrap of paper, with miscellaneous calculations by TJ.

To Louis Sébastien Mercier

Sir Washington Feb. 6. 1803.

I recieved by mr Paine the letter of 12th. Fructidor which you were so kind as to write me. I some time ago testified, in a letter to the President of the National institute, my grateful sense of the honor done me by that society: and in reply to your obliging expressions on the same subject, I can only reiterate assurances of my thankfulness for the partial light in which they have been pleased to view me. with every affection for science, & every disposition to promote it which can animate the [heart] of man, it has been my fortune to be obstructed from it by circumstances, and to be destined to pass my life in labours less pleasing to my natural propensities: labours too which, however well intended, do not always leave the mind as well satisfied with their result, as with that of a geometrical problem.

Madame Bonneville has not yet arrived. should she visit this part of our republic, be assured, Sir, that I shall [...] [shew her] those attentions which her [merits] and your recommendation entitle her [to expect]. long acquainted with your distinguished work as a writer, often nourished by information from your pen, I have peculiar satisfaction in being furnished with an occasion of expressing to you the sentiments of my esteem and assurances of my high respect and consideration. TH: JEFFERSON

P.S. Feb 10. on conversing with mr Paine I find I was mistaken in a supposing Made. Bonneville not arrived. she is in New Jersey, and was the bearer of your letter, which mr Paine delivered me, and I thought he had recieved it from you.

RC (DLC); blurred; at foot of text: "M. Mercier."

LETTER OF 12TH. FRUCTIDOR: that is, 30 Aug. (Vol. 38:320-2). TJ's letter to the NATIONAL INSTITUTE of France is printed in this volume at 14 Nov.

See Mercier's letter cited above for Marguerite Brazier de BONNEVILLE.

To J. P. G. Muhlenberg

DEAR SIR Washington Feb. 6. 1803.

Monsr. d'Yrujo, the Spanish minister here, has been so kind as to spare me 200. bottles of Champagne, part of a larger parcel imported for his own use, & consequently privileged from duty. but it would be improper for me to take the benefit of that. I must therefore ask the favor of you to take the proper measures for paying the duty, for which purpose I inclose you a bank check for $22\frac{1}{2}$ dollars the amount of it. if it could be done without mentioning my name, it would avoid ill-intended observations, as in some such way as this 'by duty paid on a part of such a parcel of wines not entitled to privilege' or in any other way you please. the wine was imported into Philadelphia, probably about Midsummer last. Accept assurances of my great esteem & respect. TH: JEFFERSON

RC (George Baer Hiester, Reading, Pennsylvania, 1949); at foot of text: "Genl. Muhlenburg." PrC (MHi); endorsed by TJ in ink on verso.

BOTTLES OF CHAMPAGNE: see Carlos Martínez de Irujo to TJ, [8 Dec. 1802] and 30 Dec. 1802.

To Thomas Newton

DEAR SIR Washington Feb. 6. 1803.

Colo. Monroe informs me you have not more than two or three pipes of your Brazil Madeira left. I must therefore pray you to send me two pipes of it, recieving paiment at 90. days if that will suit. for my demands here are such as to keep me in that predicament. if you import this wine annually, it is probable I shall annually call for two or three pipes.

I have recieved 6. barrels of Crab cyder 2. or 3. days ago, which I take for granted comes from you. a line as to the cost being dropped to myself or mr Barnes, he will immediately remit the amount. Accept assurances of my constant esteem & high respect.

TH: JEFFERSON

PrC (MHi); at foot of text: "Colo. Thos. Newton"; endorsed by TJ in ink on verso. Recorded in SJL with notation "2. pipes Madeira."

To Daniel Trump

DEAR SIR Washington Feb. 6. 1803

Two or three years ago I informed you that mr Divers, a neighbor of mine, who was building a good house, would want his windows from you. he is much later about his building than was expected: however he is now ready for the windows. I must pray you therefore to have them executed according to the memorandum subjoined, and to forward them to Messrs. Picket, Pollard & Johnson Richmond for mr George Divers, and with as little delay as possible. mr Joseph [Higbee] of Philadelphia will recieve orders from mr Divers to pay for them as soon as delivered. let me pray you to have them done in the best [manner]. the circular windows you had made for me, [all gave way]. they have cost me a great deal of work in repaining, and I am afraid will [never] be made to stand at all. Accept my best wishes & respects.

TH: JEFFERSON

[8]. windows 9 f.—7 I. high, 3 f.—4$\frac{3}{4}$ I. wide in the clear between the rabbets, divided into 3. [equal] sashes for each window, & glazed with best glass 12. by 18. I.

9. circular sashes 3 f—6$\frac{3}{4}$ I diameter finished. glazed with best glass.

2. sashes 3 f—4$\frac{3}{4}$ I square, to be placed over doors. glazed with 12. by 18. I. panes best glass.

1. semicircular sash 4 f—3 I long on the straight edge when finished, being the half of a circle of 4 f—3 I diam. glazed with best glass.
1. semicircular window sash 6 f—7 I long on the strait edge, glazed as above

[all] the sashes to be $1\frac{1}{2}$ I. thick, that being the width of the rabbets.
24. panes window glass 12. by 10 I. for repaining
1. pane plate glass 18[$\frac{3}{4}$] by $22\frac{1}{2}$ I. for the window of a carriage.

PrC (MHi); faint and blurred; at foot of text: "Mr. Trump"; endorsed by TJ in ink on verso. Recorded in SJL with notation "G. Divers sashes."

A letter of 27 Jan. from George DIVERS to TJ, recorded in SJL as received 2 Feb., has not been found. On 21 Feb., TJ wrote to Divers, probably to report information contained in Daniel Trump's letter of 12 Feb., recorded in SJL as received 19 Feb. Neither of these letters has been found.

RABBETS were long grooves cut at right angles and used to join two wooden objects together (Carl R. Lounsbury, ed., *An Illustrated Glossary of Early Southern Architecture and Landscape* [New York, 1994], 303).

To Volney

DEAR SIR Washington Feb. 6. 1803.

The opportunity of sending you a line safely by mr Monroe is so favorable that I cannot [intermit] it, altho' we have little from this side of the water interesting to you. he goes on a mission of great importance to our future destinies. the occurrence which has lately happened at New Orleans of suppressing our right of deposit, stipulated by treaty, and without which the navigation of the Missisipi is useless, shews the necessity of placing that right on a footing subject to no accidents. believing that the property of it has passed to France, we propose to take timely arrangements with her to prevent it's ever disturbing our friendship, and on the event of this negotiation will depend whether we are to be a people consigned? to peace and friendship with all nations, not meddling in the affairs of Europe, or are to take part in their broils, and become a spiteful? unhappy nation.

[Of science] you are of course to expect nothing from us. business is our general pursuit. I engage mr Monroe to take from Philadelphia the last volume of our Philosophical transactions, and deliver them to you on my part. you may find here and there something which may interest you. we have been long expecting your petit format translation of the Ruines. mr Pougens bookseller of Paris, having established a commercial connection with Duane here, might be a convenient agent in that business.

As you are a member of a deliberative body, and might sometimes wish to know the rules of the oldest deliberative body we are acquainted with, I send you a copy of a Parliamentary Manual which I compiled for the use of the Senate, while I presided over them. a bee will extract honey from any plant; so possibly may you from this.

The revolution of public opinion here has been what I have always predicted to you. it was in a fevered state while you were here, affected by artifice. the people in mass have got back to the principles which separated us from England. their leaders, too far committed to retract, and the mercantile inhabitants of the great & [port] towns, being able [...], make a good deal of noise: but when the people come out to elections, they are as unanimous as a large body can ever be. three only of the Eastern states are not yet with us; but they are fast advancing towards majorities in sentiment with the other fourteen states. the Federalists therefore, whom you know, are sinking fast into [...] and, at the ensuing session of Congress, will scarcely be seen in that body. our nation thus tranquilized within, our only remaining [wish] is to secure tranquility abroad.

Is there any thing in which I can be useful to you here? it will give me great pleasure to be so. the days are past which watched our correspondence, & I am happy in the freedom of now indulging in [manifestations] of the [...] I bear you, and of tendering you assurances of constant & sincere attachment, & high respect.

TH: JEFFERSON

PrC (DLC); blurred; at foot of first page: "M. Volney." Enclosure: *A Manual of Parliamentary Practice. For the Use of the Senate of the United States* (Washington, D.C., 1801).

From James Ash

SIR, Baltimore 7th. February 1803

I send you, inclosed, proposals for a work, which shall be published, when money is received to pay the expence of printing.

The encouragment which you are disposed to contribute, be pleased to return by next post.

I have the honor to be, Sir, your mo. ob: Hble: Servt.

JAMES ASH

RC (MHi); at foot of text: "Thomas Jefferson President of the United States"; endorsed by TJ as received 9 Feb. and so recorded in SJL. Enclosure not found, but see below.

James Ash moved from Winchester, Virginia, in 1795, and settled in Baltimore, where he became a clerk of the superior court of Maryland. In 1798, he applied to be one of George Washington's aides and also submitted a proposal for printing a digest of the laws of the state. The following year he petitioned the Maryland General Assembly as an insolvent debtor and initiated legal proceedings (*Laws of Maryland, Made and Passed at a Session of Assembly, Begun and Held at the City of Annapolis on Monday the Fourth of November, in the Year of Our Lord One Thousand Seven Hundred and Ninety-Nine* [Annapolis, 1800], chap. 88; Washington, *Papers, Ret. Ser.*, 2:121, 464-5; Ash to TJ, 12 Jan. 1807 and enclosure).

PROPOSALS FOR A WORK: Ash planned to publish "The American Law of Merchants," but failed to gain sufficient subscriptions.

To Stephen Cathalan, Jr.

DEAR SIR Washington Feb. 7. 1803.

I will not look back to my letter files to see when I wrote to you or you to me, last. we are both men of business, and have not much time for any thing else. your letters are often recieved by the Secretary of state on business, which is the most important concern. we delay taking any measure respecting your office until you shall have had time enough to remove the obstacles opposed by your own government. what cannot be obtained at one moment may at a more favorable one. when you despair you will tell us so. Mr. Monroe being on his departure for Paris, I could not omit so safe an opportunity of recalling myself to your recollection. the change of neighbors at New Orleans, and some late occurrences there have rendered it expedient to join mr Monroe to mr Livingston to make arrangements for the preservation of peace & friendship with France under our new situation as neighbors. I have understood from our officers who have visited Marseilles in their cruizes that your father & mother are still living. I pray you to present me to them respectfully, & to assure them I always recollect with sensibility the civilities I recieved from them at Marseilles. make my compliments acceptable too to Made. Cathalan, and to my young friend your daughter, who is now, I suppose, a mater-familias. your kindness in furnishing me, while I was at Paris, with the productions of the South of France of the best quality, has encouraged me to ask the same favor of you here, where we can get only the very worst. we have now so many merchant vessels trading to the Mediterranean that I imagine you have frequent opportunities to New York, Philadelphia, or the ports of the Chesapeak. I therefore take the liberty of sending an invoice on the back hereof of the articles & quantities desired. my Maitre d'hotel who makes it out, is confident you will understand what he means by caisse, boete, panier &c. should you be at a loss, you may be enabled to conjecture what he means, by knowing that he intends this for a year's supply. not being able to guess the amount of these things I have thought you would be so kind as to forward them, sending me at the same time a bill of the cost by different conveyances, and within two months after the reciept of your letter I will place the money in Paris subject to your order, or if you have any correspondent here, I will pay it to your order on sight, as shall be most convenient to you. to this invoice I would have added 100. bottles of *White* hermitage wine of the crops of M. de Meuse, de Loche, Berger avocat, le chanoine Monron, Gaillet, or de Beausace. when I was at Tains in 1787. on my way to Marseilles, I examined the vineyards of Hermitage, and the cellars at Tains, and found that the whole of the white wine of Hermitage of first quality was made in the vineyards of these individuals. some of them are doubtless dead, but some living, and the same vineyards & management if continued, probably produce the same qualitied wine. I say I should have added this to my request, but that I know the difficulty of communication from Tains to Marseilles, and that in so obscure a village as Tains you may not have a correspondent. I always have found it safest to address my orders for wine to the proprietor of the vineyard himself, who will send it faithfully for the credit of his vineyard. I leave this matter to your own convenience.—as a number of small packages are liable to egarements on the way, it is best to put a number of the small cases, boxes, & baskets together into large ones. Accept my apologies for this trouble, and assurances of my constant esteem and respect. TH: JEFFERSON

RC (Archives municipales, Marseilles, France); at foot of first page: "M. Cathalan"; endorsed by Cathalan and a clerk as received 1 May. PrC (DLC).

WHEN I WROTE TO YOU OR YOU TO ME: Cathalan's last letter, written in February 1802, had come to TJ in April. TJ's most recent letter to Cathalan was in 1796 (Vol. 29:368, 369n; Vol. 36:559-62).

French citizens, by a provision in the nation's constitution, could not hold appointments under foreign governments. Cathalan encountered OBSTACLES in his effort to obtain an exequatur from the French government that would allow him to serve as the U.S. commercial agent at Marseilles (Vol. 34:334n; Vol. 35:494, 495n; Vol. 36:561, 562n).

CIVILITIES: TJ visited Marseilles in 1787. While there he made the acquaintance of Cathalan's family, including Cathalan's DAUGHTER, Eulalie, "little Lalie," who was about three years old at the time. In 1797, Eulalie's parents sent her to Paris to complete her education at an English convent school (Vol. 11:247-8, 516; Vol. 12:198, 321; Vol. 14:287; Vol. 29:369; Vol. 31:108; Cathalan to TJ, 31 May 1803).

MAITRE D'HOTEL: Étienne Lemaire.

For TJ's interest in obtaining WHITE HERMITAGE WINE, see his List of French Wines, [on or before 7 Feb.], below.

EGAREMENTS: getting lost.

ENCLOSURE

List of Groceries Wanted from Marseilles

50. ℔ de Maccaroni.
50. ℔ de meme composition de differentes façons pour les potages.
6. paniers d'huile de la meilleure qualité.
8. caisses d'olives.
4. idem de capres fines.
2. idem d'Anchois.
20. ℔ de thon mariné.
8. douzaines de petites boetes historiés[1] de 6. ou 7. fruits.
3. caisses de pruneaux.
3. idem de belles figues.
1. idem de dattes.
30. ℔ d'amandes douces, sans coquilles.
25. ℔ idem avec leurs coquilles.
10. ℔ d'amandes amers.
6. caisses de fruits assortis à l'eau de vie.
26. ℔ de queües d'artichaux secs.
4. ℔ de truffes du Perigord.

EDITORS' TRANSLATION

50 pounds of macaroni.
50 pounds of the same composition, in different shapes for soups.
6 panniers of oil of the best quality.
8 cases of olives.
4 cases of fine capers.
2 cases of anchovies.
20 pounds of pickled tuna.
8 dozen small decorated cans of preserves of 6 or 7 fruits.
3 cases of prunes.
3 cases of fine figs.
1 case of dates.
30 pounds of sweet almonds, shelled.
25 pounds of the same, unshelled.
10 pounds of bitter almonds.
6 cases of assorted fruits in brandy.
26 pounds of dried artichokes on their stalks.
4 pounds of Périgord truffles.

MS (Archives municipales, Marseilles, France); entirely in TJ's hand; with notations by Cathalan, not printed above, recording quantities of items from the list shipped on 9 May, 27 Dec. 1803, and 21 Apr. 1804 (see also Cathalan to TJ, 31 May 1803, 25 Apr. 1804); Cathalan added an unspecified quantity of "Pistaches" (pistachio nuts) at foot of list. PrC (MHi); endorsed by TJ in ink on verso. MS (MHi); undated; in Étienne Lemaire's hand, in French; at head of text: "Etat des provisions a fair venir de Marseille"; at foot of text, Lemaire's estimate of total expenditure to be about 86.2.3 livres; with one interlineation in TJ's hand (see note 1) and with list of wines in TJ's hand at foot of text (see the next document); endorsed by TJ: "LeMaire. groceries from Marseilles."

[1] In MS in Lemaire's hand, TJ interlined this word above "istorrié."

List of French Wines

[on or before 7 Feb. 1803]

A year's stock of French wines

250. bottles	white Hermitage de M. Meuse, M. de Loche. M. Berger avocat. M. Chanoine Monron. M. Gaillet. M. de Beausace.
400. do.	Champagne non mousseux d'Aij de M. d'Orsay
<*250. do.*	*Clos de Vougeau or Chambertin*>
250. do.	Rozan-Margau from Made. de Rozan. or Medoc
250. do.	Sauterne de M. Salus.
	brandy

MS (MHi); entirely in TJ's hand; undated; written at foot of list by Étienne Lemaire of groceries wanted from Marseilles (see note to enclosure to preceding document).

TJ drew this list of wines and their vintners from a memorandum he composed either near the end of his stay in France or shortly after his return to the United States in 1789. He subsequently obtained WHITE HERMITAGE through Stephen Cathalan, Jr., the American consul in Marseilles; still champagne and burgundy from CHAMBERTIN through Fulwar Skipwith, the consul at Paris; and Rausan Margaux and sauterne through William Lee, the consul at Bordeaux (MB, 2:1116-17; Vol. 27:761-3; TJ to Fulwar Skipwith, 4 May 1803; TJ to William Lee, 14 June 1803; TJ to Stephen Cathalan, Jr., 20 Nov. 1803).

From Thomas McKean

DEAR SIR, Lancaster Febry. 7th. 1803.

Since the commencement of the sessions of the Legislature of this State, my public & private engagements have prevented my paying my respects to you until now: having little to communicate, and nothing that required speed; and knowing how your time must be employed with Congress, & by visits on business and of ceremony, must constitute my appology.

The last general election in Pennsylvania has been very fortunate for liberty & republicanism; the sense of the people has been unequivocally declared in favor of our democratic representative government and its present administration. This cannot be doubted, when it shall be told that the opponents exerted their whole power & influence, in most of the counties, as much as they did in 1799. The uncommon change in the public mind, in the space of three years, cannot be attributed merely to a conviction of former errors, to personal attachments or good management, but permit me to say in no small degree to the President of the United States, and his patriotic, just & wise measures: besides, the President and the numerous officers under him (with about twenty exceptions in the whole State) were friendly in 1802; whereas all of this description, together with a considerable majority in both Houses of Congress, were, in 1799, as zealously engaged against us (without its being foreknown or even suspected) and exerted every power & influence, that office, wealth, character & individual industry could accomplish, inasmuch as if their temporal & eternal salvation had depended on the event. They then suffered a defeat, but now a total overthrow, and are in a state of despair.

After the 4th. of March next you will have, Sir, two Senators and eighteen Representatives in the more numerous House in Congress, all Republicans, from this State. I know every one[1] of them personally, and you may depend upon them; altho' I should be more gratified, if some of them had a little more learning & knowledge, or a little more diffidence than what is attributed to them; indeed, there is not a shining star among them, but their intentions & conduct will, I trust, render them useful legislators. I have reason to believe, that Messieurs Adams & Pinkney will be again proposed as candidates for the presidency (a forlorn hope) but I entertain not a doubt, Sir, from my thorough knowledge of this State, that in 1804 the twenty electors of President & Vice-President will give their unanimous vote for the present Chief Magistrate: at the same time, I believe, they will surrender the choice of Vice-President to the Tories, unless Congress will propose an amendment to the Constitution for discriminating the characters to be voted for.

The people do not always know their own good; and when they do, it is not always pursued: their late conduct however in this State has not depreciated them, nor do I believe that it will in the next election of President.

The time of our legislature has been engrossed for ten or twelve days on the trial of a Judge Addison, who was impeached for arbitrary & despotic conduct in office: he has been convicted, "removed from his station and disqualified to hold or exercise the office of judge in any court of law within the Commonwealth of Pennsylvania." He was a favorite of Mr; Liston, the British Minister, the transmontane Goliah of federalism in this State, a remarkable political apostate; and, in my opinion, federalism will fall with him in the six Western counties. Neither Messrs. Ross, Woods, Wilkins, nor any of the party have taken an open part in his behalf. So you find, Sir, we know how to get ride of obnoxious judges as well as the Congress. In fact, the Tories in Pennsylvania are not only humbled but subdued; but we have to dread the effects of vanity, jealousy, ambition & envy among the Republicans; no small share of vigilance must be kept up for a few years more to prevent their running riot.—

With the best intentions in the world our legislators are attempting innovations; but as their Bills have been generally without limitations, and some of them appeared to be too dangerous even for an experiment, I have been too frequently compelled to interpose my qualified negative. I wish for a few Gentlemen of science in law, history, & government &c. in each House, but in my day I despair of being so gratified, and must therefore submit to my destiny.

The infamous & seditious libels, published almost daily in our news-papers, are become intolerable. If they cannot be altogether prevented, yet they may be greatly checked by a few prosecutions: I have had it for some time in contemplation to make the experiment; but as the President, Congress and several of the principal officers of the U.S. have been frequently implicated, I have declined it until I should obtain your advice & consent. This vice is become a national one, and calls aloud for redress.—

The mission on which you have sent Governor Munroe has afforded singular pleasure to the Republicans, not less with respect to the measure than the person: I do not entertain a doubt of his success.

A thirst for office is still prevalent in Pennsylvania. I have been beset with Applicants to recommend them to Your Excellency for office, but have had fortitude enough to resist nineteen out of twenty. From humanity, I cannot help naming Thomas Rodney Esquire of the State of Delaware and Mr; Blair Mc.Clenechan; the former was a member of Congress with me, during the Revolutionary war, the latter must be known to you. A Mr; Lovitt Harris, of Philadia. Merchant is well spoken of, and as a young Gentleman qualified for a Consul or commercial Agent.

After the present session of Congress, I am confident, you will have smooth seas and fine weather, and that you will pilot the national ship with ease & honor to yourself, and glory & happiness to your country, as long as it shall please God to prolong your life. That this may be your fate is the ardent prayer of, dear Sir,

Your Excellency's Most obedient humble servant

THOS M:KEAN

RC (DLC); at head of text: "Private"; at foot of text: "His Excellency Thomas Jefferson"; endorsed by TJ as received 11 Feb. and so recorded in SJL. Tr (PHi).

The impeachment TRIAL of Judge Alexander ADDISON extended from 17 to 26 Jan., when he was found guilty by a 20 to 4 vote of the charges that his actions against fellow judge John B. C. Lucas had led to the "obstruction of the free, impartial and due administration of justice" and produced a sentiment "contrary to the public rights and interests" of the commonwealth. In this way, the Republican legislators unseated Addison by using the "dangerous tendency" argument of English common law embraced by Federalists. James ROSS, John WOODS, and William WILKINS, as attorneys and residents of Pennsylvania's fifth district court, signed a certificate noting that Addison, as president of the circuit, was "honest, impartial, upright," and "dignified." They were "perfectly satisfied" with his judicial demeanor and had the highest confidence "in his integrity, learning, and abilities." They concluded: "our clients, and the citizens in general, have respect for his character, and repose great confidence in his opinions and decisions." Addison was not allowed to use the certificates as evidence (*Trial of Alexander Addison, Esq. President of the Courts of Common-Pleas in the Circuit Court Consisting of the Counties of Westmoreland, Fayette, Washington and Allegheny, on an Impeachment, by the House of Representatives, before the Senate of the Commonwealth of Pennsylvania. To which is Affixed the Certificates Offered by Mr. Addison in His Defence, but by the Senate Refused a Reading* [Lancaster, 1803], 16-17, 21, 121-6, 150-4, Appendix, p. 15, 20-1; Shaw-Shoemaker, No. 4848; Peter Charles Hoffer and N. E. H. Hull, *Impeachment in America, 1635-1805* [New Haven, 1984], 191-205; Alexander Addison to TJ, 7 Oct. 1802).

COMPELLED TO INTERPOSE MY QUALIFIED NEGATIVE: on 9 Dec. McKean vetoed the "Act for the recovery of debts not exceeding one hundred dollars," which extended the powers of the justices of the peace to settle small claims and furthered the principle of arbitration in the state courts (Samuel Hazard and others, eds., *Pennsylvania Archives. Selected and Arranged from Original Documents in the Office of the Secretary of the Commonwealth*, 119 vols. [Harrisburg, 1852-1935], 4th ser., 4:496-500). For the division in Republican ranks on how to carry out judicial reform and McKean's resort to his veto power, see Rowe, *McKean*, 333-6, 338-9, and Higginbotham, *Pennsylvania Politics*, 51-3, 65-6.

LATTER MUST BE KNOWN TO YOU: see Blair McClenachan to TJ, 6 Jan. and 29 Nov. 1802. LOVITT HARRIS: that is, Levett Harris (see Andrew Ellicott to TJ, 24 Dec. 1802).

[1] Word supplied by Editors.

From J. P. G. Muhlenberg

Collector's office - Philadelphia
SIR Febry. 7th. 1803

Three Boxes, directed To The President of the United States, were imported into this District, in the Ship Pennsylvania, Captn. York, from Hamburg, in December 1801—The contents are unknown, & they have since their importation, remaind in the Custom House—Any directions the President may be pleasd to give me, with regard to them, shall be imediately complied with.

I have the Honor to be with great Respect Sir Your Most Obedt Servt P MUHLENBERG

RC (MHi); at foot of text: "The President of The U.S."; endorsed by TJ as received 10 Feb. and so recorded in SJL.

To John Joseph Rey

SIR Washington Feb. 7. 1803.

I have perused the statement of grievances and impositions which you left with me, and find they are not of the class which the constitution has placed within Executive cognisance. their redress can only be obtained from the judiciary establishments, and through the accustomary instrumentality of the Attornies at law, who would be able to point out to you the measures which the law has placed within your own power for obtaining redress. I return the statement with my best wishes & respects. TH: JEFFERSON

PrC (DLC); at foot of text: "Mr. Rea." Recorded in SJL as a letter to "Rey John Joseph." Enclosure not found.

From Edward Savage

SIR New York Feby. 7—1803

Since my Residence in this City I have added meany Europen Paintings to the collection which you Saw in Philadelphia. Last Spring I Bought the Collection of Natural Curosities known by the Name of the Tammany Museum in this City which I Have added to the Paintings the Collection Now is Large and fills a Large Space I have taken the Liberty to Enclose to you a Discription of an non Descript animal. Likewise one of my Proposals for Publishing the Print of the Declaration of Independence which I intend to finish as soone as Possable Should you be pleased to incourage the work and will be kind enough to send to Either of the Door keepers of Congress, I have Furnished them with Printed Recipts to be given for money advanc'd.

I am Sir with great Respect your Most Humble Sert.

EDWARD SAVAGE

RC (DLC); at foot of text: "Thomas Jefferson President of the united States"; endorsed by TJ as received 11 Feb. and so recorded in SJL. Enclosures: see below.

TAMMANY MUSEUM: in 1802, Savage acquired the natural history collection of the American Museum, founded by the Tammany Society in 1791, and renamed his New York institution the Columbian Gallery of Painting and City Museum (ANB).

I HAVE TAKEN THE LIBERTY TO ENCLOSE: the enclosures mentioned by Savage above apparently miscarried. TJ informed the painter of this in his reply on 4 Mch., and Savage resent his description of a mountain ram and a copy of his proposal on 10 Mch.

Savage began advertising his proposal to publish a PRINT OF THE DECLARATION OF INDEPENDENCE in February 1803. The engraving was to be based on an 11 foot by 8 foot painting of the signing, which Savage declared to be "nearly completed" and possessing "Striking likenesses of the principal characters who composed the Congress of that day." The print would measure 26 inches by 19 inches and include an index to the portraits contained in the picture (ANB; New York *Morning Chronicle*, 26 Feb. 1803; New York *Daily Advertiser*, 1 Mch. 1803).

From William Wingate, with Jefferson's Note

SIR, Haverhill Feb 7, 1803

I am drove *unexpectedly* Also through *necessity* for to Communicate to you the inclosed papers and Information, I wish you to begin and examine them in the following order, to Wit, paper marked No. 1. 2. & 3. These I offer as Evidence to Sattisfy You that I am Considered a true Friend to the Republican Cause—

No. 4. 5. 6. 7. 8. 9. 10. all these except No. 5. respects *Ephraim Emery* who Col Varnum informs me has been Appointed by the President of the United States, Also, that the Appointment of Mr. Ephraim Emery has not Yet been Confirmed by the Senate—

Sir, You may rest assured that all the Charges I have alledged Against *Emerys Moral* and *Political Charector* are *Sacredly true* and well known by *many* of his intimate Acquaintance in *this* and *other Towns*—I Still hope for those reasons mentioned in *my letter* to *Mr. Varnum* that the President will not Suffer *my name* to be *known as*

Complainent—Notwithstanding, I Shall Cheerfully Submit to Your Judgment.

Sir, I have requested Mr. Varnum to deliver to the President all the letters I have Sent him and *not found here inclosed*, if Mr. Varnum Should either neglect or refuse to deliver them, I will furnish you with attested Copies if requested, not doubting but that Mr. Varnum will readily deliver them, also readily Join with you in adjusting every thing they respect in the *most Just* and *honorable* manner—Therefore will thank the President to present Mr. Varnum with my best regards, also; receive the papers if wanted—

Sir, Believe me to be with Sentiments of the most Sincere Esteem & Respect

Your most devoted Humble Servant William Wingate

Note, Sir, I wish you to inclose No. 2. 3. 7. & 9 in a *wrapper* and request your Private Secretary to direct them to me *after* the business is adjusted—

[*Note by TJ*:]

Nos 1. 2. 3. 7. 8. 9. came

4. 5. 6. did not come

RC (DNA: RG 59, LAR); at head of text: "To the President of the United States of America"; endorsed by TJ as received 21 Feb. and "against Ephraim Emery" and so recorded in SJL. Enclosures not found, but see TJ to Wingate, 25 Feb. 1803; Wingate resent copies of enclosures 2 and 5 in his letter to TJ of 15 Feb. 1804.

William Wingate (1745-1821) was a younger brother of former New Hampshire congressman Paine Wingate. During the 1790s, he briefly served as postmaster at Haverhill, Massachusetts. Wingate wrote TJ several times during his first term as president, offering his views on foreign and diplomatic affairs and seeking an appointment. After a hiatus of more than a decade, Wingate recommenced his letters to TJ in 1815 and 1816, enclosing religious manuscripts and asking the former president's assistance in disseminating their contents in Washington. TJ declined the requests (Madison, *Papers, Pres. Ser.*, 5:544n; Stets, *Postmasters*, 147; Vol. 35:754; Vol. 36:681; Wingate to TJ, 15 Feb. 1804, 31 Mch., 3, 14 Apr. 1815, 8 Apr. 1816; TJ to Wingate, 25 Apr. 1815, 4 May 1816).

For the nomination and rejection of EPHRAIM EMERY, see TJ to the Senate, 11 Jan. 1803 (third letter).

From William, Benjamin, and W. L. Bakewell

SIR New Haven 8 Feby 1803

Although we are unknown to you, permit us to express our sense of the benefits resulting from your administration of the affairs of this Country; benefits the more valued, when contrasted with the state of other nations, which but for the happy example that America affords, might induce the friends of liberty, to despair of any amelioration of the political condition of mankind.

To you, Sir, it is needless to enlarge on this subject. In the sensations of your own mind, & in the thanks of a free people, you will doubtless find abundant compensation for the abusive fabrications of your enemies, of which we are concerned to observe several in this neighbourhood; though we hope & believe that the more candid & intelligent part of them, are becoming sensible of the mistaken principle on which their enmity is founded; but all arguments are useless upon those men, whose only object is, to be supported in idleness at the public expence; & with whom *that* government is the *best*, which has the greatest number of *offices*, *pensions*, & *sinecures*.

Having established a Brewery in this City, we have sent by the from NYork a Barrel of Ale, of which we beg your acceptance, as a small token of our esteem & gratitude. It may be either drawn wholly from the Cask, or if not all drawn off by the middle of April, will be best kept in bottles after that time.

With best wishes for your health & happiness, we remain, Sir, Your obedt. Servts. WM, BENJ, & W L. BAKEWELL

PS. We forward this by an English Gent of our acquaintance traveling to the southern states.

RC (DLC); in William Bakewell's hand and signed by him; endorsed by TJ as received 4 Apr. from "Bakewell, Wm Benj. & W.L." and so recorded in SJL.

Benjamin Bakewell (1767-1844), a native of Derby, England, and an importer of French dry goods in London, immigrated to the United States in 1793 and became a merchant in New York City. With the financial backing of his older brother, William (1762-1821), he opened a brewing business in New Haven in 1798. One week after sending this letter and ale to TJ, the Bakewell brewing business was destroyed in a fire and was not resumed. Upon the expiration of the partnership of William, Benjamin, & William Luccock Bakewell sometime before 15 Apr. 1806, W. L. Bakewell handled the settlement with their debtors. Benjamin Bakewell set up a dry goods shop in New York and later established a glassworks in Pittsburgh, which was renowned for its cut and engraved wares and whose products were used in the White House during the presidencies of James Monroe and Andrew Jackson. William Bakewell settled on a farm in Montgomery County, Pennsylvania, where his daughter met and married the naturalist John James Audubon (ANB; New York *Daily Advertiser*, 2 Mch. 1803; Hartford *American Mercury*, 17 Mch. and 7 Apr. 1803; New Haven *Connecticut Journal*, 1 May 1806; Arlene Palmer, *Artistry and Innovation in Pittsburgh Glass, 1808-1882: From Bakewell & Ensell to Bakewell, Pears & Co.* [Pittsburgh, 2004], 15-20; *The Family Book of Bakewell, Page, Campbell* [Pittsburgh, 1896], 25-9, 47).

ENGLISH GENT OF OUR ACQUAINTANCE: see Theophilus Harris to TJ, 12 Apr.

From James Brobson and John Warner

SIR Wilmington Feby 8th. 1803

We enclose you a recommendation signed by ourselves & a number of respectable Republican Inhabitants of this Borough in favor of Conl. Nehemiah Tilton, to which we beg leave to draw your attention; being well convinced that his appointment will give the most general satisfaction to the Republicans of this place. at the same time we believe it will meet the approbation of our fellow citizens of the same sentiment in other parts of the State (The Town of NewCastle from local views excepted) for any further information however on this subject we woud refer you to the Govenor who is decidedly in favor of Conl. Tilton and has taken much pain to collect the public sentiment on this point, his official station as the Chief Executive magistrate of the State enables him to give that advice which may we respectfully apprehend be relied on, Shoud additional weight be necessary, we have no doubt but that our Representative (elect) (who has from motives of peculiar delicacy relative to this business declined interfering with the nomination of a suitable person) woud unite with us in opinion in case of a vacancy

we are Sir with sincere regard Your Obedt. Servts.

JAS BROBSON
JOHN WARNER

RC (DLC); in Brobson's hand, signed by Brobson and Warner; at foot of text: "Thomas Jefferson Prest. of the United States"; endorsed by TJ as received 10 Feb. and "Nehemiah Tilton to be Collector, vice Mc.lane" and so recorded in SJL. Enclosure not found.

James Brobson (1759-1833) and John Warner (1773?-1825) were Wilmington merchants active in the West Indies trade. Guided by Caesar A. Rodney's recommendation, TJ appointed them bankruptcy commissioners in early July 1802. They both supported the erection of a drawbridge in Wilmington, a project vigorously opposed by merchants in New Castle from 1802 to 1807, when the Wilmington Bridge Company was incorporated, with Warner as a director. Brobson periodically served as chief burgess of Wilmington between 1801 and 1826. In that capacity he joined Nehemiah Tilton in 1801 to congratulate TJ on his election.

Madison appointed Brobson U.S. marshal for the district of Delaware in May 1809, a position he held for many years, receiving his last nomination for a four-year-term in December 1825. In 1802, Rodney described Warner as "our most influential, active politician." He was a director of the Bank of Delaware, a founding director of the Farmers' Bank of Wilmington, and a member of the Delaware Abolition Society. In 1815, Madison appointed him U.S. consul to Puerto Rico. He was serving as U.S. commercial agent at Havana at the time of his death. As a public officer, it was observed, "his conduct was marked by a distinguished charity and attention to the unfortunate" (John A. Munroe, *Federalist Delaware, 1775-1815* [New Brunswick, N.J., 1954], 135, 246, 252-3; J. Thomas Scharf, *The History of Delaware, 1609-1888*, 2 vols. [Philadelphia, 1888], 2:637, 639, 671, 733-4, 739, 758-9; Benjamin Ferris, *A History of the Original Settlements on the Delaware: From Its Discovery by Hudson to the Colonization under William Penn* [Wilmington, Del., 1846], 274; JEP, 2:122, 3:96, 109, 258, 273, 448, 457; *Daily National Intelligencer*, 19 May 1825; Madison, *Papers, Pres. Ser.*, 1:192-3; James F. Hopkins and others, eds., *The Papers of Henry Clay*, 11 vols. [Lexington, Ky., 1959-92], 4:119, 216-17n; Vol. 33:211-12; Vol. 37:678, 680n, 705, 709).

REFER YOU TO THE GOVENOR: for David Hall's endorsement of Nehemiah Tilton as collector, see Vol. 37:518.

OUR REPRESENTATIVE (ELECT): Caesar A. Rodney.

To George Jefferson

DEAR SIR Washington Feb. 8. 1803.

I now inclose you eleven hundred and seventy dollars, and shall this day draw on you in favor of Colo. Charles L. Lewis for 200.

Charles L. Lewis	200.
Lilburne Lewis	400.
Christopher Smith	400.
Charles Smith	66.67[1]
Joseph Moran	98.
	1164.67

I expect that you have recieved for me some nail rod from Jones & Howell Phila. 4. casks of cyder from Colo. Newton, Norfolk
2. hhds of wine from Smith & Buchanan, Balt.
and that you will shortly recieve 7½ ~~Cwt~~ bar iron from Jones & Howell and several packages of groceries &c. not yet gone from hence. all to be forwarded to Monticello. be pleased also to send there by the first *safe boatmen* a hogshead of molasses. I say *safe boatmen*, because nothing is so liable to adulteration by them as molasses. the wine should also be confided to trustworthy hands. Accept my affectionate esteem and best wishes. TH: JEFFERSON

PrC (MHi); at foot of text: "Mr. George Jefferson"; endorsed by TJ in ink on verso. Recorded in SJL with notation "1164.67."

George Jefferson's reply has not been found but was recorded in SJL as a letter of 12 Feb. received 17 Feb. with the notation "1170. D. rods. hoops. cyder. molasses." A letter of 12 Jan. from TJ to LILBURNE LEWIS has also not been found. In his financial memoranda, TJ recorded payments to the "Lewises for corn," to Christopher and Charles SMITH for the hire of slaves, and Joseph Moran "in full." A letter of 8 Feb. from TJ to Moran, who had performed stone work at Monticello, has not been found but was recorded in SJL with the notation "98" (MB, 2:1092; Vol. 38:651-2).

[1] MS: "166.67."

To James Madison

TH:J. TO J.M. Feb. 8. 1803.

I had before heard this matter spoken of, but did not suppose it seriously intended. if there be any danger of it, the Secretary at war will be desired to give orders at Massac & Fort Adams to stop them by force. but would it not be well to write to the Govr. of Kentucky to have the persons arrested & bound to their good behavior or the peace?

RC (DNA: RG 59, NL); addressed "The Secretary of State" below a canceled address in Jacob Wagner's hand to "The President of the United States" from the State Department. Not recorded in SJL. Enclosure: Carlos Martínez de Irujo to Madison, 5 Feb.; he understands that inflammatory statements in newspapers in recent weeks have created considerable agitation in the western part of Pennsylvania along the banks of the Ohio River; according to reports, a desperate individual intends to collect a number of volunteers, who with others from the states of Kentucky and Tennessee will attack Louisiana as a means of exacting justice for their complaints against the intendant at New Orleans; it is likely that enemies of the United States and Spain have fostered this foolhardy expedition by secret means, and although they cannot accomplish the object they desire, they will embarrass the U.S. government and undermine the just, circumspect, and prudent measures that have brought so much honor to American justice and enlightenment; convinced of the good faith and constructive policies of the president, Irujo has no doubt that the government of the United States has heard with due indignation of these plans to create contempt for the laws and the Constitution; he is certain that the U.S. will take—as he asks in the name of the king—action to stop an enterprise so contrary to the internal peace of the United States and to a monarch who has given proof of his good faith and sincere friendship; Madison, recognizing that this spark will ignite a fire fueled by ambition and intrigue in the western country, will see that prompt and decisive measures are the only way to frustrate the sinister designs of a party that is attempting to bring itself to power on the public ruin; Irujo hopes that everything necessary has been done to preserve order and friendship with foreign powers and to confirm the justified reputation of TJ's administration as a government based on virtue and justice (RC in same, in Spanish; see Madison, *Papers*, *Sec. of State Ser.*, 4:303).

IF THERE BE ANY DANGER: Irujo repeated his entreaties to Madison on 14 Feb. (same, 4:321). For orders given by the secretary of WAR a few days after that, see Topics for Consultation with Heads of Departments, at 10 Feb. below.

WRITE TO THE GOVR: Madison wrote to the governors of Pennsylvania, Kentucky, and Tennessee on 18 Feb., noting the Spanish minister's concern about the reports of an armed force being raised to "proceed with hostile intentions" against Louisiana. "As such a procedure would be not only incompatible with the authority and dignity of the Government but dangerous to our peace with foreign nations," Madison informed each of the governors, "the President entertains the fullest confidence, that your Excellency will take the most early and efficient measures to restrain such an attempt" (Madison, *Papers*, *Sec. of State Ser.*, 4:327).

To Craven Peyton

DEAR SIR Washington Feb. 8. 1803.

In my letter of Nov. 2. I expressed a hope I might be able to pay you 1000. D. the 1st. week of this month, 1000. D. in March, & the balance in the summer. in my letter of the 20th. of Nov. I still thought it might be but suggested a possibility that the paiments might be a month later. it is with sincere concern I am obliged, by a rigorous view of my affairs, to say, not only that I cannot begin the paiments till next month, but that instead of paiments of 1000. D. each month, I shall be able only to make paiments of 500. D. a month for Mar. Apr. May & June, with 600. D. in Aug. to mr Carr according to my assumpsit, & the balance the month after I wish I could have done more; but it is out of my power and it is better for me to say so, that you may be enabled to make your arrangements for the best in this state of things. I should be very willing, if it would be of any advantage, to give you my notes of 500. D. each payable as above; altho' if not inconvenient I would rather not have paper of mine at market. but in this I will conform to your wish. I shall be at home about the 9th. of March to make a short stay, when I shall hope to see you. Accept these my apologies, with assurances of the regret with which I am obliged to make them, and of my esteem and best wishes for you. TH: JEFFERSON

PrC (ViU); at foot of text: "Mr. Craven Peyton"; endorsed by TJ in ink on verso.

For TJ's payment to Dabney CARR, see Peyton to TJ, 16 Dec. 1802.

From Thomas Hobbes Scott

SIR/ London Feby 8th. 1803—

Tho' a Stranger to your person yet not so to your fame, I have taken the liberty of forwarding to Mr Paine a small pamphlet accompanied with a letter under the protection of your Excellency. I am induced to trouble you in this manner, because its being directed to him wou'd occasion the curiosity of the officers of our Government to open & stop it; tho' it contains nothing upon politicks, this I shou'd not wish to be done as I have requested him to send me some books from America—

I congratulate yourself & the *true* friends of liberty both of America & England on the accession of your Excellency to chair of government of the United States

From your known principles & your late addresses to Congress, there is every reason to beleive how much the country will flourish under your administration.

I trust your Excellency will pardon this intrusion upon your time & the liberty I have taken—

I have the honor to be Your Excellency's most obedt. Servt.

THOS. HOBBES SCOTT

RC (MoSHi: Jefferson Papers); endorsed by TJ as received 6 May and so recorded in SJL. Enclosure not identified.

An English native, Thomas Hobbes Scott (1783-1860) matriculated at Oxford at the age of 30, and subsequently received his degrees from there. At some point between 1794, when his father died without leaving him an inheritance, and matriculating at Oxford, he served as vice-consul at Bordeaux and was also a wine merchant there. Ordained as an Anglican priest, he accepted appointment in 1824 as first archdeacon of New South Wales, where he drew public attention to the need for colonial education (*Australian Dictionary of Biography*, 17 vols. [Melbourne, 1966-2007], 2:431-3).

To Charles Smith

SIR Washington Feb. 8. 1803.

I have this day remitted to messrs. Gibson & Jefferson of Richmond 66⅔ Dollars for you, for which I now inclose you an order. Accept my best wishes & respects TH: JEFFERSON

PrC (MHi); at foot of sheet: "Mr. Charles Smith"; endorsed by TJ in ink on verso. Recorded in SJL with notation "66.67." Enclosure: Order on Gibson & Jefferson to pay Smith $66⅔ for value received (same; pressed on same sheet as letter above; at foot of text: "66⅔ D." and "Messrs. Gibson and Jefferson Richmond").

Charles Smith (1778-1815), a resident of Louisa County, may have been known to TJ through shared connections to the Lewis family. He and his brother Christopher rented slaves to TJ (Sarah Travers Lewis Scott Anderson, *Lewises, Meriwethers and Their Kin: Lewises and Meriwethers with Their Tracings through the Families Whose Records Are Herein Contained* [Richmond, 1938], 359, 391; MB, 2:1092, 1119, 1121, 1134; Vol. 36:21).

On this day, TJ wrote an identical letter to Christopher Smith, indicating a remittance of $400 (PrC in MHi; at foot of sheet: "Mr. Christopher Smith"; endorsed by TJ in ink on verso; recorded in

SJL with notation "400"). TJ enclosed an order on Gibson & Jefferson to pay Christopher Smith $400 for value received (same; pressed on same sheet as letter to Smith; at foot of text: "400. D." and "Messrs. Gibson & Jefferson Richmond").

From Robert Smith

SIR, Feb. 8. 1803

Mr Nicholson's letter respecting the Marine Corps I have well considered and since I had the pleasure of conversing with you upon the Subject I have had some Communication with Mr Nicholson. The result is the letter herewith sent to you for your Consideration. It is little more than a Statement of facts for the Committee to form their own Opinion. As to the insufficiency of a Captain to be the Commandant of a Corps in which there is more to do than in any regiment whatever all Military men must concur. And therefore I believe that nothing is hazarded in the Opinion I have expressed upon that point. But in my apprehension I should hazard much, were I to express a different Opinion or even a doubt upon such a question.

Mr Nicholson is desirous of having this Communication soon.

With great Respect, I am Sir Your Obedt Serv RT SMITH

RC (DLC); at head of text: "*private*"; endorsed by TJ as received from the Navy Department on 9 Feb. and "Marine corps" and so recorded in SJL. Enclosure: probably Smith to Joseph H. Nicholson, 8 Feb. 1803, in reply to Nicholson's letter of 5 Feb.; to assist the House committee in determining whether or not to reduce the Marine Corps, Smith forwards a statement of the current distribution and employment of its officers and privates in the Mediterranean, on ships in ordinary, and at the barracks, as well as estimates of the numbers needed for the next relief squadron and for the proposed guards at the six navy yards; the statement calculates the need for 25 commissioned officers and 624 noncommissioned officers and privates, but the present corps contains only 453 of the latter, leaving a deficiency of 171 men that could be reduced to 46 if the frigates *Chesapeake*, *Constellation*, and *Adams* return before the next relief squadron is sent out; Smith adds his opinion respecting the grade of the commandant, stating that no competent military gentleman would undertake the arduous duties of the office for the pay and emoluments of a captain, which amount to $649.72 per annum, while those of a major and lieutenant colonel commandant amount to $826.80 and $1,722.90, respectively (NDBW, 2:357-8).

On 27 Jan., the House of Representatives appointed Joseph H. Nicholson, Roger Griswold, and Andrew Gregg to a committee to examine whether alterations were needed to the MARINE CORPS and to the rank and pay of its commanding officer (JHR, 4:306).

From Albert Gallatin

DEAR SIR [9 Feb. 1803]

Will you be good enough to let me see the recommendations for the enclosed nominations? If my memory serves me right, the two last were recommended by Crowningshield. The name of the new collector of Portland I never heard before—

With respect Your affecte. Servt. ALBERT GALLATIN

NB. I do not intend answering Tracy, as I think the request from a *committee* to a *head of dept* improper, but will communicate to our friends

RC (DLC); endorsed by TJ as received from the Treasury Department on 9 Feb. and "nominations" and so recorded in SJL. Enclosure not found, but see below.

ENCLOSED NOMINATIONS: Uriah Tracy sought the recommendations for Isaac Ilsley, Zachariah Stevens, and Joseph Story, all 2 Feb. nominations to replace customs officers at Massachusetts ports. Their nominations were among those postponed by the Senate and referred to a committee headed by Tracy (see TJ to the Senate, 2 Feb.). Robert Wright of Maryland was the only Republican on the committee (*Biog. Dir. Cong.*).

From John Barnes

SIR Geo: Town 10th: Feby 1803.

I have already packed the undermentioned viz. Coffee—powdered & loaf Sugar. tea Pearl Barley and Rice.—not a Cask of good Philada porter to be had! I have therefore—℔ last nights Mail—forwarded Money & order to my Correspondent Mr Ladd at Alexandria for 8 Casks 3 doz each, of Mr Hares best, as well 25. ℔ Jamesons Crackers to be ready to put on Board, Mr Sprogalls Vessel when called for—in a day or two—and should you wish for any Other Article—to Morrow or Saturday will be in time for this favblr: Opportunity.

I am Sir mst Respectfully your very Obedt: JOHN BARNES

I have by me fresh Muscatile Raisins, Olives, Capers Anchovies best Sweet Oil & fine Spices.

T. flour Cask, Containing
loaf Sugar, Coffee, & tea in Cannister well secured
Also, your large tin Scale—at Bottom of Cask—

large Keg 114. ℔ white Sugar, the only one
to be met with here—

Small Keg. 25. ℔ Clean Rice
and 10. ℔ Pearl Barley well secured
in treble stout paper—

NB. if any packages with you, they may be sent directly on board at Mr Lears Wharf. those with me will not be sent before Saturday—in Case any other should Offer—and one porterage will suffice

RC (ViU); at foot of first page: "The President UStates"; endorsed by TJ: "forwarded to Monticello Feb. 1803.

1. flour cask.	loaf sugar. coffee. tea. steelyard scales
1. large keg.	114 ℔ sugar
1. small do.	rice. barley."

Alexandria merchant John G. LADD had previously received and forwarded articles for TJ (Vol. 35:734, 740, 746).

HARES BEST: the popular porter manufactured by Philadelphia brewer Robert Hare since the 1770s included George Washington among its consumers (Edgar Fahs Smith, *The Life of Robert Hare, An American Chemist, (1781-1858)* [Philadelphia, 1917], 3; *Poulson's American Daily Advertiser*, 17 Apr. 1802; Georgetown, D.C., *Olio*, 5 Aug. 1802; Washington, *Papers*, *Confed. Ser.*, 6:387, 442; *Pres. Ser.*, 6:44, 606-7, 635).

JAMESONS CRACKERS: probably a product of Andrew Jamieson's biscuit bakery in Alexandria (T. Michael Miller, comp., *Artisans and Merchants of Alexandria, Virginia, 1780-1820*, 2 vols. [Bowie, Md., 1991-92], 1:232).

MR SPROGALLS VESSEL: Thomas Y. Sprogell's schooner *Dolphin* (*Washington Federalist*, 7 July 1802, 11 Feb. 1803; Vol. 38:53-4; TJ to George Jefferson, 18 Feb. 1803).

From John Breckinridge and Others

February 10th. 1803 Washington

The States of Kentucky, Georgia, & Tennissee, having been for some time impressed with a belief, that it would redound greatly to their mutual interests, if an easy land communication could be opened between Danville in Kentucky, & Augusta in Georgia, have made some attempts to ascertain its practicability. These attempts altho' not very considerable, have produced full conviction that a good waggon road may be made between those two places. But as it must necessarily pass through the lands of the Cherokee Indians, permission must consequently be obtained from them by the U. States for that purpose.

The extent of Indian Country through which this road must pass, is so considerable, that the principal advantages to be derived from it would be defeated, unless the U. States would also procure from the Indians more land than was barely sufficient for the road. One mile on each side of this road, (or perhaps less), or two or three miles square upon the road at convenient distances, would we apprehend be sufficient. As the distance from Danville to Augusta is, it is believed, 200 Miles short of the distance from Danville to any other Atlantic commercial town or navigable water, much of the Produce of Kentucky & Tennissee could be carried to markett in Waggons, which it is well known cannot carry in them, supplies of forage & provisions, but for very short distances.

To obtain the nearest & best road is of the utmost importance; and the undersigned beg leave respectively to suggest the propriety of appointing one or more persons from each State to view minutely the Country through which the road ought to pass.

The States which they represent would have long since procured, (under laws and resns. passed by them for that purpose), this information: but the commissioners appointed by the State of Kentucky were prohibited by the officers of the U. States, from entering the Indian lands for that purpose.

The undersigned therefore, on behalf of the several States they respectively represent, earnestly request the President of the United States, that he would as early as convenient, take the foregoing under consideration, and if approved of by him, procure for the people of the said States an Object conceived by them to be of very high Importance, not only in a pecuniary point of view, but of great political consideration, in cementing & binding together by every practicable tie, the Atlantic and Western States.

John Breckinridge
Jos: Anderson
Abr Baldwin
Jas Jackson
John Fowler
Wm Cocke
Thos. T. Davis
Peter Early
Wm. Dickson
D. Meriwether

RC (PHi); in Breckinridge's hand, signed by all; addressed: "The President of the U. States"; endorsed by TJ as received 11 Feb. and so recorded in SJL with notation "Kentucky, Tenissee & Georgia."

For earlier correspondence regarding a proposed road between DANVILLE and AUGUSTA, and the refusal of the CHEROKEE INDIANS to allow roads through their lands, see Vol. 34:456-8 and Vol. 36:190-1, 543-4. Prior to writing the above letter, members of the Georgia and Tennessee congressional delegations met in the Senate chamber and chose Breckinridge, Joseph Anderson, and Peter Early as a committee to draw up an address to the president "upon the subject of the road from Kentucky through Tennessee to Georgia" (Anderson and Early to Breckinridge, 31 Jan. 1803, in DLC: Breckinridge Family Papers).

From Robert Eastburn

RESPECTED FRIEND   2d mo 10th 1803 N Brunswick N Jersey

I take the freedom to Adress thee as Sutch being pleased with thy Government

I Rote thee A few lines about one year past butt did nott desire thy Condesention to Answer it

I have Taken Notice of Some proposition Relative to A dry dock for the preservation of Shiping butt the vast Cost Attending as well as doubts of its utility may have Arisen to defer it.

Butt as it Appears thy desire to do the Best for the General Good of the Great Bodies of people overwhom thou presides

I therefore take the Liberty to Convey my mind on that Great & Interesting Subject of the use of meanes to prevent that Rapid decay of those highly vollewable Machines & on A Vew of our Timber Growing Scarse Except at Considerable distances from us & when our Ships & other vessels are Built witch mutch hard Labour & Cost it is pitiable to observe there Short duration as well as the Eminent danger to witch man & property is Exposed Even many Times before the danger is discovered destruction is Fast at hand: then A Natureal Inquiry Arises what shall be done as A Remedy the Answer is at hand plain & Easy to perform: that is to me Beyond a doubt that will preserve the plank as well as Timber perhaps Sundry fold or many yeares Longer than otherwise & the article is Salt & if the president only desires it I will Indevour if Spared to Convey the perticular manner of Applying it with Evidences of its utility

I am with Sinseer Respect thy friend   ROBERT EASTBURN

my former ocapation was that of A Ship Carpenter & have Evidently discovered from my own Experiment & may be witnessed by Sundry persons of Reputation of the true State of what is known Relative thereto

RC (MHi); endorsed by TJ as received 16 Feb. and so recorded in SJL.

I ROTE THEE A FEW LINES: Eastburn to TJ, 2 Mch. 1802.

From John Wayles Eppes

DEAR SIR,   Eppington Feb: 10th: 1803.

From the want of time your last letter received a few days before I left Richmond was not acknowledged. Maria arrived here just one week before the Legislature finally adjourned. She was in good health herself but was very near loosing our little Francis on the road between Edge hill and this place. From cold or cholick or some other cause he became lifeless in an instant in the carriage and most probably would have expired but for the friendly aid of mr. Randolph who hastened back with him in his arms to a house and procured a warm bath by which he was gradually restored.

By a letter from Mr Lilly I learn that he has failed in hiring hands for the levelling at Pant-Ops. The terror of Pages name he says prevented the possibility of hiring them. This shall not in future be a bar to our operations there—It has been long my wish to part with Page notwithstanding his skill and industry—& nothing but my being unable to procure a suitable character last year would have caused me to continue him longer. I will however at any rate part with him at the end of the present year, and indeed if I was myself perfectly satisfied with his conduct, such an evidence of the publick sentiment against him would induce me to give him up.

We shall meet you at Monticello early in March—The necessity of my being at the different Courts of the district in the month of March will prevent my seeing much of you while at Monticello. It is probable I shall have no competitor in the District as no one has as yet come forward.

I enclose you the Report of the committee appointed to ascertain the amount of the debt due from the Commonwealth of Virginia on which subject you made some inquiry during the last year—

accept for your health & happiness the warm wishes of Maria & myself—

Yours sincerely JNO: W: EPPES

When you write direct to city point as we shall be at home in a few days and continue there until we set out for Edge-hill—

RC (ViU: Edgehill-Randolph Papers); endorsed by TJ as received 16 Feb. and so recorded in SJL. Enclosure not found, but see below.

The Virginia LEGISLATURE FINALLY ADJOURNED on 29 Jan. (*Journal of the House of Delegates of the Commonwealth of Virginia*, Dec. 1802-Jan. 1803, 71).

TERROR OF PAGES NAME: William Page, overseer of Eppes's plantation at Pantops, had a reputation as a cruel manager who needed to be moderated (Stanton, *Free Some Day*, 39, 42, 43; Vol. 30:56).

REPORT OF THE COMMITTEE: on 18 Dec. 1802, the Virginia House of Delegates appointed a committee "to enquire into the state of the debts due from the commonwealth," to determine the amount of revenue and expenditures for the past year, and estimate the appropriations needed for the ensuing year. Daniel Sheffey submitted a report on behalf of the committtee on 8 Jan. 1803, with the caveat that the lack of proper records prevented precise reporting. He calculated the probable amount of the public debt as of 1 Oct. 1802 as $184,399, with revenue for 1801 of $296,289 and expenditures exceeding revenue by $23,529. For the year beginning on 30 Sep. 1802, the committee anticipated expenses of $308,443 and resources of $511,201 to meet those obligations. The committee did not recommend raising taxes and ordered 250 copies of the report to be printed for the use of members of the general assembly (*Journal of the House of Delegates of the Commonwealth of Virginia*, Dec. 1802-Jan. 1803, 19, 47-9).

To Albert Gallatin

TH:J. TO MR GALLATIN Feb. 10. 1803.

I inclose you Crowninshield's and Gibaut's letters recommending Stevens & Storer. Storer was also recommended by mr Lincoln. Illsley by Genl. Dearborne. the circumstance of exhibiting our recommendations, even to our friends, requires great consideration. recommendations, when honestly written should detail the bad as well as good qualities of the person recommended. that gentlemen may do freely, if they know their letter is to be confined to the President or the head of a department. but if communicated further it may bring on them troublesome grounds. in Gl. Washington's time he resisted every effort to bring forth his recommendations. in mr Adams's time I only know that the republicans knew nothing of them. I have always considered the controul of the Senate as meant to prevent any bias or favoritism in the President towards his own relations, his own religion, towards particular states &c. and perhaps to keep very obnoxious persons out of offices of the first grade. but in all subordinate cases I have ever thought that the selection made by the president ought to inspire a general confidence that it has been made on due inquiry & investigation of character, and that the Senate should interpose their negative only in those particular cases where something happens to be within their knolege, against the character of the person & unfitting him for the appointment. to mr Tracy at any rate no exhibition or information of recommendation ought to be communicated. he may be told that the President does not think it regular to communicate the grounds or reasons of his decision. friendly salutations & respect.

P.S. to exhibit recommendations would be to turn the Senate into a court of honor, or a court of slander, and to expose the character of every man nominated to an ordeal, without his own consent, subjecting the Senate to heats & waste of time, [of] which those who were present at the nomination of Colo. W. S. Smith, have seen an example. there a committee sat weeks in judgment on him, [raising? up] scandal from every quarter.

PrC (DLC); blurred and torn. Recorded in SJL as a letter to the Treasury Department with notation "Stevens. Storer. Illsley." Enclosure: perhaps Jacob Crowninshield to Levi Lincoln, 26 Nov., recommending Joseph Story (see enclosure described at Lincoln to TJ, 13 Dec. 1802). Other enclosures not found.

STORER: that is, Joseph Story. For Lincoln's recommendation, see his letter to TJ of 13 Dec.

President Adams's nomination of his son-in-law William Stephens SMITH to be surveyor and inspector for the district of New York was referred to a COMMITTEE on 10 Dec. 1800. The committee did not report until 16 Feb. On 24 Dec., Smith presented TJ, as president of the Senate, with documents he had assembled to support his nomination, which TJ delivered to Gouverneur Morris, chairman of the committee "instructed to seek testimony" and report (Vol. 32:351-2).

From Thomas Newton

DEAR SIR Norfolk. Febry. 10—1803

After two months session I have got home & hope you have received the Cyder, which Mr Taylor informs me he shipped to you & that it may please as it is said to be good & well racked—some was shipped agreeable to your order to Mr. Jefferson at Richmond. Our harbour is full of shipping & daily more ariving but they bring nothing new, except the dreadful situation of the French in St. Domingo, no quarters is given, the accounts are that several white people have been found hanging, with labels fixed on their breasts that all taken would meet the same fate. I am wishing you health

Yrs respectfully THOS NEWTON

RC (DLC); endorsed by TJ as received 23 Feb. and so recorded in SJL.

Newton was senator for Nansemond, Norfolk, and Princess Anne Counties during the Virginia General Assembly SESSION lasting from 6 Dec. 1802 to 29 Jan. 1803 (Leonard, *General Assembly*, 230).

From Clement Storer and Others

SIR Portsmouth N.H. Feby 10th. 1803

Expecting that the Office of District Judge for the New-Hampshire District will soon be vacant, and sensible of the difficulty of distinguishing suitable Characters at this distance from the Seat of Government. We the undersign'd beg leave to recommend Jonathan Steele of Durham in said District Esquire to fill that Office. We believe it has been usual where the merits of the Candidates have been in other respects equal, for the District Attorney to succeed to the

Office of District Judge but there is no person in this District in whose abilities integrity and principles the community will place greater confidence than in those of Mr Steele his education and profession, being a Lawyer, have been suitable for a Candidate to that Office. You may be assured Sir that in makeing this recommendation we are not influenced by partial motives but as well from a wish that no person may be appointed to that Office in whose integrity the people cannot place confidence as from a conviction that Mr Steele will be more acceptable to the friends of Government and at the same time less obnoxious to others than any other Candidate.—

With high Respect We are Sir Your Mot. Ob. Servts.

Clement Storer
Elijah Hall
Edward Cutts
John Goddard
John McClintock
Charles Cutts

RC (DNA: RG 59, LAR); in an unidentified hand, signed by all; at head of text: "Thomas Jefferson—President of the United States"; endorsed by TJ as received 1 Mch. and "Steele to be district judge; not Sherburne" and so recorded in SJL.

A physician and merchant in Portsmouth, New Hampshire, Clement Storer (1760-1830) was elected as a Democratic Republican to serve in the House of Representatives from 1807 to 1809 and in the U.S. Senate from 1817 to 1819, where he chaired the Committee on the Militia. He became a major general in the state militia and was commander of the First Militia Brigade in 1812. He served as sheriff of Rockingham County from 1818 to 1824 (*Biog. Dir. Cong.*; Lynn Warren Turner, *The Ninth State: New Hampshire's Formative Years* [Chapel Hill, 1983], 270, 290; Charles M. Wiltse and others, eds., *The Papers of Daniel Webster: Correspondence*, 7 vols. [Hanover, N.H., 1974-86], 1:103n). In 1802, Storer and Elijah Hall were elected as Republicans to the state house of representatives and John Goddard to the senate. Hall and Edward Cutts were selectmen at Portsmouth in 1802 and 1803. Later, Hall served as Republican councillor from Rockingham County. Edward Cutts, Goddard, and Jonathan Steele were among those recommended by John S. Sherburne, the district attorney, as bankruptcy commissioners at Portsmouth. John Langdon recommended Goddard, John McClintock, and Charles Cutts. TJ appointed Goddard and McClintock (Portsmouth *New-Hampshire Gazette*, 2 Mch., 31 Aug. 1802, 5 Apr. 1803; Turner, *Ninth State*, 282; Vol. 37:462-3, 577, 621, 689, 698, 703, 707).

For the appointments after the removal of John Pickering as DISTRICT JUDGE, see note at John Langdon to TJ, 20 Jan. 1803.

Topics for Consultation with Heads of Departments

[on or after 10 Feb. 1803]

Sy. War. Wafford's settlemt. qu. if Indns. wd accept rent?
instruct Meigs to bring settlemt. of Cherokee road to an end
settle Wafford's affair.
Wilkinson & Dinsmore to purchase above Yazoo of Choctaws
to examine our rt betw. Tombigbee, Alibama
Harrison to buy of Kaskaskias
of the Pioria chief
to settle bounds with Kickapoos, Poutewatamies & Weauhs.
gallies at Fort Adams.
ord. to posts on Ohio & Missi to stop persons going down with hostile views.

Sy. Treasy. Genl. Dearborne's case.
Ellicot's case.
Natchez. Acts. 1801-2. pa. 145.

Sy. Navy. guncarriages Marocco.

Council. Removals. Boston.
Tripoli.

Sy. of state. Lincoln's opn on Danish ship. case of War onskan. 2. Rob. 299.

MS (DLC: TJ Papers, 234:41852); entirely in TJ's hand, apparently consisting of notes of subjects for discussion with members of the cabinet; undated, but not completed before 10 Feb., the date of Levi Lincoln's opinion on the *Hendrick* case (see below); TJ did not fill all the space he allowed for some sections of the document.

SY. WAR: for the matters pertaining to Indian affairs, see also TJ to Dearborn, 15 Feb.

WAFFORD'S SETTLEMT.: on 19 Feb., Dearborn asked Return Jonathan MEIGS, the U.S. agent for the Cherokees, to seek some accommodation that would let William Wofford and his neighbors remain on land within the Cherokees' boundary. If the Cherokees would not agree to sell the land, Meigs was to try to obtain their consent to a seven-year lease. Dearborn also instructed Meigs to hold a conference with the Cherokees to get permission for a ROAD from the vicinity of Southwest Point in Tennessee to the headwaters of the Oconee River. It would be well if the agent could also obtain agreement for the establishment of public houses along the route—but, Dearborn insisted, "at all events we must have a road." All nations allowed other countries access through their territories in time of peace, Dearborn stated, "and we shall not consider the Cherokees as good neighbours unless they will allow, their best friends who are taking every means in their power to make them happy, to make a road at their own expense to pass through their Country from one settlement to another" (Dearborn to Meigs, 19 Feb., in DNA: RG 75, LSIA; Josiah Tattnall, Jr., to TJ, 20 July 1802).

Dearborn wrote to James WILKINSON

on 18 and 21 Feb. about measures to obtain lands between the YAZOO and Mississippi Rivers. Acquisition of land in that area was of higher priority, Dearborn indicated, than on the TOMBIGBEE River. Silas Dinsmoor, the agent for the Choctaws, was to begin talks with the upper Choctaw towns for the tract west of the Yazoo (Dearborn to Wilkinson, 18 Feb., in DNA: RG 107, LSMA, and 21 Feb., in DNA: RG 75, LSIA; Vol. 37:447).

For Dearborn's instructions of 21 Feb. to William Henry HARRISON, see the Memorandum for Henry Dearborn on Indian Policy, 29 Dec. In addition to asking Harrison to begin negotiations for land at Kaskaskia and at the junction of the Mississippi and Ohio Rivers, Dearborn in February and March issued orders for the establishment of an army post at the mouth of the Illinois River with one company of soldiers. There were existing posts with small garrisons at Massac on the Ohio River and at Kaskaskia (Dearborn to Amos Stoddard, 19 Feb., in DNA: RG 107, LSMA; Dearborn to Matthew Lyon, 9 Mch., in DNA: RG 107, MLS).

Dearborn took steps to put two additional companies of soldiers at FORT ADAMS by summer (Dearborn to Daniel Vertner, 9 Mch., in DNA: RG 107, MLS).

ORD. TO POSTS ON OHIO & MISSI: on 19 Feb., Dearborn initiated orders to the army's officers at Pittsburgh, Massac, Chickasaw Bluffs, and Fort Adams "to use all prudent means in their power to prevent the passage of any armed force, not authorised by the Government," that might attempt to pass downriver with HOSTILE intent against New Orleans. To Wilkinson on the 18th, Dearborn confided that he did not think there was "any good reason to fear such a movement." He referred to the reports of an armed force being recruited in western Pennsylvania as a "rumour" and did not mention Carlos Martínez de Irujo's representation to Madison on the matter. It was, however, "thought advisable" to issue the orders (Dearborn to Wilkinson, 18 Feb., and to Thomas H. Cushing, 19 Feb., in DNA: RG 107, LSMA; TJ to Madison, 8 Feb.).

GENL. DEARBORNE'S CASE: see Dearborn to TJ, 5 Feb.

ELLICOT'S CASE: see Gallatin to TJ, 8 Jan.

See Thomas Marston Green to TJ, 3 Feb., on making NATCHEZ a port of entry and deposit; TJ in the document printed above repeated Green's citation to a page in the ACTS of Congress.

MAROCCO: although the prospect of war with Morocco prompted a decision in September to stop the shipment of gun carriages to Mawlay Sulayman, following the resolution of the dispute the sultan still expected to receive the gift. TJ discussed the matter with Robert Smith, probably in the first week of March, and the navy secretary suggested that it would be cheaper for the United States, and perhaps more satisfactory to Sulayman, to send money that the sultan could use to purchase gun mounts made to his specifications (Madison, *Papers*, *Sec. of State Ser.*, 3:608n; 4:222; Madison to TJ, 22 July 1802; TJ to Smith, 6 Sep.; Smith to TJ, 12 Mch. 1803; Madison to TJ, 17 Mch.; TJ to Madison, 19 Mch.; TJ to Smith, 29 Mch.).

REMOVALS: TJ may have wanted to discuss with the cabinet Uriah Tracy's demand for information regarding certain nominations; see Gallatin to TJ, [9 Feb.], and TJ to Gallatin, 10 Feb.

TJ probably intended to consult with his advisers about the projected use of smaller vessels in the ongoing war with TRIPOLI. According to the plan he favored, the squadron in the Mediterranean would consist of one or two frigates and four schooners (TJ to Smith, 29 Mch.). News of Sweden's peace treaty with Tripoli had arrived during December. William Eaton's project of using Ahmad Qaramanli against his brother Yusuf, the dey of Tripoli, had gone awry when Ahmad accepted an offer from Yusuf—who held Ahmad's wife and children hostage—to become the governor of the province of Derna. Ahmad's agents remained in contact with the U.S. naval commander Richard V. Morris, however, urging that with support from the United States, Ahmad could raise an army against his brother. Stating that he had no authority to grant the requested assistance, Morris advised Ahmad to write to Washington and explain "the specific sum that may be wanted, and the probability of success that will attend the undertaking." Accordingly, Ahmad addressed a letter dated 20 Jan. 1803 to "his Excellency the President of the United States of America." Calling himself "the lawful Bashaw of Tripoli" and declaring his intention to raise 100,000 men, Ahmad asked that the United States "advance me Forty thousand spanish Dollars, also some Guns, Powder &ca. for which I promise to repay them whenever we take Tripoli." He pledged that he would "always remain the faithful friend" of the Americans. It is likely that TJ never saw the appeal for aid, which is not in his papers and not recorded in SJL. A copy is in the papers of Edward Preble, who took over as commander of the Mediterranean squadron in September 1803. Richard Farquhar, a merchant on the island of Malta, acted as Ahmad Qaramanli's intermediary in this attempt to communicate with TJ. A letter from Farquhar to TJ of 15 Nov. 1803 is also in Preble's papers and did not reach TJ (Ahmad Qaramanli to TJ, 20 Jan., Tr in DLC: Edward Preble Papers, in English with signature in Arabic, endorsed; Farquhar to TJ, 15 Nov. 1803, in same; NDBW, 2:317, 347; 3:222; Madison, *Papers*, *Sec. of State Ser.*, 3:45, 519, 557, 576; 4:389; New York *Morning Chronicle*, 15 Dec. 1802; Christopher McKee, *Edward Preble: A Naval Biography, 1761-1807* [Annapolis, Md., 1972], 141-2, 187; Madison to TJ, 3 Sep. 1802; Farquhar to TJ, 18 Mch. 1804, in DNA: RG 59, CD, Tripoli; TJ to Madison, 7 Aug. 1804).

LINCOLN'S OPN ON DANISH SHIP: in 1799, a French privateer in the West Indies captured a Danish brig, the *Hendrick*. The U.S. revenue cutter *Pickering* then captured the *Hendrick* from the French and had it condemned by a British admiralty court. Applying a rate of salvage from U.S. law, the court awarded the American captors half the value of the vessel and its cargo. In June 1801, Swedish consul general Richard Söderström, who at the time also represented Denmark's interests in the United States, protested that the U.S. law of salvage did not apply to neutral ships or cargoes. He argued too that the matter should have been handled by an American court rather than by a British tribunal in the West Indies. By February 1803, Söderström acted as attorney for the owners of the *Hendrick* and asked Peder Blicher Olsen to submit a claim to the U.S. government. After receiving the documents on 9 Feb., Madison referred the matter to the attorney general. Replying with a "hastely formed" opinion on the 10th, Lincoln ventured that the actions of the British court were "binding, untill reversed by a Judicial proceeding." He added that it "would be dangerous for the legislature or the Executive of the U States to adopt a different principle." Lincoln believed that the claimants should seek redress from individuals, not from the United States government. The *Hendrick* and its cargo were subject to salvage not under U.S. law, he contended, but by "general principles" of laws of salvage, and rulings by British courts, as well as by American courts in "one or two instances," justified the recapture of a neutral vessel from a belligerent nation. "I know of no principle by which the U.S. are bound to compensate for the injuries complained of," Lincoln stated (Lincoln to Madison, 10 Feb., in DNA: RG 59, LOAG; Madison, *Papers*, *Sec. of State Ser.*, 1:293-5, 296n; 4:312-13, 318; enclosure to TJ to the Senate and the House of Representatives, 23 Feb.).

In the case of the WAR ONSKAN, a Swedish ship that had been captured in 1799 first by the French, then by the British, the British High Court of Admiralty upheld the granting of salvage on neutral property. Salvage awarded a portion of the value of property to those who saved the property from perishing; the court held that the likelihood of condemnation of the *War Onskan* by capricious French prize courts had presented a danger of total loss that had been averted by the British capture of the ship. "When these lawless and irregular practices are shewn to have ceased," Sir William Scott wrote of the French prize tribunals in his ruling in the case, "the rule of paying salvage for the liberation of neutral property must cease likewise" (Christopher Robinson, *Reports of Cases Argued and Determined in the High Court of Admiralty; Commencing with the Judgments of The Right Hon. Sir William Scott, Michaelmas Term 1798*, 6 vols. [1799-1808], 2:299-302).

To Cornplanter and Others

BROTHERS Washington Feb. 11. 1803.

I have recieved your letter of January 18. and observe the dissatisfaction you express at the sale of lands made by your nation to the state of New York. it was the act of your nation, which the United States would not pretend to controul: they had no interest in it; yet they sent a commissioner to watch over your interests and to see that you understood the transaction, & gave free consent to it. the determination you express to sell no more of your lands is perfectly agreeable to me; as our wish is that you remain in a situation to support yourselves happily & plentifully. but, brothers, when you consider the diminution of the game on your lands, you must be sensible you cannot feed & clothe yourselves but by working your lands more, and manufacturing cloaths for yourselves. in this way the lands you hold will abundantly maintain you from generation to generation. your leaving off the use of spirituous liquors is a wise measure, and will leave you much more capable of taking care of yourselves & families. with respect to the lands on the Alleganey river which you wish to have given to the Handsome lake, I am not informed whether the right to them has been purchased from you by Pensylvania, in which case they belong to that state, and are not subject to our gift, or whether they still belong to your nation, in which case they can give them themselves to the Handsome lake as they please. I am very glad you are pleased with your new agent and hope he will continue to give you satisfaction. Accept brothers my best wishes for your health and happiness.

TH: JEFFERSON

RC (NBuHi); at head of text: "To the Cornplanter, the Stinking fish and Gachgewashe" and so recorded in SJL. PrC (DLC).

BROTHERS: Stinking Fish (Kenjauaugus), one of the recipients of this letter, was among the Seneca leaders who signed a treaty negotiated by Timothy Pickering at Canandaigua in 1794 (Charles J. Kappler, comp. and ed., *Indian Affairs: Laws and Treaties*, 5 vols. [Washington, D.C., 1975], 2:37).

The LETTER of 18 Jan. has not been found and is not recorded in SJL. Handsome Lake addressed a document to TJ on the same day (see TJ to Handsome Lake, 12 Feb.). A Seneca now commonly known as Governor Blacksnake probably carried the letters to Washington. Other people traveled with him, but nothing is known of the size or composition of the group. Blacksnake, also called The Nephew, was a relative of Cornplanter and Handsome Lake and a supporter of their revitalization program. He passed through Pittsburgh late in January on his way to the capital. There is no indication that he addressed TJ in a conference or acted as anything except a courier for the written communications. He and his group were ready to depart Washington on 14 Feb., when they received a pass from Dearborn for their return journey (pass for The Nephew, 14 Feb., in DNA: RG 75, LSIA; Georgetown *Olio*, 10 Feb.; Thomas S. Abler, *Chainbreaker: The Revolutionary War Memoirs of Governor Blacksnake* [Lincoln, Neb., 1989], 20-1, 82, 217; Anthony F. C. Wallace, *The Death and Rebirth of the Seneca* [New York, 1969], 240-1, 285).

The letters from Cornplanter and Handsome Lake followed a Seneca council held in January at Cornplanter's Town (Jenuchshadago) or Burnt House, which was on a tract on the Allegheny River granted to Cornplanter in 1795 by the state of Pennsylvania. The meeting protested the recent SALE OF LANDS on the Niagara River, announced that Cornplanter's Town would become the site for meetings of the council of the Six Nations confederation—of which Handsome Lake was a member—and attempted to decree that Buffalo Creek, where Red Jacket, the political rival of Cornplanter and Handsome Lake, lived, would no longer be a council site. According to a newspaper report, Blacksnake was also "the bearer of information to the President respecting overtures of an unfriendly nature towards the United States made to the Seneca Nation of Indians, by French emissaries" (Georgetown *Olio*, 10 Feb.; Wallace, *Death and Rebirth*, 171-2, 285-6; Thomas S. Abler, *Cornplanter: Chief Warrior of the Allegany Senecas* [Syracuse, N.Y., 2007], 57, 83; Vol. 37:30, 35n).

THE ACT OF YOUR NATION: another delegation, connected to Red Jacket—who supported the recent land cessions and had no role in the January council—was in Washington at the same time as Blacksnake's group (see TJ to Farmer's Brother and Others, 14 Feb.).

PLEASED WITH YOUR NEW AGENT: Callender Irvine was the U.S. agent for the Six Nations. Red Jacket had objected to the replacement of Israel Chapin with Irvine (Dearborn to TJ, 22 Aug. 1802).

From Samuel Hanson

SIR, Feby 11th. 1803

It is believed, generally, that John M. Gantt, one of the Commissioners of Bankruptcy for this county, will be appointed to a Judgeship in one of the districts of Maryland. In case of this event, I beg leave to recommend as a candidate for the place of Commissioner of Bankruptcy, Nicholas King, of this city—.

Presuming that you are acquainted with Mr. King's character and pretensions, I have only to solicit you to excuse the liberty I take in his behalf; a liberty to which I am prompted merely by my desire to serve a worthy man, in indigent circumstances.

with great respect, I am, Sir, Your most obedt.

S HANSON OF SAML

RC (DNA: RG 59, LAR); endorsed by TJ "King Nichs. to be Commr. bkrptcy v. Gantt" and so recorded in SJL on 11 Feb.

On 23 Feb., JOHN M. GANTT wrote Madison offering his resignation as bankruptcy commissioner for the District of

Columbia. Maryland law required that upon accepting the appointment as a state judge, he resign any federal commissions he held. Gantt requested that Madison notify the president of his decision (RC in DNA: RG 59, RD; endorsed by TJ: "Gantt J. M. to mr Madison. resigns as Commr. bkrptcy"). TJ appointed James S. Morsell, a Georgetown lawyer, to fill the vacancy with a commission dated 3 June. Two days later Morsell returned the commission to Madison, noting that his professional duties occupied "so great a portion" of his time that he could not "render an attention to the execution of the trusts" required by the office (RC in same, endorsed by TJ: "Morsell to mr Madison declines as Commr bkrptcy"; Madison, *Papers, Sec. of State Ser.*, 5:61; list of commissions in Lb in DNA: RG 59, MPTPC). In October, TJ appointed William O. Sprigg to join Hanson and William Thornton as bankruptcy commissioners (same; Vol. 37:709).

In August 1802, TJ endorsed the appointment of NICHOLAS KING as surveyor for the city of Washington. The State Department issued the commission on 4 Mch. 1803 (FC in Lb in DNA: RG 59, MPTPC; Vol. 38:234, 287-8, 327).

Letter of Credence for James Monroe

CITIZEN FIRST-CONSUL,

Desirous of improving and perpetuating, by every arrangement calculated for mutual advantage, the good correspondence which so happily prevails between the united States and the French Republic,[1] I have for this purpose, with the advice and consent of the Senate, given full powers to Robert R. Livingston,[2] now our Minister Plenipotentiary at Paris,[3] and to James Monroe, lately Governor of the State of Virginia, who repairs thither[4] in the character of Minister Extraordinary and Plenipotentiary. The special objects with which they are charged, are regarded as intimately connected with the welfare of the two nations, and will evince the disposition of the United States to consolidate their amicable relations with the French Republic. From the knowledge I have of the fidelity, probity, and just views of these distinguished citizens, I have entire confidence that they will render themselves acceptable to you in this charge. I beseech you, therefore, to give full credence to whatever they shall say to you on the part of the United States, and most of all when they shall assure you of our friendship and wishes for the prosperity of France.[5] And I pray God, to have you, Citizen First Consul,[6] in his safe and holy keeping.

Written at the city of Washington the eleventh day of February in the year of our Lord one thousand eight hundred & three

TH: JEFFERSON

FC (Lb in DNA: RG 59, Credences); in a clerk's hand; at head of text: "Thomas Jefferson, President of the United States of America, To the First-Consul of the French Republic"; below signature: "By the President of the United States" and "James Madison, Secretary of State." FC (Lb in same); in a clerk's hand; at head of text: "Thomas Jefferson, President of the United States of America, To His Majesty Don Carlos by the grace of God King of Castile, of Leon, of Arragon, of the two Sicilies, of Jerusalem, of Navarre, of Granada, of Toledo, of Valencia, of Galicia, of Mallorca, of Seville, of Sardinia, of Cordova, of Corcega, of Murcia, of Jaen, of the Algarves, of Algeciras, of Gibraltar, of the Canary Islands, of the East & West Indies, of the Islands and Main Land, of the Ocean—Arch-Duke of Austria, Duke of Burgoña, of Brabant, and of Milan, Count of Apsburg, of Flanders, of Tirol, and of Barcelona, Lord of Biscay and Molina &c."; salutation: "Great and Good Friend"; variations in wording as noted below. Not recorded in SJL.

[1] 2d FC: "Spain."
[2] 2d FC: "Charles Pinckney."
[3] 2d FC: "to your Majesty."
[4] 2d FC: "to Madrid."
[5] 2d FC: "Spain."
[6] 2d FC: "Great and Good Friend."

From J. P. G. Muhlenberg

Philadelphia Febry. 11th. 1803

Last Evening I was honor'd with The Presidents favor of the 6th. inst— The business therein alluded to has this morning been transacted, agreeably to direction, & perfectly consonant with former usage—In this stage of business, after the Entries have been made, the insertion of names is unnecessary—It was only requisite to Credit the U.S with $22.50—for Duties received, & to endorse the Rect. on the Original Entry.

I have the Honor to be with Perfect Respect Sir your most Obedt

P Muhlenberg

RC (DLC); at foot of text: "The President of The. U.S."; endorsed by TJ as received 16 Feb. and so recorded in SJL; also endorsed by TJ: "paimt. of duty on 200. bottles Champagne bot from M. de Casa Yrujo."

From Elisha Bennett

Kinderhook State New York
feby. the 12th. 1803

Honoured Sir I wish to inform your Excellency of the Cruell intreatment which I Have Met with in Regard to wages Being Due to Me for Servisses Dun In the Continantal Servis in the Late american war. May it Please your Excellency, I Enterd on Board the Continantal frigate: Trumbull, Dudley Saltonstall Esqr Commander: on the 7th. of jany. 1777 and Continued on Board until the 13th of februay 1778—as Second Mate—it Being 13 Months & 6 Days at 15 Dollars Per Month—My wages amounted to one Hundred & Ninty Eight

Dollars—& I Received 72 Dollars whilst Belonging to the Ship for the youse of My family & Have Never Reced. one farthing from that time to this—May it Please your Excellency—when I was Dischargd from the Trumbull I amedeately went to Sea & Had the Misforting of Being taken Prisoner four times going So that I Had Not an oppertunity of apploying for My wages until the war Endd. and when the Honourable Congress was Pleased to advertis threw out the United States for all Soldiers & Seamen who Had Served in the Continantal Servis in the Late war & Had Not Reced. their wages—if they apployd after a Ragaler Manner they Should Receive their wages—and in the year 1792 I apployd to Congress in Philadelphia, But Could Have Nothing Don for Me, where as their was So many which Had apployd Befour Me—May it Please your Excellency I Have Producd a Certificate which I Reced from one of the Principle officers Belonging to the Trumbull—who Made oath that I was the Identacle Man, and the Certificate Sind By the Mare of the City of New York—But all in Vain—May it Please your Excellency I Have traveld since November—1792—2530 Miles in Persute of the Ballance of My just wages and am Denied of it, without knowing for what Reason—My Name is in the Trumbulls Books where I Stand open unpaid at the Auditor office—I Hombly Beg that your Excellency will Be So well Pleasd as to Inquire into this Matter, and to know the Reason why the Honourable Congress Refuses to allow Me the Ballance of My just wages—for which favour I Shall for Ever Be with Much thankfullness your Excellencys Most obediant Servent—

Elisha Bennett

RC (DLC). Recorded in SJL as received 21 Feb.

A resident of Kinderhook, New York, since 1788, Elisha Bennett (ca. 1732-1821) sent several unsuccessful petitions to Congress seeking compensation for his naval service during the American Revolution (Virgil D. White, *Genealogical Abstracts of Revolutionary War Pension Files*, 4 vols. [Waynesboro, Tenn., 1990-92], 1:237; JS, 1:459, 2:41; JHR, 2:389, 430-1, 4:63, 157; Syrett, *Hamilton*, 16:60-2).

To Handsome Lake

Brother Handsome Lake Washington Feb. 12. 1803.

I have recieved your letter of January 18th. wherein you suppose that in my former answer to you of Nov. 3. I had not fully understood what you had communicated to me; and you repeat a complaint that the state of New York had purchased lands from your nation to which some part of the nation did not consent. this is exactly what I understood, and then answered so fully that I need here repeat only in general, that if no nation can do an act till every individual of it, or even every town of it, consents, it will never do any act as a nation, because such an universal consent of all it's members can never be obtained. therefore it is a rule with all nations that what the great body of their people agree to is valid, and binds the smaller part tho' they disagree. deputies from the great body of your nation attended at Albany and made the sale to New York. the United states were not interested, but we sent a Commissioner there to see that the transaction was fair, and that no fraud should be practised on you. he found it fair, and we consented to the sale. you say, brother that the great spirit has forbidden you to sell any more of your land. if your people are satisfied of this, no doubt they will obey the great spirit, and sell no more. and if they do not chuse to sell, I repeat my assurances that they shall be protected in their possessions, and shall not be forced to sell. but if they are not satisfied that the Great Spirit has forbidden them to sell, and they shall find it advantageous at times to sell a part, the Great Spirit has not forbidden us to purchase. they have a right over their own lands, to keep or to sell them; and we will not controul them either way.

Brother, I observe what you say as to a tract of land ten miles square which your brother the Cornplanter claims from Thomas Morris. we will have the matter enquired into, and we will authorise some person to pursue your brother's right, as far as it can be by our laws, and have justice done him. you shall accordingly know what shall be doing on this subject. I am glad you disapprove of the violent proceedings of some of your chiefs, at Buffalo creek, to defraud our revenue, and give to a British trader the advantage of introducing his goods duty free, while our traders are obliged to pay duties. I am in hopes they will never repeat this act, as we shall be obliged to maintain the authority of our laws, and see that they are duly obeyed.

Brother I wish to yourself and all your people every happiness in this world and in the world to come. TH: JEFFERSON

PrC (DLC).

The LETTER from Handsome Lake has not been found and is not recorded in SJL; see also TJ to Cornplanter and Others, 11 Feb.

For the agreements made at ALBANY in August, see Vol. 38:342-4 and TJ to the Senate, 27 Dec.

When Cornplanter and Handsome Lake saw TJ in Washington in March 1802, Cornplanter said that THOMAS MORRIS had promised him a tract of land (Vol. 37:38).

VIOLENT PROCEEDINGS: in the spring of 1802, after a customs officer sequestered the goods of a Canadian woman who wanted to trade with the Senecas, Red Jacket, Farmer's Brother, and Young King broke into a storehouse to give the woman her goods back despite the "repeated remonstrance" of the revenue officer. Dearborn, who threatened to assess damages against the Senecas' annuity, insisted that the offenders must learn to "pay all deference to the Laws of the U. States, and the State in which they live" (Dearborn to Israel Chapin, 14 June 1802, in DNA: RG 75, LSIA; Christopher Densmore, *Red Jacket: Iroquois Diplomat and Orator* [Syracuse, N.Y., 1999], 60; Vol. 38:275n).

From Thomas Mendenhall

Paradise, (near Wilmington, Del:)
February 12th. 1803

DEAR SIR,

No one can more seriously regret the Existance of a necessaty for this intrusion than I do; But it is imposible to obtain the object of my solicitude by any other means; as I trust my application will not be considered indecorous in point of motive, neither can I despair of its successful issue:—it is not merely to my friend, but, to the friend of Justice, I make my claim.

The Remonstrance of Nehemiah Tilton, Isaac Hendrickson & others, presented to you by Ceasar A Rodney in July 1801; (and which was not made known to me until about the first of August last,)[1] is the object of my prayer.—a duplicate of that instrument does exist with its authors; but it is imposible for me, or my friends to obtain a Copy on any terms.

Nevertheless, the artifice & collusion of the parties;—their resorting to obscure and uninteresting Characters to obtain signatures;—the uncommon secrecy & precipitancy with which the measure was conducted;—the Extraordinary care taken to conceal it from persons who it was beleived were my friends;—with the subsequent insidious conduct of Certain prominent Characters in the Junto;—to me, are proofs "strong as holy writ," that both my private Character, & *personal Interest*, were intended to be involved in its operations.—this being the fact, You will my dear Sir, I hope readily grant me a Copy of that *original*, and if I cannot humanize its *Principals*, I may posibly Neutralize its Powers.—But however unsuccessful I may be, in the pursuit of individual Justice; be assured my dear Sir, that Reason, & not resentment, shall be my rule of action. No ingratitude from the Public, no injustice from Individuals, what ever their Political professions may be; shall ever lessen my reverence, for those immutable principles, which has hitherto been the Standard of my Moral & political life.—and in conformity to which, I have removed with my little flock to this farm, (which I lately purchased,) with the pleasing Expectation of spending the Remnant of my days in agricultural pursuits,—the Education of a Daugter & Eight sons;—Brightning occasionally the links of that great political Chain, which binds down our Political Adversaries; and discharging as far as I may possess the means, all the Social duties of domestic life.—Relying on Example as the strongest argument in contradiction to those who may have been pleased to say we, "are Republicans, *only* while in pursuit of office."—many are the considerations I might offer in Extenuation of this delay; but with you they are unnecessary; you will Sir, readily conceive the degree of reluctance I must ever have felt, at entering on the pursuit of so unseemly an object;—especially, as its influence with You gave me little concern, for confident I was, that you must readily have recognized the features of the Parents, in the countenance of this ofspring of insincerity & fraud.

But as the Political relations of our State are adjusted for the time being; and I am retired on my farm, enjoying the energies of an independent mind, (tho confined at this time to my room with the Influenza, & my nerves & spirits deprest, a little below their usual tone,) still solicitous to Rescue a Pilfer'd Reputation from the hands of the depredators: and impeld by a sense of the propriety as well as necessaty of the measure, I have thus endeavoured, with a pure heart, & hallowed hands, to approach the Presidential Sanctuary;—and indeed, my dear Sir, My feeble effort will much need the Kind indulgence of a generous friend.

Tho', I have already dwelt to long on this dreary Subject, the folowing incidents may not be deemed unworthy notice. A little previous to the date of my application, in familiar conversation with Ceasar A Rodney on the subject, I prest him gently on that side where Sincerity had yet her stand, and he verry courteously observed; "Capt. Mendenhall, what little Interest I may have, which indeed can be but Small, I should most cheerfully exercise in your favour; But Capt Bennett has previously Spoken to me on that subject, & I have pledged myself to him,"—this Sir was the fact, Ceasar was candid, Bennet had Spoken to him, and he had made his election in his favour, I believe, from the best of motives.—he knew the Service's Capt Bennet had rendered his Country during our revolutionary Struggle, he also knew his Intrinsick Merit: and nothing at that time had presented, to divert the natural Current of his Benevolence; But how far Ceasar A Rodney has acquited himself of this moral obligation with good faith, you can best determine; as no Evidence of the fact, not even of a presumptive nature has appeared in his favor here. nevertheless, "*Ceasar is an honourable man*," and had my vote & interest to go to Congress, tho not with quite so good a grace as I could have wished.—

I pray you accept Sir My best wishes for your personal & political Welfare, & believe me with much sincerity, your devoted friend, [& Hble] Sevt. THOMAS MENDENHALL

RC (DLC); torn; addressed: "Thomas Jefferson Esqr. President of the United States Washington"; endorsed by TJ as received 24 Feb. and so recorded in SJL.

TO MY FRIEND: Mendenhall saw TJ in Washington in January 1801 (Vol. 32:496-7).

The REMONSTRANCE OF NEHEMIAH TILTON has not been found, but in the summer of 1801 James Tilton and others persuaded Caesar A. Rodney to visit the president in Washington "for the express purpose of representing the true interest of republicanism in Delaware" against the misrepresentations of the Federalists and the "intrigues of selfish & insidious friends" (Vol. 34:487-8).

DATE OF MY APPLICATION: Mendenhall applied for the collectorship at Wilmington on 27 Apr. 1801. Jesse S. Zane, of Wilmington, actively supported his candidacy. Caleb Prew BENNETT applied for the same office in July 1801, but Rodney's endorsement of him has not been found (Vol. 33:644-6; Vol. 34:348-9, 566-7). In late 1802, Rodney informed the president that "Capt: Mendenhall did all he could to injure my election" (Vol. 38:638).

[1] Opening parenthesis supplied by Editors.

From Robert Leslie

SIR Philada Feby 13th 1803

your favour of the 27th ult was duly received, I Should have acknoledged the recipt imediately, but wished at the same time, to make as near an estimate of the expence as my knoledge of the subject would permit, I know nothing of the situation of the place but what I see in Mr Latrobes report, and as it is impossible to form a corect opinion of a piece of ground from a printed discreption my Ideas of it may be but imperfect, as to the machanical parts, I consider myself in some measure able to form an opinion from experience, having since my return from england, superentended two buildings, tho of a privet nature, and not on so large a scale as the Pennsylvania Bank, or Philada water works, has served to give me a perfect, knoledge of the expence of both Wood and Stone work, in every form that can be required for Dry Docks. and after a deliberate and careful investigation of the subject am confirmed in my first opinion, that less than one half of the sum reported by Mr L will be sufficent to compleat the work.

In your letter to me you say you presume I do not wish to make a secret of the particular defect I suppose to exist &c. I certainly did not. I never had, nor never shall have, any secret in the arts, or any machanical subject, that I would not gladly communicate to you, the information you ware pleased to ask for, I took the liberty of forwarding Pr Post on the 26th which was the day before your letter was wrote,

The drawing and description was done in great hast, and so imperfect that I fear it will hardly give a clear Idea of what I wish, but if from what you see, you can form such an opinion as to say wheather in its present form, or by any alteration or improvements, it can be made to answer I shall be extreamly gratifyed, if it should in no way meet your aprobation, I shall not feel myself disappointed as I know I am as likely to be mistaken in my opinion as others. but wheather your opinion should be in favour or aganst the plan, I shall be extreamly gratifyed to have a line on the subject when you are perfectly at leasure, as I think it a subject of the utmost consequence to the United States, and if my first plan is defective I should wish to turn my attention to another. and if favoured with your assistence, I have no doubt but a plan can be formed that will answer every wished for purpose, and at very moderate expence,

I was much surprised to find in the debates of congress, that a lerned gentleman, should express his doubts wheather Timber that had been once wet through for any length of time, would ever be perfectly dryed agane. the opinion and practice of ship Builders in I belive all parts of the world, is, that Timber seasons and drys much better after laying a long time under water, the timber intended for the ships of War to be built in this City is now under water. and as for the fears of foul air having a bad effect in a dry Dock, thay are eaqually groundless as the air may be kept as pure in a Dry Dock as in the open field. every other objection that has been offered may be easely set a side by a candid inspection of the true operations of nature,

I did intend to have viseted your City during this session of Congress, but have now give it up, as I am engaged in makeing arangements for quiting the Clock & watch business, I am compelled to do it, on account of having lost the use of my left hand, by a Rhumatic complaint in the wrist and sholder. and as I have been in the same situation every winter for the last four years, I have little hopes of ever getting the better of it, I am tharefore no longer able to do any thing at the mechanical parts of the business, and before I went to england I experienced too much of the evil of imploying Apprentices and journimen, to have recource to it agane, one strikeing proof of it, came within your knoledge, and which hurt my feeling more than all the rest. it was the employing the man who made your large Clock, and the small one intended for you (and who by you letter of last spring I find was knave enough to charge both you and my Partner for doing the same work.) as both of those Clocks ware made on a plan different from the common, and neither of them answerd, it must have been natural for you to suppose the defect lay in the construction, which was not the case, as I have since had several made on the same plan which answers every purpose wished for. These circumstances with a veriety of simuler ones, have long ago convinced me of the impossiblity of extending the working part of the Clock & Watch business to any degree in this Country at present, and as for the selling imported articles in that line, it is not worth attending to, as I am certain thare is not one man in that line, that has sold in Philada during the last twelve months, half as much as would pay his house rent. my situation may tharefore be described in few words. Viz. A man with a Wife and five Children to mentain, with one hand, and one head, neither of them worth much. the head stuffed full of what he once thought usefull knoledge, colected in various places, and at great expence, dureing the last fifteen years, but which is now of so little value that it would not purches a Beef stake, or a loaf of Bread, in the Market,

Notwithstanding the above is a true picture of my present situation I do not despair but I shall spend the remainder of my days more hapy than those that are past. in your notes, you say, Farmers are the only hapy people, and I intend to try to get a little farm in some agreable neighbourhood whare I can live without want of the common necessarys of life, I want no more,

I am quite ashamed to trouble you with so much scribleing, but if you will pander me this time, I will not trouble you agane, unless the situation of the Country should call your attention to Ship Building, if that should hapen, I am afrade I should be tempted to trouble you with some observations on that art, as it has been one of my hobby horses ever since I was five years of age

I am with respect your very humble Servt Robert Leslie

RC (DLC); at head of text: "To the President of the United States"; endorsed by TJ as received 19 Feb. and so recorded in SJL.

A LERNED GENTLEMAN: Samuel L. Mitchill. During the debate in Congress over the proposed dry dock at Washington, Mitchill stated it was "very questionable" whether the dampness acquired by navy vessels "could ever be so thoroughly dried out as to prevent putrefaction" (*Annals*, 12:404).

THE MAN WHO MADE YOUR LARGE CLOCK: Peter Spurck. For TJ's 1802 correspondence with Leslie regarding Spurck's clocks and his overcharging for the work, see Vol. 37:347-8, 394.

YOUR NOTES: that is, TJ's *Notes on the State of Virginia*, in which he asserted that "Those who labour in the earth are the chosen people of God" (*Notes*, ed. Peden, 164-5).

From Jean Vermonnet

EXCELLENCE Havane le 13 Fevrier 1803.

L'occasion que je rencontre d'un Officier de la Marine Francaise qui se rend aux Etats unis est pour moi une circonstance trop heureuse, puisque par elle je me trouve à même de me rappeller à V.E. de laquelle j'ai reçu des Politesses, et des marques de bonté lorsque j'eu l'honneur de la visiter à la City federal il y a environ deux Ans. Elle eut même à cette Epoque la bonté de m'annoncer que s'il se formoit un Corps d'Ingénieurs, Elle n'oubliroit pas que par mes Services passés j'aurai des droits à réclamer sa protection, et ce fut par cet espoir que je m'occupé de former un Plan de la Baye de Hampton, du même que des environs de Norfolk à fin d'y decrire un Sisteme de defence tel que je l'appercevois utile. Mais la Situation de ma famille et la Lenteur du Secretaire de la Guerre à m'honorer d'une reponse pendant 8. mois à cinq Lettres que je lui avois écrit me devint un garant de son refus à m'affirmer la protection que V.E. m'avoit temoigné. Je pris alors le parti de quitter les Etats unis, ou j'avois residé pendant 27. Ans, et ou j'avois servi 13. ans comme Ingénieur, pour visiter un Domaine Francais ou j'avois des grands Intérêts en terre, &c. Depuis ayant l'avantage d'être connû par le Gouvernement Francais, j'ai été invité à me rendre dans les Possessions Espagnoles pour y remplir une Mission, et y prendre aussi une Fonction qui me lie au Gouvernement qui m'a accuilli. Etant dans ce moment ci à la Havane j'ai eu la Satisfaction d'y rencontrer votre chargé d'affaires Vincent Gray Esquire homme trés estimable, et qui a acquis la consideration à bien juste titre des personnes en place, et respectables du Pays ou il est. Dans le Cas qu'il seroit agreable à V.E. de recevoir quelques objets d'histoire naturelle comme aussi de toute autre chose dans les Pays Espagnols ou ma place me donne des relations, et me met à même de voyager, je la prie de croire que ce seroit pour moi un plaisir égal à celui que j'éprouve à l'assurer du respecteux attachement avec le quel j'ai l'honneur d'être

De V.E. Son tres humble et tres obeissant Serviteur

VERMONNET
Comisaire et agent G.
pour lisle de cube l'a louisianne
Campêche &c

EDITORS' TRANSLATION

Your Excellency, Havana, 13 Feb. 1803

A French naval officer who is traveling to the United States provides me with an unhoped for occasion to send greetings to Your Excellency who was particularly kind to me when I had the honor of visiting you in the capital city some two years ago. At that time you generously pledged that if you were to create a corps of engineers, you would remember that I could seek your support, given my past service. Inspired by this hope, I worked on formulating a plan for Hampton Bay and the area around Norfolk, designing a system of defense that I judged useful. But after writing five letters to the secretary of war and not receiving any response in eight months, I concluded that he was unwilling to confirm the support Your Excellency had promised. Given my family situation, I thus decided to leave the United States, where I had lived for 27 years, including 13 as an engineer, and to visit a French territory where I had significant land interests, etc. Since then, benefiting from being known by the French government, I have been invited to the Spanish possessions to fulfill a mission and perform a function that links me to the government that has welcomed me. In Havana, where I am now, I was pleased to meet your chargé d'affaires, Vincent Gray, Esquire, a very worthy man, who has deservedly earned respect from the officials and notable citizens of the country.

If Your Excellency would like some specimens of natural history, or any other objects from the Spanish territories where my position leads me to travel and meet people, I assure you that fulfilling your wish would be a pleasure equal to the one I have in assuring you of the respectful attachment with which I have the honor of being Your Excellency's very humble and obedient servant

Vermonnet
Commissary and General Agent
for the island of Cuba,
Louisiana, Campeche, etc.

RC (DLC); in a clerk's hand, signed by Vermonnet; endorsed by TJ as a letter of 13 Jan. received 21 Mch. and so recorded in SJL.

Jean Arthur Marie de Vermonnet (or Vermonet), also known as John Vermonnet, was born in France in 1750 and served as a junior officer in the royal army from 1768 to 1775. In America in 1776, he received, with George Washington's endorsement, a brevet appointment as an officer in the Continental Army and served as an engineer. Afterward he was in Saint-Domingue. Beginning in 1792, he offered himself as a painter of miniature portraits in several American cities, and he and his wife, whom he married in Boston, advertised a school for young ladies in Baltimore. In 1794, he sought engineering work from the commissioners of the Federal District before receiving an appointment from Secretary of War Henry Knox to direct the construction of fortifications at Annapolis and Alexandria. Vermonnet lived in East Florida in 1806 and provided TJ with information about St. Augustine. The next year the French government made him its commissary for commercial relations for Kentucky, to reside at Natchez (André Lasseray, *Les Français sous les treize etoiles, 1775-1783* [Paris, 1935], 480-1; Gilbert Bodinier, *Dictionnaire des officiers de l'armée royale qui ont combattu aux États-Unis pendant la guerre d'Indépendance, 1776-1783*, 4th ed. [Versailles, 2005], 460; Leonard W.

Labaree and others, eds., *The Papers of Benjamin Franklin*, 40 vols. [New Haven, 1959-], 36:203n; Washington, *Papers, Rev. War Ser.*, 5:67n; *Pres. Ser.*, 15:423-4, 459-60; ASP, *Military Affairs*, 1:93-5; RCHS, 9 [1906], 113-14; New York *Daily Advertiser*, 25 July 1792; *Baltimore Daily Intelligencer*, 28 Oct. 1793; Alexandria *Columbian Mirror*, 19 Apr. 1794; Abel Poitrineau, "Demography and the Political Destiny of Florida during the Second Spanish Period," *Florida Historical Quarterly*, 66 [1988], 439; Heitman, *Register*, 560; Notes on St. Augustine, 27 Feb. 1806, in DLC; exequatur, 21 Apr. 1807, FC in Lb in DNA: RG 59, Exequaturs, and Tr in KyU, endorsed).

À LA CITY FEDERAL IL Y A ENVIRON DEUX ANS: Vermonnet probably visited the capital city in the spring of 1801, when he asked Mann Page to write a letter of introduction to TJ (Vol. 34:207). Vermonnet, in hopes of obtaining an appointment to lay out fortifications near the mouth of Chesapeake Bay, also solicited support from John Dawson. The engineer addressed two letters to the War Department on the subject, one from Norfolk in March 1801 and another from Portsmouth, Virginia, in July of that year. Vermonnet enclosed a plan with the second communication and also discussed the establishment of a school of engineering. A War Department clerk answered that letter, informing Vermonnet in Henry Dearborn's absence that the fortification plans had been brought to the president's attention (Vermonnet to the War Department, 28 Mch., 16 July 1801, noted in DNA: RG 107, RLRMS; chief clerk to Vermonnet, 27 July 1801, in DNA: RG 107, MLS).

Since the summer of 1802, VINCENT GRAY, the former deputy collector of customs at Georgetown, had been acting U.S. consul at Havana (Madison, *Papers, Sec. of State Ser.*, 4:62; Roy F. Nichols, "Trade Relations and the Establishment of the United States Consulates in Spanish America, 1779-1809," *Hispanic American Historical Review*, 13 [1933], 305; Vol. 35:43, 46n).

From J. P. P. Derieux

MONSIEUR Du Hâvre de Grace ce 14. Fevrier 1803.

Je viens d'arriver au Havre aprés une Traversée de 52. Jours, qui fut trés orageuse. J'ose prendre la liberté Sachant combien ma famille doit avoir d'inquietudes à mon Egard, de vous adresser cy joint une Lettre pour ma Femme, a fin d'eviter Les retards, qui resultent Souvent de La négligence des Capitaines pour les mettre a la poste, quand elles ne Sont pas adressées a des personnes de Consideration. Veuilléz je vous en Supplie, Monsieur m'accorder votre indulgence dans cette nouvelle importunité, et etre persuadé que ma reconnaissance en tous points, ne Cessera jamais d'Egaler Les Sentiments du Respectueux attachement avec Les qu'els J'ay L'honneur d'être

Monsieur Votre trés humble et trés Obeissant Serviteur

P. DERIEUX

P.S. Je trouve La France bien changée a son grand avantage, Et le peuple de cette Nation paroit avoir acquis avec Leur liberté Cet Esprit de hardiesse et de Caractere que je ne leur avois jamais connu.

J'aurai peut-etre Loccasion a Paris d'entendre parler de mon cher affectioné beau pere Mazzei, qui paroit avoir pris bien tard le parti de se marier, et de se donner en outre le titre de pere, quil n'eut jamais dans sa Jeunesse. J'aurois toujours cru que son grand age, nous donnoit Lieu d'en attendre toutte autre nouvelle. Ma femme il en faut Convenir Est bien malheureuse en bons parents, et je crains que nous sommes, Lun et L'autre destinés a L'être de tous les cotés.

EDITORS' TRANSLATION

SIR Le Havre, 14 Feb. 1803

I just arrived at Le Havre after a very stormy 52-day crossing. Knowing how worried my family must be, I dare take the liberty of enclosing a letter for my wife, to avoid the delays that often result from sea captains' negligence in mailing envelopes that are not addressed to eminent people. I beg you, Sir, to indulge this latest imposition and to be persuaded that my gratitude in all things will never cease matching the sentiments of respectful attachment with which I have the honor of being, Sir,

Your very humble and obedient servant. P. DERIEUX

P.S. I find France much changed for the better. With their liberty, the people of this nation seem to have acquired a boldness and spirit that I had never seen in them before.

In Paris I may have news of my beloved father-in-law Mazzei, who seems to have decided belatedly to marry and acquire the title of father, which he never had in his younger years. I always believed that his advanced age would lead us to expect quite different news. I must say that my wife is very unhappy about family matters and I fear we are both destined for unhappiness on all sides.

RC (DLC); endorsed by TJ as received 22 Apr. and so recorded in SJL. Enclosure not found.

Philip MAZZEI had married Antonia Antoni in 1796, and in 1798 their daughter Elisabetta was born. Mazzei had a strained relationship with his first wife, Marie Hautefeuille Martin, whom he called "scoundrelly." She died in 1788 and was, by a previous marriage, the mother of Maria Margarita Martin, Derieux's wife (Margherita Marchione, ed., *Philip Mazzei: My Life and Wanderings*, trans. S. Eugene Scalia [Morristown, N.J., 1980], 205-6, 226-7, 256-7, 271, 275, 283-4, 366-70; Vol. 7:388; Vol. 8:676, 677, 679n; Vol. 12:538; Vol. 13:415-16; Vol. 29:83; Vol. 32:279n).

To Nicolas Gouin Dufief

SIR Washington Feb. 14. 1803.

I observe in your printed catalogue les Sermons de Massillon 15. tom. 12mo. 15. D. be pleased to forward them to me with the others, and accept my best wishes & respects. TH: JEFFERSON

PrC (DLC); at foot of text: "Dufief"; endorsed by TJ in ink on verso.

Dufief was offering a mixed edition of 15 volumes of collected sermons of Jean Baptiste MASSILLON printed by various publishers between 1776 and 1801 (Sowerby, No. 1571).

From Nicolas Gouin Dufief

MONSIEUR, Le 14 de Février. 1803

Vous verrez par le Certificat-ci joint que je n'ai pu recevoir qu'aujourd'hui la Lettre dont vous m'avez honoré le 4—Je vous envoie cette piece, d'abord, pour me justifier du Soupçon de manquer d'exactitude à votre égard, vous qui donnez dans la place éminente que vous occupez, un exemple si Glorieux, & en même tems si rare d'une régularité à laquelle rien n'échappe; & ensuite pourque si vous le jugiez à propros, l'on pût faire des recherches dans le Bureau de la poste de Washington, au sujet d'une négligence qui pourrait être quelquefois fatale au service public.

Lorsque Monsieur le Colonel *Monroe*, passera par Philadelphie, j'irai lui présenter mes respects & remplir la Commission agréable dont vous me chargez auprès de lui—Aussitôt la lecture de votre lettre j'ai fait mettre à part les trois ouvrages de votre choix—Je vous les adresserai à la premiere occasion favorable, avec la philosophie d'Epicure en Latin, par Gassendi—J'augmenterai cet envoi d'un petit Helvetius, en 10 volumes qui me serait parvenu de New York depuis un mois, si la Navigation de notre rivière n'eut eté interceptée par les Glaces—

J'ai cru sentir en lisant votre lettre que vous seriez charmé de posseder les seules *Reliques* littéraires qui nous restent probablement de l'immortel Franklin, *Saint* bien plus Grand qu'aucun de ceux du Calendrier du peuple le plus dévot, puisqu'il a contribué par ses *miracles* à fonder une Nation, où Dieu est adoré suivant la Conscience, & où ses interpretes ne sont que ce qu'ils devraient être partout de simples ministres de la Religion; veuillez donc les accepter malgré le desir religieux de les garder qu'elles m'avaient inspiré, & pour que vous ayez un *reliquaire* complèt, J'y Joindrai un ouvrage en 3 volumes intitulé *Miscellanies of America*, ou se trouvent dans le 1er Tome plusieurs notes Marginales au crayon & à la plume, que je crois être du même Grand Homme c'est une offrande que vous fais & qui vous est du puisque vous êtes l'ami & l'un des Collaborateurs de l'illustre mort. Aucun Grec ne fut surpris de voir Philoctète posseder les armes d'Hercule—

Recevez avec votre bonté ordinaire l'assurance respectueuse d'une estime profondément sentie

Votre tres devoué Serviteur N. G. Dufief

EDITORS' TRANSLATION

Sir, 14 Feb. 1803

You will see from the enclosed certificate that the letter with which you honored me on the 4th did not arrive until today. I am sending you this evidence, first to vindicate myself from any suspicion that I might lack punctuality toward you, who, in your eminent position, give so glorious and at the same time so rare an example of punctuality from which nothing escapes; and second so that, if you judge it appropriate, you can request an investigation of negligence in the Washington post office that could endanger public welfare.

When Colonel Monroe comes through Philadelphia, I will present my respects and render the pleasant service you entrusted to me. Upon receiving your letter, I immediately set aside the three books you chose. I will send them on the first possible occasion, along with Gassendi's work in Latin on Epicurus's philosophy. I will include a small Helvetius, in 10 volumes, which would have reached me from New York a month ago if ice had not impeded navigation on our river.

Reading your letter, I sensed that you would enjoy owning what are probably the only remaining literary relics from the immortal Franklin, who was a much greater saint than any of those on the calendar of the most devout believers, since his miracles helped found a nation where God is worshipped by following one's conscience and where his interpreters are no more than what they should be everywhere: simple ministers of religion. Please accept these books despite my own fervent desire to keep them for myself. For you to have a complete reliquary, I will include a three-volume work entitled *Miscellanies on America*, whose first volume contains several marginal notes, in pencil and pen, that I believe to be from the same Great Man. This is a gift; it is rightfully yours, since you are the friend and collaborator of the illustrious deceased. No Greek was surprised to see Philoctetes inherit the arms of Hercules—

Receive with your usual kindness the respectful assurance of a deeply felt esteem.

Your devoted servant N. G. Dufief

RC (DLC); at foot of text: "Thomas Jefferson, President of the United States"; endorsed by TJ as received 19 Feb. and so recorded in SJL. Enclosure not found.

For the three works (TROIS OUVRAGES) that TJ wanted to purchase from Benjamin Franklin's library, see TJ to Dufief, 4 Feb.

In March 1802, TJ had asked Dufief to obtain some books from France, including a work by Pierre GASSENDI on the philosophy of Epicurus and a small-format edition of the works of Claude Adrien Helvétius (Vol. 37:113-14).

RELIQUES LITTÉRAIRES: the pamphlets by Matthew Wheelock and Allen Ramsay from Franklin's collection; see Dufief's letter of 31 Jan. and TJ's reply of 4 Feb.

INTITULÉ MISCELLANIES OF AMERICA: in three volumes he called *Miscellanies on America*, Franklin collected 13 printed tracts by various authors that had been published in the period from 1775 to 1781 and related to the colonies' break from Great Britain. The volumes, which were among the books that TJ sold to the Library of Congress in 1815, contain notations by Franklin (Sowerby, Nos. 3056-3068).

DE VOIR PHILOCTÈTE POSSEDER LES ARMES D'HERCULE: in Greek mythology, when no one else would light a pyre to put Hercules, who was slowly dying of poison, out of his misery, Philoctetes agreed to do it. In gratitude, Hercules gave Philoctetes his bow and arrows (Richard Stoneman, *Greek Mythology: An Encyclopedia of Myth and Legend* [London, 1991], 91).

From Rolfe Eldridge

Subpœna Buckingham
14th. February 1803

DEAR SIR

I have lately seen two Gentlemen from the State of North Carolina who informed me that the Heirs of Lord Granville had commenced a Suit in the Grand Federal Court against that State to recover a large body of Land there, which Suit will come on Tryal at the next Court which will be held in the Fedral City. My Wife and her Sisters, claim a right to five thousand acres of Land in that State called the Han or Sasapahan fields Tract a Moiety of ten thousand acres granted by Lord Granville to Sir Richard Everard who was father to Susanna Meade their Grand Mother under whom she claims and who devised the above Land to them by her last Will and Testament, they informed me that my Wife and her Sisters Title depended on Lord Granvilles and advised me not to Sue the Tenants on their Lands until that Suit was determined, as the State of North Carolina had granted Patents for their Lands to the People who were tenants of Mrs. Meade on rent. Patrick Henry Esqr. was employed by me to commence Suits against the Tenants in possession who had all the Title papers and informed me that the Title was very good but as he was groing old & had lost his Son Edward who he depended on to assist him declined the prosecution and nothing done since. If it will not be too much trouble for you to have an enquiry made at the Clerks Office of the Federal Court respecting that Suit and inform me what you think would be the best way my Wife and her Sisters shou'd proceed in order to recover their Land shall esteem it a singular favour and hope you'll excuse my freedom

I am your real friend & obedt. servt. ROLFE ELDRIDGE

P.S. all the Title papers I expect are at Mrs. Henrys if Mr. Henry did not send them to Andrew Meades except the Grant from the Crown of England to Lord Granville under whom Sir Richard Everard claims which I expect is in the Clerks Office of the Federal Court & which I expect will be necessary to support my Wife & her Sisters claim. R:E

RC (DLC); endorsed by TJ as received 26 Feb. and so recorded in SJL; also endorsed by TJ: "to enquire if the suit of Ld Granville v. Davie be on the docquet of the Supreme court, & when it will be tried."

Rolfe Eldridge (b. 1744) had served as clerk of Buckingham County, Virginia, since 1770. He married Susanna Everard Walker in 1773. His wife was the granddaughter of Susanna Everard Meade and the great-granddaughter of Sir Richard Everard, who served as the last proprietary governor of North Carolina from 1725 to 1731 (VMHB, 46 [1938], 176; WMQ, 1st ser., 18 [1910], 290-1; 20 [1912], 206; William S. Powell, ed., *Dictionary of North Carolina Biography*, 6 vols. [Chapel Hill, 1979-96], 2:171-2).

HEIRS OF LORD GRANVILLE HAD COMMENCED A SUIT: John Carteret, first earl of Granville, was a descendant and heir of the original Lords Proprietors of Carolina created by Charles II of England in the 1660s. When the remaining Proprietors sold their shares in Carolina back to the crown in the late 1720s, Granville refused and instead received one-eighth of the land, consisting of much of the northern half of North Carolina. Granville administered this estate, the Granville District, from England through agents, who granted lands to new immigrants and collected modest quitrents from existing settlers. The American Revolution brought title to the land into dispute and the state of North Carolina began making grants in the district by its own authority after the war. In 1801, devisees of Lord Granville brought ejectment actions against Nathaniel Allen, Josiah Collins, and William R. Davie, each of whom had received grants in the Granville District from the state in the 1780s. News of the suit against Davie began appearing in newspapers in June 1802 and the case of *Granville's Devisee v. Allen* came before the federal circuit court in North Carolina in 1805, where the jury found in favor of the defendants. The case was then appealed to the United States Supreme Court and lingered on its docket until 1817, when it was dismissed with the consent of both parties (A. Roger Ekirch, *"Poor Carolina": Politics and Society in Colonial North Carolina, 1729-1776* [Chapel Hill, 1981], 127-33; Henry G. Conner, "The Granville Estate and North Carolina," *University of Pennsylvania Law Review and American Law Register*, 62 [1914], 671-97; Marshall, *Papers*, 6:400-1; William S. Powell, ed., *Encyclopedia of North Carolina* [Chapel Hill, 2006], 524-5; *Philadelphia Gazette*, 19 June 1802; *National Intelligencer*, 22 Oct. 1802).

Patrick Henry's SON EDWARD died in 1793 (Charles P. Blunt, IV, *Patrick Henry: The Henry County Years, 1779-1784* [Danville, Va., 1976], 11).

To Farmer's Brother and Others

BROTHERS OF THE SENECA, ONEIDA & ONONDAGUA NATIONS Feb. 14. 1803.

I give you a hearty welcome on your arrival at the Seat of our Government, where I am glad to take you by the hand and to renew the Chain of Friendship between us: and I am thankful to the Great Spirit who has preserved you in health during your long journey at this inclement season of the year, and am hopefull his protection will cover you on your return.

I sincerely lament with you, Brothers, the unfortunate murder which was committed by one of your people on one of ours at Buffaloe Creek—It has been one of the many evils produced by the abuse of spiritous liquors—and it is with sincere pleasure I learn that your people have in a great measure[1] abandoned the use of them—You ask an explanation how it has happened, that, our Treaty having provided that injuries done by either party to the other shall be settled by Commissioners, the murderer, in this case, should be tried by the Laws of New York; to which laws you say you never gave your consent and therefore are not subject to them—The words of the Treaty, Brothers, are, "that for injuries done by individuals on either side, no private revenge or retaliation shall take place, but, instead thereof, complaint shall be made by the party injured to the other, by the six nations, or any of them, to the President of the U.S. or the Superintendant by him appointed, and, by the Superintendant or other person appointed by the President, to the principal Chiefs of the six nations, or of the nation to which the offender belongs: and such prudent measures shall then be pursued as shall be necessary to preserve our peace & friendship unbroken, *until the Legislature or Great Council of the U. States shall make other equitable provision for the purpose.*" In pursuance of this agreement in the Treaty, the Great Council of the U.S. have made provision by a law that, where any murder shall be committed by any of our people on yours, or of yours on ours, the murderer shall be punished with death—In this case the murder was committed within the lands belonging to New York, and therefore the judges of New York are the persons authorised to enquire into the truth of the fact, and to punish it, if true—And had the murder been committed at the same place by an Englishman, a Frenchman, a Spaniard[2] an American, or a person of any other nation the same judges would have tried it, by the same rules, and subject to the same punishment; So that you are placed on the same footing, in this respect, as the most powerful & the most friendly nations are, and as we are ourselves. As the State authority, where the murder was committed, is appointed to enquire into the fact & to punish it, so they are entrusted to remit the punishment, if they[3] find it was committed under circumstances which entitle the murderer to mercy. And I have great hopes, Brothers, that those who enquire into the case may find grounds for pardoning the offender, and that he may again be safely restored to you.

You ask that the Lands which you hold at Buffaloe Creek, Allegany and all other reserves, now in your possession, may remain yours, and descend to your children, and that we will confirm your title to these lands, and oppose any chief who may in future come forward to sell. These lands are yours, Brothers, we confirm the title to them for yourselves and your children, against our people, and all others, except yourselves. No person shall ever take one foot of them by any bargain with one or a few unauthorised chiefs, nor any otherwise than[4] with the consent of your nation, fully[5] given by your deputies, according to your own rules & customs—When the nation at large[6] shall see an interest in making any bargain respecting their own lands,[7] they certainly would not chuse we should oppose what they judge for their own interest.[8] All we can rightfully do is to maintain them in the exercise of all their rights over the country they possess; and this we will do against fraud and force.

With respect to the residence of our Superintendant, or an assistant, at Konon-daigua, to the payment of your monies at Albany, the delivery of the goods for the Oneidas, Onondaiguas & Stockbridge Indians at Konon-daigua, and the continuance of the blacksmiths and gunsmiths, the Secretary of War will consult with you, & will endeavor to accomodate these matters to your and our convenience. Whatever he says to you on that subject, you are to consider as if said by myself.

We hope with you, Brothers, that the tomahawk is for ever buried between us; never more to be taken up. Peace and friendship is our best interest.[9] By war we can injure one another: but no good man can receive pleasure from doing injuries. We wish to see you advance in the cultivation of the earth, in manufacturing clothes, and in whatever may contribute to feed & clothe your people, and make them comfortable & happy. In this way your numbers will increase, & the hardships & wants you now experience, from the uncertain pursuit of wild beasts, will be exchanged for plentiful living, produced by less labor from the soil you live on.

I pray you, Brothers to carry for me to your nation, assurances of the constant friendship & protection of the United States to them.

TH: JEFFERSON

RC (NPV: Jasper Parrish Papers); in a clerk's hand, signed and dated by TJ. FC (Lb in DNA: RG 75, LSIA); in a clerk's hand; dated 12 Feb.; at head of text: "A talk delivered by the President to a deputation from the Six-nations of Indians." Dft (DLC); dated 14 Feb. Recorded in SJL as to "Farmer's brother et al. of Senecas, Oneidas & Onondagues."

Farmer's Brother (d. 1814), who may have been born in the 1730s or as early as 1725, was a Seneca sachem, or civil leader, and had been a prominent warrior. He,

Red Jacket, and Young King were leaders of the Buffalo Creek Senecas, frequently in political opposition to Cornplanter and Handsome Lake. Farmer's Brother joined Red Jacket in bringing about the sale of the tract on the Niagara River and in breaking into the customs storehouse in 1802 (see TJ to Handsome Lake, 12 Feb.). He participated in meetings with Timothy Pickering, Robert Morris, and missionaries, often acting as moderator or introductory speaker at councils in which Red Jacket was the primary orator. Farmer's Brother had made at least one visit to Philadelphia, where his oldest grandson had gone for an education, and he later reported that he had found the young man's schooling in the city to be primarily in the arts of gentlemanly debauchery (Granville Ganter, ed., *The Collected Speeches of Sagoyewatha, or Red Jacket* [Syracuse, N.Y., 2006], xxvi, 4, 6, 9, 14, 15, 42, 74-5, 87, 93, 97, 105, 281-2; Anthony F. C. Wallace, *The Death and Rebirth of the Seneca* [New York, 1969], 131, 137, 145, 172-3, 180-3, 205; Thomas S. Abler, *Cornplanter: Chief Warrior of the Allegany Senecas* [Syracuse, N.Y., 2007], 147, 151; Christopher Densmore, *Red Jacket: Iroquois Diplomat and Orator* [Syracuse, N.Y., 1999], 58-9, 84; Alan Taylor, *The Divided Ground: Indians, Settlers, and the Northern Borderland of the American Revolution* [New York, 2006], 271, 274).

GLAD TO TAKE YOU BY THE HAND: Farmer's Brother and his delegation probably received permission before traveling to Washington, Dearborn having corresponded with Callender Irvine during the autumn about a pass for four unnamed chiefs (Dearborn to Irvine, 19 Nov., in DNA: RG 75, LSIA). The other Seneca group in the capital city in February, representing the council held on the Allegheny in January, would not have had time to wait for permission before setting off for Washington—and apparently did not get to have a formal conference with TJ and Dearborn (see TJ to Cornplanter, 11 Feb., and to Handsome Lake, 12 Feb.).

The UNFORTUNATE MURDER was the case of Stiff-Armed George, which had been a source of discontent among the Senecas for several months. On 14 Feb., Dearborn wrote to George Clinton on TJ's authority, urging the governor to pardon the man (see Vol. 38:274n).

An article of a 1794 TREATY between the United States and the Six Nations contained the clauses about INJURIES DONE BY EITHER PARTY. Farmer's Brother signed the treaty (along with Red Jacket, Cornplanter, and Handsome Lake). PROVISION BY A LAW: articles on punishment of crimes committed by Indians and by whites against Indians appeared in acts of Congress of May 1796 and March 1802 (Charles J. Kappler, comp. and ed., *Indian Affairs: Laws and Treaties*, 5 vols. [Washington, D.C., 1975], 2:36; U.S. Statutes at Large, 1:469-74; 2:139-46).

AS IF SAID BY MYSELF: Dearborn addressed Farmer's Brother's delegation on the 14th. "In addition to what your Father, the President of the United States has said to you in his answer to your talk made before him since your arrival at this place," Dearborn stated, he was authorized by TJ to say that they were appointing Jasper Parrish, who had experience as an interpreter, as a subagent. Dearborn made that appointment the following day, instructing Parrish to reside at Canandaigua but to spend at least three months each year among the Oneidas, Onondagas, Stockbridge Mohicans, Cayugas, and Indians who lived along the Genesee River. Irvine would continue as principal agent, residing part of each year at Buffalo Creek and spending time in other towns of the Six Nations tribes. Dearborn would arrange for future payments of money, clothing, and farming implements to be made in a way that would be convenient for each Indian nation. Those annuities must be distributed by the government's agents, he indicated (and deductions would be made to cover the expenses of making the distributions). Because of "the friendly disposition of your father the President towards his Red Children," blacksmithing operations would be established at Buffalo Creek, in the Oneidas' territory for them and neighboring tribes, and among the Senecas on the Allegheny River. Smiths at Niagara and Canandaigua would serve smaller tribes. The secretary of war authorized Irvine to use $2,500 of the annuities of the Six Nations tribes for tools, farm implements, and payments to blacksmiths. As Irvine and Parrish circulated among the Indians' towns in the course of a year, they would help to advance "improvements in husbandry and domestic manufactories" and resolve disputes. Perhaps in response to rumors of French intrigue among the Indian tribes, Dearborn warned that "evil designing people often attempt to fill your ears with stories calculated to excite uneasiness in your minds." Such attempts should be reported to the government's Indian agents, he urged, "as the most sure means of preserving the friendship which so happily exists at present between your Nations and your father the President." Dearborn also acknowledged the divisions among Seneca leaders. "As peace and friendship among yourselves as well as with your white neighbours is essential to your general happiness," he stated, "permit me to advise you to avoid all party quarrels and disputes between your respective Nations and Towns and to use every means in your power to heal any differences or jealousies which may now exist between any of your Nations or parts of Nations, and especially between those who live near Buffaloe Creek and those who live on the Allegany river." He declared that "without harmony among yourselves you can never be happy" (Dearborn address, 14 Feb.; Dearborn to Parrish, 15 Feb.; and to Irvine, 15 Feb., in DNA: RG 75, LSIA; Vol. 36:634n; Vol. 37:31).

[1] Preceding four words interlined in Dft in place of "entirely."

[2] Here in Dft TJ canceled "or any other."

[3] Here in Dft TJ canceled "think."

[4] Preceding passage beginning "by any bargain" interlined in Dft in place of "but."

[5] Word interlined in Dft.

[6] Preceding two words interlined in Dft.

[7] Here in Dft TJ canceled "we ought not."

[8] Here in Dft TJ canceled "but as long."

[9] Here in Dft TJ canceled "war may do great injur."

From James Jackson

SIR Washington Feby 14th 1803

When I did myself the honor of waiting on you on Saturday, I was in hopes of finding you disengaged and that I could be indulged with a few moments of private attention—I wished to have shewn you two or three letters from Men who are true Republicans—have been warm and Zealous advocates for your gaining the Presidency and continue firm supporters of your administration—They express their fears that a change in the sentiments of the people is gaining ground in Georgia and all impute it to one cause—the not obtaining as the deed of Cession between the United States and Georgia promised them the whole of the Okmulgee fork—the failure of which at the late Treaty they say was the fault of Mr Hawkins—that he gives private talks whilst he wears an open countenance to the wishes of the Government—and that they consider him as the Chief of the Indian tribes more connected with them than the White people and therefore not as the Superintendant of the United States or the friend of the State of Georgia or her Citizens—that in short—they give up all hopes of procuring an extension of boundary to the Okmulgee as well as the lands left out by the line of 1798 which Mr Hawkins officiously run with the Creeks who had no claim to them whilst he continues or unless he has positive orders to procure those lands in a given time or leave the nation—The Federalists they inform me persuade the people and too many are easily led away by them in every State—that no intention of procuring a further extension to the Okmulgee, or for the lands so left out exists—that the small slip along the Oconee altogether out of shape for any publick purpose it being impossible to form it into a County not being above sixteen miles wide is all they will ever obtain under the present administration or the boasted Cession—that even their Senators are not friendly to an extension, and that they would have stood a better chance under the resolution of Congress passed under the former administration—to restore Talassee County altogether or to procure the Okmulgee fork in lieu of it—That myself and others had duped them by teaching them to believe that the effect of a change[1]—of the Administration would be the obtaining the Okmulgee fork & Talassee County immediately for them and that this was evident from the slips only being obtained after the Cession had made it an express stipulation—Such Sir are the contents of the letters I meant to have shewn you and must beg indulgence in having been thus prolix in relating them—Two of those Gentlemen who have written me were Electors who voted for you as President with myself when Mr Adams was elected our vote joined Governor Clinton with you—As to Mr Hawkins—I acknowledge that I not only voted for him but warmly supported your nomination of him as a Commissioner and I believe I might add saved him from rejection as well as General Pickens, and which may appear strange when I say that I saw enough of Mr Hawkins at the treaty of Coleraine—I know that he there with the then Agent Seagrove held private talks and know further that whilst the Commissioners of Georgia were preparing their talks and proposals for a Cession the Women of the Neighbourhood were collected—and whilst the talk delivered by myself was given the Indians the Ladies were introduced into the square with the Commissioners of the U States & those of Georgia—which of itself would have blasted all our expectations if they had been ever so much disposed to sell the land we asked—considering a talk where a Woman is present as altogether an old Womans story not worth minding—That the Indians were disposed to sell I can bring proof and most sincerely believe it would have taken place had it not been for Mr Hawkins, his Colleagues and the Agent who used every means even in enhancing the value of the lands in the minds of the Indians in their power to frustrate it—I have published all I have here said about the Coleraine treaty in the Publick Newspapers—so that I care not who knows it—It maybe asked indeed if I knew all this how I came to support him—I reply—Because, I did not wish at so early a day that any of your nominations should afford a triumph to your enemies by a rejection, and the Federalists all stood ready to seize every opening and I further thought that gratitude to you—for the nomination in the first place and to the Senators from Georgia for supporting it in the second would have induced other conduct than that at Coleraine and that he would have aided in the mutual interest of the General and State Governments that of extending the boundary South and South West of the U States as far as practicable—But if I had been actuated by Friendly motives to Mr Hawkins in his support—I should have reasons now for a change So many lift up their voices against him not only from Georgia but Tenessee and Kentucky I understand has complaints that I must believe him hostile to any extension of boundary or the procuring any road in that quarter as interfering with his Sovereignty—for such the people view his power as a chief of the tribes and as is certainly alluded to in the Notes of Messrs Carnes Eensly & Harris, by the expressions of another Agent—that the Indians can dispose of no lands without the consent of their friend & agent, which must mean Mr Hawkins, whilst the President of the United States is not even hinted at.

I am sorry to observe from the conversation of Saturday that the Secretary of War seems to me to be taking the ground of his predecessors—to support Indian Agents against Independent States—Had I not interfered, a remonstrance against the proceedings of the Commissioners at the late treaty and the Superintendant would have taken place at the last Session of the State Legislature—I prevailed on several zealous Republicans to drop it assuring them of the good intentions of the present administration towards the State and that I had no doubt of a further extension by another treaty this Summer—should this not take place, however light it may be viewed as respects the whole continent, I dread the consequence as respects Georgia, if her Legislature becomes warm and it will meet in May—the people will follow—I confess I did not expect the Secretary to be so warm in favor of Mr Hawkins and the Agents against the poor Georgians who seem always to be placed by the War department as respects Indians in the background—I cannot account for it at present unless a Mr Hill Mr Hawkins's foreman in all business has been giving him some wonderful stories in favor of his Master & against the poor Georgians and as he is here with one or two others of Hawkins's partizans from Greene County I have little doubt but that the bridge story over the Oconee and the other of the declaration of a Member of the Georgia Legislature's declaration that all the fork belonged to Georgia and she would take it came from him—the one of which I believe as much as I do the other and am of opinion they are both fabricated for the occasion—Should however the first be true the Indians have now no right to complain as the land belongs to the State on both sides the Okonee—and it must be considered as a silly apology in Mr Hawkins—to say, that the silly speech of a silly Member should be of that consequence either to prevent his using his influence to obtain a further Cession or the Indians to make one or that the silly speech should be considered as the voice of the State of Georgia

Pardon me Sir for this length and the candor I have exercised—I cannot act otherwise where I feel the interest I do in the welfare of the general Administration and the State I represent—I must be further indulged to beseech you Sir to consider the present critical moment France is certainly about to possess herself of Louisiana—She may abide by the existing Treaties and she may not—she is at any rate a subtle and a very politic power she will naturally wish when she is so close a neighbour to prevent as much as possible an extension of our temporary boundaries in order to prevent the increase of our population towards her frontier—Her emissaries which find their way into every Court & among all the hordes of the eastern World will be found among the Indian tribes here and even if they should not reach the Creeks altho Hill says one is daily expected there yet if they persuade the Chickasaws and Choctaws not to part with their lands—Runners from them will immediately inform the Creeks and Cherokees and the Federalists will triumph at a failure—it strikes me Sir that the present is the moment to secure what lands and roads can be obtained from all those tribes—and on it depend in a great measure in my humble opinion not only Republican principles in that quarter united with a love of the present administration but a lasting and never to be eradicated affection for the general Government and the most steady determination at the hazard of life and fortune to meet any event should it be the lot of the United States to be visited by that scourge of Nations War

Assuring you of my unfeigned attachment to our common country and personally to yourself I have the honor to be Sir Yr most Obed Servt

JAS JACKSON

You sometime since enquired of me if another set of Commissioners of bankruptcy was necessary for Augusta or rather Louisville district—I deem another set necessary and beg leave to recommend

Thomas Collier Merchant } Louisville
Cowles Mead Attorney } Augusta

the other two I must leave to Mr Baldwin & the Representatives

Mr B has agreed to those

RC (DLC); above postscript: "The President of the U States"; endorsed by TJ as received 14 Feb. and so recorded in SJL.

Jackson wrote on a Monday; the previous SATURDAY was 12 Feb.

DEED OF CESSION: for the agreement on Georgia's western bounds negotiated by federal and state commissioners and the TREATY to clear the Creek Indians' title, see TJ's second message to the Senate on 27 Dec.

LINE OF 1798: Jackson was governor of Georgia in 1798, when the legislature recalled the state's commissioners from a survey by Benjamin Hawkins to mark a section of the boundary between Georgia and the Creeks' territory. Commissioners from the Creek nation participated in the demarcation, which Hawkins completed without the Georgia delegates. At the time, Hawkins presumed that anyone from Georgia found to be living on the Indians' side of the line would have to relocate (Thomas Foster, ed., *The Collected Works of Benjamin Hawkins, 1796-1810* [Tuscaloosa, Ala., 2003], 242-3, 287-8, 294, 300; Merritt B. Pound, *Benjamin Hawkins—Indian Agent* [Athens, Ga., 1951], 130-1).

In February 1799, a RESOLUTION approved by the House of Representatives in response to a memorial from the Georgia legislature called for a treaty between the United States and the Creeks to enable Georgia to recover the lands it claimed as Tallassee County "or other lands on the frontier of the said State, which may be deemed equivalent thereto" (JHR, 3:461; Vol. 33:178n).

TWO OF THOSE GENTLEMEN: Jackson, Edward Telfair, Charles Abercrombie, and William Barnett were the presidential ELECTORS for Georgia in 1796. They all cast their votes for TJ and George Clinton (Savannah *Columbian Museum*, 6 Dec. 1796; *Philadelphia Gazette*, 29 Dec. 1796).

VOTED FOR HIM: in the Senate in January 1802, Jackson voted to confirm a number of TJ's interim appointments, including Hawkins, James Wilkinson, and Andrew PICKENS as commissioners for treaties with the Creeks and other tribes. The vote in the Senate on the collective nominations was 16 in favor and 14 opposed. TJ had made the appointments of Hawkins and the others months earlier, in the spring of 1801 (JEP, 1:405; Vol. 34:130n; Vol. 36:332, 336n).

Hawkins was a commissioner for the United States and Jackson a commissioner for Georgia at treaty talks with the Creeks at Colerain (COLERAINE) on the Saint Marys River in 1796. The federal and state delegations were at odds through the course of the negotiations, which concerned land cessions. The Creeks were unwilling to yield land to the state but signed a treaty with the U.S. commissioners, leaving Georgians bitterly dissatisfied with the outcome of the conference. At the time, James SEAGROVE was the U.S. agent for the Indians in the region (Pound, *Hawkins*, 84-98; Florette Henri, *The Southern Indians and Benjamin Hawkins, 1796-1816* [Norman, Okla., 1986], 54-8; ASP, *Indian Affairs*, 1:586-616; Vol. 36:155n).

EMISSARIES: the first French official to reach Louisiana, the civil prefect Pierre Clément Laussat, sailed from France on 10 Jan. and did not arrive in New Orleans until 26 Mch. However, according to one hearsay account that reached the Choctaws by mid-February, "the French are in New-Orleans," a Chickasaw leader had talked to them there, and a conference between Chickasaw chiefs and French officials was expected in the spring (*Charleston Courier*, 14 May; E. Wilson Lyon, *Louisiana in French Diplomacy, 1759-1804* [Norman, Okla., 1974], 137-8; Madison, *Papers*, *Sec. of State Ser.*, 4:130n).

Thomas Collier and Cowles Mead received appointments as COMMISSIONERS OF BANKRUPTCY on 1 Mch. (list of commissions, in Lb in DNA: RG 59, MPTPC; TJ to Madison, 1 Mch.; Vol. 37:711; Appendix I).

[1] MS: "chang."

From Charles Willson Peale

DEAR SIR Museum Feby. 14th. 1803

The enclosed essay on health is dressed to render it more worthy of your acceptance, and in this neither seeking compliments on it, or supposing it can give you any light, but knowing you will appreciate my Motive for making the Publication, that of bringing some of my acquaintance to reflection and then reformation. Should that be the case in a single instance my labour will not be thrown away, I shall be well paid for my trouble.

No letter from my Sons since the 14th of Octr. last, I am more than anxious about their success—Rembrandt will not write to give me pain if he can help it. They may be too much engaged to seek for conveyances, and but little acquainted with the various ways of sending to America. As their next letters will be the most interresting, I will not fail to send you notice as soon as I can.

The Trees in the State-House-Garden are in Mourning; with fallen leaves, not crape—Their founder Mr. Vaughan Senr. has departed this life! The Philosophical Hall would not have been reared but through the Industry & perseverance of the good old man!

May you Dr Sir long enjoy good health & america be thankful for your Services— C W PEALE

RC (DLC); at foot of text: "His Excelly. Thos Jefferson Esqr."; endorsed by TJ as received 19 Feb. and so recorded in SJL. PoC (PPAmP: Peale-Sellers Papers). Enclosure: Charles W. Peale, *An Epistle to a Friend on the Means of Preserving Health, Promoting Happiness; and Prolonging the Life of Man to its Natural Period* (Philadelphia, 1803); Sowerby, No. 912; Shaw-Shoemaker, No. 4829.

ESSAY ON HEALTH: Peale probably had copies of his *Epistle to a Friend* in hand from the Philadelphia printer Jane Aitken—daughter of the deceased Robert Aitken—by 14 Feb., for on that day he sent the treatise to Madison as well as to TJ, and in neither case did he refer to it as an unpublished manuscript. He advertised the pamphlet in the *Aurora* beginning 1 Mch. Although Peale framed the tract as an "epistle" to an unnamed friend "in a public station" and gave it a dateline, closing, signature, and postscript, he was following a literary convention rather than publishing an actual letter. He did begin writing the piece as a letter to TJ dated 3 Mch. 1802, but did not send it. Peale stated in a preface that he had been moved to write upon "hearing of the indisposition" of the intended receiver of the letter, and he opened the epistle with the declaration: "I have heard my dear Friend, that your health is much impaired." He may have been reacting to unspecified reports about TJ's health—Gallatin, for example, heard in January 1802 that TJ had been "unwell"—or perhaps had learned something from Benjamin Rush, to whom TJ confided, in a letter of 20 Dec. 1801, that he was concerned about a "flaw" in his health. Rush's own letter to TJ in response to that revelation was dated 12 Mch. 1802. Peale related in his preface that after he set out to write a letter to his friend, his thoughts "naturally led to reflections that were not necessary to communicate to the person it was intended for" and he decided to make the piece a longer work for a broader audience. As published, the essay with the preface was 46 pages long (Peale, *Papers*, v. 2, pt. 1:474n, 489, 491; Peale, *Epistle to a Friend*; Madison, *Papers*, *Sec. of State Ser.*, 4:321; Philadelphia *Aurora*, 1 Mch.; ANB, s.v. Robert Aitken; Vol. 36:178, 368; Vol. 37:68).

APPRECIATE MY MOTIVE: "I have made innumerable experiments on the means of preserving health," Peale declared in his essay. He argued that personal habits detrimental to health were the result of a lack of rational analysis of alternatives. A person could "live to extreme old age, without disease," he wrote, by "*enjoying* every good gift and *abusing* none." Peale advocated "not a life of privation, but rather of every enjoyment." In his discourse he commented on diet, methods of preparing food, posture, exercise, and the relationship of mind, character, and physical health. In a postscript written after his initial composition of the essay, Peale discussed his son Raphaelle's experiments with water filtration, a recipe for making bread, and methods for cooking with steam (Peale, *Papers*, v. 2, pt. 1:489-513; Dft in PPAmP: Peale-Sellers Papers).

The British merchant Samuel VAUGHAN, the father of John and Benjamin Vaughan, died in England in 1802. In the mid-1780s, he had resided in Philadelphia, where he designed the landscaping of the yard adjoining the State House, was responsible for the plantings at Gray's Gardens, raised funds for the American Philosophical Society, and helped promote the completion of the society's building, Philosophical Hall. Vaughan was born in 1720 (Sarah P. Stetson, "The Philadelphia Sojourn of Samuel Vaughan," PMHB, 73 [1949], 459-74; Mary Vaughan Marvin, *Benjamin Vaughan, 1751-1835* [Hallowell, Me., 1979], 1).

To the Senate

GENTLEMEN OF THE SENATE

I nominate Aaron Vale of New York to be commercial agent of the United States at L'orient in France.

TH: JEFFERSON
Feb. 14. 1803.

RC (DNA: RG 46, EPEN; 7th Cong., 2d sess.); endorsed by Senate clerks. PrC (DLC). Recorded in SJL with notation "nomination of Vale."

Meriwether Lewis delivered this nomination to the Senate on 14 Feb. and the next day it was read and ordered to lie for consideration. A week later it was referred to Uriah Tracy, Robert Wright, and Dwight Foster, the same committee considering eight of TJ's nominations of 2 Feb. The Senate approved the appointment of Vail (VALE) on 1 Mch. (JEP, 1:442-3, 445, 446).

To the Senate and the House of Representatives

GENTLEMEN OF THE SENATE AND OF THE HOUSE OF REPRESENTATIVES.

In obedience to the Ordinance for the government of the territories of the United States, requiring that the laws adopted by the Governor & judges thereof shall be reported to Congress from time to time, I now transmit those which have been adopted in the Indiana territory from January 1801. to February 1802. as[1] forwarded to the office of the Secretary of State.

TH: JEFFERSON
Feb. 14. 1803.

RC (DNA: RG 233, PM, 7th Cong., 2d sess.); endorsed by a House clerk. PrC (DLC); lacks emendation (see note below). RC (DNA: RG 46, LPPM, 7th Cong., 2d sess.); endorsed by a Senate clerk. Both letters recorded in SJL and connected by a brace to notation "laws of Indiana." Enclosures: copies of 12 laws and resolutions passed by the governor and judges of the Indiana Territory from 19 Jan. 1801 to 3 Feb. 1802 (Trs in DNA: RG 233, PM, endorsed by a House clerk; Trs in DNA: RG 46, LPPM, endorsed by a Senate clerk).

ORDINANCE FOR THE GOVERNMENT OF THE TERRITORIES: that is, the Northwest Ordinance of 1787, the terms of which were adopted by the act of Congress of 7 May 1800 creating the Indiana Territory (*Terr. Papers*, 2:42-3; U.S. Statutes at Large, 2:58-9).

TJ's message and its accompanying papers were received by the House of Representatives on 14 Feb. and by the Senate the following day. The House ordered them to lie on the table, while the Senate referred them to a committee consisting of Joseph Anderson, John Breckinridge, and DeWitt Clinton (JHR, 4:341; JS, 3:265). They were subsequently printed as *Message from the President of the United States, Transmitting the Laws of the Indiana Territory of the United States, from January, 1801, to February, 1802* (Washington, D.C., 1803; Shaw-Shoemaker, No. 3365).

[1] Word altered from "and." RC in RG 46: "as."

From James Burnham

SIR, Beverly February 15—1803

Having been informed by my Friend the Hon. Mr Cutler that he had shewn you some specimens of our Manufacture, and that you had asked him some questions, particularly respecting the Wadding, which he could not answer, I observed to him in reply that I would do myself the honor of writing you on the subject.—The cotton is carded in an entire fleece (as we call it), then laid on a board & wet with gum, and set aside until it is dry—My intention was when writing Mr. Cutler to have enclosed several samples of different kinds of our

Manufacture, but find they will make a Package too large to incumber the Mail with, and shall embrace the first conveyance by water from this neighborhood—I requested of Mr. Cutler to lay in a Claim for a Patent for making the wadding: altho' I cannot claim the invention of it originally, yet I can say that I made the first ever made in the United States, and without having seen a piece of imported larger than a cent— Large quantities have been imported within two years and some of it retailed at the enormous price of 80 cents pr. piece. We should be very glad to make almost any given number of Pieces, & sell them at a price which would afford the retailer a handsome profit at 33 cents—

As it is not convenient to send the samples by the mail as contemplated, I omit any observations which might otherwise be made on the several articles which we manufacture—

I flatter myself Sir, that any communications I may make respecting the subject will not be esteemed as troublesome—

I am Sir respectfully your humble Servant

James Burnham

RC (DLC); at foot of text: "Thomas Jefferson Esquire President of the United States"; endorsed by TJ as received 2 Mch. and so recorded in SJL.

James Burnham served for a number of years as superintendent of the Beverly (Massachusetts) Cotton Manufactory, among the earliest cotton mills in the United States. He represented Beverly in the Massachusetts House of Representatives for a term and in 1801 erected the water-powered Bass River Cotton Manufactory, which he ran until selling off his interest in October 1803. After this, he appears to have moved to Newburyport for a short time before settling in Portland, Maine (Robert W. Lovett, "The Beverly Cotton Manufactory: Or Some New Light on an Early Cotton Mill," *Bulletin of the Business Historical Society*, 26 [1952], 227; William R. Bagnall, *The Textile Industries of the United States Including Sketches and Notices of Cotton, Woolen, Silk, and Linen Manufactures in the Colonial Period* [Cambridge, Mass., 1893], 267-8; John J. Currier, *History of Newburyport, Mass. 1764-1909*, 2 vols. [Newburyport, Mass., 1906-09], 2:405; Brookfield *Political Repository*, 10 June 1800; *Newburyport Herald*, 23 Jan. 1807; *Portland Gazette, and Maine Advertiser*, 13 Mch. 1809, 19 Mch. 1810).

Manasseh cutler, a Federalist congressman, recounted a visit he paid to the President's House on New Year's Day, 1803, and the interest shown by TJ and many of the women present in the textile samples he had left during a previous visit. "As soon as I came in," Cutler wrote, "the President applied to me for further information respecting the piece of wadding on his table" and "the two samples of bed-ticking, which I had shown him, and which I had in my pocket-book." The textiles "afforded the ladies much satisfaction" and "were pronounced much preferable and cheaper than that imported from Europe" (William Parker Cutler and Julia Perkins Cutler, *Life, Journals, and Correspondence of Rev. Manasseh Cutler, LL.D.*, 2 vols. [Cincinnati, 1888; repr. Athens, Ohio, 1987], 2:115).

From Madame de Corny

a paris le 15 fevrier 1803.

bien peu de jours apres la lettre que vous m'avez ecrit et a laquelle je me fesois un grand plaisir de repondre, jay eprouvé un cruel accident c'est une chutte qui ma cassé los du femeur de la Cuisse juste le même malheur que m de la fayette, je commence le 7eme mois je ne quitte presque jamais mon lit, et pour quelques pas dans ma chambre je souffre encor beaucoup, et boette si fort que je ne me flatte daucune guerison et quoique lon veuille me laisser quelques esperances pour lété prochain moi, je pense que le tems de lesperance cet passé, sans doute a la vie que je mene habituellement, ce n'est pas une grande privation de ne pas sortir, mais la sujettion a laquelle je suis reduitte, ne pouvant remuer sans aucun secour, et ce quil me reste de douleur quoiquelles soient bien diminuees, rend ma vie tres penible, encor si vous menvoyez Mde church je reprendrois de la vie car celle du coeur est la veritable.

jay lue avec bien de linteret votre dernier discours. jy trouve votre esprit et prudence accoutumee je ne suis pas assurée quavec toute votre habilete la louisiane ne vous donne quelquembaras, combien je désiré que tout autour de vous, et par vous, soit bien, que chaque difficulte sapplanisse et que votre vie ne soit pas trop agitee, mais, quelque gloire qui puisse etre votre partage, pardonnez a lamitie craintive dune femme le desir de vous savoir A montechéllo je voudrois hater la fin de votre presidence Cest avec une amitie bien sincere mon cher monsieur qu'on fait un pareil souhait cependant quel etat de situation florissant! payer ses dettes, augmenter son comerce. il est permi d'etre fier en rendant un tel compte, puisque vos retour de chine sont si nombreux souffrez que je vous demande du thé c'est mon dejeuner Constant il me sera agreable de vous le devoir chaque jour, que votre bon esprit ne trouve pas cette demande familiere je vous assure quelle nest que Sentimatalle—mais en grace prenez un comissionaire fidel et croyez que je vous aurai toute sorte dobligation de satisfaire ce desir.

Vos filles sont près de vous je lespere elles promettoient beaucoup et les jeunes plantes cultivées par vous ont surement bien proffittee je suis Contente de ce que vous aprouvez le mariage de Kitty je [minteresse] beacoup a son bonheur. cetoit un tems heureux que celuy ou je lavois près de moi ou je vous voyois souvent. helas quand je regarde autour de moi, que tout y est bien desert. le coeur se serre et on se demande que fais je dans cette vallée?

adieu mon cher monsieur jaimerois a recevoir quelques fois de vos nouvelles je vous recommande mon souvenir. DE CORNY

EDITORS' TRANSLATION

Paris, 15 Feb. 1803

Just a few days after receiving your letter, which I looked forward to answering, I had a terrible accident, a fall that broke my hip bone, exactly the same misfortune as Monsieur de Lafayette. This is the beginning of the seventh month in which I have almost never left my bed. It still causes me great pain just to take a few steps in my bedroom and I limp so seriously that I have no illusions about healing. Although they would like to give me some hope for next summer, I think the time for hope has passed, at least for my normal life. It is not a great deprivation not to go out, but being reduced to subjection, not being able to move without help, and the lingering pain, although much diminished, make my life very laborious. If you could send me Madame Church, however, I would come back to life, since the true life is that of the heart.

I read your last speech with much interest. I find in it your spirit and your characteristic prudence. I am not sure that Louisiana is not giving you problems, despite all your skill. I have so wished that everything around you, and through you, would work out well, that every difficulty would be smoothed out, and that your life would not be too tumultuous. But whatever glory may come to you, forgive the solicitous friendship of a woman who would like to know that you are at Monticello. I would like to hasten the end of your presidency. Such a wish, my dear sir, springs from very sincere affection. Yet what a flourishing situation when one's debts are paid and one's commerce is thriving. You can be proud of this. Since the goods you receive from China are so abundant, permit me to ask you for some tea. It is my daily breakfast. I would be pleased to owe it to you each morning. May your good will not find this request out of place. I assure you that it comes straight from the heart. Please choose a reliable messenger and know that I would be much indebted to you for fulfilling this wish.

I hope your daughters are with you. They were so promising and the young plants have surely benefited from being cultivated by you. I am happy that you approve of Kitty's marriage and am eager for her to be happy. It was a happy period when I had her near me and often saw you. Alas, when I look around me, at this emptiness, my heart aches and I wonder what I am doing in this valley.

Farewell, my dear sir. I would like to have news from you sometimes. You are in my thoughts. DE CORNY

RC (DLC); torn; addressed: "Monsieur de Jefferson President des Etats-Unies Amerique"; franked; postmarked New York, 30 Apr.; endorsed by TJ as received 2 May and so recorded in SJL.

LA LETTRE QUE VOUS M'AVEZ ECRIT: TJ wrote to Madame de Corny on 23 Apr. 1802 (Vol. 37:308-10).

LE MÊME MALHEUR QUE M DE LA FAYETTE: the Marquis de Lafayette had recently fallen on ice in Paris and severely fractured his upper thigh (Harlow Giles Unger, *Lafayette* [Hoboken, N.J., 2002],

333; Elizabethtown *Maryland Herald*, 27 Apr.; Lafayette to TJ, 17 May; Monroe to TJ, 20 Sep. 1803).

DERNIER DISCOURS: TJ's second annual message.

Catherine Church Cruger was KITTY.

To Henry Dearborn

TH:J. TO GENL. DEARBORNE. Feb. 15. 1803.

The inclosed were sent to me by mr Bacon with permission to keep them. they may therefore be filed in the War office. as we percieve that a light[1] French breeze has already reached most of the Indians, it will be well for us to keep our eye on all their movements. I have therefore asked the favor of mr Bacon to continue to send me this correspondence. as I have no doubt the arrival of the French at New Orleans will entirely stiffen the Indians against the sale of lands, I think the present moment critical to press for all we want immediately. viz. from

1. the Creeks, the residue of the Oakmulgee fork
2. the Cherokees Wafford's settlement & the Southeastern road.
3. the Choctaws, their lands between the Yazoo & Missisipi.
4. the Kaskaskias & Piorias,[2] their lands between the Wabash & Missisipi.
5. the Kickapoos, Poughtewatamies & Weauhs a settlement & extension of boundary.

the 1st. article I suppose must be charged on Hawkins.

the 2d. on Wilkinson & Meigs.

the 3d. on Wilkinson & Dinsmore, and qu. if it would not be better to give up the purchase between Tombigbee & Alabama, and treat only for the lands on Missisipi. their great debt to Panton & Leslie is an immediate instrument to obtain what we want immediately[3] and ought not to be wasted on a less important object. it will be a long time before debts, still to be contracted with us, will produce any effect towards obtaining land.

the 4th. & 5th. to be charged on Govr. Harrison with instructions to lose no time.

should we not immediately begin to prepare & send instructions? those to Wilkinson & Dinsmore[4] are the most pressing.

when will the Chickasaw Agent repair to his post?

RC (PHi); TJ first wrote the list without numbering the items, then added the numbers alongside to delineate the five items; endorsed by Dearborn as dated 14 Feb. and "relating to Indian affairs." PrC (DLC). Recorded in SJL with notation "Indian purchases &c." Enclosures not found, but see below.

Congressman John BACON of Massachusetts had transmitted two letters he received from John Sergeant, a missionary with the Stockbridge Mohican Indians in central New York State. Through members of that "New Stockbridge" community who traveled on religious missions, Sergeant obtained information from as far west as the Mississippi River (Alan Taylor, "Captain Hendrick Aupaumut: The Dilemmas of an Intercultural Broker," *Ethnohistory*, 43 [1996], 440-1; Bacon to TJ, 11 Apr. 1803; Sergeant to TJ, 25 June 1803).

LIGHT FRENCH BREEZE: see note to TJ to Owl and Others, 8 Jan.; note to TJ to Cornplanter and Others, 11 Feb.; and James Jackson to TJ, 14 Feb.

RESIDUE OF THE OAKMULGEE FORK: on 19 Feb., Dearborn instructed Benjamin Hawkins to "exert all the influence you possess to induce the Creeks to make the Oakmulgee the boundary line by extending the cession made the last summer as far as that River." Noting complaints from the Indians about incursions of livestock from outside their territory, Dearborn suggested that the Creeks might be persuaded to prefer "a strong natural boundary" such as the Ocmulgee River to the current boundary, which was "a mere mathematical line in the woods" (Dearborn to Hawkins, 19 Feb., in DNA: RG 75, LSIA). Dearborn expected James Wilkinson to join in the negotiations over changes in the boundary with the Creeks (Dearborn to Wilkinson, 18 Feb., in DNA: RG 107, LSMA).

Dearborn advised Wilkinson that the Choctaws' collective debts to the PANTON, Leslie firm might provide leverage for land cessions. "If no other consideration will induce the Chocktaws to part with any of their lands but that of paying off the debt they owe Panton & Co.," the secretary of war stated, the upper Choctaw towns might be willing to cede lands between the Yazoo and the Mississippi for that purpose and the lower towns might give up territory between the Tombigbee and Alabama Rivers. In 1805, the Choctaws' indebtedness to the company was about $46,000; at that time, Dearborn anticipated that in exchange for relieving the Choctaws of the obligation, the United States might acquire as much as 4,500,000 acres of land (Dearborn to Wilkinson, 21 Feb., in DNA: RG 75, LSIA; William S. Coker and Thomas D. Watson, *Indian Traders of the Southeastern Spanish Borderlands: Panton, Leslie & Company and John Forbes & Company, 1783-1847* [Pensacola, Fla., 1986], 255-6).

SEND INSTRUCTIONS: for the orders to Wilkinson, Return Jonathan Meigs, Silas Dinsmoor, and William Henry Harrison, see TJ's memorandum for Dearborn at 29 Dec. and Topics for Consultation with Heads of Departments, [on or after 10 Feb.].

Samuel Mitchell was the agent for the CHICKASAW Indians. A party from that tribe visited Washington in November 1802 and probably met TJ. Their only interpreter, however, was a young boy, who according to Dearborn spoke "but very little english." Dearborn and the president, "unable to converse" with the group "understandingly," could not ascertain the purpose of the visit. The secretary of war reminded Mitchell and Meigs, the agent for the Cherokees, that delegations traveling to Washington must receive prior authorization, carry passes, and be accompanied by skilled interpreters. The lack of an interpreter, Dearborn informed Mitchell, was "dangerous" and could "produce misunderstandings, that may lead to the most serious consequences" (Dearborn to Meigs, 23 Nov., and to Mitchell, 27 Nov., in DNA: RG 75, LSIA; James R. Atkinson, *Splendid Land, Splendid People: The Chickasaw Indians to Removal* [Tuscaloosa, Ala., 2004], 181, 184).

[1] TJ first wrote "slight" before altering the word.

[2] Ampersand and word interlined.

[3] Remainder of sentence interlined.

[4] Ampersand and name interlined.

From Albert Gallatin

DEAR SIR Feby. 15th 1803

Mr Miller commissioner of the revenue applied to me to know whether there was any impropriety in his acting as one of the directors of the Branch Bank in this city. To him personally it is of no importance; but the mother Bank seems very desirous that he should accept. They are much at a loss to find proper directors & wish to fill the vacancy caused by the refusal of John T. Mason to serve any longer.

As the office was established here by the Bank for our convenience & at our request, I do not wish to make any unreasonable objections, or to throw any embarrassment in their way; and as the office of Comr. of the revenue will soon expire, a decision in this case is not very important. I would not, however, give my assent without having consulted you.

Be good enough to let me know your opinion.

With great respect Your obedt. Servt. ALBERT GALLATIN

I feel extremely sorry for Gen. Dearborn's peculiar situation in the contract; but the more I reflect on it the less do I like any interference whatever on your part. I think the principle to alter contracts on the part of the public wrong; whenever it has come before Congress, and a very hard case I recollect to have seen before them, they have rejected the application: but, in the case of a public officer it is infinitely worse; and, if an allowance should be made in this case, where not even an account of expences has been kept, it hardly ever can be refused in any other contract. It is proper to add that should we even think fit to authorize an additional allowance, the subject must come before Congress for the purpose of authorizing an appropriation. Nay, as it would have been illegal to form a contract for the erection of that light house for a sum greater than had been appropriated, it must be illegal at present to authorize An allowance greater than the appropriation. I feel the most perfect conviction that if it shall come before Congress, it will be rejected. Gen. D. may flatter himself that if he was out of office & could with propriety urge his application there, it would succeed; but, rely upon it, that he is altogether mistaken.

If it is certain that, when presented to Congress, it will fail, it seems inexpedient that you should assume the responsibility of presenting the claim before their view. A. G.

RC (DLC); at foot of text: "The President"; endorsed by TJ as received from the Treasury Department on 15 Feb. and so recorded in SJL with notation "Miller. Dearb."

At the 1 Feb. meeting of the president and directors of the Bank of the United States, William MILLER was elected director of the office of discount and deposit in Washington for the term beginning 7 Mch. 1803. William Brent, JOHN T. MASON, Thomas Munroe, and Tristram Dalton were among the twelve others elected. In 1801, only nine directors were required at the Washington branch (*Washington Federalist*, 7 Feb. 1803; Vol. 35:132, 133-4n).

AT OUR REQUEST: see Vol. 35:135-6n.

For Henry DEARBORN'S PECULIAR SITUATION, see Dearborn to TJ, 5 Feb. and enclosure.

From Philip Mazzei

Pisa, 15 Febb., 1803.

Rispondendo il 10 Aprile 1802 alle sue pervenutemi da Milano coll'istesso corriere, una del 29 Aprile 1800 e l'altra del 17 Marzo 1801, Le dissi le ragioni che m'inducevano ad intraprendere il viaggio di Pietroburgo. Da, Venezia Le scrissi pochi versi, il 17 do.[1] e dopo quella dei 6 xbre 1800, la quale Ella dice nella sua dei 17 Marzo d'aver ricevuto, Le avevo scritto il 5 Febb., il 2 e il 30 Luglio, il 28 7bre, e il 15 9bre 1801. Con quella del 28 7bre le mandai dei noccioli di varie qualità di pesche. Gradirei di sapere per mia regola se tutte le lettere le son pervenute, o quali. Dall'annessa lettera del Piattoli Ella vedrà la sua dolente istoria, e come sia terminata. Ora il Principe Adamo Czartoryski figlio ed io tentiamo di farlo rimpatriare, con qualche impiego qui, e si ordisce una tela per fargli aver col tempo una corrispondenza letteraria coll'Imp. di Russia, Principe stimabile per le facoltà della mente, e adorabile per la qualità del cuore. Tal corrispondenza non à finora esistito. Cz. vuol proporla, e non dubito dell'effetto. Egli è amato e stimato (al par d'ogni altro *almeno*) dall'Imperatore e dalle 2 Imp. madre e moglie, 3 degne persone che si amano reciprocamente; ed à un'ottimo posto ancora nell'opinion pubblica. Le dirò su questo proposito una cosa che Le farà gràn piacere, cioè, che i buoni patriotti pollacchi sono adesso molto favorevolmente accolti in tutta la Russia, e specialmente a Pietroburgo, e quei pochi malcontenti, che ne suscitarono le ostilità contro la Patria vi sono sommamente disprezzati.

Non mi ricordo se io Le feci conoscere il do. Pr. Cz. in Parigi, dove giunse in età di 17 anni l'anno 1787. Il Duca della R., M., C., e tutti gli altri, ai quali lo introdussi, lo riguardarono allora come un prodigio per le vaste e profonde sue cognizioni e chiare vedute, per il retto giudizio, e per l'eccessiva modestia. In bontà di cuore pochissimi l'uguagliano, e niuno piò superarlo. Il pazzo, crudele, furibondo, e barbaro Paolo, che odiava il virtuoso figlio primogenito come pure la virtuosa moglie ai quali dava tutti i dispiaceri che poteva, lo mandò presso il detronato Rè di Sardigna, unicamente per allontanarlo dal figlio, sapendo che si amavano svisceratamente. Egli è adesso Vice Gran Gran gran Cancelliere di Russia, ed in gran parte in un'ottimo piano di riforme generali per il governo di quell'Impero[...] che io ò veduto. Due giovani signori, N. e Str., amici veri anch'essi dell'Imperatore, dotati pure di ottime qualità di mente e di cuore, vi ànno egualmente cooperato. L'imperatore è il più giovane dei 4. Queste 4 persone si amano, vanno d'accordo in tutto, e (per quanto mi è parso) incammineranno le cose in guisa da svergognare gli altri governi Europei. Cat. 2da. ꝑ supplire allo smoderato fasto, e alle profusioni a favor dei suoi drudi, e s'è recorso alla Cartamoneta. Lo stravagantissimo Paolo e le contrafazioni inglesi ne ànno impestato tutto l'Impero. La carta e il rame formano la sola moneta in corso. Il rublo d'argento è divenuto mercanzia, che scema e cresce di prezzo a norma delle circostanze, come lo zecchino d'Olanda. Prima dell'introduzion della Cartamoneta lo zecchino valeva circa 250 copcek: Quando montò nel Trono Alessandro ne valeva 495. Le apparenze che si ebbero d'un buon governo, e l'economia nella quale si messe Alessandro, fecero megliorare il cambio immediatamente. Quando io arrivai in Russia ne valeva circa 440, e quando venni via, 418. Sento che va continuamente scemando il prezzo dello zecchino, cosa vantaggiosa ꝑ me, poichè l'Imperatore mi à accordato una pensione di 1200 rubli per il suo terzo di quel che mi era dovuto dal Defunto Rè di Pollonia, i quali mi produrranno più o meno denaro effettivo, a norma del cambio. 3000 rubli, che il sopradetto Prno. Cz. volle mandare al nostro Piattoli, a motivo delle sofferte disgrazie, produssero 702 zecchini, che ebbi la dolce consolazione di portargli io stesso. 2. Se fossero stati ridotti in zecchini al tempo de la mia partenza, un mese e $\frac{1}{2}$ più tardi; ne avrebbero prodotti circa 720. 3. Quanto al mio credito col Conte G.D., nè ò ricevuto circa il quarto (che non à bilanciato le gravi spese del duro, e disastroso, e ꝑicoloso viaggio) e per gli altri $\frac{3}{4}$ ci è ora maggior probabilità di ricevergli che non ci era prima.

Io scrissi al principio del 92, ꝑ ordine del buono Stanislao (che mai cesserò d'amare) un opuscolo sulla natura della moneta e del cambio del quale furon pubblicate 2 traduzioni in Varsavia, una pollacca, e l'altra francese. Il supradetto Ni. Sagre: intimo delle cose personali dell'Imperatore, che si è occupato più degli altri di ciò che riguarda la moneta, non potendosi trovare in D.go. alcuno esemplare della 2da. traduzione, volle vedere il mio originale; ma non essendo molto franco nella lingua, e riescendogli consequentemente difficile la lettura del manoscritto, gli promessi di stamparle e di mandargliene un'esemplare per la posta. Sarà pronto tra pochi giorni, cio è prima che parta la presente. Mi prendero la libertà di mandarne uno anche a Lei, e La prego di osservare alla pagina 51, linea ultima, quel che segue dopo *ostinazione*; aggiunta ch'io feci dopo d'aver conosciute le sorprendenti risorse interne dell'Impero Russo, all'investigazione delle quali m'indusse il vedere, [...] commerciante (non ostante le inevitabili continove perdite nel cambio) [...] aversi colla carta centinaia di migliaia di zecchini e di rubli d'argento, cosa che non avrei creduta senza vederla.

Oltre il do. opuscolo prenderò la libertà di mandarle un'esemplare d'un altro sui mali della questua e sui mezzi di curarli che stampai 4 anni sono, lusingándomi che l'amicizia l'indurrà a dare un'occhiata ad ambedue, quantunque sieno totalmente superflui ꝑ Lei, e spero che saranno sempre tali ꝑ codesto Paese. Aggiungerò ai 2 opuscoli 2 grossi volumi d'un Tableau Hist. e Statistique de l'Empire de Russie tradotto del tedesco, perchè contengono dei fatti tendenti a dar dei lumi, che possan (ꝑ quanto mi pare) divenir molto utili costà, subito che il paese sarà più popolato. Il terzo vol. non era comparso quando lasciai Pietroburgo, e credo che non sia ꝑ anche pubblicato. Se Ella non avesse disposto di tutti gli esemplari delle *Notes on Virginia*, che aveva destinati per gli Amici, Le sarei molto grato di un altro, perchè quello che mi favorí, mi è stato portato via, e non ò alcuna speranza di recuperarlo.

Mediante le ripetute contrarietà e disgrazie accadutemi per viaggio, il mio ritorno qui sarebbe stato troppo tardo per poterle mandar quest'anno la piante che Ella desidera, quando ancora le perfide stagioni non avessero fatto, in tutti il regno vegetabile, una strage molto superiore a tutto ciò che su questo punto ci suggerisce la memoria, e ci dice l'istoria. In una mia precedente Le dissi, che, quando nell'atmosifera manca la requisita dose di umido per renderla salubre, una lunga esperienza mi aveva convinto, che l'innaffiatura, per quanto sia copiosa, può bastare a mantener la pianta in vita ma non a farla vegetare. In quella parte della Lombardia, che Ella vedde quando fù a Milano, si possono irrigar le prata quando e quanto si vuole, como Ella sa, colle acque delle nevi che si struggono sulle Alpi ogni anno tutta la State senza eccezione. Non ostante, a motivo di non esser mai piovuto, vi è mancata interamente la raccolta del fieno. Tanto basta per farle congetturare il grave danno di quel paese, e quanto maggiore debba assere stato negli altri. Son mancate le raccolte ꝑ i $\frac{3}{4}$ circa sul totale dei grani, delle biade, delle civaie, dell'Olive, delle castagne, dei funghi, e della ghiande intieramente in alcuni luoghi, e circa $\frac{3}{4}$ sul totale. Gli ortaggi sono stati scarsi, e di poco sapore. Pochissime e di poco sapore le frutte d'inferior qualità, punte delle megliori. Le sole viti ànno resistito; il vino è stato non abondante, ma buono. Un danno che si risentirà per degli anni è la mortalità delle piante fruttifere, soprattutto dei peschi, e la debol salute di quelle che ànno sopravvissuto. Alla da. siccità è succeduta una pioggia copiosissima e quasi continova, nell'Autunno, per cui non si son potute per anche fare in vari luoghi le semente. Le inondazioni ànno fatto un danno immenso. Io sono stato trattenuto una volta per 18 giorni senza poter procedere nel mio viaggio. Le strade son rese quasi impassabili. Tra Tortona e la Bocchetta, e di qua da Genova, ò dovuto più volte farmi accompagnare da 12 uomini ℘ parecchie miglia, scender di tanto in tanto dal carrozzino, fare staccare i cavalli, e stare in distanza col cuor palpitante, vedendo alcuni uomini o in pericolo di precipitare dalle strade dirupate col carrozzino addosso, o di esser trasportati dalla rapidità dei torrenti e dal rotolamento di ciottoli di smisurata mole. Quanto ai pericoli che ò corso, Le dirò tra gli altri, che fra Tortona e Novi solamente ò dovuto passare di dove, 15 giorni avanti, era stato assassinato e sepolto un viandante e un'altro giorno ℘ una strada dove erano stati arrestati e rubati 2 giorni prima i viandanti che viaggiavano insieme in 3 carrozze. Nell'istesso luogo fù ferito e rubato il corrier di Spagna il giorno dopo. Questi son frutti delle desolazioni causate dalle armate, non meno gravi di quelle provenienti dalle pessime stagioni. Le miserie son grandissime, e generali, e il caro prezzo di tutti i generi di prima necessità le rende superiori alle forze di molti, assuefatti a vivere in qualche affluenza. Io sarò contento se la pensione accordatami dall'Imp. Alessandro potrà supplire al deficit ℘ la pura sussistenza.

Un invernata senza punto freddo à causato dei ben fondati timori per i futuri prodotti della terra. Otto giorni sono successe, ad un tratto un rigidissimo freddo, e cadde pei tre giorni continovi tanta neve, che mai n'e caduta una terzia parte (per quanto è noto) in questo paese. Per un vecchio statuto l'Università di Pisa à vacanza quando cade la neve. Ciò dinota che era ben rara. I vecchi dicono, che nella lor gioventù passavano molti anni senza vederne l'ombra. In oggi cade quasi gradualmente più spesso, o in maggior quantità.

È già del tempo che i fenomeni del nostro globo son maggiori o più frequenti di quel che solevano essere (per quanto sappiamo dall'istorie veridiche) e vanno continovamente crescendo. Non potrebbero presagire qualche gran cambiamento, e forse in tutto il sistema solare? Fin dall'anno 1790 mi avveddi, al mio pmo. ritorno in Italia, d'una gran diminuzione di caldo nella State. Avanti ch'io partisse nel

1752 non si portava in queste parti altro che mantino e taffettà, o tela finissima, dal Maggio all'8bre, e si desiderava di poter trovar qualcosa di più leggiero ancora. Adesso non son molti i giorni in tutta la state, che il panno di lana paia troppo grave alla più fervida gioventù. Per un antica etichetta ò veduto alla Corte di Francia gli abiti di mantino appena terminata la primavera, il che dinota che là pure anticamente la stagione lo richiedeva. A mio tempo, avrebbero sofferto gran freddi, se non avessero avuto sotto il mantino dei vestimenti più caldi. Per un'antichissimo statuto la Citta di Cracovia era obbligata di portare al Vescovo un pane di grano nuovo, in un tempo che ora il grano appena vi comincia a mostrar la spiga. In Inghilterra nei tempi antichi vi si faceva il vino; adesso raramente vi matura l'uva lugliola. Perchè non potrebbe avverarsi la supposizione di Newton, che le Comete sieno Corpi destinati ad alimentare il sole, rifondendogli di tanto in tanto la perdita causatagli dalle continove esalazioni, e che quella smisurata cometaccia che fa il giro ogni 300 anni, e che nel prossimo, (cioè tra un secolo circa) gli passerà tanto vicina da esser nel caso di cadervi dentro, mediante l'irresistibil forza dell'attrazione? Il desiderio di trattenermi seco vedo che attrarrebbe anche me, a segno da farmi scrivere un libro in vece d'una lettera. Termino dunque, senza per altro aver perduta la speranza di riveder Monticello, nonostante i 72 anni, e quasi 2 mesi. Mi conservi la sua cara benevolenza, e mi creda con i piu fervidi sentimenti del cuore. Suo Devmo. Servo ed Affmo. Amico, F. M.

EDITORS' TRANSLATION

Pisa, 15 Febb., 1803.

In replying on 10 April 1802 to your letters, which I received from Milan by the same courier, one from 29 April 1800 and the other from 17 March 1801, I explained my reasons for embarking on the trip to St. Petersburg. From Venice I wrote you a few lines on the 17th and after the letter of 6 December 1800, which you say in your letter of 17 March you have received, I wrote you on 5 February, on 2 and 30 July, on 28 September, and on 15 November 1801. Along with my letter of 28 September I sent some seeds of various qualities of peaches. I would like to know, for my records, whether all the letters have reached you, and if not, which ones have. From the attached letter by Piattoli you will see his sorrowful story and its outcome. Now Prince Adamo Czartoryski, the son, and I are trying to have him go back to his country and get some form of employment here. We are planning to have him establish a literary correspondence with the Emperor of Russia, a monarch endowed with remarkable intellectual faculties, and adored for the qualities of his heart. Such correspondence has yet to be. Cz. wants to propose it, and I have no doubt about the outcome. He is loved and highly regarded (at least just as much as anybody else) by the emperor and the two empresses, his mother and his wife, three worthy persons bound by mutual love. Furthermore, he still enjoys a remarkably good position in public opinion. To this let me add something that will certainly please you; namely, that the good Polish patriots are now very favorably treated throughout Russia, and especially in St. Petersburg; the few disgruntled ones who stirred its hostility toward their homeland are held in great contempt.

I cannot remember whether I introduced the aforesaid Pr. Cz. to you in Paris, where he arrived when he was 17, in the year 1787. The Duke of R., M., C., and all the others to whom I introduced him regarded him at that time as a wonder for his vast and deep knowledge, as well as for his clear mind, power of judgment, and his incredible modesty. Very few equal him in kindness of heart; none can outdo him. The mad, cruel, deranged and barbaric Paul, who hated his firstborn son as well as his own virtuous wife, both of whom he vexed in any way he could, sent him to stay with the dethroned King of Sardinia, simply in order to distance him from his son, knowing that they loved one another most dearly. He is now Vice Grand Chancellor of Russia, and a great part of a remarkable plan to introduce general reforms into the government of that Empire which I have seen. Two young men, N. and Str., they too true friends of the Emperor, likewise endowed with remarkably good minds and hearts, have also collaborated on it. The emperor is the youngest of the four. These four people love one another, agree on everything, and—as far as I have been able to observe—they will set in motion things which will shame all other European governments. Cat. 2da., in order to support her immoderate luxury and her expenditures in favor of her lovers, has made the recourse to paper money necessary. The most extravagant Paul and the British counterfeits have plagued the whole empire. Paper and copper are the only circulating currency. The silver ruble has become a commodity, the price of which decreases and increases according to the circumstances, the same as the Dutch Sequin. Before paper money had been introduced, the Sequin was worth around 250 kopeck. When Alexander ascended to the throne, it was worth 495. What appeared to be a good government, and the tight economic measures adopted by Alexander, immediately produced a better exchange rate. When I arrived in Russia, it was worth about 440, when I left, 418. I hear that the value of the Sequin is steadily decreasing; something that actually turns to my advantage, since the Emperor has granted me a pension of 1,200 rubles for the third of the money the late king of Poland owed me. This pension will produce more or less actual money, based on the exchange rate. 3,000 rubles, which the aforementioned Young Prince Cz. sent to our Piattoli, on account of the misfortunes he suffered, produced 702 sequins, which I had the sweet consolation of personally delivering to him myself. 2. Had they been changed into sequins at the time of my leaving—one and a half months later—they would have yielded about 720. 3. As far as my credit with Count G.D., I have been paid about a quarter (which has not made up for the heavy expenses for the harsh, troubled, and dangerous journey); for the remaining three quarters, there is now a better chance to recover them than there was before.

I wrote at the beginning of 92, upon request from the good Stanislaus (whom I will never cease to love) a short work on the nature of currency and exchange, of which two translations were published in Warsaw, one in Polish and the other in French. The aforementioned Ni. Sagre: who has intimate knowledge of the emperor's personal matters, and who has worked more than anybody else on what pertains to currency, being unable to find in D.go. any copy of the second translation, asked to see my original. Not having advanced knowledge of the language, however, and thus having difficulties in reading the manuscript, I promised him I would print it and send him a copy by mail. It will be ready in a few days, that is, before this letter shall be sent out. I will take the liberty to send one copy to you as well and I would like to draw your attention to what I write on p. 51, last line, after the word *ostinazione*; this is something I have added after coming to know the incredible internal resources of the Russian Empire, to the investigation of which I was drawn by seeing that [. . .], businessman (in spite of the inescapable losses in the exchange) [. . .] had along with paper money hundreds of thousands of sequins and silver rubles, something I would have never believed, had I not witnessed it.

In addition to that little work, I will take the liberty to send you a copy of another work on the evils of begging and the ways to cure them, which I published four years ago, hoping that you might honor our friendship and take a quick look at both, though they are both utterly superfluous for you and I hope will keep being such for your Country. I will add to these two little works two large volumes of a Historical and Statistical Description of the Russian Empire, translated from German, since they contain interesting data and explanations, which may turn out to be (it seems to me) very useful over there, as soon as the country will be more densely populated. The third volume had not yet appeared when I left St. Petersburg, and I believe it still is unpublished. In case you have not yet disposed of all the copies of the Notes on Virginia, which you had destined for your friends, I would be very grateful for another one, since the one you were so kind to give me has been taken away from me, and I have no hope at all to recover it.

Notwithstanding the frequent accidents and misfortunes I have suffered in my journey, my return here would have not been too late in the year for me to be able to send you the plants that you would like to receive, had the treacherous weather not wreaked a much larger havoc through the whole realm of vegetation than memory and history have recorded. In one of my previous letters, I wrote you that my long experience has convinced me that—when the atmosphere lacks the required amount of moisture to make it salubrious— artificial watering, however copious, may help to keep the plant alive but not to make it grow. In the part of Lombardy that you saw when you were in Milan, one may irrigate the fields as much as one wants, as you know, with the water from the snow from the Alps, which regularly melts in the summer every year. Yet since it never rained, in those areas the hay harvest was entirely lost. This may enable you to estimate the great damage suffered by that area and how in the others it has been even greater. About three quarters of the whole harvest is lost for grains, forage, legumes, olives, chestnuts, mushrooms, and acorns (in some places completely, in other ones about three quarters of the whole). Produce has been scant and of little flavor; very few and of little flavor low-quality fruit; none of the high-quality. Only vineyards have prevailed: wine has been good, though not plentiful. A loss that will have repercussions for years is that of fruit trees, especially of peach trees, and the poor health of the trees that survived. After the drought a most copious rain succeeded, almost uninterrupted through the fall, resulting in many places without new sowing. The floods have brought immense devastation. Once during my journey, I had been stuck for eighteen days. The roads are made almost impassable: between Tortona and Bocchetta and past Genoa, on many occasions, I have had to be escorted by twelve men for many miles, some times get off my small coach, have the horses unharnessed, and stand back with my heart racing, seeing some of the men in danger of falling from the crumbling roads crushed by the coach or of being dragged away by the torrents' current or hit by the huge rolling boulders in the stream. As for the dangers I have run, let me tell you that just between Tortona and Novi I have had to pass where fifteen days before a wayfarer had been killed and buried, and another day through a road where two days before the wayfarers who were traveling together in three coaches had been stopped and robbed. In that very place the Spanish courier was wounded and robbed the next day. These are the effects of the devastations brought about by the armies, which are no less inferior than those caused by the bad seasons. Poverty is great and general, and the high price of first necessities is beyond the endurance of many, since all are used to living in some affluence. I will be happy that the pension granted to me by the Emperor Alexander will make up for the deficit to my subsistence.

A winter without any cold has raised well-grounded fears for the future crops. Eight days have elapsed and all of a sudden the most rigid cold, and for three days so much snow fell uninterrupted that a third as much had never fallen (so far as is known) in this country. According to an old statute, the University in Pisa is closed when snow falls. This suggests that it must have been a quite rare event. The old people say that in their youth several years would pass in which they would not see any snow. In these days, it falls more often or in greater amounts.

For some time now, the phenomena in our globe have been greater or more frequent than what they used to be (from what we can gather from recorded history), and they are continuously growing. Could it be possible that they are foreshadowing some great change, perhaps in the whole solar system? Since the year 1790 I noticed, upon my first return to Italy, that the heat had diminished considerably. In the summer I left in 1752 in these areas one would only wear satin, taffeta, or very light fabric, between May and October, and one would actually have wished to find something even lighter. Now there are not many days in the whole summer when wool would feel too heavy to the hottest youth. In observance of an old custom, I have seen at the French Court the garments in satin come into fashion right at the end of spring, which too suggests that in those places the climate required that. In my days, they would have suffered great cold, had they not worn warmer clothing under the silk. According to an ancient statute, the City of Kraców was bound to present the Bishop with a loaf of bread made of new grain, and this in a time of the year when nowadays grain is just about starting to show its ear. In England, in the ancient times, wine was made; now the July grapes barely reach ripeness. Why couldn't what Newton supposes come true? Namely, that Comets are bodies destined to feed into the sun, reimbursing it, from time to time, of the loss caused by its continued exhalations? And that that enormous bad comet that every 300 years does its round, and that next time around (that is, in about a century), will come so close that it might fall into it, on account of the irresistible force of attraction? I see that the desire to continue being with you would attract me too, to the point of making me write a book rather than a letter. I stop here, thus, though without having lost hope of seeing Monticello again, notwithstanding my age of 72 years and almost two months. I wish you will remain dearly benevolent to me and believe that I am your most fervidly affectionate devoted servant and dearest friend,

F. M.

Dft (Archivio Filippo Mazzei, Pisa, Italy); part of a conjoined series of Mazzei's drafts of letters to TJ, where it precedes Mazzei's letter of 15 Apr. 1803 (see Margherita Marchione and Barbara B. Oberg, eds., *Philip Mazzei: The Comprehensive Microform Edition of his Papers*, 9 reels [Millwood, N.Y., 1981], 5:0387-91). RC recorded in SJL as received from Pisa on 5 Mch. 1805, but not found. Enclosures: (1) Mazzei, *Riflessioni sulla natura della moneta e del cambio* (Pisa, 1803; Sowerby, No. 2855). (2) Mazzei, *Riflessioni su i mali provenienti dalla questua e su i mezzi di evitargli* (Pisa, 1799). (3) Heinrich Friedrich von Storch, *Tableau historique et statistique de l'Empire de Russie à la fin du dix-huitième siècle*, 2 vols. [Basel, 1801], a translation of *Historisch-statistisches Gëmalde des russischen Reiches am Ende des achtzehnten Jahrhunderts*, first published in Riga in 1797. Other enclosure not found, but see below.

SE TUTTE LETTERE LE SON PERVENUTE: for Mazzei's earlier attempts to account for TJ's receipt of his correspondence, see Vol. 37:201-4.

LETTERA DEL PIATTOLI: Scipione Piattoli's letter has not been identified, but for Mazzei's attempt in 1803 to help him find employment, see Margherita Marchione, ed., *Philip Mazzei: Selected Writings and Correspondence*, 3 vols. (Prato, Italy, 1983), 3:271-2. For information on Piattoli, an Italian priest who became active in Polish politics, see *Encyclopaedia Judaica*, 2d ed., 22 vols. (Detroit, 2007), 16:143.

Polish prince, Adam Jerzy CZARTORYSKI, was an adviser and close friend of the Russian heir apparent, Alexander. The Duke de la Rochefoucauld, Jean François Marmontel, and the Marquis de Condorcet considered him a prodigy. Rumored to have been the lover of Alexander's wife, Elizabeth Alekseevna, Czartoryski was banished from Russia in 1799, when Emperor Paul appointed him minister to the exiled king of Sardinia, Charles Emanuel IV. After Alexander I assumed the throne in 1801, Czartoryski remained in the czar's esteem and became his deputy foreign minister in September 1802 (Marchione, *Mazzei: Writings*, 3:291; Patricia Kennedy Grimsted, *The Foreign Ministers of Alexander I: Political Attitudes and the Conduct of Russian Diplomacy, 1801-1825* [Berkeley, Calif., 1969], 106-11; Howard R. Marraro, "Philip Mazzei and His Polish Friends," *Quarterly Bulletin of the Polish Institute of Arts and Sciences in America* [1944], 52-4).

IN PARIGI: Maria Cosway introduced TJ to Czartoryski sometime in the fall of 1787, when she was in Paris (Vol. 12:69, 387, 415, 459-60).

DUE GIOVANI SIGNORI, N. AND STR.: Nikolai Novosiltsov, Paul Stroganov, and Czartoryski collaborated with Alexander in planning reforms for Russia's government. Together with Victor Pavlovich Kochubei, they became the emperor's "Secret Committee" of advisers when he came to power in 1801 (Janet M. Hartley, *Alexander I* [London, 1994], 39-40).

CAT. 2DA.: Catherine the Great.

STANISLAO: Stanislaus Augustus, king of Poland from 1764 to 1795, for whom Mazzei had been an agent and privy councilor (Marraro, "Mazzei and His Polish Friends," 15-16).

UN OPUSCOLO: Mazzei's *Reflections on the Nature of Money and Exchange*, a protest against the impact of inflationary schemes on Poland's finances, was written in Italian in 1792 and was first published in Polish, selling 14,000 copies in the first week. Soon thereafter translated into French, it was not published in Italy until 1803 (Richard Cecil Garlick, Jr., *Philip Mazzei, Friend of Jefferson: His Life and Letters* [Baltimore, 1933], 129).

NI. SAGRE: Nikolai Novosiltsov.

OSSERVARE ALLA PAGINA 51, LINEA ULTIMA: at this place in his *Reflections on the Nature of Money and Exchange*, Mazzei commented that a country with natural resources greater than other countries would be less impoverished by exchange losses in a negative balance of trade (Marchione, *Mazzei: Writings*, 3:285).

Mazzei had lent a copy of TJ's NOTES ON VIRGINIA to Nicolas & Jacob van Staphorst in February 1786 (Vol. 9:275).

LA PIANTE CHE ELLA DESIDERA: Mazzei sent TJ a box of plum, apricot, and peach stones as well as some grapevine root and stem cuttings and a vase of strawberries that, because of shipping delays, did not leave Pisa until January 1804 (Marchione, *Mazzei: Writings*, 3:311-13, 341; Mazzei to TJ, 28 Dec. 1803 and 27 Jan. 1804; TJ to Mazzei, 18 July 1804).

IN UNA MIA PRECEDENTE: Mazzei to TJ, 6 Dec. 1800.

UN'ANTICHISSIMO STATUTO: in 1421, the bishop of Krakow gave his cook a parcel of land and obligated the inhabitants of the village of Pradnik to provide bread for his table. Another tradition held that the first loaf of pradnicki was made on the day the first rye harvest of the season was presented to the king. Pradnicki bread, a brown bread made with fermented rye, is still noted for its quality, size, thick crust, and long-lasting freshness (John Irving, ed., *Terra Madre, 1,600 Food Communities* [Bra, Italy, 2007], 401; *Official Journal of the European Union*, 53 [10 July 2010] c 187/16-19).

[1] Mazzei here canceled "relativamente all'incombenza d'approvisionar la flottiglia degli S. U. nel Mediterraneo, data (per quanto intesi) a persona privata, invece d'affidarla al console," meaning "about the task of poisoning the U.S. fleet in the Mediterranean entrusted (from what I heard) to a private person rather than to the consul."

To James Jackson

DEAR SIR Washington Feb. 16. 1803

Your favor of the 14th. was recieved on the same day, and will be duly attended to in the course of our affairs with the Creeks. in keeping Agents among the Indians two objects are principally kept in view. 1. the preservation of peace. 2. the obtaining lands. towards effecting the latter object we consider the leading the Indians to agriculture as the principal means from which we can expect much effect in future. when they shall cultivate small spots of earth & see how useless their extensive forests are, they will sell from time to time to help out their personal labour in stocking their farms, & procuring clothes & comforts from our trading houses. towards the attainment of our two objects of peace, & lands, it is essential that our agent acquire that sort of influence over the Indians which rests on confidence. in this respect I suppose no man has ever obtained more influence than Colo. Hawkins. towards the preservation of peace he is omnipotent. in the encouragement of agriculture among them he is indefatigable, & successful. these are important portions of his duty. but doubts are entertained by some whether he is not more attached to the interests of the Indians, than of the US. whether *he* is willing they should cede lands, when *they* are willing to do it. if his own solemn protestations can command any faith he urges the ceding lands as far as he finds it practicable to induce them. he only refuses to urge what he knows cannot be obtained. he is not willing to destroy his own influence by pressing what he knows cannot be obtained. this is his representation. against this I should not be willing to substitute suspicion for proof; but I shall always be open to any proofs that he obstructs cessions of land which the Indians are willing to make: and of this, Sir, you may be assured that he shall be placed under as strong a pressure from the Executive to obtain cessions, as he can feel from any opposite quarter to obstruct. he shall be made sensible that his value will be estimated by me in proportion to the benefits he can obtain for us. I am myself alive to the obtaining lands from the Indians *by all honest & peaceable means*, and I believe that the honest and peaceable means adopted by us will obtain them as fast as the expansion of our settlements with due regard to compactness will require. the war department, charged with Indian affairs, is under the impression of these principles and will second my views with sincerity. and, in the present case, besides the official directions which will go to Colo. Hawkins immediately to spare no efforts from which any success can be hoped to obtain the residue of the Oconee & Oakmulgee fork, I shall myself write to Colo. Hawkins and possess him fully of my views and expectations; and this with such explanations as I trust will bring him cordially into them, as they are unquestionably equally for the Interest of the Indians and ourselves.

I have availed myself of the occasion furnished by your letter of explaining to you my views on this subject with candor, and of assuring you they shall be pursued unremittingly—when speaking of the Oakmulgee fork, I ought to have added that we shall do whatever can be done properly in behalf of Wafford's settlement; and that as to the South-Eastern road, it will be effected; as we consider ourselves entitled on principles acknoleged by all men to an innocent passage through the lands of a neighbor, and to admit no refusal of it. Accept assurances of my great esteem and high consideration.

TH: JEFFERSON

PrC (DLC); at foot of first page: "Genl. Jackson."

EXPLAINING TO YOU MY VIEWS: in April, Jackson made an extract of TJ's letter, from "I am myself alive" in the first paragraph to the end of the second paragraph, and sent it to John Milledge, the governor of Georgia (Tr in G-Ar).

From Thomas Newton

Dr Sir Norfolk Febry 16—1803

Your favor of the 6th I received and am glad the Cyder had got to hand. I have not the acct. of it at present or should forward it. two pipes of Brazil wine shall be sent you the first good opty. if you wou'ld say how many you wou'd take yearly, I would order them with my own, of superior quality—my intentions are to send only for as many pipes as my freinds want & import none for promiscuous sales, My Corespondents are Portugese they inform me they will send wines to my order, for my freinds & myself of better quality than we have been used to, I shall try them for some, as I wish to have the best.—

My son's in Law Js Taylor & Theo Armistead have a ship that has made only one Voyage particularly built, copered to light water marks, Composition bound, & in every respect well built, & calculated for a ship of war; with making ports & laying the lower Decks, which they would sell & could fit out compleated in a short time; she is built on the Construction of a Brittish 20 gun Ship & sails fast, it is probable she would suit Government for one of the 4 to be fitted out, I do not beleive a better vessel can be built, for the purpose, as she was built to be kept & not intended for sale, but the fall of freights induce them to part with her, if they can obtain the value. we have nothing new here. a very heavy Snow is now falling from the Sea board, which I suppose does not reach far up the country. health &c attend you are the wishes of yr obt Servt Thos Newton

RC (DLC); addressed: "Thos Jefferson Esquire President Washington"; franked; postmarked 17 Feb.; endorsed by TJ as received 25 Feb. and so recorded in SJL.

To John Breckinridge

Th: Jefferson to mr. Brackenridge Feb. 17. 1803.

I think the inclosed may properly furnish grounds for an amendment to the judiciary law, whenever it is before Congress; to be proposed by a member. Judge Innis inclosed it to me with an idea that the proposition might go from me to Congress: but this is hardly within the regular compass of message. I therefore turn it over to you.

RC (DLC: Breckinridge Family Papers); addressed: "The honble Mr. Breckenridge." Not recorded in SJL. Enclosure not found, but see Harry Innes to TJ, 14 Jan. 1803.

From Daniel Carroll Brent

Sir/ Feby. 17th. 1803

It is difficult to ascertain the quantity of stone that can be raised in a given time by a given number of hands—because the rock is buried in the earth from 6 to 16 feet, & it cannot be known whether it is good or will cut well, untill the earth is removed, the removeing of which constitutes a considerable portion of the labour in quarrying; & it not unfrequently happens that the rock either is not good or will not cut, & the labour & time taken up in removeing the earth is lost—

In the year 1797 a company I was concerned in delivered at the City wharf 900 Tons of stone, & I think more than 100 Tons remained in the quarry—this was done by about 26 hands hired by the year, including, in that number, 2 Overseers, 1 blacksmith & his striker, 1 cooke, 1 skipper & 3 watermen; in addition to this labour we, in the summer, hired hands by the month—not haveing the weekly returns of the hands here, I cannot state the amount of this labour, but from my best recollection I am *confident* it did not exceed that of 10 hands by the year, & I think less than that of five—

It is proper to observe that every thing was well prepared to commence with the year—no time was lost, that the hands hired by the year were well experienced in quarrying & were chosen from the best of those who had been accustomed to this work—that I think as many equally good hands cannot be got at present, that more stone cou'd then be raised in that quarry, than any other on aquia creek, as there was less dirt to remove, & the stone cut better—I have written to Virginia on this subject & so soon as the answers return you shall know the result—

I have to apologize for not sending in this sooner, but, I was kept up almost the whole of Tuesday night—with real respect I am Sir yr. obt. Sevt.

Daniel C Brent

RC (DLC); endorsed by TJ as received 17 Feb. and so recorded in SJL.

Brent, with members of his family and in partnership with John Cooke, was involved in several quarries on AQUIA CREEK, Virginia, which supplied sandstone for the public buildings in Washington (Bryan, *National Capital*, 1:169, 231, 411; *Federal Gazette & Baltimore Daily Advertiser*, 18 Oct., 12 Dec. 1797; Georgetown *Centinel of Liberty*, 9 Apr., 29 Oct. 1799; Latrobe, *Correspondence*, 1:262n, 426n, 497-9; Benjamin H. Latrobe to TJ, 15 Jan. 1804; Thomas Munroe to TJ, 18 Feb. 1804).

From Joseph Coppinger

Pittsburgh 18th February 1803

I did myself the honour of addressing your Excellency on the 3d of January last, enclosing a letter to your neighbour the Rigt. Revd. Doctor Carroll forwarded in the view of establishing character, If such might be eventually useful, in my position towards obtaining the contemplated patent right in preserving animal and vegetable substances, both in their natural, and a cuit State. But on reflection this was perhaps a liberty I should not have taken as possibly thereby I have given your Excellency offence—If such should unfortunately be the case I am really sorry for it. the more as nothing could be more foreign to my views or wishes than such a result, In that case do me the Justice to believe that Ignorance and not want of respect for your Excelly was the true cause. Neither could I now prevail on my self to address you again (having received no answer to my former letter) If the importance of the subject did not appear to Justify me in doing so. By a late act of Congress I perceive aliens will not be granted patent rights untill by residence they have become citizens of the United States; this of course renders the probation indispensible and induces me to make your Excellency the following proposal which will at once give Government and the Country the full and unrestrained benefit of whatever advantages my discoverys are found to possess, and I trust that on a fair and patient trial they will be found numerous and many, whether regarded in a political, commercial, or agriculturel point of view.

And of this If I am permitted, and encouraged so to do, your Excellency will if you please be constituted the sole Judge. or If more agreeable to your wishes to call in such other characters as you may think proper to Select in order to assist your Judgment in determining what quantum of compensation I may be Justly entitled to. In that case let me receive it to what amount, and in what manner, and time you may think Proper to determine and direct. But If it should so happen that you do not think me entitled to any in that case let me go empty for I can with truth declare that I do not desire to possess myself, of one single Dollar either of Publick or private property that I have not a fair and honourable claim to. were I actuated by any other motive your Excellency will readily perceive I would not make this Proposal. expecting an answer at what time and in what way you may think proper to direct I am with real respect your Excellencys

Most Obt. & Very Hble. Servt. JOSEPH COPPINGER

P.S. your answer should I be honoured with one will determine my sending you the memorial containing the Principles and application of this theory and I hope its simplicity and easy practability will be its best recommendation

RC (DLC); endorsed by TJ as received 24 Feb. and so recorded in SJL.

LATE ACT OF CONGRESS: for the patent law of 1793, see Vol. 38:535.

To Benjamin Hawkins

DEAR SIR Washington Feb. 18. 1803.

Mr. Hill's return to you offers so safe a conveyance for a letter that I feel myself irresistably disposed to write one, tho' there is little to write about. you have been so long absent from this part of the world, and the state of society so changed in that time, that details respecting those who compose it are no longer interesting or intelligible to you. one source indeed of great change in social intercourse arose while you were with us, tho' it's effects were as yet scarcely sensible on society or government. I mean the British treaty which produced a schism that went on widening and rankling till the years 98. 99. when a final dissolution of all bonds civil & social appeared imminent. in that awful crisis the people awaked from the phrenzy into which they had been thrown, began to return to their sober & antient principles, &[1] have now become, five sixths, of one sentiment to wit, for peace, economy, and a government bottomed on popular election in it's legislative & Executive branches. in the public councils the Federal party hold still one third. this however will lessen, but not exactly to the standard of the people; because it will be for ever seen that of bodies of men, even elected by the people, there will always be a greater proportion aristocratic than among their constituents. The present administration had a task imposed on it, which was unavoidable, and could not fail to excite the bitterest hostility in those opposed to it. the preceding administration left 99. out of every hundred in public office of the Federal sect. Republicanism had been[2] the mark on Cain which had rendered those who bore it exiles from all portion in the trusts & authorities of their country. this description of citizens called imperiously & justly for a restoration of right. it was intended however to have yielded to this in so moderate a degree as might conciliate those who had obtained exclusive possession. but as soon as they were touched, they endeavored to set fire to the four corners of the public fabric and obliged us to deprive of the influence of office several who were using it with activity and virulence to destroy the confidence of the people in their government, and thus to proceed in the drudgery of removal farther than would have been had not their own hostile enterprises rendered it necessary in self-defence. but I think it will not be long before the whole nation will be consolidated in their antient principles, excepting a few who have committed themselves beyond recall, and who will retire to obscurity & settled disaffection.

Altho' you will receive[3] thro' the official channel of the war office every communication necessary to develope to you our views respecting the Indians and to direct your conduct, yet supposing it will be satisfactory to you, and to those with whom you are placed, to understand my personal dispositions & opinions in this particular, I shall avail myself of this private letter to state them generally. I consider the business of hunting as already become insufficient to furnish clothing and subsistence to the Indians. the promotion of agriculture therefore and houshold manufacture are essential for their preservation, and I am disposed to aid and encourage it liberally. this will enable them to live on much smaller portions of land, and indeed will render their vast forests useless, but for the range of cattle,[4] for which purpose also, as they become better farmers, they will be found useless and even disadvantageous. while they are learning to do better on less land, our increasing numbers will be calling for more land, and thus[5] a coincidence of interests will be produced between those who have lands to spare and want other necessaries,[6] and those who have such necessaries to spare and want lands. this commerce then will be for the good of both, and those who are friends to both ought to encourage it. you are in the station peculiarly charged with this interchange, and who have it peculiarly in your power to promote among the Indians a sense of[7] the superior value of a little land well-cultivated over a great deal unimproved, and to encourage them to make this estimate truly. the wisdom of the animal which amputates & abandons to the hunter the parts for which he is pursued, should be theirs, with this difference that the former sacrifices what is useful. the latter what is not. in truth the ultimate point of rest & happiness for them is to let our settlements and theirs meet and blend together, to intermix and become one people, incorporating themselves with us as citizens of the US. this is what the natural progress of things will of course bring on, and it will be better to promote than to retard it. surely it will be better for them to be identified with us, and preserved in the occupation of their lands, than be exposed to the many casualties which may endanger them while a separate people. I have little doubt but that your reflections must have led you to view the various ways in which their history may terminate, and to see that this is the one most for their happiness. and we have already had an application from a settlement of Indians to become citizens of the US. it is possible, perhaps probable that this idea may be so novel as that it might shock the Indians were it even hinted to them. of course you will keep it for your own reflection. but convinced of it's soundness, I feel it consistent with pure morality to lead them towards it, to familiarize them to the idea that it is for their interest to cede lands at times to the US. and for us thus to procure gratifications to our citizens from time to time by new acquisitions of land. from no quarter is there at present so strong a pressure on this subject as from Georgia for the residue of the fork of Oconee & Oakmulgee; and indeed I believe it will be difficult to resist it. as it has been mentioned that the Creeks had at one time made up their minds to sell this, and were only checked in it by some indiscretions of an individual, I am in hopes you will be able to bring them to it again. I beseech you to use your most earnest endeavors for it. it will relieve us here from a great pressure, and yourself from the unreasonable suspicions of the Georgians which you notice, that you are more attached to the interests of the Indians than of the US. and throw cold water on their willingness to part with lands. it is so easy to excite suspicions, that none are to be wondered at: but I am in hopes it will be in your power to quash them by effecting the object.

Mr. Madison enjoys better health since his removal to this place, than he had done in Orange. mr Giles is in a state of health feared to be irrecoverable, altho' he may hold on for some time, and perhaps be reestablished. Browse Trist is now in the Missisipi territory forming an establishment for his family which is still in Albemarle, & will remove to the Missisipi in the spring. mrs Trist his mother begins to yield a little to time. I retain myself very perfect health having not had 20. hours of fever in 40. years past. I have sometimes had troublesome headachs, and some slight rheumatic pains. but, now sixty years old nearly, I have had as little to complain of in point of health as most people. I learn you have the gout. I did not expect that Indian cookery or Indian fare would produce that. but it is considered as a security for good health otherwise. that it may be so with you I sincerely pray, and tender you my friendly and respectful salutations.

TH: JEFFERSON

RC (Francis W. Taylor, Pensacola, Florida, 1966, on deposit at University of West Florida, Pensacola); at foot of first page: "Colo. Hawkins." PrC (DLC).

MR. HILL'S RETURN TO YOU: see Hawkins to TJ, 15 Jan. 1803.

SO LONG ABSENT: since his appointment as Indian agent by George Washington in 1796, Hawkins had resided almost exclusively among the Southwestern tribes, primarily with the Creeks (ANB).

BRITISH TREATY: Jay Treaty.

For the most recent pressure from GEORGIA to extinguish Indian title in the FORK OF OCONEE and Ocmulgee Rivers, as well as criticism of Hawkins's alleged attachment TO THE INTERESTS OF THE INDIANS, see James Jackson to TJ, 14 Feb. 1803.

[1] Preceding word and ampersand interlined.

[2] Preceding two words interlined in place of "was."

[3] TJ here canceled "all."

[4] TJ first wrote "which parcels, as they become better farmers, will be found useless and disadvantageous," before altering the remainder of the sentence.

[5] TJ here canceled "produce."

[6] Word interlined in place of "comforts."

[7] Preceding three words interlined.

To George Jefferson

DEAR SIR Washington Feb. 18. 1803.

I inclose you the reciept of Capt Sprogell of the Sloop Dolphin who sailed from Alexandria the 15th. inst. and having had fair winds is now probably in James river. besides the boxes & hampers No. 1. to 18. he was to recieve at Alexandria a cask or keg of crackers, and some packages of porter. I will thank you to forward these, when recieved, by a trustworthy boatman to Milton. I expect to be at Monticello myself about the 9th. of March, to stay there a fortnight only. Accept my affectionate salutations. TH: JEFFERSON

PrC (MHi); at foot of text: "Mr. George Jefferson"; endorsed by TJ in ink on verso. Recorded in SJL with notation "things for Monticello sailed from Alexa. 15th."

For the shipment to Monticello that included CRACKERS and PORTER, see John Barnes to TJ, 10 Feb. Also likely included in the shipment was a large quantity of sherry, 424 bottles of Pedro Ximenes, a sweet variety, and 278 bottles of different quality sherries, which Étienne Lemaire recorded packing "pour Monteselo" on 13 Feb. (MS in ViU, entirely in Lemaire's hand; MB, 2:1115).

From Joseph Anderson, William Cocke, and William Dickson

SIR, Feby 19th. 1803

Some days ago, we had the honer to adress you, in Conjunction with the Members of Congress from Georgia and Kentucky; upon the Subject of a Road, from Danville, through Tennessee, to Augusta in Georgia—In Support of that adress, we now beg leave to present some resolutions pass'd by our Legislature and inclos'd to us by the Governor—from the Tenor of those *Resolutions*, it will appear that the State we have the honer to represent, is particularly Anxious to Obtain this desireable Object—And as its Utility to the Citizens of our State, will much depend upon the part of the Indian Country through which it may pass, it will be of great moment to have the most Skillful Judicious Woodsmen, that can be Obtaind (and who have a knowledge of the Country) to explore the ground, and point out the most Eligible Way—for that purpose, on the part of Tennessee, we take the liberty of recommending Mr Isaac Thomas (of Sevierville) in the County of Sevier—

As the Legislature of our State will at their next meeting be anxious to know,—what attention we have paid to their resolutions, and what prospect there will be of Obtaining their Object, we request the favor of a Written Answer to this adress—

With Sentiments of due Consideration

JOS: ANDERSON
WM. COCKE
WM. DICKSON

RC (PHi); in Anderson's hand, signed by Anderson, Cocke, and Dickson; addressed: "The President of the United States"; endorsed by TJ as received 22 Feb. and so recorded in SJL. Dft (T); in Anderson's hand; endorsed by Anderson: "Upon the Subject of a Road from Danville to Augusta." Enclosures not found.

SOME DAYS AGO: John Breckinridge and Others to TJ, 10 Feb. 1803.

A native of Virginia and former Indian trader, ISAAC THOMAS served as a military scout for John Sevier and others against the Cherokee before retiring to his farm in Sevier County (James Grant Wilson and John Fiske, eds., *Appleton's Cyclopædia of American Biography*, 6 vols. [New York, 1888], 6:82; John R. Finger, *Tennessee Frontiers: Three Regions in Transition* [Bloomington, Ind., 2001], 59, 61, 65).

From Samuel J. Cabell

DEAR SIR

Feby. 19h. 1803

It is with the utmost difficulty that I can prevail upon myself to make application to you for the appointment to office of any person, however dear to me, as my confidence in your wisdom and Patriotism is so great, as to impress me with the most satisfactory belief, that your circumspection will ever produce the best selection of Characters—

yet under my present impressions, I can not forego recommending to your attention. Col. Greene, the present Member of Congress from the Mississippi Territory, as a Gentleman well and ably qualified to discharge the duties of a Brigadier General in case you should deem one proper therefor—indeed, Sir, I conceive that his address and Talents united with his Zealous and firm Republican principles peculiarly mark him out as a character by far the best fitted to fill that Station of any person within that Territory that has come within my notice—which concludes me with the highest consideration

Dear Sir yours truly SAM: J CABELL

RC (DNA: RG 59, LAR); at foot of text: "The President of the U States"; endorsed by TJ as received 19 Feb. and "Greene to be Brigadr. Genl." and so recorded in SJL.

Samuel J. Cabell (1756-1818) of Amherst County attended the College of William and Mary and attained the brevet rank of colonel during the American Revolution. He was a member of the Virginia House of Delegates from 1785 to 1792 and also represented Amherst County at the state ratifying convention in 1788, where he voted against ratification. Elected to Congress in 1795, Cabell was a solid Republican whom TJ supported when his circular letters to his constituents were criticized by James Iredell and a federal grand jury. However, TJ was also critical of his absences from Congress in 1798 and sought unsuccessfully to replace him with James Monroe the following year. Cabell was defeated for reelection in 1803 by TJ's son-in-law, Thomas Mann Randolph, and thereafter retired from public life (DVB, 2:494-5; Vol. 29:418-19n, 491-504, 594; Vol. 30:279, 363, 641-2).

COL. GREENE: Thomas Marston Green.

From Henry Dearborn

War Department
19. February 1803

SIR,

I take the liberty of proposing to your consideration the following promotions (viz)

2d. Lieut: Bartholomew D. Armistead, 2d. Regt. of Infantry, to be 1st. Lieut: vice, 1st. Lieut. Samuel Lane, resigned 12th. August 1802.

2d. Lieut: Benjamin Wilkinson, 2d. Regt. of Infantry, to be 1st. Lieut: vice, 1st. Lieut: G. Barde dismissed the service

Ensign Josiah Taylor 2d. Regt. of Infantry, to be 2d. Lieutenant vice, 2d. Lieut: B. D. Armistead promoted.

Ensign William L. Chew, 2d. Regt. Infantry, to be 2d. Lieutenant, vice, 2d. Lieut: Benja. Wilkinson promoted.

Should the above suggested promotions meet your approbation, I have to request that the names of Cordiah N. Daniel, and Jonathan H. Sparhawk, who were appointed during the last recess of Congress, Surgeons Mates in the Army, may be added to the list to be sent to the Senate for confirmation.

I am, Sir, with great respect, Yr: Obt: Servant

H. Dearborn

RC (DLC); in a clerk's hand, signed by Dearborn; at foot of text: "The President of the U. States"; endorsed by TJ as received from the War Department on 22 Feb. and so recorded in SJL; also endorsed by TJ: "Nominations"; on verso in another clerk's hand: "Sparhawk—N. Hampshire Daniel—Mississippi Territory." FC (Lb in DNA: RG 107, LSP).

TJ included the above promotions and nominations in his message to the Senate of 1 Mch. 1803.

To Thomas McKean

Dear Sir Washington Feb. 19. 1803.

Your's of the 7th. inst. has been duly recieved. the late election in Pensylvania has to be sure been a triumphant proof of the progress of the republican spirit: and must afford great consolation to yourself personally, as a mark of the public approbation of your administration. I believe we may consider the mass of the states South & West of Connecticut & Massachusets as now a consolidated body of republicanism. in Connecticut, Massachusets & N. Hampshire there is still a federal ascendancy: but it is near it's last. if we can settle happily the difficulties of the Missisipi, I think we may promise ourselves smooth seas during our time. the federal candidates for the general government I believe are certainly to be mr King & Genl. Pinckney. of this I believe you may be assured. mr Ross, so strongly marked by popular rejection in his late competition with you, and to retire from the Senate within a few days by a like rejection by the representatives of his state, is setting himself up by his war-movements here as if he were their[1] friend, & the only person who has their confidence. I have been told he has declared the people of his quarter would go of their own authority & take N. Orleans, & that he would head them himself. but I rather suppose it sufficient, that a measure has his approbation, to produce their distrust of it. mr Harris has been informed that a consulship (I believe it is at Rotterdam) is vacant, if it will suit him. for mr T. Rodney I should certainly be glad to do any service; but really do not foresee any vacancy likely to happen where he could be employed. so also as to mr Mc.lanachan. the fact is that we have put down the great mass of offices which gave such a patronage to the President of the US. these had been so numerous, that presenting themselves to the public eye at all times & places, office began to be looked to as a resource for every man whose affairs were getting into derangement, or who was too indolent to pursue his profession, and for young men just entering into life. in short it was poisoning the very source of industry, by presenting an easier resource for a livelihood, and was corrupting the principles of the great mass of those who cast a wishful eye on office. the case is now quite changed. we have almost nothing to give. in such a state as Pensylvania for instance, I recollect but 6. offices within my appointment, 3. of which are of the law, & 3. in the customs. for I do not count the commissioners of bankruptcy, who will so soon be put down with the law. while the habit of looking for office therefore continues, the means of gratifying it have been given up.

On the subject of prosecutions, what I say must be entirely confidential, for you know the passion for torturing every sentiment & word which comes from me. the Federalists having failed in destroying the freedom of the press by their gag-law, seem to have attacked it in an opposite form, that is by pushing it's licentiousness and it's lying to such a degree of prostitution as to deprive it of all credit. and the fact is that so abandoned are the tory presses in this particular that even the least informed of the people have learnt that nothing in a newspaper is to be believed. this is a dangerous state of things, and the press ought to be restored to it's credibility if possible. the restraints provided by the laws of the states are sufficient for this if applied: and I have therefore long thought that a few prosecutions of the most eminent offenders would have a wholsome effect in restoring the integrity of the presses. not a general prosecution, for that would look like persecution: but a selected one. the paper I now inclose appears to me to offer as good an instance in every respect to make an example of, as can be selected. however of this you are the best judge. I inclose it lest you should not have it. if the same thing be done in some other of the states it will place the whole band more on their guard. Accept my friendly salutations & assurances of my high respect & consideration. TH: JEFFERSON

RC (PHi); at foot of first page: "Govr. Mc.Kean"; endorsed: "Private." PrC (DLC). Enclosure not found, but see below.

LATE COMPETITION: McKean overwhelmingly won the 1802 gubernatorial election with 47,879 votes to James Ross's 17,037. The Pennsylvania Federalists won no seats in the state senate and only 9 out of 86 in the house of representatives. The general assembly elected Republican Samuel Maclay to succeed Ross in the U.S. Senate when it met in December 1802 (Higginbotham, *Pennsylvania Politics*, 46; *Kline's Carlisle*

Weekly Gazette, 22 Dec. 1802). WAR-MOVEMENTS: on 14 Feb., Ross addressed the Senate for two hours, noting that he could not go home to his constituents without making an effort "to avert the calamity which threatened the Western country." He was convinced "that more than negotiation was absolutely necessary" to regain the right of deposit at New Orleans. Congress should give the president the power to vindicate "the wounded honor and the best interests of the country." Two days later, Ross brought forward a set of resolutions, which asserted that the United States had an indisputable right to the free navigation of the Mississippi River and to a "convenient place of deposit" at New Orleans. The late infraction of this right by Spain indicated that it was inconsistent with the safety of the Union "to hold a right so important by a tenure so uncertain." The resolutions authorized the president to call into service up to 50,000 militiamen from South Carolina, Georgia, Ohio, Kentucky, Tennessee, or the Mississippi Territory to augment U.S. military and naval forces and together take immediate possession of a site or sites deemed fit for a place of deposit. Ross proposed a $5,000,000 appropriation to carry the resolutions into effect. During the debate, which began on 23 Feb. and continued through the 25th, William H. Wells and Samuel White of Delaware, Jonathan Dayton of New Jersey, Gouverneur Morris of New York, and Ross presented lengthy arguments in support of the resolutions, while John Breckinridge of Kentucky, William Cocke and Joseph Anderson of Tennessee, DeWitt Clinton of New York, Robert Wright of Maryland, and James Jackson of Georgia led the opposition. On the last day of debate, Stevens Thomson Mason observed: "Here we see a number of people from the Eastern States and the seaboard, filled with the most extreme solicitude for the interest and rights of the western and inland States; while the representatives of the Western people themselves appear to know nothing of this great danger, and to feel a full confidence in their government." The resolutions were defeated by a 15 to 11 vote, Ross being the only western member to vote for them. The Senate went on to adopt resolutions proposed by Breckinridge, which gave the president the authority, if he judged it expedient, to cooperate with all of the states in organizing, arming, equipping, and holding in readiness a militia of up to 80,000 men and a corps of volunteers. Congress appropriated $1,500,000 to cover the expenses and $25,000 to construct and furnish one or more arsenals on the western waters at such place or places as the president thought proper. Congress had also authorized the president to have up to 15 gunboats built and used as the "public service may require" (*Annals*, 12:83-97, 105-206, 208-56; *Biog. Dir. Cong.*; Arthur Preston Whitaker, *The Mississippi Question, 1795-1803: A Study in Trade, Politics, and Diplomacy* [New York, 1934], 215-17; U.S. Statutes at Large, 2:206, 241; Robert Smith to TJ, 19 Jan. 1803).

Debate on repeal of the bankruptcy LAW took place in the House of Representatives on 13 Jan. and 16 and 18 Feb., when it was decided to postpone the question until the next session of Congress. The act was repealed in December soon after Congress reconvened (*Annals*, 12:375-9, 530-3, 546-65; Vol. 37:702).

PAPER I NOW INCLOSE: TJ perhaps sent McKean a recent copy of Joseph Dennie's *Port Folio*. The 15 Jan. 1803 issue included satirical references to James T. Callender's "stories of black Sall and Mrs. Walker"; to the Barbary powers, who "having heard that we had sold our Navy" are "excluding our vessels from the Mediterranean"; to the entertainment of Thomas Paine in Washington by "our religious chief," with introductions "to the mammoth cheese, Mr. Duane, Mr. Gallatin, and the rest of the royal family"; and an article defending Callender and freedom of the press. It also included the first installment of "Progress of Democracy." In July 1803, Pennsylvania authorities brought libel charges against Dennie for a passage in the 23 Apr. issue of *The Port Folio*, describing the "futility" of democracy and predicting, "It is on its trial here, and the issue will be civil war, desolation, and anarchy" (Philadelphia *Port Folio*, 15, 22, 29 Jan., 23 Apr. 1803; Rowe, *McKean*, 337-8; Pasley, *Tyranny of Printers*, 251-2, 256, 264-5). For Dennie, see Vol. 34:517n.

[1] TJ here canceled "only."

From Craven Peyton

DEAR SIR Stump Island 19. Feby 1803

yours of the 8th. has Just come to hand, and am much hurt at being compeled to send my ovarseer with this request but am in hopes to be excused when I inform you it is from pure necessity, which is from security ship. And if a considerable sum is not paid by the twenty sixth of the month a considerable sacrafice must be made in proparty and no chance for me to be reimbursd. again, after giveing you the real situation I am fully assured that if you can possibly make it convenient to give a draft on Geo. Jefferson & Co. payable the Tenth of march for 1000 D. you will relieve me. this will be receavd. as cash by the sherriff as it cant be demand. of him untill about that time, respecting the othar payments every exertion in my power shall be used to make them as distant as possible,

I am with much Respt. Yr. mst. Obt. C PEYTON

RC (ViU); endorsed by TJ as received 23 Feb. and so recorded in SJL.

BY THE SHERRIFF: probably William Michie, who served as sheriff of Albemarle County in 1803 (Woods, *Albemarle*, 274).

From Robert Smith

[19 Feb. 1803]

The Secretary of the Navy has not deemed it expedient to write the proposed letter to Jacob Bauldin because he cannot ascertain that such a person is in the City or in Geo. Town. It is, besides, believed that such a person, if worthy of attention, would present himself in person—He certainly ought to do so—

RC (DLC); undated; addressed: "The President"; endorsed by TJ as received from the Navy Department on 19 Feb. and "Bauldin" and so recorded in SJL as a letter of 19 Feb.

A letter from JACOB BAULDIN to TJ, dated 15 Feb. 1803 from Washington, is recorded in SJL as received 17 Feb. with the notation "N," but has not been found.

From James Taylor, Jr.

SIR Norfolk Febry 19. 1803

I am directed by Col: Newton to furnish you with two pipes of wine, which I have this day shipped on board the sloop Maria Capt: O'Meara, to the address of Mr: John Barnes, of George Town—the account is annexed—The quality is similar to that I sent before & I hope will give equal satisfaction—

I am respectfully Yr: ob: servt. JAS TAYLOR JR

T. Jefferson Esqr. to James Taylor jr.		Dr.
2 pipes Brazil Wine	350—	700 —
Drayage		25
5 gallons apple Brandy put into the Cyder shippd last year.		6 25
		706=. 50

RC (MHi); endorsed by TJ as received 3 Mch. and so recorded in SJL with notation "2. pipes wine 706.50."

A bill of lading intended for John Barnes likely accompanied the shipment of BRAZIL quality Madeira wine (MS in ViU; being a printed form dated 21 Feb. 1803, filled out by James Taylor, Jr., and signed by Francis O. Meara, describing a shipment of two pipes of wine branded with Thomas Newton's mark on the *Maria* bound for Alexandria, "OMeara," master, with subsequent shipment to Georgetown; endorsed on verso by Barnes as payment for freight from Norfolk to Alexandria for $4.25, from Alexandria to Georgetown for $1.33, and from Georgetown to the President's House for $1.00, for a total of $6.58).

From John Carroll

SIR Baltimore Feb. 20– 1803

The papers inclosed, which I have the honour to transmit to you, have been for some time in my hands. Mr. Joseph Coppinger, now, or lately at Pittsburg, from whom I received them, requests that they may be submitted to your inspection, informing me at the same time, that he has already been honoured by some communications to and from you. This gentleman is personally unknown to me; but brought two letters for me from Ireland from most respectable characters there; both of which represent him as a person of great integrity, ingenuity, & agricultural knowledge, as well as possessing an intimate acquaintance with some useful manufactures.

I have the honour to be with the highest respect, Sir, Your most obedt. servt. J. CARROLL

RC (DLC). Recorded in SJL as received 21 Feb. Enclosures not found, but see Joseph Coppinger to TJ, 3 Jan.

PERSONALLY UNKNOWN TO ME: while Carroll, the Roman Catholic bishop of Baltimore, was not familiar with Joseph Coppinger, he was undoubtedly acquainted with his brother, William, a bishop from County Cork, Ireland (Vol. 35:202-3n; Vol. 38:508n).

From Thomas Rodney

DEAR SIR Dover February 20th. 1803.

Being distant from the seat of government, and unacquainted with the business of the Cabinet, it is with reluctance that I Take the Liberty of Troubling you with this letter, or of advising any thing respecting public appointments in any case, but on the present Occasion have been prevailed on by a number of leading Republicans to write a few lines respecting the Collectorship of the Port of Wilmington in this State—about which there appears to be considerable adgitation at this time—Yet being unacquainted with the official conduct of the present Collector I can Say nothing on that head—but can assure the government that So far as I have heard the Sentiments of the Republicans of this State, they are Unanimous in disiring that the present Officer Should be removed—but they are Not Equally Unanimous in pointing out a Successor, however I believe a Majority of them are in favor of *Col. Nehemiah Tilton* (brother of the Doctor) who is Considered as a firm Republican, and a Steadfast friend of the Present administration, and a person Who has held Several respectable offices in this State—But without Saying any thing more on this Occasion I Submit it to your own wisdom and better information to do what you May think best and beg leave to Conclude with assurances of My verry high respect and Esteem.

Your Most Obedient THOMAS RODNEY

RC (DNA: RG 59, LAR); endorsed by TJ as received 26 Feb. and so recorded in SJL with notation "Tilton to be Collector."

PRESENT COLLECTOR: Allen McLane. According to SJL, TJ received another recommendation from Dover, Delaware, on 18 Mch. expressing SENTIMENTS in favor of Nehemiah Tilton in place of McLane, but it has not been found.

BROTHER OF THE DOCTOR: Rodney's political connections with Dr. James Tilton went back to the Revolution. In 1775, both were elected to the Kent County Committee of Correspondence, with Rodney serving as chairman (William Baskerville Hamilton, *Anglo-American Law on the Frontier: Thomas Rodney & His Territorial Cases* [Durham, N.C., 1953], 11).

For Rodney's earlier correspondence with TJ, see Vol. 17:547-51 and Vol. 29:249n. For Caesar A. Rodney's description of his father, see Vol. 32:370-1.

From Elize Winn

Hail Louisville Ky Feby 20th 1803

Father of the nations our emperor the man we love
Next heaven if I said more twere scarce a Sin
You are all thats good and god like
In the full vintage of thy flowing honours Sat Still
And saw it presst by other hands fortune Came Smileing
To thy youth an wood it and purple greatness met thy
Ripend years
When first you Cam to Empire was borne on tides of people
To thy triumph the wish of nations and the willing word
Received as thy pledge of futer peace
O peace sweet union of States what else but thou gives
Strength and glory to a people me think again I see those gentle
days renewd that blessd our isle I see our
plains unbounded waveing with the gifts of harvest
Our Seas with Commerce Throng our busey ports
with Cheerful toil
Our nymphs and Shepherds Sporting in each vale inspire
New song and wake the pastoral reed—Come my Sons I long
To See this prince of whom the world Speaks largely
Well whose name Ile teach you to lisp whose fortunes
You shall follow
His cause thy nerveous arms shall defend and may those
wings that spreds from Shore to Shore Vouchsaf to Shelter me and
My little familey … and long may he live to rule america
O may he be blessd as he deserves is the prayers of his most Humbl
and obedient Servt

Except as a pledge of my love and ready obedience a few peccans they were sent to me by a french lady from St vincenes I never opend them but send them On to you with my preyers and beg you may recieve them I am Dear Sir your ever faithful Servt Elize Winn

RC (DLC); at foot of text: "Thomas Jefferson Presedt. of the U.S."; endorsed by TJ as received 16 Mch. and so recorded in SJL.

To John Daly Burk

SIR Washington Feb. 21. 1803.

Your favor of the 2d. has been duly recieved. in the early part of my life I paid a good deal of attention to the state papers of Virginia, and in some degree, to those of the other states. the result of my enquiries is contained in the list of statepapers at the end of the Notes on Virginia, and so far as I possessed any of these papers they were communicated to mr Hazard to be published in his Collection of statepapers. independent of these I possess a tolerably compleat set of the printed laws of Virginia. this being the only set in existence, (for they are lost from the offices) and being now resorted to from all parts of the state as the only resource for laws not to be found in the late publications, I have been obliged to decline letting the volumes go out of my possession further than Milton or Charlottesville, because the loss of a volume would be irreparable. the consequence is that the courts instead of requiring the volume itself to be produced to them as evidence, accept a copy from me; so that they are substantially a deposit of records. I mention this as a reason why I cannot offer them to be taken to a distance. I possess also a file of Virginia newspapers from about 1733 to about 1775. these are all the materials in my possession, and to a free use of which you shall be perfectly welcome, & to every other service I can render to your undertaking, to which I ask leave to become one of the subscribers. I doubt whether the laws furnish any thing material or interesting to the historian. the laws of England for instance, scarcely enter at all into the history of England. I pray you to accept my best wishes & respects TH: JEFFERSON

PrC (DLC); at foot of text: "Mr. John D. Burk."

For TJ's collection of the STATE PAPERS OF VIRGINIA, see Susan Myra Kingsbury, ed., *The Records of the Virginia Company of London*, 4 vols. (Washington, D.C., 1906-35), 1:41-54. For the results of his ENQUIRIES about the papers of other states, see his list of more than 200 documents from 1496 to 1768 in *Notes*, ed. Peden, 177-96, 269n. TJ was a subscriber to the 1774 proposal of Ebenezer HAZARD to publish a collection of American state papers and in 1775 TJ offered to assist in gathering the records for Hazard's *Historical Collections; Consisting of State Papers, and Other Authentic Documents; Intended as Materials for an History of the United States of America*, published in two volumes in Philadelphia in 1792 and 1794 (Sowerby, No. 3044; Vol. 1:144-9, 164-5, 176; Vol. 19:284-5, 287-8; Vol. 22:294).

To John Wayles Eppes

Dear Sir Washington Feb. 21. 1803.

Your's of the 10th. was recieved on the 16th. I shall leave this about the 6th. of March, unless unexpected business, bad roads or bad weather should delay it a little. I am happy to learn that I shall meet Maria & yourself at Monticello. my stay there will be of two or three weeks, the visit being for the purpose of planting trees, in order that they may be growing during my absence. as Lilly hired 15. hands for me this winter, I am not without hopes he will be able to accomplish my canal, and perhaps your levelling both. but as the latter must be postponed to the former, it will of course be autumn before the levelling will be begun, which will throw the building into the next year. I am in hopes Maria's visit in March is intended to continue till the sickly season of the autumn is over. in your letter of Nov. 27. you mentioned that the receipt of the 400. D. in March would be quite sufficient, or even later if it should be inconvenient to me. I am not yet certain how that will be; but either then, if I have it not in hand, or at any other moment when your calls require it, I can get it from the bank here; but that being in the hands of federalists, I am not fond of asking favors of them. however I have done it once or twice when my own resources have failed, and can do it at all times. the approach of my meeting with yourself and Maria makes me look with impatience to the 6th. of March. present her my tenderest affections. make short journies as you travel that you may never be out in the night; and accept my affectionate salutations and sincere esteem

Th: Jefferson

RC (Mrs. Francis Shine, Los Angeles, California, 1946); addressed: "John W. Eppes Bermuda H. near City point"; franked and postmarked. PrC (CSmH); endorsed by TJ in ink on verso.

my canal: see TJ to James Walker, 1 Oct. 1802.

Eppes's letter of 27 Nov., recorded in SJL as received 3 Dec. from Bermuda Hundred has not been found.

i can get it from the bank here: for TJ's experiences with notes on the Bank of Columbia, see Vol. 37:439-40n, 459.

From James Madison

[21 Feb. 1803]

The inclosed report as altered is acquiesced in by Mr. L. In two instances recurred to Congs have already interposed; one of them the Paoli—at last Session. The judgmt. of the Court agst Capt. Maley was pd. by Congs—Several Dutch & British precedts. can also be cited. The 7 Art: of the British Treaty & 21 of the Span: go on the responsibility of those Govts. for irregular acts of Officers under their authy. or *colour* of it—our instructions relative to Spanish Spoliations have the same implication. If the principle be tenable, it is evidently & greatly in favor of the U.S. in a general view. Two correct copies will be sent to the P. in the Morning—The present one is sent that if approved, he may accomodate his message to it without further delay—

RC (DLC); in pencil on verso of an address sheet with remnant text: "of the U. States"; undated; endorsed by TJ as received from the State Department on 21 Feb. and "Danish Brig Henrich. from Hambg to Cape François" and so recorded in SJL. Enclosure: Dft, not found, of Madison's report on the *Hendrick* case (see enclosure to TJ to the Senate and the House of Representatives, 23 Feb.).

ACQUIESCED IN BY MR. L.: for Levi Lincoln's opinion on the *Hendrick* question, see Topics for Consultation with Heads of Departments at 10 Feb.

PD. BY CONGS: Peder Blicher Olsen had contacted Madison on 17 Feb., urging action by Congress in the case of the *Hendrick* and observing that the session would end soon. In April 1802, Congress authorized a payment to Paolo Paoly, the master of a Danish merchant ship that had been captured by a U.S. armed schooner under the command of William Maley. A U.S. district court condemned the Danish ship as a French armed vessel and lawful prize, but the circuit court overturned the decision and Congress agreed to award Paoly more than $7,000 in damages (Madison, *Papers*, *Sec. of State Ser.*, 3:46-7; 4:326-7, 335; U.S. Statutes at Large, 6:47).

Article 7 of the 1794 TREATY with Great Britain established a process for compensation to U.S. citizens for "irregular or illegal Captures or Condemnations of their vessels and other property under Colour of authority or Commissions from His Majesty." Article 21 of the 1795 treaty with Spain concerned compensation to Americans for captures of ships and cargoes by subjects of the Spanish crown. The treaty with Spain did not use the phrase "color of authority," but in INSTRUCTIONS to Charles Pinckney in June 1801 and February 1802, Madison referred to losses "for which Spain is held responsible" and to captures that had been made "under colour of authority from his Catholic Majesty" (Miller, *Treaties*, 2:252, 335; Madison, *Papers*, *Sec. of State Ser.*, 1:274; 2:441-2).

IN THE MORNING: see TJ to Madison, 22 Feb.

To J. P. G. Muhlenberg

DEAR SIR Washington Feb. 21. 1803.

The three boxes mentioned in your letter of the 7th. inst. were addressed to me by mr Arnold Oelrichs of Bremen, through Borger, Kramer & Rump merchts. of Hamburg to Wachsmith & Soullier of Philadelphia. they contain 3. busts of value intended as a present to me; but as I have made it a rule to accept no presents while in office, I have declined having any thing to do with them. mr Oelrichs is an entire stranger to me. he wrote me a letter describing the contents of the boxes, and informed me that his friend mr James Zwisler of Baltimore would transmit me another. this last I never received, nor any letter from messrs. Wachsmith & Soullier. but I presume these last are the proper persons to direct what is to be done with them now, observing that my taking them is out of the question. accept my friendly & respectful salutations. TH: JEFFERSON

P.S. A bill of lading is inclosed.

PrC (DLC); endorsed by TJ in ink on verso. Enclosure not found.

For the PRESENT, see Arnold Oelrichs to TJ, 28 Dec. 1802.

To Thomas Jefferson Randolph

Washington, Feb. 21st. 1803.

I have to acknowledge the receipt of your letter of the 3d, my dear Jefferson, and to congratulate you on your writing so good a hand. By the last post I sent you a French Grammar, and within three weeks I shall be able to ask you, "Parlez vous Français, monsieur?" I expect to leave this about the 9th, if unexpected business should not detain me, and then it will depend on the weather and the roads how long I shall be going—probably five days. The roads will be so deep that I can not flatter myself with catching Ellen in bed. Tell her that Mrs. Harrison Smith desires her compliments to her. Your mamma has probably heard of the death of Mrs. Burrows.[1] Mrs. Brent is not far from it. Present my affections to your papa, mamma, and the young ones, and be assured of them yourself. TH: JEFFERSON

Printed in Sarah N. Randolph, *The Domestic Life of Thomas Jefferson, Compiled from Family Letters and Reminiscences by His Great-Granddaughter*, 3d ed. (Cambridge, Mass., 1939), 249.

A LETTER OF THE 3D from Thomas Jefferson Randolph, recorded in SJL as received 11 Feb., has not been found.

[1] *Domestic Life*: "Barrows."

To the Senate

GENTLEMEN OF THE SENATE

The Tuscarora Indians, having an interest in some lands within the state of North Carolina, asked the superintendence of the Government of the US. over a treaty to be held between them & the state of North Carolina respecting these lands. William Richardson Davie was appointed a Commissioner for this purpose, and a treaty was concluded under his superintendance. this, with his letter on the subject, is now laid before the Senate for their advice & consent whether it shall be ratified.

TH: JEFFERSON
Feb. 21. 1803.

RC (DNA: RG 46, EPIR, 7th Cong., 2d sess.); endorsed by clerks. PrC (DLC). Enclosures: (1) Treaty between the United States and the Tuscarora Indians, concluded at Raleigh, North Carolina, on 4 Dec. 1802, agreeing that the Tuscaroras, with the cooperation of the legislature, will lease out their lands in Bertie County until July 1816 and then give up all claim to the land (printed copy in DNA: RG 46, EPIR; endorsed by a clerk). (2) William R. Davie to Henry Dearborn, 3 Feb. 1803, enclosing the treaty and the act of the state legislature for carrying it into effect; he explains that the reason for the leasing arrangement rather than for an outright cession of the land is that the Tuscaroras do not have title, but only rights of use (RC in same). (3) Act of the General Assembly of the state of North Carolina, 16 Dec. 1802, authorizing the Tuscaroras to continue existing lease agreements until their expiration, including an agreement made in 1766; the act authorizes changes in the leases to facilitate the Tuscaroras' collection of rents, and the governor is to appoint commissioners to protect the Indians' interests; in 1816, the lands allotted in 1748 for the use of the Tuscaroras will revert to the state (Tr in same). Message and enclosures printed in ASP, *Indian Affairs*, 1:685-6.

For the desire of the TUSCARORA INDIANS to dispose of lands in North Carolina and use the proceeds to augment their reservation in New York State, see Vol. 36:635n. TJ appointed William R. DAVIE to act as commissioner for the United States in the negotiations (Vol. 33:677; Vol. 36:332; Vol. 38: Appendix I).

ADVICE & CONSENT: the Senate received the message and papers from Meriwether Lewis on 21 Feb. and unanimously approved the treaty on 1 Mch. (JEP, 1:443-4, 445-6).

Statement of Account with George Andrews

[on or before 22 Feb. 1803]

1803 Februy. The President of the United States to George Andrews

Dr

				s	d
[lo] 73	Setts of Corinthian frieze ornaments	@ 4s/10d ℔	£17	12	10
130	pair of Scrolls for Corinthian Blocks	a 5 ℔	2	14	2
130	leaves for Do	a 4½ ℔	2	8	9
104	lenths of large egg & dart moulding	a 10 ℔ lenth	4	6	8
200	lenths of oyer moulding	a 7 ℔ d	6	5	0
43	ox Sculls	a 1/6 ℔	3	4	6
36	round pattras	a 1/4 ℔	2	8	0
130	Small pattras	a 3½	1	17	11

1	large pattra	0 1 $10\frac{1}{2}$
do	a frieze ornament for a Chimney piece	0 12 6
Cash	Paid for turning 130 Nuckles for Blocks	0 15 0
		£42 7 $2\frac{1}{2}$
	Credit for Cash Recd on acct	9 7 6
		87.96 = £32 19 $8\frac{1}{2}$

MS (ViU); partially dated; in George Andrews's hand, with figures in italics in TJ's hand; endorsed at foot of text by TJ: "Feb. 22. 1803. gave order J. Barnes."

Andrews was making composition ORNAMENTS and pateras for interior decorative work at Monticello (TJ to James Dinsmore, 1 Dec. 1802; Notes on Composition Ornaments, 17 Mch. 1803). According to TJ's financial records, on 21 Feb. he gave Andrews an order on John Barnes for $87.96 for "composition ornaments in architect" (MB, 2:1092).

To James Madison

TH:J. TO J.M. Feb. 22. 1803.

I return you the report, and have prepared a message, tho' I confess myself not satisfied on the main question, the responsibility of the government in this case, and with our taking wholly on ourselves the risk of the decision. for to enable Congress to judge for themselves the record must go; & the printing that would prevent it's being taken up this session. if we do not send in the record they must decide solely on our statement & throw the whole responsibility on us. it is certainly not known to us to be an entirely clear case. honest opinions may be given both ways, & have been given as we see by Grotius & Bynkershoek. the sum is very large. how much more clear & expedient was the case of the Berceau, & yet how much dust has it enabled the disaffected party to throw in the eyes of the nation. I acknolege that where cases are doubtful I would always decide on the liberal side. but time for full consideration & enquiry into the practice of nations it seems prudent to take in a precedent of such consequences as this may produce in future cases. how would it do for Congress to authorise the advancing a certain sum for the present relief & support of the capt. and to refer the final decision to their next meeting, on the professed ground of want of time? however if you are perfectly satisfied, I shall be in readiness to send in the report on recieving it.

I return you Monroe's instructions which are entirely right. one circumstance only might perhaps as well be left out. I mean the mention of my letter to Dupont. as that correspondence will make no part of the public records, perhaps it is as well it should not be spoken of in them. affectionate salutations.

RC (DLC: Madison Papers, Rives Collection). PrC (DLC). Enclosures: (1) Dft of Madison's report on the *Hendrick* (see Madison to TJ, [21 Feb.], and TJ to the Senate and the House, 23 Feb.). (2) Dft of Madison's instructions to Robert R. Livingston and James Monroe (see TJ to Livingston, 3 Feb.).

MY LETTER TO DUPONT: as Madison sent them under date of 2 Mch., the instructions to Livingston and Monroe referred only obliquely to TJ's correspondence with Pierre Samuel Du Pont de Nemours about New Orleans and the Floridas, without details or naming Du Pont (Madison, *Papers*, *Sec. of State Ser.*, 4:366; note to TJ to Livingston, 3 Feb.).

From Joseph H. Nicholson

SIR Feb. 22. 1803

I take the liberty to enclose you the Bill to reduce the Marine Corps, together with the Communication from the Secretary of the Navy to the Committee.

This communication exhibits an apparent necessity for the Continuance of the whole number of Lieutenants now in service, and may possibly induce some Difficulty in passing the Law—I wish therefore to know whether you have any Objection to my stating that "I have reason to believe three of the Frigates now in the Mediterranean, will return in the Course of two or three months, and that no relieving Squadron will be sent out (except the four small Vessels) unless there is reason to apprehend more extensive Hostility with the Barbary Powers"—These Facts you mentioned to me, but I conceived under an Injunction not to repeat them as coming from you with a View to the Reduction of the Marine Corps—If permitted to state them as above, I think we shall have no Difficulty.

Annexed to the Secretary's Communication, you will find such a Distribution of the Officers and Privates, as I mean to make use of in discussing the Bill—

I have the Honor to be, Sir most respectfully Yr. Ob. Servt.

JOSEPH H. NICHOLSON

RC (DLC); endorsed by TJ as received 22 Feb. and so recorded in SJL. Enclosures: (1) "A Bill To reduce the Marine Corps of the United States," 18 Feb. 1803, limits the total officers to no more than one captain and twelve lieutenants but allows the president to increase the number of lieutenants if necessary to an amount not exceeding the total authorized by existing laws, repeals the 22 Apr. 1800 act fixing the rank and pay of the Marine Corps commandant, does not revive the rank of major, and grants three months' pay to each officer discharged from the service by virtue of the act (Washington, D.C., 1803). (2) Robert Smith to Nicholson, 14 Feb. 1803, replying to Nicholson's letter of 7 Feb. regarding the duties performed by the lieutenant colonel commandant of the Marine Corps; Smith states that the commandant is responsible for recruiting men and seeing that they are supplied with clothing and provisions, for distributing Marines agreeably to the requirements of the service, for keeping guards on ships in ordinary and at navy yards, and for overseeing discipline on shore and seeing that arms are kept in order; the commandant has to correspond with the secretary of the navy, marine officers, and others; he supervises the actions of the paymaster, although all requisitions and payments pass through the commandant and on his responsibility; all accounts of expenditures by the corps are settled with him; "From this detail," Smith states, "the committee will be able to judge what rank the commanding officer of the marine corps, ought to bear," and from his enclosed statement of the present distribution of officers and men, the committee may also "determine upon the expediency or inexpediency of reducing the marine corps" (ASP, *Naval Affairs*, 1:110). (3) "Statement of the distribution and employment of the officers and privates of the marine corps" (same; see note at Smith to TJ, 8 Feb. 1803).

Nicholson's committee submitted its BILL TO REDUCE THE MARINE CORPS to the House of Representatives on 18 Feb. 1803. After discussion and amendments, the House passed the bill on 28 Feb., but the Senate withheld its concurrence and voted to postpone further discussion of it until the next session of Congress (JHR, 4:352, 368, 371, 373, 383; JS, 3:277, 279, 281, 282; Robert Smith to TJ, 8 Feb. 1803).

From Lyman Spalding

SIR, Portsmouth, Feby. 22nd 1803

Be pleased to accept a few copies of my bill of mortality for Portsmouth, N.H. for 1802.

With great respect Sir, I have the honour to be your humble Servt.

L. SPALDING

RC (DLC); at foot of text: "The President of the United States"; endorsed by TJ as received 3 Mch. and so recorded in SJL. Enclosure: Lyman Spalding, "Bill of Mortality, For Portsmouth, Newhampshire, for A.D. 1802," a printed table recording the number and causes of death, as well as the ages of the victims (same, TJ Papers, 128:22155).

For the previous year's BILL OF MORTALITY, see Vol. 36:626.

To Joseph Anderson, William Cocke, and William Dickson

GENTLEMEN Washington Feb. 23. 1803.

It is upwards of a twelvemonth since my attention was drawn to the importance of a road which should enable the inhabitants of Tenissee & Kentucky to seek a market on the Savannah, and instructions were immediately given to our Commissrs. Genl. Wilkinson & others to negotiate with the Cherokees for permission to the states interested to open the road through their country. it was stiffly rejected at first; but they have been made sensible of the urgency of the case, and have latterly shewn better dispositions. instructions have been given to bring it to a close, and when obtained we shall adopt the best means we can for having it judiciously conducted. you may assure your government that no unnecessary delay will be admitted so far as our operation is necessary. Accept my friendly salutations & assurances of respect. TH: JEFFERSON

RC (T); at foot of text: "The Senators & representative of Tenissee"; addressed: "The honble Mr. Anderson." PrC (DLC). Recorded in SJL with notation "Road."

From Nicolas Gouin Dufief

MONSIEUR. 23 février. 1803

Je me suis acquitte Vendredi dernier, de votre Commission à l'égard du Colonel Monroe—J'aurais bien voulu pouvoir accompagner d'une lettre le présent flatteur que vous faites à Mr Volney, mais le départ précipité du Colonel, qui n'a resté qu'une heure à Philadelphie, m'a empêché de remplir ce désir de mon Cœur—J'ai ajouté les sermons du Racine de la Chaire française à vos autres livres—Le tout vous sera adressé cette semaine, par eau—J'aurai l'honneur de vous écrire à ce sujet

Je suis avec les Sentimens les plus inébranlables d'estime et de respect, Votre très humble Serviteur N. G. DUFIEF

EDITORS' TRANSLATION

SIR, 23 Feb. 1803

Last Friday I fulfilled your errand regarding Colonel Monroe. I would have liked to enclose a letter with the generous gift you are sending Mr. Volney, but the hasty departure of the colonel, who stayed in Philadelphia for only an hour, prevented me from accomplishing this heart-felt wish. I added the sermons of the Racine of the French pulpit to your other books. They will all be sent to you this week, by ship. I will have the honor of writing to you about this.

With deepest feelings of respect and admiration, I am your very humble servant. N. G. DUFIEF

RC (DLC); at foot of text: "Le Président des Etats-Unis"; endorsed by TJ as received 27 Feb. and so recorded in SJL.

RACINE DE LA CHAIRE FRANÇAISE: Jean Baptiste Massillon was known as the Racine of the pulpit for the style of his sermons (*Oeuvres complètes de Massillon, évêque de Clermont*, 14 vols. [Paris, 1829], 14:xvi, 156).

To Joseph H. Nicholson

DEAR SIR Washington Feb. 23. 1803.

It may be stated with truth, I believe, that the Secretary of the Navy has made his estimate on the present state of things in the Mediterranean,[1] and the possible necessity of keeping that up, by sending a relieving squadron in place of the three frigates which are under orders to return. tho' this could only be necessary in case our warfare there should become much more extensive, yet prudence required him to be prepared for that. but as there is not the smallest ground for believing that any other of the Barbary powers thinks of breaking with us, (for as to the demands some of them are making, there is never a moment they are not demanding) the relieving squadron in place of the three frigates ordered to return, will be the three small vessels which, with the Enterprize, will be employed there, under the protection of the two remaining frigates, and will be a much more effective force than the present one, against the Tripolitans alone. and it may be said that this is plainly to be inferred from the statement of this subject in the message on the opening of Congress, where it will be seen that the vessels in the Mediterranean were reinforced only in a moment when war with other powers was expected, that this apprehension had ceased already at the opening of Congress, and orders were given for the return of a part of the force, & a proposition made to Congress to furnish smaller vessels: it may be said with truth that the Executive has[2] freely explained these ideas to such gentlemen as have made enquiries on the subject, and that it is perfectly understood to be their purpose to keep only 2 frigates & the 4. small vessels in the Mediterranean this summer: that this therefore is the only force which need be absolutely provided for, only giving power to add to it, should the present state of things be changed, contrary to present probabilities. certainly neither economy nor prudence permits to keep in actual service all the force which might be necessary in the worst state of things; for then we ought to keep a large standing army. you will of course percieve that this letter is not intended to be communicated to any body, but is confidentially for yourself. Accept my friendly and respectful salutations.

TH: JEFFERSON

RC (NNFoM); addressed: "The honble Joseph H. Nicholson." PrC (DLC); in ink at foot of text: "Joseph Nicholson esq." Recorded in SJL with notation "marine corps."

MESSAGE ON THE OPENING OF CONGRESS: Annual Message to Congress, 15 Dec. 1802.

[1] Preceding three words interlined.

[2] Word interlined.

To Craven Peyton

Dear Sir Washington Feb. 23. 1803.

Before I ventured to write you my letter of the 8th. inst. I entered into arrangements with my banker in Georgetown to be sure that I could punctually comply with what was therein undertaken. immediately on the reciept of yours to-day I went to him again to see if he could throw the two paiments of 500. D. each promised for March & April into one of 1000. D. for March. on examining the state of his affairs he undertook[1] to do it. I therefore am able now to inclose you a draught on Gibson & Jefferson as you desire for 1000. D. payable at their counting house the 10th. of March, & shall inform them that the money shall be in their hands by the post of that evening. I shall be happy if the accomplishment of this object shall render the arrangements of the letter of the 8th. instant suitable to your purposes. Accept my best wishes & respects. Th: Jefferson

RC (Mrs. G. T. Errickson, Lexington, Kentucky, 1956); addressed: "Mr. Craven Peyton Albemarle" and "by mr Hunter." PrC (ViU); pressed on same sheet as enclosure; endorsed by TJ in ink on verso. Recorded in SJL with notation "1000. D." Enclosure: Order on Gibson & Jefferson, dated Washington, 23 Feb., noting, "Pay to Craven Peyton or order one thousand dollars on the tenth day of March ensuing for value recieved" (PrC in same; at foot of text: "1000. D." and "Messrs. Gibson & Jefferson").

my banker in georgetown: John Barnes.

inform them: see TJ to George Jefferson, 25 Feb. TJ recorded this $1,000 order in his financial records at 23 Feb. as "part paimt. land" (mb, 2:1093).

[1] Interlined in place of "agreed."

From Benjamin Reynolds

Sir/ Phila: Feby 23d: 1803

Fully impressed with the importance of Your Station, and proportionately enjoying the Blessings derived under Your mild, benevolent and wise Administration, by the people of these United States: I feel myself emboldened to assume what You have acknowledged a "Right" but which in a former time would have been termed "an insolent liberty" That Sir, of personally addressing You; and upon the following facts.

On the 1st. June 1799. I addressed a Letter to oliver Woolcott Esquire the then Secretary of the Treasury, containing several allegations against the Conduct of Allen McLane Esqr. Collector of the Port of Wilmington in the State of Delaware of which Port I had been the Gauger for upwards of seven Years, and from which Station

I was dismissed by Mr McLane.— This Letter also contained a certificate signed by thirty one of the most respectable Merchants and Traders of that Port, expressing their satisfaction with and approbation of my conduct.

On the 27th June 1799. Mr Woolcott sent me an official Letter informing "that Mr McLane had transmitted a fully reply dated the seventh instant" (June 1799) and concluding with "he could not consistently with a sense of Justice and duty omit to declare that his vindication appeared to him satisfactory."[1]

I shall offer no comment upon this Novel way of dismissing a complaint; my accusations and Mr McLanes defence are filed in the Secretarys office.

On Mr Gallatins succeeding Mr Woolcott, I conceived a proper time presented to renew my complaint and that a period was arrived when delinquency in official conduct (however remote) would not so easily be passed over.

Accordingly on the 23d april 1801—I addressed a Letter to the present Secretary, restating my charges against Mr McLane, attended with some few remarks upon the popular prejudices and fixed opinions of the Citizens of Delaware; and requesting a Copy of McLanes defence, or reply to my charges.

On the 22d May following, Mr Gallatin acknowledged the receipt of my Letter inclosing therein, "such parts of Mr McLanes Reply to Mr Woolcott as relate to those charges" and further informing that my Letter would be speedily laid before Your Excellency.

On the 28th of the same Month, I again addressed Mr Gallatin and cursorily observing upon the equivocal and shifting defence of Mr McLane: His artifices, His intrigues, His notorious oppression in official relations, His subornation of Testimony, His Reprimand from Mr Bedford the district Judge for his improper conduct &c. &c. I inclosed the Secretary an affidavit of a Mr James Welsh establishing three of my principal allegations; and on the seventh of June following I forwarded the affidavits of Thomas Moore, James Bevins and Lewis R. Brown in further proof.

Mr Gallatin with his wonted promptitude on the 18th June 1801, inclosed me Your Excellencys direction that an inquiry should immediately be instituted in the proof of my charges, and that James Tilton and George Read Junior Esquires were selected for that purpose.

On the 6th: July following, I again applied to the Secretary of the Treasury, requesting from him, official information in my complaint against McLane, and particularly whether Mr McLane had charged the United States *thirty Dollars* per Month for his Bargemen, and more particularly for the Month of april 1797—Perhaps, the extreme pressure of Business in Mr Gallatins department at that time prevented his complying with my request—It was to me a very necessary and important obtainment—I was disappointed.

Messrs Tilton and Reed very readily accepted Your Excellencys appointment; and proceeded in their inquiry with equal candour and correctness.

But even here the evil Genius of Federalism prevailed—The stale trick of corruption was successfully applied; and my Evidence James Welsh, who could have proven the principal part of my charges, was with wonderful dexterity placed out of my reach, and this too, after I had advanced him four Dollars to pay his expences from Philadelphia to Wilmington, while there, and on his return.—The friends of Mr McLane openly boasted of this proof of their perception and ingenuity.

The Gentlemen appointed, however persevered in their examination; and maugre the united talents and exertions of Seven Lawyers on the part of the Collector (I stood alone for some time[2]) have, as I am by them informed, reported his culpability upon two of my charges.

On the contrary Mr McLane reports, That they have unequivocally declared He is innocent of all the charges: I have applied to the Secretary of the Treasury for a copy of their report, and of his Letter to McLane confirming the same—I have not obtained it.

From these considerations I have been induced to step out of the common official tract of application, and to apply directly to Your Excellency.—I know that the possession of that report and Letter is at this moment essentially material: not as to myself, but as to the progressing of Democratic Republicanism in the State of Delaware.—The Port of Wilmington is its sheet anchor therein; and the moment the Federalists can shew an increase of Number, we shall be shaken to our Centre, We stand on a pivot now.—I most solemnly repeat that the conduct of Mr McLane is held in more general dislike than that of any Man in the district—That the democratic Republicans view with regret, if not with disgust his continuance in an office which he has not only abused but disgraced—They consider that they have persevered and by firmly persevering, conquered a Political opponent, base, malignant, and vindictive only for the purpose of destroying the head; while the most poisnous of his ramifacations hold their power: They remember that these Men have been represented as devoid of Political Honesty: restrained by no consideration in their political purposes: the friends of Monarchy and its attendants—They believed this—They opposed—They conquered, and they Yet See the most active, persevering, hyprocital and influential of them, retain their stations—This for Delaware at least is dangerous.

But Sir, the Federalists themselves, sneer at and insult us—They say we (meaning the Government) dare not remove McLane and altho the Citizens of wilmington have by a Petition and remonstrance testified their disapprobation of this Mans continuance in this o[ffice.] Yet with their wonted insolence, they have set up a Counter Petition and severely smarting under a knowledge of Mr McLanes want of popularity and respect in that Port, have with singular (but appropriate) dexterity grounded their confidence in success, by procuring the signatures of the Merchants of Philadelphia: I am informed a few republicans have been caught in the Snare. But the Citizens of Delaware will not thank either party, for interfering in their local appointments.

Concluding Sir, with an assurance that I am induced hereto by no other consideration than the public good, that no pecuniary hope is attached, or any personal resentment towards Mr McLane for his conduct toward me, an auxilary. I most respectfully sollicit a copy, by Your direction, from the Treasurer of the said Report of Messrs Tilton and Reed & of His Letter to McLane thereon.

With my best wishes for Your continuance in Health and that our common Country may long enjoy the advantages of Your Wisdom and Patriotism as Her chief Director. I am sir Yr. Hble Svt.

BENJN REYNOLDS

RC (DLC); torn at seal; addressed: "The President of the United States. Washington"; endorsed by TJ as received 4 Mch. and "Mc.lane to be remvd" and so recorded in SJL.

For Benjamin Reynolds's ALLEGATIONS AGAINST Wilmington collector ALLEN MCLANE, see Vol. 34:170-1. THEIR REPORT: the report by James Tilton and George Read, Jr., has not been found, but see Vol. 36:182-3 for the conclusion by the Treasury Department, approved by TJ, that "no grounds for a removal" were found.

TESTIFIED THEIR DISAPPROBATION: addresses by Delaware Democratic Republicans against the Wilmington collector are printed in Vol. 37:116-18 and 542-4. For the petition and SIGNATURES on McLane's behalf, see Philadelphia Merchants and Others to TJ, 2 Feb.

[1] Closing quotation mark supplied by Editors.

[2] Preceding three words interlined.

To the Senate and the House of Representatives

GENTLEMEN OF THE SENATE AND
OF THE HOUSE OF REPRESENTATIVES

I lay before you a report of the Secretary of state on the case of the Danish brigantine Henrich, taken by a French privateer in 1799. retaken by an armed vessel of the US. carried into a British island, and there adjudged to be neutral, but under allowance of such salvage and costs as absorbed nearly the whole amount of sales of the vessel & cargo. indemnification for these losses occasioned by our officers is now claimed by the sufferers, supported by the representations of their government. I have no doubt the legislature will give to the subject that just attention and consideration which it is useful as well as honourable to practise in our transactions with other nations, and particularly with one which has observed towards us the most friendly treatment and regard.

TH: JEFFERSON
Feb. 23. 1803.

RC (DNA: RG 46, LPPM, 7th Cong., 2d sess.); endorsed by a clerk. PrC (DLC). RC (DNA: RG 233, PM, 7th Cong., 2d sess.); endorsed by a clerk.

ATTENTION AND CONSIDERATION: Meriwether Lewis delivered the message and the accompanying documents to the House and the Senate on 23 Feb., but each chamber was busy with other matters and put off formally receiving the papers until the 24th. On 1 Mch., the House passed a bill from the Committee of Claims "to enable the President of the United States to make restitution" to the *Hendrick*'s owners. The session ended before the Senate voted on the bill. The House of Representatives took up the matter again in the next Congress, again without ultimate success. The *Hendrick* claim remained unresolved (JHR, 4:363, 374, 377-8; JS, 3:271, 281, 285; Madison, *Papers, Sec. of State Ser.*, 1:296n; 4:338n; 6:245).

ENCLOSURE

Madison's Report on the *Hendrick*

The Secretary of State has the honor to report to the President of the United States, upon the note of the Minister of his Danish Majesty, Dated on the 9th. inst, as follows.

That it appears that the Danish Brigantine Henrich, Capt. Peter Scheele, sailing from Hamburg, loaded with an assorted Cargo, and bound to Cape Francois, was captured on the 3d. of Octr. 1799 by a French Privateer, and on the 8th. of the same month she was recaptured by an American public armed vessel called the Pickering, and carried to the British Island of St. Christopher, where she arrived on the 10th.

That from an authenticated transcript of the proceedings in the case of the said Vessel, had before the Court of Vice Admiralty at the said Island, it appears that the said Court took cognizance of the case, and awarded one half of the gross amount of the sales of the Brig and her Cargo to be paid to the recaptors, and the other half after deducting costs and expences to be restored to the owners. That this rate of Salvage appears to have been adopted from the laws of the United States, as then applicable to recaptures of American property and of such as belonged to belligerent powers in amity with the United States; but it is believed that these laws had, according to decisions of our own Courts, no reference to recaptures of Neutral property. That admitting, what has received the sanction of some recent authorities, that in certain peculiar cases of danger of a neutral being condemned by a belligerent, the recaptors are entitled to a proportionate Salvage, there is much reason to believe this is not such a case, as the Vessel was bound from a neutral to a french port, the whole of the property being neutral, and according to the assurance of Mr. Lindemann, the Governor of the Danish West India Islands most of the Danish Vessels carried into Guadaloupe for a year before this capture, were released, and some of them with damages. That the Courts of the United States have in cases much more strongly marked by circumstances indicating a danger of the neutral being condemned allowed much smaller rates of salvage.

That the laws of the United States required Vessels captured under their authority to be brought within their jurisdiction; and it is conceived that it was the duty of the American Officers in this case to repel the attempt of the foreign judicatory to take cognizance, much less ought they to have directly submitted their recapture to its decision, which as it could not be revised or rectified, in case of error, by the tribunals of their own Country, might tend to involve it in claims on its responsibility from others.

That, according to the representation of the Agent for the owners of the Danish Vessel, of the sum of $44.500.– the value of the Vessel, freight and Cargo, there remained, after satisfying the decree for Salvage and expences no more than $8,374\frac{41}{100}$.

That as the policy and interest of the United States lead them in a special manner to respect and promote the rights and facilities of Neutral commerce; as the sentence in this case was permitted, if not procured by Officers of the United States, to be made in a foreign and therefore improper tribunal, as there remains no doubt but that a Court of the United Staes, pronouncing thereon, would either have rejected the claim for salvage altogether or reduced it to the most moderate scale as the declared basis of the sentence, Viz: the law of the United States was inapplicable to the case; and as it is understood, that a remedy is now unattainable, in the ordinary judicial course, it is the opinion of the Secretary of State, that under all the circumstances, the case ought to be referred to the just provisions of Congress thereon.

All which is respectfully submitted

James Madison
Department of State
22 February 1803

MS (DNA: RG 46, LPPM, 7th Cong., 2d sess.); in a clerk's hand, signed by Madison, who inserted day of month in place of erased "19"; endorsed by a clerk. FC (Lb in DNA: RG 59, DL). Recorded in SJL as received from the State Department on 22 Feb. and "Danish brig Henrich." Enclosure: copy of records pertaining to the *Hendrick* in the Court of Vice Admiralty on the island of St. Christopher (St. Kitts), October 1799, including statements regarding the capture, the ownership of the vessel and cargo, and the court's ruling (PrC of Tr in DNA: RG 46, LPPM, in clerks' hands; printed, with TJ's message and Madison's report, in ASP, *Foreign Relations*, 2:483-6).

NOTE OF THE MINISTER: Peder Blicher Olsen submitted the claim of the *Hendrick*'s owners to Madison on 9 Feb. (Madison, *Papers*, *Sec. of State Ser.*, 4:312).

From Anne Cary Randolph

DEAR GRAND PAPA [before 24 Feb. 1803]

Your letters give me so much pleasure that I accept with joy the proposal you made me in your last to become your correspondant. I am very much obliged to you for the profile and verses you sent me. I am reading Thucydidies in english and ancient history in french and am learning arithmetic but I am going on very slowly in my french for want of a dictionary if Mr Duane has got me one will you be so good as to forward it by the first opportunity he promised MaMa that it should be in Washington before she left it but as it had not arrived Papa left money with Captain Lewis to pay for it Elen gives her love to you and says she hopes to be able to write to you soon herself as she is now learning little Cornelia has Just come to beg that I will give her love to you adieu Dear Grand Papa your affectionate Grand daughter

A C RANDOLPH

RC (ViU: Coolidge Deposit); addressed in Martha Jefferson Randolph's hand: "Thomas Jefferson President of the United States Washington City"; endorsed by TJ as received 24 Feb. and so recorded in SJL.

YOUR LAST: a letter from TJ to his granddaughter, recorded in SJL at 6 Feb., has not been found.

From Thomas Jefferson Randolph

DEAR GRAND PAPA [before 24 Feb. 1803]

We have been expecting the measles but have escaped it as yet. Virginia has learnt to speak very well. Ellen is learning french. Cornelia sends her love to you I would be very much obliged to you if you would bring me a book of geography adieu Dear Grand Papa your affectionate Grand son

THOMAS JEFFERSON R

RC (ViU); undated; endorsed by TJ as received 24 Feb. and so recorded in SJL.

To Lacépède

Dear Sir Washington Feb. 24. 1803.

I have just recieved from mr Paine the copy of your Discours d'ouverture de l'an IX. which you were so good as to send me. a rapid view of parts of it only assures me of the pleasure I shall recieve from a deliberate perusal of the whole the first moment I have to spare. I was struck with the prophetic spirit of the passage pa. 10. 11. 'bientot de courageux voyageurs visiteront les sources du Missisipi et du Missouri, que l'oeil d'un European n'a pas encore entrevues' &c. it happens that we are now actually sending off a small party to explore the Missouri to it's source, and whatever other river, heading nearest with that, runs into the Western ocean; to enlarge our knolege of the geography of our continent, by adding information of that interesting line of communication across it, and to give us a general view of it's population, natural history, productions, soil & climate. it is not improbable that this voyage of discovery will procure us further information of the Mammoth, & of the Megatherium also, mentioned by you page 6. for you have possibly seen in our Philosophical transactions, that, before we had seen the account of that animal by mr Cuvier, we had found here some remains of an enormous animal incognitum, whom, from the disproportionate length of his claw, we had denominated Megalonyx, and which is probably the same animal; and that there are symptoms of it's late and present existence. the route we are exploring will perhaps bring us further evidence of it, and may be accomplished in two summers.

I have long been fatigued with the eternal repetition of the term '*Man in the state of nature*', by which is meant man in his savage and stupid state, with his faculties entirely undeveloped. if this be his natural state, then the foetus in embryo exhibits it in it's utmost perfection. as if the improvement of the senses of man, the strengthening and developing his reasoning faculties, any more than the growth of his body, rendered him an unnatural being, and placed him beyond the limits of his nature! I was pleased therefore to observe your luminous correction of this idea, pa. 8. 'parmi tous les etres vivans et sensibles, *l'art de l'espece est sa nature*. l'industrie qui ne vient que d'elle, celle qu'elle n'a reçue d'aucune espece etrangere, est *le complement de ses attributs naturels*. on n'aurait qu'une idée bien imparfaite de son essence, si on ignorait jusqu'on peut aller le developpement de ses facultés.' the examination of the different races of men, which you propose, under this point of view, will produce an arrangement of them which has not hitherto been sufficiently admitted.

In the writings of M. de Buffon he has supposed the Moose of America to be the Renne of Europe, the deer of America to be the Chevreuil, and what we call a panther (tho' it is certainly not one) to be a Cougar. I procured for him the skeleton, skin & horns of a Moose 7. feet high, the horns of our deer, and the skin of our falsely called panther. he was perfectly satisfied. he had been misinformed as to them all; & told me he would correct those articles in the first volume he should publish. however I think he did not live to publish another volume. has any thing posthumous of his been published? & particularly the corrections abovementioned? I presume the specimens I gave him of the animals are still in the Cabinet, the care of which has been so fortunately confided to you. You will no doubt have heard that a tolerably compleat frame of the Mammoth has been carried by mr Peale to London, and he intends carrying it to Paris: so that you will have an opportunity of seeing this colossal subject, and of comparing it with the elephant. returning to the principal object of my letter, I thank you for the friendly communication of your discourse, & for the occasion it has given me of turning for a moment from the barren field of politics to the rich map of nature: and I pray you to accept assurances of my great consideration and respect.

TH: JEFFERSON

PrC (DLC); at foot of first page: "M. de Cepede." Enclosed in TJ to James Monroe, 25 Feb.

DISCOURS D'OUVERTURE: TJ and Bernard Germain Étienne de La Ville-sur-Illon, the Comte de Lacépède, had not corresponded since TJ was U.S. minister to France and Lacépède assisted the Comte de Buffon in the preparation of his multivolume survey of natural history. During the interim, TJ had made an effort to keep up with the volumes that Lacépède wrote to complete the *Histoire naturelle* after Buffon's death in 1788. During the French Revolution, Lacépède, who was born in 1756, served in the Legislative Assembly but left Paris during the Terror. After his return in 1794, he held a chair in zoology at the museum of natural history and was also, beginning in 1799, a member of the Conservative Senate of France. The opening and closing lectures of his course in zoology at the museum were published in Paris in 1801 as *Discours d'ouverture et de clôture du cours de zoologie: Donné dans le Muséum national d'Histoire naturelle, l'an IX de la République*. Lacépède was one of the original members of the National Institute in 1795 (DSB; *Dictionnaire*, 18:1475-7; Sowerby, Nos. 1029, 1044; Vol. 12:287-8; Vol. 28:358; Vol. 32:178).

PASSAGE PA. 10. 11: the lectures in Lacépède's *Discours* had separate pagination. In the closing lecture, Lacépède referred to some explorers of northern North America such as Alexander Mackenzie and commented that no European had yet seen the source of the Mississippi or Missouri River (Lacépède, *Discours*, closing lecture, 11).

Lacépède knew of the MEGATHERIUM from the skeletal remains found in South America and described by Georges Cuvier. Lacépède speculated that perhaps the animal still lived in some remote part of that continent (Lacépède, *Discours*, closing lecture, 6-7; Vol. 29:300n). He expressed that view again in his volume on whales in the *Histoire naturelle*, first published in 1804. There, Lacépède observed that while humans had found their way to every part of the ocean where whales could exist, there were still places in the Americas where large land animals such as the mammoth and the megatherium could live, unknown as yet to science. In a footnote to that statement, Lacépède paraphrased and quoted (in French) much of the first paragraph of TJ's letter printed above (Anselme-Gaëtan Desmarest, ed., *Histoire naturelle de Lacépède, comprenant les cétacées, les quadrupèdes ovipares, les serpents et les poissons*, 2 vols. [Paris, 1844], 1:42).

IN OUR PHILOSOPHICAL TRANSACTIONS: TJ's and Caspar Wistar's descriptions of the Virginia megalonyx appeared in APS, *Transactions*, 4 (1799), 246-60, 526-31.

PA. 8: among living and sentient beings, Lacépède declared in his *Discours*, the distinctive feature of a species was its "art," the skills that could have come from that species alone and complemented its innate attributes. One could have only an imperfect idea of a species without understanding the development of its faculties through time. In Lacépède's view, THE DIFFERENT RACES OF MEN were distinguished by the adaptations they had made of the properties that nature had granted to the human species—"L'usage que chaque race de l'espèce humaine a fait des qualités que la Nature lui a départies" (Lacépède, *Discours*, opening lecture, 8).

In Paris in 1787, TJ obtained the bones and hide of a MOOSE from northern New England, along with antlers of North American moose, caribou, elk, and deer, for Buffon. RENNE is the French word for reindeer. Earlier TJ gave the naturalist the stuffed skin of an American COUGAR. "I have convinced him that our deer is not a Chevreuil," TJ wrote during his campaign to educate Buffon about American fauna (DSB; Vol. 9:130-1; Vol. 10:625; Vol. 12:194-5).

FROM THE BARREN FIELD OF POLITICS: the *Magasin encyclopédique*, a French periodical, published a French translation of TJ's letter to Lacépède in the spring of 1803. That translation differs from the extracts quoted by Lacépède in the *Histoire naturelle* the following year (see above). At least one other publication in France printed the full translation. In November 1804, the *Port Folio* of Philadelphia published TJ's letter in the form of a retranslation into English of the French-language version. In the text published in France, TJ's sentence beginning "the examination of the different races of men" appeared as "L'examen des différentes races d'hommes que vous proposez sous ce point de vue, produira un classement dont on n'a point jusqu'ici suffisamment tenu compte," rendered in the *Port Folio* as "The examination of the *different races of men*, which you propose, under this point of view, will produce a classification, which has not hitherto been sufficiently valued." TJ's passage beginning "if this be his natural state" and running through "correction of this idea" became, in the *Port Folio*, "If such is the state of nature, the fœtus, in its embrio state, would be its highest term or degree, for then is discovered its least developement. Surely there is nothing more contrary to nature, in the developement of the faculty of perception and thinking, than in the increase of its body. You will hence perceive *how greatly I have been charmed* to see this false idea combatted by you." The *Port Folio* translation was by someone identified only as "An Observer," who also provided several paragraphs of commentary. Those remarks admonished TJ for holding "the infidel philosophy which supposes different races of man." Such "classification," declared "Observer," would "establish the inequality of men, and thereby destroy not only one of the elements of our proclamation of independence, which declares that all men are born equal, but the authenticity of the Scriptures, which inform us, that all men are descended from Adam." In the French translation, TJ's report that the western expedition "will perhaps bring us further evidence" of the megalonyx became "éclaircira probablement ce fait," translated in the *Port Folio* as "will, we hope, illuminate this fact." Taking the "fact" in question to be the survival of the megalonyx into the current era rather than its relationship to the megatherium, "Observer" avowed that Americans "of common sense" did not believe TJ's "*scientific voyagers*" would encounter a living megalonyx. Mocking the president's interest in natural history, "Observer" warned that "the philosophers of Europe, who are entitled to that name, will laugh at seeing him eternally mounted upon the mammoth, and his ridiculous inquiries after his moose's skeleton, his deer's horns, and panther's skin." "Observer" went on to criticize portions of TJ's 8 Nov. 1804 annual message to Congress. Several newspapers reprinted the *Port Folio*'s version of the letter to Lacépède—some with and some without the commentary (*Magasin encyclopédique, ou Journal des sciences, des lettres et des arts*, 9th year, 1 [1803], 254-7; *Port Folio*, 24 Nov. 1804; Richmond *Enquirer*, 4 Dec.; Norwich, Conn., *True Republican*, 26 Dec.; New York *Evening Post*, 28 Jan. 1805; *New-York Herald*, 30 Jan.; Dover, N.H., *Sun*, 2 Feb.; Bennington *Vermont Gazette*, 11 Feb.; Peacham, Vt., *Green Mountain Patriot*, 12 Feb.).

To John Carroll

Washington Feb. 25. 1803.

Th: Jefferson presents his respects to Bishop Carroll acknoleges the reciept of his letter of the 20th. and of the letters therein inclosed, which he this day re-inclosed to mr Coppinger at his particular request. he tenders his friendly salutations.

PrC (DLC); endorsed by TJ in ink on verso.

LETTERS THEREIN INCLOSED: for the letters from Nehemiah Bartley to Joseph Coppinger, see Coppinger to TJ, 3 Jan. TJ's letter to Coppinger of THIS DAY is recorded in SJL but has not been found.

Circular to the Governors of the States

Washington City
February 25th. 1803

SIR

In compliance with a request of the House of Representatives of the US. as well as with a sense of what is necessary, I take the liberty of urging on you the importance and indispensible necessity of vigorous exertions, on the part of the state governments, to carry into effect the militia system adopted by the national legislature, agreeably to the powers reserved to the states respectively, by the constitution of the US. and in a manner the best calculated to ensure such a degree of military discipline, & knowledge of tactics, as will, under the auspices of a benign providence, render the militia a sure and permanent bulwark of national defence.

None but an armed nation can dispense with a standing army. to keep ours armed and disciplined, is therefore at all times important. but especially so at a moment when rights the most essential to our welfare[1] have been violated, and an infraction of treaty committed without colour or pretext. and altho' we are willing to believe that this has been the act of a subordinate agent only, yet it is wise to prepare for the possibility that it may have been the leading measure of a system. While therefore we are endeavoring, and with a considerable degree of confidence, to obtain by friendly negociation a peaceable redress of the injury, and effectual provision against it's repetition, let us array the strength of the nation, and be ready to do with promptitude & effect whatever a regard to justice & our future security may require.

In order that I may have a full and correct view of the resources of our country in all it's different parts, I must desire you, with as little delay as possible, to have me furnished with a return of the militia, & of the arms & accoutrements of your state, and of the several counties, or other geographical divisions of it.

Accept assurances of my high consideration and respect.

Dft (DLC); in TJ's hand, except for dateline added in an unidentified hand. RC (VtMS); dated 25 Feb. 1803; in a clerk's hand, signed by TJ; at foot of text: "Vermont"; endorsed: "In General Assembly Octr. 15th. 1803. Read and referred to the Committee appointed to enquire into the state of the Militia" and "In Council 15th. Octr. 1803. Read and Concurred." RC (Vi); dated February 1803; in a clerk's hand, signed by TJ; at foot of text: "Virginia"; endorsed. RC (CSmH); dated February 1803; in a clerk's hand, signed by TJ. RC (Christie's, New York City, 1995); dated February 1803; in a clerk's hand, signed by TJ; at foot of text: "Georgia." RC (Christie's, New York City, 2004); dated February 1803; in a clerk's hand, signed by TJ; at foot of text: "Maryland"; endorsed. Recorded in SJL at 25 Feb. 1803 with notation "Governors. circular. resoln. of Congress."

REQUEST OF THE HOUSE: on 7 Feb. 1803, the House committee considering the portion of TJ's annual message that related to the militia made its report. It concluded with a resolution requesting that the president write the state governors "urging the importance and indispensible necessity of vigorous exertions, on the part of the state governments," to carry into effect the militia system adopted by Congress, "in a manner the best calculated to ensure such a degree of military discipline and knowlege of tactics, as will under the auspices of a benign providence, render the militia a sure and permanent bulwark of national defence." The House agreed to the resolution on 14 Feb. and appointed Joseph B. Varnum and William Butler to present it to the president (*Report of the Committee, Appointed on so Much of the President's Message, of the 15th of December Last, "As Relates to the Militia Institution of the United States"* [Washington, D.C., 1803], 5; JHR, 4:340).

INFRACTION OF TREATY COMMITTED: the termination by the Spanish intendant of the right of deposit at New Orleans.

[1] Word interlined in place of "existence."

From Pierpont Edwards

SIR Hartford Feby 25h 1803

Mr George Wolcott of Windsor in Hartford county, in this state, brother of Alexander Wolcott Esqr., is desirous of being appointed surveyor of the port of Saybrook, in the district of Middletown, should Mr Dickinson, the present holder of that office be displaced, an event which I presume must soon take place. George Wolcott has been as essentially injured by the persecution of the federalists, during the reign of terror as any man in connecticutt—He was a deputy sheriff for Hartford county, an office which yielded him and his family a handsome support; he was, by a law of this state made purposely to reach him, displaced by the county Court for this county—He is a man not in affluent circumstance, and his dismissal distressed him. He is, in my opinion capable, honest, and friendly to the constitution, and in all respects a very reputable citizen—I am with sentiments of very high respect & esteem

Your Obed Servt PIERPONT EDWARDS

RC (DNA: RG 59, LAR); at foot of text: "His Excellency Thomas Jefferson"; endorsed by TJ as received 4 Apr. and "Woolcott George to be Surveyor Saybrook" and so recorded in SJL. Enclosed in Alexander Wolcott to TJ, 18 Mch. 1803.

GEORGE WOLCOTT, a cousin of former secretary of the Treasury Oliver Wolcott, Jr., received a commission as surveyor of Saybrook in December 1803 and continued in the position until his death in 1822. George's brother, ALEXANDER WOLCOTT, was a Republican leader in Connecticut and collector of Middletown. Richard DICKINSON had been surveyor of Saybrook since 1795 (JEP, 1:180, 460, 461; Hartford *American Mercury*, 22 Mch. 1804; New Haven *Connecticut Herald*, 12 Feb. 1822; Kline, *Burr*, 1:419; Vol. 31:543, Vol. 36:323).

To George Jefferson

DEAR SIR Washington Feb. 25. 1803.

Having occasion to pay 1000. D. in Richmond on the 10th. of March ensuing I have drawn on you for that sum payable then to Craven Peyton, for which you shall be duly provided. mr Barnes will put the money into the mail here on the 8th. and you will consequently recieve it on the 9th.

Two small boxes, not ready in time for Capt Sprogall, will follow by the first vessel to be forwarded to Monticello. accept my affectionate salutations. TH: JEFFERSON

PrC (MHi); at foot of text: "Mr. George Jefferson"; endorsed by TJ in ink on verso.

For the SUM PAYABLE, see TJ to Craven Peyton, 23 Feb.

From Levi Lincoln

SIR Feby 25th. 1803

It may be gratifying to learn the temper of friends, in distant parts of the Country. By the enclosed you will perceive one I hope, in which, the spirit of republicanism is about to exhibit, itself, in Massachusetts. Similar preparations, it is said, are making in other parts of that State—Such things have a double effect—to animate on the one hand, on the other, to depress—All my late letters, speak of Government measures, with approbation, & confidence of their success—The lawyers are coming around—the Clergy, becoming mute, and I suspect the Worcester celebration will be without prayers, for the want of a priest to make them

Most respectfully yours, L LINCOLN

RC (DLC); at foot of text: "President of US"; endorsed by TJ. Recorded in SJL as received 28 Feb. Enclosure: probably a notice addressed "To All True Republicans and Friends of the Federal Union," dated 16 Feb., announcing a public celebration to be held in Worcester on 4 Mch. for all "desirous of rejoicing in our glorious return to the first principles of our Revolution, at the commencement of the present Administration"; the event includes a discharge of cannon, a procession to the South Meeting House to hear an address by Levi Lincoln, Jr., "appropriate Music," and a public dinner; with the request that officers and members of the Worcester Artillery Company join in the celebration "and perform the Military Honors of the day"; tickets are available for $1 through the committee of arrangements, which includes Samuel Flagg, Abraham Lincoln, Francis Blake, and four others (Worcester *National Aegis*, 16 Feb.; *Massachusetts Spy, or Worcester Gazette*, 16 Feb.).

WORCHESTER CELEBRATION: see enclosure described above and Lincoln to TJ, 15 Mch.

From Schuyler Livingston

SIR Friday Morg [25 Feb. 1803]

Presuming that the Convention with Spain will be carried into effect and understanding that Commissioners are to be appointed to adjust the Claims for Spoliations &c—I take the liberty to signify to you, that the appointment of a Commissioner would be agreeable to me—For any Information which the President may require, I beg leave to refer to the Republican part of the Delegation from New York.

I am with high Consideration yr. very obd. Servt.

SCHUYLER LIVINGSTON

RC (DNA: RG 59, LAR); partially dated; endorsed by TJ as received 25 Feb. and so recorded in SJL; also endorsed by TJ: "to be Commr. to Spain."

Peter Schuyler Livingston (1772-1809), son of Walter and Cornelia Schuyler Livingston, was born at the upper Livingston Manor in New York. He graduated from Columbia College in 1788 and from Yale a year later. In 1796, he married Eliza Barclay, the daughter of Thomas and Susanna DeLancey Barclay. Eliza's father, a loyalist during the American Revolution, was serving as British consul at New York. Livingston had an office on Greenwich Street, first as an attorney and then as a merchant, and resided in Harlem, New York. In early 1801, Burr had recommended him for the consulship at Madeira (Cuyler Reynolds, comp., *Genealogical and Family History of Southern New York and the Hudson River Valley*, 3 vols. [New York, 1914], 3:1316; Dexter, *Yale*, 4:645-6; Alfred F. Young, *The Democratic Republicans of New York: The Origins, 1763-1797* [Chapel Hill, 1967], 8, 25, 71; *Longworth's American Almanac, New-York Register, and City-Directory, for the Twenty-Eighth Year of American Independence* [New York, 1803], 197; *Longworth's American Almanack, New-York Register, and City Directory. For the Thirtieth Year of American Independence* [New York, 1805], 300; New York *Republican Watch-Tower*, 11 July 1809; Madison, *Papers, Sec. of State Ser.*, 3:613n; Vol. 33:666).

COMMISSIONERS ARE TO BE APPOINTED: see Joseph H. Nicholson to TJ, 19 Nov. 1802.

To Thomas Mendenhall

SIR Washington Feb. 25. 1803.

I recieved last night your favor of the 12th. I can say with truth that I do not remember ever to have recieved such a paper as is the subject of your letter. I might ascertain this by a recurrence to my files; but it is unnecessary for another reason. it is so important to the public service that I should be the center of information as to whatever concerns them, that in order to induce it to be freely given I am obliged to let it be understood that whatever I recieve is sacredly confidential, and shall not under any circumstances be given up. this imposes on me the obligation to suffer no impression to be made on me by any secret information, nor to act on it, until I verify it by further & sufficient enquiry. for this reason had I such a paper as you suppose I could not communicate it without a breach of trust, but I repeat my assurance that I have not the smallest recollection of having recieved such an one. Accept my best wishes & respects. TH: JEFFERSON

RC (Seth Kaller, Inc., White Plains, New York, 2005); at foot of text: "Mr. Mendenhall." PrC (DLC).

To James Monroe

Dear Sir Washington Feb. 25. 1803.

I inclose you another letter for mr Cepede keeper of the National cabinet. I have not superscribed the titles of the gentlemen on my letters, because I know them not. perhaps some apology may be necessary for this omission. Congress having passed the two million bill, you will recieve by this mail your last dispatches. others will follow you about the 2d. week of April, before which time I shall be returned from Monticello. I set out for that place on the 6th. of March. Congress has given authority for exploring the Missisipi, which however is ordered to be secret. this will employ about 10. persons two years. present my friendly respects to mrs Monroe & Eliza, and accept my best wishes for a pleasant voyage, happy result, and assurances of my constant & affectionate attachment

Th: Jefferson

RC (Thornton H. Brooks, Greensboro, North Carolina, 1947); addressed: "James Monroe Min. Extr. & Plenipo. to France at New York." PrC (DLC); endorsed by TJ in ink on verso. Enclosure: TJ to Lacépède, 24 Feb.

two million bill: on 22 Feb. the Senate passed a bill "making further provision for the expenses attending the intercourse between the United States and foreign nations." The bill, which became law on 26 Feb., appropriated $2,000,000 "for the purpose of defraying any extraordinary expenses which may be incurred in the intercourse between the United States and foreign nations." It authorized the president to borrow part or all of the sum at six percent interest, allowed the Bank of the United States to lend the money, and provided for the application of surpluses of duties on imports and tonnage as necessary to pay the interest and principal of the loan. The Senate on 22 Feb. also passed the appropriation of $2,500 for "extending the external commerce of the United States"—the funds for exploring beyond the Mississippi that TJ requested in his confidential message to Congress on 18 Jan. The House of Representatives had prepared and passed both bills in closed sessions under the injunction of secrecy on its proceedings relating to TJ's confidential message. The House conveyed the two bills to the Senate on 15 Feb. with an explanation that the appropriation for foreign intercourse expenditures was "to enable the President of the United States to commence, with more effect, a negotiation with the French and Spanish governments, relative to the purchase of the Island of New Orleans, and the provinces of East and West Florida. The nature and importance of the measure contemplated, have induced us to act upon the subject with closed doors." An amendment that would have designated the appropriation for "the cession of the island of New Orleans, or other territories, to the United States, as may be stipulated by the President of the United States, by treaty with foreign nations claiming the jurisdiction and sovereignty thereof," rather than for unspecified "extraordinary expenses," failed in the Senate on 21 Feb. (U.S. Statutes at Large, 2:202, 206; JEP, 1:443-5; JHR, 4:269; TJ to the Senate and the House of Representatives, 18 Jan., first message).

To James B. Richardson

SIR Washington. Feb. 25. 1803.

Having found it difficult to obtain here the names of gentlemen proper for the office of Commissioners of bankruptcy, and who are willing to accept it, and the non-acceptances & re-appointments at such a distance consuming much time, while the service is on sufferance, I take the liberty of inclosing four blank commissions which I ask the favor of you to fill up with the names of gentlemen whom you think proper for the office, & who shall have previously signified to you that they will accept. when filled up, I have still to request you to give me information of the names, that they may be entered in the records of the Secretary of State's office. the interest which I am sure you feel in whatsoever relates to the state over which you preside, will apologize for the liberty I take in asking you to perform for me a duty which you can perform so much more advantageously for your state. I pray you to accept assurances of my high consideration & respect.

TH: JEFFERSON

PrC (DLC); in ink at foot of text: "Governor Richardson."

James Burchell Richardson (1770-1836), son of the Revolutionary War general Richard Richardson, was a South Carolina planter who lived at Big Home plantation in Clarendon District. He owned plantations and urban property throughout the state, including a summer residence with a course for horse racing in the Sand Hills. He had almost 400 slaves at the time of his death. Between 1792 and 1817, Richardson served seven terms in the South Carolina House of Representatives and four terms in the senate. The general assembly elected him governor in 1802. He served one term. In December 1812, he was elected director of the Bank of the State of South Carolina and he served as a trustee of South Carolina College (*S.C. Biographical Directory, House of Representatives*, 4:475-6). For Richardson's initiation of penal reform while governor, see John M. Bryan, "Robert Mills, Benjamin Henry Latrobe, Thomas Jefferson and the South Carolina Penitentiary Project, 1806-1808," in *South Carolina Historical Magazine*, 85 (1984), 2-3.

For the previous appointment of COMMISSIONERS OF BANKRUPTCY in South Carolina, several of whom had declined or resigned the appointment, see Vol. 37:512-13, 706-7, 711. GIVE ME INFORMATION OF THE NAMES: a letter from Richardson to TJ of 2 Apr., recorded in SJL as received on the 17th with the notation "S," has not been found, but on his list of appointments at 25 Feb., TJ recorded the names of South Carolina's four new bankruptcy commissioners with the notation to see Governor Richardson's answer of 2 Apr. TJ had sent the letter to the State Department, where the commissions for Simon McIntosh, William Lee, Jr., Guilliam Aertsen, and Francis Mulligan were recorded (list of commissions in DNA: RG 59, MPTPC; Appendix I: List of Appointments). On 5 Apr., William Moultrie, an earlier South Carolina appointee, wrote Madison and returned his commission noting, "as tis a business that requires much time and attention, it will be very inconvenient for me." He recommended the appointment of John Webb in his place (RC in DNA: RG 59, LAR, endorsed by TJ: "Moultrie Wm. to mr Madison. resigns as Commr bkrptcy Webb John recommended to succeed him"; Vol. 37:513n, 699). On the same day, Webb wrote Madison offering himself as a candidate to fill the vacancy (RC in DNA: RG 59, LAR; endorsed by TJ: "to be Commr. bkrptcy S. Carola.). For Webb's previous applications and TJ's hesitation to appoint him, see Vol. 37:450n, 706.

On 23 Sep. 1802, Mulligan informed Gallatin that Daniel Stevens, supervisor of the revenue in South Carolina, intended to resign. He applied for the position, noting his experience as collector of the revenue under the Direct Tax law. He referred to a previous letter of recommendation from Governor John Drayton and other respectable citizens of the state. Mulligan asserted that he was known for his efforts "in the cause of liberty, and republicanism, under many disadvantages" (RC in DNA: RG 59, LAR; endorsed by TJ: "Mulligan Francis to be Supervisor of S.C. vice Stevens who means to resign"). Writing the Treasury secretary again on 17 Nov. 1802, Mulligan enclosed Stevens's resignation. Noting that his service would always be marked by "Integrity, Zeal, and Fidelity," Mulligan again applied for the position of supervisor (RC in same; endorsed by TJ: "Mulligan Francis to mr Gallatin to be Supervisor of S.C."; TJ also questioned: "has Stevens resigned?" and is Mulligan "a republican & otherwise qualified & approved by mr Gallatin?"). TJ did not appoint an official replacement for Stevens (TJ to the Senate, 11 Jan., second letter, 2 Feb. 1803; Gallatin to TJ, 30 June 1803).

To William Wingate

SIR Washington Feb. 25. 1803.

Your favor of the 7th. was duly recieved, and I now return you the papers No. 1. 2. 3. 7. 8. 9. as you desired. Nos. 4. 5. 6. tho' mentioned in your letter, were not inclosed in it. the business has been settled in the Senate, as my nomination had been previously given in, before I had recieved any information on the subject. Accept my thanks for the communication which has rendered useful service to the public, and be assured of my best wishes & respects. TH: JEFFERSON

PrC (DLC); in ink at foot of text: "Mr. William Wingate Haverhill"; endorsed by TJ in ink on verso.

MY NOMINATION: Ephraim Emery.

From Peter Hughes

State of New York Coy: of Cayuga
Ovid, Februy: 26. 1803.

SIR,

I am induced from a Principle of filial Duty to say that I am the Son of the late Col. Hugh Hughes of this State who served under the United States as Dy Qr Master General in this State & who failed in getting his Pay of Congress for his Services during the War, which were zealously & disinterestedly performed for Sir, had not that been the Case he would not have left my Mother & five Sisters two of whom are Widows & three single[1] in a pennyless State.—Nor would I ever have troubled you Sir, on this Occasion, were it in my Power to afford the necessary Relief without sacraficing my little Property which I have earned by Industry part of which has gone to the Support of my Parents during the Life of my Father.

It is true Governor Clinton on his accession to Office presented me with the Sheriffalty of this County, but which as the County is new is very unproductive & great Responsibilty Attached to it & my Farm is small & New—I must confess I feel Chagrined at seeing a Foreigner enjoying the Sweets of an Office in this Country who knew nothing of him in the Day of her Adversity, while those who have borne the Heat of the Day are in modest Silence labo[ring] for a Living at an humble distance from Honours and Office—I mean the Office in the Customs of the City of New York lately enjoyed by Col. B. Walker but now Sir by an Englishman.—Sir, I do not ask any Thing on own Merit, altho' I served in the three northern Campaigns, one against Quebec & the second two in General Gates's Family (at his Invitation) this is well known to Genl Van Cortlandt now in Congress who can as would Govr Clinton & Genl Gates give every just recommendation if necessary.—I have the more fully to convince you Sir, of the Truth of my preceding Remarks & the Justice with which I have called for your Attention Sir, enclosed a Letter from my Mother now in the 78th Year of her Age & who has nothing to Support her save the Labours of her Children.—If it is consistent with the Honor of your Administration Sir, to enable me by conferring the Appointment alluded to to Yield That Comfort & Support to my venerable & afflicted Parent, you will also add a great Consolation to a Son,

Who is with great Respect Your Well Wisher

PETER HUGHES

RC (DNA: RG 59, LAR); torn; addressed: "His Excellency Thomas Jefferson Esqr." with "City of Washington" canceled and "near Milton Virginia" written below and marked "private"; franked; postmarked Cayuga Bridge, 7 Mch.; endorsed by TJ as received 25 Mch. and "to be vice Rogers" and so recorded in SJL. Enclosure: Charity Hughes to Peter Hughes, 27 Jan. 1803, informing him of the death of his brother, James Miles Hughes; "the dispensations of Gods providence are just," she writes, "I have no wright to murmur against his will but my loss is great he was my only help he was Allways Redy to Asist me but Alass my recorce is Cut of"; Miles died of a "fit of the Apoplexy" and he passed from life "without a groan or a struggle"; Mrs. Hughes believes she will go to Hackensack with "Mrs. Gamble," who will take charge of a school there (same; Anna M. Holstein, *Swedish Holsteins in America From 1644 to 1892* [Norristown, Pa., 1892], 84, 93).

Peter Hughes (1751-1817) served briefly as aide-de-camp to Horatio Gates during the American Revolution. He was appointed sheriff of Cayuga County in 1801 and county clerk in 1804 (Holstein, *Swedish Holsteins*, 93; Heitman, *Register*, 307; Franklin B. Hough, *The New York Civil List* [Albany, 1860], 430, 440; *Albany Advertiser*, 15 Jan. 1817).

A deputy quartermaster general during the American Revolution, HUGH HUGHES spent the postwar years pressing a series of unsuccessful claims on Congress for payment of his wartime accounts (E. Wayne Carp, *To Starve the Army at Pleasure: Continental Army Administration and American Political Culture, 1775-1783* [Chapel Hill, 1984], 134-5).

AN ENGLISHMAN: Richard Rogers, a former Loyalist and the naval officer at New York City since replacing Benjamin Walker in 1797. For efforts by New York Republicans to secure his removal, see Vol. 34:126-7, 316-17; Vol. 35:62, 100-1, 272-4.

[1] Preceding two words and ampersand interlined.

To Anne Cary Randolph

MY DEAR ANNE Washington Feb. 26. 1803.

Davy Bowles is to call on me this morning, and if he can carry your dictionary I will deliver it to him, having recieved it yesterday from mr Duane. if he cannot, I will endeavor to carry it when I go. in the latter case you will recieve it about the 9th. or 10th. of March, or as soon after as health, weather & roads will permit. tell Jefferson that there is not a book of geography to be had here, but I will give him one I have at Monticello. tell Ellen, Cornelia & Virginia how d' ye,[1] give my affectionate esteem to your Papa & to your Mama my constant love. for yourself I deliver numberless kisses to this letter which you are to take from it. I hope in a few days we shall all be happy together at Monticello. TH: JEFFERSON

PrC (CSmH); at foot of text: "A. C. Randolph"; endorsed by TJ in ink on verso.

[1] TJ here canceled one or two illegible words.

To Benjamin Smith Barton

DEAR SIR Washington Feb. 27. 1803.

I inclose you a copy of two discourses sent you by mr La Cepede through the hands of mr Paine, who delivered them with some sent me. what follows in this letter is strictly confidential. you know we have been many years wishing to have the Missouri explored, & whatever river, heading with that, runs into the Western ocean. Congress, in some secret proceedings, have yielded to a proposition I made them for permitting me to have it done. it is to be undertaken immediately with a party of about ten, & I have appointed Capt

Lewis, my secretary, to conduct it. it was impossible to find a character who to a compleat science in botany, natural history, mineralogy & astronomy, joined the firmness of constitution & character, prudence, habits adapted to the woods, & a familiarity with the Indian manners & character, requisite for this undertaking. all the latter qualifications Capt Lewis has. altho' no regular botanist &c. he possesses a remarkeable store of accurate observation on all the subjects of the three kingdoms, & will therefore readily single out whatever presents itself new to him in either: and he has qualified himself for taking those observations of longitude & latitude necessary to fix the geography of the line he passes through. in order to draw his attention at once to the objects most desirable, I must ask the favor of you to prepare for him a note of those in the lines of botany, zoology, or of Indian history which you think most worthy of enquiry & observation. he will be with you in Philadelphia in two or three weeks, & will wait on you and recieve thankfully such a paper, and any verbal communications which you may be so good as to make to him. I make no apology for this trouble, because I know that the same wish to promote science which has induced me to bring forward this proposition, will induce you to aid in promoting it. Accept assurances of my friendly esteem & high respect. TH: JEFFERSON

RC (PHi); at foot of text: "Dr. Barton"; endorsed by Barton as received 3 Mch. PrC (DLC).

For Lacépède's DISCOURSES, see TJ's letter to him of 24 Feb. In November, Barton had written to the French naturalist on behalf of the American Philosophical Society. The society received the printed lectures in a meeting on 4 Mch. (APS, *Proceedings*, 22, pt. 3 [1884], 327, 334).

To William Henry Harrison

DEAR SIR Washington Feb. 27. 1803.

While at Monticello in August last I recieved your favor of Aug. 6. and meant to have acknoleged it on my return to the seat of government at the close of the ensuing month. but on my return I found that[1] you were expected to be on here in person, & this expectation continued till winter. I have since recieved your favor of Dec. 30. In the former you mentioned the plan of the town which you had done me the honour to name after me, and to lay out according to an idea I had formerly expressed to you. I am thoroughly persuaded that it will be found handsome, & pleasant, and I do believe it to be the best means of preserving the cities of America from the scourge of the yellow fever which being peculiar to our country must be derived from some peculiarity in it. that peculiarity I take to be our cloudless skies. in Europe, where the sun does not shine more than half the number of days in the year which it does in America, they can build their towns in a solid block with impunity. but here a constant sun produces too great an accumulation of heat to admit that. ventilation is indispensably necessary. experience has taught us that in the open air of the country the yellow fever is not only not generated, but ceases to be infectious. I cannot decide from the drawing you sent me, whether you have laid off streets round the squares thus or only the diagonal street therein marked. the former was my idea, and is, I imagine, most convenient.

You will recieve herewith an answer to your letter as President of the Convention: and from the Secretary at War you recieve from time to time information & instructions as to our Indian affairs. these communications being for the public records are restrained always to particular objects & occasions. but this letter being unofficial, & private, I may with safety give you a more extensive view of our policy respecting the Indians, that you may the better comprehend the parts dealt out to you in detail through the official channel, and observing the system of which they make a part, conduct yourself in unison with it in cases where you are obliged to act without instruction. our system is to live in perpetual peace with the Indians, to cultivate an affectionate attachment from them, by every thing just & liberal which we can do for them within the bounds of reason, and by giving them effectual protection against wrongs from our own people. the decrease of game rendering their subsistence by hunting insufficient, we wish to draw them to agriculture, to spinning & weaving. the latter branches they take up with great readiness, because they fall to the women, who gain by quitting the labours of the field for those which are exercised within doors. when they withdraw themselves to the culture of a small piece of land, they will percieve how useless to them are their extensive forests, and will be willing to pare them off from time to time in exchange for necessaries for their farms & families. to promote this disposition to exchange lands which they have to spare & we want, for necessaries, which we have to spare & they want, we shall push our trading houses, and be glad to see the good & influential individuals among them run in debt, because we observe that when these debts get beyond what the individuals can pay, they become willing to lop th[em off] by a cession of lands. at our trading houses too we mean to sell so low as merely to repay us cost and charges so as neither to lessen or enlarge our capital. this is what private traders cannot do, for they must gain; they will consequently retire from the competition, & we shall thus get clear of this pest without giving offence or umbrage to the Indians. in this way our settlements will gradually circumbscribe & approach the Indians, & they will in time either incorporate with us as citizens of the US. or remove beyond the Missisipi. the former is certainly the termination of their history most happy for themselves. but in the whole course of this, it is essential to cultivate their love. as to their fear, we presume that our strength & their weakness is now so visible that they must see we have only to shut our hand to crush them, & that all our liberalities to them proceed from motives of pure humanity only. should any tribe be fool-hardy enough to take up the hatchet at any time, the seizing the whole country of that tribe & driving them across the Missisipi, as the only condition of peace, would be an example to others, and a furtherance of our final consolidation.

Combined with these views, & to be prepared against the occupation of Louisiana by a powerful & enterprising people, it is important that setting less value on interior extension of purchases from the Indians, we bend our whole views to the purchase and settlement of the country on the Missisipi from it's mouth to it's Northern regions, that we may be able to present as strong a front on our Western as on our Eastern border, and plant on the Missisipi itself the means of it's own defence. we now own from 31.° to the Yazoo, & hope this summer to purchase what belongs to the Choctaws from the Yazoo up to their boundary, supposed to be about opposite the mouth of Acanza. we wish at the same time to begin in your quarter, for which there is at present a favorable opening. the Cahokias being extinct, we are entitled to their country by our paramount sovereignty. the Piorias we understand have all been driven off from their country, & we might claim it in the same way; but as we understand there is one chief remaining, who would, as the survivor of the tribe, sell the right, it will be better to give him such terms as will make him easy for life, and take a conveyance from him. the Kaskaskias being reduced to a few families, I presume we may purchase their whole country for what would place every individual of them at his ease, & be a small price to us. say by laying off for each family wherever they would chuse it as much rich land as they could cultivate, adjacent to each other, inclosing the whole in a single fence, and giving them such an annuity in money or goods for ever as would place them in happiness. and we might take them also under the protection of the US. thus possessed of the rights of these three tribes, we should proceed to the settling their boundaries with the Poutewatamies & Kickapoos; claiming all doubtful territory, but paying them a price for the relinquishment of their concurrent claim, and even prevailing on them if possible to cede for a price such of their own unquestioned territory as would give us a convenient Northern boundary. before broaching this, and while we are bargaining with the Kaskaskias, the minds of the Poutewatamies & Kickapoos should be soothed[2] & consiliated by liberalities and sincere assurances of friendship. perhaps by sending a well qualified character to stay some time in Decoigne's village as if on other business, and to sound him & introduce the subject by degrees to his mind & that of the other heads of families, inculcating in the way of conversation all those considerations which prove the advantages they would recieve by a cession on these terms, the object might be more easily & effectually obtained than by abruptly proposing it to them at a formal treaty. of the means however of obtaining what we wish you will be the best judge; and I have given you this view of the system which we suppose will best promote the interests of the Indians & of ourselves, & finally consolidate our whole country into one nation only, that you may be enabled the better to adapt your means to the object. for this purpose we have given you a general commission for treating. the crisis is pressing. whatever can now be obtained must be obtained quickly. the occupation of New Orleans, hourly expected, by the French, is already felt like a light breeze by the Indians. you know the sentiments they entertain of that nation. under the hopes of their protection, they will immediately stiffen against cessions of land to us. we had better therefore do at once what can now be done.

I must repeat that this letter is to be considered as private & friendly, & is not to controul any particular instructions which you may recieve through the official channel. you will also percieve how sacredly it must be kept within [your] own breast, and especially how improper to be understood by the Indians. [for] their interests & their tranquility it is best they should see only the present age of their history. I pray you to accept assurances of my esteem & high consideration.

TH: JEFFERSON

PrC (DLC); faint; words in brackets supplied from Tr; at foot of first page: "Governor Harrison." Tr (ViW); in an unidentified hand.

YOUR FAVOR OF DEC. 30: no letter from Harrison to TJ dated 30 Dec. 1802 has been found or is recorded in SJL. TJ probably refers to the memorial and petition of the Indiana Territory convention, dated 28 Dec. 1802, which Harrison signed as president and delegate from Knox County. TJ may also be conflating this letter with one of 30 Dec. 1802 from Edmund Harrison.

PLAN OF THE TOWN: Jeffersonville, in the Indiana Territory, adopted a modified version of a checkerboard town plan suggested by TJ, which left every other square unoccupied in the belief that it prevented the spread of yellow fever (Vol. 38:165-7).

ANSWER TO YOUR LETTER AS PRESIDENT OF THE CONVENTION: see TJ to Harrison, 28 Feb. 1803.

ACANZA: Arkansas River.

DECOIGNE'S VILLAGE: Jean Baptiste Ducoigne.

GENERAL COMMISSION FOR TREATING: see TJ to the Senate, 2 Feb. 1803.

[1] MS: "the."
[2] MS: "sothed."

From Justus Erich Bollmann

SIR, Philada. February 28th 1803

Your Excellency's Letter of the 6th Inst. did not come to Hand untill the 11th, and the Bottle of Wine to which it refers, and which it was necessary to receive in Order to reply to it with Precision was only delivered to me a few Days ago.—I observe that the Wine in this Bottle was very thick and cloudy; should it have been in this State when You received it from Mr. Olsen I apprehend You will have formed a less favourable Idea of it than it deserves, since it was perfectly bright when it was sent from home. This however does not apply to the Tokay which never fines completly on Account of its Richness.

The whole Family of the Hungarian Wines are more or less sweet, but they are notwithstanding held in high Estimation among those who are in the Habit of drinking them, and are reputed to partake in some Degree of the Quality of Tea, as they exhilerate, when genuine, without intoxicating.

I have taken Notice of the Qualtity which You prefer and it is agreable to me to find that one Box of it, containing Twelve Bottles remains still unopened, which, if you desire it, I can forward to Washington by Water with the first Opportunity. This Kind costs $18 pr. Dozen and it will give me a particular Pleasure to procure You any Quantity of it You may direct.—The sweeter Wine, which was contained in the other long-necked Quart bottles, costs double the Price of the former.

I remain with great Respect Your Excellency's most obt. humble St. J. ERICH BOLLMANN

RC (MHi); at foot of text: "The President of the United States"; endorsed by TJ as received 3 Mch. and so recorded in SJL.

The imperfect, THICK AND CLOUDY finish of the wine TJ had ordered may account for his estimation of its relative sweetness, as opposed to the opinion of Danish minister Peder Blicher OLSEN, who had sent this and other Hungarian vintages to him (Peder Blicher Olsen to TJ, [23 Jan.]; TJ to Bollmann, 6 Feb.).

From Matthew Clay

SIR Congress Hall 28th Feby: 1803

There is now before the Senate a Bill for opening two land Offices in the Mississippi Territory which among other things impowers the President of the United States to appoint two Receivers of Public monies, one to be in the county of Adams, for this Office I beg leave to name Abner Green a person in all respects qualified to fill that place—Mr. Green is admited to be one of the best Accomptants in the Territory—he stands high in the confidence of the people of that Country—he is a man of integrity—attached to the republican party; & is an admirer of the measures of the present Administration—

Not having noticed the appointment of Secretary in that Territory since Mr. Steel's time expired beg leave to recommend Cato West—this gentleman's literary talents are inferior to none in that quarter, he stands high in the confidence of the Republican party—he is a man of integrity warmly attached to the Constitution & the measures of the present Administration—

I trust I shall stand excused with the President of the United States for the part which I take in the nomination of those Gentleman when he is informed that it is solicited by both the gentlemen & the Republican party of the Territory—

With sentiments of high respect I am yr Ob: Servt.

MAT. CLAY

RC (DNA: RG 59, LAR); endorsed by TJ as received 1 Mch. and so recorded in SJL with notation "Abner Greene & Cato West to office"; also endorsed by TJ: "Green Abner to be Reciever public monies West Cato to be Secretary."

Matthew Clay (1754-1815) of Virginia was a veteran of the American Revolution who served in the House of Representatives from 1797 to 1813. As a freshman congressman, he boarded with TJ and earned the vice president's praise for being "firm as a rock" in his Republican loyalty (ANB; Vol. 29:422, 469n).

The BILL mentioned by Clay was passed into law by Congress on 3 Mch. 1803 as "An Act regulating the grants of land, and providing for the disposal of the lands of the United States, south of the state of Tennessee." Among its provisions, the act authorized the president to establish two land offices in the Mississippi Territory, one in Adams County and the other in Washington County, to dispose of lands lying west and east of Pearl River, respectively. A register and receiver of public monies was to be appointed for each land office (U.S. Statutes at Large, 2:229-35).

ABNER GREEN was treasurer general of the Mississippi Territory and a justice of the peace for Adams County. He did not receive an appointment from TJ. His brother-in-law, CATO WEST, was nominated secretary of the territory by TJ in his 1 Mch. 1803 message to the Senate (*Terr. Papers*, 5:191n, 529).

TJ had previously received recommendations for the new Mississippi offices from Kentucky representative Thomas T. Davis. Writing James Madison on 23 Feb., Davis asked the secretary "to inform the President" that Congressmen Abram Trigg of Virginia and Robert Williams of North Carolina "will be pleased to obtain the appointment of Commissioners under the Act for disposing of the Lands in Mississippi Terretory" (RC in DNA: RG 59, LAR; addressed: "Mr Madison"; endorsed by TJ as received 23 Feb. and "Abram Trigg Robert Williams to be Western commissioners" and so recorded in SJL).

From Albert Gallatin

Tr. Dep. 28th Feby. 1803

Joel Burt Collector of customs for the district of Oswego and Inspector of the revenue for the port of entry in the said district

---

Thomas Dudley Surveyor of the port of Swansborough in the district of Newbern *vice Alexander Carmalt dead.*

The above seem to be the only nominations which it is necessary to make, although several other removals will be officially submitted in cases where the vacancy has not yet taken place: unless some mistake has been made in the Vermont nomination which does not yet appear very clear & on the subject of which, I have written to Mr Bradley.

The place of collector for the district of Oswego has never been filled. The enclosed recommendation from Governor Clinton may be depended upon, as he has not given it until he had consulted & enquired for near nine months. The port of entry is designated generally in the nomination of inspector, as it is not fixed by the law, & must be fixed by an act of the President. I think Sodus must be the place, but will make a report on the subject before the commission shall be transmitted.

The surveyorship of Swansborough became vacant during the session; it is difficult to obtain recommendations from that quarter; but upon the whole Dudley seems, in the opinion of the members of that State to be the most proper.

If it shall be necessary to do any thing in Vermont, it shall be transmitted this evening—

With respect ALBERT GALLATIN

Note—The President will not forget that the Secretaryship of the Mississipi territory must also be filled—and whether upon the whole Mr Triest is not better calculated for that than for the collectorship Must be determined

RC (DLC); with emendation by TJ supplied in italics; at foot of text: "The President of the United States"; endorsed by Gallatin: "Nominations to be made before the adjournment of the Senate"; endorsed by TJ as received from the Treasury Department on 28 Feb. and "Nomns" and so recorded in SJL. Enclosure not found.

JOEL BURT: for the establishment of the Oswego collection district and the appointment of the first collector, see Gallatin to TJ, 17 July and 9 Sep. 1802.

On 18 Jan., Francis Hawks, collector at New Bern, North Carolina, informed Gallatin of the death of the surveyor at Swansboro and the interim appointment of THOMAS DUDLEY to discharge the duties until the president appointed a replacement. When Dudley applied to Hawks for the surveyorship, Hawks requested recommendations. On 20 Nov. 1802, Dudley supplied a certificate signed by 12 people, who noted that Dudley was an honest man, possessing "property that would afford a Security to the United States," with the capability of performing the duties of the office. Two others, who were better educated than Dudley, applied for the position, but they were strangers to Hawks. Swansboro had so little business that the collector did not personally have the opportunity to judge Dudley's performance (RC in DNA: RG 59, LAR). On 18 Jan., Dudley applied to Gallatin directly for the surveyorship, noting that Hawks was writing the Treasury secretary on the subject (RC in same; endorsed by TJ: "Dudley Thos. to mr Gallatin. Surveyor of Swansboro' Newbern").

VERMONT NOMINATION: probably that of Jabez Penniman in place of David Russell as collector at Alburg on Lake Champlain (see the first three enclosures at Gallatin to TJ, 18 Jan., and TJ to the Senate, 2 Feb.).

To William Henry Harrison

SIR — Washington Feb. 28. 1803.

Your letter of Dec. 28. written as President of the Convention at Vincennes, was recieved on the 23d. inst. by the hands of mr Parke: and I derive great satisfaction from it's expressions of confidence in my attention to the interests of the territory of Indiana; attentions which my duties call for, and which certainly never will be intermitted on my part.

Instructions which were sent you some time ago will have informed you of the measures we are contemplating for laying the foundations of lasting peace with the several Indian tribes, by a settlement of boundaries with them; and will have shewn you that the matter particularly addressed to me by the letter of the Convention had been anticipated before it's reciept. for those addressed by their memorial to the legislature of the US. I must refer to the proceedings of that body.

Accept, Sir, for yourself, and the members who composed the convention, assurances of my high consideration and respect.

TH: JEFFERSON

PrC (DLC); at foot of text: "Governor Harrison."

Benjamin PARKE was a Vincennes attorney and protégé of Harrison, who later served as the territorial delegate to Congress and a federal judge (ANB; Vol. 38:138-40).

INSTRUCTIONS: see TJ's Memorandum for Henry Dearborn on Indian Policy at 29 Dec. 1802.

To Lewis Harvie

DEAR SIR Washington Feb. 28. 1803.

When I came into my present office you were so kind as to offer your aid as secretary to it; but having a considerable time before that proposed it to Capt Lewis, I could not avail myself of it. some object in the Western country which will probably employ him a year or two, will so long withdraw him from his post. altho' the progress you have made in the mean time in preparing yourself for entering on the scene of public life, may make that not acceptable now which would have been so two years ago, yet from duty as well as inclination I make you the tender. how far, by taking a station here, and a broader survey of the field you are to enter on, you may be enabled to do it with better preparation, you can best judge. the office itself is more in the nature of that of an aid de camp than a mere secretary. the writing is not considerable, because I write my own letters & copy them in a press. the care of our company, execution of some commissions in the town occasionally, messages to Congress, occasional conferences & explanations with particular members, with the offices, and inhabitants of the place where it cannot so well be done in writing, constitute the chief business. they do not in the whole encroach much on the hours of study before dinner, and admit of the afternoon & evening being entirely given to study at home or the society of the place. the salary of 600. D. a year serves for clothes & pocket money. a servant of the house to render you the offices you may need, and a horse in the stable always at your service, unless attachment to a particular servant or horse of your own should induce you to prefer bringing them, in which case they will be taken into the family. should it be your object to pursue the study of the law, I have no doubt mr Mason will give you any aid in his power. this, my dear Sir, is a brief state of the nature of the position placed at your command and I wish you to consider it solely with a view to your own objects. if these can be promoted by it, my wishes will be doubly fulfilled. if you think they would not, say so with frankness, as I should be sorry to see [one] hour of your time uselessly employed. your aid would be acceptable to me in the highest degree, but not on the condition of obstructing or retarding more useful pursuits. I shall leave this place for Monticello on the 6th. of March, where I would wish to recieve your answer soon after my arrival there; as, should you not find it eligible to take the stand proposed, it will be necessary for me to think of another person. about the 1st. of April it would be convenient to me to have the place occupied. Accept assurances of my sincere esteem.

TH: JEFFERSON

PrC (DLC); torn; at foot of first page: "Lewis Harvie esq."; endorsed by TJ in ink on verso.

Some day previous to this, TJ offered the post of SECRETARY to William Brent, who, like Harvie, had sought the position when TJ was elected president. In a response to Meriwether Lewis, however, Brent declined the offer, citing his efforts to establish himself as a merchant (William Brent to Meriwether Lewis, 25 Feb., RC in DLC, endorsed by TJ; Vol. 33:241-2).

From Alexander Moultrie

Feb: 28th: 1803.

Col: Moultrie's Respects to the President;—has been Advised by Mr: John Randolph, to commit to his Care, the within; which contains a Letter from Doctr: Moultrie of South Carolina (Col: M's Son in Law & relative) to his old Friend & Fellow-Student, Mr: Th: M. Randolph, which he begs his Attention to.—

RC (DLC); endorsed by TJ as received 28 Feb. and so recorded in SJL. Enclosure not found.

Alexander Moultrie (ca. 1750-1807) of South Carolina, a colonel at the close of the American Revolution, lost his post as state attorney general in 1792 following his impeachment for embezzling public money. His daughter Catherine was married to Dr. James Moultrie of Charleston, who earned his medical degree in 1788 from the University of Edinburgh, where Thomas Mann Randolph also studied from 1784 to 1788 (*S.C. Biographical Directory, House of Representatives*, 3:515-17; Joseph Ioor Waring, *A History of Medicine in South Carolina, 1670-1825* [Charleston, 1964], 337, 344, 347; William H. Gaines, Jr., *Thomas Mann Randolph: Jefferson's Son-in-Law* [Baton Rouge, 1966], 14-24; Vol. 34:15n).

To Benjamin Rush

DEAR SIR Washington Feb. 28. 1803.

I wish to mention to you in confidence that I have obtained authority from Congress to undertake the long desired object of exploring the Missouri & whatever river, heading with that, leads into the Western ocean. about 10. chosen woodsmen headed by Capt. Lewis my secretary, will set out on it immediately & probably accomplish it in two seasons. Capt. Lewis is brave, prudent, habituated to the woods, & familiar with Indian manners & character. he is not regularly educated, but he possesses a great mass of accurate observation on all the subjects of nature which present themselves here, & will therefore readily select those only in his new route which shall be new. he has qualified himself for those observations of longitude & latitude necessary to fix the points of the line he will go over. it would be very useful to state for him those objects on which it is most desireable he should bring us information. for this purpose I ask the favor of you to prepare some notes of such particulars as may occur in his journey & which you think should draw his attention & enquiry. he will be in Philadelphia about 2. or 3 weeks hence & will wait on you.

I have owed, now a twelvemonth, an answer to your very friendly letter of Mar. 12. 1802. but when certain things press, & others will bear delay, we naturally take up the former, & the latter lie over. after all my life having enjoyed the benefit of well formed organs of digestion & deportation, I was about 2. years ago taken with a diarrhoea, after having dined moderately on fish which had never affected me before. in the course of 2. or 3. weeks it wore me down by the frequency of calls, but then got so much better as to call on me but once a day, but still of watery consistence, and distressing me with troublesome borborygmi. for a twelvemonth past however, these circumstances are more favorable, and tho' they continue to a certain degree, I enjoy good health. in the course of it I have made experiment of every kind of diet, drink & regimen: and I find that fish is the only article which affects me; & what is remarkeable while fish & sturgeon affect me powerfully, neither oysters nor crabs do. I find it important too to be moderate in the quantity of food. the stomach has never failed in the least, but performs it's functions most perfectly: the bowels alone are weak and labour in their operations. I have troubled you with these details because your friendship called for them. I have found that riding is my remedy. a journey brings me to my antient habits for some days, and daily rides of an hour or two keep me free from inconvenience from the visceral weakness. I see at present nothing more in it than a liability to a return whenever an unfavorable affection occurs in any part of my system. I doubt the effect of medecine in chronical[1] cases of this kind at any period of life, & still more so at mine. the system however may perhaps gradually recover it's strength. but these unlettered ideas are laid at your feet: your information & experience will regard nothing but the facts; and certainly my confidence not only in your skill but your friendship will render truly valuable to me any ideas which you can without trouble throw on paper, for my government in the event of a return of the complaint to a troublesome degree: for at present it exists only[2] in a perfectly innocent state. I pray you to accept assurances of my affectionate friendship & sincere respect. TH: JEFFERSON

RC (CU-BANC); at foot of first page: "Dr. Rush." PrC (DLC); endorsed by TJ in ink on verso.

Rush opened his FRIENDLY LETTER of 12 Mch. 1802, which touched on several subjects, by asking for more information about the "flaw" in TJ's health that TJ had mentioned in a letter of 20 Dec. 1801 (Vol. 36:177-8; Vol. 37:68-9).

[1] Word interlined.
[2] Word interlined.

From Robert Smith

Nav. Dep
28 Feb 1803

SIR!

There are eight vacancies in the Navy, of Lieutenants—The Gentlemen mentioned in the accompanying List, are the eldest in rank of the Midshipmen—

I have the honor to be respectfully, Sir, your mo ob: st:

RT SMITH

RC (DLC); in a clerk's hand, signed by Smith; at foot of text: "President of the United States"; endorsed by TJ as received from the Navy Department on 28 Feb. and "Nominns" and so recorded in SJL. FC (Lb in DNA: RG 45, LSP). Enclosure: undated list addressed to the "Gentlemen of the Senate," nominating Michael B. Carroll of Maryland, Abner Woodruff and Theodore Hunt of New Jersey, James Decatur and George W. Reed of Pennsylvania, Benjamin Smith of Rhode Island, Samuel Elbert of Georgia, and William Mallet Livingston of New York to be lieutenants in the navy (MS in same; in a clerk's hand; endorsed by TJ).

TJ included the names on the ACCOMPANYING LIST in his nominations to the Senate of 1 Mch. 1803.

Abstract of Warrants from Robert Smith

Navy Department
February 28th 1803

Abstract of Warrants on the Treasurer by the Secretary of the navy for navy purposes, shewing also the Balance on hand for the Week ending the 26th. day of February 1803

Date	no.	In whose favor & for what purpose	amot. of Warrants	amot. of Deposits & Balance
1803		Balance from last Report		1758.47
Feby 22	2041 / 1078	Daniel Murray—Pay & Continge.	115.87	
26	2042 / 1079	George Merrill—Pay &c.	55.80	
		Balance on hand	1586.80	
		Drs.	1758.47	1758.47

Rt Smith

MS (DLC); in a clerk's hand, signed by Smith; endorsed by TJ as received from the Navy Department with notation "Warrts."

last report: Smith had prepared weekly abstracts for TJ of warrants drawn for navy purposes throughout January and February 1803. For the week ending 1 Jan. 1803, the secretary drew two warrants totaling $1,700, leaving a balance on hand of $1,741.78. For the week ending 8 Jan. 1803, the secretary drew one warrant for $79.68, leaving a balance on hand of $1,662.10. For the week ending 15 Jan. 1803, the secretary received a deposit of $90,000 and drew 23 warrants totaling $56,575.42, leaving a balance on hand of $35,086.68. For the week ending 22 Jan. 1803, the secretary drew eight warrants totaling $11,710.61, leaving a balance on hand of $23,376.07. For the week ending 29 Jan. 1803, the secretary drew eight warrants totaling $14,130.46, leaving a balance on hand of $9,245.61. For the week ending 5 Feb. 1803, the secretary received a deposit of $10,000 and drew six warrants totaling $12,917.38, leaving a balance on hand of $6,328.23. For the week ending 12 Feb. 1803, the secretary drew eight warrants totaling $4,375.66, leaving a balance on hand of $1,952.57. For the week ending 19 Feb. 1803, the secretary drew three warrants totaling $195.10, leaving a balance on hand of $1,758.47 (all in DNA: RG 59, Records of the Bureau of Rolls and Library; all in a clerk's hand; all signed by Smith except abstract for week ending 29 Jan. 1803; abstract for week ending 5 Feb. 1803 addressed: "The President"; all endorsed by TJ).

daniel murray and george merrill were midshipmen in the navy (ndbw, *Register*, 37, 39).

To Caspar Wistar

Dear Sir Washington Feb. 28. 1803

The inclosed sheets may contain some details which perhaps may be thought interesting enough for the transactions of our society. they were forwarded to me by mr Dunbar with a couple of vocabularies which I retain to be added to my collection.

What follows is to be perfectly confidential. I have at length succeeded in procuring an essay to be made of exploring the Missouri & whatever river, heading with that, runs into the Western ocean.

Congress by a secret authority enables me to do it. a party of about 10. chosen men headed by an officer will immediately set out. we cannot in the US. find a person who to courage, prudence, habits & health adapted to the woods, & some familiarity with the Indian character, joins a perfect knolege of botany natural history, mineralogy & astronomy, all of which would be desireable. to the first qualifications Capt Lewis my secretary adds a great mass of accurate observation made on the different subjects of the three kingdoms as existing in these states, not under their scientific forms, but so as that he will readily sieze whatever is new in the country he passes thro, and give us accounts of new things only; and he has qualified himself for fixing the longitude & latitude of the different points in the line he will go over. I have thought it would be useful to confine his attention to those objects only on which information is most deficient & most desireable: & therefore would thank you to make a note on paper of those which occur to you as most desireable for him to attend to. he will be in Philadelphia within two or three weeks & will call on you. any advice or hints you can give him will be thankfully recieved & usefully applied. I presume he will compleat his tour there & back in two seasons. Accept assurances of my sincere esteem & high respect.

TH: JEFFERSON

PrC (DLC); at foot of text: "Dr. Wistar." Enclosure: Martin Duralde to William Dunbar, 24 Apr. 1802 (see Enclosure No. 1 listed at Dunbar to TJ, 5 Jan.).

From Joseph Croswell

Plymouth (State of Massachusetts)
Feby 1803,

SR

Nothing could tempt me to intrude on your important moments but imperious circumstances, of which I shall only mention a partial detail, It is constitutional in my family to adhere invariably to those political doctrines that appear just & righteous and the more powerfully they are oppos'd, to oppose the more zeal in their defence, consequently I have suffer'd an uncommon share of persecution from the Tories previous to Our Revolution & latterly from the same sort of Men stiled Federalists, who improv'd as an advantage some losses I had sustaind at Sea and seem'd determin'd to ruin me, they overperswaded men who had sent private adventures in My Vessell to the care of the Captain (who committed Baratry) to prosecute me & used their influence with Referees which induc'd them allways to give in

their awards against me & I could get no relief as every Judge attorney & Officer pertaining to our Courts are Federal—It would require a volume to mention all the persecution I suffer'd purely on account of my Republican principles, for they knew that I was zealous in the Cause & the only person in this Country that wrote in the News paper's against them.—My Brother, a man of some note & a Magistrate, also suffer'd their resentment & was defrauded of some property for the same cause. He died soon after, Wm. Davis (a leader of the federal band & brother to the judge in Boston) told me soon after, when perswading me to join his party, "that if my brother had been of their side in politic's, he would now be living"—My troubles afflicted my Family, My Wife Died soon after, or about five years ago, I was also sick myself but providentially recover'd—my Daughter of 22 years old was sick & died, during this distress the Tories would often send a savage deputy sheriff into the room where my daughter was sick to heighten my trouble—however I have discharg'd all demands just & unjust & trade a little on my own property but find I am unavoidably diminishing of it yearly—[1]
Chosen for this district, General Warren having previously consulted with one or two of his friends & with me about the propriety of introducing his Son Henry as a Candidate, We objected on account of his political principles, as he wore the black Cockade & appear'd a zealous federalist, strictly observing Mr Adams's birth day, & afterwards sign'd the Plymouth address approving of his whole administration—a number of Whigs afterwards set me up as a Candidate, soon after a Caucus meeting was hel'd at *Abington*, Genl Warren who is esteem'd as a *Nestor* for wisdom by some, perswaded our two delegates that my loosing my property was a rational bar to my being chosen into office & sent his mandates into the Country recommending his Son, but if he would not do, another person was propos'd, which finally caused a Schism amongst the Whigs & facilitated the choice of Mr Read, the oppinion prevailing in some degree that a Man is not Eligible to any Office that is not rich[2] serves to keep me in the back ground—& the Warren family who are rich, in real property, have lately brought forward the Son, but some jaolousy remaining amongst the Whigs as Peter was of [...] amongst the *deciples* respecting *Paul*, who was c[...] and the federalists being inveterate against him for deserting them, made a powerfull opposition so [that?] a Mr Mitchell, a moderate federalist, not very pop[ular] nor powerfull, easily obtain'd his Election—I must [be] as brief as possible to extenuate in part the freedom I take I am a Widower about 60,

Son of a Minister formerly of Boston who was a zealous friend to Liberty & well known to Govr Adams & to the late Govr Hancock & I believe he is still remember'd by Docr Eustis & by Mr Bacon. I have 5 Children 2 youngest with me—If it was meritorious amongst the antient Romans to save the life of a Citizen is it not equally so to relieve a faithfull Zealous Unfortunate & persecuted Republican. If the Collectors Office in this Town, which is now fill'd by Wm Watson (father in law to Judge Davis) a bitter federalist, strongly suspected of winking at the frauds of his party, should become vacant, I think I could discharge the duties of it with honesty (a property the federalists will all acknowledge I possess) it might smooth the latter part of my path of life that has been fill'd with bryars & thorns,

Tho' I cannot say it will add to the oppinions I have of the personage I now address—I herewith use the freedom to enclose a book, it may show somthing of the Author, I expected to receive some benefit by its being Acted in Boston, but it has not, perhaps it's being tinctur'd with Republicanism has prevented—I could enumerate many pieces of mine publish'd in the Boston news papers, in support of liberty, previous to Our Revolution to the present time, occasionally, but shall only mention two—one on your accession to the seat of Goverment—begining

"Behold fair freedoms banners rise"
(in the Boston Chronicle)

& one entitled "the Mammoth Cheese" (publishd in the same paper) The Hudibrastic verse[3] design was to stop the nonsense of the federalists on that subject & to turn the ridicule upon them & I think it had that effect—

The federalists are so sinsible of my exertions in the cause of Liberty that one of their principal men told me lately "if I had been on their side & done so much I should have had [an] [...] before now—I think they would be better satified, [...] I was promoted (as they esteem me as an honest man) than they would to see a new convert put into Office—"The calm Sea wonder's at the wrecks it made"—

I do not wish to injure Genl Warren or his family, nor do I wish they should take undue advantages. I have wrote *sparingly*, I thought it was proper you should have some Idea of the Characters of men at a great distance from You, I wish it might not be known that I have wrote You, it might excite[4] annimosities that never tend to establish the truth or falshood of any point—there is not any man of Note in this county I believe but know's what I say of H W. is true—Mr Smith has been caress'd by them lately—

I have now to make my apology for this intrusion, If[5] it is tho't to be an act of temerity, the excuse may be, If oppression makes a wise man mad, it may make one of my description act imprudently—Or that Thirty years combating the Enemies of the Country ought to give a right to address the first Man in it, Or if necessity hath no law, my circumstances ought to paliate for transgresing the rules of decorum I do not wish to give You the trouble to write me any reply to this, but shall rest satisfied that your wisdom will prompt you to act right on all occasions, with profound respect & esteem I am Sr your Humble Servt

JOSEPH CROSWELL

RC (DNA: RG 59, LAR); torn at seal; addressed: "Thomas Jefferson President of the United States att Washington"; endorsed by TJ as received 16 Mch. and "to be Collector vice Watson" and so recorded in SJL. Enclosure: Joseph Croswell, *A New World Planted; or, The Adventures of the Forefathers of New-England; Who Landed in Plymouth, December 22, 1620, An Historical Drama—in Five Acts* (Boston, 1802; Shaw-Shoemaker, No. 2102).

Joseph Croswell (b. 1742?) of Plymouth, Massachusetts, was the son of Andrew Croswell, a radical separatist minister of a Congregational church in Boston. Joseph Croswell became a shopkeeper in Plymouth as well as a writer, and in 1772 married Lucy Allen in Boston. He witnessed the Boston Massacre in 1770 and was deposed at the trial for his recollections of the event. He served as a constable for Plymouth in 1778. One of his compositions, "An Ode to Liberty," was sung at a civic feast in Plymouth on 24 Jan. 1793 (*New England Historical and Genealogical Register*, 59 [1905], 247-8; Boston *Independent Chronicle*, 31 Jan. 1793; *Proceedings of the Massachusetts Historical Society*, 3 [1886-87], 430-1; *Records of the Town of Plymouth*, 3 vols. [Plymouth, 1903], 3:339; Chandler Robbins, *An Address Delivered at Plymouth, on the 24th Day of January, 1793, to the Inhabitants of That Town; Assembled to Celebrate the Victories of the French Republic over Their Invaders* [Boston, 1793], 19-20; Croswell to TJ, 15 July 1803).

NESTOR: in Greek mythology, an older Homeric hero known for his wisdom and speaking ability (OED).

SCHISM AMONGST THE WHIGS: several individuals, including Croswell, Daniel Snow, Josiah Smith, and William Crow Cotton, were potential Republican candidates in the 1800 Massachusetts congressional elections. The *Independent Chronicle* reported the candidates and announced the qualifications of General James Warren's SON, Henry, who had been clerk of the Massachusetts House of Representatives since 1792. The party split after a caucus held at Abington, ultimately contributing to the election of Federalist representative Nathan READ, who had assumed the seat vacated by Samuel Sewall (Boston *Independent Chronicle*, 20-23 and 27-30 Oct. 1800; *Biog. Dir. Cong.*). Warren, an unsuccessful candidate for state senate in May 1802, on 1 Nov. ran as the Republican candidate from Plymouth district for one of the 17 seats from Massachusetts in the Eighth Congress. He lost to the Federalist Nahum MITCHELL, 1,002 votes to 1,400 (*Salem Gazette*, 7 Feb. 1802; Boston *Columbian Centinel*, 29 May 1802; New Bedford *Columbian Courier*, 8 Oct. 1802; *Windham Herald*, 11 Nov. 1802; Vol. 37:555-6; Vol. 38:313-14; Appendix I: List of Appointments).

William WATSON, the father-in-law of JUDGE John DAVIS, the United States attorney for Massachusetts, was head of a local Federalist junto in Plymouth as well as its customs official (Prince, *Federalists*, 25-6; Vol. 37:555-6; Vol. 38:661-3).

BEHOLD FAIR FREEDOMS BANNERS RISE: the first line in a six-verse poem titled "Ode, on the Fourth of March, 1801" appeared in the Boston *Independent Chronicle* issue of 16-19 Mch. 1801.

THE MAMMOTH CHEESE, a satirical piece written in HUDIBRASTIC VERSE or octosyllabic couplets, was published in the Boston *Independent Chronicle* on 8 July 1802.

THE CALM SEA WONDER'S AT THE WRECKS IT MADE: "after a tempest, when the winds are laid, the calm sea wonders at the wrecks it made," lines delivered by the king in Act 5 of "The Maid's Tragedy Alter'd" by Edmond Waller (*Poems, &c. Written upon Several Occasions and to Several Persons* [London, 1722], 212).

[1] Canceled: "sometime after or the last time Mr Read was."

[2] Preceding four words interlined.

[3] Preceding two words interlined by Croswell without symbol for insertion.

[4] Word interlined in place of "stir up."

[5] Croswell here canceled "this address."

From Abraham Baldwin

ABR BALDWIN TO THE
PRESIDENT OF THE UNITED STATES — March 1st. 1803

Agreeably to your request I have consulted my colleague and the Representatives respecting recommending two persons to be Commissioners of Bankruptcy we have concluded to recommend Robert Walker and George Watkins of Augusta

RC (DNA: RG 59, LAR); addressed: "Thomas Jefferson President of the United States"; endorsed by TJ as a letter of 1 Mch. received 28 Feb. and recorded in SJL as a letter of 28 Feb. received the same day; also endorsed by TJ: "Robert Walker George Watkins } Commrs. bkrptcy Augusta."

MY COLLEAGUE: Senator James Jackson. Peter Early and David Meriwether were Georgia's REPRESENTATIVES (*Biog. Dir. Cong.*). Robert Walker and George Watkins received appointments as COMMISSIONERS OF BANKRUPTCY on 1 Mch. (list of commissions in Lb in DNA: RG 59, MPTPC; Vol. 37:706, 707n, 711; Appendix I: List of Appointments). For two other candidates from Georgia who were appointed at the same time, see Jackson to TJ, 14 Feb.

From Isaac Briggs

Sharon, near Brookeville, Maryland,
1st. of the 3rd. Month 1803.

RESPECTED FRIEND,

Agreeably to my promise, I have investigated thy Problem for finding the longitude by lunar observation. In reducing the operation to a practical formula, in every modification which I have been able to give it, a knowledge of the *time* of observation appears essential.

Without a knowledge of the time, the Moon's right ascension, or longitude may be found, and, from the Nautical Almanac, the time at Greenwich, of that observation; but these are not sufficient data for finding the terrestrial longitude. Assuming, therefore, the time, as one of the data, I have labored faithfully, for two days, in order to simplify the process; yet, in every view, it appears to me too intricate and troublesome, for any but an adept in Astronomy, and one who has, by practice, acquired considerable expertness in making observations.

In the course of my attention to this subject a very simple method of finding the longitude has occurred to me. It requires no instruments but a good watch giving seconds, and a Portable Transit such as our friend Andrew Ellicott can easily furnish. The observations require but little skill, and, without unnecessary inattention, this method admits not of an error, in longitude, greater than 6½ miles when the moon is in her Apogee, and when in her Perigee not greater than 4 miles. By taking a mean of several observations, and by a regular course of similar observations made in the City of Washington, the probability of error will be greatly diminished. On account of the uncertainty which still exists in the best lunar calculations, a regular course of observations made at the Zero of American longitude, as a standard of comparison for similar observations made in different places, would, in my opinion, furnish incomparably the best means of improving the Topography of America.

A Method of finding the Longitude, by the Moon's Culmination.

Observations.

Note the instant of time when the moon's enlightened limb is on the meridian. Note also the instant of culmination of several known fixed Stars, as near the time of the moon's culmination as can be obtained, either before, or after it, or both, for ascertaining the correctness of the watch.

A scientific traveller should multiply these observations as much as possible, keep an accurate list of them and of the places to which they correspond, and defer the calculations to his leisure, or the skill of Astronomers.

Formula.

1. By the estimated longitude, reduce the time of observation to Greenwich time; which call, G.

2. Take, from the Nautical Almanac, the difference between the moon's right ascension for the time next after and next before G. which difference call D.

3. Take the Moon's Semidiameter answering to G. which call S.

4. As D : 12 hours :: S : C.

5. When the moon's enlightened limb is west, add C to, when east, subtract it from, the time of observation, and the sum or remainder will be the time of her centre passing the meridian, which call T.

6. Take the time of the moon's passage over the meridian of Greenwich, for the same day (M) and for the following day (N.)

7. N—M (: 360° :: / : 24^h ::) T—M (: The Longitude, in degrees &c. / : The Longitude, in Time.

N.B. This formula is adapted solely to West longitude.

Example.

Admit that on the 4th. of the 3rd. Month 1803, the appulse of the Moon's enlightened limb to the meridian was observed at 9 h. 9 m. 12 sec. apparent time,—Longititude estimated to be 5 hours West.

	H M S			
	9. 9.12	Moon's R. Asc. Mar. 5. Noon		134.° 37'
Est. Long. +	5		Mar. 4. Midnight	128. 34
G =	14. 9.12		D =	6. 3
S =	14.' 57"		Time of observation	9. 9. 12
	6.° 3' :	12 hours :: 14.' 57" :	C =	+ 29. 38
N =	$10.^h$ 15^m		T =	9.38. 50
M =	9. 29		M =	9.29. —
	46			9. 50

46^m (: 360° :: / : 24^h ::) $9.^m$ 50^s (: 77° / : $5.^h$ 8^m) Longitude West of Greenwich. This is the longitude of the Capitol.

The practice of this method would be greatly facilitated by two tables, one, of the moon's passage over the meridian of Washington, true to a second; and the other, the time of her semidiameter passing the meridian, also true to a second, for every noon and midnight. These would, perhaps, if calculated for a few years to come, furnish the best substitute for a course of actual observations at that place.

RC (DLC); unsigned, in Briggs's hand; endorsed by TJ as received 6 Mch. and so recorded in SJL.

Briggs probably made his PROMISE to TJ on a visit to Washington. The two had not corresponded since June 1802 (Vol. 37:688). TJ hoped to find a way to determine LONGITUDE on an overland journey when transporting a chronometer might not be practical, such as Meriwether Lewis's exploration up the Missouri River. Briggs confirmed one method proposed by TJ, but not before Lewis set off on his expedition (Bedini, *Statesman of Science*, 359-60; TJ to William Dunbar, 25 May 1805).

To Nicolas Gouin Dufief

SIR Washington Mar. 1. 1803.

I communicated your manuscript catalogue to the member of Congress charged with the purchase of books, and they have returned it to me with information that they had already exhausted their funds, and that therefore it was unnecessary for them to take the subject into consideration. it is now reinclosed to you with assurances of my esteem & respect.

TH: JEFFERSON

PrC (DLC); at foot of text: "M. Dufief"; endorsed by TJ in ink on verso. Enclosure: Dufief's list of books from Benjamin Franklin's library; see Dufief to TJ, 31 Jan.

COMMUNICATED: TJ to Abraham Baldwin, 4 Feb.

From Nicolas Gouin Dufief

MONSIEUR, 1er de Mars. 1803

J'ai fait mettre à bord du Sloop *Harmony* Cap. Ellwood, une Caisse à votre adresse, contenant les livres mentionés dans le mémoire ci-inclus.

J'aurais bien desiré vous procurer un Gassendi en français, & d'une format tel que vous l'aimez, mais il parait d'après les recherches que mon Libraire a faites, qu'on ne trouve en France que cette édition, & que la philosophie d'Epicure n'est point séparée des autres Œuvres de Gassendi—Le dictionnaire des Grands hommes en 4 vol 8vo, fait mention de l'édition que je vous envoye ainsi elle doit etre la bonne—

J'ai l'honneur d'être avec les Sentimens que l'amérique entière vous doit, & en particulier avec ceux que vous m'avez inspirés Votre très dévoué Serviteur

N. G. DUFIEF

EDITORS' TRANSLATION

SIR, 1 Mch. 1803

I dispatched a box to your address, on the sloop *Harmony*, under Captain Ellwood, containing the books listed on the enclosed invoice.

I would have wished to procure a Gassendi for you in French and in your preferred format, but according to my bookseller's inquiries, this is the only edition available in France, and Epicurus's philosophy is not separate from Gassendi's other works. The dictionary of great men in 4 octavo volumes mentions the edition I have sent you, so it must be the right one.

I have the honor of sharing the sentiments that all America owes you, and especially those you have inspired in your very devoted servant

N. G. DUFIEF

RC (DLC); at foot of text: "Thomas Jefferson, Président des E.U."; endorsed by TJ as received 4 Mch. and so recorded in SJL with notation "books 55.50."

John ELLWOOD gave Dufief a bill of lading at Philadelphia on 26 Feb. for a box shipped to TJ on the sloop *Harmony* (MS in DLC).

QU'ON NE TROUVE EN FRANCE QUE CETTE ÉDITION: Dufief referred to an edition of the works of Pierre Gassendi that contained six volumes in folio size published in Lyons in 1658 (J. C. F. Hoefer, *Nouvelle biographie générale depuis les temps les plus reculés jusqu'a nos jours*, 46 vols. [Paris, 1855-66], 19:587; Sowerby, No. 4914).

ENCLOSURE

Invoice for Books

Thos. Jefferson. President of the U. S.

To N. Gouin Dufief—	Dr.
To Philosophie d'Epicure par Gassendi, 6 vol. fol. ℔	24. "
" Athenaei Dipinosophistarum &c. folio	1.50
" Philostratus concerning the life of Apollonius the Tyanaean, fol.	1. "
" Derham's physico-astro-Theology 2 vol. 8o.	3. "
" Sermons de Massillon, 15 vol. 12mo.	15. "
" OEuvres d'Helvétius, 10 vol. petit format, br.	6. "
" Philosophical Transactions, 4to. in board. bgt. at Dobson's for Cl. Munroo.	4. "
	54.50
Box.	1. "
	55.50

RC (DLC); in a clerk's hand; at foot of text in Dufief's hand: "Recd the above in full N. G. Dufief."

The "br." in Dufief's invoice entry for the works of Claude Adrien HELVÉTIUS is for *broché*, meaning paperbound. TJ had the volumes bound in calf leather (Sowerby, No. 1242; Statement of Account with John March, 10 July).

BGT. AT DOBSON'S: Thomas Dobson of Philadelphia published the fifth volume of the American Philosophical Society's *Transactions*.

From Christopher Ellery

March 1st. 1803

C. Ellery intended to have conversed, this morning, with the President, on the subject of the forged letters—but having been prevented by the presence of a third person—he begs to be permitted to observe to the President, that he will be very happy to receive, from the President, through Captain Lewis, any advice or direction relative to the subject—if indeed the President has any communication whatever to make

RC (DLC); endorsed by TJ as received 1 Mch. and so recorded in SJL.

FORGED LETTERS: presumably the two letters TJ received in August 1801 from Nicholas Geffroy, which Ellery attributed to Federalist congressman John Rutledge, Jr. See Vol. 35:3-6; Vol. 38:527-9.

To the House of Representatives

Gentlemen of
the House of Representatives

According to the request stated in your resolution of December 20th. I communicated to you such returns of the Militia of the different states as had then been recieved. since that date returns have been recieved from New Hampshire, Massachusets, Connecticut, New York, North Carolina, Georgia and Kentucky, which are now transmitted to you.

Th: Jefferson
Mar. 1. 1803.

RC (DNA: RG 233, PM, 7th Cong., 2d sess.). PrC (DLC). Recorded in SJL with notation "militia." Enclosure: "Return of the Militia of those States from which Returns have been received at the War Office since the 20th of December, 1802," dated War Department, 1 Mch. 1803, and signed by Henry Dearborn, consisting of returns made by the states of New Hampshire, Massachusetts, Connecticut, New York, North Carolina, Georgia, and Kentucky, and compiling them into tables for general and field staff, field officers and regimental staff, artillery, cavalry, grenadiers, infantry, light infantry, riflemen, and arms, ammunition, and accoutrements (printed in ASP, *Military Affairs*, 1:163-7).

I COMMUNICATED TO YOU: TJ to the House of Representatives, 5 Jan. 1803.

The House received TJ's message and its accompanying papers on 1 Mch. and ordered both to lie on the table (JHR, 4:378).

From Michael Leib

Sir, Washington March 1st. 1803

The name of the gentleman about whom I convers'd with you is John Harrison—Permit me to suggest, that in addition to his fitness for the office of a commissioner of Bankruptcy, he has an additional recommendation in having been an uniform whig, and having sustained persecution on account of his unshaken adherence to our cause—As he is of a respectable quaker family and extensively connected with the society of friends, it may be of use and be gratifying to them to find a member of their body noticed by you—

If, Sir, such an appointment can be made without an interference with your arrangements, I need not say, how much many of your friends would be gratified by the appointment of Mr. Harrison

I am, Sir, With sentiments of sincere respect and regard Your obedt Servt.

M Leib

RC (DNA: RG 59, LAR); endorsed by TJ as received 1 Mch. and "Harrison John to be Commr. bkrpts vice Vancleve" and so recorded in SJL.

JOHN HARRISON, a chemist, druggist, and Michael Leib's brother-in-law, was also recommended by congressman-elect Joseph Clay, a Philadelphia bankruptcy commissioner, but Harrison did not receive the appointment. QUAKER FAMILY: Harrison's parents were married at the Philadelphia meeting of the Society of Friends in 1764. His mother, Sarah Richards Harrison, was an eloquent speaker who traveled extensively as a Quaker minister (William Welsh Harrison, *Waples and Allied Families: Being the Ancestry of George Leib Harrison of Philadelphia and of His Wife Sarah Ann Waples* [Philadelphia, 1910], 10-18, 27; *Biog. Dir. Cong.*; Vol. 38:119-20; Clay to TJ, 29 Mch. and 19 Oct. 1803; John Harrison to TJ, 1 Nov. 1808, in DLC).

Memorandum to James Madison

Commissions to be issued to the following persons under the bankrupt law.

John Mussey at Portland vice Joseph Boyd who has not qualified (to be so expressed)

Simeon Thomas at New London for Connecticut

Charles Ludlow at New York for New York.

John Stephen at Baltimore for Maryland.

Cowles Meade, Robert Walker & George Watkins at Augusta } for Georgia

Thomas Collier at Louisville } for Georgia

TH: JEFFERSON
Mar. 1. 1803.

MS (ViU); entirely in TJ's hand; check marks later added by each name; addressed: "The Secretary of State." Not recorded in SJL.

On 18 Feb., Salmon Chase wrote the secretary of state from PORTLAND, noting that the resignation of Joseph McLellan and the absence of JOSEPH BOYD meant that only he and William Widgery remained as commissioners to take care of the bankruptcy cases. He feared that a great inconvenience would arise if either became indisposed. Chase recommended Isaac Ilsley, noting his appointment would be "very acceptable" to the friends of the administration and to the present commissioners (RC in DNA: RG 59, LAR; endorsed by TJ: "Chase Salmon to Mr. Madison. Illsley to be Commr. bkrptcy Portland").

Jacob DeWitt, finding it "inconvenient to attend to the duties of Commissioner of Bankruptcy," wrote Madison from Norwich, CONNECTICUT, on 8 Feb., to submit his resignation. He would finish the cases appointed to him (RC in DNA: RG 59, LAR; endorsed by TJ: "DeWitt Jacob to mr Madison declines Commn. bkrptcy Simeon Thomas put in his place"). On a separate sheet of paper, TJ wrote: "Jacob Dewitt of Norwich Commr. bkrptcy will resign <*Ebenezer*> Simeon Thomas to be appd in his place" (MS in DNA: RG 59, MCL; entirely in TJ's hand).

JOHN STEPHEN was appointed in place of Henry Payson (Vol. 37:709).

Commissions for all designated above were dated 1 Mch. 1803 (list of commissions in Lb in DNA: RG 59, MPTPC).

To Joseph H. Nicholson

DEAR SIR Washington Mar. 1. 1803.

You recommended to me some time ago mr Thos. Rodney of Delaware for an appointment. nothing has yet turned up. in your letter you do not say whether he is a lawyer or not. if he is, it is possible he may suit as a Commissioner for the Missisipi land titles, and we might give him the most favorable berth which will be in the Eastern district, where the business will be short, & probably finished in the winter. will you be so good as to inform me on this subject, & favor me with your opinion? at the same time I must pray that not a word may be said to him or any other on the subject, as very serious embarrassments have sometimes occurred from a previous knolege of a designation to office. Accept my friendly salutations & assurances of high respect. TH: JEFFERSON

PrC (DLC); blurred; at foot of text: "Joseph H. Nicholson esq."; endorsed by TJ in ink on verso.

YOU RECOMMENDED: see Nicholson to TJ, 19 Nov.

COMMISSIONER FOR THE MISSISIPI LAND TITLES: the 3 Mch. legislation, which provided for the establishment of two land offices in Mississippi Territory, also called for the settlement of land claims in each district by having the land office register join with two commissioners appointed by the president to hear the cases. They were to meet on or before 1 Dec. 1803 to 1 Apr. 1804, or until the business was completed (U.S. Statutes at Large, 2:229-35; Matthew Clay to TJ, 28 Feb.).

To Philip Pearson

SIR Washington Mar. 1. 1803.

Your favor of the 19th. inst. was recieved by General Winn and I feel with due sensibility the testimony of approbation given me by the name you have been pleased to affix to your institution. sincerely a friend to science, I am happy to see it rising in every quarter. I am a friend to it because I believe it the only agent which can hold tyranny & bigotry in check. the people themselves are the only safe deposit of their own rights; and to make them safe, they must be informed to a certain degree. no instance I believe is known of an ignorant people remaining free after they were organised into a government. while un-organised, as our Indians, they are free because they have no magistrates, nor any laws which these magistrates can wield till they raise themselves above them. I sincerely wish you may be able either from public or private patronage, to maintain your institution in a flourishing state. I beg leave to present through General Winn such an aid as the extensive contributions under which I am laid in behalf of similar institutions in every part of the union leave at my disposal, and I pray you to accept for yourself & your associate trustee assurances of my great respect & consideration. TH: JEFFERSON

PrC (DLC); at foot of text: "Philip Pearson esq."

To the Senate

GENTLEMEN OF THE SENATE

I nominate Bartholomew D. Armistead now a 2d. Lieutent of Infantry in the 2d. regiment to be 1st. Lieutenant vice Saml. Lane resigned Aug. 12. 1802.

Benjamin Wilkinson, a 2d. Lieutt. in the 2d. regiment of infantry to be 1st. Lieutt. vice G. Barde dismissed the service.

Josiah Taylor now an ensign in the 2d. regimt of infantry to be 2d. Lieutt. vice B. D. Armistead promoted.

William L. Chew now an ensign in the 2d. regimt of infantry to 2d. Lieutt vice Benj. Wilson promoted

Cordiah N. Daniel of Missisipi to be a surgeon's mate in the army

Jonathan H. Sparhawk of N. Hampshire to be a surgeon's mate in the army.

Michael B. Carroll of Maryland,
Abner Woodruff of New Jersey
Theodore Hunt of New Jersey
James Decatur of Pensylvania
Benjamin Smith of Rhode island
Samuel Elbert of Georgia
Wm. Mallet Livingston of New York
George W. Reed of Pensylvania
} now midshipmen, to be Lieutenants in the Navy of the US.

Thomas Lovell of Boston to be commercial agent at La Rochelle

Levitt Harris of Pensylvania to be Consul at Rotterdam.

Isaac Dayton of New York to be Surveyor & Port inspector of Hudson vice J. C. Ten Broeck removed.

Joel Burt of New York to be Collector of customs and Inspector of the revenue for the district of Oswego.

Thomas Dudley of North Carolina to be Surveyor of the port of Swansborough in the district of Newbern, vice Alexander Carmalt deceased.

Charles Willing Byrd of Ohio, to be judge of the district of Ohio.

Michael Baldwin of Ohio to be Attorney for the US. in the district of Ohio.

David Zeigler of Ohio to be Marshal for the district of Ohio.

Cato West of the Missisipi territory to be Secretary of the territory, vice John Steele whose term has expired. TH: JEFFERSON

Mar. 1. 1803.

RC (DNA: RG 46, EPEN; 7th Cong., 2d sess.); endorsed by Senate clerks. PrC (DLC).

BENJ. WILSON: that is, Benjamin Wilkinson (see Henry Dearborn to TJ, 19 Feb.).

On 24 Feb., William Eustis sent the secretary of state communications advocating the appointment of THOMAS LOVELL as consul or commercial agent at La Rochelle. The first, dated 12 Jan. 1803, was from James Lovell, naval officer at Boston and father of the applicant. He enclosed an unsigned, undated sketch by Benjamin Homans, a merchant sea captain familiar with the ports of France. Homans noted the commercial importance of La Rochelle and lamented that it and surrounding ports were under the jurisdiction of the consul at Bordeaux, who had appointed Frenchmen "who could speak more or less of our language, but whose private interests have often militated with the Duty, & in many instances to my knowledge they have been prejudicial to our Countrymen." Homans advocated the appointment of an American and noted that Thomas Lovell's "Education, abilities, information, judgement & good disposition" made him "inferior to no One already appointed to similar Offices in France." His French connections by marriage would also be helpful in carrying out his duties. "Mr Lovell in obtaining this appointment," Homans thought, "would have greater advantages than any other Man" (RC and enclosures in DNA: RG 59, LAR, endorsed by TJ: "Lovell Thos. to be Consul La Rochelle"; Madison, *Papers, Sec. of State Ser.*, 4:346; Vol. 35:60n).

One of the leading advocates of Ohio statehood, MICHAEL BALDWIN served as the state's first U.S. attorney until October 1804, when he resigned to run for a seat in the state assembly. Baldwin noted that he had received the appointment without any solicitation on his part. Senator Abraham Baldwin, his half-brother, supported the nomination (Andrew R. L. Cayton, *The Frontier Republic: Ideology and Politics in the Ohio Country, 1780-1825* [Kent, Ohio, 1986], 83-8; Madison, *Papers, Sec. of State Ser.*, 8:143; Vol. 36:458; Thomas Worthington to TJ, 18 Sep. 1804). Another statehood advocate, Cincinnati Republican DAVID ZEIGLER served as U.S. marshal until March 1805, when he resigned for health reasons (Donald J. Ratcliffe, *Party Spirit in a Frontier Republic: Democratic Politics in Ohio, 1793-1821* [Columbus, Ohio, 1998], 26-7, 55-6; Madison, *Papers, Sec. of State Ser.*, 9:103-4; Vol. 37:636n).

On 1 Mch., Meriwether Lewis delivered TJ's message to the Senate, where it was immediately read and ordered to lie for consideration. The Senate consented to the appointments on 3 Mch. (JEP, 1:446-7).

From Benjamin Waterhouse

SIR, Cambridge March 1st. 1803.

I here transmit for your acceptance, a copy of my Treatise on the Kine Pock, which, though dated Novr. 1802 is just out of the press. The first part contains the history of the progress of this new inoculation in America; The second contains the theory of morbid poisons, together with practical rules & observations.—

Being aware that this first narrative would probably be referred to, in time to come, I was desirous to give it all the dignity in my power, by recording the patrons of this new discovery & practice. The unreserved applause which some of its most distinguished patrons have received in *all* the newspapers in this part of the Union, has given us high satisfaction. The same strain of eulogium pervades many of the British publications, especially the volume of public characters for 1803 just come to my hands, in sheets. In Jenner's character page 47, a paragraph begins thus,—"This beneficial practice is patronised by *Jefferson* in the New world, & by the *Emperor of Germany*, the *Empress Dowager of Russia* in the old." Then follows a copy of the letter from the Empress to Dr Jenner, dated Panlowsky Augt. 10th. 1802.

A second edition of this Treatise will I believe follow in a few months, before which I hope to receive from my friends & correspondents such corrections, hints for additions, or omissions as will make it less exceptionable to the scholar & physician. With high respect, I am

your very humble servt. BENJN. WATERHOUSE

RC (DLC); at foot of text: "President Jefferson"; endorsed by TJ as received 18 Mch. and so recorded in SJL. Enclosure: Waterhouse's *A Prospect of Exterminating the Small Pox, Part II, Being a Continuation of a Narrative of Facts Concerning the Progress of the New Inoculation in America; Together with Practical Observation on the Local Appearance, Symptoms, and Mode of Treating the Variola Vaccina, or Kine Pock* (Cambridge, Mass., 1802; Sowerby, No. 946).

The second part of Waterhouse's TREATISE included a narrative of his efforts to spread the cow pox vaccine throughout the United States and some of his communications with TJ and other DISTINGUISHED PATRONS (*Prospect of Exterminating the Small Pox, Part II*, 5-74).

To Richard Winn

Washington Mar. 1 1803.

Th: Jefferson presents his compliments to General Winn and asks the favor of him to take the trouble of recieving the amount of the inclosed order for the use of the academy on Broad river in S. Carolina which mr Pearson informs him the General patronised together with the letter to mr Pearson in answer to that of which the General was the bearer.

PrC (DLC); endorsed by TJ in ink on verso. Enclosure: Order on John Barnes for payment of $100 to Richard Winn "for value received," Washington, 1 Mch.

(PrC in same; in TJ's hand and signed by him; pressed on same sheet as letter above).

Richard Winn (ca. 1750-1824), a native of Fauquier County, Virginia, moved to South Carolina, where he established himself as a surveyor, merchant, and planter in Camden District. A Revolutionary War veteran who became a major general in the state militia, he served in the general assembly from 1779 to 1786. He donated 100 acres in 1777 to the Mount Sion Society for the establishment of a school and was an ex-officio trustee of South Carolina College from 1801 to 1802. Among the many public offices he held were United States Superintendent for Indian Affairs in the Southern Department, justice of the peace for Camden District and Fairfield County, commissioner for the purchase and laying out of Columbia, South Carolina, in 1786 and lieutenant governor from 1800 to 1802. He represented South Carolina in the United States Congress from 1793 to 1797 and again from 1803 to 1813 before moving to Maury County, Tennessee (ANB; *S.C. Biographical Directory, House of Representatives*, 3:779-81; *Biog. Dir. Cong.*; Vol. 36:262n).

FOR THE USE OF THE ACADEMY: TJ's financial records for 28 Feb. note this transaction with Barnes as "charity to Jefferson Monticello academy in S. Carolina" (MB, 2:1093).

LETTER TO MR PEARSON: TJ to Philip Pearson, 1 Mch.

From John Page

SIR, Richmond March 2d. 1803.

I received last night your letter of February 1803, to the Governor of Virginia, written in compliance with a request of the House of Representatives of the United States, that you should urge on the Executive of each state the importance and indispensible necessity of vigorous exertions on the part of the State governments to carry into effect the militia System adopted by the national Legislature, and I hasten to assure you, that I intirely accord in opinion with the House of representatives respecting the importance and necessity of the exertions they require, and with you, that none but an armed nation can dispense with a standing Army; and that nothing shall be wanting on my part, as far as the powers vested in me will permit, to render the militia a sure and permanent bulwark of national defence.

I have given orders, which, as soon as they can be executed, will enable me to transmit to you the return which you require of the militia, and of the arms and accoutrements of this state, and of the several counties or other geographical divisions of it.

Accept Sir, assurances of my high respect. JOHN PAGE

FC (Vi: Executive Letterbook); in a clerk's hand; at head of text: "The President of the United States." Recorded in SJL as received 16 Mch. with notation "W."

YOUR LETTER: Circular to the Governors of the States, 25 Feb.

To Robert Patterson

Dear Sir Washington Mar. 2. 1803.

I am now able to inform you, tho' I must do it confidentially, that we are at length likely to get the Missouri explored, & whatever river heading with that, leads into the Western ocean. Congress by a secret act has authorised me to do it. I propose to send immediately a party of about ten men with Capt Lewis, my secretary, at their head. if we could have got a person perfectly skilled in botany, natural history, mineralogy, astronomy, with at the same time the necessary firmness of body & mind, habits of living in the woods & familiarity with the Indian character, it would have been better. but I know of no such character who would undertake an enterprise so perilous. to all the latter qualities Capt. Lewis joins a great stock of accurate[1] observation on the subjects of the three kingdoms which are found in our own country but not according to their scientific nomenclatures. but he will be able to seize for examination & description such things only as he shall meet with new. he has been for some time qualifying himself for taking observations of longitude & latitude to fix the geographical points of the line he will pass over. but little means are possessed here of doing that; and it is the particular part in which you could give him valuable instruction, & he will recieve it thankfully & employ it usefully. the instruments thought best to be carried for this purpose are a good theodolite & a Hadley. he will be in Philadelphia 2. or 3. weeks hence to procure instruments & will take the liberty to call on you; and I shall be particularly obliged to you for any advice or instruction you can give him. I think it adviseable that nothing should be said of this till he shall have got beyond the reach of any obstacles which might be prepared for him by those who would not like the enterprise. Accept assurances of my sincere esteem & great respect.

Th: Jefferson

RC (CtY-BR); addressed: "Mr. Robert Patterson Philadelphia. S. 4th. str."; franked; postmarked 4 Mch. PrC (DLC).

TJ was familiar with both the THEODOLITE and the HADLEY reflecting quadrant, which was an instrument similar to a sextant. He had owned a theodolite (also called a universal equatorial instrument) for some time, and in the spring of 1802, Patterson helped him obtain a Hadley's quadrant (Bedini, *Statesman of Science*, 344-5; Vol. 37:107-8, 254, 327, 329n, 598).

[1] Word interlined in place of "scientific."

Statement of Account with Rapine, Conrad & Co.

The President of the United States—} To Rapine, Conrad & Co.

1802				
May 4	To 1	Aitkin's Letters		$1.
		Franklin's works		1.
		Volney's Lectures		.75
		Adams' Anacdotes		.87½
		Flowers of modern history 2 Vols		2.
		Burton's Lectures		.75
		Columbian Orator		.75
		Lyttleton's Dialogues		.87½
		Looking Glass for the mind		.75
		Moral Library		.75
		La Perous' Voyage		1.
		American Preceptor		.50
		Life of French		.25
	5	Foy books		.21
		An Almanac from Balto.		.10
Augt. 7		Willes' Reports, as ℔ Subscription		4.50
Decr. 16	2	Almanacs from Baltimore	10	.20
1803				
Jany. 1	1	Map of Maryland		5.
		Pike's Arithmetic		2.25
				$23.51

If it is convenient for the President to discharge the above bill he will much oblige his

Mo. Obt. Servts.

Rapine, Conrad & Co.
March 2d. 1803

MS (MHi); in Daniel Rapine's hand and signed by him; endorsed by TJ: "Acct 23.51. D pd. by ord. on J. Barnes Mar. 5. 1803."

AITKIN'S LETTERS: John Aikin's *Letters from a Father to His Son, on Various Topics, Relative to Literature and the Conduct of Life. Written in the Years 1792 and 1793*, was published in London in 1793 and in Philadelphia the following year (Evans, No. 26541).

TJ owned a copy of FRANKLIN'S WORKS published in London in 1779 as *Political, Miscellaneous, and Philosophical Pieces*. This was the only edition of Franklin's writings, besides his scientific works, published with his consent during his lifetime (Sowerby, No. 3053). Several editions of his works were published posthumously, including *The Works of the Late Dr. Benjamin Franklin; Consisting of His Life, Written by Himself. Together with Essays, Humorous, Moral and Literary, Chiefly in the Manner of the Spectator. To which is added, not in any other Edition, An Examination, before the British House of Lords, respecting the*

Stamp-Act, 2 vols. in 1, printed and published in Philadelphia in 1801 (Shaw-Shoemaker, No. 515).

VOLNEY'S LECTURES: Constantin François Chasseboeuf Volney, *Lectures on History*, was an English translation of *Leçons d'Histoire, prononcées a l'École Normale*, which first appeared in Paris in 1799 (Sowerby, No. 133).

ADAMS' ANACDOTES: Reverend John Adams, *Anecdotes, Bon-Mots, and Characteristic Traits of the Greatest Princes, Politicians, Philosophers, Orators, and Wits of Modern Times*, was printed in London in 1789. TJ also purchased Adams's *The Flowers of Modern History; Comprehending on a New Plan, The Most Remarkable Revolutions and Events, As Well as the Most Eminent and Illustrious Characters, of Modern Times*, which was published in London in 1788 and in Philadelphia in 1796, and was "designed for the improvement and entertainment of youth" (Evans, No. 29950).

BURTON'S LECTURES: J. Burton's *Lectures on Female Education and Manners* was published in London in 1793 and reprinted in New York in 1794 (Evans, No. 26723).

COLUMBIAN ORATOR: Caleb Bingham, *The Columbian Orator: Containing a Variety of Original and Selected Pieces; Together with Rules Calculated to Improve Youth and Others in the Ornamental and Useful Art of Eloquence*, was published in Boston in 1797 and designed as a second part to the *American Preceptor* (Evans, No. 31827).

LYTTLETON'S DIALOGUES: George Lyttelton, *Dialogues of the Dead*, was published in London in 1760 with the first American edition printed in Worcester, Massachusetts, in 1797 (Sowerby, No. 4621).

LOOKING GLASS FOR THE MIND: Arnaud Berquin, *The Looking-Glass for the Mind; or, Intellectual Mirror. Being an Elegant Collection of the Most Delightful Little Stories and Interesting Tales: Chiefly Translated from That Much Admired Work* L'Ami des Enfans, published in Yorkshire, England, in 1794.

The MORAL LIBRARY, published in Boston in 1796, consisted of three separate titles: *Principles of Virtue and Morality; or Essays and Meditations on Various Subjects* by David Macbride; *Essay on the Happiness of the Life to Come* by Charles-Michel Villette; and *On the Immortality of the Soul* translated by Soame Jenyns (Evans, No. 30813).

LA PEROUS' VOYAGE: Jean André Perreau, *Le Roi voyageur ou examen des abus de l'administration de la Lydie*, printed in London in 1784 (Sowerby, No. 2342).

AMERICAN PRECEPTOR: Caleb Bingham, *American Preceptor; Being a New Selection of Lessons for Reading and Speaking. Designed for the Use of Schools*, appeared in a second edition from Boston in 1794 and 1795.

Several ALMANACS FROM BALTIMORE were printed and sold for the year 1803 including the *Town and Country Almanac* and the *Citizen and Farmer's Almanac* by Bonsal and Niles, and the *Town and Country Almanac* and *The Annual Visitor; or, Almanac*, produced by Thomas, Andrews & Butler (Shaw-Shoemaker, Nos. 1765, 1922, 3173, 50278; Vol. 38:498).

MAP OF MARYLAND: not identified, but William Duane, writing from Washington in 1802, previously told TJ that "no map of Maryland is to be had here" (Sowerby, No. 3848; Vol. 37:311).

DISCHARGE THE ABOVE BILL: on 5 Mch., TJ gave an order on John Barnes to pay Rapine, Conrad & Co. $23.51 for books (MS in MHi, in TJ's hand and signed by him, signed by Rapine, Conrad & Co. acknowledging payment, endorsed by Barnes as paid on 26 Mch.; MB, 2:1093).

From Robert Smith

Nav Dep
2nd March 1803

SIR!

I enclose Warrants for
Laurence Keene
Francis Hall
Lewis Hunt
Walter G Anderson
Francis Mitchell
Wm. Ballard &
Wm. R Nicholson.

to be Midshipmen in the Navy. These young gentleman have all been well recommended—and should you approve their appointment, the enclosed Warrants will require your Signature.

I have the honor to be with the greatest respect Sir yr ob st

RT SMITH

RC (DLC); in a clerk's hand, signed by Smith; at foot of text: "President U States"; endorsed by TJ as received from the Navy Department on 3 Mch. and "Nominns" and so recorded in SJL. FC (Lb in DNA: RG 45, LSP).

WELL RECOMMENDED: for recommendations in favor of Francis Mitchell, including one from TJ, see Vol. 38:410, 428, 533. William R. Nicholson, a relative of Congressman Joseph H. Nicholson, was killed in a duel in 1804 (NDBW, 5:42, 376).

From Joseph Anderson

Senate Chamber
4 OClock 3rd March 1803

SIR

In pursueance of an act regulating the grants of land, and provideing for the disposal of the lands of the United States, South of the State of Tennessee—Commissioners are to be appointed to determine Certain Individual claims therein Specify'd—Some Considerations induce me to inform you—that I will accept the appointment of one of the Commissioners, who are to set on that business, in the *County* of *Adams*, shou'd you think me qualify'd therefor—My time as a Senator expires with this Session—As my arrangements after I return home, will depend on the information, I may receive from you, upon this Subject—I will wait on you to morrow morning, for an answer—and in the mean time pirmit me to assure you, (If I know myself) that whatever your decision may be—my high respect and esteem for you, will remain undimenishd

With Sentiments of the Most Respectful Consideration—

Jos: Anderson

RC (DNA: RG 59, LAR); endorsed by TJ as received 3 Mch. and "to be Commr. Missipi" and so recorded in SJL.

For the appointment of commissioners under the act, see TJ to Joseph H. Nicholson, 1 Mch. 1803.

From John Bacon

March 3d. 1803.

J Bacon presents his respectful regards to the President of the United States—wishes him a long, a useful, and a happy life—that he may be richly endowed with that wisdom which is from above, with that prudence which is profitable to direct, and with that integrity and uprightness which shall still preserve him; and that as his day is, so may his strength be.

RC (DLC); addressed: "The President of the United States"; endorsed by TJ as received 3 Mch. and so recorded in SJL.

A native of Connecticut, John Bacon (1738-1820) graduated from the College of New Jersey in 1765 and worked as an itinerant Presbyterian minister before assuming the pulpit of Boston's Old South Church in 1771. His short tenure there was marred by controversies over his orthodox Calvinism and suspicions that he was a Tory sympathizer. Denied another pulpit, Bacon settled in Stockbridge, Massachusetts, where he prospered as a farmer, became a successful politician, and trained in the law. He represented Stockbridge in the state house of representatives and senate for many terms and served for four years as chief justice of the court of common pleas for Berkshire County. During the 1778 convention called to draft a state constitution, he delivered a long, forceful address opposing a clause that barred Indians and citizens of African descent from voting. When the Massachusetts legislature debated Virginia's resolutions against the Alien and Sedition Acts in February 1799, Bacon was the lone senator to vote against the legislature's final report in support of the Acts, a stance that prompted one Federalist newspaper to dub him derisively "the *Nay*" and that likely contributed to his defeat in the state elections held two months later. In 1801, he won a runoff election to represent Massachusetts's first western district in the Seventh Congress, his only term in federal office (James McLachlan, *Princetonians, 1748-1768: A Biographical Dictionary* [Princeton, 1976], 479-82; ANB; George H. Moore, *Notes on the History of Slavery in Massachusetts* [New York, 1866], 187-91; Northampton, Mass., *Hampshire Gazette*, 20 Feb. 1799; Boston *Columbian Centinel*, 24 Apr. 1799; Michael J. Dubin, *United States Congressional Elections, 1788-1997: The Official Results of the Elections of the 1st through 105th Congresses* [Jefferson, N.C., 1998], 22-3).

To William Dunbar

Dear Sir Washington Mar. 3. 1803.

Your favor of the 5th. of Jan. has been duly recieved, and I have to return you thanks for the two vocabularies. the memoir of mr Durald has been forwarded to the Philosophical society. we shall be happy to see your history of the Missisipi compleated, as it is becoming one of the most interesting parts of our country, the only one where some of the Tropical productions can be numbered among ours. mrs Trist had only a little mistaken the information I gave her; which was, not that you were removing altogether, but that you meant shortly to take a trip to England, which I had understood from some other person, if not from yourself.

The late interruption of our commerce at New Orleans by the Spanish Intendant, combined with the change of proprietors which Louisiana certainly, and the Floridas possibly, are immediately to undergo, have produced a great sensation here. while some[1] have wished to make it the immediate cause of war which might derange our finances & embarras the administration of the government, which in the state of their political passions would be a countervail for the most serious public[2] calamities; we have pursued what we believe a more certain, & more speedy means of reestablishing permanently the rights & conveniences of our commerce. whether we may succeed in the acquisition of the island of N. Orleans & the Floridas peaceably for a price far short of the expence of a war, we cannot say. but that we shall obtain peaceably an immediate & firm reestablishment of all our rights under the Spanish treaty every circumstance known to us leads us to believe. if contrary to expectations, war should be necessary to restore our rights, it is surely prudent to take a little time for availing ourselves of the division of Europe to strengthen ourselves for that war. nothing but the failure of every peaceable mode of redress, nothing but dire necessity, should force us from that path of peace which would be our wisest pursuit, to embroil in broils and contentions of Europe, and become a satellite to any power there. yet this must be the consequence, if we fail in all peaceable means of reestablishing our rights. were we to enter into the war alone the Missisipi would be blockaded at least during the continuance of that war, by a superior naval power, and all our Western states be deprived of their commerce unless they would surrender themselves to the blockading power. great endeavors have been used from this quarter to inflame the Western people to take possession of New Orleans, without looking forward to the use they could make of it with a blockaded river: but I trust they will be sensible that a peaceable redress will be the quickest & most for their interests. we shall endeavor to procure the Indian right of soil, as soon as they can be prevailed on to part with it, of the whole left bank of the Missisipi to a respectable breadth, and encourage it's prompt settlement; and thereby plant on the Missisipi itself the means of it's own defence, and present as strong a frontier on that as on our Eastern border.   I pray you to accept assurances of my great esteem and respect.

TH: JEFFERSON

PrC (DLC); in ink at foot of first page: "Mr. Dunbar." Not recorded in SJL.

FORWARDED TO THE PHILOSOPHICAL SOCIETY: see TJ to Caspar Wistar, 28 Feb.

[1] Interlined in place of "one party."

[2] Word interlined in place of "[government]."

From Pierre Samuel Du Pont de Nemours

MONSIEUR LE PRÉSIDENT, Paris 3 Mars 1803.

Je vous remercie, comme Philosophe pacifique, comme Français, et comme ami très chaud des Etats unis d'avoir mis en négociation l'affaire de la Louisiane.

Je pense qu'elle sera terminée à votre satisfaction, même avant l'arrivée de Mr. Munroë.

J'en ai raisonné fortement de vive voix et par écrit plusieurs fois avec Mr. de Talleyrand et en dernier lieu avec le Consul Le Brun.

Le Gouvernement n'a pas intention de priver vos Etats de la navigation du Fleuve, ni de l'entrepôt dans la Ville. Le Consul m'a dit que: "cette question était décidée par les Principes du droit civil qui veut lorsqu'un héritage ne peut être exploité sans passer sur un autre que le Passage ne soit pas refusé."

Mais on désire quelque compensation: telle par exemple que la Franchise absolue de tout droit de Douane à l'entrée de votre territoire par le Mississipi et l'ohio pour les Marchandises francaises.—Et, sous cette condition, je suis persuadé qu'on établira pour vous la Nouvelle Orleans en Port franc à la descente du Fleuve et à sa sortie par le bas.

Il ne serait cependant pas impossible qu'on désirât un leger droit d'*un* ou *un et demi* pour *cent* en cas d'entrepôt applicable à l'entretien des quais. C'est un objet de négociation.

Ce qui regarde les Florides en sera un autre que je crois qu'on pourra régler par les mêmes principes. Et quant à l'acquisition du Territoire interieur qui peut vous convenir dans cette partie, je pense encore que, si vos Propositions sont suffisantes, elles ne seront point rejettées.

Je resterai ici tant que je croirai pouvoir y être utile à l'entretien ou au rétablissement de la bonne Harmonie entre les deux Nations, qui me sont toutes deux si cheres—sous cet aspect, il me parait que mon voyage convenait, que mon séjour convient encore, et qu'il conviendra peut-être longtems.

Je vous remercie de vos bontés pour mes Fils.

Vous connaissez mon profond respect. Soyez certain de mon attachement inviolable pour Vous, pour votre Patrie.

Du Pont (de Nemours)

EDITORS' TRANSLATION

Mister President, Paris, 3 Mch. 1803

As a peace-loving philosopher, a Frenchman, and a fervent friend of the United States, I thank you for having begun negotiations about the Louisiana affair. I think they will conclude to your satisfaction, even before Mr. Monroe's arrival.

I have discussed this several times with Mr. Talleyrand, in person and by mail, and most recently with Consul Lebrun.

The government has no intention of depriving your states of navigation on the river or of warehouses in the city. The consul told me that "this issue has been settled according to the principles of civil law which establish that when one property can be enjoyed only by passing through another one, such passage cannot be refused."

But we wish some compensation, for example a total exemption from tariffs for French goods entering your territory from the Mississippi and Ohio Rivers. Under this condition, I am certain we would establish a free port for you in New Orleans at the mouth of the river.

It is not impossible, however, that we would request a small tax of one or one and a half percent for warehouses, in order to maintain the piers. This is a topic for negotiation. Another will be Florida, which I think we can resolve according to the same principles. As for the acquisition of interior territories in the region that might suit you, I also believe that if your propositions are adequate, they will not be refused.

I shall stay here as long as I feel I can be useful in preserving or restoring harmony between the two nations, both of whom are so dear to me. In this light, I feel my trip was worthwhile, remains worthwhile, and may be so for a long time.

Thank you for your kindness to my sons.

You know the deep respect I have for you. Be certain of my inviolable devotion to you and your country. Du Pont (de Nemours)

RC (DLC); at head of text: "A Son Excellence Monsieur Jefferson Président des Etats unis"; endorsed by TJ as received 21 May and so recorded in SJL.

CONSUL LE BRUN: Charles François Lebrun was the third consul of France. He was particularly involved in matters of finance (Tulard, *Dictionnaire Napoléon*, 1043).

From Joseph Hamilton

HON'D SR Hudson March 3rd. 1803.

The motives Which induce me at this time to take the Liberty to present to you the two enclosed Pamphlets are first that if the Sentiments contained in either of them Should be approved of by you, it's Publicity may be thereby Increased, and Secondly to make known my earnest Desire that you would be Pleased to accept of them as a Tribute paid to a Character that I have most Sincerely Loved and revered ever Since the year '76.—perhaps at Some leisure moment they may afford Some little Amusement, and perhaps also be Convenient among your Neighbours.—

Would wish to Say much more; But This I wrote from my Bed (being Sick with the gout),[1] therefore beg your Indulgence while I take the Libery to Subscribe myself with every Sentiment of Esteeme, & Consideration

Your Humble Servt. JOS HAMILTON

RC (DLC); at foot of text: "His Excellency Thos. Jefferson"; postmarked Hudson, N.Y., 4 Mch., and Washington, 14 Mch.; endorsed by TJ as received 18 Mch. and so recorded in SJL. Enclosures: see below.

Originally from Connecticut, Joseph Hamilton (ca. 1738-1805) was a doctor who lived for many years in Hudson, New York. Having inherited a large stake in the Susquehannah Company, Hamilton played a leading role in reviving the company in the 1780s and in its attempt to reassert the claims of Connecticut settlers in the Wyoming Valley area of Pennsylvania. In 1804, he publicized his plan to establish a consortium of botanical gardens, where doctors throughout the country could collect seeds and attempt to grow exotic plants (John L. Brooke, *Columbia Rising: Civil Life on the Upper Hudson from the Revolution to the Age of Jackson* [Chapel Hill, 2010], 185; *Petersburg Intelligencer*, 10 Jan. 1804; *Albany Gazette*, 7 Mch. 1805; Julian P. Boyd and Robert J. Taylor, eds., *The Susquehannah Company Papers*, 11 vols. [Ithaca, N.Y., 1930-71], 8:310-13).

Hamilton was likely enclosing two of his own PAMPHLETS, the 1800 Hudson publication, *A Certain Bar against the Approach of the Yellow Fever, Written for the Good of the Public* (Evans, No. 37574), and *Occasional Reflections on the Operations of the Small-Pox, or, the Traveller's Pocket-Doctor*, originally published in New York City in 1798 (Syrett, *Hamilton*, 24:85).

On 21 Mch., TJ responded from Monticello, writing, "Th: Jefferson presents his respectful salutations to Doctr. Hamilton, and his thanks for the pamphlets accompanying his letter of the 3d. inst. which he recieves & shall have the pleasure of perusing here where he is on a visit of a fortnight only" (PrC in DLC; endorsed by TJ in ink on verso).

[1] Closing parenthesis supplied by editors.

From Craven Peyton

DEAR SIR Richmond 3d March 1803.

I recvd. the draft on Mesrs. Gibson & Jefferson for One Thousand Dollars. which answerd my purpose Just as Cash the arrangement I have made in this place with Mr. Robt. Burten for the ballance which is due him, is to obtain a Draft from you on Gibson & Jefferson in his favour payable the first week in July Next for 1300 $. this he has been goodenough to receave although he might open an execution Next Month for his Money. now sir if you will be so Obligeing as to execute the draft Directed to Gibson & Jefferson, in a letter you will releave me much, & I hope you will perceave my wish to accomodate you inforcing the payment as far off[1] as possible. please forward the draft by return mail as I shall be compeled to stay hear untill it is Negotiated.

With real Esteem Yr. mst. Obt. C PEYTON

RC (ViU); endorsed by TJ as received 16 Mch. and so recorded in SJL.

DRAFT ON MESRS. GIBSON & JEFFERSON FOR ONE THOUSAND DOLLARS: see TJ to Peyton, 23 Feb.

Robert Burton (BURTEN) was a partner in the Richmond and London mercantile firm of Donald & Burton (Vol. 12:347; Vol. 24:461).

[1] MS: "of."

To William Short

DEAR SIR Washington Mar. 3. 1803.

As you talked of coming on here in the month of February I have been expecting you, without writing. I am in hopes however the inclosed letter from mr Lilly will reach you at New York. there is not in the world a lighter or more unprincipled talker than Henderson: and as to any offer from him he is entirely bankrupt. still I have no doubt that eight dollars could be got for your whole tract, deducting perhaps one third of the price of the 70. or 80. acres held by Price at a rent so much below it's value. I set out in three days for Monticello, and shall be absent about three weeks. I will make enquiry what can be got. it is not probable that prompt paiment can be had. but interest, & a detention of the title till the whole price is paid will make a sale secure.

On the day after tomorrow mr Barnes will recieve for you from my funds a first sum of 500. D. and thenceforward 500. D. monthly without interruption till the discharge of the whole sum principal & interest in my hands. it is probable that after some time the paiments may be considerably increased, so as to accomplish the whole in two years. as I shall be back here by the last of the month, & the coldness of the season will probably prevent your getting into motion earlier, I shall be in hopes of seeing you here after my return, in transitu at least. Accept assurances of my affectionate attachment & respect.

TH: JEFFERSON

RC (DLC: Short Papers); at foot of text: "Mr. Short"; endorsed by Short. Enclosure not found.

DISCHARGE OF THE WHOLE SUM: for TJ's plan to repay the funds he had used from Short's accounts, see Vol. 38:468, 469n.

From David Thomas

DEAR SIR Washington March 3rd. 1803

Permit me to request your Excellency to examine the enclosed letters—the one addressed to yourself was forwarded to me previous to my leaving home last fall for this City, which I intended to present immediately on my arrival here, had not I learnt that you had made it a principle not to appoint general Commissioners of Bancruptcey except in the commercial Towns, but when an instance of Bancruptcey should happen in a port remote from the residence of the General Commissioners, you would on the case being represented appoint special Commissioners for the particular case, and therefore I wrote Mr. McCrea giving him this information, to that letter I received the one inclosed from Mr. Cuyler who is Clerk of the County in which he lives and whose information may be relied on, as well as Mr. McCreas

It appears the person to whom it is wished that the benefit of the Bancrupt. law may be extended, is Alman Phillips and if this case is sufficiently represented, I wish your Excellency to appoint special Commissioners, and recommend as proper persons Peter Sailly of the County of Clinton and Stephen Cuyler and James McCrea of the County of Essex in the state of New York.—

Should this appointment be made the Commission may be for[...] to

Your Excellencys Most [...] Humble servt DAVID THOMAS

P.S. having recd. this letter from Mr. Cuyler since I had the honor of seeing you today I thought it incumbent on me to made this application [...] in this way—

RC (DNA: RG 59, LAR, 11:0082-3); torn; endorsed by TJ as received 3 Mch. and "Commrs bkrptcy. at Willsborough. N.Y." and so recorded in SJL. Enclosures: (1) Stephen Cuyler to David Thomas, Willsboro, 8 Feb. 1803, regarding a letter of 12 Jan. from Thomas to "your friend" James McCrea, on the "Subject of Commissioners of Bancruptcy"; McCrea remains interested in the case and Cuyler agrees the case merits a bankruptcy commission (RC in same, 11:0086). (2) James McCrea to David Thomas, Willsboro, 13 Dec. 1802, on the "situation of an unfortunate man, imprisoned in this county on an Execution in favour of a person deceased and against whose Estate he holds a demand nearly Equal to the Debt against himself"; a commission serving the northern New York counties would benefit the individual in this case and also others who might subsequently apply; he has written to the president on the subject but retains the letter in anticipation of getting Thomas's opinion on the matter; the persons agreed upon by him and the individual in question are Peter Sailly, Stephen Cuyler, and himself but "should any other person in this Quarter meet more fully the approbation & the wishes of Genl Thomas he will please to have him named in my Stead" (RC in same, 11:0088-9).

David Thomas (1762-1831) was born in Massachusetts and served as an infantryman in Massachusetts regiments during the Revolution. He settled in Washington County, New York, where he kept a tavern, worked as a merchant, and became an officer in the state militia. After holding some local offices and serving in the state assembly, he was elected as a Republican to the Seventh Congress. Reelected three times, he resigned his seat in 1808, after which he served a couple of stints as state treasurer of New York. During the 1804 New York elections, he appears to have supported Aaron Burr, having been one of the Republicans seeking assurances of TJ's neutrality in the gubernatorial race and subsequently communicating those assurances in the press. Rufus King identified him as one of the "democratical Members of Congress from the East" who agreed with the opinion Burr had shared with Federalist congressman Roger Griswold, that "the northern States must be governed by Virginia, or govern Virginia" (*Biog. Dir. Cong.*; Worcester *National Aegis*, 30 Nov. 1831; Kline, *Burr*, 2:853, 863, 865).

On the following day, TJ appointed as bankruptcy COMMISSIONERS for Willsboro, Peter Sailly, Stephen Cuyler, and James McCrea (Vol. 37:709, 711n; Appendix I: List of Appointments).

ENCLOSURE

From James McCrea

SIR Willsborough September 13th. 1802

Permit me to State to you the Situation of a person now in Confinement on Execution in the prison of the county of Essex on Lake champlain in the State of Newyork about one hundred and forty five Miles North of Albany from which Situation he can find no immeadiate mode of relief but through the medium of the Bankrupt Act which to him is rendered very difficult and Almost beyond his reach by reason of the great distance he is placed at from the commissioners lately appointed and the great expence That must necessarily attend the execution of their commission in this Quarter would nearly exhaust The remainder of the property now possessed by the unfortunate Debtor. Unfortunate because having a Just demand—Against the principle Creditor which he can derive no advantage from on account of his Absence in Europe his return very uncertain and none to whom he can appeal for an adjustment of his claim And consequently the result must be the loss of his whole demand with the addition of a tedious imprisonment, Under an impression of the Truth of this Statement I have Just reason to hope your Excellency will feel no reluctance in complying with the request of the unfortunate which is that three persons may be appointed in this Northern Quarter of the State to Act as generall Commissioners of Bankruptcy as it will not only tend much to alleviate the present situation of the present Applicant but that of others who Still reside much Farther to the North of this State, The expence which is now required in procureing the attendance of the present Commissioners is more than persons of this description Can well bear, The Names of the persons proposed to fill these officess in case it meets the approbation of your Excellency will accompany this Letter Together with such Authority to Satisfy your Excellencys Mind on the Subject as will I presume be deemed Sufficient With the Fullest Assurance of your Excellencys compliance I remain with great respect

Your Excellencys Most Obedt & very Humble Sert

James McCre'a

RC (DNA: RG 59, LAR, 11:0084-5); at head of text: "To his Excellency Thomas Jefferson Esquire President of the United States &c"; endorsed by TJ as received 3 Mch. 1803 and "to be Commr. bkrptcy Willsboro'" and so recorded in SJL.

James McCrea was a lawyer and operated a land office in Willsboro, Essex County, New York. He served as surrogate for Essex and after moving to Saratoga County was a judge of the court of common pleas (New York *American Citizen*, 4 Nov. 1801; *Albany Centinel*, 5 May 1801; *Albany Argus*, 23 Nov. 1819; Alden Chester, *Courts and Lawyers of New York: A History, 1609-1925*, 4 vols. [New York, 1925], 3:1108, 1112; Robert O. Bascom, *The Fort Edward Book, Containing Some Historical Sketches, with Illustrations, and Family Records* [Fort Edward, N.Y., 1903], 58).

An advertisment from the supervising judge in the case against the UNFORTUNATE DEBTOR, Alman Phillips, identified Stephen Taylor as the petitioning CREDITOR (*Albany Register*, 17 Apr. 1804). In his letter of 8 Feb. to David Thomas, Stephen Cuyler identified John Cochran as the "Acting Creditor" (Enclosure No. 1 above).

Appendix I

EDITORIAL NOTE

Jefferson kept an ongoing list of appointments and removals that extended throughout his two terms as president, with entries extending from 5 Mch. 1801 to 23 Feb. 1809. For the first installment of this list, from 5 Mch. 1801 to 14 May 1802, see Vol. 33, Appendix I, List 4. Subsequent installments have appeared as Appendix I in Volumes 37 and 38. This installment continues at 13 Nov. 1802, with the president's recording of Jehu Nichols's appointment at 20 Nov. It includes the entries for the period covered by this volume with the addition of 4 Mch., because the appointees at that date appear between a set of entries for 1 Mch. This was a working list, which Jefferson updated, often wholly or partially canceling a name—for example, Thomas Webber at 24 Nov.—when he learned an appointee had declined the office. Jefferson left a space for the South Carolina bankruptcy commissioners at 25 Feb., the day he sent James B. Richardson blank commissions to complete after the governor found people who would accept the appointment. Jefferson returned to the space and entered, in a smaller hand than usual, the names of the new commissioners after he received Richardson's letter of 2 Apr. The president entered Gabriel Duvall's name twice on the list below. The first entry, at 10 Dec., is the date Jefferson informed John Steele that his resignation had become effective, as his replacement's commission was being issued that day. In fact, the president sent Duvall's nomination to the Senate on 15 Dec. It was immediately approved and the commission issued the same day, the date of the second entry on the list. A lapse in communication with the State Department probably explains why Jefferson recorded the appointment of the Tennessee bankruptcy commissioners at 7 Jan., the day he received the recommendations from the state's congressional delegation; the commissions from the State Department, however, are dated 28 Mch. 1803. Two bankruptcy commissions for replacements in Massachusetts, those for Edward Jones and David Tilden, are also dated 28 Mch. but are on the list below at 4 Mch. The president recorded all of the other appointments of bankruptcy commissioners on the date the State Department issued the commissions (lists of commissions in Lb in DNA: RG 59, MPTPC; TJ to Steele, 10 Dec.; TJ to the Senate, 15 Dec.; Joseph Anderson, William Cocke, and William Dickson to TJ, 6 Jan. 1803; TJ to Richardson, 25 Feb.).

While Congress was in session, Jefferson, for the most part, entered his appointments that required Senate approval at the date the nominees were confirmed by the Senate. Of those he nominated on 2 Feb., seven were approved by the Senate and recorded at 8 Feb. Four civil appointments that had been referred to committee and Aaron Vail, whose nomination was submitted on 14 Feb., were approved and recorded by the president at 1 Mch. Jefferson did not record on his list Joseph Story's appointment as naval officer at Salem and Beverly, Massachusetts, approved by the Senate on 1 Mch. Perhaps he already knew that Story had declined the appointment when he made the entries. At 3 Mch., the president entered the nominations submitted and approved by the Senate on the last day of the session. He included three other nominees at that date—Hore Browse Trist, Henry Warren, and Joseph Turner—whose nominations were not submitted to the Senate until the next session of Congress. They became interim appointments. Jefferson's check marks at 3 Mch. indicate those nominees approved by the Senate (Madison, *Papers*, *Sec. of State Ser.*, 4:504n; TJ to the Senate, 2, 14 Feb., 3 Mch. 1803).

List of Appointments

[13 Nov. 1802-4 Mch. 1803]

20. Jehu Nichols of N.C. Inspector of the Revenue & Surveyor of the port of Tombstone N.C. vice James Clarke resigned

24. James Nimmo Commr. bkrptcy Norfolk. Virga.
Edward Harriss
William Blackledge
<*Thos. Webber.*> declines
Samuel Gerock
} Newbern[1] N.C. commrs bkrptcy

Dec. 7. William Judd [Farmington] Commr. bkrptcy Connecticut

10. Gabriel Duval of Maryland Comptroller of the Treasury v. John Steele. resd.

13. John Postel Williamson
Edward Stebbins
Joseph Welscher
Wm. B. Bullock
} of Savanna. to be Commrs. bkrptcy[2] of Georgia

14. James L. Shannonhouse of N.C. who is surveyor of the port of Newbegun creek in N.C. to be Inspector of the revenue for the same

Benjamin Cheney of N.C. who is surveyor of the port of Beaufort in N.C. to be Inspector of the revenue for the same.

15. Gabriel Duval of Maryland Comptroller of the Treasury[3] of the US. v John Steele resigned. approvd.

17. Wm. Peck of R.I. reappointed Marshal of R.I.

20 Joshua Potts
Christopher Dudley
Caleb D. Howard
James Walker
} of Wilmington N.C. to be Commrs. bkrptcy.

22. John Spence West of N.C. reappointed Marshal of N.C.

29. Henry Seymour at Hartford to be commmr. bkrptcy for Connecticut v.

Obadiah Hodgkiss at New Haven. do. vice John Nichols declined

Samuel Motte at Preston do. vice Elisha Hyde declined.

1803

Jan. 7. Edward Scott, John Crozier } Knoxville; Moses Fish, George Mc.Deaderick } Nashville. } Commrs. bkrptcy Tennissee

17. Hopley Yeaton of N.H. master of a revenue cutter vice removed to restore Yeaton

Benjamin Gunnison. of N.H. 1st. mate of do. vice

22. James Monroe Minr. Exty Plen. to France & Spain with R.R.L. in the former & C.P. in the latter.

Feb. 16. do. do. Spain

8. Marien Lamar. Maryland. Consul of Madeira.

Brewer Wm. Surveyor of Nixinton N.C. & Inspector v. Knox resigned

Jabez Pennyman Collector & Inspector of Alburg in L. Champlain. vice David Russell removd

John Heard Inspector of Perth Amboy

Tho. T. Davis of Kentuckey Chief justice of Indiana. vice William Clarke decd. qu. Ch. Just?

Wm. H. Harrison. Govr. of Indiana territory for 3. y. from May 13.

do. Commr. of the US. to treat with Indns. N.W. of Ohio within US.

Jesse Spencer of Ohio. Register of Land office at Marietta. v. Thos. Worthington resd.

25. Horatio Seymour. Middleburg Verm. Commr. bkrptcy v. Darius Chipman resd.

Simon MacIntosh, Wm Lee junr., Guilliam Aertsen, Francis Mulligan } Charleston. Commrs. bkrptcy. a blank commn. was sent to Govr. Richardson. see his answer Apr. 2.

28. Francis Brooke, Stephen Winchester, Robert Patton } Fredsbg. Commrs. bkrptcy

Mar. 1.	John Mussey. vice Joseph Boyd. at Portland.		Commrs. bkrptcy
	Simeon Thomas.	New London	
	Charles Ludlow	New York	
	John Stephen	Baltimore	
	Cowles Meade	Louisville[4]	
	Robert Walker, George Watkins	Augusta.	
	Thomas Collier	Louisville	

Mar. 4.	Peter Sailly of Clinton cty.		Willsborough. Commrs. bkrptcy for N.Y.
	Stephen Cuyler, James Mc.rea	of Essex cty.	
	Edward Jones. Boston. vice S. A. Otis; Daniel Tilden do.		Commrs. bkrptcy

Mar. 1. Zachariah Stevens. of Mass. Surveyor & Inspector of Gloucester vice Saml. Whittermore

Isaac Illsley jnr. of Mass. Collector of district of Portland vice Fosdyck delinquent

√ Aaron Vale of New York Commercl. Agent Lorient vice William Patterson who goes to Nantes

William Patterson. New York. Commercl. Agent Nantes vice Thos. T. Gantt

John Martin Baker. of New York. Consul of Majorca Minorca Yvica

√3. Charles Willing Byrd of Ohio a judge of the district court of Ohio

√ Michael Baldwin of Ohio Atty of the US. for the district of Ohio

√ David Zeigler of Ohio Marshal of the Ohio district

√ Cato West of Missisipi Secretary for the Missipi territory vice John Steele whose time expired.

Hore Browse Trist of Missipi Collector at Fort Adams vice Carmichael removd for delinquency[5]

√ Joel Burt of N. York Collector & Inspector distr. Oswego new.

√ Thomas Dudley of N. Carola. Surveyr Swansboro' v. Alexr. Carmelt dead.

√ Isaac Dayton of N.Y. Surveyor & Inspector port of Hudson vice Tenbroeck removd for delinquency

√ Thomas Lovell Mass. Commercl. agent La Rochelle

Henry Warren inspector of the revenue for the port of Plymouth Mass. & Collector of the customs for the district of Plymouth v. William Watson remvd for malconduct[6]

√ Levitt Harris Pensva. to be Consul Rotterdam.

Joseph Turner Collector of Brunswick Georgia vice Claud Thompson insane.[7]

MS (DLC: TJ Papers, 186:33096); entirely in TJ's hand, including brackets, check marks, and cancellations and emendations made at later sittings; being the continuation of a list that extends from 5 Mch. 1801 to 23 Feb. 1809; for the installment immediately preceding this one, see Vol. 38: Appendix I.

The State Department issued a commission for "John" instead of JEHU NICHOLS. On 13 Nov., Samuel Tredwell, collector of the district at Edenton, North Carolina, informed John Steele at the Treasury Department of the mistake. Gallatin, in an undated note on the address sheet, wrote: "The Secretary of State is requested to have a new commission made out in the name of Jehu Nichols by his obedt. Servt. Albert Gallatin" (RC in DNA: RG 59, LAR; endorsed by TJ: Nichols Jehu. Tredwell's lre to mr Gallatin for Commn").

HENRY SEYMOUR was appointed in place of John Dodd, who declined the appointment as bankruptcy commissioner (Vol. 37:708; Vol. 38:173, 174n, 224).

TJ commissioned HOPLEY YEATON and BENJAMIN GUNNISON to take charge of the newly built revenue cutter at Portsmouth in September 1802, and it is not clear why he recorded the appointments at this late date (Vol. 38:243n, 373, 403). For Yeaton's dismissal from the old cutter in 1798, see Vol. 35:653n, 654-5.

R.R.L.: Robert R. Livingston. C.P.: Charles Pinckney.

FREDSBG. COMMRS. BKRPTCY: on 20 Feb. 1803, William S. Stone, a Fredericksburg merchant, wrote John Dawson that he perhaps would be "compeled to resort to the Bankrupt Law" to settle a debt and that it was "very inconvenient" and expensive to conduct the business in Richmond. Stone requested that Dawson use his influence to have two or three commissioners appointed immediately. He recommended three of "Our friends," including Francis T. Brooke and William W. Hening (RC in DNA: RG 59, LAR, endorsed by TJ: "Brooke & al. to be Comrs. bkrptcy Fredsbg."; Madison, *Papers*, 17:147-8; Vol. 37:710). Stephen Winchester was among those Dawson had recommended at Fredericksburg in 1802, but TJ declined to make the appointments at that time. Hening had recently declined to serve as a bankruptcy commissioner at Charlottesville. On 5 Feb. 1803, he returned his commission to Madison, noting that since his appointment he had been "consulted as counsel in every case of Bankruptcy" prosecuted "in this part of the state." He declined to serve, "deeming it incompatible with the judicial functions of a commissioner of bankruptcy, to exercise the duties of a lawyer, in the same cause" (RC in DNA: RG 59, RD, endorsed by TJ: "Hening Wm. W. to mr Madison declines as Commr. bkrptcy"; Vol. 37:699, 710; Vol. 38:221n, 233).

Jonathan L. Austin, a bankruptcy commissioner at Boston, requested that replacements be found for Samuel A. OTIS and Samuel Brown, who had not formally accepted their commissions, which were issued in July 1802. There would then be two sets of commissioners in Boston to hear the increasing number of bankruptcy cases in the district. Austin recommended Edward Jones for his "mercantile abilities & moral & political Character" (Austin to Madison, 3 Jan. 1803, RC in DNA: RG 59, LAR, endorsed by TJ; Vol. 37:707).

[1] Interlined in place of "Wilmington."
[2] Interlined.
[3] Interlined in place of "[Senate]."
[4] Partially erased.
[5] Entry interlined.
[6] Entry interlined.
[7] Entry interlined.

Appendix II

Letters Not Printed in Full

EDITORIAL NOTE

In keeping with the editorial method established for this edition, the chronological series includes "in one form or another every available letter known to have been written by or to Thomas Jefferson" (Vol. 1:xv). Most letters are printed in full. In some cases, the letter is not printed but a detailed summary appears at the document's date (for an example, see E. T. Hadwen to TJ, 3 Jan. 1803). Other letters have been described in annotation. For the period covered by this volume, these are listed in this appendix. Arranged in chronological order, this list includes for each letter the correspondent, date, and location in the volumes where it is described. Among the letters included here are brief letters of transmittal, multiple testimonials recommending a particular candidate for office, repetitive letters from a candidate seeking a post, and official correspondence that the president saw in only a cursory way. In other instances, documents are described in annotation due to the near illegibility of the surviving text. Using the list in this appendix, the table of contents, and Appendix III (correspondence not found but recorded in Jefferson's Summary Journal of Letters), readers will be able to reconstruct Jefferson's chronological epistolary record from 13 Nov. 1802 to 3 Mch. 1803.

To Robert Bridges, 23 Nov 1802. Noted at John Stuart Kerr to TJ, 24 Dec. 1801.

To Caspar Wistar, 23 Nov. Noted at John Stuart Kerr to TJ, 24 Dec. 1801.

From Robert Smith, 10 Dec. Noted at Smith to TJ, 10 Dec. 1802.

To Samuel Elliot, 20 Dec. Noted at Elliot to TJ, Nov. 1802.

From Thomas C. James, 7 Jan. 1803. Noted at TJ to James, 21 Jan. 1803.

To Albert Gallatin, [on or after 10 Jan.]. Noted at Ephraim Kirby to TJ, 3 Jan. 1803.

From Albert Gallatin, 17 Jan. Noted at TJ to the Senate and the House of Representatives, 18 Jan. 1803 (third letter).

To Carlos IV, King of Spain, 29 Jan. Noted at Carlos IV to TJ, 9 Sep. 1802.

To Christopher Smith, 8 Feb. Noted at TJ to Charles Smith, 8 Feb. 1803.

Appendix III

Letters Not Found

EDITORIAL NOTE

This appendix lists chronologically letters written by and to Jefferson during the period covered by this volume for which no text is known to survive. Jefferson's Summary Journal of Letters provides a record of the missing documents. For incoming letters, Jefferson typically recorded in SJL the date that the letter was sent and the date on which he received it. He sometimes included the location from which it was dispatched and an abbreviated notation indicating the government department to which it pertained: "N" for Navy, "S" for State, "T" for Treasury, and "W" for War.

From Benjamin Brown, 13 Nov. 1802; received 19 Nov. from Charlottesville.
From David Higginbotham, 15 Nov.; received 19 Nov. from Milton.
From Jones & Howell, 15 Nov.; received 19 Nov. from Philadelphia; notation: "for Roberts & Jones."
From William Bache, 16 Nov.; received 21 Nov. from Edgehill.
From John Wayles Eppes, 17 Nov.; received 21 Nov. from Edgehill.
To Lilburne Lewis, 17 Nov.
To Gabriel Lilly, 17 Nov.
From John Perry, 17 Nov.; received 21 Nov. from Shadwell.
From Thomas Cooper, 18 Nov.; received 25 Nov. from Wilkes-Barre; notation: "N."
From Anonymous; received 19 Nov. from Baltimore; notation: "Yundt & Brown. printers."
From Robert Bridges, 19 Nov.; received 22 Nov. from Philadelphia.
From William Short, 20 Nov.; received 20 Nov.
To William Stewart, 21 Nov.
From William Jackson, 24 Nov.; received 27 Nov. from Philadelphia; notation: "T."
From James Dinsmore, 25 Nov.; received 30 Nov. from Monticello.
To Gabriel Lilly, 25 Nov.
From John Bartram, Jr., 26 Nov.; received 1 Dec. from Kingsessing.
From John Wayles Eppes, 27 Nov.; received 3 Dec. from Bermuda Hundred.
From Benjamin Seymour, 27 Nov.; received 8 Dec. from Plymouth; notation: "N."
From Dabney Carr, 30 Nov.; received 7 Dec. from Charlottesville.
From John Wayles Eppes, 1 Dec.; received 7 Dec. from Bermuda Hundred.
To Gabriel Lilly, 1 Dec.
From William Short, 2 Dec.; received 2 Dec. from Georgetown.
From Marten Wanscher, 2 Dec.; received 3 Dec. from Alexandria; notation: "30. D."
From William Jackson, 3 Dec.; received 6 Dec. from Philadelphia.
From Thomas C. James, 4 Dec.; received 9 Dec. from Philadelphia.
From James Oldham, 4 Dec.; received 7 Dec. from Monticello.
From Edward Tiffin, 4 Dec.; received 22 Dec. from Chillicothe.

From Hugh Chisholm, 5 Dec.; received 10 Dec.
To Gabriel Lilly, 7 Dec.; notation: "150."
To Joseph Moran, 7 Dec.; notation: "200."
To Henry Sheaff, 8 Dec.
From Mathew Carey; received 10 Dec. from Philadelphia; notation: "Tenche Coxe to be employed."
From Gabriel Lilly, 10 Dec.; received 14 Dec. from Monticello.
To Hugh Chisholm, 11 Dec.
To Christopher Ellery, 13 Dec.
From Christopher Ellery, 13 Dec.; received 14 Dec.; connected by a brace with letter received the same day from Theodore Foster of 13 Dec., with notation: "Wm. Peck to be contd. Marshal R.I."
To Theodore Foster, 13 Dec.
From Theodore Foster, 13 Dec.; received 14 Dec.; for notation, see from Christopher Ellery, 13 Dec., above.
From David Higginbotham, 13 Dec.; received 17 Dec.
From the Treasury Department; received 13 Dec.; notation: "nominations."
From Burgess Griffin, 14 Dec.; received 21 Dec. from Poplar Forest.
From Tadeusz Kosciuszko; received 14 Dec. from Paris.
From John Smith, 14 Dec.; received 15 Dec. from Washington; notation: "of N.Y."
From Christopher Ellery, 15 Dec.; received 16 Dec.; notation: "Newan to be officer in army."
To Gabriel Lilly, 15 Dec.; notation: "35 D. P. Carr."
To William Stewart, 15 Dec.
From John Perry, 18 Dec.; received 24 Dec. from Shadwell.
From Thomas T. Davis, 19 Dec.; received 29 Dec.
From Samuel Hanway, 23 Dec.; received 8 Jan. 1803 from Morgantown.
To Burgess Griffin, 25 Dec.
To Benjamin H. Latrobe, 25 Dec.
To Gabriel Lilly, 25 Dec.
From Phebe Baldwin, 27 Dec.; received 18 Jan. 1803 from Paterson.
From John Wayles Eppes, 27 Dec.; received 1 Jan. 1803 from Richmond.
From John and Thomas, 27 Dec.; received 2 Jan. 1803 from Philadelphia; notation: "N."
From Rufus Law, 27 Dec.; received 1 Jan. 1803 from New York; notation: "N."
From Benjamin H. Latrobe, 29 Dec.; received 1 Jan. 1803 from Philadelphia.
From Edmund J. Lee, et al., 30 Dec.; received 1 Jan. 1803 from Alexandria.
From James Dinsmore, 31 Dec.; received 5 Jan. 1803 from Monticello.
From Gabriel Lilly, 1 Jan. 1803; received 7 Jan. from Monticello.
From Mrs. August Konig, January; received 2 Jan. from Baltimore.
To Lee, Powell, & McLean, 2 Jan.
From James Oldham, 2 Jan.; received 7 Jan. from Monticello.
From Lilburne Lewis, 3 Jan.; received 7 Jan. from Mt. Gallatin.
From Jones & Howell, 4 Jan.; received 8 Jan. from Philadelphia.
From Marten Wanscher, 7 Jan.; received 9 Jan. from Alexandria.
From Edmund J. Lee, et al., 8 Jan.; received 9 Jan. from Alexandria.
From John Stanley, 8 Jan.; received 16 Jan. from Halifax, Va.

From Gabriel Lilly, 9 Jan.; received 14 Jan.
From Thomas Mann Randolph, 10 Jan.; received 15 Jan. from Gordon's Tavern.
From William Bradley, 11 Jan.; received 12 Jan. from Washington.
To Joseph Brand, 11 Jan.; notation: "124.25."
"Indiana petition"; received 11 Jan.; notation: "to continue Govr. Harrison."
To Gabriel Lilly, 11 Jan.; notation: "513.33. Overton. Chisolm. Johnson."
To Joseph Moran, 11 Jan.; notation: "200."
From John Perry, 11 Jan.; received 22 Jan. from Shadwell.
To Lilburne Lewis, 12 Jan.
To Gabriel Lilly, 12 Jan.
From James Dinsmore, 13 Jan.; received 22 Jan. from Monticello.
From St. George Tucker, 13 Jan.; received 18 Jan. from Williamsburg; notation: "Blair to be judge Indiana."
"Eastriver petn"; received 15 Jan.; notation: "to change port."
From Benjamin H. Latrobe, 15 Jan.; received 19 Jan. from Philadelphia.
From John Jacob Ulrich Rivardi, 15 Jan.; received 20 Jan. from Philadelphia; notation: "W."
From David Higginbotham, 17 Jan.; received 22 Jan. from Milton
From William Short, 20 Jan.; received 24 Jan. from New York.
From William Stewart, 20 Jan.; received 26 Jan. from Monticello.
From Philip R. Thompson, 20 Jan.; received 20 Jan.; notation: "Gregg for a place. W."
From John Campbell White, 22 Jan.; received 24 Jan. from Baltimore.
To Benjamin H. Latrobe, 23 Jan.
From Gabriel Lilly, 23 Jan.; received 28 Jan.
From Gouveneur Morris "& other members N.Y.," 24 Jan.; received 7 Feb. from Washington.
From William Pickering; received 24 Jan.; notation: "jail. pardon."
From Phebe Baldwin, 25 Jan.; received 29 Jan. from Paterson; notation: "N."
From George Divers, 27 Jan.; received 2 Feb. from Farmington.
From James Dinsmore, 30 Jan.; received 4 Feb. from Monticello.
From James Oldham, 30 Jan.; received 4 Feb. from Monticello.
From Thomas Mann Randolph, 31 Jan.; received 4 Feb. from Richmond.
From Thomas Jefferson Randolph, 3 Feb.; received 11 Feb.
From Philippe Reibelt; received 3 Feb.
From J. P. G. Muhlenberg, 4 Feb.; received 8 Feb. from Philadelphia; notation: "Mc.Lane to remain in office."
To James Dinsmore, 6 Feb.
From Benjamin H. Latrobe, 6 Feb.; received 9 Feb. from Philadelphia.
To Gabriel Lilly, 6 Feb.; notation "150. D."
To Anne Cary Randolph, 6 Feb.
To Gabriel Lilly, 8 Feb.
To Joseph Moran, 8 Feb.; notation: "98."
From David Higginbotham, 11 Feb.; received 16 Feb. from Milton.
From John Walker, 11 Feb.; received 19 Feb. from Belvoir.
From George Jefferson, 12 Feb.; received 17 Feb. from Richmond; notation: "1170. D. rod. hoop. cyder. molasses."

From Jones & Howell, 12 Feb.; received 19 Feb. from Philadelphia; notation: "47.45."
From Daniel Trump, 12 Feb.; received 19 Feb. from Philadelphia.
From Jacob Bauldin, 15 Feb.; received 17 Feb. from Washington; notation: "N."
From Saquiricia, 15 Feb.; received 16 Mch. from Windsor, N.C.; notation: "W."
From DeWitt Clinton, 18 Feb.; received 18 Feb. from Washington; notation: "Dayton v. Ten Broeck."
From James Dinsmore, 18 Feb.; received 25 Feb. from Monticello
From William Fitzhugh, 18 Feb.; received 19 Feb. from Alexandria.
From Martha Jefferson Randolph, 18 Feb.; received 24 Feb. from Edgehill.
From John Bird, 21 Feb.; received 26 Feb. from New Castle; notation: "to be Collector."
To George Divers, 21 Feb.
To Joseph Coppinger, 25 Feb.
"Delaware memorial"; received 25 Feb.; notation: "John Bird to be collector."
From William Pechin & Co., 25 Feb.; received 26 Feb. from Baltimore.
From Joseph T. Scott, 25 Feb.; received 5 Mch. from Philadelphia.
From James Dinsmore, 26 Feb.; received 16 Mch. from Monticello.
To Andrew Ellicott, 26 Feb.
From John Bird, 28 Feb.; received 28 Feb. from Washington; notation: "to be collector v. Mc.lane."
From Christopher Ellery, 28 Feb.; received 28 Feb.; notation: "Durfey Survr. Tiverton R.I."
From Joseph Stanton, 28 Feb.; received 1 Mch.; notation: "Durfee to be Surveyor Tiverton."
From Daniel L. Hylton, 1 Mch.; received 5 Mch. from Richmond; notation: "Watson for lighthouse."
From Henry Sheaff, 1 Mch.; received 18 Mch. from Philadelphia.
From DeWitt Clinton, 3 Mch.; received 3 Mch.; notation: "removal Ludlow. Rogers. Smith."
To William Fitzhugh, 3 Mch.
From John Lambert, 3 Mch.; received 16 Mch. from Trenton; notations: "Govr." and "W."

Appendix IV

Financial Documents

EDITORIAL NOTE

This appendix briefly describes, in chronological order, the orders and invoices pertaining to Jefferson's finances during the period covered by this volume that are not printed in full or accounted for elsewhere in this volume. The orders for payments to Étienne Lemaire and Joseph Dougherty pertain, for the most part, to expenses associated with running the President's House. The *Memorandum Books* are cited when they are relevant to a specific document and provide additional information.

Order on John Barnes for payment of $13.10½ to Joseph Dougherty, 14 Nov. 1802 (MS in Philip D. Sang, Chicago, Illinois, 1960; in TJ's hand and signed by him; signed by Dougherty acknowledging payment; endorsed by Barnes as paid on 16 Nov.). TJ recorded this transaction as payment of Dougherty's accounts for provender, saddlers, smiths, utensils, and "flower pots & trowel" (MB, 2:1086).

Order on John Barnes for payment of $101.10 to Étienne Lemaire, Washington, 16 Nov. (MS in Hugh Hood Davenport, Birmingham, Alabama, 1994; in TJ's hand and signed by him; unidentified signature acknowledging payment). TJ recorded this transaction as payment of Lemaire's accounts from Nov. 7 to 13 for provisions, charcoal, and contingencies (MB, 2:1086).

Order on John Barnes for payment of $94.23 to Étienne Lemaire, Washington, 23 Nov. (MS in Gallery of History, Las Vegas, Nevada, 1994; in TJ's hand and signed by him; unidentified signature acknowledging payment; endorsed by Barnes as paid on 26 Nov.). TJ recorded this transaction as payment of Lemaire's accounts from Nov. 7 to 13 for provisions, wine, servants, furniture, and contingencies. TJ probably intended the date of Lemaire's account to have been the week of Nov. 14 to 20 (MB, 2:1087).

Order on John Barnes for payment of $48.67 to Peter Lenox, Washington, 7 Dec. (MS in MHi; in TJ's hand and signed by him; signed by Lenox acknowledging payment; endorsed by Barnes as paid on 8 Dec.). TJ recorded this transaction as payment for building a shed (MB, 2:1088).

Order on John Barnes for payment of $10 to Mr. Tobine, Washington, 9 Dec. (MS in MHi; in TJ's hand and signed by him; signed by Tobine acknowledging payment; endorsed by Barnes as paid 9 Dec.). TJ recorded this transaction as charity (MB, 2:1088).

Invoice submitted by Henry Ingle to TJ for $3.62½ for purchase on 30 Sep. of steelyards, pincers, and a "Sockett Chissel," Washington, 14 Dec. (MS in MHi; signed by William Huber for Ingle acknowledging payment; addressed: "Presidents House"; endorsed by TJ: "Ingle Henry. hhd furn. pd by mr Lemaire 3.625").

Order on John Barnes for payment of $10 to Mrs. Ann Jones, Washington, 14 Dec. (MS in MHi; in TJ's hand and signed by him; signed by Jones acknowledging payment; endorsed by Barnes as paid on 15 Dec.). TJ recorded this transaction as charity (MB, 2:1088).

Order on John Barnes for payment of $40 to Thomas Carpenter, Washington, 16 Dec. (MS in ViU: Edgehill-Randolph Papers; in TJ's hand and signed by him; signed by Carpenter acknowledging payment; endorsed by Barnes as paid on 18 Dec.). TJ recorded this transaction as a payment on account of Meriwether Lewis (MB, 2:1088).

Order on John Barnes for payment of $20 to Étienne Lemaire, Washington, 16 Dec. (MS in CtY; in TJ's hand and signed by him; signed by Lemaire acknowledging payment; endorsed by Barnes as paid on 16 and 23 Dec.). TJ recorded this transaction as a payment on account of Meriwether Lewis (MB, 2:1088).

Order on John Barnes for payment of $10 to Charles McLaughlin, Washington, 16 Dec. (MS in ViU: Edgehill-Randolph Papers; in TJ's hand and signed by him; signed by Edgar Patterson acknowledging payment; endorsed by Barnes as paid on 16 Dec.). TJ recorded this transaction as payment for his subscription to the Georgetown balls (MB, 2:1088).

Order on John Barnes for payment of $125.72 to Étienne Lemaire, Washington, 20 Dec. (Typescript from George A. Van Nosdall, New York City, 1954; in TJ's hand and signed by him; signed by Lemaire acknowledging payment). TJ recorded this transaction as payment of Lemaire's accounts from Dec. 12 to 18 for provisions, servants, and contingencies (MB, 2:1088).

Order on John Barnes for payment of $91.12 to Étienne Lemaire, Washington, 29 Dec. (MS in R. M. Smythe & Co., Inc., New York City, 1997; in TJ's hand and signed by him; signed by Lemaire acknowledging payment; endorsed by Barnes as paid on 31 Dec.). TJ recorded this transaction as payment of Lemaire's accounts from Dec. 19 to 25 for provisions and contingencies (MB, 2:1089).

Order on John Barnes for payment of $5.50 to Marie Ann Pic, 29 Dec. (MS in CSmH; in TJ's hand and signed by him; endorsed as paid on 28 Dec.). TJ recorded this transaction as payment for tippets (MB, 2:1089).

Invoice submitted by George F. Hopkins to TJ for $6 for purchase on 5 Jan. 1803 of "one copy of the Federalist, gilt" (MS in MHi; order by TJ at foot of text: "Mr. Barnes will be pleased to pay this"; endorsed by John Barnes as paid on 5 Jan.). See MB, 2:1090.

Order on John Barnes for payment of $94.37 to Étienne Lemaire, Washington, 9 Jan. (MS in NjHi; in TJ's hand and signed by him; signed by Lemaire acknowledging payment; endorsed by Barnes as paid on 14 Jan.). TJ recorded this transaction as payment of Lemaire's accounts from Jan. 2 to 8 for provisions and contingencies (MB, 2:1090).

Order on John Barnes for payment of $18.60 to Joseph Dougherty, 11 Jan. (MS in CSmH; in TJ's hand and signed by him; written on invoice from Dougherty, dated 10 Jan., for expenses incurred in filling the icehouse, including $12 for carts, $3 for laborers, $2 for "Mr Belts Attendance," and $1.60 for two gallons of whiskey; signed by Dougherty acknowledging payment). See MB, 2:1090.

Order on John Barnes for payment of $10 to "mr Barney's driver," Washington, 14 Jan. (MS in FMU; in TJ's hand and signed by him, with note at foot of text: "to be delivered to mr Barney's driver who brought mrs R. & mrs E. here"; signed by Joseph Dougherty acknowledging payment; endorsed by Barnes as paid on 14 Jan.). See MB, 2:1090.

Order on John Barnes for payment of $88 to Charles McLaughlin, 1 Feb. (MS in CSmH; in TJ's hand and signed by him; written on invoice from McLaughlin to TJ, dated January 1803, for eleven days hire of a carriage and four horses at $8 per day; signed by McLaughlin acknowledging payment on 22 Feb.). TJ recorded this transaction as payment for coach hire for "R. & E." (MB, 2:1091).

Order on John Barnes for payment of $41.14 to Joseph Dougherty, Washington, 14 Feb. (MS in CU-BANC; in TJ's hand and signed by him; signed by Dougherty acknowledging payment; endorsed by Barnes as paid on 14 Feb.). TJ recorded this transaction as payment of Dougherty's accounts for forage, saddlery, smiths, and utensils (MB, 2:1092).

Order on John Barnes for payment of $100 to James Hamilton and John Campbell, Washington, 25 Feb. (MS in ViU: Edgehill-Randolph Papers; in TJ's hand and signed by him; signed by Hamilton on verso acknowledging payment; endorsed by Barnes as paid on 1 Mch.). TJ recorded this transaction as charity toward rebuilding Dickinson College (MB, 2:1093).

R. & E.: presumably Martha Jefferson Randolph and Mary Jefferson Eppes.

INDEX

INDEX

INDEX

INDEX

INDEX

A comprehensive index of Volumes 1-20 of the First Series has been issued as Volume 21. Each subsequent volume has its own index, as does each volume or set of volumes in the Second Series.

THE PAPERS OF THOMAS JEFFERSON are composed in Monticello, a font based on the "Pica No. 1" created in the early 1800s by Binny & Ronaldson, the first successful typefounding company in America. The face is considered historically appropriate for The Papers of Thomas Jefferson because it was used extensively in American printing during the last quarter-century of Jefferson's life, and because Jefferson himself expressed cordial approval of Binny & Ronaldson types. It was revived and rechristened Monticello in the late 1940s by the Mergenthaler Linotype Company, under the direction of C. H. Griffith and in close consultation with P. J. Conkwright, specifically for the publication of the Jefferson Papers. The font suffered some losses in its first translation to digital format in the 1980s to accommodate computerized typesetting. Matthew Carter's reinterpretation in 2002 restores the spirit and style of Binny & Ronaldson's original design of two centuries earlier.

✧